# Explanatory Nonmonotonic Reasoning

## Advances in Logic

Series Editor: Dov M Gabbay FRSC FAvH
Department of Computer Science
King's College London
Strand, London WC2R 2LS
UK
dg@dcs.kcl.ac.uk

---

*Published*

Vol. 1 Essays on Non-Classical Logic
*by H. Wansing*

Vol. 2 Fork Algebras in Algebra, Logic and Computer Science
*by M. Frias*

Vol. 3 Reasoning about Theoretical Entities
*by T. Forster*

Vol. 4 Explanatory Nonmonotonic Reasoning
*by A. Bochman*

Advances in Logic – Vol. 4

# Explanatory Nonmonotonic Reasoning


**Alexander Bochman**

Holon Academic Institute of Technology, Israel



World Scientific

NEW JERSEY • LONDON • SINGAPORE • BEIJING • SHANGHAI • HONG KONG • TAIPEI • CHENNAI

*Published by*

World Scientific Publishing Co. Pte. Ltd.

5 Toh Tuck Link, Singapore 596224

*USA office:* 27 Warren Street, Suite 401-402, Hackensack, NJ 07601

*UK office:* 57 Shelton Street, Covent Garden, London WC2H 9HE

**British Library Cataloguing-in-Publication Data**
A catalogue record for this book is available from the British Library.

**EXPLANATORY NONMONOTONIC REASONING**
**Advances in Logic — Vol. 4**



ISBN 981-256-101-3

Printed in Singapore by World Scientific Printers (S) Pte Ltd

To Jonathan Stavi and my family.

# Preface

Like my preceding book, [Bochman, 2001], the present study is also a systematic attempt to answer the question 'what is nonmonotonic reasoning?'. It complements the previous book by giving a logical formalization to the original approach to nonmonotonic reasoning that includes default logic, autoepistemic and modal nonmonotonic logics, and logic programming. We call this approach *explanatory* nonmonotonic reasoning, since the notion of explanation can be seen as the ultimate and unifying basis behind these nonmonotonic formalisms.

Three aspects distinguish this book from previous studies in this area. First, the book provides a uniform generalized theory of explanatory nonmonotonic reasoning rather than a description of existing nonmonotonic logics. Though the latter are shown to be covered by this theory, the formalism of biconsequence relations, taken as a logical basis of this study, suggests a powerful generalization going in most cases far beyond existing nonmonotonic formalisms. Second, the book shifts attention to some relatively recent, non-epistemic approaches to nonmonotonic reasoning, such as four-valued biconsequence relations, causal reasoning and argumentation theory. These formalisms actually fill the gap between logic programming, on the one hand, and traditional nonmonotonic logics, on the other. Accordingly, default and modal nonmonotonic logics are covered only in the last two chapters, and only as parts of the more general formalism of epistemic biconsequence relations. Last but not least, the book focuses on the logical, monotonic basis of explanatory nonmonotonic reasoning. In this sense, it is as much about logic as it is about nonmonotonic reasoning. As the main benefit of this approach, it will be shown that different formalisms of explanatory nonmonotonic reasoning are based on essentially the same principles and models, the main distinction being the underlying logical formalisms that host such a reasoning.

The intended audience of this book consists of graduate students and researchers in AI, on the one hand, and general logicians, on the other. In fact, one of the aims of the book consists in persuading the former about the need of logic, and the latter that nonmonotonic reasoning should be an integral part of general logical research.

*A. Bochman*

# Contents

# Chapter 1

# Introduction

In this introductory chapter I will delineate the subject of this study, and the questions it is going to answer.

## 1.1 Two Theories of Nonmonotonic Reasoning

Studies in nonmonotonic reasoning have given rise to two basically different approaches that will be called, respectively, *preferential* and *explanatory* nonmonotonic reasoning, with little interaction between them[1]. The first approach encompasses nonmonotonic inference relations of [Kraus *et al.*, 1990], and a general theory of belief change [Alchourrón *et al.*, 1985]. A detailed description of this approach can be found in [Bochman, 2001]. The second, explanatory approach is older, and it includes default and modal nonmonotonic logics, as well as logic programming with negation as failure. In fact, all the papers in the famous 1980 issue of the Artificial Intelligence Journal on nonmonotonic reasoning could be seen as belonging to this latter camp (though McCarthy's circumscription is covered also by the preferential approach). The aim of this study consists of providing a systematic logical theory for this explanatory approach to nonmonotonic reasoning.

It might well be (and I certainly hope so) that both these approaches will some day become parts of a single future theory of nonmonotonic reasoning. Nevertheless, I also believe that a proper basis for a future unification should consist in a careful separation between these approaches. Such a separation, however, is not a trivial matter.

The difference between the two approaches can be found on a number

[1] They have been called, respectively, *classical* and *argumentative* nonmonotonic reasoning in [Bochman, 2001].

of levels. To begin with, there are two different senses in which a logical formalism, or a reasoning system, may be called nonmonotonic. First, it may be nonmonotonic in that its rules do not admit addition of new premises, that is, the system does not allow Strengthening the Antecedent. Second, it may be nonmonotonic in the sense that adding further rules to the system may possibly invalidate some of the conclusions obtained earlier. Now, it turns out that these two kinds of nonmonotonicity are largely independent. Thus, preferential inference relations (see [Kraus *et al.*, 1990]) are nonmonotonic in the first sense, since strengthening the antecedent does not hold for them (*Birds fly* does not imply *Penguins fly*). However, they are monotonic in the second sense, since addition of new preferential conditionals does not invalidate previous conclusions. On the other hand, default logic (see [Reiter, 1980]) exemplifies monotonicity of the first kind and nonmonotonicity of the second kind. Indeed, we will see that any default theory can be safely extended with default rules obtained from existing ones by strengthening their pre-requisites and justifications; such additional rules will not change the set of extensions. On the other hand, adding arbitrary new rules to the default theory may result in creating new extensions, so nonmonotonic conclusions made earlier will not, in general, be preserved.

Taken by itself, however, the above distinction is a purely formal difference between formalisms, and it still does not necessarily imply that the two approaches are essentially different. Actually, one of the main incentives behind the preferential approach, already explicitly expressed in [Shoham, 1988], was the hope that default logic and other explanatory nonmonotonic formalisms can be subsumed by some generalized version of the preferential approach in the sense that extensions could be viewed as preferred models under some generalized notion of preference. Unfortunately, subsequent studies have raised grave doubts about this hope. Thus, the nonmonotonic semantics of default logic has turned out to violate even the most basic postulates of cumulative inference (see [Makinson, 1989]). A similar situation has been found in logic programming (see [Dix, 1991]).

In a hindsight, this outcome should have been expected, since the selection of intended models in an explanatory approach is not preferential in a usual sense. Namely, the explanatory approach determines the intended models as models satisfying certain closure conditions with respect to the rules (see below). On a most abstract level, such models are usually expressible as fixed points of some operator which is not even monotonic. Accordingly, the supposed preference that singles out these models appears to be a trivial, zero-one preference that basically differentiates only right models from bad ones. In this sense, the above formal difference can be viewed only as a symptom of deeper conceptual distinctions between the two approaches.

Both preferential and explanatory nonmonotonic reasoning can be seen as theories of a reasoned use of assumptions. Now, preferential reasoning treats such assumptions as *defaults*, namely as normality assumptions we can use whenever there is no evidence to the contrary. This understanding is combined with a general principle that a problem situation should be assumed as normal as it is consistently possible, given the known facts. This naturally creates a preferential setting, in which the normality of models is measured by the set of defaults they support (see [Bochman, 2001] where such a preferential order is formally described).

It turns out, however, that the explanatory nonmonotonic reasoning implicitly assigns a different role to assumptions. Using the name adopted by David Poole (see [Poole, 1989; Poole, 1990]) it makes such assumptions *conjectures*. Conjectures are assumptions that we make in order to explain observations. The supposition of normality (or abnormality, for that matter) is not essential for such conjectures. A certain combination of symptoms may lead to a conjecture about a rare and unusual disease, while in other cases some 'ordinary' illness will suffice for explaining the observations; it seems beside the point in this case to order diseases with respect to their 'normality'. As was rightly noted by Poole, we make conjectures only if there is evidence that requires them for explanation, in contrast to defaults that can be freely assumed, unless they contradict the facts and other assumed defaults. It was also strongly argued by Poole that the distinction between normality defaults and conjectures is closely related to the distinction between prediction and explanation: while we use defaults in order to predict facts that are yet unknown, conjectures are invoked when we have to explain known facts.

Unfortunately, the above presumably clear distinction has been obscured in the short history of nonmonotonic reasoning. The reason was that, from the very beginning, the main formalisms of nonmonotonic reasoning, including default logic, modal nonmonotonic logics and circumscription, have claimed their rights and responsibility on representation of normality defaults. Thus, Ray Reiter has suggested in [Reiter, 1980] that we can identify such normality assertions with a special case of default rules of the form $A{:}B/B$, appropriately called normal default rules[2].

It is the author's conviction that the preferential approach provides a more adequate analysis of the notion of normality and, in particular, of normal defaults. All the examples in the literature that reveal a discrepancy between Reiter's normal defaults $A{:}B/B$ and corresponding preferential conditionals $A \mid\!\sim B$ point out in favor of the latter. In this respect, the criticism raised against default logic in the preferential camp (see, e.g., [Kraus *et al.*, 1990; Lehmann, 1995]) seems perfectly justified, so far as we are talking only about which notion better reflects our understanding of normality. Still, there is nothing wrong or nonintuitive about having both $A : B/B$ and $A : \neg B/\neg B$ in a default theory, though it is certainly counterintuitive to treat such rules simultaneously as normality defaults. In the setting of default logic, such rules say simply that, when $A$ holds, both $B$ and $\neg B$ are equally admissible assumptions, or conjectures. This indicates, however, that default logic has a subject of its own that should not be extrapolated to the entire field of nonmonotonic reasoning.

The above picture is of course incomplete, mainly because it stresses the differences and ignores numerous similarities and connections between the two approaches. Note, for example, that McCarthy's circumscription (with abnormality predicates) can be easily understood in both ways, which might explain why it constitutes a borderline case covered by both approaches. Speaking more generally, many reasoning tasks actually involve both these forms of nonmonotonic reasoning. Still, I believe that a clear understanding of explanatory nonmonotonic reasoning can be achieved only if it is considered as an independent reasoning paradigm with a subject, goals and principles of its own.

## 1.2 Explanatory Nonmonotonic Reasoning

As the name indicates, explanation can be seen as a basic notion of an explanatory approach. Propositions and facts may be not only true or false in a model of a problem situation, but some of them are explainable by other facts and rules that are accepted. In the objective setting, some of the facts are *caused* by other facts and causal rules acting in the domain. Furthermore, explanatory nonmonotonic reasoning is based on very strong principles of *Explanation Closure* ([Schubert, 1994]) and *Causal Complete-*

[2]Poole himself implicitly considered such rules as primary examples of normality defaults.

*ness* ([Reiter, 2001]), according to which any fact holding in a model should be explained, or caused, by the rules that describe the domain. Incidentally, it is these principles that make explanatory reasoning nonmonotonic.

By the above description, *abductive reasoning*, that is, reasoning from facts to their possible explanations, can be seen as an integral part of explanatory nonmonotonic reasoning. Ultimate explanations, or abducibles, correspond in this sense not to normality defaults, but to conjectures representing base causes that are viewed as facts that do not require explanation; we assume the latter only if we have evidence that requires them for explanation.

In some domains, explanatory formalisms adopt additional, simplifying assumptions that exempt, in effect, certain classes of propositions from the burden of explanation. Reiter's *Closed World Assumption* (see [Reiter, 1978]) can be seen as one of the most important assumptions of this kind. According to the latter, negated propositional atoms do not require explanation. Nonmonotonic reasoning in databases and logic programming are domains for which such an assumption turns out to be most appropriate. It is important to note in this respect that the well-known *minimization principle* is actually a result of combining Explanation Closure with the Closed World Assumption. Indeed, we will see in what follows that semantics of logic programming, that are commonly viewed as based on the minimization principle, can be obtained directly from the combination of these two assumptions. An interesting aspect of this claim is that the minimization principle need not be viewed as a principle of scaled preference of negative information; rather, it is a by-product of the plain assertion that negated atomic propositions can be accepted without any further explanation, while positive assertions always require an explanation.

As we will show in this study, the above principles will be sufficient for establishing a formal logical framework for explanatory nonmonotonic reasoning. The above description presupposes, however, a drastic departure from traditional logical representations, since it draws a richer picture of what is in the world than what is usually captured in logical models of the latter.

The traditional understanding of possible worlds in logic can be traced back to Wittgenstein's *Tractatus* [Wittgenstein, 1961]. The atomic facts of the Tractatus' metaphysics are independent: '*[e]ach item can be the case or not the case while everything else remains the same*'. Consequently, there is no possible way of making an inference from one fact to another, entirely different fact, and there is no causal nexus to justify such an inference. The only restriction on the structure of the world is based on the principle of non-contradiction. As a result, Wittgenstein's worlds leave no place in it for dependencies among facts and related notions, in particular for causation. Accordingly, Wittgenstein concluded that belief in such dependencies is a 'superstition'.

This book is not a philosophical study, so I will refrain from indulging the reader with philosophical considerations. Still, it should be kept in mind that this book presupposes a different picture of the world, according to which the world is not a mere assemblage of unrelated facts, but something which has a structure. This structure determines dependencies among occurrent facts, while the latter serve as a basis for our explanatory and causal claims. It is this structure that makes the world intelligible and, what is especially important for this study, controllable. The picture implies, in particular, that explanatory and causal relations form an integral part of understanding of and acting in the world. Consequently, such relations should form an essential part of knowledge representation, at least in Artificial Intelligence.

## 1.3 Explanatory Nonmonotonic Reasoning and Logic

One of the main presuppositions of this book is that nonmonotonic reasoning should give us a more direct and adequate description of the actual ways we think about the world. In this respect, preferential nonmonotonic reasoning has had a definite advantage over traditional nonmonotonic logics in that it provided a direct semantic representation for its inference rules, namely default conditionals 'If $A$, then normally $B$'. This semantic representation allows us to assess our default claims and determines, ultimately, the actual choice of default assumptions made in particular circumstances.

For a number of reasons, discussed below, the basic syntactic objects of default logic and its relatives have lacked such a clear and direct semantic interpretation. As a result, a representation of nonmonotonic reasoning problems in such systems has been largely a syntactic enterprize. Thus, in default logic the user is required to provide explicit information about when one default rule can 'block' another default (by specifying appropriate justifications in premises of such rules). This information is used as a sole factor in determining acceptable combinations of defaults. This strategy can be remarkably successful in resolving difficult cases of default interaction, which can be seen as the main reason why the explanatory nonmonotonic reasoning so far has had a greater impact on practical applications of nonmonotonic reasoning in AI than its preferential counterpart. Still, such a methodology puts sometimes a heavy burden on the user by requiring from him to foresee and control the results of default interaction. In other words, it does not give us a transparent and systematic way of representing empirical data, and this makes the task of knowledge representation in such systems really an art.

As I see it, the main reason of these shortcomings amounts to the absence of an adequate logical basis in such nonmonotonic systems.

The majority of nonmonotonic formalisms have two components. The first is an ordinary, monotonic logical framework, e.g., classical logic in circumscription, or some modal logic in modal nonmonotonic logics. The second, nonmonotonic, component involves a stipulation about which potential models should be considered as intended ones. In other words, the nonmonotonic component is built in these systems *on top* of a monotonic inference system.

Unfortunately, such important nonmonotonic formalisms as default and autoepistemic logics, and semantics of logic programming, are usually described in a shortcut way, namely as pairs consisting of syntax and nonmonotonic semantics. To put it shortly, they are built in accordance with the following identity:

$$\textit{Nonmonotonic Logic} = \textit{Syntax} + \textit{Nonmonotonic Semantics}.$$

The very name 'Nonmonotonic Logic' conveys in such cases similarity with ordinary monotonic logical systems, for which the above equality is clearly appropriate. The analogy is clear, but unfortunately misleading. In ordinary logical systems, the semantics determines, of course, the set of logical consequences of a given theory, but also, and most importantly, it provides a semantic interpretation for the syntax itself. In other words, it provides propositions and rules of a syntactic formalism with *meaning*, and its theories with *informational content*. By its very design, however, nonmonotonic semantics is defined as a certain *subset* of the set of possible models, and consequently does not determine, in turn, the meaning of the propositions and rules of the syntax. For example, radically different theories may have the same nonmonotonic semantics. Furthermore, such a difference cannot be viewed as apparent, since it may well be that by adding further rules or facts to both these theories, we obtain new theories that already have different nonmonotonic models.

Thus, the above 'shortcut' definition of Nonmonotonic Logic leaves us without an exact or even clear meaning of the source syntax. Default rules do not bear on their heads information about when and how they can be applied. This is the main reason why the relevant knowledge representation methodology in such systems is essentially an art based on accumulated experience. All these shortcomings have become especially vivid in logic programming.

### 1.3.1 *Logic in logic programming*

From its very beginning, logic programming was based on the idea that program rules should have both a procedural and declarative (logical) meaning. This dual interpretation was purported to elevate the programming process by basing it on a transparent and systematic logical representation of real world information.

A declarative meaning of a definite (Prolog) program rule was commonly taken to be the meaning of the corresponding classical implication, despite the fact that the (unique) minimal model was singled out as determining the set of conclusions (answers to queries) of the program [van Emden and Kowalski, 1976]. Note that already this setting involved a certain discrepancy, since the *logical* meaning of a program (viewed as a set of implications) is not determined uniquely by the minimal model, but rather by the set of all its models.

This double understanding was further challenged with the introduction of negation as failure as a replacement of the classical negation in logic programs. Clark's completion [Clark, 1978] was commonly accepted as giving more adequate interpretations of logic programs and deductive databases. Nevertheless, for some time these developments peacefully coexisted with an opinion that they reflect a purely pragmatic concession, and an ideal solution should still consist in the full use of classical negation in programs and queries (cf. [Shepherdson, 1988]).

Things have changed, however, with the discovery that logic programs with negation as failure allow us to represent significant parts of nonmonotonic reasoning. Moreover, general nonmonotonic formalisms inspired a new kind of semantics for logic programs, the stable and answer set semantics [Gelfond and Lifschitz, 1988; Gelfond and Lifschitz, 1991]. These developments have advanced logic programming to the role of a general computational mechanism for knowledge representation and nonmonotonic reasoning (see the overviews [Apt and Bol, 1994;

Baral and Gelfond, 1994], and especially [Baral, 2003]).

The idea of a dual interpretation of logic programs, procedural and declarative, persisted in all these developments. However, the original question *'What is a declarative meaning of a program rule?'* has been replaced with the global question *'What is a declarative meaning of a logic program?'*, and an answer to this latter question has been commonly thought settled by assigning logic programs some nonmonotonic semantics. Of course, there were reasons for this shift, since already the completion of a logic program does not allow us to single out a modular meaning of a program rule.

Unfortunately, the above solution to the problem of determining a declarative meaning of logic programs has turned out to be problematic. To begin with, as was rightly noted already in [Shepherdson, 1988], this solution does not allow us to see the written text of a program as its declarative meaning. For example, adding new rules to a program does not necessarily mean that the extended program contains more information. Worse still, quite diverse programs can have the same 'meaning' according to this understanding, witness such programs as $\{p \leftarrow q\}$ and $\{q \leftarrow p\}$ (both have the empty least model). As a result, the association of logic programs with a meaning of this kind turns out to be useless for most purposes we could possibly have in invoking the notion of meaning (be it knowledge representation or the problem of updating programs).

The absence of a clear and uniform logical basis behind logic programs with negation as failure has resulted in an unbridled proliferation of semantics suggested for such programs. In part, this was due to the fact that there were no clear grounds for evaluating such semantics, apart from their computational virtues, existence for all programs, or coincidence with 'respectable' semantics in special cases. In addition, the absence of a systematic representation methodology behind logic programming created obvious difficulties for viewing the latter as a canonical knowledge representation formalism.

### 1.3.2 *A logical basis of nonmonotonic logics*

As we argued above, nonmonotonic semantics does not determine the meaning of propositions or rules of a nonmonotonic formalism. Actually, this situation is quite similar to the well-known distinction between meaning (intension) and extension of logical names, a distinction that is fundamental for modern logic. Namely, nonmonotonic semantics provides, in a sense, the extensional content of a theory in a particular context of its use. In order to determine the meaning, or informational content, of a theory, we have to consider the underlying monotonic logic. As we will see, the meaning will determine also the extension, namely associated nonmonotonic semantics, but not vice versa.

The way out of the above problem that will be suggested in this study amounts to a *clear separation of logical and nonmonotonic aspects of nonmonotonic reasoning.* The separation suggests the following modified understanding of the concept of Nonmonotonic Logic:

*Nonmonotonic Logic = Logic + Nonmonotonic Semantics*

Logic and its associated monotonic semantics should be responsible for providing the meaning of the rules and other components of the formalism, while nonmonotonic semantics will provide us with nonmonotonic consequences of a given default theory. As the main benefit of this separation, it will be shown in this book that common kinds of explanatory nonmonotonic reasoning are reducible, in effect, to different kinds of logical reasoning with respect to a single nonmonotonic semantics.

It should be noted that some explanatory nonmonotonic formalisms have actually been based on this understanding all the time. Thus, McCarthy's circumscription was explicitly based on classical logic. Similarly, [McDermott, 1982] has considered the influence of the underlying modal logic on the nonmonotonic semantics. Subsequent studies have made this connection explicit (see [Marek *et al.*, 1993]). Moreover, though Moore's autoepistemic logic has been designed initially according to the 'shortcut' scheme as independent of any particular logic, it has later been shown (in [Schwarz, 1990]) that the modal logic KD45 provides an exact underlying monotonic logic for autoepistemic reasoning.

Furthermore, it will be shown in this book that in most cases of interest, the underlying logic can be restored. Thus, for both default logic and modal nonmonotonic logics, we will find logical rules and postulates that preserve a given nonmonotonic semantics. Such rules can be considered as providing a logical basis for the corresponding system of nonmonotonic reasoning. As with ordinary inference rules, for default rules this information can be embodied in the form of 'meta-rules' that produce new default rules from given ones (this is actually the main idea behind various sequent calculi). Such rules will make the underlying formalism of default logic a *logical* system.

A more precise description of such a 'reverse engineering' is as follows. Suppose we are given a nonmonotonic logic in its virgin sense, namely some syntactic formalism $\mathbb{F}$ coupled with a nonmonotonic semantics $\mathbb{S}$. Specifically, the syntactic formalism $\mathbb{F}$ determines the basic informational units, for which the semantics $\mathbb{S}$ supplies the nonmonotonic interpretation (i.e., a set of models). Such informational units could be plain logical theories (sets of propositions), as in circumscription or modal nonmonotonic logics, or sets of (default) rules, as in default logic. Let us call such informational units *default theories*. In addition, for a default theory $\Delta$, let us denote by $\mathbb{S}(\Delta)$ the nonmonotonic semantics of $\Delta$, namely the set of models assigned to $\Delta$ by $\mathbb{S}$. Then the nonmonotonic semantics $\mathbb{S}$ imposes the following primary notion of equivalence on default theories:

**Definition 1.1** Default theories $\Gamma$ and $\Delta$ will be called *(nonmonotonically) $\mathbb{S}$-equivalent*, if $\mathbb{S}(\Delta) = \mathbb{S}(\Gamma)$.

Thus, two default theories are nonmonotonically equivalent if they have the same nonmonotonic interpretation. As has been argued earlier, however, this notion of equivalence does not determine the logical meaning of default theories. Note in this respect that, precisely due to the nonmonotonicity of $\mathbb{S}$, two nonmonotonically equivalent theories may become non-equivalent when we extend them with additional rules or propositions. In other words, we may have $\mathbb{S}(\Delta) = \mathbb{S}(\Gamma)$, though $\mathbb{S}(\Delta \cup \Phi) \neq \mathbb{S}(\Gamma \cup \Phi)$, for some default theory $\Phi$. This means that nonmonotonic equivalence is not the notion reflecting a logical meaning (or informational content) of default theories.

Still, the above considerations suggest a simple solution. Recall that a standard definition of the meaning of a logical notion in logic amounts to a stipulation that two notions have the same meaning if and only if they determine the same extension in all contexts (e.g., in all possible worlds). In our case, a context can be seen simply as a larger theory that includes a given one. This immediately leads us to the following notion:

**Definition 1.2** Default theories $\Gamma$ and $\Delta$ will be called *strongly $\mathbb{S}$-equivalent*, if $\mathbb{S}(\Delta \cup \Phi) = \mathbb{S}(\Gamma \cup \Phi)$, for any default theory $\Phi$.

As a matter of fact, the above notion of strong equivalence has been suggested in the framework of logic programming (see [Lifschitz *et al.*, 2001]), but it turns out to have a general significance. Note in this respect that strong equivalence is already a monotonic, logical notion, since strongly equivalent theories are interchangeable in any larger theory without changing the associated nonmonotonic semantics. This suggests that there exists a (monotonic) logic $\mathbb{L}$ formulated directly in the syntax $\mathbb{F}$ such that default theories are strongly equivalent if and only if they are logically equivalent in $\mathbb{L}$. In this case, the logic $\mathbb{L}$ can be viewed as the underlying logic adequate for the nonmonotonic semantics $\mathbb{S}$. The logic $\mathbb{L}$ will determine then the logical meaning of default theories and, in particular, the intended meaning of the rules and propositions of the syntactic framework $\mathbb{F}$. Fortunately, it will be shown that, for practically all nonmonotonic formalisms considered in this study, such an underlying logic can be found.

### 1.3.3 *Objective vs. epistemic formalisms*

Special attention given in this study to the underlying logics behind nonmonotonic reasoning will also be rewarded with a better understanding of the possible range of such logics that are appropriate for explanatory nonmonotonic reasoning. A systematic approach to this question will reveal, in particular, that the traditional map of such a reasoning is patently incomplete, and that it should be completed with a number of important formalisms such as four-valued biconsequence relations, production and causal inference, and argumentation theory. Adding these components to the map will give us a continuous range of nonmonotonic formalisms starting with logic programming and ending with modal nonmonotonic logics.

A distinctive feature of both default and modal nonmonotonic logics is that they are inherently *epistemic* formalisms. Namely, they are essentially based on such notions as belief and knowledge, and consequently the intended semantic models of these formalisms represent possibly incomplete sets of beliefs one can have, while their rules allow us to make inferences based on absence of belief, or consistency, with respect to candidate belief sets (cf. the introductory sections of [Reiter, 1980]). It seems that this modal, epistemic formulation of the main nonmonotonic formalisms (with McCarthy's circumscription again as an important exception) was mainly created due to historical reasons: at the time these formalisms emerged, modal logics already reigned in the literature as a standard paradigm of logical representation. The epistemic interpretation also strongly influenced logic programming in that the negation as failure has often been formulated as absence of knowledge (or derivation).

Due to its modal character, default logic has turned out to be a logically weak formalism that does not support many classical inference principles (such as reasoning by cases). It also has other well-known shortcomings, and numerous variants of default logic have been suggested in attempts to overcome them and make it more in accord with our intuitions. On our opinion, however, relatively modest success of these attempts has shown that it is impossible to radically improve default logic without abandoning its underlying epistemic interpretation.

The relation between logic programming, on the one hand, and default and modal nonmonotonic logics, on the other, is especially relevant for our discussion. As I already mentioned, the main semantics for logic programs have been inspired by these nonmonotonic logics. Moreover, logic programs under these semantics can be faithfully translated, or embedded, into these formalisms, *though not vice versa*. This makes logic programming a separate nonmonotonic formalism with the logic of its own. More precisely, as in other parts of logic, the embedding means that logic programming constitutes a more specific formalism with a richer underlying logic. This formalism has to be accounted for in the general theory of explanatory nonmonotonic reasoning, and, as we will see, such an account can be given in the formalism of biconsequence relations, described in Chapter 3. Namely, the formalism of biconsequence relations can be viewed as a straightforward formalization of the logic(s) behind logic programs. In this way we will restore the connection between Logic and Logic Programming that has been lost with the introduction of logic programs involving negation by failure.

New nonmonotonic formalisms have emerged also in one of the primary application fields of nonmonotonic reasoning, a formal representation of actions and change. It was realized quite early on that classical logic alone cannot provide an efficient representation for reasoning about change due to the famous *frame problem*, a problem of giving an efficient description for the state of the world after performing an action that would avoid computationally unbearable reproduction of all the facts that remain unaffected (see [Shanahan, 1997]). There was also a related *ramification problem* of determining the indirect effects (ramifications) of actions that arise due to the laws of the domain. And it was only natural to expect that nonmonotonic reasoning should help in resolving these problems.

After some less successful attempts to formalize temporal nonmonotonic reasoning in existing nonmonotonic logics, a dominant recent approach to solving these problems has been based on causal reasoning. The causal approach constitutes yet another instance of explanatory nonmonotonic reasoning and employs the already mentioned distinction between facts that hold in a situation versus facts that are caused (explained) by other facts and the rules. The corresponding explanation closure assumption asserts that all facts that hold in a situation should be either caused by other occurrent facts, or else preserve their truth-values in time (due to the associated *inertia assumption*). A natural formalization of these principles has been given in the framework of causal theories, introduced in [McCain and Turner, 1997]. A detailed description of this formalism will be given in Chapter 8.

Causal reasoning constitutes an important turning point in the development of nonmonotonic reasoning, since from its very beginning it was designed as a formalism that should provide an objective description of factual and causal (explanatory) information about action domains. In other words, it has shown that an epistemic view of explanatory nonmonotonic reasoning is not the only possibility. As we will see, the corresponding logical formalism of causal inference relations will form a most natural and immediate generalization of classical logic that allows for nonmonotonic reasoning. Moreover, it will be shown to constitute a general-purpose formalism that covers significant parts of nonmonotonic reasoning. In this respect, it forms a viable non-epistemic alternative to default and modal nonmonotonic logics.

## 1.4 Overview of the Book

Chapter 2, *Scott Consequence Relations*, describes the general logical tools used in this book, namely Scott and Tarski consequence relations. However, as in [Bochman, 2001], this chapter provides only a biased survey of the facts and properties relevant for the main content of the study. Nevertheless, the reader will see that many of the well-known results about nonmonotonic formalisms will find their ultimate justification in this chapter.

Chapter 3, *Biconsequence Relations*, describes the basic logical formalism adopted in this book as a logical framework for nonmonotonic reasoning. A biconsequence relation is a product, or fibring, of two Scott consequence relations that gives a representation of reasoning with respect to a pair of contexts. Accordingly, a semantic representation of biconsequence relations is given in terms of *bimodels* which correspond to pairs of ordinary models. This bi-context framework will turn out to provide a most general setting for representing explanatory nonmonotonic reasoning.

Two important interpretations of the relevant contexts will be used in this study. The first is a four-valued interpretation, which makes biconsequence relations a general logical formalism of reasoning with possibly incomplete and inconsistent information. The second is an assumption interpretation that is tailored already to the representation of explanatory nonmonotonic reasoning. By this latter interpretation, the first context represents ordinary, objective inferences, while the second one specifies assumptions under which the objective inferences can be made.

A distinctive feature of biconsequence relations is a possibility of imposing additional structural rules on them. Such structural rules describe different ways in which the two component contexts can be correlated. Rules of this kind will play an important role in describing the logics that are appropriate for different nonmonotonic semantics.

In Chapter 4, *Four-Valued Logics*, biconsequence relations will be shown to provide a structural description of four-valued reasoning. Thus, it will be shown that any four-valued connective can be defined in biconsequence relations using appropriate introduction and elimination rules. We will single out a set of four-valued connectives that will be used later, and study their properties. It will be shown, in particular, that having these connectives at our disposal, bisequents can be transformed into ordinary inference rules, and even into logical formulas in a four-valued language. Finally, structural rules for biconsequence relations will be shown to be expressible as particular instances of a general *coherence principle* formulated in different four-valued languages. This principle will also play an important role later in describing semantics for general logic programs.

In Chapter 5, *Nonmonotonic Semantics*, we finally turn to the main subject of this study, the nonmonotonic semantics. Three semantics will turn out to be important for representing common nonmonotonic formalisms, namely semantics based on exact theories, extensions and expansions. All these semantics will embody some form of explanation closure principle. Among the three semantics, the exact nonmonotonic semantics will turn out to be the primary one. Roughly, an exact model is 'self-explanatory', namely it allows to explain all its propositions when the model itself is taken as an assumption context. In this sense, an exact model will give a strongest expression to the principle of explanation closure. Furthermore, it will be shown that the other two semantics can be obtained by relaxing the latter principle, namely restricting it, respectively, to positive propositions, and to single propositional atoms.

In accordance with the general strategy of this book, for each of the above semantics, we will find a maximal underlying logic that is adequate for it. Then it will turn out that both the extension- and expansion-based nonmonotonic semantics coincide with the exact semantics for some stronger underlying logics. This fact will give us an opportunity to study the relations between these nonmonotonic semantics, as well as describe situations in which these semantics coincide. In addition, we will describe reductions of these nonmonotonic semantics to ordinary models of certain classical *completions* of the source theory. Such completions allow to reduce the computation of these nonmonotonic semantics to solving classical satisfiability problems.

After that, we introduce partial generalizations of the above three semantics. The resulting partial nonmonotonic semantics will correspond to well-known partial semantics for logic programs. Finally, we will consider in this chapter a general correspondence between biconsequence relations and logic programs with negation as failure. It will turn out that program rules are directly representable as bisequents, and the above nonmonotonic semantics of biconsequence relations will correspond to well-known semantics for logic programs. Moreover, the correspondence will turn out to be bi-directional in the sense that any bisequent theory is representable by some logic program. In addition, we describe a general scheme for defining semantics for logic programs that is based on forming a nonmonotonic completion of the associated biconsequence relation. Many alternative, weaker semantics for logic programs will be shown to be covered by this scheme.

Chapter 6, *Default Consequence Relations*, describes a derived formalism of default consequence relations that is based on rules of the form $a{:}b \vdash A$ that correspond, in particular, to rules of Reiter's default logic. The formalism will allow to give a rather simple description of extensions and expansions, and provide a convenient logical framework for studying their properties. As before, we find maximal logics of default rules that are adequate, respectively, for extensions and expansions. Unlike the case of biconsequence relations, however, these two monotonic default logics will be incompatible. Finally, we show that default consequence relations provide an exact logical counterpart of normal logic programs under the main semantics for the latter.

Chapter 7, *Argumentation Theory*, describes an apparently different, but actually closely related theory, namely theory of argumentation. The chapter describes a generalization of Dung's argumentation theory, called collective argumentation, in which the attack relation is defined directly on sets of arguments, or abducibles. The formalism is shown to be related to biconsequence relations, as well as to semantics of disjunctive logic programs. It also forms a mediating link between the preceding formalism of biconsequence relations, and systems of production and causal inference described in the next chapter.

Chapter 8, *Production and Causal Inference*, introduces a first full-fledged logical formalism of this study that is based on the classical language. Production inference relation is an inference system for causal rules of the form $A \Rightarrow B$ that originates in input/output logics of [Makinson and van der Torre, 2000]. The latter are assigned, however, a natural nonmonotonic semantics, which gives rise to an important new system of explanatory nonmonotonic reasoning. The formalism of production inference can be viewed as a most natural and immediate generalization of classical logic that allows to express nonmonotonic reasoning. Basically, the generalization amounts to dropping the Reflexivity postulate of classical inference.

As a first application, a special kind of *abductive* production inference relations will be shown to provide a logical, syntax-independent representation of abductive reasoning. It will be shown, in particular, that in many regular cases such inference relations are sufficient for describing the nonmonotonic semantics of causal theories.

As a next step, we will consider a particular kind of production inference, called *causal inference relations.* Such inference relations already admit an objective interpretation as reasoning systems about the world. Accordingly, the nonmonotonic semantics for such inference relations will also be based on worlds. The resulting nonmonotonic formalism will provide a complete characterization of the reasoning with causal theories of [McCain and Turner, 1997]. In addition, causal inference relations will be shown to correspond to biconsequence relations in a particular four-valued language. Finally, it will be shown that causal inference relations provide also a natural logical representation for logic programs under a broad range of declarative semantics for the latter.

Chapter 9, *Epistemic Consequence Relations*, describes epistemic generalizations of the formalisms studied earlier. At the semantic level, the generalization amounts to moving from single interpretations (worlds) to sets of interpretations (epistemic states) as representations of the two underlying contexts. Accordingly, epistemic biconsequence relations can already be seen as formalisms of reasoning about knowledge and/or beliefs. Syntactically, the generalization amounts to considering consequence relations that subsume classical entailment. The corresponding supraclassical default consequence relations are shown to correspond to Reiter's default logic. Extended logic programs with a second, classical negation also belong to this level. Supraclassicality requires, however, a modification of the notion of expansion. The resulting formalism of classical autoepistemic consequence relations, together with the modified notion of expansion, will constitute an exact non-modal counterpart of Moore's autoepistemic logic.

Finally, Chapter 10, *Modal Nonmonotonic Logics*, describes the modal extension of our formalisms. Modal biconsequence and default consequence relations are defined as consequence relations in a modal language that satisfy certain reflection and introspection postulates for the modal operator. Traditional modal nonmonotonic logics, including the autoepistemic logic, are shown to belong to this level. Moreover, modal (bi)consequence relations allow to transform bisequents into ordinary modal formulas, so the corresponding nonmonotonic formalisms are actually reducible to these traditional modal nonmonotonic logics. On the other hand, the modal formalisms will also be shown to be reducible to their non-modal epistemic counterparts.

* * *

Throughout the book, propositions will be denoted by $A, B, C, \ldots$, finite sets of propositions by $a, b, c, \ldots$, and arbitrary such sets by $u, v, \ldots$. For propositional languages involving connectives, the letters $p, q, r, \ldots$ will be reserved for denoting propositional atoms. $Pr$ will stand for the set of all propositions of the language. Also, for a set $u$ of propositions, $\overline{u}$ will denote the complement of $u$, that is, $Pr \backslash u$.

For a finite set $a$ of propositions, $\bigwedge a$ ($\bigvee a$) will denote the classical conjunction (respectively, disjunction) of all propositions from $a$. As a special case, $\bigwedge \emptyset$ ($\bigvee \emptyset$) will denote an arbitrary tautology $\mathbf{t}$ (resp., contradiction $\mathbf{f}$). In addition, $\neg a$ will denote the set of classical negations of all propositions from $a$. The latter notation will also be used without further ado for all the other unary logical connectives that will be introduced in what follows.

# Chapter 2

# Scott Consequence Relations

As we will see throughout our exposition, many important facts and results concerning nonmonotonic reasoning are based, ultimately, on purely logical properties of the underlying formalisms. So in this chapter I will present the main facts about the most general such formalism, namely Scott consequence relations that will form an ultimate logical basis for subsequent constructions. Many claims are made in this chapter without proofs. Most of them can be found, however, in [Bochman, 2001].

Scott consequence relations [Scott, 1974; Gabbay, 1976], known also as multiple-conclusion consequence relations (see [Segerberg, 1982; Shoesmith and Smiley, 1978]), have as their origin Gentzen's sequent calculus, and are based on the idea of taking a consequence relation to be a binary relation between sets of propositions. Accordingly, such consequence relations involve rules, or sequents, of the form $a \vdash b$, where $a$ and $b$ are finite sets of propositions, having the following informal reading:

> *If all propositions from a are accepted, then one of the propositions from b should also be accepted.*

Thus, in contrast to ordinary, single-conclusion Tarski consequence relations, Scott sequents involve sets of conclusions that are interpreted as sets of alternatives implied by the premises.

## 2.1 Basic Definitions

A set of sequents is called a *Scott consequence relation* if it satisfies the following conditions:

**(Reflexivity)** $A \vdash A$.

**(Monotonicity)** If $a \vdash b$ and $a \subseteq a'$, $b \subseteq b'$, then $a' \vdash b'$;
**(Cut)** If $a \vdash b, A$ and $a, A \vdash b$, then $a \vdash b$.

In what follows we use ordinary terminological conventions and write, e.g., $a, A \vdash b, B$ instead of $a \cup \{A\} \vdash b \cup \{B\}$ and $\vdash a$, $a \vdash$ instead of $\emptyset \vdash a$ and $a \vdash \emptyset$, respectively.

The notion of a sequent can be extended to infinite sets of premises and conclusions by requiring that, for any sets of propositions $u$ and $v$,

**(Compactness)** $u \vdash v$ if and only if $a \vdash b$, for some finite $a \subseteq u, b \subseteq v$.

This extension retains all the rules of a Scott consequence relation. Moreover, the resulting extended consequence relations could be characterized alternatively as Scott consequence relations on arbitrary sets of formulas satisfying the Compactness requirement.

The following definition describes the basic notion of a theory for a Scott consequence relation.

**Definition 2.1** A set $u$ of propositions is a *theory* of a Scott consequence relation $\vdash$ if $u \nvdash \overline{u}$.

Thus, theories are defined as sets of propositions that do not imply propositions outside them. The following lemma shows that theories can be seen as sets of propositions that are closed with respect to the sequents of a consequence relation.

**Lemma 2.1** *A set $u$ is a theory of a Scott consequence relation $\vdash$ iff, for any sequent $a \vdash b$ from $\vdash$, if $a \subseteq u$, then $u \cap b \neq \emptyset$.*

Theories of a Scott consequence relation naturally generalize theories of a Tarski consequence relation, though they do not have all the properties of the latter. Most importantly, intersections of Scott theories are not in general theories. Nevertheless, they still have the property of completeness with respect to directed sets, stated below.

A set of theories $\mathcal{T}$ will be called *upward (downward) directed*, if for any $u_1, u_2 \in \mathcal{T}$ there is $u \in \mathcal{T}$ that includes (resp., is included in) both $u_1$ and $u_2$.

**Lemma 2.2** *If $\mathcal{T}$ is an upward (downward) directed set of theories of a Scott consequence relation $\vdash$, then $\bigcup \mathcal{T}$ (respectively, $\bigcap \mathcal{T}$) is also a theory of $\vdash$.*

The above property implies, in particular, existence of inclusion minimal theories containing some set of propositions, and inclusion maximal theories disjoint from a set of propositions:

**Theorem 2.3**

*(1) If $u$ is a theory of $\vdash$, and $v$ a set of propositions such that $v \subseteq u$, then $u$ contains a minimal theory $u'$ including $v$.*
*(2) If $u$ is a theory of $\vdash$, and $u \subseteq v$, then $u$ is contained in a maximal theory $u'$ included in $v$.*

As a special case, we obtain the following useful property:

**Corollary 2.4** *Any theory of $\vdash$ is included in a maximal theory and contains a minimal theory of $\vdash$.*

### 2.1.1 *Tarski consequence relations*

Usual *Tarski consequence relations* can be considered as a special case of Scott consequence relations that are determined by rules of the form $a \vdash A$, where $A$ is a proposition. A Tarski consequence relation can also be described using the associated *provability operator* Cn defined as follows: $\mathrm{Cn}(u) = \{A \mid u \vdash A\}$. A *theory* of a Tarski consequence relation is a set of propositions $u$ such that $u = \mathrm{Cn}(u)$. As is well-known, the set of theories of any Tarski consequence relation is closed with respect to arbitrary intersections.

In many applications discussed in this book, it is convenient to use also a slight generalization of Tarski consequence relations that allows for *constraints*, that is, rules of the form $a \vdash$. Such generalized Tarski consequence relations still possess practically all the characteristic properties of ordinary Tarski consequence relations[1]. Note, in particular, that for languages having a falsity constant $\mathbf{f}$, such a generalization becomes unnecessary, since the rule $a \vdash$ can be safely identified with $a \vdash \mathbf{f}$.

A sequent $a \vdash b$ will be called *singular*, if $b$ contains no more than one proposition. The set of all singular sequents of a Scott consequence relation constitutes a generalized Tarski consequence relation that will be called its *Tarski subrelation*. The following lemma describes the set of its theories.

[1]Except that now the set of all propositions is not always a theory of a consequence relation.

**Lemma 2.5** *Theories of the Tarski subrelation of a Scott consequence relation* $\vdash$ *are precisely intersections of theories of* $\vdash$.

Actually, generalized Tarski consequence relations can be identified with singular Scott consequence relations, defined later in this section.

### 2.1.2 *Representation theorem*

Any set of sets of propositions $\mathcal{T}$ determines a Scott consequence relation $\vdash_{\mathcal{T}}$ defined as follows:

$$a \vdash_{\mathcal{T}} b \quad \equiv \quad \text{For any } u \in \mathcal{T}, \text{ if } a \subseteq u, \text{ then } b \cap u \neq \emptyset. \qquad \text{(GS)}$$

Actually, the above construction is quite general, since any Scott consequence relation can be generated in this way by the set of its theories – this is precisely the basic result about Scott consequence relations, called Scott Completeness Theorem in [Gabbay, 1981].

**Theorem 2.6** (**Scott Completeness Theorem**) *If* $\mathcal{T}_{\vdash}$ *is the set of all theories of a Scott consequence relation* $\vdash$, *then* $\vdash$ *coincides with* $\vdash_{\mathcal{T}_{\vdash}}$.

An important consequence of the above representation theorem is that Scott consequence relations are uniquely determined by their theories. Moreover, for more expressive languages the above representation theorem can serve as a basis of constructing full-fledged semantics. In this case the set of theories of a consequence relation will serve, eventually, as its canonical semantics.

The following simple lemma shows that inclusion among consequence relations is equivalent to inverse inclusion for their sets of theories. So, extending a consequence relation amounts to reducing the set of its theories.

**Lemma 2.7** $\vdash \subseteq \vdash_1$ *iff any theory of* $\vdash_1$ *is a theory of* $\vdash$.

### 2.1.3 *Compact sets of theories*

If a family $\mathcal{T}$ of sets of propositions generates a Scott consequence relation $\vdash$, any set from $\mathcal{T}$ will be a theory of $\vdash$. However, $\vdash$ will have in general other theories as well. Thus, the correspondence between Scott consequence relations and sets of theories is not in general one-to-one.

**Definition 2.2** A family of sets $\mathcal{T}$ will be called *compact*, if it coincides with the set of all theories of $\vdash_{\mathcal{T}}$.

The following lemma shows that compactness of $\mathcal{T}$ amounts to the validity of the corresponding 'generating' definition of $\vdash_{\mathcal{T}}$ for all sequents, not only for finite ones.

**Lemma 2.8** *$\mathcal{T}$ is compact iff for any sets $u, v$ of propositions,*

$$u \vdash_{\mathcal{T}} v \textit{ iff } (\forall w \in \mathcal{T})(u \subseteq w \rightarrow v \cap w \neq \emptyset).$$

The above lemma implies that there is a one-to-one correspondence between Scott consequence relations and compact sets of theories. Still, the following important result shows that we have a perfect match between *finite* sets of theories and their associated Scott consequence relations.

**Lemma 2.9** *Any finite set of theories is compact.*

Note that the above property does not hold for Tarski consequence relations, since their sets of theories are always closed with respect to intersections.

### 2.1.4 *Sequent theories*

By a *sequent theory* we will mean an arbitrary set of sequents.

Due to the 'Horn' form of the rules characterizing a Scott consequence relation, intersection of a set of Scott consequence relations is again a Scott consequence relation. This implies, in particular, the following

**Lemma 2.10** *For any sequent theory there exists a least Scott consequence relation containing it.*

The least Scott consequence relation that contains a sequent theory $\Delta$ will be denoted by $\vdash_{\Delta}$. The latter consists of all the sequents that can be inferred from $\Delta$ using the rules of consequence relations. Hence, it describes, in a sense, the logical content of $\Delta$. Accordingly, we will extend the notion of a theory to arbitrary sequent theories:

**Definition 2.3** A set of propositions will be called a *(propositional) theory of a sequent theory* $\Delta$, if it is a theory of $\vdash_{\Delta}$.

The next result seems almost obvious, but it is worth being stated. It says that propositional theories of a sequent theory $\Delta$ are precisely the sets of propositions that are closed with respect to the sequents from $\Delta$.

**Lemma 2.11** *A set $u$ of propositions is a theory of $\Delta$ if and only if, for any sequent $a \vdash b$ from $\Delta$, if $a \subseteq u$, then $b \cap u \neq \emptyset$.*

***Proof.*** The direction from left to right follows from Lemma 2.1 and the fact that $\Delta$ is included in $\vdash_\Delta$.

Let $\mathcal{T}$ denote the set of all theories that satisfy the condition of the lemma. This set of theories generates a consequence relation $\vdash_\mathcal{T}$. By the definition of the latter, every sequent from $\Delta$ belongs to $\vdash_\mathcal{T}$ (since all theories from $\mathcal{T}$ are closed with respect to it). Consequently, $\vdash_\Delta \subseteq \vdash_\mathcal{T}$, since $\vdash_\Delta$ is a least such consequence relation. Hence by Lemma 2.7, any theory from $\mathcal{T}$ will be a theory of $\vdash_\Delta$. This gives us the direction from right to left. □

Since any sequent theory determines a unique Scott consequence relation, we acquire a useful tool for constructing special consequence relations by restricting the corresponding sets of generating sequents. For example, the next definition introduces a class of Scott consequence relations that correspond to (generalized) Tarski consequence relations.

**Definition 2.4** A Scott consequence relation will be called *singular*, if it is generated by a singular sequent theory.

The following consequence of Lemma 2.5 describes such consequence relations in terms of their theories.

**Lemma 2.12** *A Scott consequence relation is singular if and only if the set of its theories is closed with respect to arbitrary intersections.*

As a consequence of the above result, any singular Scott consequence relation will always have a least theory.

#### 2.1.4.1 *Dependencies*

A more fine-grained description of sequent theories can be obtained by using the induced dependence relations among propositions. Such descriptions play an important role in logic programming.

Let us say that a proposition $B$ *depends* on a proposition $A$ with respect to a sequent theory $\Delta$ (notation $A \lhd_\Delta B$), if $\Delta$ contains a sequent of the form $a, A \vdash b, B$. A *dependency graph* of a sequent theory $\Delta$ is the directed graph $G_\Delta$ such that the nodes of $G_\Delta$ are the propositions occurring in $\Delta$, while the arcs are the pairs of propositions $(A, B)$ such that $A \lhd_\Delta B$.

Let us denote by $\leq_\Delta$ the transitive and reflexive closure of $\lhd_\Delta$.[2] Clearly, $A \leq_\Delta B$ holds if and only if either $A = B$, or there is a path from $A$ to $B$ in the dependency graph $G_\Delta$. In addition, $<_\Delta$ and $\approx_\Delta$ will denote,

[2]that is, the least pre-order containing $\lhd_\Delta$.

respectively, the corresponding strict partial order and induced equivalence relation:

$$A <_\Delta B \;\equiv\; A \leq_\Delta B \;\&\; B \not\leq_\Delta A,$$
$$A \approx_\Delta B \;\equiv\; A \leq_\Delta B \;\&\; B \leq_\Delta A.$$

For a set $u$ of propositions, $\lhd^u_\Delta$ will denote the restriction of $\lhd_\Delta$ to propositions from $u$. The restriction corresponds to the sub-graph of $G_\Delta$ that is induced by $u$. Similarly, we will use $\leq^u_\Delta$ to denote the transitive reflexive closure of $\lhd^u_\Delta$, while $<^u_\Delta$ will denote the corresponding strict order. Clearly, $A \leq^u_\Delta b$ holds if and only if either $A = B$, or $u$ contains a $\lhd$-path from $A$ to $B$.

From now on, we will suppress the index $\Delta$ in $\lhd_\Delta$ and derived relations whenever it will be clear from the context.

A set $u$ of propositions will be said to form a *loop* with respect to a sequent theory $\Delta$, if $u$ is an equivalence class of $\approx^u$. In other words, $u$ is a loop when the sub-graph of $G_\Delta$ that is induced by $u$ is strongly connected. Note that any singleton set of propositions $\{A\}$ is a (trivial) loop by this definition.

The following definition employs the above notions in describing some useful finiteness constraints on sequent theories.

**Definition 2.5** A sequent theory $\Delta$ will be called

- *locally finite*, if each node of $G_\Delta$ has no more than a finite number of incoming arcs;
- *acyclic*, if $\lhd$ is a well-founded relation: there is no infinite sequence $\{A_i \mid i \geq 0\}$ of propositions such that $A_{i+1} \lhd A_i$, for any $i$.
- *well-founded*, if $<^u$ is well-founded, for any set $u$ of propositions;
- *finitely well-founded*, if it is locally finite, and there is no infinite sequence $\{A_i \mid i \geq 0\}$ of *distinct* propositions such that $A_{i+1} \lhd A_i$, for any $i$.

As can be seen, a sequent theory $\Delta$ is locally finite if and only if, for any proposition $A$, $\Delta$ has no more than a finite number of sequents containing $A$ in their conclusions. This constraint will turn out to be essential for a 'classical' description of minimal and supported theories (see below).

An acyclic sequent theory has an especially simple structure. Thus, any such theory does not have nontrivial loops. A well-known alternative characterization of acyclicity is provided in the next proposition.

**Proposition 2.13** *A sequent theory $\Delta$ is acyclic if and only if there exists a ranking function $r$ from propositions to ordinals such that, for any sequent $a \vdash c$ from $\Delta$, $r(A) < r(C)$, for any $A \in a$ and $C \in c$.*

It is easy to verify that any acyclic theory will be well-founded, though not vice versa. An alternative description of well-foundedness in terms of 'initial' loops is given below.

**Lemma 2.14** *A sequent theory is well-founded if and only if any set $u$ of propositions contains a loop $l$ such that, for any $A \in u$, if $A \lhd B$, for some $B \in l$, then $A \in l$.*

***Proof.*** Assume first that a sequent theory is well-founded. Then any set $u$ of propositions must contain a minimal element with respect to $<^u$. Let $l$ be an equivalence class of $\approx^u$ that contains such a minimal element. Then $l$ is clearly a loop that satisfies the above condition. In the other direction, if $u$ contains such a loop $l$, then it is easy to verify that all propositions from $l$ are minimal with respect to the order $<^u$. Consequently, $<^u$ is well-founded. □

Turning to finitely well-founded theories, note first that if a sequent theory is not well-founded, it must have an infinite decreasing $\lhd$-path consisting of distinct propositions. Consequently, we immediately obtain

**Lemma 2.15** *Any finitely well-founded sequent theory is well-founded.*

An additional important property of finitely well-founded sequent theories is that they cannot have infinite loops (by the König Lemma). Finally, it should be clear that any finite sequent theory will be finitely well-founded (though not vice versa).

### 2.1.5 *Relativized consequence relations*

We will describe now relativization of the notions of a consequence relation and a sequent theory with respect to a given set of propositions. These relativized notions will turn out to be useful in what follows.

Given a Scott consequence relation $\vdash$ and a set $u$ of propositions, we will define the following consequence relation $\vdash^u$:

$$a \vdash^u b \;\equiv\; a \cap b \neq \emptyset \text{ or } a \cap u \vdash b, \overline{u}.$$

It can be easily verified that $\vdash^u$ is also a Scott consequence relation. It will be called a *restriction*, or *relativization*, of $\vdash$ with respect to $u$.

The effect of relativization of consequence relations amounts to restricting the inferences to propositions from $u$. Thus, the following lemma shows that only the latter propositions matter in determining theories of $\vdash^u$.

**Lemma 2.16** *A set $v$ of propositions is a theory of $\vdash^u$ if and only if $v \cap u$ is a theory of $\vdash$.*

***Proof.*** $v$ is a theory of $\vdash^u$, if and only if $v \nvdash^u \overline{v}$, that is, $v \cap u \nvdash \overline{u}, \overline{v}$. The latter means that $u \cap v$ is a theory of $\vdash$. □

It should be noted that the restricted consequence relation is not a subrelation of the source consequence relation. In fact, the two consequence relations are in general incomparable with respect to set inclusion.

The above relativization can be extended to sequent theories. Thus, the *restriction (or relativization) of a sequent theory* $\Delta$ with respect to a set $u$ of propositions will be defined as the following sequent theory $\Delta^u$:

$$\Delta^u = \{a \vdash b \cap u \mid a \vdash b \in \Delta \;\&\; a \subseteq u\}.$$

The above relativization of a sequent theory amounts to restricting its sequents to propositions from $u$. Note, in particular, that $u$ is a theory of $\Delta$ if and only if $\Delta^u$ does not contain sequents of the form $a \vdash$.

The following lemma shows that the relativization of sequent theories agrees with our earlier definition of relativization for consequence relations.

**Lemma 2.17** *$\vdash_{\Delta^u}$ coincides with the restriction of $\vdash_\Delta$ with respect to $u$.*

***Proof.*** A set $v$ of propositions is a theory of $\Delta^u$ if and only if it is closed with respect to the sequents from $\Delta^u$. As can be verified, the latter holds iff $u \cap v$ is closed with respect to the sequents of $\Delta$. But by the preceding lemma these are precisely the theories of the restriction of $\vdash_\Delta$ with respect to $u$. Hence the result. □

In view of the above lemma, $\Delta^u$ provides an adequate constructive description of relativization. In particular, we immediately obtain that a set $v$ is a theory of $\Delta^u$ if and only if $u \cap v$ is a theory of $\Delta$.

It can be easily verified that the dependency relation $\lhd_{\Delta^u}$ coincides with the restriction $\lhd^u_\Delta$ of the dependency relation for $\Delta$ with respect to $u$. Consequently, we immediately obtain also that $\leq_{\Delta^u}$, $<_{\Delta^u}$ and $\approx_{\Delta^u}$ coincide, respectively, with $\leq^u_\Delta$, $<^u_\Delta$ and $\approx^u_\Delta$. This suggests also the following convenient relativization of the notions of acyclicity and well-foundedness:

**Definition 2.6** A sequent theory $\Delta$ will be called *acyclic (resp. well-founded) on a set* $u$ of propositions, if $\Delta^u$ is acyclic (respectively, well-founded).

### 2.1.6 *The classical sequent calculus*

The distinctive role of Scott consequence relations in studying classical logical inference is based on the fact that they do not depend on a particular choice of connectives. Moreover, any classical connective is definable in them by introduction and elimination rules.

Let $\alpha \models A$ denote the fact that the proposition $A$ is true in an interpretation $\alpha$. Then any classical connective $\#(A_1, \dots, A_n)$ can be described by the following condition:

$$\alpha \models \#(A_1, \dots, A_n) \equiv \mathcal{F}_\alpha[A_1, \dots, A_n] \qquad (D(\#))$$

where $\mathcal{F}_\alpha[A_1, \dots, A_n]$ is a classical propositional formula in the meta-language generated by elementary propositions of the form $\alpha \models A_i$. As is well-known, an axiomatization of this connective can be always given in the form of introduction and elimination rules:

$$(\#E) \qquad \frac{\{a, a_i \vdash b, b_i\} \qquad (1 \leq i \leq k_1)}{a, \#(A_1, \dots, A_n) \vdash b}$$

$$(\#I) \qquad \frac{\{a, a_i \vdash b, b_i\} \qquad (1 \leq i \leq k_2)}{a \vdash b, \#(A_1, \dots, A_n)}$$

where $a_i$ and $b_i$ are subsets of $\{A_1, \dots, A_n\}$.

The above rules satisfy the *subformula property*, and allow to reduce any sequent involving classical connectives to a set of sequents containing atomic propositions only, without the use of the Cut rule.

Yet another description of classical connectives in the framework of Scott consequence relations (see [Gabbay, 1981; Segerberg, 1982]) can always be given using a plain set of sequents having one of the following forms:

$$(\#E_0) \qquad a, \#(A_1, \dots, , A_n) \vdash b$$

$$(\#I_0) \qquad a \vdash b, \#(A_1, \dots, , A_n)$$

where $a$ and $b$ are subsets of $\{A_1, \dots, A_n\}$.

Finally, the well-known correspondence between the classical sequent calculus and usual (Hilbert-type) formalizations of classical logic is established by translating any sequent $a \vdash b$ into a classical formula $\bigwedge a \to \bigvee b$. By this correspondence, derivability among sequents reduces to classical entailment, and hence Scott consequence relations correspond precisely to deductively closed theories.

## 2.2 Minimal and Supported Theories

In this section we will provide a detailed description for two special kinds of theories of Scott consequence relations. To begin with, we will give a syntactic characterization for minimal theories.

**Lemma 2.18** *A set $u$ of propositions is a minimal theory of a Scott consequence relation $\vdash$ if and only if $u = \{A \mid \vdash \overline{u}, A\}$, and either $u \neq Pr$, or $Pr$ is the only theory of $\vdash$.*

***Proof.*** Assume first that $u$ is a minimal theory. If $\nvdash A, \overline{u}$, there must exist a theory $v$ such that $v \subseteq u$ and $A \notin v$. But $u$ is minimal, and hence $A \notin u$. In addition, if $A \notin u$, then $u \nvdash \overline{u}$ implies $\nvdash A, \overline{u}$ by Monotonicity.

Assume now that the above conditions are satisfied. Note first that if $u \neq Pr$, then there exists $A \notin u$, and hence $\nvdash A, \overline{u}$. This implies $\nvdash \overline{u}$, which means that there exists a theory $v$ of $\vdash$ such that $v \subseteq u$. Moreover, if $u = Pr$, the same claim follows from the fact that $Pr$ is a theory. Now, the inclusion $u \subseteq \{A \mid\vdash \overline{u}, A\}$ says that if $A \in u$, and $v$ is a theory of $\vdash$ such that $v \subseteq u$, then $A \in v$. Consequently, $u \subseteq v$, and therefore $u$ is a minimal theory. □

Clearly, if a Scott consequence relation has only one minimal theory, it will be its *least theory*. Then it can be verified that the latter will coincide with the set of propositions that are provable in a consequence relation. Note, in particular, that singular Scott consequence relations always have such a least theory.

In the general case, a similar description of minimal theories can be obtained with respect to relativized consequence relations. Indeed, if $u$ is a minimal theory of $\vdash$, it will be a least theory of $\vdash^u$ (see Lemma 2.16). Consequently, we immediately obtain

**Corollary 2.19** *A theory $u$ of a Scott consequence relation $\vdash$ is minimal if and only if $\vdash^u A$, for any $A \in u$.*

The above result suggests a relatively straightforward procedure for checking the minimality of theories. Recall first that $u$ is a theory of a sequent theory $\Delta$ if and only if $\Delta^u$ does not contain sequents of the form $a \vdash$. Now, by the above result, a theory $u$ of $\Delta$ is minimal if and only if every proposition from $u$ is derivable from $\Delta^u$. Thus, due to the correspondence between sequent theories and classical propositional theories (see above), checking minimality of theories is reducible by this construction to a standard unsatisfiability problem.

The next result provides an important characterization of minimal theories in the well-founded case. As a matter of fact, this characterization constitutes a logical basis for many computational algorithms in logic programming.

**Theorem 2.20** *If $u$ is a theory of $\Delta$, and $\Delta$ is well-founded on $u$, then $u$ is a minimal theory if and only if it does not contain a loop $l$ such that $u \backslash l$ is also a theory of $\Delta$.*

***Proof.*** The direction from left to right is immediate. Assume that $u$ is a non-minimal theory of $\Delta$, that is, there is a theory $v$ of $\Delta$ such that $v \subset u$. By Lemma 2.14, the set $u \backslash v$ contains some initial loop $l$. Suppose that $u \backslash l$ is not a theory of $\Delta$. Then $\Delta$ must contain a sequent $a \vdash b$ such that $a \subseteq u \backslash l$ and $b \subseteq \overline{u} \cup l \subseteq \overline{v}$. Moreover, since $u$ is a theory of $\Delta$, we have $b \nsubseteq \overline{u}$, and consequently $b \cap l \neq \emptyset$. Clearly, if $B \in b \cap l$, then $A \lhd B$, for any $A \in a$. But $l$ is an initial loop in $u \backslash v$, and $a$ is disjoint from $l$, hence $a$ must be disjoint from $u \backslash v$. Consequently, $a \subseteq v$. But we have also $b \subseteq \overline{v}$, which contradicts the assumption that $v$ is a theory of $\Delta$. Thus, $u \backslash l$ is also a theory of $\Delta$. This completes the proof. □

Now we will describe a generalization of the notion of a minimal theory that will play an important role in what follows.

**Definition 2.7** A theory $u$ of a Scott consequence relation $\vdash$ will be called *supported* (or *pointwise minimal*), if, for any $A \in u$, the set $u \backslash \{A\}$ is not a theory of $\vdash$. A theory $u$ of a sequent theory $\Delta$ will be called *supported*, if it is a supported theory of $\vdash_\Delta$.

Supported theories are theories that do not permit removals of single propositions without violating the closure with respect to the sequents of a consequence relation. Such theories correspond to the models of pointwise circumscription [Lifschitz, 1987]. As we will see, they will correspond also to supported models of logic programs, as well as to a number of other familiar nonmonotonic formalisms.

Clearly, any minimal theory of a consequence relation will be supported, though not vice versa. Non-minimal supported theories may arise due to loops in the dependency relation. For example, $\{A, B\}$ may be a supported theory of a consequence relation containing $A \vdash B$ and $B \vdash A$, even when the empty set is also a (minimal) theory.

The next lemma provides a syntactic description of supported theories.

**Lemma 2.21** *A set $u$ of propositions is a supported theory of a Scott consequence relation $\vdash$ if and only if $u = \{A \mid u\backslash\{A\} \vdash \overline{u}, A\}$, and either $u \neq Pr$, or $Pr$ is a theory.*

***Proof.*** If $u$ is a supported theory, and $u\backslash\{A\} \nvdash A, \overline{u}$, there must exist a theory $v$ such that $u\backslash\{A\} \subseteq v \subseteq u$ and $A \notin v$. This is possible only if $u = v$, and hence $A \notin u$. In addition, if $A \notin u$, then $u \nvdash \overline{u}$ amounts to $u\backslash\{A\} \nvdash \overline{u}, A$.

Assume now that the above conditions are satisfied. If $u \neq Pr$, then there exists $A \notin u$, and hence $u\backslash\{A\} \nvdash A, \overline{u}$, which amounts to $u \nvdash \overline{u}$. Thus, $u$ is a theory of $\vdash$. Moreover, if $u$ is not proper, the same claim follows from the fact that $Pr$ is a theory. Now, the inclusion $u \subseteq \{A \mid u\backslash\{A\} \vdash \overline{u}, A\}$ says that if $A \in u$, then $u\backslash\{A\}$ is not a theory $\vdash$. Therefore $u$ is a supported theory. □

As for minimal theories, the above description of supported theories can be simplified by using relativized consequence relations.

**Corollary 2.22** *A theory $u$ of a consequence relation $\vdash$ is supported if and only if $u \setminus \{A\} \vdash^u A$, for any $A \in u$.*

***Proof.*** Immediate from the preceding lemma and the fact that $u\backslash\{A\} \vdash^u A$ is equivalent to $u \setminus \{A\} \vdash A, \overline{u}$. □

The above description says, in effect, that a theory $u$ of a sequent theory $\Delta$ is supported if and only if any proposition from $u$ is provable from $\Delta^u$, given the rest of the propositions from $u$.

As was mentioned earlier, non-minimal supported theories arise in sequent theories that involve inferential loops. This claim can be made precise as follows.

**Lemma 2.23** *If $u$ is a supported theory of $\Delta$, and $\Delta$ is acyclic on $u$, then $u$ is a minimal theory of $\Delta$.*

***Proof.*** By Theorem 2.20, a non-minimal theory $u$ of $\Delta$ must contain some loop $l$ such that $u\backslash l$ is also a theory. Since $\Delta$ is acyclic on $u$, $l$ can only by a trivial loop $\{A\}$, for some $A \in u$. But then $u\backslash\{A\}$ is a theory, and consequently $u$ is not a supported theory of $\Delta$. □

The above lemma will serve as a logical basis for many subsequent results in this book. A most immediate consequence of the lemma is

**Corollary 2.24** *Supported theories of an acyclic sequent theory coincide with its minimal theories.*

### 2.2.1 *Completion and loop-completion*

Now we are going to show that supported and minimal theories of a sequent theory $\Delta$ correspond to the classical models of certain classical logical theories that will be called *completions* of $\Delta$.

In what follows, we will always assume that the sequents of a sequent theory do not contain repeated occurrences of propositions. Note that since sequents $A, a \vdash A, b$ are trivial, while, e.g., $a \vdash A, A, b$ is reducible to $a \vdash A, b$, any sequent theory can be safely assumed to be of this form.

We will begin with the description of supported theories. For any locally finite sequent theory $\Delta$, we will define its *completion*, $comp(\Delta)$, as the set of all classical formulas of the form

$$A \leftrightarrow \bigvee\{\bigwedge(a \cup \neg b) \mid a \vdash b, A \in \Delta\},$$

plus the set $\{\neg \bigwedge a \mid a \vdash \in \Delta\}$.

If we will treat propositions of the underlying language as propositional atoms, it should be clear that the classical models of the above classical propositional theory will stand in one-to-one correspondence with certain sets of propositions. Moreover, the following result shows that they will correspond in this sense precisely to the supported theories.

**Theorem 2.25** *If $\Delta$ is a locally finite sequent theory, then the classical models of $comp(\Delta)$ correspond exactly to supported theories of $\Delta$.*

***Proof.*** Assume first that $\alpha$ is a model of $comp(\Delta)$, and $u_\alpha$ is the set of propositional atoms that hold in $\alpha$. Then the right-to-left implications corresponding to the equivalences from $comp(\Delta)$ secure that $u_\alpha$ is closed with respect to all sequents from $\Delta$, and therefore it is a theory of $\Delta$. Moreover, if $A \in u_\alpha$, then $\Delta$ must contain a sequent $a \vdash b, A$ such that $\bigwedge(a \cup \neg b)$ holds in $\alpha$. The latter means that $a \subseteq u_\alpha \backslash \{A\}$ and $b \subseteq \overline{u_\alpha}$. Consequently, we obtain $u_\alpha \backslash \{A\} \vdash \overline{u_\alpha}, A$, which implies that $u_\alpha \backslash \{A\}$ is not a theory of $\Delta$. Therefore, any model of $comp(\Delta)$ corresponds to a supported theory of $\Delta$.

Assume now that $u$ is a supported theory of $\Delta$, and $\alpha_u$ its associated classical interpretation. Since $u$ is closed with respect to $\Delta$, all right-to-left implications from $comp(\Delta)$ hold in $\alpha_u$. Suppose now that some left-to-right implication from $comp(\Delta)$ does not hold in $\alpha_u$. Then there exists $A \in u$ such that, for any sequent $a \vdash b$ from $\Delta$, either $a \not\subseteq u$, or $A \in a$, or $u \cap (b \backslash \{A\}) \neq \emptyset$. But by Lemma 2.11, this is exactly what is required for $u \backslash \{A\}$ being a theory of $\Delta$, contrary to our assumption that $u$ is a supported theory. Hence, $\alpha_u$ is a model of $comp(\Delta)$. □

Now we will turn to minimal theories. Recall first that a theory $u$ of a well-founded sequent theory $\Delta$ is minimal if and only if it does not contain a loop $l$ such that $u \backslash l$ is also a theory of $\Delta$ (see Theorem 2.20). Hence, the corresponding definition of completion should be extended to cover also nontrivial loops. In addition, in order to obtain a finitary syntactic description, we will consider only sequent theories that are finitely well-founded. Accordingly, given a finitely well-founded sequent theory $\Delta$, we will define its *loop-completion*, $lcomp(\Delta)$, as the deductive theory containing the following classical formulas:

- $\bigwedge a \to \bigvee b$, for any sequent $a \vdash b$ from $\Delta$;
- $\bigwedge l \to \bigvee \{\bigwedge (a \cup \neg(b \backslash l)) \mid a \vdash b \in \Delta \ \& \ l \cap b \neq \emptyset \ \& \ l \cap a = \emptyset\}$, for any loop $l$ of $\Delta$.

As can be seen, finite well-foundedness is required to secure the correctness of this definition, since it implies finiteness of both loops and the disjunctions in the formulas of the second kind.

Then we have

**Theorem 2.26** *If $\Delta$ is a finitely well-founded sequent theory, then the classical models of $lcomp(\Delta)$ correspond exactly to minimal theories of $\Delta$.*

***Proof.*** Assume first that $\alpha$ is a model of $lcomp(\Delta)$, and $u_\alpha$ is the corresponding set of propositional atoms. Then the formulas of a first kind in $lcomp(\Delta)$ secure that $u_\alpha$ is closed with respect to all sequents from $\Delta$, and therefore it is a theory of $\Delta$. Moreover, if $l \subseteq u_\alpha$, for some loop $l$, then the corresponding formula of the second kind implies that $\Delta$ must contain a sequent $a \vdash b$ such that $l \cap a = \emptyset$, and $\bigwedge (a \cup \neg(b \backslash l))$ holds in $\alpha$. The latter means that $a \subseteq u_\alpha \backslash l$ and $b \subseteq \overline{u_\alpha \backslash l}$, which implies that $u_\alpha \backslash l$ is not a theory of $\Delta$. Therefore, by Theorem 2.20, any model of $lcomp(\Delta)$ corresponds to a minimal theory of $\Delta$.

Assume now that $u$ is a minimal theory of $\Delta$, and $\alpha_u$ its associated classical interpretation. Since $u$ is closed with respect to $\Delta$, all the formulas of the first kind in $lcomp(\Delta)$ hold in $\alpha_u$. Suppose that some formula of the second kind does not hold in $\alpha_u$. Then there exists a loop $l \subseteq u$ such that, for any sequent $a \vdash b$ from $\Delta$, either $a \not\subseteq u \backslash l$, or $b \cap l = \emptyset$, or $u \cap (b \backslash l) \neq \emptyset$. Note also that, since $u$ is a theory of $\Delta$, if $a \vdash b \in \Delta$, $a \subseteq u$, and $b \cap l = \emptyset$, then $u \cap (b \backslash l) \neq \emptyset$. Consequently, for any $a \vdash b$ from $\Delta$, if $a \subseteq u \backslash l$, then $u \cap (b \backslash l) \neq \emptyset$. But by Lemma 2.11, this is exactly what is required for $u \backslash l$ to be a theory of $\Delta$, contrary to our assumption that $u$ is a minimal theory. Hence, $\alpha_u$ is a model of $lcomp(\Delta)$. □

In subsequent chapters, the above completions will be extended to bi-consequence relations.

## 2.3 Unitary Consequence Relations and Their Theories

As we will see in due course, an important class of nonmonotonic models can be described in terms of Scott consequence relations and sequent theories that have a unique theory. We will call such consequence relations *unitary* ones.

**Definition 2.8**

- A Scott consequence relation $\vdash$ will be called *unitary*, if, for any proposition $A$, either $\vdash A$, or $A \vdash$.
- A sequent theory $\Delta$ will be called *unitary*, if $\vdash_\Delta$ is a unitary consequence relation.

Thus, in a unitary consequence relation, any proposition is either proved, or refuted. The properties of such consequence relations are summarized in the next lemma.

**Lemma 2.27**

- *A nontrivial Scott consequence relation is unitary if and only if it has a single theory.*
- *A set $u$ of propositions is the only theory of a Scott consequence relation if and only if, for any proposition $A$,*

$$A \in u \quad \textit{iff} \quad \vdash A$$
$$A \notin u \quad \textit{iff} \quad A \vdash .$$

***Proof.*** Assume first that $\vdash$ is a nontrivial unitary consequence relation, and let $u = \{A \mid \vdash A\}$. Suppose that $u$ is not a theory of $\vdash$, that is $u \vdash \overline{u}$. By compactness, there are finite sets $a \subseteq u$ and $b \subseteq \overline{u}$ such that $a \vdash b$. Now, all propositions in $a$ are provable, so applying Cut a finite number of times, we obtain $\vdash b$. But all propositions in $b$ are refutable, so a finite number of applications of Cut will give us $\emptyset \vdash \emptyset$, contrary to our assumption that $\vdash$ is non-trivial. Thus, $u$ is a theory of $\vdash$. Suppose now that some other set $v$ is a theory of $\vdash$, and assume first that $A \in u \backslash v$, for some $A$. Then we have $\vdash A$, and consequently $v \vdash \overline{v}$ by Monotonicity, contrary to the assumption that $v$ is a theory of $\vdash$. Similarly, if $A \in v \backslash u$, then we have $A \vdash$, and therefore again $v \vdash \overline{v}$ (since $A \in v$). Hence $v$ should coincide with $u$, and therefore $u$ is the only theory of $\vdash$.

Assume now that $u$ is the only theory of $\vdash$. If $A \in u$, then $A$ belongs to all theories of $\vdash$ (since $u$ is the only theory), and therefore $\vdash A$. Moreover, since $u$ is a theory of $\vdash$, we have $u \nvdash \overline{u}$, and therefore $A \nvdash$ by Monotonicity. Now suppose that $A \notin u$. Then no theory of $\vdash$ contains $A$, and therefore $A \vdash$. In addition, $u \nvdash \overline{u}$ implies in this case $\nvdash A$ by Monotonicity.

Finally, assume that the above two conditions are satisfied for some set $u$, and suppose first that $\vdash$ is trivial. Then $\vdash A$, for any $A$, and therefore $u$ should include all propositions by the first condition. But we have also $A \vdash$, for any $A$, and therefore $u = \emptyset$ by the second condition. The obtained contradiction shows that $\vdash$ is nontrivial. In addition, the two conditions immediately imply that, for any proposition $A$, either $\vdash A$, or $A \vdash$, and therefore $\vdash$ is a unitary consequence relation. This completes the circle and shows that both the above claims hold. □

Thus, unitary consequence relations are precisely consequence relations that have a unique theory. Accordingly, in the general correspondence between consequence relations and classical deductively closed theories, unitary consequence relations correspond exactly to *complete* theories.

The importance of unitary consequence relations for our study creates the need for a more constructive description. To this end, we will extend the notion of a dependency graph of a sequent theory to literals.

Let $\mathcal{L}$ be the set of propositions appearing in a sequent theory $\Delta$. Below we will treat these propositions as propositional atoms. Accordingly, by a *literal* we will mean a formula of the form $A$ or $\neg A$, where $A \in \mathcal{L}$. Sets of literals will be represented as unions $x \cup \neg y$, where $x, y \subseteq \mathcal{L}$. In addition, for a literal $L$, we will denote by $\neg L$ the complementary literal. The notation $\neg l$, where $l$ is a set of literals, will have a similar meaning.

A *literal dependency relation* determined by $\Delta$ will be defined as a relation $\tilde{\lhd}_\Delta$ on the corresponding set of literals determined the following conditions:

$A\tilde{\lhd}_\Delta B$ holds, if $\Delta$ contains a sequent $a, A \vdash b, B$;
$\neg A\tilde{\lhd}_\Delta B$ holds, if $\Delta$ contains a sequent $a \vdash b, A, B$;
$A\tilde{\lhd}_\Delta \neg B$ holds, if $\Delta$ contains a sequent $a, A, B \vdash b$;
$\neg A\tilde{\lhd}_\Delta \neg B$ holds, if $\Delta$ contains a sequent $a, B \vdash b, A$.

As can be seen, the above dependency relation stems from a symmetric treatment of positive and negative literals, when a sequent $a \vdash b$ is viewed, in effect, as a disjunctive clause $\bigvee(\neg a \cup b)$. Note, in particular, that this relation is contrapositive in the sense that, for any literals $L_1$ and $L_2$, $L_1\tilde{\lhd}_\Delta L_2$ holds if and only if $\neg L_2\tilde{\lhd}_\Delta \neg L_1$.

All the notions defined earlier for atom dependency relations, namely derived orders, equivalence and loops, can be directly extended to literal dependency relations. Note, however, that loops will now be sets of literals, and hence they will be called *literal loops*, in order to distinguish them from atom loops, defined earlier. Also, due to the above contraposition property, if a set $l$ of literals is a loop, then the set $\neg l$ of complementary literals will also form a loop. In particular, we will have now that, for any proposition $A$, the singular sets $\{A\}$ and $\{\neg A\}$ will always form trivial literal loops.

Since the literal dependency relation is in some sense symmetric, the corresponding finiteness constraints can now be strengthened as follows:

**Definition 2.9** A sequent theory $\Delta$ will be called

- *strongly locally finite*, if each proposition occurs in no more than a finite number of sequents from $\Delta$;
- *strongly acyclic*, if $\tilde{\lhd}$ does not have infinite chains;
- *strongly well-founded*, if $\tilde{<}^u$ does not have infinite chains, for any consistent set $u$ of literals;
- *finitary*, if it is strongly locally finite, and $\tilde{\lhd}$ does not have infinite chains of *distinct* literals.

As before, strong well-foundedness is equivalent to existence of initial literal loops.

**Corollary 2.28** *A sequent theory is strongly well-founded if and only if any consistent set $u$ of literals contains a literal loop $l$ such that, for any $L \in u$, if $L\tilde{\lhd}L_0$, for some $L_0 \in l$, then $L \in l$.*

Finally, finitary sequent theories are strongly well-founded, and do not have infinite loops.

With the above notions at our disposal, we can give the following loop-based description of unitary sequent theories.

**Theorem 2.29** *If $\Delta$ is a strongly well-founded sequent theory, then a set $u$ of propositions is the only theory of $\Delta$ if and only if the set of literals $u \cup \neg\overline{u}$ does not contain a literal loop $l \cup \neg m$ such that $(u \backslash l) \cup m$ is also a theory of $\Delta$.*

***Proof.*** The direction from left to right is immediate. Assume now that $u$ is not the only theory of $\Delta$, and $v$ is another such theory. By Corollary 2.14, the set of literals $(u\backslash v) \cup \neg(v\backslash u)$ contains some initial loop $l \cup \neg m$. Suppose that $(u\backslash l) \cup m$ is not a theory of $\Delta$. Then $\Delta$ must contain a sequent $a \vdash b$ such that $a \subseteq (u\backslash l) \cup m$ and $b \subseteq \overline{(u\backslash l) \cup m}$. The first condition reduces to $a \subseteq u \cup m$ and $a \cap l = \emptyset$, whereas the second one—to $b \subseteq \overline{u} \cup l$ and $b \cap m = \emptyset$. Now, since $u$ is a theory of $\Delta$, either $a \not\subseteq u$, or $b \cap u \neq \emptyset$. Consequently, the preceding conditions give us that either $a \cap m \neq \emptyset$, or $b \cap l \neq \emptyset$.

Suppose first that $b \cap l \neq \emptyset$. Clearly, if $B \in b \cap l$, then $A \tilde{\lhd} B$, for any $A \in a$. But $l \cup \neg m$ is an initial loop in $(u\backslash v) \cup \neg(v\backslash u)$, and $a$ is disjoint from $l$, hence $a$ must be disjoint from $u\backslash v$. Consequently, $a \subseteq v$. But $v$ is a theory of $\Delta$, and therefore $b \cap v \neq \emptyset$. By the preceding conditions, this implies that there exists $B_1 \in b \cap (v\backslash u)$. Clearly $\neg B_1 \tilde{\lhd} B$ (since both belong to $b$). But since $l \cup \neg m$ is an initial loop, we obtain $\neg B_1 \in \neg m$, contrary to the condition $b \cap m = \emptyset$.

Suppose now that $A \in a \cap m$, for some $A$. Then $\neg B \tilde{\lhd} \neg A$, for any $B \in b$, and hence, by the same argument as before, $b \subseteq \overline{v}$. Since $v$ is a theory of $\Delta$, we have $a \not\subseteq v$, and consequently there exists $A_1 \in a \cap u\backslash v$. Clearly, $A_1 \tilde{\lhd} \neg A$ (since both belong to $b$). But since $l \cup \neg m$ is an initial loop, we obtain $A_1 \in l$, contrary to the condition $a \cap l = \emptyset$. The obtained contradiction shows that $(u\backslash l) \cup m$ should be a theory of $\Delta$. □

Just as for minimal and supported theories, the above theorem can be used for a characterization of unitary sequent theories in terms of some classical completion. Namely, a *literal loop-completion*, *llcomp*($\Delta$), of a finitary sequent theory $\Delta$ will be defined as a deductive theory containing the following classical formulas:

- $\bigwedge a \to \bigvee b$, for any sequent $a \vdash b$ from $\Delta$;
- $\bigwedge l \to \bigvee\{\bigwedge((a \cup \neg b)\backslash \neg l) \mid a \vdash b \in \Delta \ \&\ l \cap (\neg a \cup b) \neq \emptyset \ \&\ \neg l \cap (\neg a \cup b) = \emptyset\}$, for any literal loop $l$ of $\Delta$.

It turns out that the above deductive theory is complete. Moreover, if it is consistent, then $\Delta$ is a unitary sequent theory such that the model of $llcomp(\Delta)$ corresponds to its unique theory.

**Theorem 2.30** *Let $\Delta$ be a finitary sequent theory. Then $u$ is the only theory of $\Delta$ if and only if the corresponding classical interpretation $\alpha_u$ is a model of $llcomp(\Delta)$.*

***Proof.*** Assume first that $\alpha$ is a model of $llcomp(\Delta)$, and $u_\alpha$ is the corresponding set of propositional atoms. Then, due to formulas of the first kind in $llcomp(\Delta)$, $u_\alpha$ is a theory of $\Delta$. Moreover, if $l \subseteq \alpha$, for some loop $l = m \cup \neg n$ (that is, $m \subseteq u_\alpha$ and $n \subseteq \overline{u}_\alpha$), then the corresponding formula of the second kind implies that $\Delta$ must contain a sequent $a \vdash b$ such that $\neg l \cap (\neg a \cup b) = \emptyset$, and $\bigwedge((a \cup \neg b) \backslash \neg l)$ holds in $\alpha$. As can be verified, these conditions are equivalent to $a \subseteq (u_\alpha \backslash m) \cup n$ and $b \subseteq \overline{(u_\alpha \backslash m) \cup n}$. Consequently, $(u_\alpha \backslash m) \cup n \vdash_\Delta \overline{(u_\alpha \backslash m) \cup n}$, and therefore $(u_\alpha \backslash m) \cup n$ is not a theory of $\Delta$. By Theorem 2.29, $u_\alpha$ is the only theory of $\Delta$, and hence $\Delta$ is a unitary sequent theory.

Assume now that $\Delta$ is a unitary sequent theory, $u$ is the only theory of $\Delta$, and $\alpha_u$ its associated classical interpretation. Since $u$ is closed with respect to $\Delta$, all the formulas of the first kind in $llcomp(\Delta)$ hold in $\alpha_u$. Suppose that some formula of the second kind does not hold in $\alpha_u$. Then, for some loop $m \cup \neg n \subseteq \alpha_u$, we obtain that, for any $a \vdash b \in \Delta$, either $a \not\subseteq (u_\alpha \backslash m) \cup n$, or $b \not\subseteq \overline{(u_\alpha \backslash m) \cup n}$. By Lemma 2.11, this is exactly what is required for $(u \backslash m) \cup n$ to be a theory of $\Delta$, contrary to our assumption that $u$ is the only theory. Hence, $\alpha_u$ is a model of $llcomp(\Delta)$. □

Since a strongly acyclic sequent theory does not have non-trivial literal loops, the above completion for such a theory can be greatly simplified. The corresponding deductive theory, that we will denote by $acomp(\Delta)$, will contain the following formulas, for any proposition $A$:

$$A \leftrightarrow \bigvee\{\bigwedge(a \cup \neg b) \mid a \vdash b, A \in \Delta\},$$

$$\neg A \leftrightarrow \bigvee\{\bigwedge(a \cup \neg b) \mid a, A \vdash b \in \Delta\}.$$

It can be easily verified that, if the literal loops are restricted to singular sets of literals $\{A\}$ and $\{\neg A\}$, then $llcomp(\Delta)$ and $acomp(\Delta)$ are logically equivalent, and hence we obtain

**Corollary 2.31** *Let $\Delta$ be a strongly acyclic and strongly locally finite sequent theory. Then $u$ is the only theory of $\Delta$ if and only if the corresponding classical interpretation $\alpha_u$ is a model of $acomp(\Delta)$.*

In Chapter 5, the above completions will be used for a constructive description of exact nonmonotonic semantics.

## 2.4 Circumscription

It turns out that the framework of Scott consequence relations and their theories allows us to give a concise formal characterization of plain circumscription.

In the context of Scott consequence relations, the circumscription principle says that only minimal theories should matter in determining what should be inferred or refuted. Accordingly, for a given Scott consequence relation $\vdash$, we will define new a consequence relation, called a *circumscription* of $\vdash$, that is determined by minimal theories of $\vdash$:

**Definition 2.10** Let $\mathcal{T}_m$ be the set of all minimal theories of a Scott consequence relation $\vdash$. Then $\vdash_{\mathcal{T}_m}$ will be called the *circumscription* of $\vdash$ and will be denoted by $\vdash^c$.

As can be seen, $A \vdash^c$ holds if and only if $A$ is false in all minimal models of $\vdash$. In this case $A$ is taken to be false according to circumscription. Generally speaking, circumscription extends the set of propositions that are seen as refuted with respect to a consequence relation. Moreover, we will see that circumscription can even be characterized as a maximal extension of this kind that still preserves information that is provable in the source consequence relations.

The following theorem gives a syntactic characterization of the circumscribed Scott consequence relation.

**Theorem 2.32** *$a \vdash^c b$ holds iff $\vdash b', b$, for any $b'$ such that $\vdash b', A$, for every $A \in a$.*

***Proof.*** If $a \nvdash^c b$, then there must exist a minimal theory $u$ of $\vdash$ such that $a \subseteq u$ and $b \subseteq \overline{u}$. Now, if $A \in a$, then $\vdash A, \overline{u}$, since otherwise there must exist a theory that is smaller than $u$. Since $a$ is finite, this implies that there is a finite set $b' \subseteq \overline{u}$ such that $\vdash b', A$, for any $A \in u$. But $b$ is also included in $\overline{u}$, and hence $\nvdash b, b'$.

In the other direction, assume that there is $b'$ such that $\vdash b', A$, for any $A \in u$, and $\nvdash b, b'$. The second condition implies that there must exist a minimal theory $u$ disjoint from $b \cup b'$. But the first condition implies then that any such $u$ should include every $A \in a$. Consequently, $a \nvdash^c b$. □

As follows from the above theorem, $\vdash^c$ is uniquely determined by sequents without premises ('provable disjunctions') that belong to $\vdash$. Accordingly, two Scott consequence relations that coincide on such sequents will produce the same circumscription. This leads us to the following

**Definition 2.1**

- Two Scott consequence relations will be called *minimally equivalent* if they have the same premise-free sequents.
- Two sequent theories will be called *minimally equivalent* if their corresponding generated Scott consequence relations are minimally equivalent.

As the next lemma shows, minimal equivalence amounts to coincidence with respect to minimal theories.

**Lemma 2.33** *Two consequence relations (or sequent theories) are minimally equivalent iff they have the same minimal theories.*

***Proof.*** Follows from the fact that $\nvdash b$ holds if and only if $b$ is disjoint from some minimal theory of $\vdash$. □

The next result states the basic properties of the circumscribed consequence relation. The proofs are immediate.

**Lemma 2.34** *For any consequence relation* $\vdash$,

*(i)* $\vdash \subseteq \vdash^c$;
*(ii)* $\vdash$ *is minimally equivalent to* $\vdash^c$;
*(iii)* $\vdash$ *is minimally equivalent to* $\vdash_1$ *iff* $\vdash^c = \vdash_1^c$;
*(iv)* $\vdash^c$ *is a greatest consequence relation among minimal equivalents of* $\vdash$.

Thus, any equivalence class with respect to minimal equivalence has a greatest element which is also a circumscription of all consequence relations in the class. In addition, the fact that any consequence relation is minimally equivalent to its circumscription means that circumscription does not change the set of premise-free sequents.

### 2.4.1 *Partial deduction*

Clearly, finding circumscription of a sequent theory amounts to finding the corresponding derived set of premise-free sequents. An important algorithm for determining this set is based on the principle of *partial deduction* that can be formulated as follows:

*Replace a sequent $A, a \vdash c$ of a sequent theory $\Delta$ with the set*

$$\{a, a_i \vdash c, c_i \mid a_i \vdash c_i, A \in \Delta\}.$$

As can be seen, partial deduction allows to eliminate propositions from the premises of sequents, and hence it can be employed for obtaining the derived set of premise-free rules. The adequacy of this principle is based on the following result stating that partial deduction preserves minimal equivalence.

**Theorem 2.35** *If a sequent theory $\Delta'$ is obtained from $\Delta$ by an application of partial deduction, then $\Delta$ is minimally equivalent to $\Delta'$.*

***Proof.*** Let us assume that $\Delta'$ has been obtained from $\Delta$ by replacing a sequent $A, a_0 \vdash c_0$ with a set of sequents

$$a_0, a_i \vdash c_0, c_i, \qquad (*)$$

for every sequent $a_i \vdash c_i, A$ from $\Delta$ containing $A$ among its conclusions.

To begin with, any sequent from (*) can be obtained from $\Delta$ by the Cut rule. Consequently, $\vdash_{\Delta'} \subseteq \vdash_\Delta$, and hence any theory of $\Delta$ will be a theory of $\Delta'$. Suppose now that $u$ is a minimal theory of $\Delta'$ that is not a theory of $\Delta$. Then $u$ is not closed with respect to the sequent $A, a_0 \vdash c_0$, which means that $\{A\} \cup a_0 \subseteq u$ and $c_0 \subseteq \overline{u}$. Since $u$ is closed with respect to the sequents from (*), we have also that, for any sequent $a_i \vdash c_i, A$ from $\Delta$, if $a_i \subseteq u$, then $c_i \cap u \neq \emptyset$. But then it can be easily seen that $u \setminus \{A\}$ is a theory of $\Delta$, since it is closed with respect to all its sequents. Consequently, $u \setminus \{A\}$ will be a theory of $\Delta'$, contrary to our assumption that $u$ is a minimal theory of $\Delta'$. Hence any minimal theory of $\Delta'$ will also be a (minimal) theory of $\Delta$, which shows that $\Delta$ and $\Delta'$ are minimally equivalent. □

In the next chapter, this result will be extended to biconsequence relations.

### 2.4.2 *Compact circumscription*

Since circumscription is an extension of the source consequence relation, any theory of the circumscribed consequence relation will also be a theory of the original consequence relation. It turns out, however, that the set of all minimal theories of a Scott consequence relation is not always compact (see Definition 2.2). This means that in some cases the circumscription of a consequence relation $\vdash$ will have theories that are not minimal theories of $\vdash$.

**Example 2.1** Consider a Scott consequence relation $\vdash$ generated by the following sequents: $\{\vdash A_i, C\} \cup \{\vdash A_i, B_i\}$, for any $i \geq 0$. Then $u = \{A_i \mid i \geq 0\}$ will be a minimal theory of $\vdash$, but $\vdash^c$ will have also $u \cup \{C\}$ as a theory.

This unpleasant fact is important, since, as we will see, some useful features of circumscription will only hold under the condition that the set of minimal theories is compact.

Somewhat abusing our terminology, we will say that a circumscription of a Scott consequence relation $\vdash$ is *compact*, if any theory of $\vdash^c$ is a minimal theory of $\vdash$.

**Definition 2.11** A Scott consequence relation will be called *min-finite*, if it has only a finite number of minimal premise-free sequents.

The following lemma shows that min-finiteness is a weaker property than finiteness.

**Lemma 2.36** *If $\Delta$ is a sequent theory such that $\bigcup\{b \mid a \vdash b \in \Delta\}$ is finite, then $\vdash_\Delta$ is min-finite.*

***Proof.*** Let $h = \bigcup\{b \mid a \vdash b \in \Delta\}$. If $u$ is a theory of $\vdash_\Delta$, then by Lemma 2.11 $u \cap h$ will also be a theory of $\vdash_\Delta$. Now if $\nvdash_\Delta b \cap h$, for some $b$, then there exists a theory $u$ that is disjoint from $b \cap h$. But then $u \cap h$ is a theory that is disjoint from $b$, and therefore $\nvdash_\Delta b$. Consequently, if $\vdash_\Delta b$, then $\vdash_\Delta b \cap h$, and therefore there exists only a finite number of minimal premise-free sequents belonging to $\vdash_\Delta$. □

Now, the following important result shows that min-finiteness is a sufficient condition for the compactness of circumscription.

**Theorem 2.37** *If $\vdash$ is a min-finite Scott consequence relation, then it has a compact circumscription.*

***Proof.*** For any proposition $A$, we will denote by $\Delta^A$ a (finite) set of all minimal sequents of the form $\vdash A, b$ from $\vdash$. In addition, if $\nvdash A$, we will denote by $\Delta_A$ the set of all minimal sequents of the form $A, a \vdash$ such that $a \cap b \neq \emptyset$, for any sequent $\vdash A, b$ from $\Delta^A$ (note that in this case $b$ is always non-empty). Finally, we will denote by $\Delta$ the union of all $\Delta^A$ and $\Delta_A$, where $A$ ranges over propositions of the language. We are going to show now that theories of $\vdash_\Delta$ coincide with the minimal theories of $\vdash$.

It is easy to show that a set $u$ is closed with respect to all $\Delta^A$ if and only if $\nvdash \overline{u}$. Consequently, there exists a theory $u_0$ of $\vdash$ such that $u_0 \subseteq u$. In addition, $u$ is closed with respect to all $\Delta_A$ iff, for any $A$, either $A \notin u$, or there is a minimal sequent $\vdash b, A$ such that $b \subseteq \overline{u}$. Consequently, if $A \in u$, then $\vdash \overline{u}, A$ by Monotonicity. Therefore, there can be no models $u'$ of $\vdash$ such that $u'$ is a proper subset of $u$. Combining this with the earlier condition, we obtain that $u$ is a minimal theory of $\vdash$.

Assume now that there is a minimal theory $u$ of $\vdash$ that is not closed with respect to some sequent from $\Delta_A$. Then $A \in u$ and consequently $\vdash \overline{u}, A$, since $u$ is minimal. Therefore there must exist a minimal sequent $\vdash b, A$ such that $b \subseteq \overline{u}$. But then we have $a \not\subseteq u$, for any sequent $A, a \vdash$ from $S_A$, contrary to the assumption that $u$ is not closed with respect to $\Delta_A$. Consequently, all minimal models of $\vdash$ are closed with respect to all the sequents determining $\vdash_\Delta$, and hence are theories of the latter.

Now, since $\vdash_\Delta$ is determined by the minimal theories of $\vdash$, it coincides with the circumscription of $\vdash$. Therefore, the theories of $\vdash_\Delta$ coincide with theories of $\vdash^c$, and we are done. □

The proof of the above theorem contains, in fact, a procedure for constructing a circumscription of a Scott consequence relation in the finite case. To this end we must find first all minimal premise-free sequents that belong to $\vdash$ and then add to them all minimal sequents of the form $a \vdash$ ('refutable conjunctions') that do not change the former set of sequents.

Min-finiteness, though sufficient, is by no means a necessary condition for compactness of circumscription.

**Example 2.2** Consider a Scott consequence relation generated by a set of sequents $\{\vdash A, B_i\}$, for any $i \geq 0$. Clearly, this consequence relation is not min-finite. It has, however, only two minimal models, namely $\{A\}$ and $\{B_i \mid i \geq 0\}$, and hence its circumscription is compact.

We will show now that a compact circumscription is always generated by adding sequents of the form $a \vdash$ to the source Scott consequence relation. This result shows clearly that the main effect of circumscribing a consequence relation consists in enlarging the set of 'refutable conjunctions'.

**Lemma 2.38** *If $\vdash^c$ is compact, it coincides with the least Scott consequence relation containing all sequents of the form $a \vdash$ and $\vdash b$ from $\vdash^c$.*

***Proof.*** Let $\vdash^*$ be the least Scott consequence relation containing all sequents of the form $a \vdash$ and $\vdash b$ from $\vdash^c$. Let $u$ be a theory of $\vdash^*$. Assume that $u \vdash^c$. Then there exists a finite set $a \subseteq u$ such that $a \vdash^c$, contrary to the fact that $u$ is closed with respect to all rules $a \vdash$ from $\vdash^c$. Therefore $u \nvdash^c$, and hence $u$ is included in some theory $v_1$ of $\vdash^c$. Similarly, it can be shown that $\nvdash^c \overline{u}$, and hence $u$ includes some theory $v_2$ of $\vdash^c$. However, due to compactness, both $v_1$ and $v_2$ are minimal models of $\vdash$, and hence $v_1 = v_2 = u$. Therefore, all theories of $\vdash^*$ are theories of $\vdash^c$, and hence $\vdash^c \subseteq \vdash^*$. But the reverse inclusion is obvious, and consequently $\vdash^*$ coincides with $\vdash^c$. □

Note that, due to the fact that $\vdash$ and $\vdash^c$ are minimally equivalent, the set of sequents of the form $\vdash b$ in the formulation of the above theorem is actually the set of such sequents that belong to the source consequence relation $\vdash$.

Unfortunately, the above result does not hold for arbitrary Scott consequence relations, as is shown by the following example of a non-compact circumscription.

**Example 2.3** Let us consider a Scott consequence relation generated by the following set of sequents (for all natural $i$):

$$\vdash A_i, B_i \qquad B_i \vdash B_{i+1} \qquad B_i \vdash C \qquad B_i \vdash D$$

Minimal theories of this consequence relation are $\{A_1, \ldots, A_i, \ldots\}$ and $\{C, D, A_1, \ldots, A_n, B_{n+1}, B_{n+2}, \ldots\}$, for each natural $n$. However, its circumscription has also a non-minimal theory $\{C, D, A_1, \ldots, A_i, \ldots\}$. In addition, the circumscription contains sequents $C \vdash^c D$ and $D \vdash^c C$ that are not deducible from the set of constraints added to $\vdash$.

## 2.5 Supraclassicality

In this last section, we will describe a general class of consequence relations that subsume classical inference. Such *supraclassical* consequence relations will turn out to be suitable for describing the logical basis of traditional nonmonotonic formalisms such as default and modal nonmonotonic logics.

We will consider below consequence relations that are based on a classical language containing the ordinary classical connectives $\{\vee, \wedge, \neg, \rightarrow\}$. As usual, $\vDash$ will denote the classical entailment relation with respect to these connectives, and Th its associated classical derivability operator.

**Definition 2.12** A Tarski consequence relation $\vdash$ in a classical language will be called *supraclassical* if it subsumes classical inference, that is, $\vDash \subseteq \vdash$.

Supraclassicality is equivalent to the requirement that all theories of a consequence relation are deductively closed sets.

**Lemma 2.39** *A Tarski consequence relation is supraclassical iff all its theories are deductively closed sets.*

Supraclassicality allows for replacement of classically equivalent formulas in premises and conclusions of the rules. In addition, it allows to replace sets of premises by their classical conjunctions: $a \vdash A$ will be equivalent to $\bigwedge a \vdash A$. Accordingly, supraclassical Tarski consequence relations can be reduced to certain binary relations on the set of classical propositions, namely to relations satisfying, for instance, the following postulates (see [Bochman, 2001]):

**Dominance** If $A \vDash B$, then $A \vdash B$.
**Transitivity** If $A \vdash B$ and $B \vdash C$, then $A \vdash C$.
**And** If $A \vdash B$ and $A \vdash C$, then $A \vdash B \wedge C$.

By a *conditional theory* we will mean in what follows an arbitrary set $\Delta$ of rules of the form $A \vdash B$, where $A, B$ are classical propositions. Slightly abusing our earlier terminology, for a conditional theory $\Delta$, we will denote by $\vdash_\Delta$ the least supraclassical Tarski consequence relation containing $\Delta$, while $\mathrm{Cn}_\Delta$ will denote its associated provability operator. It can be easily verified that theories of $\vdash_\Delta$ are precisely deductively closed sets that are closed also with respect to the rules from $\Delta$. The following lemma gives a convenient alternative description of this consequence relation.

**Lemma 2.40** *If $\vdash_\Delta$ is a least supraclassical Tarski consequence relation containing a conditional theory $\Delta$, then, for any set $u$ of propositions, and any $A$, $u \vdash_\Delta A$ holds iff $A$ is derivable from $u$ by the rules from $\Delta$ and the classical entailment.*

It should be noted that provable equivalence with respect to a supraclassical consequence relation does not imply that the corresponding formulas are interchangeable in all contexts. For example, even if $A \vdash B$ and $B \vdash A$ hold, this does not imply, in general, $\neg A \vdash \neg B$ or $A \vee C \vdash B \vee C$. This property will hold, however, for 'fully' classical consequence relations described below.

**Definition 2.13** A Tarski consequence relation will be called *classical* if it is supraclassical and satisfies the deduction theorem:

**Deduction** If $a, A \vdash B$, then $a \vdash A \to B$.

Classical consequence relations already satisfy all the familiar rules of classical inference, such as Contraposition and Disjunction in the Antecedent. Moreover, each of the latter rules is sufficient for classicality.

Note that even classical consequence relations still do not coincide, in general, with the classical entailment $\vDash$; the latter can be described as the least classical (or, equivalently, least supraclassical) consequence relation. There is, however, an intimate connection between the classical entailment and classical consequence relations. Note that any rule $A \vdash B$ of a classical consequence relation is equivalent to $\vdash A \to B$. Consequently, any classical consequence relation can be seen as a classical entailment with some set of propositions added as additional, nonlogical axioms. And in this respect arbitrary supraclassical consequence relations allow additional freedom in that they permit the use of auxiliary nonlogical *inference rules* $A \vdash B$ that are not reducible to the corresponding material implications.

The following definition provides a two-step extension of supraclassicality to Scott consequence relations.

**Definition 2.14** A Scott consequence relation will be called *weakly supraclassical*, if it satisfies:

**Supraclassicality** If $a \vDash A$, then $a \vdash A$.

and *(strongly) supraclassical*, if it satisfies, in addition,

**Falsity** $\mathbf{f} \vdash$.

As can be seen, a Scott consequence relation is weakly supraclassical if and only if its Tarski subrelation is supraclassical. And just as for the latter, this requires all theories of a Scott consequence relation to be deductively closed. Strong supraclassicality amounts, in addition, to exclusion of the inconsistent theory $Pr$ from consideration. In the supraclassical case, such a model does not have a useful meaning (at least for our study), precisely because it is classically inconsistent. Accordingly, a Scott consequence relation is supraclassical if and only if all its theories are *consistent* deductively closed sets.

Just as for Tarski consequence relations, supraclassicality allows for replacement of classically equivalent formulas in premises and conclusions of sequents, as well as replacement of sets of premises by their classical conjunctions: $a \vdash b$ will be equivalent to $\bigwedge a \vdash b$. Multiple conclusions, however, cannot be replaced in this way by their classical disjunctions. Taking the simplest case, a sequent $\vdash B, C$ is not reducible to $\vdash B \vee C$; the latter says that any theory should contain $B \vee C$, while the former asserts a stronger constraint that any theory should contain either $B$ or $C$.

Finally, in order to obtain a classical sequent calculus, we need only to add the following postulate:

**Completeness** $\vdash A, \neg A$.

Let us say that a Scott consequence relation is *classical*, if it is supraclassical and satisfies Completeness. Any theory of a classical Scott consequence relation will contain either $A$, or $\neg A$, for any proposition $A$, and hence it will be a world. Consequently, such a relation will satisfy already all the postulates of a sequent calculus. In particular, we will have that any sequent $a \vdash b$ of such a consequence relation will be reducible to $\bigwedge a \vdash \bigvee b$, so it will be equivalent also to a classical Tarski consequence relation.

Completeness is equivalent to each of the following rules:

**(Disjunction$_1$)** $A \vee B \vdash A, B$.
**(Disjunction$_2$)** If $A, a \vdash b$ and $B, a \vdash b$, then $A \vee B, a \vdash b$.

As a general agreement for what follows, for a sequent theory $\Delta$ in a classical language, we will denote by $\overrightarrow{\Delta}$ the set of classical implications corresponding to the sequents from $\Delta$:

$$\overrightarrow{\Delta} = \{\bigwedge a \to \bigvee b \mid a \vdash b \in \Delta\}.$$

Then it can be easily verified that a proposition $A$ is provable in the least classical consequence relation containing $\Delta$ if and only if $\overrightarrow{\Delta} \vDash A$.

### 2.5.1 *Minimal and classically supported theories*

The definition of a minimal theory of a consequence relation can be directly extended to supraclassical relations. Moreover, its syntactic description (cf. Lemma 2.18) for the (strongly) supraclassical case can now be simplified by excluding the case of $Pr$:

**Lemma 2.41** *A set $u$ of propositions is a minimal theory of a supraclassical Scott consequence relation if and only if $u = \{A \mid \vdash \overline{u}, A\}$.*

The definition of a supported (pointwise-minimal) theory, however, was essentially syntactic, and hence it cannot be transferred directly to the supraclassical case due to the requirement of deductive closure. Still, a proper modification of this notion can be obtained as follows.

In the structural setting of general Scott consequence relations, a minimal change of a theory (= set of propositions) $u$ has been achieved simply by a removal of a single proposition. In a deductively closed setting, however, the corresponding change can be defined as a transition from a deductively closed theory to some its *maximal* proper sub-theory. Note that, for any deductive theory $u$, there always exist maximal deductive theories that are properly included in $u$. The set of all such sub-theories (plus $u$ itself) is usually denoted by $u\bot$; it plays an important role in the AGM theory of belief change (see [Alchourrón *et al.*, 1985; Bochman, 2001]). A similarity with the notion of pointwise minimality can be established if we identify deductively closed sets of propositions with the associated sets of worlds. Then every maximal sub-theory of a given theory $u$ can be obtained by adding a single new world to the set of worlds corresponding to $u$. In other words, these theories from $u\bot$ can be obtained as sets of the form $u \cap \alpha$, where $\alpha$ is a world that does not include $u$ (this is precisely the *Grove connection* [Grove, 1988]).

The following notion of a classically supported theory embodies this understanding of minimality.

**Definition 2.15** A theory $u$ of a supraclassical Scott consequence relation $\vdash$ will be called *classically supported* if $u$ is the only theory of $\vdash$ in $u\bot$.

Clearly, any minimal theory of a supraclassical consequence relation will be classically supported, though not vice versa. The next lemma provides a syntactic description of classically supported theories.

**Lemma 2.42** *A theory $u$ of a supraclassical Scott consequence relation $\vdash$ is classically supported if and only if $\alpha \cap u \vdash \overline{\alpha \cap u}$, for any world $\alpha$ that does not include $u$.*

***Proof.*** The above condition says, in effect, that no set of the form $u \cap \alpha$ is a theory of $\vdash$. Due to the Grove connection, this means that $u$ is classically supported. □

The above description of supported theories can be simplified by using relativized consequence relations. Note that if $\vdash$ is a supraclassical consequence relation, and $u$ is a deductively closed set, then the relativized consequence relation $\vdash^u$, as defined earlier, will also be a supraclassical consequence relation.

For a deductively closed set $u$, let us denote by $\vdash^u_c$ the least *classical* consequence relation containing $\vdash^u$. Then we have

**Corollary 2.43** *A theory $u$ of a consequence relation $\vdash$ is classically supported if and only if $\vdash^u_c A$, for any $A \in u$.*

***Proof.*** Note first that theories of $\vdash^u_c$ are precisely theories of $\vdash^u$ that are worlds. Consequently, the above condition says that $u \subseteq \alpha$, for any world $\alpha$ that is a theory of $\vdash^u$, that is, $\alpha \nvdash^u \overline{\alpha}$. By Lemma 2.16, $\alpha$ is a theory of $\vdash^u$ if and only if $\alpha \cap u$ is a theory of $\vdash$. Hence the result follows from the preceding lemma. □

The above description can be transformed into a relatively simple algorithm of checking whether a theory is classically supported. Recall that $A$ is provable in the least classical consequence relation containing $\Delta$ if and only if $\overrightarrow{\Delta} \vDash A$. Consequently, we obtain

**Corollary 2.44** *A theory $u$ of a sequent theory $\Delta$ is classically supported if and only if $\overrightarrow{\Delta^u} \vDash A$, for any $A \in u$.*

Finally, we will give two sufficient conditions for coincidence of minimal and classically supported theories of a sequent theory. These conditions will play an important role in Chapter 9.

**Definition 2.16** A sequent theory in a classical language will be called

- *premise-free*, if it contains only sequents of the form $\vdash a$;
- *literal*, if it contains only sequents of the form $l \vdash m$, where $l, m$ are sets of classical literals.

**Theorem 2.45** *Classically supported theories of a premise-free or literal sequent theory coincide with its minimal theories.*

***Proof.*** Assume first that $\Delta$ is a premise-free sequent theory, and suppose that $u$ is a non-minimal theory of $\Delta$, that is, there is a theory $v$ of $\Delta$ such that $v \subset u$. Let $\alpha$ be an arbitrary world that includes $v$, but does not include $u$. Then $u \cap \alpha$ will also be closed with respect to all the sequents from $\Delta$, and hence $u$ will not be classically supported. Indeed, if $\vdash a \in \Delta$, then $A \in v$, for some $A \in a$ (since $v$ is a theory). Consequently $A \in \alpha \cap u$, and hence $a \cap (\alpha \cap u) \neq \emptyset$.

Assume now that $\Delta$ is a literal sequent theory, and let $\alpha$ be a world that contains all literals from $v$, negations of all literals from $u \backslash v$, and $u \nsubseteq \alpha$ (the latter condition is needed only if the second set of literals is empty). Now, if $a \vdash b \in \Delta$ and $a \subseteq u \cap \alpha$, then $a \subseteq v$ (since $a$ is a set of literals), and hence $A \in v$, for some literal $A \in b$. Consequently $A \in \alpha \cap u$, and hence $b \cap (\alpha \cap u) \neq \emptyset$. Thus, $u \cap \alpha$ is closed with respect to all the sequents from $\Delta$, and hence $u$ is not classically supported. □

The following simple example shows that, when the above conditions are not satisfied, a sequent theory may have classically supported models that are not minimal.

**Example 2.4** The sequent theory $\Delta = \{p \vdash q;\ q \vdash p;\ \vdash p \vee q\}$ is neither a premise-free, nor a literal one. Using Corollary 2.44, it can be verified that $\mathrm{Th}(p, q)$ is a supported theory of $\Delta$, but it is not minimal, since $\mathrm{Th}(p \vee q)$ is a least theory of $\Delta$.

This completes our description of the facts and properties of ordinary consequence relations that will be used in subsequent chapters.

# Chapter 3

# Biconsequence Relations

Speaking generally, biconsequence relations, introduced below, are specialized consequence relations for reasoning with respect to a pair of contexts. On the interpretation suitable for nonmonotonic reasoning, one of these contexts is the main one, while the other context provides assumptions, or explanations, that justify inferences in the main context. It is precisely this separation of inferences and their justifications that will create a possibility of explanatory nonmonotonic reasoning.

As we will see, however, quite a diverse understanding of the role and nature of such explanations will arise in our study. Accordingly, remaining uncommitted about such differences, in this chapter these two contexts will be termed, respectively, the *context of truth* and the *context of falsity.* In the truth context the propositions will be evaluated as being either true or non-true, while in the falsity context they will be evaluated as being false or non-false. These notions will be used, however, only as convenient generic terms, the first sign being that we will freely admit situations in which propositions are both true and false, or neither true nor false.

As a first benefit of the above terminological decision, we obtain that a 'bi-context' reasoning can also be interpreted as a reasoning with possibly inconsistent and incomplete information. Furthermore, as has been observed first by Belnap (see [Belnap, 1977]), reasoning with independent truth and falsity assignments is nothing other than a four-valued reasoning. This will tightly connect our study to the latter. Accordingly, biconsequence relations will provide a language-independent, structural description of four-valued reasoning.

In contrast to ordinary consequence relations, biconsequence relations turn out to permit introduction of additional structural rules. In this way, for instance, a formalization of partial logic, as well as of different kinds of three-valued logics, can be obtained. A number of such rules will be described in what follows; they will provide us later with a formal description of logics adequate for different nonmonotonic semantics.

Though the formalism of biconsequence relations will later provide a logical basis for nonmonotonic reasoning and logic programming, the main content of the next two chapters is independent of these applications (though they certainly contribute to the significance of dealing with these issues).

## 3.1 Biconsequence Relations

By a *bisequent* we will mean an inference rule of the form:

$$a : b \Vdash c : d,$$

where $a, b, c, d$ are finite sets of propositions.

In accordance with the above informal description, we will employ in what follows two equally useful informal interpretations of bisequents. According to the *explanatory* (or *assumption*) *interpretation*, the above bisequent is interpreted as follows:

> *'If no proposition from b is assumed, and all propositions from d are assumed, then all propositions from a hold only if one of the propositions from c holds'.*

According to the second, *four-valued interpretation*, the above bisequent is interpreted as

> *'If all propositions from a are true and all propositions from b are false, then either one of the propositions from c is true or one of the propositions from d is false'.*

In accordance with this latter interpretation, propositions from $a$ and $b$ will be called, respectively, *positive* and *negative premises*, while that from $c$ and $d$—*positive* and *negative conclusions.*

The following definition provides a primary characterization of such bisequents; it will agree with both the interpretations above.

**Definition 3.1** A *biconsequence relation* is a set of bisequents that satisfies the following rules:

**Monotonicity** $\dfrac{a : b \Vdash c : d}{a' : b' \Vdash c' : d'}$, if $a \subseteq a'$, $b \subseteq b'$, $c \subseteq c'$, $d \subseteq d'$;

**Positive Reflexivity** $A : \Vdash A :;$

**Negative Reflexivity** $: A \Vdash : A;$

**Positive Cut** $$\frac{a : b \Vdash A, c : d \quad A, a : b \Vdash c : d}{a : b \Vdash c : d};$$

**Negative Cut** $$\frac{a : b \Vdash c : A, d \quad a : A, b \Vdash c : d}{a : b \Vdash c : d}.$$

As follows from the above description, a biconsequence relation can be seen as a fusion, or *fibring*, of two Scott consequence relations in the sense of [Gabbay, 1998]. This fusion gives a syntactic expression to combining two independent contexts.

**Remark 3.1** *Bisequents are quite similar to* quadrants, *introduced in [Langholm, 1996] for representing general reasoning with inconsistency and incompleteness (cf. also [Muskens, 1999]). Quadrants are also sequents having four structural positions, but they allow to define, in addition, different possible 'flows of inference' between them.*

In what follows, we will use the symbol $\Vdash$, possibly with indices, also for denoting biconsequence relations themselves.

The definition of a biconsequence relation is also extendable to arbitrary sets of propositions by accepting the *compactness requirement*:

**Compactness** $u : v \Vdash w : z$ iff $a : b \Vdash c : d$,

for some finite sets $a, b, c, d$ such that $a \subseteq u$, $b \subseteq v$, $c \subseteq w$ and $d \subseteq z$.

For a set $u$ of propositions, a *positive $u$-reduct* of a biconsequence relation $\Vdash$ will be defined as the following consequence relation $\Vdash^+_u$:

$$a \Vdash^+_u c \;\equiv\; a : \overline{u} \Vdash c : u.$$

It is easy to verify that the above description determines a Scott consequence relation. This simple fact will allow us to reduce many proofs below to the properties of ordinary consequence relations.

The following definition introduces the basic notions of a bitheory and theory of a biconsequence relation.

**Definition 3.2**

- A pair of sets of propositions $(u, v)$ will be called a *bitheory* of a biconsequence relation $\Vdash$ if $u : \overline{v} \nVdash \overline{u} : v$.

- A set $u$ of propositions will be called a *(propositional) theory* of $\Vdash$, if $(u, u)$ is a bitheory of $\Vdash$.

As can be seen, $(u, v)$ is a bitheory of $\Vdash$ if and only if $u$ is a theory of the positive $v$-reduct $\Vdash^+_v$. Similarly, $u$ is a theory of $\Vdash$ iff it is a theory of $\Vdash^+_u$. Propositional theories of a biconsequence relation will play an important role later in our study. For now, we will restrict our attention to bitheories.

The following lemma describes bitheories as pairs of sets that are closed with respect to the bisequents of a biconsequence relation:

**Lemma 3.1** *$(u, v)$ is a bitheory of a biconsequence relation $\Vdash$ if and only if, for any bisequent $a : b \Vdash c : d$ from $\Vdash$, if $a \subseteq u$ and $b \subseteq \overline{v}$, then either $c \cap u \neq \emptyset$ or $d \cap \overline{v} \neq \emptyset$.*

***Proof.*** If the above condition is not satisfied for some bisequent $a : b \Vdash c : d$, then we obtain $u : \overline{v} \Vdash \overline{u} : v$ by Monotonicity and Compactness, and hence $(u, v)$ is not a bitheory. In the other direction, if $u : \overline{v} \Vdash \overline{u} : v$, then, due to Compactness, there are finite sets $a, bc, d$ such that $a \subseteq u$, $b \subseteq \overline{v}$, $c \subseteq \overline{u}$, $d \subseteq v$ and $a : b \Vdash c : d$. □

By an *assumption theory* of a biconsequence relation $\Vdash$ we will mean any set of propositions $v$ such that $(u, v)$ is a bitheory of $\Vdash$, for some $u$. Thus, an assumption theory is an assumption component of some bitheory. Clearly, $v$ is an assumption theory of $\Vdash$ if and only if the positive $v$-reduct $\Vdash^+_v$ is a nontrivial Scott consequence relation.

### 3.1.1 *Semantics*

Now we are going to describe a generic semantics for biconsequence relations.

By a *bimodel* we will mean a pair of sets of propositions. A set of bimodels will be called a *binary semantics*. Note that a binary semantics can also be viewed as a *binary relation* on sets of propositions.

**Definition 3.3** A bisequent $a : b \Vdash c : d$ will be said to be *valid* in a binary semantics $\mathcal{B}$, if, for any bimodel $(u, v) \in \mathcal{B}$, if $a \subseteq u$ and $b \subseteq \overline{v}$, then either $c \cap u \neq \emptyset$, or $d \cap \overline{v} \neq \emptyset$.

For a binary semantics $\mathcal{B}$, let $\Vdash_{\mathcal{B}}$ denote the set of all bisequents that are valid in $\mathcal{B}$. Then a straightforward check of the rules for biconsequence relations gives us the following

**Lemma 3.2** *$\Vdash_{\mathcal{B}}$ is a biconsequence relation.*

Thus, any binary semantics determines a biconsequence relation. In order to prove completeness, we will show now that any biconsequence relation $\Vdash$ is determined in this sense by its *canonical semantics* defined as the set of bitheories of $\Vdash$.

Let $\mathcal{B}_{\Vdash}$ be the set of all bitheories of a biconsequence relation $\Vdash$. Clearly, this set constitutes a binary semantics in the above sense. Moreover, the following Representation Theorem shows that the source biconsequence relations is determined by this semantics.

**Theorem 3.3** **(Representation Theorem)** *If $\Vdash$ is a biconsequence relation, then it coincides with $\Vdash_{\mathcal{B}_{\Vdash}}$.*

***Proof.*** The inclusion $\Vdash\subseteq\Vdash_{\mathcal{B}_{\Vdash}}$ follows from Lemma 3.1. Assume now that $a_0 : b_0 \nVdash c_0 : d_0$. Fixing $a_0$ and $c_0$, we can define the following Scott consequence relation:

$$d \vdash b \quad \equiv \quad a_0 : b \Vdash c_0 : d.$$

Then the Completeness Theorem for Scott consequence relations implies that there is a set $v$ such that $d_0 \subseteq v$, $b_0 \subseteq \overline{v}$ and $a_0 : \overline{v} \nVdash c_0 : v$. Now, the positive $v$-reduct of $\Vdash$ is also a Scott consequence relation, and therefore there is a set $u$ such that $a_0 \subseteq u$, $c_0 \subseteq \overline{u}$, and $u : \overline{v} \nVdash \overline{u} : v$. Clearly, $(u, v)$ is a bitheory of $\Vdash$, and hence $a_0 : b_0 \nVdash_{\mathcal{B}_{\Vdash}} c_0 : d_0$. Thus, $\Vdash$ coincides with $\Vdash_{\mathcal{B}_{\Vdash}}$. □

Since biconsequence relations are determined by their bitheories, we immediately obtain that inclusion among biconsequence relations is equivalent to reverse inclusion for the sets of their respective bitheories.

**Lemma 3.4** $\Vdash \subseteq \Vdash_1$ *if and only if any bitheory of* $\Vdash_1$ *is a bitheory of* $\Vdash$.

***Proof.*** The direction from left to right is immediate. Let $a : b \Vdash c : d$ but $a : b \nVdash_1 c : d$, for some $a, b, c, d$. Then there is a bitheory $(u, v)$ of $\Vdash_1$ such that $u$ includes $a$ and disjoint from $c$, while $v$ is disjoint from $b$ and includes $d$. But $u : \overline{v} \Vdash \overline{u} : v$ by Monotonicity, and hence $(u, v)$ is not a bitheory of $\Vdash$. □

The next definition introduces an important class of bitheories.

**Definition 3.4** A bitheory $(u, v)$ of $\Vdash$ will be called *positively minimal*, if there is no bitheory $(u', v)$ of $\Vdash$ such that $u' \subset u$.

$(u, v)$ is a positively minimal bitheory of $\Vdash$ if and only if $u$ is a minimal theory of its positive $v$-reduct $\Vdash_v^+$. Consequently, Corollary 2.4 implies

**Lemma 3.5** *For any bitheory $(u, v)$ of $\Vdash$ there exists a positively minimal bitheory $(u_0, v)$ of $\Vdash$ such that $u_0 \subseteq u$.*

The following technical lemma provides a syntactic description of positively minimal bitheories. The proof is immediate from Lemma 2.18.

**Lemma 3.6** *A pair $(u, v)$ is a positively minimal bitheory of $\Vdash$ if and only if $: \overline{v} \nVdash : v$ and, for any proposition $A$,*

$$A \in u \text{ iff } : \overline{v} \Vdash A, \overline{u} : v.$$

As in Lemma 2.18, the condition $: \overline{v} \nVdash : v$ is unnecessary if $u$ is not the set of all propositions of the language. So it is required only in the latter, extreme case.

### 3.1.2 *Duality*

For a bisequent $\sigma = a : b \Vdash c : d$, we will denote by $\sigma^\circ$ the *dual* bisequent $d : c \Vdash b : a$. Similarly, for a biconsequence relation $\Vdash$, we will denote by $\Vdash^\circ$ the set of bisequents that are dual to that of $\Vdash$. It can be verified that $\Vdash^\circ$ is also a biconsequence relation; we will call it a biconsequence relation *dual* to $\Vdash$. Actually, it is easy to check that $(u, v)$ is a bitheory of $\Vdash^\circ$ if and only if $(v, u)$ is a bitheory of $\Vdash$.

The above notion of duality imposes derived duality relations on all the objects, conditions and constructions associated with biconsequence relations. Such duality considerations will save us much effort in what follows.

### 3.1.3 *Bisequent theories*

By a *bisequent theory* we will mean an arbitrary set of bisequents. Just as for ordinary consequence relations, for any bisequent theory $\Delta$ there exists a least biconsequence relation that contains it. We will denote this biconsequence relation by $\Vdash_\Delta$. The latter comprises of all the bisequents that can be inferred from $\Delta$ using the postulates of biconsequence relations.

The biconsequence relation $\Vdash_\Delta$ can be seen as describing the logical content of a bisequent theory $\Delta$. Accordingly, bisequent theories that generate the same biconsequence relation will be considered as logically equivalent.

Since $\Vdash_\Delta$ determines the logical content of $\Delta$, we will extend the notions of a bitheory and propositional theory to arbitrary bisequent theories:

**Definition 3.5**

- A pair of sets $(u, v)$ will be called a *bitheory of a bisequent theory* $\Delta$, if it is a bitheory of $\Vdash_\Delta$.
- A set of propositions $u$ will be called a *propositional theory of a bisequent theory* $\Delta$, if $(u, u)$ is a bitheory of $\Delta$.

As could be expected, the next result shows that the bitheories of $\Delta$ are precisely pairs of sets of propositions that are closed with respect to bisequents from $\Delta$. Actually, the proof repeats almost literally that of Lemma 2.11.

**Lemma 3.7** *A pair $(u, v)$ of sets of propositions is a bitheory of a bisequent theory $\Delta$ if and only if, for any bisequent $a : b \Vdash c : d$ from $\Delta$, if $a \subseteq u$ and $b \subseteq \overline{v}$, then either $c \cap u \neq \emptyset$, or $d \cap \overline{v} \neq \emptyset$.*

***Proof.*** The direction from left to right follows from Lemma 3.1 and the fact that $\Delta$ is included in $\Vdash_\Delta$.

Let $\mathcal{B}$ denote the set of all bitheories that satisfy the condition of the lemma. This set of bitheories generates a biconsequence relation $\Vdash_\mathcal{B}$. By the definition of the latter, every bisequent from $\Delta$ belongs to $\Vdash_\mathcal{B}$ (since all bitheories from $\mathcal{B}$ are closed with respect to it). Consequently, $\Vdash_\Delta \subseteq \Vdash_\mathcal{B}$, since $\Vdash_\Delta$ is a least such biconsequence relation. Hence by Lemma 3.4, any bitheory from $\mathcal{B}$ will be a bitheory of $\Vdash_\Delta$. This gives us the direction from right to left. □

As a consequence of the above result, we obtain the following description of propositional theories corresponding to bisequent theories:

**Corollary 3.8** *A set $u$ of propositions is a propositional theory of a bisequent theory $\Delta$ if and only if, for any bisequent $a : b \Vdash c : d$ from $\Delta$, if $a, d \subseteq u$, then $(b \cup c) \cap u \neq \emptyset$.*

As a general agreement for what follows, we will assume by default (whenever relevant) that bisequents $a{:}b \Vdash c{:}d$ of a bisequent theory do not contain repeated occurrences of propositions in the sense that $a, b, c, d$ are sets of propositions (rather than multi-sets), $a$ is disjoint from $c$, and $b$ is disjoint from $d$. In particular, if a bisequent of a bisequent theory is described as having the form $a{:}b \Vdash C, c{:}d$, we will presuppose that $C \notin c$ (and, of course, $C \notin a$). Such an agreement will simplify a lot of qualifications in what follows. Note in this respect that, since the logical content of a bisequent theory is determined by the generated biconsequence relation, any bisequent theory is reducible to an equivalent theory of this form.

For a set $v$ of propositions, a *positive $v$-reduct* of a bisequent theory $\Delta$ will be defined as the following sequent theory:

$$\Delta_v^+ = \{a \vdash c \mid a : b \Vdash c : d \in \Delta \ \&\ b \subseteq \overline{v} \ \&\ d \subseteq v\}.$$

As can be seen, $\Delta_v^+$ is obtained from $\Delta$ by fixing the assumption context to $v$. Accordingly, the following fact can be easily verified:

**Lemma 3.9** *A set $u$ of propositions is a theory of $\Delta_v^+$ if and only if $(u, v)$ is a bitheory of $\Delta$.*

By a *positive reduct* of a bisequent theory $\Delta$ we will mean the plain sequent theory, denoted by $\Delta^+$, that is obtained by removing the assumption context of bisequents from $\Delta$:

$$\Delta^+ = \{a \vdash c \mid a : b \Vdash c : d \in \Delta\}.$$

It turns out that many useful kinds of bisequent theories can be described using their positive reducts. In particular, the *(positive) dependency graph* of a bisequent theory $\Delta$ will be defined as the dependency graph of $\Delta^+$. Moreover, most of the derived notions and constraints defined earlier for sequent theories (see Definitions 2.5 and 2.9) will be transferred in this way to bisequent theories. In particular,

**Definition 3.6** A bisequent theory $\Delta$ will be called *(strongly) locally finite*, *(strongly) acyclic*, *(strongly) well-founded*, *finitely well-founded*, or *finitary*, if $\Delta^+$ is such.

### 3.1.4 *Four-valued representation*

To begin with, guided by Belnap's idea, we can identify the four truth-values $\top, \mathbf{t}, \mathbf{f}, \bot$ of a four-valued interpretation with the four possible subsets of the set of classical truth-values $\{t, f\}$, namely $\{t, f\}$, $\{t\}$, $\{f\}$ and $\emptyset$. Accordingly, $\top$ will mean that a proposition is both true and false (i.e., contradictory), $\mathbf{t}$ will mean that it is 'classically' true (that is, true without being false), $\mathbf{f}$ will mean that it is classically false (without being true), while $\bot$ will mean that it is neither true nor false (undetermined). This representation allows us, in turn, to see any four-valued interpretation as a pair of ordinary classical interpretations, corresponding, respectively, to assignments of truth and falsity to propositions. To be more exact, for any four-valued interpretation $\nu$ (under the above representation), we can define the following two satisfaction relations:

$$\nu \models A \quad \text{iff} \quad t \in \nu(A)$$
$$\nu \dashv A \quad \text{iff} \quad f \in \nu(A).$$

Clearly, the source 4-assignment can be restored from the above two valuations as follows:

$$\nu(A) = \top \quad \text{iff} \quad \nu \models A \text{ and } \nu \dashv A$$
$$\nu(A) = \mathbf{t} \quad \text{iff} \quad \nu \models A \text{ and } \nu \not\dashv A$$
$$\nu(A) = \mathbf{f} \quad \text{iff} \quad \nu \not\models A \text{ and } \nu \dashv A$$
$$\nu(A) = \bot \quad \text{iff} \quad \nu \not\models A \text{ and } \nu \not\dashv A.$$

The equivalence of these two representations shows that the 'binary' representation is fairly general and does not restrict the set of possible four-valued interpretations.

Taking into account the above representation of the four truth-values, a four-valued reasoning in general can be seen as reasoning about truth and falsity of propositions, the only distinction from classical reasoning being that the assignments of truth and falsity are independent of each other. Consequently, inference rules for such a reasoning could have a form of constraints on possible assignments, e.g., 'If $A$ is true, then $B$ is either true or false', *etc.* As can be seen, any constraint of this kind is expressible by a bisequent, which leads us to the following definition.

**Definition 3.7** A bisequent $a : b \Vdash c : d$ will be said to be *valid* with respect to a four-valued interpretation $\nu$, if $\nu \models A$, for every $A \in a$, and $\nu \dashv B$, for every $B \in b$, imply that either $\nu \models C$, for some $C \in c$, or $\nu \dashv D$, for some $D \in d$.

If $\mathbf{I}$ is a set of 4-interpretations, we will denote by $\Vdash_{\mathbf{I}}$ the set of all bisequents that are valid with respect to every interpretation in $\mathbf{I}$. It is easy to show that this set forms a biconsequence relation.

Finally, any bimodel $(u, v)$ can be identified with a four-valued interpretation by taking $u$ to be the set of true propositions and $v$ the set of propositions that are not false. Then the Representation Theorem immediately implies that any biconsequence relation is determined by some set of 4-interpretations.

**Corollary 3.10** *$\Vdash$ is a biconsequence relation if and only if $\Vdash = \Vdash_{\mathbf{I}}$, for some set of 4-interpretations* $\mathbf{I}$.

This shows that biconsequence relations provide an adequate formalization of the four-valued semantics. In the next chapter this representation will be extended to fully fledged four-valued logics.

## 3.2 Structural Rules

A distinctive feature of four-valued reasoning, a feature that does not hold for classical logic, is a possibility of imposing some nontrivial structural constraints on the set of possible four-valued interpretations. For example, we can restrict our valuations to those that do not assign the value $\top$ to propositions, and in this way will obtain, in effect, a system of three-valued reasoning. Similarly, we can exclude both non-classical values $\bot$ and $\top$ and thus obtain ordinary classical valuations. In this way, both three-valued and classical two-valued reasoning will be shown below to be special cases of our formalism.

On a syntactic side, the above mentioned constraints can be imposed by adding certain *structural* rules to biconsequence relations. In this section we will consider the constraints and their associated rules that will play an important role in our study of nonmonotonic reasoning. But though we will restrict our attention only to the constraints that will be relevant to the latter, the resulting picture will nevertheless be quite rich.

### 3.2.1 *Consistency*

Let us begin with biconsequence relations of the following kind:

**Definition 3.8** A biconsequence relation will be called *consistent*, if it satisfies the following rule:

**Consistency** $A : A \Vdash$

Consistency is equivalent to the following Import rules that allow to transfer propositions from positive conclusions to negative premises, and from negative conclusions to positive premises:

**(Positive Import)** $$\frac{a : b \Vdash c, A : d}{a : b, A \Vdash c : d}$$

**(Negative Import)** $$\frac{a : b \Vdash c : d, A}{A, a : b \Vdash c : d}$$

**Lemma 3.11** *Consistency is equivalent to each of the two Import rules.*

***Proof.*** We will show only the equivalence of Consistency and Positive Import, since the proof of the second equivalence is completely analogous.

Assume first that Consistency holds. Then $C, a : C, b \Vdash c : d$ by Monotonicity, and hence if $a : b \Vdash c, C : d$, we can infer $a : b, C \Vdash c : d$ by Positive Cut. Hence Positive Import holds. In the other direction, Consistency follows directly from Positive Import and Positive Reflexivity. □

The following definition gives us a semantic counterpart of Consistency.

**Definition 3.9** A bimodel $(u, v)$ will be called *consistent*, if $u \subseteq v$. A binary semantics will be called *consistent* if all its bimodels are consistent.

From the point of view of the four-valued representation, consistency amounts to the requirement that, for any four-valued interpretation $\nu$, $\nu \models A$ is incompatible with $\nu \dashv A$. In other words, any such interpretation must be consistent in the sense that no proposition can be both true and false. Note also that the basic semantic setting of *partial logic* (see, e.g., [Blamey, 1986]) can be identified with this interpretation, since it usually deals only with possible incompleteness of information.

The next theorem is actually a representation theorem for consistent biconsequence relations.

**Theorem 3.12** *A biconsequence relation is consistent if and only if it has a consistent binary semantics.*

***Proof.*** It is easy to verify that a consistent binary semantics validates Consistency, and hence determines a consistent biconsequence relation. In the other direction, it is sufficient to show that if $\Vdash$ is a consistent biconsequence relation, then all its bitheories are consistent. Indeed, suppose that $(u, v)$ is a bitheory of $\Vdash$ such that $u \not\subseteq v$. Then there exists a proposition $A$ such that $A \in u \cap \overline{v}$. But $A : A \Vdash$ by Consistency, and therefore $u : \overline{v} \Vdash \overline{u} : v$ by Monotonicity, contrary to our assumption that $(u, v)$ is a bitheory of $\Vdash$. Hence $u \subseteq v$, and consequently all bitheories of $\Vdash$ are consistent. □

As we will show in the next chapter, consistent biconsequence relations turn out to correspond to three-valued logics based on truth as the only distinguished value.

### 3.2.2 *Completeness*

We will briefly consider now biconsequence relations that are dual to consistent ones.

**Definition 3.10** A biconsequence relation will be called *complete*, if it satisfies the following rule:

**Completeness** $\Vdash A : A$

As can be easily seen, $\Vdash$ is a complete biconsequence relation if and only if its dual, $\Vdash^{\circ}$ is a consistent biconsequence relation. Accordingly, all the properties and results below can be obtained from those for consistent biconsequence relations by duality considerations.

To begin with, Completeness is equivalent to the Export rules that allow to transfer propositions from premises to conclusions:

**(Negative Export)** $$\frac{a : b, A \Vdash c : d}{a : b \Vdash c, A : d}$$

**(Positive Export)** $$\frac{A, a : b \Vdash c : d}{a : b \Vdash c : d, A}$$

A bimodel $(u, v)$ will be called *complete*, if $v \subseteq u$. A binary semantics will be called *complete* if all its bimodels are complete. Then we have

**Theorem 3.13** *A biconsequence relation is complete if and only if it has a complete binary semantics.*

In a four-valued setting, Completeness amounts to the requirement that, for any four-valued interpretation $\nu$, either $\nu \models A$, or $\nu \dashv A$. In other words, any such interpretation must be complete in the sense that any proposition should be either true or false in it (though it still can be both true and false). Such interpretations can also be considered as three-valued ones, though the third value is 'inconsistent' rather than 'undetermined'. As we will see in the next chapter, complete biconsequence relations will correspond to three-valued logics based on a *weak notion of truth* or *non-falsity*: instead of one distinguished value **t**, the latter use the two truth-values distinct from **f** as distinguished values.

### 3.2.3 *Scott biconsequence relations*

Now we will consider biconsequence relations that are both consistent and complete. As we will see, such biconsequence relations are reducible to ordinary Scott consequence relations.

**Definition 3.11** A biconsequence relation will be called a *Scott biconsequence relation* if it is both consistent and complete.

Scott biconsequence relations satisfy both the Import and Export rules. Accordingly, the joint effect of such rules amounts, in effect, to identification of positive premises with negative conclusions and negative premises with positive conclusions. In particular, we have that an arbitrary bisequent $a{:}b \Vdash c{:}d$ is equivalent to a reduced bisequent $a, d{:} \Vdash b, c{:}$. But the bisequents of the form $a{:} \Vdash b{:}$ determine a Scott consequence relation, so we immediately obtain

**Lemma 3.14** *A biconsequence relation* $\Vdash$ *is a Scott one if and only if there exists a Scott consequence relation* $\vdash$ *such that, for any* $a, b, c, d$,

$$a : b \Vdash c : d \text{ if and only if } a, d \vdash b, c.$$

***Proof.*** If the above equivalence holds, then both Consistency and Completeness are clearly valid for $\Vdash$, so it is a Scott biconsequence relation. In the other direction, if a biconsequence relation $\Vdash$ is a Scott one, then the above equivalence holds for a Scott consequence relation defined as follows:

$$a \vdash b \;\equiv\; a : \Vdash b :$$

□

Turning to semantic considerations, the joint effect of Consistency and Completeness amounts to restricting possible bimodels and bitheories to that of the form $(u, u)$.

**Definition 3.12** A bimodel of the form $(u, u)$ will be called a *Scott bimodel.* A binary semantics will be called a *Scott* one, if all its bimodels are.

Then, as a direct consequence of the representations for consistent and complete biconsequence relations, we obtain

**Theorem 3.15** *A biconsequence relation is a Scott one if and only if it has a binary Scott semantics.*

Scott biconsequence relations constitute, in a sense, the strongest kind of reasonable biconsequence relations. Thus, all the rules for biconsequence relations that will be considered in what follows will be valid also for Scott biconsequence relations.

### 3.2.3.1 *Scott-equivalence*

Recall that a set $u$ of propositions is a theory of a biconsequence relation $\Vdash$, if $(u, u)$ is a bitheory of $\Vdash$. Such 'Scott' bitheories will play an important role in our applications. In particular, we will be especially interested in transformations of biconsequence relations that preserve theories. The following notion of equivalence will turn out to be useful in this respect.

**Definition 3.13** Biconsequence relations will be said to be *Scott-equivalent*, if they have the same theories.

The above equivalence relation imposes a partition on the set of biconsequence relations. It turns out that each equivalence class contains a greatest element, namely the Scott biconsequence relation determined by the relevant set theories.

We will denote by $\Vdash^s$ the least Scott biconsequence relation containing a biconsequence relation $\Vdash$. Then we have

**Lemma 3.16** *The set of bitheories of* $\Vdash^s$ *coincides with the set of Scott bitheories of* $\Vdash$.

***Proof.*** $\Vdash^s$ is actually a least biconsequence relation that contains $\Vdash$ and all bisequents of the form $A{:}A \Vdash$ and $\Vdash A{:}A$. Consequently, by Lemma 3.7, bitheories of $\Vdash^s$ are precisely bitheories of $\Vdash$ that are closed with respect to the latter two sets of bisequents. As can be seen, such bitheories are precisely the Scott bitheories of $\Vdash$. □

The above result has a number of useful consequences. To begin with, we immediately obtain

**Corollary 3.17** $\Vdash$ *is Scott-equivalent to* $\Vdash_1$ *if and only if* $\Vdash_1^s = \Vdash^s$.

Yet another important consequence of the above lemma follows from the fact that the set of theories of a Scott biconsequence relation coincides with the set of theories of some Scott consequence relation. This implies that such a set is always chain-complete, and therefore we have

**Corollary 3.18** *Any theory of a biconsequence relation contains some minimal theory and is contained in some maximal theory of a biconsequence*

*relation.*

### 3.2.4 *Ordering*

Now we will describe biconsequence relations that can be seen as a 'common part' of consistent and complete biconsequence relations.

**Definition 3.14** A biconsequence relation $\Vdash$ is *ordered* if it satisfies the following rule:

**Ordering** $A : A \Vdash B : B$.

Ordering also has a number of equivalent reformulations, for example the following rule:

$$\frac{a : b \Vdash b : d \qquad a : c \Vdash c : d}{a : b \Vdash c : d}$$

Clearly, both consistent and complete biconsequence relations are ordered in the above sense. Moreover, the semantic condition corresponding to ordering is that each four-valued interpretation should be either consistent or complete:

**Definition 3.15** A binary semantics will be called *ordered* if it contains only consistent or complete bimodels.

**Theorem 3.19** *A biconsequence relation is ordered if and only if it has an ordered binary semantics.*

***Proof.*** It can be verified that an ordered semantics validates Ordering. So, it is sufficient to show that any bitheory of an ordered biconsequence relation is either consistent, or complete.

Let $(u, v)$ be a bitheory of an ordered biconsequence relation, and suppose that it is not consistent, that is, there exists a proposition $A \in u \cap \overline{v}$. But $(u, v)$ should be closed with respect to bisequents of the form $A : A \Vdash B : B$, and therefore, for any $B$ we have either $B \in u$, or $B \in \overline{v}$. The latter implies $v \subseteq u$, and therefore $(u, v)$ is a complete bitheory. Hence, any bitheory of $\Vdash$ is either consistent, or complete. □

As a direct consequence of the above theorem, we obtain

**Corollary 3.20** *A biconsequence relation is ordered if and only if it is an intersection of a complete and a consistent biconsequence relation.*

***Proof.*** Clearly, if a biconsequence relation is an intersection of a complete and a consistent biconsequence relation, then it is ordered, since Ordering holds in both. Now if $\Vdash$ is an ordered biconsequence relation, we will denote by $\Vdash^{\mathbf{t}}$ and $\Vdash^{\mathbf{f}}$ biconsequence relations determined, respectively, by all consistent and all complete bitheories of $\Vdash$. Then it is easy to see that $\Vdash$ is an intersection of these two biconsequence relations. □

### 3.2.5 *Regularity*

Now we will describe biconsequence relations that will play an especially important role in nonmonotonic reasoning.

**Definition 3.16** A biconsequence relation will be called *regular* if it satisfies

**Regularity** $$\frac{b : a \Vdash a : b}{: a \Vdash : b}$$

Regularity is a kind of an assumption coherence constraint. It says that a good set of assumptions should be such that it is compatible with taking these assumptions as actually holding. This feature is even more vivid in the following condition that is equivalent to Regularity:

**Reduction** $$\frac{a : b \Vdash c : d}{: b, c \Vdash : a, d}$$

The above condition implies, in particular, that any bisequent imposes a constraint on admissible sets of assumptions.

The next rule, which is also equivalent to Regularity, shows that Regularity supports some non-trivial derivability relations among bisequents:

**R-Cut**
$$\frac{a : b \Vdash c : d \quad \{a_0 : b, A \Vdash c_0 : d \mid A \in a\} \quad \{a_0 : b \Vdash c_0 : d, C \mid C \in c\}}{a_0 : b \Vdash c_0 : d}$$

As will be shown in Chapter 8, the above postulate will directly correspond to an ordinary Cut rule in a system of production inference.

**Lemma 3.21** *Regularity is equivalent to Reduction and to R-Cut.*

***Proof.*** *Regularity implies Reduction.* If $a : b \Vdash c : d$, then $a, d : b, c \Vdash b, c : a, d$ by Monotonicity, and hence $: b, c \Vdash : a, d$ by Regularity.

*Reduction implies R-Cut.* Assume that all the premises of R-Cut hold. Then we have $: b, c \Vdash : a, d$ by Reduction from the first premise. Combining the latter with $a_0 : b \Vdash c_0 : d, C$, for every $C \in c$, we obtain $a_0 : b, c \Vdash c_0 : d$ by applications of Negative Cut. Similarly, combining the last bisequent with $a_0 : b, A \Vdash c_0 : d$, for every $A \in a$, we derive $a_0 : b \Vdash c_0 : d$ by applications of Positive Cut.

*R-Cut implies Regularity.* By Negative Reflexivity, $: a, B \Vdash : b$, for any $B \in b$, and $: a \Vdash : b, A$, for any $A \in a$. Consequently, $a : b \Vdash b : a$ implies $: b \Vdash : a$ by R-cut. □

For consistent biconsequence relations, Regularity can be replaced with the following structural rule

**(C-Regularity)** $$\frac{A, a : b \Vdash : d}{a : b \Vdash : A, d}$$

C-Regularity is a special case of a Positive Export rule for bisequents that do not have positive conclusions. It implies, in effect, that, for consistent regular biconsequence relations, bisequents $a : b \Vdash : d$ are equivalent to both $: b \Vdash : a, d$ and $a, d : b \Vdash$. This property turns out to be quite useful in logic programming.

**Lemma 3.22** *A consistent biconsequence relation is regular if and only if it satisfies C-Regularity.*

***Proof.*** Assume first C-Regularity, and suppose that $b{:}a \Vdash a{:}b$. Then $b{:}a \Vdash {:}b$ by Negative Import, and hence ${:}a \Vdash {:}b$ by a number of applications of C-Regularity. Hence, Regularity holds.

Now assume Regularity, and suppose that $A, a{:}b \Vdash d$. Then ${:}b \Vdash {:}A, a, d$ by Reduction, and hence $a{:}b \Vdash {:}A, d$ by Positive Import. □

A semantic counterpart of Regularity is provided in the next definition.

**Definition 3.17** A binary semantics $\mathcal{B}$ will be called *quasi-reflexive* if, for any bimodel $(u, v)$ from $\mathcal{B}$, $(v, v)$ is also a bimodel in $\mathcal{B}$.

The following representation theorem shows that the quasi-reflexive semantics is adequate for regular biconsequence relations.

**Theorem 3.23** *A biconsequence relation* $\Vdash$ *is regular if and only if it has a quasi-reflexive binary semantics.*

***Proof.*** If $\mathcal{B}$ is a quasi-reflexive semantics, and the bisequent ${:}a \Vdash {:}b$ is not valid in $\mathcal{B}$, then there exists a bimodel $(u, v)$ such that $b \subseteq v$ and $a \cap b = \emptyset$. But $(v, v)$ is also a bimodel, and it invalidates $b{:}a \Vdash a{:}b$. Hence, Regularity holds for $\mathcal{B}$.

Suppose now that $\Vdash$ is a regular biconsequence relation with a bitheory $(u, v)$ such that $(v, v)$ is not a bitheory. Then by compactness $a{:}b \Vdash c{:}d$, for some $a, d \subseteq v$ and $b, c \subseteq \overline{v}$. Consequently, $:b, c \Vdash :a, d$ by Reduction, and therefore $u : \overline{v} \Vdash \overline{u} : v$ by Monotonicity, contrary to the assumption that $(u, v)$ is a bitheory of $\Vdash$. Thus, the set of bitheories of $\Vdash$ determines a quasi-reflexive canonical semantics. □

As a particular implication of the above semantic characterization, note that a set of propositions is a theory of a regular biconsequence relation $\Vdash$ if and only if it is an assumption theory of $\Vdash$. In other words, we have

**Corollary 3.24** *A set $u$ is a theory of a regular biconsequence relation $\Vdash$ if and only if $:\overline{u} \nVdash :u$.*

For a bisequent theory $\Delta$, we will denote by $\Vdash^r_\Delta$ the least regular biconsequence relation containing $\Delta$. Bitheories of $\Vdash^r_\Delta$ will be called *regular bitheories of* $\Delta$. Our next result describes such bitheories.

**Lemma 3.25** *A pair $(u, v)$ is a regular bitheory of $\Delta$ if and only if both $(u, v)$ and $(v, v)$ are bitheories of $\Delta$.*

***Proof.*** Let $\mathcal{B}$ denote the set of bitheories satisfying the above condition. Clearly, $\mathcal{B}$ is quasi-reflexive, and hence $\Vdash_\mathcal{B}$ is a regular biconsequence relation that includes $\Delta$. Therefore, $\Vdash^r_\Delta \subseteq \Vdash_\mathcal{B}$, and consequently any bitheory of $\mathcal{B}$ is a regular bitheory of $\Delta$. In the other direction, any regular bitheory of $\Delta$ should be closed with respect to $\Delta$, and hence it is a bitheory of $\Delta$. In addition, by Reduction, it should be closed with respect to all bisequents $: b, c \Vdash : a, d$ such that $a{:}b \Vdash c{:}d$ belongs to $\Delta$. By Corollary 3.8, this means that $v$ should also be a propositional theory of $\Delta$, and therefore any regular bitheory of $\Delta$ should belong to $\mathcal{B}$. □

Regularity constitutes a certain strengthening of the logic of bisequents determined by the rules of biconsequence relations. It turns out, however, that the effect of this strengthening can be captured directly by adding certain bisequents to a bisequent theory.

For a bisequent theory $\Delta$, we will denote by $\Delta^r$ the set of bisequents $\{: b, c \Vdash : a, d \mid a{:}b \Vdash c{:}d \in \Delta\}$. The bisequents of $\Delta^r$ could be called *assumption constraints* imposed by the corresponding bisequents from $\Delta$. Then we obtain that regular derivability among bisequents amounts to adding such assumption constraints to a bisequent theory.

**Corollary 3.26** $\Vdash^r_\Delta = \Vdash_{\Delta \cup \Delta^r}$.

***Proof.*** As can be verified, $(u, v)$ is a bitheory of $\Delta^r$ if and only if $v$ is a propositional theory of $\Delta$. Consequently, a pair $(u, v)$ is a regular bitheory of $\Delta$ if and only if it is a bitheory of $\Delta \cup \Delta^r$. Hence the result. □

### 3.2.6 *Semi-classicality and tightness*

We will now describe rather unusual biconsequence relations that will be very useful in the analysis of certain nonmonotonic semantics.

**Definition 3.18** A biconsequence relation will be called *semi-classical*, if it is regular, ordered and, for any two *different* propositions $A, B$, contains the following bisequents:

**Quasi-Consistency** $A, B : A, B \Vdash$ ;
**Quasi-Completeness** $\Vdash A, B : A, B$.

Clearly, if we remove the restriction that $A$ and $B$ are different propositions, we will obtain precisely the Consistency and Completeness postulates. With the restriction, however, these conditions state that no more than one proposition can be non-classical (that is, neither classically true, nor classically false). Accordingly, the following binary semantics will turn out to be adequate for such biconsequence relations.

By $v \triangle u$ below we will denote the symmetric difference of $u$ and $v$.

**Definition 3.19**

- A bimodel $(u, v)$ will be called *semi-classical*, if $v \triangle u$ contains no more than one proposition.
- A binary semantics $\mathcal{B}$ will be called *semi-classical* if it is regular, and all its bimodels are semi-classical.

A bimodel $(u, v)$ is semi-classical if it is 'almost classical': no more than one proposition may have the value distinct from truth **t** or falsity **f** in the associated four-valued interpretation. As will be shown in what follows, this pointwise deviation from classicality allows to model most regular kinds of nonmonotonic models.

The next theorem establishes a correspondence between semi-classical biconsequence relations and their associated semantics.

**Theorem 3.27** *A biconsequence relation is semi-classical if and only if it has a semi-classical semantics.*

***Proof.*** It can be easily verified that any semi-classical semantics validates the conditions for semi-classical biconsequence relations. In the other direction, it is sufficient to show that any bitheory $(u, v)$ of a semi-classical biconsequence relation $\Vdash$ is semi-classical in the above sense. Since $\Vdash$ is ordered, we have either $u \subseteq v$, or $v \subseteq u$. Assume that $u \subseteq v$, the other case can be proved similarly. If $v \neq u$, there exists $A \in v \backslash u$. Suppose that $v \backslash u$ contains also another proposition, $B$. Since $\Vdash A, B{:}A, B$, we will have then $\Vdash \overline{u} : v$, and therefore $u : \overline{v} \Vdash \overline{u} : v$, contrary to the assumption that $(u, v)$ is a bitheory. Hence $v \Delta u = \{A\}$, and therefore $(u, v)$ is semi-classical. □

The following properties of semi-classical biconsequence relations will play an important role in what follows.

**Lemma 3.28** *If* $\Vdash$ *is a semi-classical biconsequence relation, then*

*(1) If* $a{:}b \Vdash c, C{:}d$ *and* $C \notin a$, *then* $a{:}b, C \Vdash c{:}d$;
*(2) If* $a, A{:}b \Vdash c{:}d$ *and* $A \notin c$, *then* $a{:}b \Vdash c{:}d, A$;
*(3) If* $c \neq \emptyset$, *then* $a : b \Vdash c : d$ *iff* $a : b, c\backslash\{C\} \Vdash C : d$, *for each* $C \in c$;
*(4) If* $a \neq \emptyset$, *then* $a : b \Vdash c : d$ *iff* $A : b \Vdash c{:}d, a\backslash\{A\}$, *for each* $A \in a$;
*(5) If* $:b \Vdash c{:}a, d$ *and* $a{:}b, c \Vdash :d$, *then* $a{:}b \Vdash c{:}d$.

The above properties can be easily verified semantically, so a syntactic proof can safely be left as an exercise for the reader. Combining these properties, we obtain that in common cases an arbitrary bisequent is reducible to a set of bisequents of an especially simple form.

**Corollary 3.29** *If* $\Vdash$ *is a semi-classical biconsequence relation, then any bisequent* $a{:}b \Vdash c{:}d$ *such that* $a \cup c \neq \emptyset$ *and* $a \cap c = \emptyset$ *is equivalent to the set*

$$\{: b, c\backslash\{C\} \Vdash C : d, a \mid C \in c\} \cup \{A : b, c \Vdash : d, a\backslash\{A\} \mid A \in a\}.$$

Bisequents that have no more than one positive premise or positive conclusion will later be called *determinate* ones. As we will see in Chapter 8, such bisequents will play much the same role as Horn rules in classical logic. Accordingly, the significance of the above result will amount to the fact that, for semi-classical biconsequence relations, any bisequent is reducible to a set of determinate bisequents.

To conclude this section, we will briefly consider the case of consistent biconsequence relations.

**Definition 3.20** A biconsequence relation will be called *tight*, if it is semi-classical and consistent.

Note first that Consistency implies both Ordering and Quasi-Consistency. Consequently, we obtain

**Lemma 3.30** *A biconsequence relation is tight if and only if it is consistent, regular and satisfies Quasi-Completeness.*

In addition, a simplified reduction of bisequents in the tight case is described in the following corollary.

**Corollary 3.31** *If* $\Vdash$ *is a tight biconsequence relation, then any bisequent* $a : b \Vdash c : d$ *such that* $c \neq \emptyset$ *and* $a \cap c = \emptyset$ *is reducible to the set of bisequents*

$$\{: b, c \backslash \{C\} \Vdash C : d, a \mid C \in c\}.$$

***Proof.*** By Lemma 3.28 (2) and the Import rule, any bisequent $a{:}b \Vdash c{:}d$ such that $a \cap c = \emptyset$ is equivalent to $:b \Vdash c{:}a, d$. Now the claim follows from (3) of Lemma 3.28. □

### 3.2.7 *Invariance*

Finally, we will consider biconsequence relations that are based on the idea that reasoning with respect to the two contexts should be invariant with respect to the mutual replacement of the two contexts.

To begin with, it should be noted that the above idea will already be inappropriate for the explanatory interpretation of bisequents, since the latter presupposes an essential difference in the role and function of the two contexts. Accordingly, the Invariance rule, introduced below, will not be valid for the logical systems used to describe nonmonotonic reasoning. Still, the invariance idea makes good sense for the second, four-valued interpretation of bisequents. Namely, it amounts to the requirement that reasoning with respect to truth should have the same properties as reasoning with respect to non-falsity—after all, both coincide for the classical logical reasoning. Moreover, it will be shown that corresponding *invariant* biconsequence relations will provide a formalization of four-valued reasoning that preserves the *truth order* among the four truth-values. In addition, we will see that such biconsequence relations will be close relatives of relevant entailment. But most importantly, the resulting formalisms of invariant four-valued reasoning will turn out to be suitable for describing partial generalizations of the main nonmonotonic semantics.

**Definition 3.21** A biconsequence relation will be called *invariant*, if it satisfies the rule

**Invariance** $\dfrac{a : b \Vdash c : d}{d : c \Vdash b : a}$

As can be seen from the above description, a biconsequence relation $\Vdash$ is invariant if and only if it coincides with its dual $\Vdash^{\circ}$.

The following definition describes a semantic counterpart of Invariance.

**Definition 3.22** A binary semantics $\mathcal{B}$ will be called *symmetric*, if, for any bimodel $(u, v)$ from $\mathcal{B}$, $(v, u)$ also belongs to $\mathcal{B}$.

Symmetric semantics provides an exact representation for the above invariance principle—it secures that if $(u, v)$ is an admissible pair of contexts, then $(v, u)$ should also be an admissible combination of contexts.

As before, we have the following representation theorem.

**Theorem 3.32** *A biconsequence relation is invariant if and only if it has a symmetric binary semantics.*

***Proof.*** Let us verify first that any symmetric binary semantics determines an invariant biconsequence relation. Suppose that a bisequent $a : b \Vdash c : d$ is valid in a symmetric binary semantics $\mathcal{B}$, though $d : c \Vdash b : a$ is not valid in $\mathcal{B}$. Then there exists a bimodel $(u, v)$ such that $d \subseteq u$, $c \subseteq \overline{v}$, $b \subseteq \overline{u}$ and $a \subseteq v$. But $(v, u)$ is also a bimodel in $\mathcal{B}$, and it invalidates $a : b \Vdash c : d$, contrary to our assumptions.

To complete the proof, it is sufficient to show that the set of bitheories of an invariant biconsequence relation $\Vdash$ is symmetric. Assume that $(v, u)$ is not a bitheory of $\Vdash$, that is, $v : \overline{u} \Vdash \overline{v} : u$. Then $a : b \Vdash c : d$, for some finite $a \subseteq v$, $b \subseteq \overline{u}$, $c \subseteq \overline{v}$ and $d \subseteq u$. But we have $d : c \Vdash b : a$ by Invariance, and therefore $u : \overline{v} \Vdash \overline{u} : v$ by Monotonicity. Consequently, $(u, v)$ is not a bitheory of $\mathcal{B}$. This shows that the set of bitheories of $\Vdash$ is symmetric. □

Invariant biconsequence relations also admit an alternative, possible worlds semantics that will be described in the next chapter.

It is interesting to note that the invariant four-valued representation associated with the symmetric binary semantics imposes a peculiar understanding of the non-classical truth-values $\bot$ and $\top$. To begin with, note that the bimodels $(u, v)$ and $(v, u)$ determine the same classically true and classically false propositions; in other words, they provide the same classical information. On the other hand, if a proposition is undetermined in $(u, v)$ (that is, it has the value $\bot$ in the associated four-valued interpretation), it will be inconsistent in $(v, u)$ (that is, it will have the value $\top$). Consequently, any proposition that is undetermined (respectively, inconsistent) in some interpretation associated with a symmetric semantics will also be inconsistent (resp., undetermined) in some other interpretation. This feature obliterates to a certain extent the distinction between $\top$ and $\bot$, and makes the corresponding semantics quite similar to a three-valued one.

For a bisequent theory $\Delta$, we will denote by $\Vdash^i_\Delta$ the least invariant biconsequence relation containing $\Delta$. Bitheories of $\Vdash^i_\Delta$ will be called *invariant bitheories of* $\Delta$. Our next result provides a useful alternative description of such bitheories.

**Lemma 3.33** *A pair $(u, v)$ is an invariant bitheory of $\Delta$ if and only if both $(u, v)$ and $(v, u)$ are bitheories of $\Delta$.*

***Proof.*** Let $\mathcal{B}$ denote the set of bitheories satisfying the above condition. Clearly, $\mathcal{B}$ is invariant, and $\Vdash_{\mathcal{B}}$ includes $\Delta$. Therefore, $\Vdash^i_\Delta \subseteq \Vdash_{\mathcal{B}}$, and consequently any bitheory of $\mathcal{B}$ is an invariant bitheory of $\Delta$. In the other direction, any bitheory of $\Vdash^i_\Delta$ should be closed both with respect to $\Delta$, and (by Invariance) with respect to the bisequents that are dual to $\Delta$. As can be verified, the latter means that $(v, u)$ should also be a bitheory of $\Delta$, and therefore any invariant bitheory of $\Delta$ should belong to $\mathcal{B}$. □

Extending our earlier terminology, we will denote by $\Delta^\circ$ the set of bisequents dual to the bisequents of $\Delta$. Then we obtain

**Corollary 3.34** $\Vdash^i_\Delta = \Vdash_{\Delta \cup \Delta^\circ}$.

***Proof.*** As can be verified, $(u, v)$ is a bitheory of $\Delta^\circ$ if and only if $(v, u)$ is a bitheory of $\Delta$. Consequently, a pair $(u, v)$ is an invariant bitheory of $\Delta$ if and only if it is a bitheory of $\Delta \cup \Delta^\circ$. Hence the result. □

The above result shows, in effect, that invariant inference amounts to an ordinary bisequent entailment with respect to a 'symmetric' bisequent theory $\Delta \cup \Delta^\circ$.

## 3.3 Restricted Kinds of Biconsequence Relations

We will describe now biconsequence relations that are generated by bisequent theories of restricted kinds.

Two kinds of bisequents will be of special interest for our study. The first are bisequents without negative conclusions $a{:}b \Vdash c{:}$. Such bisequents will be called *default* ones, due to the obvious connection with the rules of default logic. The second are bisequents without positive premises ${:}b \Vdash$

$c{:}d$. Such bisequents will be called *autoepistemic* ones, again due to strong connections with autoepistemic logic that will be revealed in the sequel.

In a nutshell, the difference between these two kinds of bisequents can be described as follows. A default bisequent $a{:}b \Vdash c{:}$ can be viewed as an inference rule $a \vdash c$ that is conditioned by a set of negative assumptions $b$. In other words, such bisequents involve full-fledged inference capabilities with respect to the main context, but permit only a restricted (namely negative) kind of assumptions. In contrast, an autoepistemic bisequent ${:}b \Vdash c{:}d$ can be seen as a plain (disjunctive) assertion $c$ that is conditioned by a set of negative assumptions $b$ and a set of positive assumptions $d$. In other words, such bisequents have rich assumption capabilities, but allow us to make only plain positive factual assertions. The difference between these two kinds of rules creates a difference in representation capabilities of the logical systems that are based on these rules. The relationship between default and autoepistemic reasoning has traditionally occupied an important place in the study of nonmonotonic reasoning. It will play an important role also in our study.

In addition to the above distinction, we will also be especially interested in bisequents having no more than one proposition as their positive conclusions.

**Definition 3.23** A bisequent $a{:}b \Vdash c{:}d$ will be called *singular*, if $c$ contains no more than one proposition. A biconsequence relation will be called *singular*, if it is a least biconsequence relation containing some set of singular bisequents.

Singular biconsequence relations can be seen as natural bisequent counterparts of Tarski consequence relations. Their main advantage consists in lowering the complexity of logical and nonmonotonic reasoning that are based on such rules.

Just as for Tarski consequence relations, a characteristic property of singular biconsequence relations is the closure of positive parts of bitheories with respect to intersections. Thus, the following result is obtainable as an immediate consequence of Lemma 2.12.

**Lemma 3.35** *A biconsequence relation $\Vdash$ is singular iff, for any set of bitheories of the form $(u_i, v)$, the pair $(\bigcap u_i, v)$ is also a bitheory of $\Vdash$.*

As a consequence of the above result, if $v$ is an assumption theory of $\Vdash$, there always exists a least set $u_0$ such that $(u_0, v)$ is a bitheory of $\Vdash$. An immediate implication from this fact is the following simplified description of positively minimal bitheories for singular biconsequence relations:

**Corollary 3.36** *A pair* $(u, v)$ *is a positively minimal bitheory of a singular biconsequence relation* $\Vdash$ *iff* $:\overline{v} \nVdash\ :v$ *and* $u = \{A \mid: \overline{v} \Vdash A : v\}$.

### 3.3.1 *Default biconsequence relations*

We will begin our description with default bisequents.

**Definition 3.24** A biconsequence relation will be called *default* one, if it is a least biconsequence relation containing some set of default bisequents.

Default biconsequence relations are sets of bisequents that are derivable from some default bisequent theory. It can be easily verified that a biconsequence relation is a default one if and only if it is a least biconsequence relation that includes all its default bisequents.

Any biconsequence relation $\Vdash$ contains a greatest default biconsequence relation, namely the least biconsequence relation containing all the default bisequents from $\Vdash$. We will call it the *default subrelation* of $\Vdash$ and denote it by ${}_d\Vdash$. Similarly, a *singular default subrelation* of $\Vdash$ will be defined as the least biconsequence relation containing all the singular default bisequents from $\Vdash$.

The following lemma provides a direct syntactic description of this default subrelation.

**Lemma 3.37** *If* ${}_d\Vdash$ *is a default subrelation of* $\Vdash$, *then*

$$a : b\, {}_d\Vdash c : d \text{ if and only if } b \cap d \neq \emptyset \text{ or } a : b \Vdash c :$$

***Proof.*** Let $\Vdash^*$ denote the set of bisequents determined by the above condition. We will show first that this is a biconsequence relation. Reflexivity and Positive Cut are trivial, so we check only the Negative Cut.

Assume that $a{:}b, A \Vdash^* c{:}d$ and $a{:}b \Vdash^* c{:}d, A$. If either $A \in b$, or $A \in d$, then $a{:}b \Vdash^* c{:}d$, as required. So assume $A \notin (b \cup d)$. Then the second bisequent gives us that either $a{:}b \Vdash c{:}$, or $b \cap d \neq \emptyset$, which amounts to $a{:}b \Vdash^* c{:}d$. Thus, Negative Cut holds for $\Vdash^*$, and therefore it is a biconsequence relation.

Note now that $\Vdash^*$ contains all the default bisequents from $\Vdash$. Moreover, all the bisequents from $\Vdash^*$ should belong to any biconsequence relation that contains the default bisequents of $\Vdash$. Hence $\Vdash^*$ is the least such biconsequence relation, and therefore it coincides with ${}_d\Vdash$. □

Using our new terminology, we can say now that a biconsequence relation is default one if and only if it coincides with its default subrelation. Accordingly, we immediately obtain

**Corollary 3.38** *A biconsequence relation* $\Vdash$ *is a default one if and only if, for any* $a, b, c, d$,

$$a : b \Vdash c : d \text{ only if } b \cap d \neq \emptyset \text{ or } a : b \Vdash c :$$

The above description shows that any nontrivial bisequent of a default biconsequence relation is reducible to its corresponding default 'reduct'.

Finally, we will give a semantic description of default biconsequence relations.

**Definition 3.25** A binary semantics $\mathcal{B}$ will be called *negatively monotonic* if, for any $(u, v) \in \mathcal{B}$, if $v \subseteq v'$, then $(u, v') \in \mathcal{B}$.

Then the following theorem shows that default biconsequence relations are complete for negatively monotonic semantics.

**Theorem 3.39** *A biconsequence relation is a default one if and only if it has a negatively monotonic binary semantics.*

***Proof.*** For the direction from right to left, we will use Corollary 3.38. Let $\mathcal{B}$ be a negatively monotonic binary semantics. Assume that a bisequent $a{:}b \Vdash c{:}$ is not valid in $\mathcal{B}$. Then there exists a bimodel $(u, v)$ in $\mathcal{B}$ such that $a \subseteq u$, $b \subseteq \overline{v}$, and $c \subseteq \overline{u}$. Assume now that $d$ is some set disjoint from $b$. Then $(u, v \cup d)$ is also a bimodel in $\mathcal{B}$, and it invalidates the bisequent $a{:}b \Vdash c{:}d$. Consequently, the set of bisequents that are valid in $\mathcal{B}$ satisfy the condition of Corollary 3.38, and therefore they form a default biconsequence relation.

In the other direction, it is sufficient to show that the set of bitheories of a default biconsequence relation is negatively monotonic. Let $\Vdash$ be a default biconsequence relation generated by a set of default bisequents $\Delta$. Recall that the bitheories of $\Vdash$ are precisely pairs of sets that are closed with respect to bisequents from $\Delta$. It is easy to see also that if $(u, v)$ is closed with respect to some default bisequents, and $v \subseteq v'$, then $(u, v')$ will also be closed with respect to these bisequents. Consequently, the set of bitheories of $\Vdash$ will be negatively monotonic. □

As a useful by-product of the above representation theorem, the following corollary describes the set of bitheories of the default subrelation of a biconsequence relation. It will be used in subsequent chapters.

**Corollary 3.40** *A pair $(u, v)$ is a bitheory of ${}_d\Vdash$ if and only if there exists $v' \subseteq v$ such that $(u, v')$ is a bitheory of $\Vdash$.*

***Proof.*** Follows from the fact that the above description determines a least negatively monotonic set of bitheories that includes the set of bitheories of $\Vdash$. □

3.3.1.1 *Positive biconsequence relations*

Default bisequents of the form $a{:} \Vdash c{:}$ will be called *positive.* Such bisequents do not contain assumptions, and hence they correspond to ordinary inference rules. Accordingly, biconsequence relations that are generated by positive bisequents constitute yet another counterpart of Scott consequence relations (distinct from Scott biconsequence relations).

**Definition 3.26** A biconsequence relation will be called *positive*, if it is a least biconsequence relation containing some set of positive bisequents.

Clearly, positive biconsequence relations constitute a very special case of default biconsequence relations. As before, any biconsequence relation $\Vdash$ contains a greatest positive biconsequence relation, namely the least biconsequence relation containing all the positive bisequents from $\Vdash$. We will call it the *positive subrelation* of $\Vdash$ and denote it by ${}_p\Vdash$. The following observation provides a syntactic description of this subrelation. The proof is similar to the general default case.

**Lemma 3.41** *If ${}_p\Vdash$ is a positive subrelation of $\Vdash$, then*

$$a : b\,{}_p\Vdash c : d \text{ if and only if } b \cap d \neq \emptyset \text{ or } a :\Vdash c :$$

As a consequence, we immediately obtain

**Corollary 3.42** *A biconsequence relation $\Vdash$ is positive if and only if, for any $a, b, c, d$,*

$$a : b \Vdash c : d \text{ only if } b \cap d \neq \emptyset \text{ or } a : \Vdash c : \ .$$

The latter description allows to establish a direct one-to-one correspondence between positive biconsequence relations and Scott consequence relations.

**Lemma 3.43** *A biconsequence relation $\Vdash$ is positive if and only if there exists a Scott consequence relation $\vdash$ such that, for any sets $a, b, c, d$,*

$$a : b \Vdash c : d \text{ iff either } b \cap d \neq \emptyset, \text{ or } a \vdash c.$$

***Proof.*** Immediate from the preceding corollary and the fact that the set of bisequents $a : \Vdash c :$ forms a Scott consequence relation. □

Finally, we will give a convenient semantic description of positive biconsequence relations.

**Lemma 3.44** *A biconsequence relation $\Vdash$ is positive when $(u, v)$ is a bitheory of $\Vdash$ if and only if $u$ is a theory of $\Vdash$.*

***Proof.*** Assume first that a biconsequence relation $\Vdash$ satisfies the above condition. If $a{:} \nVdash c{:}$, then there exists a bitheory $(u, v)$ of $\Vdash$ such that $a \subseteq u$ and $c \subseteq \overline{u}$. Assume now that $b, d$ are two disjoint sets. Then $(u, d)$ is also a bitheory of $\Vdash$, and it invalidates the bisequent $a{:}b \Vdash c{:}d$. Consequently, $\Vdash$ satisfies the condition of Corollary 3.42, and therefore it is positive. In the other direction, it is easy to see that $(u, v)$ is closed with respect to a set of positive bisequents if and only if $(u, u)$ is closed with respect to them. Consequently, if $\Vdash$ is positive, it satisfies the above condition. □

### 3.3.2 *Autoepistemic biconsequence relations*

Now we will turn to autoepistemic bisequents.

**Definition 3.27** A biconsequence relation will be called *autoepistemic*, if it is a least biconsequence relation containing some set of autoepistemic bisequents.

As can be verified, $\Vdash$ is an autoepistemic biconsequence relation if and only if its dual $\Vdash^\circ$ is a default biconsequence relation. Due to this duality, we will omit all the proofs in this section, since they can be easily restored from the proofs given earlier.

Any biconsequence relation $\Vdash$ contains a greatest autoepistemic biconsequence sub-relation, namely the least biconsequence relation containing all the autoepistemic bisequents from $\Vdash$. We will call it the *autoepistemic subrelation* of $\Vdash$ and denote it by ${}_a\Vdash$. Similarly, a *singular autoepistemic subrelation* of $\Vdash$ will be defined as the least biconsequence relation containing all the singular autoepistemic bisequents from $\Vdash$.

A syntactic description of the autoepistemic subrelation is given below.

**Lemma 3.45** *If ${}_a\Vdash$ is an autoepistemic subrelation of $\Vdash$, then*

$$a : b\,{}_a\Vdash c : d \text{ if and only if } a \cap c \neq \emptyset \text{ or } : b \Vdash c : d.$$

Clearly, a biconsequence relation is autoepistemic if and only if it coincides with its autoepistemic subrelation. Accordingly, we obtain

**Corollary 3.46** *A biconsequence relation* $\Vdash$ *is autoepistemic if and only if* $a : b \Vdash c : d$ *holds only if* $a \cap c \neq \emptyset$ *or* $: b \Vdash c : d$.

The above description shows that any nontrivial bisequent of a autoepistemic biconsequence relation is reducible to its corresponding autoepistemic 'reduct'. Finally, a semantic description of autoepistemic biconsequence relations is given in the next definition.

**Definition 3.28** A binary semantics $\mathcal{B}$ will be called *positively monotonic* if, for any $(u, v) \in \mathcal{B}$, if $u \subseteq u'$, then $(u', v) \in \mathcal{B}$.

Then the following theorem shows that autoepistemic biconsequence relations are complete for positively monotonic semantics.

**Theorem 3.47** *A biconsequence relation is autoepistemic if and only if it has a positively monotonic binary semantics.*

3.3.2.1 *Minimal equivalence*

Coincidence on autoepistemic bisequents determines an important equivalence relation on general biconsequence relations and bisequent theories.

**Definition 3.29**

- Two biconsequence relations will be called *minimally equivalent* if they have the same autoepistemic bisequents.
- Bisequent theories $\Gamma$ and $\Delta$ will be called *minimally equivalent*, if $\Vdash_\Gamma$ is minimally equivalent to $\Vdash_\Delta$.

As can be expected, minimal equivalence amounts to coincidence of positively minimal bitheories (cf. Lemma 2.33).

**Lemma 3.48** *Two biconsequence relations or bisequent theories are minimally equivalent iff they have the same positively minimal bitheories.*

The equivalence class of an arbitrary biconsequence relation $\Vdash$ with respect to minimal equivalence always contains a least element, namely the autoepistemic subrelation of $\Vdash$. In addition, it always has a greatest element, namely the biconsequence relation determined by all positively minimal bitheories of $\Vdash$. For reasons that will be made clear in what follows, this latter biconsequence relation will be called a circumscription of $\Vdash$.

**Definition 3.30** A *circumscription* of a biconsequence relation $\Vdash$ (denoted by $\Vdash^{cir}$) is a biconsequence relation determined by all positively minimal bitheories of $\Vdash$.

The next lemma summarizes the properties of minimal equivalence.

**Lemma 3.49** *Biconsequence relations* $\Vdash$ *and* $\Vdash_1$ *are minimally equivalent if and only if one of the following conditions holds:*

*(1)* ${}_a\Vdash \subseteq \Vdash_1 \subseteq \Vdash^{cir}$;
*(2)* $\Vdash^{cir} = \Vdash_1^{cir}$;
*(3)* ${}_a\Vdash = {}_a\Vdash_1$.

Circumscription of biconsequence relations will be studied later in this chapter.

### 3.3.2.2 *Autoepistemic reduction and GPPE*

Finding the autoepistemic sub-theory of a bisequent theory will turn out to be an important stage in determining practically all nonmonotonic semantics of bisequent theories. Accordingly we describe below a general algorithm for computing such an autoepistemic sub-theory. It is based on the *Generalized Principle of Partial Evaluation (GPPE)* used in logic programming (see [Brass and Dix, 1995a; Dix and Müller, 1994; Sakama and Seki, 1994]).

GPPE for bisequent theories amounts to the following transformation:

> *Replace a bisequent* $A, a : b \Vdash c : d$ *of a bisequent theory* $\Delta$ *with the set of bisequents*
>
> $$\{a, a_i : b, b_i \Vdash c, c_i : d, d_i \mid a_i : b_i \Vdash c_i, A : d_i \in \Delta\}.$$

As can be easily seen, GPPE constitutes a straightforward generalization of the principle of partial deduction to biconsequence relations. Accordingly, the following consequence of Theorem 2.35 shows that GPPE preserves minimal equivalence.

**Corollary 3.50** *If a bisequent theory* $\Delta'$ *is obtained from* $\Delta$ *by an application of GPPE, then* $\Delta$ *is minimally equivalent to* $\Delta'$.

Clearly, GPPE can be used to eliminate bisequents containing positive premises. For instance, if $A$ does not occur in heads of bisequents from $\Delta$ at all, any bisequent containing $A$ among its positive premises can be simply eliminated. Speaking more generally, if a bisequent theory $\Delta$ does not contain trivial bisequents $a{:}b \Vdash c{:}d$ such that $a \cap c \neq \emptyset$, then applying GPPE to all bisequents of $\Delta$ that contain $A$ among their positive premises, we obtain a bisequent theory in which $A$ does not appear as a positive premise. Further details, as well as possible optimizations of this procedure can be found in [Brass and Dix, 1995b].

### 3.3.3 *Simple biconsequence relations*

Finally we will briefly describe biconsequence relations that are generated by bisequents of the form $:b \Vdash c:$. We will call them *simple bisequents.* Such biconsequence relations are both default and autoepistemic ones, and hence they have especially simple properties. We will omit almost all the proofs in this section also, leaving them as an exercise for the reader.

**Definition 3.31** A biconsequence relation will be called *simple*, if it is a least biconsequence relation containing some set of simple bisequents.

Simple biconsequence relations are sets of bisequents that are derivable from some set of simple bisequents. As before, any biconsequence relation $\Vdash$ contains a greatest simple biconsequence sub-relation; we will call it the *simple subrelation* of $\Vdash$ and denote it by ${}_s\Vdash$. Similarly, a *singular simple subrelation* of $\Vdash$ will be defined as the least biconsequence relation containing all the singular simple bisequents $:b \Vdash C:$ from $\Vdash$. The following lemma provides a syntactic description of the simple subrelation.

**Lemma 3.51** *If ${}_s\Vdash$ is a simple subrelation of $\Vdash$, then, for any $a, b, c, d$,*

$$a : b \; {}_s\Vdash c : d \text{ iff } a \cap c \neq \emptyset \text{ or } b \cap d \neq \emptyset \text{ or } : b \Vdash c :$$

Clearly, a biconsequence relation is simple if and only if it coincides with its simple subrelation. Accordingly, we immediately obtain

**Corollary 3.52** *A biconsequence relation $\Vdash$ is simple iff $a : b \Vdash c : d$ holds only if $a \cap c \neq \emptyset$ or $b \cap d \neq \emptyset$ or $: b \Vdash c :$.*

Thus, any nontrivial bisequent of a simple biconsequence relation is reducible to its corresponding simple 'reduct'. Actually, simple bisequent theories are simple also in the sense that they are almost devoid of an implicit (derived) content:

**Lemma 3.53** *If $\Delta$ is a simple bisequent theory, then, for any $a, b, c, d$,*

$$a : b \Vdash_\Delta c : d \text{ iff } a \cap c \neq \emptyset \text{ or } b \cap d \neq \emptyset \text{ or } : b_0 \Vdash c_0 :\in \Delta,$$

*for some* $b_0 \subseteq b$ *and* $c_0 \subseteq c$.

The proof of the above result follows immediately from the fact that the above description determines a simple biconsequence relation. As a consequence, a simple bisequent $: b \Vdash c :$ is derivable from a simple bisequent theory $\Delta$ if and only if it is subsumed by some bisequent $: b_0 \Vdash c_0 :$ from $\Delta$.

The following important result shows that simple biconsequence relation actually *coincide* with biconsequence relations that are both default and autoepistemic.

**Lemma 3.54** *A biconsequence relation is simple if and only if it is both a default and autoepistemic one.*

***Proof.*** The direction from left to right is immediate. Assume that $\Vdash$ is both default and autoepistemic, and we have $a{:}b \Vdash c{:}d$. Since $\Vdash$ is default, we infer that either $b \cap d \neq \emptyset$, or $a{:}b \Vdash c{:}$. But the latter bisequent implies that either $a \cap c \neq \emptyset$, or $:b \Vdash c:$ (since $\Vdash$ is also autoepistemic). Therefore, $\Vdash$ is simple by the preceding corollary. □

Finally, a semantic description of simple biconsequence relations is given in the next definition.

**Definition 3.32** A binary semantics $\mathcal{B}$ will be called (fully) *monotonic* if it is both positively and negatively monotonic.

Then the following theorem shows that simple biconsequence relations are complete for monotonic semantics.

**Theorem 3.55** *A biconsequence relation is simple if and only if it has a monotonic binary semantics.*

## 3.4 Circumscribed Biconsequence Relations

A *circumscription* $\Vdash^{cir}$ of a biconsequence relation $\Vdash$ was defined above as a biconsequence relation determined by all positively minimal bitheories of $\Vdash$. This notion of circumscription was suggested, in effect, in [Przymusinski, 1991a; Yuan and You, 1993] in the framework of logic programming.

Since positively minimal bitheories always exist, any non-trivial biconsequence relation has circumscription. As was shown earlier, it is the greatest biconsequence relation that is minimally equivalent to the source one.

Circumscription of a biconsequence relation can be seen as a *parameterized* circumscription that does not vary the assumption context. This view can be described formally using positive reducts of a biconsequence relation. Namely, let $\vdash^c_v$ denote the circumscription of the positive $v$-reduct $\Vdash^+_v$ of $\Vdash$. Then we have

**Lemma 3.56** *If* $\Vdash^{cir}$ *is a circumscription of* $\Vdash$*, then* $a : b \Vdash^{cir} c : d$ *holds iff* $a \vdash^c_v c$*, for any assumption theory* $v$ *of* $\Vdash$ *such that* $b \subseteq \overline{v}$ *and* $d \subseteq v$*.*

***Proof.*** $a : b \Vdash^{cir} c : d$ does not hold iff there exists a positively minimal bitheory $(u, v)$ of $\Vdash$ such that $a \subseteq u$, $b \subseteq \overline{v}$, $c \subseteq \overline{u}$ and $d \subseteq v$. As can be seen, in this case $v$ is an assumption theory of $\Vdash$ and, moreover, $u$ is a minimal theory of $\Vdash^+_v$. Consequently, the latter condition amounts to the fact that $a \vdash^c_v c$ does not hold. Hence the result. □

As a consequence of the above result, the basic facts about circumscription of biconsequence relations, stated below, are completely analogous to the corresponding facts for Scott consequence relations, including their proofs.

The following corollary from the above lemma provides a direct syntactic description of the circumscribed biconsequence relation. The proof is immediate from Theorem 2.32.

**Corollary 3.57** $a{:}b \Vdash^{cir} c{:}d$ *holds iff* $:b, b' \Vdash c, c'{:}d, d'$*, for any* $b', c', d'$ *such that* $:b' \Vdash c', A{:}d'$*, for every* $A \in a$*.*

As can be seen from this description, the circumscription is uniquely determined by the autoepistemic bisequents belonging to a biconsequence relation.

Practically all the results about circumscription of Scott consequence relations are extendable to biconsequence relations. This pertains also to *compact* circumscriptions, for which any theory of $\Vdash^{cir}$ is a positively minimal theory of $\Vdash$. The following results are straightforward extensions of the corresponding results for Scott consequence relations, stated in Chapter 2.

**Definition 3.33** A bisequent theory will be called *min-finite*, if, for any proposition $A$, it contains no more than a finite number of minimal bisequents of the form $: b \Vdash c, A : d$.

**Theorem 3.58** *If* $\Vdash$ *is a min-finite biconsequence relation, then it has a compact circumscription.*

Moreover, just as for Scott consequence relations, for compact circumscription only bisequents of the 'constraint' type $a : b \Vdash : d$ need to be added to $\Vdash$ in order to obtain $\Vdash^{cir}$.

**Lemma 3.59** *If $\Vdash^{cir}$ is compact, it is the least biconsequence relation containing all bisequents of the form $a : b \Vdash : d$ and $: b \Vdash c : d$ from $\Vdash^{cir}$.*

As before, this result does not hold for arbitrary biconsequence relations. A suitable counterexample can be easily obtained from the corresponding example given earlier for Scott consequence relations.

The above lemma suggests a general method of circumscribing a biconsequence relation. To this end we must find first all minimal autoepistemic bisequents that belong to $\Vdash$, and then add to them all (minimal) bisequents of the form $a : b \Vdash : d$ that do not change the former set of bisequents.

For default biconsequence relations, the above characterization of circumscription can be strengthened as follows:

**Lemma 3.60** *If $\Vdash^{cir}$ is a compact circumscription of a default biconsequence relation, then it is the least biconsequence relation containing all bisequents of the form $a : \Vdash : d$ and $: b \Vdash c :$ from $\Vdash^{cir}$.*

***Proof.*** Let $\Vdash_*$ be the least biconsequence relation containing all sequents of the form $a : \Vdash : d$ and $: b \Vdash c :$ from $\Vdash^{cir}$. Clearly, $\Vdash_* \subseteq \Vdash^{cir}$. Let $(u, v)$ be a bitheory of $\Vdash_*$. Then $: \overline{v} \nVdash_* \overline{u} :$. But $: b \nVdash_* c :$ holds only if $: b \nVdash^{cir} c :$. Consequently, $: \overline{v} \nVdash^{cir} \overline{u} :$, and therefore there exists a bitheory $(u_1, v_1)$ of $\Vdash^{cir}$ such that $u_1 \subseteq u$ and $v_1 \subseteq v$. Similarly, $u : \nVdash_* : v$ implies $u : \nVdash^{cir} : v$, and therefore there is a bitheory $(u_2, v_2)$ of $\Vdash^{cir}$ such that $u \subseteq u_2$ and $v \subseteq v_2$. Now, since $\Vdash$ is a default biconsequence relation, and $(u_1, v_1)$ is a positively minimal bitheory of $\Vdash$, both $(u_1, v)$ and $(u_1, v_2)$ are bitheories of $\Vdash$. But $(u_2, v_2)$ is also positively minimal in $\Vdash$, and consequently $u_1 = u_2 = u$. Moreover, $(u, v)$ is positively minimal in $\Vdash$, since otherwise $(u_2, v_2)$ would not be positively minimal. Thus, any bitheory of $\Vdash_*$ is a bitheory of $\Vdash^{cir}$, and therefore $\Vdash^{cir}$ coincides with $\Vdash_*$. □

The above strengthening considerably reduces the 'search space' for constructing circumscription by reducing it to bisequents of the form $a : \Vdash : d$. Note, however, that the circumscription of a default biconsequence relation need not be a default biconsequence relation by itself.

# Chapter 4

# Four-Valued Logics

This chapter can be seen as a general introduction to a theory of four-valued reasoning based on the formalism of biconsequence relations. The latter formalism has an important advantage in this respect in that it does not depend on a particular choice of four-valued connectives. Moreover, we will show that any such connective is definable in it via introduction and elimination rules as in the classical sequent calculus, with the only distinction that we will have a pair of introduction rules and a pair of elimination rules corresponding, respectively, to the two contexts forming a four-valued interpretation. In this way we will obtain also formal representations for a number of important four-valued logics that will be used in the sequel.

## 4.1 Introducing Connectives

Due to the correspondence between four-valued interpretations and bimodels, any four-valued connective $\#(A_1, \ldots, A_n)$ can always be determined by a pair of conditions describing, respectively, when it is true and when it is false. Consequently, it can be described by a pair of definitions:

$$\begin{aligned} \nu \models \#(A_1, \ldots, A_n) &\equiv \mathcal{F}^+_\nu[A_1, \ldots, A_n] \\ \nu \mathrel{=\!\!|} \#(A_1, \ldots, A_n) &\equiv \mathcal{F}^-_\nu[A_1, \ldots, A_n] \end{aligned} \qquad (D\#)$$

where $\mathcal{F}^+_\nu[A_1, \ldots, A_n]$ and $\mathcal{F}^-_\nu[A_1, \ldots, A_n]$ are classical logical formulas in the meta-language generated by elementary propositions of the form $\nu \models A_i$ and $\nu \mathrel{=\!\!|} A_i$.

We will show that introduction and elimination rules for such a connective can be always given in the following form:

$$(\#E^+) \quad \frac{\{a, a_i : b, b_i \Vdash c, c_i : d, d_i\} \qquad (1 \le i \le k_1)}{a, \#(A_1, \dots, A_n) : b \Vdash c : d}$$

$$(\#I^+) \quad \frac{\{a, a_i : b, b_i \Vdash c, c_i : d, d_i\} \qquad (1 \le i \le k_2)}{a : b \Vdash c, \#(A_1, \dots, A_n) : d}$$

$$(\#E^-) \quad \frac{\{a, a_i : b, b_i \Vdash c, c_i : d, d_i\} \qquad (1 \le i \le k_3)}{a : b \Vdash c : d, \#(A_1, \dots, A_n)}$$

$$(\#I^-) \quad \frac{\{a, a_i : b, b_i \Vdash c, c_i : d, d_i\} \qquad (1 \le i \le k_4)}{a : b, \#(A_1, \dots, A_n) \Vdash c : d}$$

where $a_i$, $b_i$, $c_i$ and $d_i$ are subsets of $\{A_1, \dots, A_n\}$.

The following theorem shows that any four-valued connective can be characterized by such rules added to a biconsequence relation. This theorem can be seen as a generic Completeness Theorem for biconsequence relations in languages containing four-valued connectives.

**Theorem 4.1** *Let $\#(A_1, \dots, A_n)$ be a four-valued connective determined by $D\#$. Then there are four rules of the above form such that any biconsequence relation satisfying these rules is generated by a set of four-valued interpretations satisfying $D\#$.*

***Proof.*** Let us assume that $\mathcal{F}_\nu^+[A_1, \dots, A_n]$ is represented in a disjunctive normal form $\mathcal{C}_1 \vee \cdots \vee \mathcal{C}_k^d$, where each $\mathcal{C}_i$ is a conjunction of 'literals' of the form $\nu \models A_j$, $\nu \not\models A_j$, $\nu \dashv A_j$, or $\nu \not\dashv A_j$. Then we will introduce a rule of the form $\#E^+$ such that $A_j$ belongs to $a_i$ (respectively, to $b_i$, $c_i$, or $d_i$) iff $\nu \models A_j$ ($\nu \dashv A_j$, $\nu \not\models A_j$, or $\nu \not\dashv A_j$) belongs to $\mathcal{C}_i$.

Assume now that $\mathcal{F}_\nu^+[A_1, \dots, A_n]$ is transformed into a *conjunctive* normal form $\mathcal{D}_1 \wedge \cdots \wedge \mathcal{D}_m$, where each $\mathcal{D}_i$ is a disjunction of the same 'literals'. Then we will introduce a rule $\#I^+$ such that $A_j$ belongs to $a_i$ (respectively, to $b_i$, $c_i$, or $d_i$) iff $\nu \not\models A_j$ ($\nu \not\dashv A_j$, $\nu \models A_j$, or $\nu \dashv A_j$) belongs to $\mathcal{D}_i$.

In the same way, a disjunctive normal form of $\mathcal{F}_\nu^-[A_1, \dots, A_n]$ generates a rule of the form $\#I^-$, while its conjunctive normal form generates a rule of the form $\#E^-$.

Assume that $\Vdash$ is a biconsequence relation satisfying the above rules, $(u, v)$ is some its bitheory and $\nu_{(u,v)}$ a four-valued interpretation corresponding to $(u, v)$. Then $\#E^+$ implies that if $\#(A_1, \dots, A_n)$ belongs to $u$, at least one of the conjuncts $\mathcal{C}_i$ of a disjunctive normal form of $\mathcal{F}_\nu^+[A_1, \dots, A_n]$ should be such that $a_i \subseteq u$, $b_i \subseteq \overline{v}$, $c_i \subseteq \overline{u}$ and $d_i \subseteq v$. Consequently, $\nu_{(u,v)} \models \#(A_1, \dots, A_n)$ implies $\mathcal{F}_\nu^+[A_1, \dots, A_n]$ for $\nu = \nu_{(u,v)}$. Similarly,

$\#I^+$ implies that if $\nu_{(u,v)} \not\models \#(A_1, \ldots, A_n)$, one of the disjuncts of a conjunctive normal form of $\mathcal{F}_\nu^+[A_1, \ldots, A_n]$ for $\nu = \nu_{(u,v)}$ should be false, and hence $\mathcal{F}_\nu^+[A_1, \ldots, A_n]$ itself is false with respect to this interpretation. Thus, $\nu_{(u,v)}$ satisfies the first condition of $D\#$. In the same way it can be shown that the other two rules imply the validity of the second condition from $D\#$ for $\nu_{(u,v)}$. Consequently, all canonical interpretations of $\Vdash$ satisfy $D\#$. Now the result follows from the Representation Theorem for biconsequence relations, since any biconsequence relation is generated by its canonical semantics. □

An implementation of the procedure given in the proof of the above theorem to a particular class of *classical* four-valued connectives will be presented below.

Just as for the classical sequent calculus, the rules corresponding to four-valued connectives satisfy the *subformula property*, and hence allow us to reduce any bisequent involving such connectives to a set of bisequents containing atomic propositions only, without the use of the two Cut rules. This is simply a syntactic expression of the fact that the value of any proposition involving only truth-functional connectives in an interpretation is uniquely determined by the values of its atomic propositions.

Bisequents that involve only atomic propositions will be called *basic* ones. Thus, for any given language containing four-valued connectives, there is a one-to-one correspondence between biconsequence relations and their restrictions to the basic bisequents. Note that the latter can be considered as biconsequence relations in their own right, namely as biconsequence relations in the language without connectives. Such biconsequence relations will also be called *basic*. Thus, any biconsequence relation involving only four-valued connectives is equivalent to some basic biconsequence relation.

Finally, we will briefly describe yet another general way of characterizing four-valued connectives in biconsequence relations, namely by a set of bisequents having one of the forms:

$$(\#E_0^+) \quad a, \#(A_1, \ldots, A_n){:}b \Vdash c{:}d \qquad (\#I_0^+) \quad a{:}b \Vdash c, \#(A_1, \ldots, A_n){:}d$$
$$(\#E_0^-) \quad a{:}b \Vdash c{:}d, \#(A_1, \ldots, A_n) \qquad (\#I_0^-) \quad a{:}b, \#(A_1, \ldots, A_n) \Vdash c{:}d,$$

where $a$, $b$, $c$ and $d$ are subsets of $\{A_1, \ldots, A_n\}$. This characterization is actually a four-valued generalization of the corresponding description of classical connectives in the framework of Scott consequence relations given in [Gabbay, 1981; Segerberg, 1982].

The next theorem shows that any four-valued connective can be characterized in this way.

**Theorem 4.2** *Let $\#(A_1, \ldots, A_n)$ be a four-valued connective determined by $D\#$. Then there are rules of the above form such that any biconsequence relation satisfying these rules is generated by a set of four-valued interpretations satisfying $D\#$.*

***Proof.*** As in the proof of the preceding theorem, let us assume first that $\mathcal{F}_\nu^+[A_1, \ldots, A_n]$ is represented in a disjunctive normal form $\mathcal{C}_1 \vee \cdots \vee \mathcal{C}_k^d$, where each $\mathcal{C}_i$ is a conjunction of literals of the form $\nu \models A_j$, $\nu \not\models A_j$, $\nu \dashv A_j$, or $\nu \not\dashv A_j$. Then, for every $\mathcal{C}_i$, we will introduce a bisequent of the form $\#I_0^+$ such that $A_j$ belongs to $a$ (respectively, to $b$, $c$, or $d$) iff $\nu \models A_j$ ($\nu \dashv A_j$, $\nu \not\models A_j$, or $\nu \not\dashv A_j$) belongs to $\mathcal{C}_i$.

Assume now that $\mathcal{F}_\nu^+[A_1, \ldots, A_n]$ is transformed into a conjunctive normal form $\mathcal{D}_1 \wedge \cdots \wedge \mathcal{D}_m$. Then, for every $\mathcal{D}_i$, we will introduce a bisequent of the form $\#E_0^+$ such that $A_j$ belongs to $a$ (respectively, to $b$, $c$, or $d$) iff $\nu \not\models A_j$ ($\nu \not\dashv A_j$, $\nu \models A_j$, or $\nu \dashv A_j$) belongs to $\mathcal{D}_i$.

In the same way, a disjunctive normal form of $\mathcal{F}_\nu^-[A_1, \ldots, A_n]$ generates bisequents of the form $\#E_0^-$, while its conjunctive normal form generates bisequents of the form $\#I_0^-$.

Assume now that $\Vdash$ is a biconsequence relation satisfying the above rules, and $\nu_{(u,v)}$ is a four-valued interpretation corresponding to some bitheory $(u, v)$. Then each bisequent $\#E_0^+$ implies that if $\nu_{(u,v)} \models \#(A_1, \ldots, A_n)$, then the corresponding disjunct $\mathcal{D}_i$ of a conjunctive normal form of $\mathcal{F}_\nu^+[A_1, \ldots, A_n]$ is true for $\nu = \nu_{(u,v)}$. Consequently, all such bisequents imply jointly that $\mathcal{F}_\nu^+[A_1, \ldots, A_n]$ is true for $\nu = \nu_{(u,v)}$. Similarly, all bisequents of the form $\#I^+$ jointly imply that if $\nu_{(u,v)} \not\models \#(A_1, \ldots, A_n)$, $\mathcal{F}_\nu^+[A_1, \ldots, A_n]$ should be false for $\nu = \nu_{(u,v)}$. Thus, $\nu_{(u,v)}$ satisfies the first condition of $D\#$. In the same way it can be shown that the bisequents of the other two kinds imply the validity of the second condition from $D\#$. Consequently, all canonical interpretations of $\Vdash$ satisfy $D\#$. Now the result follows from the Representation Theorem for biconsequence relations. □

### 4.1.1 *Classical four-valued connectives*

A particular class of four-valued functions turns out to be of special interest in our intended use of biconsequence relations. Since we will be primarily interested in what information a bi-context (four-valued) reasoning can give us about ordinary, classical truth and falsity, that is, about **t** and **f**, we should require that the corresponding four-valued reasoning must agree with the classical one in cases when the context does not involve inconsistent or incomplete information. To secure this requirement, we should restrict our attention to connectives that are *classical* in the sense that they are conservative on the subset $\{\mathbf{t}, \mathbf{f}\}$ of classical truth-values. In other words, such connectives should give classical truth-values when their arguments receive classical values $\mathbf{t}$ or $\mathbf{f}$.

The set of classical connectives is actually well-known in the literature on many-valued logics, and it can be described in a number of ways. A most important 'global' property of this set is that it is functionally pre-complete in the class of all four-valued functions (see [Hendry, 1983]): adding an arbitrary non-classical function to this set allows to express any four-valued connective whatsoever.

It turns out that there are four natural and mutually independent connectives that are jointly sufficient for defining all classical four-valued functions. The first is the well-known *conjunction* connective:

$$\begin{aligned} \nu \models A \wedge B \quad &\text{iff} \quad \nu \models A \text{ and } \nu \models B \\ \nu \mathrel{=\!\!|} A \wedge B \quad &\text{iff} \quad \nu \mathrel{=\!\!|} A \text{ or } \nu \mathrel{=\!\!|} B. \end{aligned} \qquad (D\wedge)$$

A conjunction of two propositions is true when both its conjuncts are true, and false when at least one of them is false. Thus, such a connective gives us a nearest four-valued counterpart of the classical conjunction.

Next, there are two unary connectives that can be seen as two alternative extensions of classical negation to the four-valued setting:

$$\nu \models \neg A \quad \text{iff} \quad \nu \not\models A \qquad \nu \mathrel{=\!\!|} \neg A \quad \text{iff} \quad \nu \not\mathrel{=\!\!|} A \qquad (D\neg)$$

$$\nu \models {\sim} A \quad \text{iff} \quad \nu \mathrel{=\!\!|} A \qquad \nu \mathrel{=\!\!|} {\sim} A \quad \text{iff} \quad \nu \models A. \qquad (D\sim)$$

Note that these are the only connectives that coincide with the classical negation on the classical truth-values and satisfy the Double Negation rule. The difference between the two is that the second one 'switches' the contexts between truth and falsity, while the first one retains the context. Accordingly, we will call $\neg$ and $\sim$ a *local* and *global negation*, respectively. Note also that each of them can be used together with the conjunction to define a natural *disjunction* connective:

$$A \vee B \;\equiv\; {\sim}({\sim} A \wedge {\sim} B) \;\equiv\; \neg(\neg A \wedge \neg B).$$

As could be expected, a disjunction is true when at least one of the disjuncts is true, and false when both disjuncts are false.

Finally, the following unary connective **A** can be seen as a kind of a modal operator. It determines a rudimentary modal logic definable in the four-valued setting (and becomes trivial in the classical context).

$$\nu \models \mathbf{A}A \quad \text{iff} \quad \nu \not\dashv A \qquad \nu \dashv \mathbf{A}A \quad \text{iff} \quad \nu \dashv A. \tag{$D\mathbf{A}$}$$

The operator **A** is closely related to the modal operator that will be used in a modal extension of our formalism (see Chapter 10).

We will use in what follows also alternative unary connectives **L** and $-$ defined below:

$$\nu \models \mathbf{L}A \quad \text{iff} \quad \nu \models A \qquad \nu \dashv \mathbf{L}A \quad \text{iff} \quad \nu \not\models A$$
$$\nu \models -A \quad \text{iff} \quad \nu \dashv A \qquad \nu \dashv -A \quad \text{iff} \quad \nu \not\dashv A$$

Given the global negation $\sim$, all these connectives are interdefinable:

$$\mathbf{L} = -\sim = \sim\mathbf{A}\sim \qquad - = \sim\mathbf{A} = \mathbf{L}\sim \qquad \mathbf{A} = \sim\mathbf{L}\sim = \sim- = --$$

The connective $-$ is similar to Heyting's intuitionistic negation, and is related to the negation of the *here-and-there* logic (see [Pearce, 1997]). Accordingly, it will be called an *ht-negation* in what follows. As can be verified, $-$ satisfies the de Morgan rules. It does not satisfy, however, the Double Negation rule, only a weaker 'Triple Negation' rule $---A \equiv -A$.

Even for the classical logic, the choice of a natural functionally complete set of 'basic' connectives is not unique. We have still less reasons for reaching agreement about what could be seen as a natural functionally complete set of classical four-valued functions. Nevertheless, the main advantage of the suggested choice of the basic connectives for our study is that it is modular in the sense that a number of important subclasses of four-valued connectives, discussed below, are obtained simply by removing some of the basic connectives.

The following proposition shows that any classical four-valued function is representable using our four basic connectives.

**Theorem 4.3** *The set* $\{\wedge, \neg, \sim, \mathbf{A}\}$ *is functionally complete for the set of all classical four-valued functions.*

***Proof.*** Let $\nu$ be a 4-interpretation restricted to atomic propositions $p_1, \dots, p_n$. We will define a proposition $A_\nu$ corresponding to $\nu$ as follows:

$$A_\nu \quad \equiv \quad \hat{p}_1 \wedge \check{p}_1 \wedge \cdots \wedge \hat{p}_n \wedge \check{p}_n,$$

where $\hat{p}_i$ is either $p_i$ or $\neg p_i$ when $\nu \models p_i$ or $\nu \not\models p_i$, respectively, while $\check{p}_i$ is either $\sim p_i$ or $\neg\sim p_i$ when, respectively, $\nu \dashv p_i$ or $\nu \not\dashv p_i$.

It is easy to check that, for any 4-interpretation $\mu$ restricted to the same atomic propositions, $\mu \models A_\nu$ iff $\mu$ coincides with $\nu$.

For a finite set of 4-interpretations $U$, we will define $A_U$ as a disjunction of all $A_\nu$, where $\nu \in U$. Then it is easy to see that $\nu \models A_U$ iff $\nu \in U$.

Now, for any classical four-valued function $F(p_1, \ldots, p_n)$, we will denote by $U_F$ ($V_F$) the set of all 4-valuations $\nu$ restricted to $p_1, \ldots, p_n$ such that $\nu \models F(p_1, \ldots, p_n)$ (respectively, $\nu \not\dashv F(p_1, \ldots, p_n)$).

Since $F$ is a classical function, if $\nu \in (U_F \setminus V_F)$, there must exist $p_i$ that has a non-classical value in $\nu$. If the value is $\top$, we will denote by $\hat{A}_\nu$ the formula $A_\nu \wedge \mathbf{L}p_i$. Otherwise $p_i$ has the value $\bot$, and $\hat{A}_\nu$ will denote the formula $A_\nu \wedge \mathbf{L}\neg p_i$. It is easy to check that in both cases $\models \hat{A}_\nu$ is equivalent to $\models A_\nu$, while $\dashv \hat{A}_\nu$ always holds. We will define also $\hat{A}_U$ similarly to $A_U$.

Finally we define a formula $A_F$ corresponding to $F$ as follows:

$$A_F \quad \equiv \quad \mathbf{L}A_{U_F \cap V_F} \vee \hat{A}_{U_F \setminus V_F} \vee \sim\neg\hat{A}_{V_F \setminus U_F}.$$

It is easy to check that $\nu \models A_F$ holds iff $\nu \models A_{U_F \cap V_F} \vee \hat{A}_{U_F \setminus V_F}$ iff either $\nu \in U_F \cap V_F$ or $\nu \in (U_F \setminus V_F)$ iff $\nu \in U_F$. Similarly, $\nu \not\dashv A_F$ holds iff either $\nu \models A_{U_F \cap V_F}$ or $\nu \not\dashv \sim\neg\hat{A}^-_{V_F \setminus U_F}$ iff either $\nu \in U_F \cap V_F$ or $\nu \in (V_F \setminus U_F)$ iff $\nu \in V_F$. Therefore $A_F$ determines the same four-valued function as $F$, and we are done. □

The following introduction and elimination rules provide a characterization of the above four connectives for biconsequence relations. Just as in the classical case, the rules are easily discernible from the definitions of these connectives, given the intended interpretation of the premises and conclusions of a bisequent.

Rules for conjunction

$$\frac{a : b \Vdash c, A : d \quad a : b \Vdash c, B : d}{a : b \Vdash c, A \wedge B : d} \qquad \frac{a, A, B : b \Vdash c : d}{a, A \wedge B : b \Vdash c : d}$$

$$\frac{a : b, A \Vdash c : d \quad a : b, B \Vdash c : d}{a : b, A \wedge B \Vdash c : d} \qquad \frac{a : b \Vdash c : A, B, d}{a : b \Vdash c : A \wedge B, d}$$

Rules for the local negation

$$\frac{a, A : b \Vdash c : d}{a : b \Vdash \neg A, c : d} \qquad \frac{a : A, b \Vdash c : d}{a : b \Vdash c : \neg A, d}$$

$$\frac{a : b \Vdash c, A : d}{a, \neg A : b \Vdash c : d} \qquad \frac{a : b \Vdash c : A, d}{a : b, \neg A \Vdash c : d}$$

Rules for the global negation

$$\frac{a, A : b \Vdash c : d}{a : \sim A, b \Vdash c : d} \qquad \frac{a : A, b \Vdash c : d}{a, \sim A : b \Vdash c : d}$$

$$\frac{a : b \Vdash c, A : d}{a : b \Vdash c : \sim A, d} \qquad \frac{a : b \Vdash c : A, d}{a : b \Vdash c, \sim A : d}$$

Rules for **A**

$$\frac{a : b \Vdash c : d, A}{a, \mathbf{A}A : b \Vdash c : d} \qquad \frac{a : b, A \Vdash c : d}{a : \mathbf{A}A, b \Vdash c : d}$$

$$\frac{a : A, b \Vdash c : d}{a : b \Vdash \mathbf{A}A, c : d} \qquad \frac{a : b \Vdash c : A, d}{a : b \Vdash c : \mathbf{A}A, d}$$

Theorem 4.1 can be used to show that the above rules provide a complete characterization of the corresponding connectives.

As we said above, there is another general way of characterizing four-valued connectives in biconsequence relations, namely via a set of bisequents taken as axioms. For the above connectives, these axioms are as follows:

Axioms for conjunction

$$A \wedge B : \Vdash A : \qquad A \wedge B : \Vdash B : \qquad A, B : \Vdash A \wedge B :$$

$$: A \Vdash : A \wedge B \qquad : B \Vdash : A \wedge B \qquad : A \wedge B \Vdash : A, B$$

Axioms for the local negation

$$\neg A, A : \Vdash \qquad \Vdash A, \neg A :$$

$$: \neg A, A \Vdash \qquad \Vdash : A, \neg A$$

Axioms for the global negation

$$\sim A : \Vdash : A \qquad A : \Vdash : \sim A$$

$$: \sim A \Vdash A : \qquad : A \Vdash \sim A :$$

Axioms for **A**

$$\mathbf{A}A : A \Vdash \qquad \Vdash \mathbf{A}A : A$$

$$: \mathbf{A}A \Vdash : A \qquad : A \Vdash : \mathbf{A}A.$$

Theorem 4.2 (to be more exact, the procedure of constructing the relevant bisequents) can be used to show that the above bisequents provide a complete characterization of the classical four-valued connectives.

### 4.1.2 *Local classical connectives*

From the 'classical' point of view, the most natural subclass of the classical four-valued connectives is formed by the connectives that satisfy the following properties:

- they have the same definitions for truth as for non-falsity;
- the truth (respectively falsity) of a compound formula is determined only in terms of truth (resp., falsity) of its arguments.

Connectives of this kind will be called *local classical* ones. They can be described as follows:

$$\nu \models \#(A_1, \ldots, A_n) \equiv \mathcal{F}[\nu \models A_1, \ldots, \nu \models A_n]$$
$$\nu \not\dashv \#(A_1, \ldots, A_n) \equiv \mathcal{F}[\nu \not\dashv A_1, \ldots, \nu \not\dashv A_n].$$

The local connectives can be seen as connectives that behave as ordinary classical connectives with respect to each of the two contexts. This property is the basis for a special role such connectives will play in our study.

Clearly, the conjunction and local negation are local connectives in this sense. Moreover, since a classical conjunction and negation form a functionally complete set for classical (two-valued) functions, we immediately obtain

**Lemma 4.4** *The set $\{\wedge, \neg\}$ is functionally complete for the set of local classical connectives.*

### 4.1.3 *Invariant connectives*

If we drop the second condition for local classical connectives, we obtain a broader class of connectives that conforms to the invariance principle introduced in the preceding chapter. Namely, such connectives behave similarly with respect to truth and non-falsity. To be more exact, the definition of a connective with respect to falsity can be obtained from that for the truth through a simultaneous replacement of $\models$ by $\not\dashv$ and vice versa. We will call such connectives *invariant*.

In order to give a formal description of invariance, we will make use of the unary *conflation* connective $*$, introduced in [Fitting, 1989] and used in many studies of Belnap's logic. It is defined as follows:

$$\nu \models *A \quad \text{iff} \quad \nu \not\dashv A$$
$$\nu \dashv *A \quad \text{iff} \quad \nu \not\models A.$$

The following identities show that any two connectives from the set $\{\neg, \sim, *\}$ commute and define the third one:

$$\neg\sim=\sim\neg=* \qquad \neg* = *\neg = \sim \qquad \sim * = * \sim = \neg.$$

As can be seen, the conflation connective switches the contexts between truth and non-falsity. This transformation is precisely what we need for describing invariance.

**Definition 4.1** A four-valued connective $F(p_1, \ldots, p_n)$ will be called *invariant* if, for any valuation $\nu$, the value of $F(p_1, \ldots, p_n)$ with respect to $\nu$ is equal to the value of $*F(*p_1, \ldots, *p_n)$.

For any 4-valuation $\nu = (\models, \dashv)$ we will denote by $\nu^*$ the unique *dual* valuation $(\not\dashv, \not\models)$. As can be seen, the latter is obtained from $\nu$ by a simultaneous replacement of $\models$ by $\not\dashv$ and $\dashv$ by $\not\models$. Now, as an immediate consequence of the above definition, we obtain the following characterization of invariant connectives:

**Lemma 4.5** *A four valued connective $F(A_1, \ldots, A_n)$ is invariant if and only if, for any valuation $\nu$, $\nu \models F(A_1, \ldots, A_n)$ iff $\nu^* \not\dashv F(A_1, \ldots, A_n)$.*

It is easy to check that any invariant connective should already be classical. Also, composition of invariant connectives gives us again an invariant connective.

Note now that all our basic connectives, except **A**, satisfy this property. Furthermore, it turns out that invariant connectives are precisely the connectives that are expressible via $\{\wedge, \neg, \sim\}$.

**Theorem 4.6** *The set $\{\wedge, \neg, \sim\}$ is functionally complete in the set of invariant connectives.*

***Proof.*** Let $F(p_1, \ldots, p_n)$ be an invariant connective, and $U$ a set of all 4-interpretations $\nu$ such that $\nu \models F(p_1, \ldots, p_n)$. Let $A_U$ be the formula corresponding to $U$ as defined in the proof of Theorem 4.3. Note that $A_U$ uses only connectives from $\{\wedge, \neg, \sim\}$. Since any composition of invariant connectives is invariant, $A_U$ determines an invariant function.

Now, $\nu \models F$ is equivalent to $\nu \models A_U$, since the latter holds iff $\nu \in U$. In addition, $\nu \mathrel{=\!\!|} F$ iff $\nu^* \not\models F$ (since $F$ is invariant) iff $\nu^* \not\models A_U$ iff $\nu \mathrel{=\!\!|} A_U$ (since $A_U$ is invariant). Consequently, $F$ is expressible as $A_U$. □

An alternative, possible worlds semantics for biconsequence relations in the invariant language will be described later in this chapter.

### 4.1.4 *Conservative connectives*

Another natural constraint on the class of four-valued connectives amounts to the requirement that they should not produce contradictions ($\top$) or incompleteness ($\bot$), unless some of their arguments are such. In other words, we could require our connectives to be *conservative* on the subsets $\{\mathbf{t}, \mathbf{f}, \bot\}$ and $\{\mathbf{t}, \mathbf{f}, \top\}$. Note that this immediately implies that such connectives are classical. It turns out that all such functions are expressible in terms of $\{\wedge, \sim, \mathbf{A}\}$.

**Theorem 4.7** *The set $\{\wedge, \sim, \mathbf{A}\}$ is functionally complete for the set of all conservative four-valued functions.*

***Proof.*** For any 4-interpretation on $p_1, \ldots, p_n$, we will denote by $A_\nu$ the following formula in the language $\{\wedge, \sim, \mathbf{A}\}$:

$$A_\nu \quad \equiv \quad \hat{p}_1 \wedge \check{p}_1 \wedge \cdots \wedge \hat{p}_n \wedge \check{p}_n,$$

where $\hat{p}_i$ is $\sim\mathbf{A}\sim p_i$ or $\mathbf{A}\sim p_i$, if, respectively, $\nu \models p_i$ or $\nu \models p_i$, while $\check{p}_i$ is $\sim\mathbf{A}p_i$ or $\mathbf{A}p_i$, if, respectively, $\nu \mathrel{=\!\!|} p_i$ or $\nu \not\mathrel{=\!\!|} p_i$.

Let $F(p_1, \ldots, p_n)$ be a conservative connective. As before, we will denote by $U_F$ ($V_F$) the set of all 4-interpretations for which $F$ is true (respectively, non-false).

Since $F$ is conservative, if $\nu \in U_F \setminus V_F$, then there must exist $p_i$ that has the value $\top$ in $\nu$. Then $\hat{A}_\nu$ will denote the formula $A_\nu \wedge p_i$. It is easy to check that $\models \hat{A}_\nu$ is always equivalent to $\models A_\nu$, while $\dashv \hat{A}_\nu$ always holds (due to the fact that both $\sim\mathbf{A}\sim p_i$ and $\sim\mathbf{A}p_i$ belong to $A_\nu$).

Similarly, if $\nu \in V_F \setminus U_F$, there must exist $p_i$ that has the value $\perp$ in $\nu$. Then $\check{A}_{nu}$ will denote the formula $A_\nu \wedge \sim p_i$. Then $\not\models \check{A}_\nu$ always holds, while $\dashv \check{A}_\nu$ is equivalent to $\dashv A_\nu$.

For a finite set of interpretations $U$, we will denote by $A_U$ the disjunction of all $A_{nu}$, where $\nu \in U$. $\hat{A}_U$ and $\check{A}_U$ will be defined similarly.

Finally, we define a $\{\wedge, \sim, \mathbf{A}\}$-proposition corresponding to $F$ as follows:

$$A_F \quad \equiv \quad A_{U_F \cap V_F} \vee \hat{A}_{U_F \setminus V_F} \vee \check{A}_{V_F \setminus U_F}.$$

Then $\nu \models A_F$ iff $\nu \models A_{U_F \cap V_F}$ or $\nu \models \hat{A}_{U_F \setminus V_F}$ iff $\nu \in U_F$. Similarly, $\nu \not\dashv A_F$ iff $\nu \not\dashv A_{U_F \cap V_F}$ or $\nu \not\dashv \check{A}_{V_F \setminus U_F}$ iff $\nu \in V_F$. Thus, $A_F$ determines the same four-valued function as $F$. □

The class of conservative connectives will turn out to be particularly useful for describing three-valued reducts of our four-valued formalism.

There exists a useful replacement for our representative set of conservative connectives (see [Arieli and Avron, 1996]), which consists in replacing the operator $\mathbf{A}$ with two connectives: the syntactic falsity constant $\mathbf{f}$ and the implication connective $\supset$ defined as follows:

$$\nu \models A \supset B \quad \text{iff} \quad \nu \not\models A \text{ or } \nu \models B$$
$$\nu \dashv A \supset B \quad \text{iff} \quad \nu \models A \text{ and } \nu \dashv B.$$

The above connective appears to be a nearest counterpart of material implication in the four-valued context. The following identities show that $\mathbf{A}$ is interdefinable with $\{\mathbf{f}, \supset\}$ in our present (conservative) setting.

$$A \supset B = \mathbf{A}\sim A \vee B \qquad \mathbf{f} = (\mathbf{A}A \wedge \sim\mathbf{A}A) \qquad \mathbf{A}A = \sim A \supset \mathbf{f}.$$

* * *

At this point it becomes easy to verify that all the connectives in the set $\{\wedge, \neg, \sim, \mathbf{A}\}$ are independent. Indeed, the conjunction is independent from the rest, since it is the only binary connective in the list, the local negation $\neg$ is independent, since it is the only non-conservative connective, the operator $\mathbf{A}$ is the only non-invariant connective, while the global negation $\sim$ is independent, since the rest of the connectives are *positively local*: the truth of a compound formula is determined only by the truth valuation on its components.

### 4.1.5 *Normal forms*

Just as in classical logic, it is convenient sometimes to reduce a logical formula in a four-valued language to an equivalent formula in a certain normal form. Fortunately, it turns out that in our four-valued case any formula can also be reduced to either a conjunctive or disjunctive normal form with respect to the local classical connectives, that is, to a conjunction of disjunctions (respectively, a disjunction of conjunctions) of literals. There are, however, two essential differences. First, we have a richer collection of literals. Second, the set of possible literals sufficient for a reduction will not be unique.

**Definition 4.2** Four-valued propositions $A$ and $B$ will be called *4-equivalent* (notation $A \equiv B$) if they receive the same values in any four-valued interpretation.

Propositions $A$ and $B$ are 4-equivalent if and only if, for any four-valued interpretation, $\nu \models A$ iff $\nu \models B$ and $\nu \dashv A$ iff $\nu \dashv B$. It is easy to show that 4-equivalent formulas are interchangeable in any larger context without changing the truth-value of a compound formula, or the validity of bisequents. In this sense, 4-equivalence constitutes a natural counterpart of classical logical equivalence.

As in the classical case, the reducibility of four-valued formulas to a disjunctive or a conjunctive normal form is based on three kinds of rules. First, we have the following distributivity equivalences:

$$A \wedge (B \vee C) \equiv (A \wedge B) \vee (A \wedge C)$$
$$A \vee (B \wedge C) \equiv (A \vee B) \wedge (A \vee C)$$

Second, all the unary connectives, described earlier in this chapter, can be distributed over disjunction and conjunction. Thus, for every negative connective $\bowtie \in \{\neg, \sim, -\}$ we have de Morgan laws:

$$\bowtie (A \wedge B) \equiv \bowtie A \vee \bowtie B \qquad \bowtie (A \vee B) \equiv \bowtie A \wedge \bowtie B,$$

while for every positive connective $\bowtie \in \{\mathbf{L}, *, \mathbf{A}\}$ we have a simple distribution:

$$\bowtie (A \wedge B) \equiv \bowtie A \wedge \bowtie B \qquad \bowtie (A \vee B) \equiv \bowtie A \vee \bowtie B.$$

As a result, any formula in our language is reducible to a conjunction of disjunctions (or a disjunction of conjunctions) of 'quasi-literals', that is, atoms with unary connectives nested in front of them. The following sets of equivalences will show, however, that such nested connectives will always be reducible to single ones.

First, we have that the local negation commutes with every positive unary connective $\{\mathbf{L}, \mathbf{A}, *\}$:

$$\neg\mathbf{A} = \mathbf{A}\neg = - \qquad \neg* = *\neg = \sim \qquad \neg\mathbf{L} = \mathbf{L}\neg.$$

As a consequence, the local negation can be 'moved out', and therefore any chain of nested unary connectives is reducible to a chain of the positive connectives, possibly preceded with the local negation. Furthermore, the following equivalences show that any two consecutive positive connectives are reducible to a single one.

$$**A \equiv A$$
$$\mathbf{LA} = \mathbf{L}* = *\mathbf{A} = \mathbf{AA} = \mathbf{A}$$
$$\mathbf{AL} = *\mathbf{L} = \mathbf{A}* = \mathbf{LL} = \mathbf{L}.$$

In what follows, by a *4-atom* we will mean any proposition of the form $p$, $\mathbf{L}p$, $*p$ or $\mathbf{A}p$, where $p$ is a propositional atom. By a *4-literal* we will mean, accordingly, a 4-atom or its local negation. Then the above equivalences show, in effect, that any quasi-literal is reducible to some 4-literal. As a result, we obtain

**Lemma 4.8** *Any four-valued proposition is 4-equivalent to a proposition in a conjunctive (resp., disjunctive) normal form built from 4-atoms.*

It turns out, however, that the above construction still does not give us maximally reduced normal forms. The reason is that any of the three positive unary connectives $\{\mathbf{L}, \mathbf{A}, *\}$ is 'clausally' definable in terms of the other two. Namely, we have the following equivalences:

$$\mathbf{L}B \equiv (*B \wedge \neg\mathbf{A}B) \vee (*B \wedge B) \vee (\neg\mathbf{A}B \wedge B)$$
$$*B \equiv (\neg B \wedge \mathbf{A}B) \vee (\mathbf{L}B \wedge \mathbf{A}B) \vee (\neg B \wedge \mathbf{L}B)$$
$$\mathbf{A}B \equiv (B \wedge \neg\mathbf{L}B) \vee (B \wedge *B) \vee (\neg\mathbf{L}B \wedge *B)$$
$$B \equiv (\mathbf{L}B \wedge \neg*B) \vee (\mathbf{L}B \wedge \mathbf{A}B) \vee (\mathbf{A}B \wedge \neg*B).$$

The last equivalence above shows that even 'pure' literals $p$ and $\neg p$ are eliminable, if we have the rest of the 4-literals.

Thus, as our final result, we obtain

**Theorem 4.9** *Any four-valued proposition is 4-equivalent to a proposition in a conjunctive (resp., disjunctive) normal form built from 4-atoms of any three kinds from the set* $\{p, \mathbf{L}p, \mathbf{A}p, *p\}$.

### 4.1.6 *Alternative representations*

Having the four-valued connectives at our disposal, we can transform bisequents into more familiar inference rules, and even to ordinary logical formulas.

Recall that $\neg u$ denotes the set $\{\neg A \mid A \in u\}$. The notation $\sim u$, $\mathbf{A}u$ and their combinations will have a similar meaning.

The following representation of bisequents can be easily obtained from the characteristic rules for the relevant connectives.

**Lemma 4.10** *Any bisequent* $a : b \Vdash c : d$ *is equivalent to each of the following:*

$$a, \sim b : \Vdash c, \sim d : \quad (1)$$

$$\Vdash \neg a, c : d, \neg b \quad (2)$$

$$\Vdash \neg a, \neg\sim b, c, \sim d : \quad (3)$$

$$\Vdash \mathbf{A}\sim a, \mathbf{A}b, c, \sim d : \quad (4)$$

$$\Vdash \neg a, \neg - b, c, -d : \quad (5)$$

Bisequents of the form (1) can be considered as ordinary sequents. In fact, this is a common 'trick' used for representing four- and three-valued logics in the form of an ordinary sequent calculus.

By a *Belnap consequence relation* we will mean a Scott consequence relation $\vdash$ in the language with a negation $\sim$ satisfying the following Double Negation rules for $\sim$:

$$A \vdash \sim\sim A \qquad \sim\sim A \vdash A.$$

Given the representation (1), it can be easily verified that Belnap consequence relations are interdefinable with biconsequence relations. It should be noted, however, that occurrences of $\sim$ are not eliminable in the setting of Belnap consequence relations.

If the underlying language contains also the four-valued conjunction (or, equivalently, disjunction), the set of premises can be replaced by their conjunction, while the set of (positive) conclusions can be replaced by their disjunction. Consequently, we can transform bisequents into usual 'Tarski-type' rules $A \vdash B$ using only the global negation and conjunction. Actually, the resulting system will coincide with a (flat) theory of *relevant entailment* (see [Belnap, 1977; Dunn, 1976]). Finally, if we add the local negation $\neg$ to the language, we obtain precisely the invariant language, and the representation (3) shows, in effect, that such a language is already sufficient for transforming bisequents into formulas. Namely, any bisequent $a : b \Vdash c : d$ is representable by a formula

$$\bigvee(\neg a \cup \neg{\sim}b \cup c \cup {\sim}d).$$

This indicates that four-valued logics in the invariant language admit a standard Hilbert-type axiomatization; it will be described later in this chapter.

An important alternative possibility arises from using the representation (2). This time we can use the local connectives $\{\wedge, \neg\}$ in order to reduce such bisequents to that of the form $\Vdash A : B$, where $A$ and $B$ are classical propositions. The latter will correspond to *production rules* $B \Rightarrow A$ that will form a basis for production and causal inference relations studied in Chapter 8. A distinctive feature of such rules is that they do not satisfy the Reflexivity postulate for consequence relations. Nevertheless, such inference relations will be shown to constitute a most immediate generalization of classical logic that allows representation of nonmonotonic reasoning. Note also that, due to representations (3) and (5), both the global negation $\sim$ and the ht-negation $-$ are sufficient in this setting for transforming bisequents into four-valued formulas.

Finally, the representation (4) shows that the conservative language $\{\wedge\ \sim, \mathbf{A}\}$ is also capable to provide such a formula-based representation. Moreover, the latter representation will also turn out to be suitable for representing three-valued logics.

### 4.1.7 *Classical translation*

Now we will show that biconsequence relations, and four-valued logics in general, can be faithfully translated into classical logic.

The translation, described below, exploits the fact that four-valued interpretations correspond to pairs of classical interpretations; the latter will be 'simulated' by using two different copies of propositional atoms. More precisely, for any propositional atom $p$, we will introduce a new propositional atom $p'$. Then, as a first step, we will describe two translations $|A|$ and $||A||$ of four-valued formulas $A$ to classical formulas in the extended language. The translations will be defined by a simultaneous recursion as follows:

$$
\begin{array}{rlrl}
|p| &= p & ||p|| &= p' \\
|A \wedge B| &= |A| \wedge |B| & ||A \wedge B|| &= ||A|| \wedge ||B|| \\
|\neg A| &= \neg |A| & ||\neg A|| &= \neg ||A|| \\
|\sim A| &= \neg ||A|| & ||\sim A|| &= \neg |A| \\
|\mathbf{A} A| &= ||A|| & ||\mathbf{A} A|| &= ||A||.
\end{array}
$$

As can be seen, the above translation steps closely follow the corresponding definitions of the four-valued connectives with respect to the truth and falsity valuations. Moreover, since the above set of connectives is functionally complete in the class of all classical four-valued connectives, any such connective could be readily included in these translations[1].

For a set $u$ of four-valued propositions, we will denote by $|u|$ and $||u||$ the sets of corresponding translations of all propositions from $u$. Finally, for a bisequent $\rho = a{:}b \Vdash c{:}d$ in an arbitrary four-valued language, we will denote by $[\rho]$ the classical formula

$$\bigwedge(|a| \cup \neg||b||) \to \bigvee(|c| \cup \neg||d||).$$

Similarly, for a bisequent theory $\Delta$, we will denote by $[\Delta]$ the corresponding set of classical translations. Then we obtain

**Theorem 4.11** *A bisequent $\rho$ is derivable from a bisequent theory $\Delta$ if and only if* $[\Delta] \vDash [\rho]$.

***Proof.*** Note first that, under the above translation, the postulates of biconsequence relations correspond to classically valid propositions and rules; this gives us the direction from left to right. In the other direction, assume that $\rho = a{:}b \Vdash c{:}d$ is not derivable from $\Delta$. Then there exists a four-valued interpretation $\nu$ that validates $\Delta$, but not $\rho$. Then we define a classical interpretation $i$ in the extended language as follows: for any propositional atom $p$,

$$i \vDash p \equiv \nu \vDash p \qquad i \vDash p' \equiv \nu \not\dashv p.$$

[1] Actually, the translations are easily extendable to arbitrary four-valued connectives.

Then, by an obvious induction on the complexity of four-valued formulas, we obtain that, for any formula $A$,

$$\nu \vDash A \text{ if and only if } i \vDash |A|$$
$$\nu \dashv A \text{ if and only if } i \nvDash ||A||.$$

As an immediate consequence of the above equivalences, we obtain that an arbitrary bisequent $\rho_0$ is valid in $\nu$ if and only if the classical formula $[\rho_0]$ is valid in $i$. Consequently, all formulas from $[\Delta]$ are valid in $i$, while $[\rho]$ is invalid in $i$, which shows that $[\Delta] \nvDash [\rho]$. This completes the proof. □

The above result shows that our construction provides a faithful and general embedding of four-valued inference into classical logic. Furthermore, using our previous results, this embedding can be extended to various special kinds of four-valued inference, described earlier. Thus, for consistent, complete, ordered and semi-classical inference, the corresponding classical translations are obtained simply by adding the translations of the corresponding postulates as additional premises in the above classical entailment. In addition, for the regular and invariant inference, the corresponding translations are obtainable using, respectively, Corollary 3.26 and Corollary 3.34.

**Corollary 4.12**

- *A bisequent $\rho$ is derivable from a bisequent theory $\Delta$ with respect to a regular inference if and only if* $[\Delta], [\Delta^r] \vDash [\rho]$.
- *A bisequent $\rho$ is derivable from a bisequent theory $\Delta$ with respect to an invariant inference if and only if* $[\Delta], [\Delta^\circ] \vDash [\rho]$.

## 4.2 Four-valued Entailment and 4-Theories

For a given four-valued language $\mathcal{L}$, we will denote by $\Vdash_{\mathcal{L}}$ the least biconsequence relation in $\mathcal{L}$. This biconsequence relation will be called the *bisequent calculus* (for $\mathcal{L}$). Clearly, $\Vdash_{\mathcal{L}}$ is similar to the classical sequent calculus in that it contains only bisequents that are derivable using the structural postulates of biconsequence relations and the introduction/elimination rules for the connectives from $\mathcal{L}$. In this sense, it represents the pure four-valued logic for the language $\mathcal{L}$.

In what follows, we will suppress the index $\mathcal{L}$ in $\Vdash_{\mathcal{L}}$ whenever it will be clear from the context, or else our results will invariably hold for any $\mathcal{L}$.

Now we will introduce a four-valued counterpart of the notion of a deductively closed theory.

**Definition 4.3** A pair $(u, v)$ of sets of propositions in $\mathcal{L}$ will be called a *4-bitheory*, if it satisfies the following two conditions, for any proposition $A$ from $\mathcal{L}$:

- If $u : \,|\!\models A : v$, then $A \in u$;
- If $u : A \,|\!\models\, : v$, then $A \in v$.

A 4-bitheory will be called *$\mathcal{L}$-consistent*, if $u : \,|\!\not\models\, : v$.

4-bitheories can be seen as bitheories that are closed with respect to the four-valued entailment. Similar to the classical case, the following lemma shows that a 4-bitheory can be viewed as an intersection of a set of four-valued interpretations.

**Lemma 4.13** *A pair $(u, v)$ is a (consistent) 4-bitheory if and only if there is a (nonempty) set $I$ of four-valued interpretations such that*

$$u = \{A \mid \nu \models A, \textit{ for any } \nu \in I\} \quad \textit{and} \quad v = \{A \mid \nu \,\not\!=\!\!\mid A, \textit{ for any } \nu \in I\}.$$

***Proof.*** Let us say that a four-valued interpretation $\nu$ is a *model* of $(u, v)$, if $\nu \models B$, for any $B \in u$, and $\nu \,\not\!=\!\!\mid C$, for any $C \in v$. Then $u\!: |\!\models A\!:\!v$ says that $\nu \models A$, for any model $\nu$ of $(u, v)$, while $u\!:\!A \,|\!\models\, :\!v$ says that $\nu \,\not\!=\!\!\mid A$, for any model of $(u, v)$. This gives us the direction from left to right, when $I$ is the set of all models of $(u, v)$) (note that $(u, v)$ is consistent iff it has a model). Assume now that $(u, v)$ is determined in the above way by a set of $I$ of interpretations, and $u\!: |\!\models A\!:\!v$. Clearly, any interpretation from $I$ will be a model of $(u, v)$, and consequently $\nu \models A$, for any $\nu \in I$. Therefore, $A \in u$. Similarly, it can be shown that if $u\!: |\!\models A\!:\!v$, then $A \in v$. Thus, $(u, v)$ is a 4-bitheory. In addition, if $I \neq \emptyset$, then it clearly will be consistent. □

It turns out that the definitions of many four-valued connectives are also preserved in the setting of 4-bitheories (provided the connectives belong to the language). The proof is straightforward, given the above lemma.

**Corollary 4.14** *If $(u, v)$ is a 4-bitheory, then*

- $A \wedge B \in u$ *iff* $A \in u$ *and* $B \in u$;
- $A \wedge B \in v$ *iff* $A \in v$ *and* $B \in v$;
- $*A \in u$ *iff* $A \in v$;
- $*A \in v$ *iff* $A \in u$;
- $\sim\!A \in u$ *iff* $\neg A \in v$;

- *$\sim A \in v$ iff $\neg A \in u$;*

*and similarly for $-$, $\mathbf{L}$ and $\mathbf{A}$.*

Note, however, that, just as for classical deductive theories, the corresponding equivalences do not hold for the local negation $\neg$ and disjunction.

The above conditions for the conflation $*$ and global negation $\sim$ imply, in particular, that, for the languages containing these connectives, the positive component of a 4-bitheory uniquely determines its negative component, and vice versa:

$$v = \{A \mid *A \in u\} \qquad u = \{A \mid *A \in v\}.$$

Accordingly, for languages of this kind, the following more usual notions will turn out to be appropriate.

**Definition 4.4** Given a four-valued language $\mathcal{L}$,

- A set $u$ of propositions *(positively) entails* a proposition $A$ (notation $u \vDash_4 A$), if $u$: $\Vdash_{\mathcal{L}} A$:.
- A set $u$ is a (positive) *4-theory*, if it is closed with respect to $\vDash_4$.

The entailment relation $\vDash_4$ can be seen as a natural extension of classical entailment to four-valued languages. In particular, local classical propositions (that is, propositions in the language $\{\wedge, \neg\}$) behave in a fully classical way with respect to $\vDash_4$.

The following simple result connects the notion of a 4-theory with the earlier notion of a 4-bitheory.

**Lemma 4.15** *A set $u$ is a positive 4-theory if and only if $(u, v)$ is a 4-bitheory, for some $v$.*

***Proof.*** Take $v$ as the set of all propositions $A$ such that $\nu \not\dashv A$, for any four-valued interpretation $\nu$ that validates $u$. □

By the above lemma, 4-theories are precisely the positive components of 4-bitheories. As a consequence, we immediately obtain that any 4-theory is an intersection of positive components of four-valued interpretations.

By a *4-world* we will mean a maximal consistent 4-theory. Just as for classical logic, 4-worlds can be given the following alternative descriptions:

**Lemma 4.16** *The following conditions are equivalent:*

- *$\alpha$ is a 4-world;*
- *$\alpha = \{A \mid \nu \vDash A\}$, for some four-valued interpretation $\nu$.*

- *$\alpha$ is closed with respect to $\vDash_4$ and* saturated*: $A \vee B \in \alpha$ only if either $A \in \alpha$, or $B \in \alpha$.*

Due to the above saturation property, any 4-world is uniquely determined by 4-atoms that belong to it.

The classical translation of four-valued languages, described earlier, extends also to $\vDash_4$. Namely, Theorem 4.11 immediately gives

**Corollary 4.17** *For any set $u$ of four-valued propositions, and any $A$,*

$$u \vDash_4 A \quad \textit{iff} \quad |u| \vDash |A|.$$

There is a useful consequence of the above equivalence that stems from the fact that validity of local classical propositions in each of the two contexts of a four-valued interpretation do not depend on each other.

**Lemma 4.18** *If $u, v$ are sets of (local) classical propositions, and $A, B$ are classical propositions, then*

$$u, *v \vDash_4 A \vee *B \textit{ iff either } u \vDash A \textit{ or } v \vDash B.$$

As a result, we obtain the following

**Corollary 4.19** *If $u, v, A$ are classical propositions, then*

$$u, *v \vDash_4 A \textit{ iff either } u \vDash A \textit{ or } v \vDash$$
$$u, *v \vDash_4 *A \textit{ iff either } v \vDash A \textit{ or } u \vDash .$$

This result will be used in what follows.

## 4.3 Invariant Logic

In this section we will give a detailed description of four-valued logic in the invariant language. This logic will be used later in this study for describing partial generalizations of nonmonotonic semantics.

### 4.3.1 *Axiomatic representation*

As we have seen earlier, invariant language allows us to transform bisequents into four-valued formulas, which means that four-valued logics in languages that include the invariant connectives can be given a standard Hilbert-type axiomatization. Moreover, since the locally classical connectives behave in a fully classical way in this setting, such axiomatizations can be constructed as extensions of classical logic with additional connectives.

A *four-valued logic* $\mathbb{L}_4^i$ in the language with the invariant connectives $\{\wedge, \neg, \sim\}$ is determined by the axioms (tautologies) and rules of classical logic for the language $\{\wedge, \neg\}$, plus the following axioms for $\sim$ (where $\leftrightarrow$ is the usual classical equivalence defined in terms of $\{\wedge, \neg\}$):

**Double Negation** $\sim\sim A \leftrightarrow A$;
**Commutativity** $\sim\neg A \leftrightarrow \neg\sim A$;
**De Morgan** $\sim(A \wedge B) \leftrightarrow \sim A \vee \sim B$.

Though the logic $\mathbb{L}_4^i$ is an extension of classical logic, it should be noted that the global negation $\sim$ lacks the usual property of replacement of provable equivalents. In particular, $A \leftrightarrow B$ does not imply $\sim A \leftrightarrow \sim B$.

By $u \vdash_4^i A$ we will denote the fact that $A$ is derivable from the set $u$ of propositions in $\mathbb{L}_4^i$. Given the correspondence between bisequents and formulas in the invariant language, established in Sec. 4.1.6, it is straightforward (though tedious) to show that the logic $\mathbb{L}_4^i$ provides a complete axiomatization of four-valued reasoning in the invariant language:

**Theorem 4.20** *For any set $u$ of propositions in the invariant language,*

$$u \vdash_4^i A \text{ if and only if } u \vDash_4 A.$$

Moreover, any additional four-valued connective can be incorporated into this logic by adding translations of the corresponding rules for this connective in biconsequence relations. For example, an axiomatization of **A** can be obtained by adding the following two axioms:

$$\mathbf{A}A \leftrightarrow \sim\neg A,$$

$$\sim\mathbf{A}A \leftrightarrow \sim A.$$

Actually, adding **A** to the invariant language results in a functionally complete set of classical four-valued connectives, so any such connective is already definable in this setting. For example, since $-A = \sim\mathbf{A}A$, the ht-negation $-$ is axiomatizable as follows:

$$-A \leftrightarrow \sim A,$$

$$\sim - A \leftrightarrow \sim\neg A.$$

Finally, it is interesting to note that the logic $\mathbb{L}_4^i$ is actually equivalent to the Nonstandard Propositional Logic (NPL) from [Fagin *et al.*, 1995].

Using our notation, NPL has been defined in the language $\{\wedge, \sim, \rightarrow\}$, where $\rightarrow$ is a material implication definable in $\{\wedge, \neg\}$. Note, however, that the local negation $\neg A$ is definable in the language of NPL as $A \rightarrow \sim(A \rightarrow A)$, and consequently the language of NPL turns out to coincide with the invariant language. Moreover, under this reformulation, the axiomatization of NPL, given in [Fagin *et al.*, 1995], will almost coincide with the above axiomatization of $\mathbb{L}_4^i$. The equivalence of the two logics will also immediately follow from the semantic interpretation, given below.

### 4.3.2 *Possible worlds semantics*

We describe now an important alternative semantic representation for biconsequence relations and four-valued logics in invariant languages. The origins of this representation are in the so-called 'Australian Plan' semantics for relevant logics (see [Routley *et al.*, 1982]), as opposed to the four-valued 'American Plan' semantics ([Dunn, 1976; Belnap, 1977]).

Using the characteristic condition of invariant connectives from Lemma 4.5, we immediately obtain that, for any valuation $\nu$ and any formula $A$ built with invariant connectives only, we have

$$\nu \dashv A \text{ iff } \nu^* \not\models A.$$

The above equivalence says that a proposition $A$ is false in a four-valued interpretation $\nu$ if and only if it is not true in the dual valuation $\nu^*$. This means, in effect, that, if the notion of a dual valuation is given, the falsity valuation for an invariant proposition can be defined in terms of truth assignments with respect to a given and/or dual valuation. This leads to the following construction:

**Definition 4.5** A *possible worlds $*$-model* is a quadruple $\mathbb{W} = (W, N, ^*, V)$, where $W$ is a set of *possible worlds*, $N \subseteq W$ is the set of *normal worlds*, $V$ is a valuation function assigning each world from $W$ a (classical) propositional interpretation, while $^*$ is a function on $W$ such that, for any $\alpha \in W$, $\alpha^{**} = \alpha$.

In what follows, $\alpha \models A$ will denote the fact that the proposition $A$ holds in the possible world $\alpha$.

By the intended understanding of the above $*$-model, $\alpha^*$ determines a valuation that is dual to $\alpha$, and therefore pairs $(\alpha, \alpha^*)$ stand in one-to-one correspondence with four-valued interpretations. Accordingly, we can give a semantic characterization of the invariant connectives in this setting. In fact, it is sufficient to give corresponding semantic definitions only for the base set of the invariant connectives $\{\wedge, \neg, \sim\}$. These are as follows:

$$\alpha \models A \wedge B \quad \text{iff} \quad \alpha \models A \text{ and } \alpha \models B$$
$$\alpha \models \neg A \quad \text{iff} \quad \alpha \not\models A$$
$$\alpha \models \sim A \quad \text{iff} \quad \alpha^* \not\models A.$$

As can be seen, the local connectives coincide with ordinary classical connectives in this setting, while the global negation coincides with the so-called *relevant negation* (see [Routley *et al.*, 1982]).

The intended interpretation of $*$-models immediately suggests also the following definition of validity for bisequents in such models.

**Definition 4.6** A bisequent $a{:}b \Vdash c{:}d$ will be said to be *valid* in a possible worlds $*$-model $\mathbb{W}$ if, for any normal world $\alpha \in N$, if $\alpha \models A$, for any $A \in a$, and $\alpha^* \not\models B$, for any $B \in b$, then either $\alpha \models C$, for some $C \in c$, or $\alpha^* \not\models D$, for some $D \in d$.

For a $*$-model $\mathbb{W}$, we will denote by $\Vdash_{\mathbb{W}}$ the set of bisequents that are valid in $\mathbb{W}$. It could be easily verified that the latter set always forms a biconsequence relation. Moreover, the following theorem establishes the corresponding completeness result.

**Theorem 4.21** *$\Vdash$ is a biconsequence relation in the invariant language if and only if $\Vdash = \Vdash_{\mathbb{W}}$, for some $*$-model $\mathbb{W}$.*

***Proof.*** We will establish a direct equivalence between $*$-models and four-valued semantics for the invariant language (cf. Sec. 3.2 in [Routley *et al.*, 1982]). For a $*$-model $\mathbb{W} = (W, N, {}^*, V)$, the associated set of four-valued interpretations $\mathbf{I}_{\mathbb{W}}$ will be the set of all interpretations $\nu_\alpha$, for $\alpha \in N$, defined as follows: for any propositional atom $p$,

$$\nu_\alpha \models p \equiv \alpha \models p \quad \text{and} \quad \nu_\alpha \dashv p \equiv \alpha^* \not\models p.$$

As can be verified (by induction on the complexity of formulas), the above equivalences are extendable to arbitrary invariant formulas. Namely, for any invariant formula $A$ we have

$$\nu_\alpha \models A \text{ iff } \alpha \models A \quad \text{and} \quad \nu_\alpha \dashv A \text{ iff } \alpha^* \not\models A.$$

As a result, we immediately obtain that $\mathbb{W}$ and $\mathbf{I}_{\mathbb{W}}$ determine the same sets of valid bisequents.

In the other direction, for a set of four-valued interpretations $\mathbf{I}$, we construct the associated $*$-model $\mathbb{W}_{\mathbf{I}}$ as follows:

- Every $\nu \in \mathbf{I}$ will determine two worlds $\nu_+$ and $\nu_-$. $W$ will be defined as the union of all such worlds, while $N$ as the set of all worlds of the form $\nu_+$.
- The function $^*$ will be defined in an obvious way:

$$\nu_+^* = \nu_- \qquad \nu_-^* = \nu_+.$$

- The valuation function $V$ on $W$ will be defined as follows:

$$\nu_+ \models p \ \equiv \ \nu \models p \qquad \nu_- \models p \ \equiv \ \nu \not\dashv p.$$

Again, it can be easily verified that the $*$-model $\mathbb{W}_\mathbf{I}$ determines the same set of valid bisequents in the invariant language as $\mathbf{I}$. This shows that the two semantics are fully equivalent for biconsequence relations in the invariant language. Due to the equivalence between the two semantics, we obtain that the possible worlds $*$-semantics is also adequate for biconsequence relations in the invariant language. □

As a consequence of the above result, we obtain also that the $*$-semantics provides an adequate interpretation of the four-valued logic $\mathbb{L}_4^i$.

**Definition 4.7** A proposition $A$ will be said to be *valid* in a $*$-model $\mathbb{W}$ if $\alpha \models A$, for any normal world $\alpha$.

Then we have

**Corollary 4.22** *For any set $u$ of propositions, $u \vdash_4^i A$ if and only if $A$ is valid in any $*$-model that validates $u$.*

To conclude this section, we will provide a direct description of the canonical possible worlds models for $\mathbb{L}_4^i$. Such canonical models will be used in subsequent chapters.

For a given 4-world $\alpha$, we will define the following set of propositions:

$$\alpha^* = \{A \mid {\sim}A \notin \alpha\}.$$

It can be verified that if $\alpha$ is determined by a four-valued interpretation $\nu$, then $\alpha^*$ will be a 4-world determined by the dual interpretation $\nu^*$.

Let $N$ be a set of 4-worlds. We will denote by $N^*$ the set of dual 4-worlds $\{\alpha^* \mid \alpha \in N\}$. Then the corresponding *canonical possible worlds $*$-model* will be defined as a $*$-model $\mathbb{W} = (N \cup N^*, N, {}^*, V)$, where the function $^*$ is defined as above, while $V$ is defined as follows:

$$\alpha \vDash p \text{ iff } p \in \alpha.$$

Then, for any formula $A$, $\alpha \vDash A$ will hold if and only if $A \in \alpha$.

### 4.3.3 *Invariant inference*

Recall that the invariance principle requires that four-valued reasoning with respect to truth should coincide with reasoning with respect to non-falsity. A formal expression of this principle has been given in the preceding chapter using the Invariance rule. In this section we will give a more detailed description for such an invariant four-valued reasoning.

To begin with, we will show that invariant four-valued reasoning amounts to preservation of a *truth order* among the truth-values: $\mathbf{f} \leq_t \bot, \top \leq_t \mathbf{t}$. Speaking informally, such a reasoning amounts to a simultaneous preservation of both truth and non-falsity (see [Muskens, 1999]).

Let $\nu$ be a four-valued interpretation. For a set $b$ of propositions we will denote by $\inf_t \nu(b)$ ($\sup_t \nu(b)$) the least upper bound (respectively, g.l.b.) of the values of $\nu$ on $b$ in the truth order. Then the following definition gives the notion of validity of bisequents that is based on preserving the truth order.

**Definition 4.8** A bisequent $a{:}b \Vdash c{:}d$ will be said to be *i-valid* in a set $\mathbf{I}$ of four-valued interpretations, if $\inf_t \nu(a \cup {\sim}b) \leq_t \sup_t \nu(c \cup {\sim}d)$, for any $\nu \in \mathbf{I}$.[2]

For a set $\mathbf{I}$ of four-valued interpretations, we will denote by $\Vdash^i_{\mathbf{I}}$ the set of all bisequents that are i-valid in $\mathbf{I}$. Then the following result shows that invariant biconsequence relations provide an adequate formalization of i-validity.

**Theorem 4.23** *$\Vdash$ is an invariant biconsequence relation if and only if $\Vdash = \Vdash^i_{\mathbf{I}}$, for some set $\mathbf{I}$ of four-valued interpretations.*

***Proof.*** To begin with, note that $\sup_t \nu(a)$ and $\inf_t \nu(a)$ are equal, respectively, to the values of $\bigvee a$ and $\bigwedge a$ in $\nu$[3]. In addition, it is easy to verify that $\nu(A) \leq_t \nu(B)$ holds if and only if $\nu \models A$ implies $\nu \models B$ and $\nu \,=\!\!| B$ implies $\nu \,=\!\!| A$, for any interpretation $\nu$. As a consequence, we have that if $\nu(A) \leq_t \nu(B)$, then $\nu({\sim}B) \leq_t \nu({\sim}A)$. These facts are sufficient for establishing that if $a : b \Vdash c : d$ is $i$-valid, then $d : c \Vdash b : a$ will also be $i$-valid. Consequently, any biconsequence relation of the form $\Vdash^i_{\mathbf{I}}$ will be invariant.

Now, let $\mathbf{I}$ be the set of four-valued interpretations corresponding to bitheories of an invariant biconsequence relation $\Vdash$, and assume that $a : b \Vdash c : d$. Let us denote propositions $\bigwedge(a \cup {\sim}b)$ and $\bigvee(c \cup {\sim}d)$ by $A$ and

[2]Note that we do *not* require that the global negation $\sim$ should actually belong to the underlying language.

[3]Again, $\wedge$ and $\vee$ are not required to belong to our language.

$B$, respectively. Then the latter bisequent is equivalent to $A :\Vdash B :$. By the Representation Theorem, this holds if and only if $\nu \models A$ implies $\nu \models B$, for any $\nu \in \mathbf{I}$. But we have also $d : c \Vdash b : a$ by Invariance. The latter bisequent is equivalent to $\sim B :\Vdash \sim A :$, and hence $\nu \models \sim B$ implies $\nu \models \sim A$, for any $\nu \in \mathbf{I}$. But this is equivalent to the condition that $\nu \Dashv B$ always implies $\nu \Dashv A$, and hence $\nu(A) \leq_t \nu(B)$. Thus, a bisequent belongs to $\Vdash$ if and only if it is $i$-valid in all interpretations from $\mathbf{I}$. □

Given the correspondence between biconsequence relations in the invariant language and the four-valued logic $\mathbb{L}_4^i$, invariant biconsequence relations will correspond to a strengthening of $\mathbb{L}_4^i$ with a formula-based counterpart of the Invariance rule. The latter amounts to the following additional inference rule:

**L-Invariance** If $\neg A$, then $\sim A$.

Indeed, it can be easily verified that, for biconsequence relations in the invariant language, the Invariance rule is equivalent to the rule $\dfrac{\Vdash \neg A :}{\Vdash \sim A :}$.

It should be noted that the above rule is only an inference rule, so it does not imply the validity of the implication $\neg A \to \sim A$. Still, by the properties of $\mathbb{L}_4^i$, this rule is equivalent to each of the following rules:

**L-Invariance$_1$** If $A$, then $\sim\neg A$;
**L-Invariance$_2$** If $\sim A$, then $\neg A$;
**L-Invariance$_3$** If $\sim\neg A$, then $A$.

These rules show, in effect, that $\neg A$ and $\sim A$ are inter-derivable, as well as $A$ and $\sim\neg A$.

A possible worlds semantics for invariant biconsequence relations can be obtained by restricting the set of $*$-models to *normal* ones in which all worlds are normal, that is $N = W$. Actually, such $*$-models could be described simply as triples $\mathbb{W} = (W, {}^*, V)$, provided the validity is defined with respect to all worlds in $W$.

The following theorem shows that such models provide a semantic characterization for invariant biconsequence relations.

**Theorem 4.24** *A biconsequence relation* $\Vdash$ *in the invariant language is invariant if and only if* $\Vdash = \Vdash_{\mathbb{W}}$, *for some normal* $*$*-model* $\mathbb{W}$.

***Proof.*** As has been shown earlier, for any set of four-valued interpretations there is an equivalent $*$-model, and vice versa. Moreover, the actual constructions of these counterparts are such that if the set of four-valued interpretations is invariant, then its associated $*$-model will be normal, and vice versa. Hence the result. □

## 4.4 Conservative and Three-Valued Logics

To begin with, conservative four-valued connectives generate isomorphic three-valued functions when the set of truth-values is restricted to either $\{\mathbf{t}, \mathbf{f}, \bot\}$ or to $\{\mathbf{t}, \mathbf{f}, \top\}$. In such a three-valued setting, the conjunction $\wedge$ and global negation $\sim$ reduce to the well-known strong Kleene connectives. Moreover, it immediately follows from the known results on functional completeness for three-valued functions (see, e.g., [Van Benthem, 1988]) that the resulting set of connectives is functionally complete for the class of all three-valued classical (closed) functions. As a result, alternative versions of three-valued logics based on classical three-valued connectives can be obtained simply by imposing appropriate structural rules on biconsequence relations in the conservative language.

It turns out that consistent biconsequence relations provide a formalization of three-valued inference that is based on treating $\mathbf{t}$ as the only distinguished value. Note first that any consistent four-valued interpretation $\nu$ naturally corresponds to a three-valued interpretation $\nu_3$ with the truth-values $\{\mathbf{t}, \bot, \mathbf{f}\}$, and vice versa. By this correspondence,

- $\nu \models A$ iff $A$ has the value $\mathbf{t}$ in $\nu_3$;
- $\nu \dashv A$ iff $A$ has the value $\mathbf{f}$ in $\nu_3$.

We will say that a bisequent is $\mathbf{t}$-*valid* with respect to a three-valued interpretation $\nu_3$ if it is valid with respect to the above four-valued interpretation corresponding to $\nu_3$ (see Definition 3.7). Let $\Vdash^{\mathbf{t}}_{\mathbf{I}_3}$ denote the biconsequence relation generated by a set of three-valued interpretations $\mathbf{I}_3$ in this sense. Then, as an immediate consequence of the representation result for consistent biconsequence relations, we obtain the following

**Corollary 4.25** *$\Vdash$ is a consistent biconsequence relation if and only if $\Vdash = \Vdash^{\mathbf{t}}_{\mathbf{I}_3}$, for some set of three-valued interpretations $\mathbf{I}_3$.*

A correspondence between the above representation and common three-valued formalisms can be established using a global negation $\sim$. Recall that any bisequent $a : b \Vdash c : d$ is equivalent to $a, {\sim}b : \Vdash c, {\sim}d :$. The latter can be considered as an ordinary (Scott) rule, and in accordance with the above three-valued representation, it has the following interpretation:

If all propositions in $a \cup \sim b$ are true, then one of the propositions in $c \cup {\sim}d$ is true.

Thus, the validity of such rules in accordance with this definition amounts to preservation of truth $\mathbf{t}$. This kind of three-valued validity amounts to taking $\mathbf{t}$ as the only distinguished value. Consequently, consistent biconsequence relations can be considered as a structural framework for this kind of three-valued logics.

Complete biconsequence relations provide a formalization for a different kind of three-valued inference that is based on a *weak notion of truth*. The latter uses the two truth-values distinct from $\mathbf{f}$ as distinguished values.

Any complete four-valued interpretation $\nu$ corresponds to a three-valued interpretation $\nu_3$ with the truth-values $\{\mathbf{t}, \top, \mathbf{f}\}$, and vice versa. By this correspondence,

- $\nu \models A$ iff $A$ has the value $\mathbf{t}$ or $\top$ in $\nu_3$;
- $\nu \dashv A$ iff $A$ has the value $\mathbf{f}$ or $\top$ in $\nu_3$.

We will say that a bisequent is $\mathbf{f}$-*valid* with respect to a three-valued interpretation $\nu_3$ if it is valid with respect to the above valuations. As can be seen, $\nu \models A$ holds iff $A$ does not have the value $\mathbf{f}$ in $\nu_3$. Thus, the notion of $\mathbf{f}$-validity corresponds to preservation of non-falsity.

Any set of three-valued interpretations $\mathbf{I}$ generates a biconsequence relation $\Vdash^{\mathbf{f}}_{\mathbf{I}}$ determined by bisequents that are $\mathbf{f}$-valid in the latter. Any such generated biconsequence relation will satisfy Completeness. Moreover, as a consequence of the representation result for complete biconsequence relations, we obtain this time

**Corollary 4.26** $\Vdash$ *is a complete biconsequence relation if and only if* $\Vdash = \Vdash^{\mathbf{f}}_{\mathbf{I}}$, *for some set of three-valued interpretations* $\mathbf{I}$.

Finally, Lemma 4.10 (4) shows that conservative connectives $\{\wedge, \sim, \mathbf{A}\}$ allow to replace bisequents by formulas, so we can define the corresponding Hilbert-type axiomatization. A natural axiomatization of this kind can be obtained using the implication connective $\supset$, introduced in Sec. 4.1.4, and its corresponding equivalence $\Leftrightarrow$ defined as $(A \supset B) \wedge (B \supset A)$.

A *four-valued logic* $\mathbb{L}^c_4$ in the language with conservative connectives can be characterized by the axioms and rules of (positive) classical logic for the language $\{\vee, \wedge, \supset\}$, and the following axioms:

$$\sim\sim A \Leftrightarrow A,$$
$$\sim(A \wedge B) \Leftrightarrow \sim A \vee \sim B,$$
$$\mathbf{L}A \Leftrightarrow A.$$

An appropriate Completeness Theorem can be easily obtained from the corresponding result for the language $\{\vee, \sim, \supset\}$ proved in [Arieli and Avron, 1996]. Moreover, this axiomatization can serve as a basis for axiomatizing three-valued logics. Indeed, the preceding representation results show, in particular, that an axiomatization for the two kinds of three-valued logics can be obtained, respectively, by adding the following formula-based equivalents of Consistency and Completeness rules to $\mathbb{L}_4^c$:

**L-Consistency** $\mathbf{A}\sim A \vee \mathbf{A}A$.
**L-Completeness** $A \vee \sim A$.

## 4.5 Coherence

It turns out that practically all structural rules for biconsequence relations, considered in the preceding chapter, are representable as particular cases of one general *coherence principle* that can be formulated as follows:

> Propositions provable in a biconsequence relation should be classically true, while refuted propositions should be classically false.

If the above principle holds for a biconsequence relation, the information we can *infer* in it will be of a usual classical kind.

Biconsequence relations satisfying the above principle will be called *coherent*. The strength of this principle depends, however, on the underlying language. Generally speaking, the more expressive is the language, the stronger is the corresponding coherence requirement. As we will see later in this study, the coherence principle will allow us to give a uniform representation for a number of semantics for logic programming, suggested in the literature.

In what follows, by a *language* $\mathcal{L}$ we will mean a set of four-valued connectives, while by a *logical rule* we will mean a rule for biconsequence relations that does not involve explicit occurrences of connectives. Clearly, the strength of such a logical rule can vary depending on the underlying language. In particular, the structural rules discussed in the preceding chapter can be seen as logical rules for basic biconsequence relations (that is, biconsequence relations in the empty language of four-valued connectives). Note, however, that the real constraint imposed by a logical rule in the language $\mathcal{L}$ can be 'measured' in terms of conditions it imposes on the associated basic biconsequence relation.

The following definition provides a formal description of the coherence principle.

**Definition 4.9** A biconsequence relation will be called *$\mathcal{L}$-coherent* if it satisfies the following two logical rules with respect to $\mathcal{L}$:

$$(Positive\ Coherence)\ \frac{\Vdash A :}{: A \Vdash} \qquad (Negative\ Coherence)\ \frac{A : \Vdash}{\Vdash : A}$$

The next two results describe some general features of coherent biconsequence relations.

**Lemma 4.27** *If $\mathcal{L}$ contains the local negation $\neg$, Positive and Negative $\mathcal{L}$-Coherence rules are equivalent.*

***Proof.*** If $A : \Vdash$, then $\Vdash \neg A :$. By Positive Coherence, we have $: \neg A \Vdash$. But the latter is reducible to $\Vdash : A$. Thus, Positive Coherence implies Negative Coherence. The reverse implication is proved similarly. □

**Lemma 4.28** *If $\Vdash$ is a coherent biconsequence relation in a language $\mathcal{L}$ with the global negation $\sim$, then, for any proposition $A$ in $\mathcal{L}$,*

- $\Vdash A :$ *if and only if* $: A \Vdash$;
- $A : \Vdash$ *if and only if* $\Vdash : A$.

***Proof.*** If $: A \Vdash$, then $\sim A : \Vdash$ in the language extended with connectives from $\mathcal{L}$, and hence $\Vdash : \sim A$ by Negative Coherence. The latter bisequent is reducible to $\Vdash A :$. Similarly, it can be shown that $\Vdash : A$ implies $A : \Vdash$. □

Thus, for biconsequence relations that are coherent in languages containing $\sim$, provable truth coincides with provable classical truth and provable non-truth (refutability) coincides with provable falsity.

In what follows, we will give a structural description of coherent biconsequence relations in different languages. As we will see, this description will cover practically all kinds of biconsequence relations described earlier.

### $\{\vee, \wedge\}$-*coherence*

If the language $\mathcal{L}$ contains no connectives, the coherence rules coincide with their structural counterparts. If the language contains disjunction,

Positive Coherence is already equivalent to a 'multiple' structural rule given below, though Negative Coherence is still reducible to its singular variant. Adding conjunction will give a corresponding multiple variant of Negative Coherence:

**Lemma 4.29** *A biconsequence relation* $\Vdash$ *is* $\{\vee, \wedge\}$*-coherent iff it satisfies the following structural rules:*

$$\frac{\Vdash a :}{: a \Vdash} \qquad \frac{a : \Vdash}{\Vdash : a}$$

***Proof.*** Since any finite set of propositions is replaceable by its conjunction in positive premises and negative conclusions, and by its disjunction in negative premises and positive conclusions, the implication from left to right is obvious. To prove the reverse implication, we will show a stronger result, namely that if the above structural rules hold for a biconsequence relation, then the corresponding logical rules in the language $\{\vee, \wedge\}$ will also hold with respect to it. This can be proved by induction on the total number of conjunctions and disjunctions occurring in these rules.

If $\Vdash a, A \wedge B :$, then $\Vdash a, A :$ and $\Vdash a, B :$, and therefore by the inductive assumption $: a, A \Vdash$ and $: a, B \Vdash$. Consequently, $: a, A \wedge B \Vdash$ by the properties of conjunction.

If $\Vdash a, A \vee B :$, then $\Vdash a, A, B :$ by the properties of disjunction. Hence $: a, A, B \Vdash$ by the inductive assumption (note that $a \cup \{A\} \cup \{B\}$ contains less connectives than $a \cup \{A \vee B\}$). But then $: a, A \vee B \Vdash$.

In the same way it can be proved that the second structural rule implies its $\{\vee, \wedge\}$-logical counterpart. Now, the relevant $\{\vee, \wedge\}$-coherence rules are simply special cases of such logical rules, and hence the implication from right to left also holds. □

### $\{\vee, \wedge, \mathbf{L}\}$-*coherence*

The following result describes structural equivalents for $\{\vee, \wedge, \mathbf{L}\}$-coherence rules.

**Lemma 4.30** $\{\vee, \wedge, \mathbf{L}\}$*-coherence rules are equivalent, respectively, to the following structural rules:*

$$\frac{\Vdash a, b :}{: a \Vdash b :} \qquad \frac{a, b : \Vdash}{a : \Vdash : b}$$

***Proof.*** We will consider only Positive Coherence here; the proof for Negative Coherence is completely analogous.

If $\Vdash a, b :$ then $\Vdash \bigvee(a \cup \mathbf{L}b) :$ by the properties of disjunction and $\mathbf{L}$. Hence $: \bigvee(a \cup \mathbf{L}b) \Vdash$ by Positive Coherence, which is equivalent to $: a \Vdash b :$. Thus, Positive Coherence implies the corresponding structural rule. To show the reverse inclusion, we will prove that this structural rule implies its $\{\vee, \wedge, \mathbf{L}\}$-logical counterpart. Again, this can be done by induction on the total number of connectives occurring in propositions of the rule. We will consider only the case of $\mathbf{L}$.

If $\Vdash \mathbf{L}A, a, b :$ then $\Vdash A, a, b :$. Applying the inductive assumption, we obtain $: a \Vdash A, b :$. Therefore, both $: \mathbf{L}A, a \Vdash b :$ and $: a \Vdash b, \mathbf{L}A :$ hold due to the properties of $\mathbf{L}$. This gives us the two cases of the rule depending on whether $\mathbf{L}A$ is adjoined to $a$ or to $b$. □

### *Local coherence*

For $\{\wedge, \neg\}$-coherence, that is, coherence with respect to the local connectives, Positive Coherence and Negative Coherence are already equivalent. Moreover, we have

**Lemma 4.31** *Local coherence is equivalent to the structural rule*

$$\frac{a : \Vdash c :}{: c \Vdash : a}$$

***Proof.*** If $a : \Vdash c :$, then $\Vdash \neg a, c :$, and hence $\Vdash \bigvee(\neg a \cup c) :$. Applying Positive Coherence, we obtain $: \bigvee(\neg a \cup c) \Vdash$, which is reducible to $: c \Vdash : a$. Thus, Positive Coherence implies the above structural rule. In the other direction, it can be proved that this structural rule implies the corresponding $\{\wedge, \neg\}$-logical rule (again, by induction on the complexity of propositions occurring in it). Since both Positive and Negative Coherence are special cases of such a logical rule, this will complete the proof. □

The above structural rule corresponds to an interesting semantic constraint on possible interpretations. It says that, for any bitheory $(u, v)$ there is a bitheory of the form $(v, w)$. In other words, any negative part of an admissible interpretation should also serve as a positive part of some other interpretation.

A strengthening of this constraint to the requirement that if $(u, v)$ is a bitheory, then $(v, u)$ is also a bitheory will give us a semantic description of invariant biconsequence relations (see below).

### *Regular coherence*

Regularity turns out to be equivalent to coherence in the intermediate language $\{\wedge, \neg, -\}$.

**Lemma 4.32** *A biconsequence relation is regular if and only if it is* $\{\wedge, \neg, -\}$*-coherent.*

***Proof.*** If $a{:}b \Vdash c{:}d$, then $\Vdash \bigvee(\neg a \cup \neg - b \cup c \cup -d)$ : (see Lemma 4.10 (5)), and hence : $\bigvee(\neg a \cup \neg - b \cup c \cup -d \Vdash$ by coherence. By the properties of $\neg$ and $-$, the latter bisequent is reducible to : $b, c \Vdash$: $a, d$, and therefore Regularity holds. As before, it can be proved also that the structural Regularity rule implies the corresponding $\{\wedge, \neg, -\}$-logical rule (by induction on the complexity of propositions), whereas the Coherence rules are just special cases of such a logical rule. □

### *Conservative coherence*

The following result shows that Consistency and Completeness are also kinds of coherence rules. More exactly, they are equivalent to coherence rules in the conservative language.

**Lemma 4.33** *A biconsequence relation is consistent (respectively, complete) if and only if it satisfies Positive (resp. Negative) Coherence with respect to the conservative language.*

***Proof.*** Since $\Vdash \sim\mathbf{L}A \vee A$ : is a valid bisequent, we have : $\sim\mathbf{L}A \vee A \Vdash$ by Positive Coherence. The latter bisequent is reducible to $A : A \Vdash$, and therefore Positive Coherence in our case implies Consistency as a logical rule in the conservative language. In the other direction, it is easy to show that consistent biconsequence relations make valid bisequents $A : A \Vdash$ for all conservative propositions $A$ (by induction on the complexity of $A$). Consequently, if $\Vdash A$ : holds, we obtain : $A \Vdash$ by Positive Cut. Thus, Positive Coherence holds.

The proof for completeness is similar. □

### *Invariant coherence*

Now we will show that Invariance is equivalent to coherence with respect to the language of invariant connectives.

**Lemma 4.34** *A biconsequence relation is invariant if and only if it is coherent in the invariant language.*

***Proof.*** If $a : b \Vdash c : d$, then $\Vdash \bigvee(\neg a \cup \neg{\sim}b \cup c \cup {\sim}d) :$ (see Lemma 4.10 (2)). Applying coherence, we obtain $: \bigvee(\neg a \cup \neg{\sim}b \cup c \cup {\sim}d) \Vdash$. But the latter bisequent is reducible to $d : c \Vdash b : a$. Thus, $\{\wedge, \neg, \sim\}$-coherence implies invariance. As before, the reverse implication follows from the fact that structural invariance implies invariance with respect to all $\{\wedge, \neg, \sim\}$-propositions. □

### *Classical coherence*

As an immediate consequence of Proposition 4.33 we obtain

**Corollary 4.35** *A biconsequence relation is a Scott one if and only if it is coherent with respect to the conservative language.*

The following result shows that full classicality is equivalent also to coherence in the language $\{\wedge, \neg, \mathbf{L}\}$.

**Lemma 4.36** *A biconsequence relation is a Scott one if and only if it is* $\{\wedge, \neg, \mathbf{L}\}$*-coherent.*

***Proof.*** Since $A : \Vdash A :$, for any $A$, we have $\Vdash \mathbf{L}\neg A \vee A :$ by the properties of the connectives involved, and hence $: \mathbf{L}\neg A \vee A \Vdash$ by Positive Coherence. The latter bisequent is reducible to $A : A \Vdash$. Consequently, we have also $\neg A : \neg A \Vdash$, and the latter bisequent is reducible to $\Vdash A : A$. Thus, Coherence for this language implies classicality. In the other direction, it is easy to show that, for a Scott biconsequence relation, $A : A \Vdash$ and $\Vdash A : A$ are logical rules with respect to the full language of classical connectives. Now, applying Positive Cut to $A : A \Vdash$ and $A : \Vdash$, we obtain Positive Coherence. But since the language contains a local negation, it satisfies also Negative Coherence. Thus, any Scott biconsequence relation is coherent with respect to the whole language of classical connectives. □

As is shown in the above proof, any Scott biconsequence relation is already coherent with respect to all the classical four-valued connectives. Thus, classical coherence is a strongest form of coherence possible: it reduces biconsequence relations to an ordinary classical sequent calculus.

# Chapter 5

# Nonmonotonic Semantics

We are finally ready to give a formalization of nonmonotonic reasoning in the logical framework of biconsequence relations. Basically, various nonmonotonic semantics of a biconsequence relation will be defined as certain structurally distinguishable subsets of their theories. Namely, theories from a nonmonotonic semantics will be *explanatory closed* in the sense that both presence and absence of propositions will be explained (i.e., derived) using the rules of the biconsequence relation when the theory itself is taken as the assumption context. This construction will provide a formal expression for the principle of explanatory closure that constitutes the basis of explanatory nonmonotonic reasoning.

## 5.1 Exact Semantics

The notion of an exact theory of a biconsequence relation will provide us with a simplest and most general kind of nonmonotonic reasoning. Moreover, practically all the other nonmonotonic semantics studied in this book will be shown to be reducible to exact theories.

**Definition 5.1** A theory $u$ of a biconsequence relation $\Vdash$ will be called *exact*, if there is no other set $v \neq u$ such that $(v, u)$ is a bitheory of $\Vdash$. The set of exact theories will be called an *exact nonmonotonic semantics* of $\Vdash$.

As can be seen from the definition, a set $u$ of propositions is an exact theory of $\Vdash$ if and only if, for any set $v$,

$$(v, u) \text{ is a bitheory of } \Vdash \text{ if and only if } u = v.$$

Thus, exact theories correspond to bitheories of a biconsequence relation, for which the assumption context determines itself as a unique objective state compatible with it. More precisely, $u$ is an exact theory, if the positive $u$-reduction of $\Vdash$, $\Vdash_u^+$, emerging from taking $u$ as an assumption theory, is a unitary consequence relation having $u$ as its only theory (see Definition 2.8). Consequently, Lemma 2.27 implies the following syntactic description of exact theories.

**Lemma 5.1** *A set $u$ of propositions is an exact theory of a biconsequence relation $\Vdash$ if and only if, for any proposition $A$,*

$$A \in u \quad \textit{iff} \quad : \overline{u} \Vdash A : u$$
$$A \notin u \quad \textit{iff} \quad A : \overline{u} \Vdash\ : u.$$

**Remark 5.1** *The nonmonotonic semantics was defined above as a certain set of propositional theories. This abstract definition leaves us much freedom in determining what can be seen as* nonmonotonic consequences *of a bisequent theory. The most obvious choice consists in taking propositions that belong to all such theories. But we can also consider propositions that do not belong to any such theory as nonmonotonically* rejected. *Both these options determine a* sceptical *nonmonotonic semantics. A* credulous *nonmonotonic semantics can be defined by considering propositions that belong (or not belong) to at least one theory.*

*An even more general understanding amounts to a view that* all *the information that can be discerned from the nonmonotonic semantics of a bisequent theory or a biconsequence relation can be seen as nonmonotonically implied by the latter. This view agrees with the so-called answer set paradigm in logic programming, according to which every nonmonotonic model can be seen as a solution to the nonmonotonic reasoning problem.*

The notion of an exact theory was defined above with respect to biconsequence relations, but it can be naturally extended to arbitrary bisequent theories by considering their associated biconsequence relations.

**Definition 5.2** A set $u$ of propositions will be called an *exact theory* of a bisequent theory $\Delta$, if it is an exact theory of $\Vdash_\Delta$. The set of exact theories of $\Delta$ will be called an *exact nonmonotonic semantics* of $\Delta$.

A more direct description of the exact nonmonotonic semantics for bisequent theories can be obtained by using positive reducts $\Delta_u^+$ of a bisequent theory $\Delta$. Recall that $v$ is a theory of $\Delta_u^+$ if and only if $(v, u)$ is a bitheory of $\Delta$ (see Lemma 3.9). Consequently, we immediately obtain the following description

**Lemma 5.2** *A set $u$ of propositions is an exact theory of a bisequent theory $\Delta$ iff it is the only theory of $\Delta_u^+$.*

In the setting of bisequent theories, it becomes especially clear that exact theories determine a truly nonmonotonic semantics due to the fact that extensions of a given bisequent theory with new bisequents may not only eliminate some exact theories, but may also add new ones (or both). In other words, the set of exact theories does not change monotonically with the growth of the set of bisequents. As a result, the set of nonmonotonic consequences of a bisequent theory is also changing nonmonotonically.

**Example 5.1** Let us consider a bisequent theory $\Delta = \{B{:}B \Vdash;\ \Vdash A{:}A\}$. Every subset of $\{A, B\}$ is a theory of $\Delta$. It has, however, only one exact theory, namely $\{A\}$. Now, if we add a bisequent $A{:} \Vdash B{:}$ to $\Delta$, we obtain two exact theories, $\{A, B\}$ and $\emptyset$. If we add, however, $\Vdash B{:}B$ to $\Delta$, we obtain a bisequent theory with exact theories $\{A\}$ and $\{A, B\}$.

The above example illustrates also an important special case when the nonmonotonic semantics even *grows* with the growth of the underlying bisequent theory, unlike the case of ordinary consequence relations, where addition of rules invariably leads to reduction of the set of theories. This unusual behavior can be explained as follows.

Suppose that the bisequents added to a bisequent theory do not change the propositional theories of the latter. Now, the addition of new bisequents amounts to removal of some of the bitheories (namely those that are not closed with respect to the new bisequents). But since the theories are preserved, any exact theory of the source bisequent theory will remain an exact theory of the new bisequent theory. In other words, in this special case, the extension of a bisequent theory may lead only to creating new exact theories, but never to elimination of the old ones. This property will be called a *restricted monotonicity property* of a nonmonotonic semantics. It will hold also for the rest of semantics described below. A formal description of this property is given in the next lemma.

**Lemma 5.3** *(Restricted monotonicity) If $\Vdash$ and $\Vdash_1$ are Scott-equivalent biconsequence relations such that $\Vdash \subseteq \Vdash_1$, then any exact theory of $\Vdash$ is an exact theory of $\Vdash_1$.*

Taking an extreme case, Scott biconsequence relations have only reflexive bitheories, and hence all of them correspond to exact theories. This means, in effect, that for such biconsequence relations, the nonmonotonic semantics coincides with the monotonic one. In the other extreme case, positive biconsequence relations may have a lot of theories, but they do not have exact theories at all.

Let $\Vdash^r_\Delta$ denote the least regular biconsequence relation containing a set of bisequents $\Delta$. As a first application of restricted monotonicity, the next result shows that the Regularity rule for biconsequence relations preserves the exact nonmonotonic semantics.

**Lemma 5.4** *$\Vdash^r$ has the same exact theories as $\Vdash$.*

***Proof.*** Clearly, bitheories of $\Vdash^r$ are precisely regular bitheories of $\Vdash$. Now, bitheories of the form $(u, u)$ are clearly regular, and therefore $\Vdash^r$ is Scott-equivalent to $\Vdash$. Consequently, any exact theory of $\Vdash$ will also be an exact theory of $\Vdash^r$ by restricted monotonicity.

Suppose now that $u$ is an exact theory of $\Vdash^r$, but is not an exact theory of $\Vdash$. Then $u$ is a theory of $\Vdash^r$, and therefore it should be a theory of $\Vdash$. Consequently it is not exact in $\Vdash$ only if there is a set $v \neq u$ such that $(v, u)$ is a bitheory of $\Vdash$. But $(v, u)$ is then a regular bitheory of $\Vdash$ (since $(u, u)$ is a bitheory of $\Vdash$), and consequently it is a bitheory of $\Vdash^r$, contrary to our assumption that $u$ is an exact theory in $\Vdash^r$. Therefore any exact theory of $\Vdash^r$ should also be an exact theory of $\Vdash$. □

The above theorem shows that Regularity is an admissible rule for reasoning with exact theories. Moreover, we will show now that regular biconsequence relations constitute in our abstract setting a maximal logic suitable for nonmonotonic reasoning with exact theories. To this end, we will use the notion of strong equivalence introduced in Definition 1.2 on page 11. Bisequent theories will play the role of default theories in our present case.

**Definition 5.3** Bisequent theories $\Gamma$ and $\Delta$ will be called *regularly equivalent*, if $\Vdash^r_\Delta = \Vdash^r_\Gamma$.

Bisequent theories are regularly equivalent, if each of these theories is obtainable from the other using the postulates of biconsequence relations and Regularity. Now, the following result shows that this equivalence coincides with strong equivalence with respect to the exact semantics.

**Theorem 5.5** *Bisequent theories are strongly equivalent with respect to the exact semantics if and only if they are regularly equivalent.*

***Proof.*** If $\Gamma$ and $\Delta$ are regularly equivalent, they determine the same regular biconsequence relation, and hence the same set of exact theories by the preceding lemma. Moreover, for any $\Phi$, we have also that $\Gamma \cup \Phi$

is regularly equivalent to $\Delta \cup \Phi$, and therefore $\Gamma$ and $\Delta$ will be strongly equivalent.

Assume now that $\Gamma$ and $\Delta$ are not regularly equivalent, and suppose for certainty that $(u, v)$ is a regular bitheory of $\Gamma$ that is not a regular bitheory of $\Delta$. Clearly, $v$ is a theory of $\Gamma$. We consider now two cases.

Suppose first that $v$ is not a theory of $\Delta$. Then we denote by $\Phi$ the following set of bisequents

$$\Phi = \{\Vdash A : \mid A \in v\} \cup \{A : \Vdash \mid A \notin v\}.$$

Note that bitheories of $\Phi$ are pairs of the form $(v, w)$, for some set $w$. Now it should be clear that $v$ is an exact theory of $\Gamma \cup \Phi$, though it is still not even a theory of $\Delta \cup \Phi$.

Suppose now that $v$ is also a theory of $\Delta$. Since $(u, v)$ is not a regular bitheory of $\Delta$, we have $u \neq v$. Now we construct $\Phi$ as a union of the following three sets of bisequents:

$$\Phi_1 = \{A, B : \Vdash \mid A \notin u, B \notin v\},$$
$$\Phi_2 = \{\Vdash A, B : \mid A \in u, B \in v\},$$
$$\Phi_3 = \{A : \Vdash B : \mid (A \notin u \,\&\, B \in v) \text{ or } (A \notin v \,\&\, B \in u)\}.$$

As can be verified, a pair $(w, x)$ is a bitheory of $\Phi$ iff either $w = u$ or $w = v$. As a result, both $(u, v)$ and $(v, v)$ are still bitheories of $\Gamma \cup \Phi$, and hence $v$ is not an exact theory of the latter. But $v$ is obviously an exact theory of $\Delta \cup \Phi$. Consequently $\Gamma$ and $\Delta$ are not strongly equivalent. □

In view of the above proof, the discriminating sets $\Phi$ of bisequents can be restricted to positive bisequents $a :\Vdash b :$. In other words, we have

**Corollary 5.6** *Bisequent theories $\Gamma$ and $\Delta$ are strongly equivalent with respect to the exact semantics iff, for any set $\Phi$ of positive bisequents, $\Gamma \cup \Phi$ is nonmonotonically equivalent to $\Delta \cup \Phi$.*

Finally, we will consider exact theories of consistent biconsequence relations. Such theories will be shown to correspond to extensions described later in this chapter.

**Lemma 5.7** *A set $u$ is an exact theory of a consistent biconsequence relation $\Vdash$ iff $u = \{A \mid :\overline{u} \Vdash A:u\}$, and either $u \neq Pr$, or $\nVdash :Pr$.*

***Proof.*** Assume first that the above conditions are satisfied. If $u \neq Pr$, then $A \notin u$, for some $A$, and hence $: \overline{u} \nVdash A : u$. Therefore $: \overline{u} \nVdash : u$. But if $u = Pr$, we have $\nVdash : Pr$, and therefore $: \overline{u} \nVdash : u$ in this case also. Now, if

$A \notin u$, we have $A : \overline{u} \Vdash : u$ by Consistency and Monotonicity, while if $A \in u$, then $:\overline{u} \Vdash A{:}u$, and therefore $A{:}\overline{u} \nVdash :u$, since otherwise $: \overline{u} \Vdash : u$ by Positive Cut. Thus, $u$ is an exact theory by Lemma 5.1. In the other direction, we have to show only that either $u \neq Pr$, or $\nVdash : Pr$. But if $u = Pr$, we have that $Pr$ is a theory of $\Vdash$, and therefore $\nVdash : Pr$. □

An important consequence of the above description is that exact theories of a consistent biconsequence relation are uniquely determined by its singular autoepistemic subrelation:

**Corollary 5.8** *For an exact nonmonotonic semantics, any consistent biconsequence relation is nonmonotonically equivalent to its singular autoepistemic subrelation.*

### 5.1.1 *Exact completions*

In this section we will show that, under certain finiteness conditions, the exact nonmonotonic semantics of a bisequent theory is reducible to a classical semantics of some its completion. This completion will be obtained from the description of unitary Scott consequence relations, given in Chapter 2. The corresponding construction will constitute a biconsequence counterpart of the description of causal theories from [Lee, 2004].

Recall that a bisequent theory $\Delta$ is finitary, if its positive Scott reduct $\Delta^+$ is finitary (see Definition 2.9). Now, by an *exact completion* of a finitary bisequent theory $\Delta$ we will mean a classical theory, denoted by $ecomp(\Delta)$, that consists of the following formulas:

- $\bigvee(\neg a \cup b \cup c \cup \neg d)$, for any bisequent $a{:}b \Vdash c{:}d$ from $\Delta$;
- For any literal loop $l$ of $\Delta^+$, the formula

  $$\bigwedge l \to \bigvee\{\bigwedge(\neg b \cup d \cup ((a \cup \neg c)\backslash\neg l))\},$$

  for all $a{:}b \Vdash c{:}d \in \Delta$ such that $l \cap (\neg a \cup c) \neq \emptyset$ and $\neg l \cap (\neg a \cup c) = \emptyset$.

The following result shows that $ecomp(\Delta)$ provides a concise description of the exact nonmonotonic semantics of $\Delta$.

**Theorem 5.9** *The exact semantics of a finitary bisequent theory corresponds precisely to the classical semantics of its exact completion.*

***Proof.*** Recall that $u$ is an exact theory of $\Delta$ iff it is the only theory of the sequent theory $\Delta^+_u$. Now let $\alpha_u$ be the propositional interpretation corresponding to a set of atoms $u$. Then it can be verified that $\alpha_u$ is a model of $ecomp(\Delta)$ if and only if it is a model of the literal loop-completion $llcomp(\Delta_u^+)$. Hence the result follows immediately from Theorem 2.30. □

Just as for sequent theories, if a bisequent theory is also strongly acyclic, then the description of its exact completion can be greatly simplified. Namely, by a *pointwise completion* of a bisequent theory $\Delta$, $pcomp(\Delta)$, we will mean the following set of formulas, for any proposition $A$:

$$A \leftrightarrow \bigvee\{\bigwedge(a \cup \neg b \cup \neg c \cup d) \mid a{:}b \Vdash c, A{:}d \in \Delta\}$$
$$\neg A \leftrightarrow \bigvee\{\bigwedge(a \cup \neg b \cup \neg c \cup d) \mid a, A{:}b \Vdash c{:}d \in \Delta\},$$

plus the set $\{\neg \bigwedge(\neg b \cup d) \mid: b \Vdash : d \in \Delta\}$. Then Corollary 2.31 implies

**Corollary 5.10** *The exact nonmonotonic semantics of a strongly acyclic and strongly locally finite bisequent theory $\Delta$ corresponds precisely to the classical semantics of $pcomp(\Delta)$.*

As an important special case, let us say that a bisequent $a : b \Vdash c : d$ is *determinate* if $a \cup c$ contains no more than one proposition. A bisequent theory will be called *determinate*, if it consists of determinate bisequents.

A bisequent is determinate, if it has one of the following forms:

$$A : b \Vdash : d \qquad : b \Vdash A : d \qquad : b \Vdash : d\ .$$

The importance of such bisequents stems immediately from Lemma 5.1 that says, in effect, that the exact semantics of a biconsequence relation is uniquely determined by its determinate bisequents.

Let us say that a bisequent theory is *definite*, if it is determinate and strongly locally finite. Clearly, any determinate bisequent theory $\Delta$ is strongly acyclic, and consequently we obtain

**Corollary 5.11** *The exact semantics of a definite bisequent theory corresponds precisely to the classical semantics of its pointwise completion.*

As can be seen, the pointwise completion of a definite bisequent theory can be described as follows:

$$A \leftrightarrow \bigvee\{\bigwedge(d \cup \neg b) \mid : b \Vdash A : d \in \Delta\}$$
$$\neg A \leftrightarrow \bigvee\{\bigwedge(d \cup \neg b) \mid A : b \Vdash : d \in \Delta\},$$

plus the set $\{\neg \bigwedge(d \cup \neg b) \mid : b \Vdash : d \in \Delta\}$.

### 5.1.2 *Minimality*

Our next result shows that the default subrelation of a biconsequence relation determines precisely the subset of the exact semantics that consists of minimal theories.

**Theorem 5.12** *A set of propositions is an exact theory of the default subrelation $_d\Vdash$ of a regular biconsequence relation if and only if it is both an exact and a minimal theory of $\Vdash$.*

***Proof.*** Recall first that bitheories of $_d\Vdash$ are pairs $(u, v)$ such that $(u, v')$ is a bitheory of $\Vdash$, for some $v' \subseteq v$ (see Corollary 3.40). Assume now that $u$ is an exact and a minimal theory of $\Vdash$. Since $u$ is a theory of $\Vdash$, it will be a theory of $_d\Vdash$. Suppose that there is $w \neq u$ such that $(w, u)$ is also a bitheory of $_d\Vdash$. Then there must exists $u' \subseteq u$ such that $(w, u')$ is a bitheory of $\Vdash$. Since $u'$ is a theory of $\Vdash$ by regularity, we have $u = u'$ due to minimality of $u$, and therefore $(w, u)$ is a bitheory of $\Vdash$, contrary to the assumption that $u$ is exact. Thus, $u$ is an exact theory of $_d\Vdash$.

Assume now that $u$ is an exact theory of $_d\Vdash$. Since $u$ is a theory of $_d\Vdash$, there exists $u' \subseteq u$ such that $(u, u')$ is a bitheory of $\Vdash$. Then $u'$ is a theory of $\Vdash$ by regularity, and therefore $(u', u)$ is a bitheory of $_d\Vdash$. But $u$ is exact in $_d\Vdash$, and consequently $u = u'$. Thus, $u$ is a theory of $\Vdash$. Moreover, if $(w, u)$ is a bitheory of $\Vdash$, it will be a bitheory of $_d\Vdash$. Consequently, $u$ is an exact theory of $\Vdash$. Finally, if $v$ is a theory of $\Vdash$ such that $v \subset u$, then $(v, u)$ will be a bitheory of $\Vdash$, contrary to our assumption that $u$ is exact in $_d\Vdash$. Thus, $u$ is a minimal theory of $\Vdash$. □

The most important consequence of the above theorem is the following

**Corollary 5.13** *If $\Delta$ is a default bisequent theory, then any exact theory of $\Delta$ will be a minimal propositional theory of $\Delta$.*

The next result gives a syntactic description of minimal exact theories. The proof is immediate from Lemmas 5.1 and 3.37.

**Lemma 5.14** *A set $u$ of propositions is an exact and minimal theory of a biconsequence relation $\Vdash$ if and only if, for any proposition $A$,*

$$A \in u \text{ iff } : \overline{u} \Vdash A :$$

$$A \notin u \text{ iff } A : \overline{u} \Vdash$$

Finally, for the consistent case the description is simplified as follows.

**Lemma 5.15** *A set $u$ is an exact and minimal theory of a consistent biconsequence relation $\Vdash$ iff $u = \{A \mid :\overline{u} \Vdash A:\}$.*

***Proof.*** Follows from Lemma 5.7, if we notice that ${}_d\Vdash\ : Pr$ holds only if $\Vdash$ is a trivial biconsequence relation (that is, contains all bisequents). □

As a consequence of the above representation, in the consistent case such theories are determined by the singular simple subrelation of a biconsequence relation.

## 5.2 Singular Semantics

In this section we will consider a broader class of nonmonotonic models that will be called singular theories. The distinction between exact and singular theories will form a basis for subsequent distinctions between extensions and expansions of nonmonotonic formalisms, and between stable and supported models of logic programs.

$u \triangle v$ below denotes the symmetric difference of the sets $u$ and $v$.

**Definition 5.4** A theory $u$ of a biconsequence relation $\Vdash$ will be called *singular*, if, for any set $v$ such that $u \triangle v = \{A\}$, for some proposition $A$, $(v, u)$ is not a bitheory of $\Vdash$. The set of singular theories will be called a *singular nonmonotonic semantics* of $\Vdash$.

Singular theories do not permit removals or additions of single propositions without violating the closure with respect to the bisequents of a biconsequence relation. Clearly, any exact theory will be singular, though not vice versa.

A syntactic description of singular theories is given in the next lemma.

**Lemma 5.16** *A set $u$ is a singular theory of $\Vdash$ if and only if, for any proposition $A$,*

$$A \in u \text{ iff } u \backslash \{A\} : \overline{u} \Vdash A, \overline{u} : u$$
$$A \notin u \text{ iff } A, u : \overline{u} \Vdash \overline{u} \backslash \{A\} : u.$$

***Proof.*** From the fact that $u$ is singular if and only if, for any $A \in u$ and $B \notin u$, neither $(u \backslash \{A\}, u)$, nor $(u \cup \{B\}, u)$ are bitheories. □

As for exact theories, we have the following restricted monotonicity property. The proof is similar to the case of exact theories, so we omit it.

**Lemma 5.17** *If $\Vdash$ and $\Vdash_1$ are Scott-equivalent biconsequence relations such that $\Vdash \subseteq \Vdash_1$, then any singular theory of $\Vdash$ is a singular theory of $\Vdash_1$.*

The notion of a singular theory can also be extended to bisequent theories in general.

**Definition 5.5** A set $u$ of propositions will be called a *singular theory* of a bisequent theory $\Delta$, if it is a singular theory of $\Vdash_\Delta$. The set of singular theories of $\Delta$ will be called a *singular nonmonotonic semantics* of $\Delta$.

Our next result shows that singular theories can be characterized as exact theories of semi-classical biconsequence relations.

**Theorem 5.18** *If $\Vdash^s$ is a least semi-classical biconsequence relation that contains $\Vdash$, then singular theories of $\Vdash$ coincide with exact theories of $\Vdash^s$.*

***Proof.*** Recall first that, if $\Vdash^r$ is a least regular biconsequence relation containing $\Vdash$, then both have the same exact theories. Now, bitheories of $\Vdash^s$ are precisely the semi-classical bitheories of $\Vdash^r$. Consequently, $u$ is an exact theory of $\Vdash^s$ precisely when it is a singular theory $\Vdash$. □

As a consequence of the above theorem, we obtain the following

**Corollary 5.19** *Singular theories of a semi-classical biconsequence relation coincide with its exact theories.*

Thus, the rules of semi-classical biconsequence relations are admissible for singular theories. Moreover, semi-classical biconsequence relations constitute a maximal logic suitable for the singular nonmonotonic semantics.

**Definition 5.6** Bisequent theories $\Gamma$ and $\Delta$ will be called *semi-classically equivalent*, if they determine the same semi-classical biconsequence relation.

**Theorem 5.20** *Bisequent theories are strongly equivalent with respect to a singular semantics if and only if they are semi-classically equivalent.*

***Proof.*** The implication from right to left is immediate. Assume now that $\Gamma$ and $\Delta$ are strongly equivalent, and let $\Sigma$ denote the set of all bisequents of the form $A, B{:}A, B \Vdash$, or $\Vdash A, B{:}A, B$, or $A{:}A \Vdash B{:}B$, for $A{\neq}B$. Since these are precisely bisequents that characterize a semi-classical biconsequence relation, $\Gamma$ and $\Delta$ determine the same singular theories only if $\Gamma \cup \Sigma$ and $\Delta \cup \Sigma$ determine the same exact theories. Consequently, $\Gamma$ and $\Delta$ are strongly equivalent with respect to a singular semantics only if $\Gamma \cup \Sigma$ and $\Delta \cup \Sigma$ are strongly equivalent with respect to an exact semantics. This gives us that $\Gamma \cup \Sigma$ and $\Delta \cup \Sigma$ are regularly equivalent (by Theorem 5.5), which is reducible to the claim that $\Gamma$ and $\Delta$ are semi-classically equivalent. □

Our next result states an instructive sufficient condition for coincidence of exact and singular semantics of a bisequent theory.

**Theorem 5.21** *Singular theories of a strongly acyclic bisequent theory coincide with its exact theories.*

***Proof.*** By Lemma 5.2, $u$ is an exact theory of $\Delta$ if and only if it is the only theory of $\Delta_u^+$. By Theorem 2.29, $u$ is the only theory of $\Delta_u^+$ iff the set of literals $u \cup \neg\overline{u}$ does not contain a loop $l \cup \neg m$ such that $(u \backslash l) \cup m$ is also a theory of $\Delta_u^+$. Now, since $\Delta_u^+$ is strongly acyclic, it does not have nontrivial loops, and therefore its loops are just singular sets $\{A\}$ and $\{\neg A\}$, for all propositions $A$. Consequently, $u$ is the only theory of $\Delta_u^+$ iff neither $u \backslash \{A\}$, for some $A \in u$, nor $u \cup \{A\}$, for some $A \notin u$, are theories of $\Delta_u^+$. □

Since determinate bisequent theories are (trivially) strongly acyclic, we immediately obtain

**Corollary 5.22** *Singular theories of a determinate bisequent theory coincide with its exact theories.*

Finally, for a singular nonmonotonic semantics, any bisequent theory is logically reducible to a certain determinate theory.

For an arbitrary bisequent theory $\Delta$, we will define $det(\Delta)$ as the union of the following three sets of determinate bisequents:

$$\{: b \Vdash : d \mid : b \Vdash : d \in \Delta\}$$
$$\{: b, c \Vdash C : a, d \mid a : b \Vdash c, C : d \in \Delta\}$$
$$\{A : b, c \Vdash : a, d \mid a, A : b \Vdash c : d \in \Delta\}.$$

Now, Corollary 3.29 shows that $\Delta$ is semi-classically equivalent to $det(\Delta)$. Consequently, we obtain

**Lemma 5.23** *For a singular semantics, any bisequent theory $\Delta$ is strongly equivalent to $det(\Delta)$.*

The above result gives us a modular reduction of bisequent theories to determinate ones under the singular semantics. Note, in particular, that, due to the strong equivalence, the corresponding determinate bisequent theory can replace the original theory in any larger context. Moreover, since $det(\Delta)$ is a determinate bisequent theory, we have also

**Corollary 5.24** *Singular semantics of $\Delta$ coincides with the exact semantics of $det(\Delta)$.*

The above corollary allows us, in particular, to compute singular models of bisequent theories as the classical models of the pointwise completion of $det(\Delta)$. Furthermore, it can be easily verified that the pointwise completion of $det(\Delta)$ coincides with the pointwise completion of $\Delta$ itself, and consequently we obtain

**Corollary 5.25** *If $\Delta$ is a strongly locally finite bisequent theory, then the singular nonmonotonic semantics of $\Delta$ corresponds exactly to the classical semantics of its pointwise completion.*

## 5.3 Default Semantics

Now we will define yet another, this time more familiar, class of nonmonotonic models. Extensions, defined below, will correspond to stable models of logic programs and extensions of default logic.

**Definition 5.7** A set $u$ will be called an *extension* of a biconsequence relation $\Vdash$, if $(u, u)$ is a positively minimal bitheory of $\Vdash$. A *default nonmonotonic semantics* of a biconsequence relation is the set of its extensions.

Any extension is a theory of a biconsequence relation. More precisely, $u$ is an extension if and only if it is a theory of a biconsequence relation such that there is no smaller set $v \subset u$ such that $(v, u)$ is a bitheory. In other words, $u$ is an extension if and only if it is a minimal theory of the positive reduction $\Vdash_u^+$. This implies the following simple observation:

**Lemma 5.26** *Any exact theory of a biconsequence relation is an extension.*

The reverse inclusion does not hold. For example, for positive biconsequence relations that do not have exact theories, extensions coincide with minimal theories.

The following lemma provides a syntactic description of extensions. It is an immediate consequence of Lemma 3.6.

**Lemma 5.27** *A set $u$ is an extension of a biconsequence relation $\Vdash$ if and only if $u = \{A \mid :\overline{u} \Vdash A, \overline{u}{:}u\}$ and either $u \neq Pr$, or $\nVdash: Pr$.*

By the above description, extensions are theories of a biconsequence relation that explain only why they have the propositions they have. In other words, for extensions we are relieved from the necessity of explaining why propositions do *not* belong to the relevant theory. This relaxation of the principle of explanatory closure constitutes the essence of Reiter's Closed World Assumption.

Another consequence of the above description is that extensions are determined by the autoepistemic subrelation of a biconsequence relation.

**Corollary 5.28** *The set of extensions of a biconsequence relation coincides with the set of extensions of its autoepistemic subrelation.*

For singular biconsequence relations, the above description of extensions can be simplified as follows.

**Corollary 5.29** *A set $u$ is an extension of a singular biconsequence relation $\Vdash$ if and only if $u = \{A \mid : \overline{u} \Vdash A : u\}$, and either $u \neq Pr$, or $\nVdash : Pr$.*

The proof follows immediately from Corollary 3.36. This description will be used in the next chapter.

As for exact theories, the notion of an extension can be naturally defined for arbitrary bisequent theories.

**Definition 5.8** A set of propositions $u$ will be called an *extension* of a bisequent theory $\Delta$, if it is an extension of $\Vdash_\Delta$. A *default nonmonotonic semantics* of a bisequent theory is the set of its extensions.

A more direct description of the default semantics for a bisequent theory is given in the next lemma in terms of its positive reducts. The proof is immediate from the fact that $(v, u)$ is a bitheory of $\Delta$ if and only if $v$ is a theory of $\Delta_u^+$.

**Lemma 5.30** *$u$ is an extension of a bisequent theory $\Delta$ if and only if it is a minimal theory of $\Delta_u^+$.*

Now we will show that extensions can be precisely characterized as exact theories of biconsequence relations augmented with the Consistency rule. Let us denote by $\Vdash^c$ the least consistent biconsequence relation that contains $\Vdash$. Then we have

**Theorem 5.31** *Extensions of $\Vdash$ coincide with exact theories of $\Vdash^c$.*

***Proof.*** The bitheories of $\Vdash^c$ are precisely consistent bitheories of $\Vdash$. Consequently, $u$ is an exact theory of $\Vdash^c$ precisely when there is no smaller set $v \subset u$ such that $(v, u)$ is a bitheory of $\Vdash$. Hence the result. □

The effect of the Consistency rule $A : A \Vdash$ amounts to an immediate refutation of any proposition that is *assumed* not to hold. That is why absence of propositions from extensions does not require explanation, only their presence. Accordingly, a general conclusion that can be made from the above result is that the default nonmonotonic semantics is precisely an exact semantics under a stronger logic of consistent biconsequence relations. This implies, in particular, that the minimality condition in the definition of extensions is not an independent 'rationality principle' of nonmonotonic reasoning, but a consequence of the logical Consistency postulate.

As a first consequence of the above theorem, we obtain the following

**Corollary 5.32** *Extensions of a consistent biconsequence relation coincide with its exact theories.*

Extensions turn out to have much the same properties as exact theories. Thus, we still have the restricted monotonicity property:

**Lemma 5.33** *If* $\Vdash$ *and* $\Vdash_1$ *are Scott-equivalent biconsequence relations such that* $\Vdash\subseteq\Vdash_1$*, then any extension of* $\Vdash$ *is an extension of* $\Vdash_1$*.*

***Proof.*** If $\Vdash\subseteq\Vdash_1$, then $\Vdash^c\subseteq\Vdash_1^c$, and therefore by Lemma 5.3, any exact theory of $\Vdash^c$ is a exact theory of $\Vdash_1^c$. Now the result follows from the preceding theorem. □

Due to the fact that extensions coincide with exact theories of the corresponding consistent biconsequence relation, we can immediately conclude that Consistency and Regularity are admissible rules for extensions.

Let $\Vdash^{rc}$ denote the least consistent and regular biconsequence relation that contains $\Vdash$. Similarly, $\Vdash_\Delta^{rc}$ will denote the least consistent regular biconsequence relation containing a bisequent theory $\Delta$.

**Corollary 5.34** $\Vdash^{rc}$ *has the same extensions as* $\Vdash$*.*

Moreover, we will show that consistent regular biconsequence relations constitute a maximal logic suitable for extensions.

In what follows, we will often say that bisequent theories are *(strongly) extension-equivalent*, if they are (strongly) nonmonotonically equivalent with respect to the default semantics. Then the following lemma is just a reformulation of our previous results in the new terminology.

**Lemma 5.35**

- *Any biconsequence relation is extension-equivalent to its autoepistemic subrelation;*
- *Any consistent biconsequence relation is extension-equivalent to its singular autoepistemic subrelation.*

**Definition 5.9** Bisequent theories $\Gamma$ and $\Delta$ will be called *default equivalent*, if they determine the same consistent and regular biconsequence relation.

The next result can be seen as a logical reformulation of the Main Theorem from [Lifschitz *et al.*, 2001].

**Theorem 5.36** *Bisequent theories are strongly extension-equivalent if and only if they are default equivalent.*

***Proof.*** Though it is possible to reduce the proof to that of Theorem 5.5, we give a direct proof based on a simplified set of discriminating bisequents.

The implication from right to left is immediate. Assume now that $\Gamma$ and $\Delta$ are not default equivalent, and assume for certainty that $(u, v)$ is a consistent regular bitheory of $\Gamma$, but not of $\Delta$. Then $u \subseteq v$, and $v$ is a theory of $\Gamma$.

Suppose first that $v$ is not a theory of $\Delta$, and let $\Phi$ denote the set of bisequents $\{\Vdash A : \mid A \in v\}$. Then $v$ will be an extension of $\Gamma \cup \Phi$, though it will not be even a theory of $\Delta \cup \Phi$.

Suppose now that $v$ is also a theory of $\Delta$. Then we define $\Phi$ as follows:

$$\Phi = \{\Vdash A :\mid A \in u\} \cup \{A : \Vdash B :\mid A, B \in v \backslash u\}.$$

A pair $(x, v)$ such that $x \subseteq v$ will be a bitheory of $\Phi$ only if $x$ is either $u$, or $v$. As a result, both $(u, v)$ and $(v, v)$ will still be bitheories of $\Gamma \cup \Phi$, and hence $v$ will not be an extension of the latter. But $v$ will obviously be an extension of $\Delta \cup \Phi$. Consequently $\Gamma$ and $\Delta$ will not be strongly extension-equivalent. □

As follows from the above proof, discriminating sets of bisequents $\Phi$ can be reduced for extensions to positive singular bisequents of the form $A :\Vdash B$: or $\Vdash B$:.

Finally, Lemma 5.7 gives us the following description of extensions in the consistent case:

**Corollary 5.37** *A set $u$ is an extension of a consistent biconsequence relation $\Vdash$ iff $u = \{A \mid : \overline{u} \Vdash A : u\}$, and either $u \neq Pr$, or $\nVdash : Pr$.*

Thus, extensions of a consistent biconsequence relation are uniquely determined by its singular autoepistemic subrelation.

### 5.3.1 *Stable completion*

Now we will show that, under some finiteness constraints, the default nonmonotonic semantics of a bisequent theory is also reducible to a classical semantics of some its completion.

By Definition 3.6, a bisequent theory $\Delta$ is finitely well-founded, if its positive Scott reduct $\Delta^+$ is such. Then by a *stable completion* of such a bisequent theory $\Delta$ we will mean a classical theory, denoted by $scomp(\Delta)$, that consists of the following formulas:

- $\bigvee(\neg a \cup b \cup c \cup \neg d)$, for any bisequent $a{:}b \Vdash c{:}d$ from $\Delta$;
- $\bigwedge l \to \bigvee\{\bigwedge(a \cup \neg b \cup d \cup \neg(c \backslash l)) \mid a{:}b \Vdash c{:}d \in \Delta \ \&\ l \cap c \neq \emptyset \ \&\ l \cap a = \emptyset\}$, for any (atom) loop $l$ of $\Delta^+$.

The following result shows that the stable completion provides a concise description of the default nonmonotonic semantics. It is a logical counterpart of the corresponding characterizations of stable semantics obtained for normal logic programs in [Lin and Zhao, 2002], and for disjunctive programs in [Lee and Lifschitz, 2003].

**Theorem 5.38** *The default nonmonotonic semantics of a finitely well-founded bisequent theory corresponds precisely to the classical semantics of its stable completion.*

***Proof.*** Recall that $u$ is an extension of $\Delta$ iff it is a minimal theory of $\Delta^+_u$. Hence the result follows immediately from Theorem 2.26, if we notice that the propositional interpretation $\alpha_u$ corresponding to a set of atoms $u$ is a model of $scomp(\Delta)$ if and only if it is a model of the loop-completion $lcomp(\Delta^+_u)$. □

### 5.3.2 *Minimal extensions*

Extensions do not always correspond to minimal theories of a biconsequence relation. However, just as for exact theories, such minimal extensions are determined by the default subrelation of a biconsequence relation.

**Theorem 5.39** *Extensions of the default subrelation ${}_d\Vdash$ of a regular biconsequence relation $\Vdash$ are precisely extensions of $\Vdash$ that are also minimal theories of $\Vdash$.*

***Proof.*** Assume first that $u$ is a minimal extension of $\Vdash$. Since $u$ is a theory of $\Vdash$, it will be a theory of ${}_d\Vdash$. Suppose that there is $w \subset u$ such that $(w, u)$ is also a bitheory of ${}_d\Vdash$. Then there must exist $u' \subseteq u$ such that $(w, u')$ is a bitheory of $\Vdash$. Since $u'$ is a theory of $\Vdash$ by regularity, we have $u = u'$ due to minimality of $u$, and therefore $(w, u)$ is a bitheory of $\Vdash$, contrary to the assumption that $u$ is an extension. Thus, $u$ is an extension of ${}_d\Vdash$.

Assume now that $u$ is an extension of ${}_d\Vdash$. Since $u$ is a theory of ${}_d\Vdash$, there exists $u' \subseteq u$ such that $(u, u')$ is a bitheory of $\Vdash$. Then $u'$ is a theory of $\Vdash$ by regularity, and therefore $(u', u)$ is a bitheory of ${}_d\Vdash$. But $u$ is an extension of ${}_d\Vdash$, and consequently $u = u'$. Thus, $u$ is a theory of $\Vdash$. Moreover, if $(w, u)$ is a bitheory of $\Vdash$, it will be a bitheory of ${}_d\Vdash$. Consequently, $u$ is an extension of $\Vdash$. Finally, if $v$ is a theory of $\Vdash$ such that $v \subset u$, then $(v, u)$ will be a bitheory of $\Vdash$, contrary to our assumption that $u$ is stable in ${}_d\Vdash$. Thus, $u$ is a minimal theory of $\Vdash$. □

As a consequence, we obtain the following well-known result.

**Corollary 5.40** *Any extension of a default bisequent theory will also be its minimal theory.*

Recall now that a biconsequence relation has the same extensions as its autoepistemic subrelation. This implies, in particular, that minimal extensions are determined by the autoepistemic subrelation of the default subrelation, which is nothing other than the simple subrelation of a biconsequence relation. In other words, we have

**Corollary 5.41**

- *Extensions of the simple subrelation of a biconsequence relation $\Vdash$ coincide with the extensions of $\Vdash$ that are minimal theories of $\Vdash$.*
- *Extensions of the simple singular subrelation of a consistent biconsequence relation $\Vdash$ coincide with the extensions of $\Vdash$ that are also minimal theories of $\Vdash$.*

In addition, as a consequence of Lemma 5.15, we obtain the following explicit description of minimal extensions:

**Lemma 5.42** *A set $u$ is an extension and minimal theory of a biconsequence relation $\Vdash$ iff $u = \{A \mid :\overline{u} \Vdash A:\}$.*

It is interesting to observe, however, that a restriction to extensions that are minimal theories does not change the underlying logic of biconsequence relations. This observation is immediate from the fact that all the counterexamples constructed in the proof of Theorem 5.36 give actually extensions that are also minimal theories.

It should be noted that being a default bisequent theory is only a sufficient, but not a necessary condition for minimality of extensions. As follows from Theorem 5.39, the question *"When all extensions of a bisequent theory are minimal?"* is actually equivalent to the question *"When a bisequent theory is extension-equivalent to a default bisequent theory?"*. An important sufficient condition for this property has been established, in effect, in [Inoue and Sakama, 1998] in the framework of logic programming.

A bisequent theory $\Delta$ will be called *negative acyclic*, if there exists a ranking function $r$ from propositions to ordinals such that, for any bisequent $a : b \Vdash c : d$ from $\Delta$, and any $A \in a$, $C \in c$ and $D \in d$, $r(A) \leq r(C)$ and $r(D) < r(C)$.

For a bisequent theory $\Delta$, we will denote by $shift(\Delta)$ the following set of default bisequents:

$$shift(\Delta) = \{a, d : b \Vdash c :|\ a : b \Vdash c : d \in \Delta\}.$$

Then the following result can be shown.

**Lemma 5.43** *If $\Delta$ is a negative acyclic bisequent theory, than it is extension-equivalent to $shift(\Delta)$.*

***Proof.*** Note first that $\Delta$ and $shift(\Delta)$ are Scott equivalent. Moreover, any bisequent $a{:}b \Vdash c{:}d$ implies $a, d{:}b \Vdash c{:}$ by Import, and therefore $\Vdash^{c}_{shift(\Delta)} \subseteq \Vdash^{c}_{\Delta}$. Hence by Lemma 5.33, any extension of $shift(\Delta)$ will be an extension of $\Delta$. In the other direction, suppose that $u$ is an extension of $\Delta$ that is not an extension of $shift(\Delta)$. Then there exists $v \subset u$ such that $(v, u)$ is a bitheory of $shift(\Delta)$. Let us denote by $x$ the set of all propositions that have a minimal rank in $u \backslash v$. Since $u$ is an extension of $\Delta$, $(u \backslash x, u)$ is not a bitheory of $\Delta$, and therefore $\Delta$ contains a bisequent $a{:}b \Vdash c{:}d$ such that $a \subseteq u \backslash x$, $b \subseteq \overline{u}$, $c \subseteq \overline{u \backslash x}$ and $d \subseteq u$. Now, if it were the case that $c \subseteq \overline{u}$, we would have $u{:}\overline{u} \Vdash_{\Delta} \overline{u}{:}u$, contrary to our assumption that $u$ is a theory of $\Delta$. Therefore $c \cap x \neq \emptyset$, and hence $c$ contains a proposition with a minimal rank in $u \backslash v$. By negative acyclicity of $\Delta$, we immediately conclude that both $d$ and $a$ are included in $v$. But we have also that the bisequent $a, d{:}b \Vdash c{:}$ belongs to $shift(\Delta)$, $a, d \subseteq v$, $b \subseteq \overline{u}$, $c \subseteq \overline{v}$ and $d \subseteq u$, which contradicts our assumption that $(v, u)$ is a bitheory of $shift(\Delta)$. Hence $u$ must be an extension of $shift(\Delta)$. □

Since $shift(\Delta)$ is a default bisequent theory, we immediately obtain

**Corollary 5.44** *Any extension of a negative acyclic bisequent theory will also be its minimal theory.*

The following example from [Inoue and Sakama, 1998] shows that negative acyclicity is essential for the above result.

**Example 5.2** A bisequent theory $\Delta = \{\Vdash A{:}A;\ A{:} \Vdash B{:};\ {:}B \Vdash\}$ is not negatively acyclic, and it has a unique (hence a minimal) extension $\{A, B\}$. However, $shift(\Delta)$ has no extensions.

It should also be noted that, though $shift(\Delta)$ is extension-equivalent to $\Delta$ for a negatively acyclic $\Delta$, the two bisequent theories are not default equivalent. This means that they can give different results when we add some other bisequents to both of them.

The above result has also a relativized version stating when a particular extension of an arbitrary bisequent theory will be minimal.

For a bisequent theory $\Delta$ and a set of propositions $u$, we will denote by $\Delta(u)$ the following subset of $\Delta$:

$$\Delta(u) = \{a : b \Vdash c : d \in \Delta \mid a, d \subseteq u, b \subseteq \overline{u}, c \cap u \neq \emptyset\}.$$

Then the following corollary can be easily discerned from the proof of the preceding theorem.

**Corollary 5.45** *An extension $u$ of a bisequent theory $\Delta$ will be a minimal theory of $\Delta$, if $\Delta(u)$ is negative acyclic.*

## 5.4 Supported Semantics

Finally, we will define the notion of an expansion that is related to supported models of logic programs and expansions of autoepistemic logic. Actually, the relation between expansions and extensions will be similar to that between singular and exact theories.

**Definition 5.10** A theory $u$ of a biconsequence relation $\Vdash$ will be called an *expansion* of $\Vdash$, if, for any proposition $A$ from $u$, the pair $(u\backslash\{A\}, u)$ is not a bitheory of $\Vdash$. A *supported nonmonotonic semantics* of a biconsequence relation is the set of its expansions.

Since an extension $u$ does not have proper subsets $v$ such that $(v, u)$ is a bitheory, we immediately obtain

**Lemma 5.46** *Any extension of a biconsequence relation is an expansion.*

The reverse inclusion does not hold. Recall, for example, that extensions of a positive biconsequence relation coincide with its minimal theories. As could be expected, however, its expansions will coincide with supported theories of the associated Scott consequence relation.

A syntactic description of expansions is given in the next lemma. The proof is straightforward.

**Lemma 5.47** *A set u is an expansion of* $\Vdash$ *if and only if it is a theory of* $\Vdash$ *and, for any proposition A,*

$$A \in u \text{ iff } u \backslash \{A\} : \overline{u} \Vdash A, \overline{u} : u.$$

As in Lemma 3.6, the auxiliary condition that u is a theory is needed only for the case when $u$ is the set of all propositions.

As before, the notion of an expansion can be extended to bisequent theories in general.

**Definition 5.11** A set of propositions $u$ will be called an *expansion* of a bisequent theory $\Delta$, if it is an expansion of $\Vdash_{\Delta}$. A *supported nonmonotonic semantics* of a bisequent theory is the set of its expansions.

The following result shows that expansions can be precisely characterized as extensions of semi-classical biconsequence relations.

**Theorem 5.48** *If* $\Vdash^s$ *is a least semi-classical biconsequence relation that contains* $\Vdash$*, then expansions of* $\Vdash$ *coincide with extensions of* $\Vdash^s$*.*

***Proof.*** Bitheories of $\Vdash^s$ are precisely regular semi-classical bitheories of $\Vdash$. Consequently, $u$ is an extension of $\Vdash^t$ precisely when there is no proposition $A \in u$ such that $(u\backslash\{A\}, u)$ is a bitheory of $\Vdash$. □

As a first consequence of the above theorem, we obtain the following

**Corollary 5.49** *Expansions of a semi-classical biconsequence relation coincide with its extensions.*

Moreover, if we combine the above correspondence with the correspondence between extensions and exact theories, we immediately obtain correspondence between expansions and exact theories of *tight* biconsequence relations, that is, biconsequence relations that satisfy Consistency, Regularity and Quasi-Completeness.

Let $\Vdash^t$ denote the least tight biconsequence relation containing $\Vdash$. Then we have

**Corollary 5.50**

- *If* $\Vdash$ *is a tight biconsequence relation, then the sets of its extensions, expansions, singular and exact theories coincide.*

- *Expansions of* $\Vdash$ *coincide with exact theories of* $\Vdash^t$.

Thus, the rules of tight biconsequence relations are admissible for expansions.

As for the other kinds of nonmonotonic semantics, we have the following already familiar restricted monotonicity property. The proof is similar to the case of extensions, so we omit it.

**Lemma 5.51** *If* $\Vdash$ *and* $\Vdash_1$ *are Scott-equivalent biconsequence relations such that* $\Vdash \subseteq \Vdash_1$, *then any expansion of* $\Vdash$ *is an expansion of* $\Vdash_1$.

Finally, we will show that tight biconsequence relations constitute a maximal logic suitable for expansions. In what follows, we will often say that bisequent theories are *(strongly) expansion-equivalent*, if they are (strongly) equivalent with respect to the supported semantics.

**Definition 5.12** Bisequent theories $\Gamma$ and $\Delta$ will be called *tightly equivalent*, if they determine the same tight biconsequence relation.

**Theorem 5.52** *Bisequent theories are strongly expansion-equivalent if and only if they are tightly equivalent.*

***Proof.*** The implication from right to left is immediate. Assume that $\Gamma$ and $\Delta$ are strongly expansion-equivalent, and let $\Sigma$ denote the set of all bisequents of the form $\Vdash A, B{:}A, B$, for $A{\neq}B$. Note that $\Gamma$ and $\Delta$ determine the same expansions only if $\Gamma \cup \Sigma$ and $\Delta \cup \Sigma$ determine the same extensions. Consequently, $\Gamma$ and $\Delta$ are strongly expansion-equivalent only if $\Gamma \cup \Sigma$ and $\Delta \cup \Sigma$ are strongly extension-equivalent. The latter gives us that $\Gamma \cup \Sigma$ and $\Delta \cup \Sigma$ are default equivalent (by Theorem 5.36), which is reducible to the claim that $\Gamma$ and $\Delta$ are tightly equivalent. □

An important problem consists in determining conditions on a bisequent theory under which expansions coincide with extensions. Our next result states an important sufficient condition. As we will see, it is actually a generalization of the well-known Fages' theorem in logic programming.

**Theorem 5.53** *Expansions of an acyclic bisequent theory coincide with its extensions.*

The proof follows immediately from Lemma 2.23. Actually, the latter lemma justifies a relativized version of the above result stating when a particular expansion of a bisequent theory is also its extension.

Recall that, for a bisequent theory $\Delta$ and a set $u$ of propositions, $\Delta(u)$ denotes the following subset of $\Delta$:

$$\Delta(u) = \{a : b \Vdash c : d \in \Delta \mid a, d \subseteq u, b \subseteq \overline{u}, c \cap u \neq \emptyset\}.$$

Then we have

**Corollary 5.54** *An expansion $u$ of a bisequent theory $\Delta$ is also an extension of $\Delta$, if $\Delta(u)$ is acyclic.*

Since autoepistemic bisequent theories are trivially acyclic, we obtain

**Corollary 5.55** *Expansions of an autoepistemic bisequent theory coincide with its extensions.*

Finally, it will be shown that, for a supported nonmonotonic semantics, any bisequent theory is logically reducible to a certain singular autoepistemic theory.

For an arbitrary bisequent theory $\Delta$, we will define $auto(\Delta)$ as the union of the following two sets of singular autoepistemic bisequents:

$$\{: b \Vdash : a, d \mid a : b \Vdash : d \in \Delta\}$$
$$\{: b, c \Vdash A : a, d \mid a : b \Vdash c, A : d \in \Delta\}.$$

Now, Corollary 3.31 shows that $\Delta$ is tightly equivalent to $auto(\Delta)$[1]. Consequently, we obtain

**Lemma 5.56** *Any bisequent theory $\Delta$ is strongly expansion-equivalent to $auto(\Delta)$.*

Moreover, $auto(\Delta)$ is an autoepistemic bisequent theory, and therefore we conclude with

**Corollary 5.57** *Supported semantics of $\Delta$ coincides with the default semantics of $auto(\Delta)$.*

The above construction gives us a modular reduction of bisequent theories to singular autoepistemic ones under the supported semantics. This reduction is important for the semantics of logic programs, since it allows to compute supported models of a general logic program as the classical models of its completion, defined in the next section (see also [Brass and Dix, 1995b]).

[1]Recall that, by our agreement, if $a{:}b \Vdash c{:}d \in \Delta$, then $a \cap c = \emptyset$.

### 5.4.1 *Completion*

As for the previous nonmonotonic semantics, the supported nonmonotonic semantics can also be reduced to the classical semantics of some its completion.

To begin with, recall that the default semantics of a finitely well-founded bisequent theory $\Delta$ is reducible to the classical semantics of its stable completion $scomp(\Delta)$. Now, if $\Delta$ is acyclic, it does not have nontrivial loops, and consequently the description of the stable completion reduces to a relatively simple deductive theory given in the next definition.

**Definition 5.13** A (plain) *completion* of a locally finite bisequent theory $\Delta$ is the set $comp(\Delta)$ of the following classical logical formulas, for any proposition $A$:

$$A \leftrightarrow \bigvee\{\bigwedge(a \cup d \cup \neg b \cup \neg c) \mid a : b \Vdash c, A : d \in \Delta\},$$

plus the set $\{\neg \bigwedge(a \cup d \cup \neg b) \mid a : b \Vdash : d \in \Delta\}$.

**Lemma 5.58** *If $\Delta$ is a locally finite acyclic bisequent theory, then the classical models of $comp(\Delta)$ correspond exactly to extensions of $\Delta$.*

Now, since autoepistemic bisequent theories are trivially acyclic, we immediately obtain

**Corollary 5.59** *The default nonmonotonic semantics of a locally finite autoepistemic bisequent theory coincides with the classical semantics of its completion.*

Clearly, the completion of an autoepistemic bisequent theory $\Delta$ is determined as the set of all classical formulas of the form

$$A \leftrightarrow \bigvee\{\bigwedge(d \cup \neg(b \cup c)) \mid : b \Vdash c, A : d \in \Delta\},$$

plus the set $\{\neg \bigwedge(d \cup \neg b) \mid : b \Vdash : d \in \Delta\}$.

Due to the fact that expansions of an acyclic bisequent theory coincide with its extensions, the above results give us, in effect, all we need in order to prove the following theorem.

**Theorem 5.60** *If $\Delta$ is a locally finite bisequent theory, then the classical models of $comp(\Delta)$ correspond exactly to expansions of $\Delta$.*

***Proof.*** Recall that any bisequent theory $\Delta$ is logically reducible under the supported semantics to the autoepistemic bisequent theory $auto(\Delta)$. Consequently, the plain completion of $auto(\Delta)$ corresponds exactly to the set of expansions of $\Delta$. Now the result follows from the fact that $\Delta$ and $auto(\Delta)$ determine the same completion. $\square$

## 5.5 Partial Nonmonotonic Semantics

In this section we are going to describe a generalization of the nonmonotonic semantics, described earlier, to partial models. Partial nonmonotonic semantics have played a prominent role in logic programming, and there have been numerous attempts to extend them to general nonmonotonic formalisms. In this section we will give a structural description of such partial semantics. In Chapter 8 we will provide these semantics with a logical basis.

All the nonmonotonic semantics, described earlier, have been defined as certain sets of *theories* of a biconsequence relation. Now, while a biconsequence relation can be viewed as a representation of a possibly incomplete and/or inconsistent information, its theories correspond to 'classical' models of the latter, since they are precisely bitheories that are both consistent and complete. In other words, while biconsequence relations are inherently partial, its nonmonotonic semantics, as defined above, are essentially classical. This conceptual incoherence naturally suggests that it is worth exploring a possibility of generalizing the nonmonotonic semantics to partial models. In other words, it seems interesting to consider generalizations of these semantics that are based on a broader set of bitheories of a biconsequence relation, instead of just its theories.

Three guiding principles will be used below in defining partial counterparts of nonmonotonic semantics. First, it is natural to require that such a semantics should subsume the corresponding 'classical' nonmonotonic semantics. Second, it should be required that partial semantics must preserve the explanatory nature of the original nonmonotonic semantics, namely, the assumption context of each partial model should explain its corresponding objective (positive) part. Third, we will require, in addition, that the intended partial models should be symmetric with respect to its components, namely they should correspond to *invariant* bitheories of a biconsequence relation. The last requirement will increase the similarity with the earlier nonmonotonic semantics. It will give us also partial models corresponding to existing semantics of logic programs.

The following definition describes the partial counterparts of the main nonmonotonic semantics that conform to the above requirements.

**Definition 5.14** An invariant bitheory $(u, v)$ of a biconsequence relation $\Vdash$ will be called

- *partial exact*, if there are no other sets $u_1 \neq u$ and $v_1 \neq v$ such that $(v_1, u)$ or $(u_1, v)$ are bitheories of $\Vdash$;
- a *partial extension*, if both $(u, v)$ and $(v, u)$ are positively minimal bitheories of $\Vdash$;
- a *partial expansion*, if $(u\backslash\{A\}, v)$ and $(v\backslash\{B\}, u)$ are not bitheories of $\Vdash$, for any $A \in u$ and $B \in v$.

In accordance with our earlier terminology, the set of partial exact bitheories will be called a *partial exact semantics* of $\Vdash$, the set of partial extensions will form a *partial default semantics* of $\Vdash$, while the set of partial expansions will form a *partial supported semantics* of $\Vdash$. As before, all these partial semantics will be extended to arbitrary bisequent theories in an obvious way.

Partial nonmonotonic semantics were defined above as certain sets of bitheories. Each such bitheory can be considered as a four-valued interpretation, which gives us yet another dimension of freedom in determining *partial nonmonotonic consequences* of a bisequent theory. Thus, if $(u, v)$ is a bitheory, then propositions from $u \cap v$ can be viewed as *classically true* (namely, both true and non-false), propositions from $\overline{u} \cap \overline{v}$ can be viewed as *classically false* (both false and non-true), propositions from $\overline{u} \cap v$ are *undetermined* (neither true, nor false), while propositions from $u \cap \overline{v}$ can be seen as *contradictory* (both true and false). In other words, while the earlier 'classical' nonmonotonic semantics, being sets of theories, determined Scott consequence relations, the informational content of partial nonmonotonic semantics is described by the biconsequence relation generated by the corresponding set of bitheories. This biconsequence relation clearly provides a more fine-grained description of the information that is nonmonotonically implied by a source bisequent theory or biconsequence relation.

A more specific feature of the definitions given to the partial semantics is that each of them forms a symmetric binary semantics:

**Lemma 5.61** *If $(u, v)$ is a partial exact bitheory (partial extension, partial expansion) of a biconsequence relation, then $(v, u)$ is also a partial exact bitheory (resp., partial extension, partial expansion).*

As a result, the biconsequence relations generated by the partial nonmonotonic semantics will always be invariant (see Sec. 3.2.7).

It is important to note that the information provided by the classical nonmonotonic semantics is not lost in this setting, and it can be restored just by restricting the corresponding set of bitheories to theories, that is, to bitheories that are both consistent and complete. This is an immediate consequence of the following simple result.

**Lemma 5.62** *A theory $u$ of a biconsequence relation is exact (an extension, an expansion) if and only if $(u, u)$ is a partial exact bitheory (respectively, partial extension, partial expansion).*

The proof of the above result can be discerned directly from the corresponding definitions of nonmonotonic semantics. It shows that restrictions of partial nonmonotonic semantics to classical models gives us precisely the corresponding classical nonmonotonic semantics. Yet another general correspondence between these nonmonotonic semantics and their partial counterparts will be established below using a doubling construction.

An additional constraint that is often imposed on partial nonmonotonic semantics consists in choosing only consistent partial models, namely bitheories $(u, v)$ such that $u \subseteq v$. Clearly, such a *consistent* partial nonmonotonic semantics will still subsume the classical nonmonotonic semantics, so it will occupy an intermediate ground between the classical and fully partial semantics in our sense. Still, such a constraint does not seem to have a systematic justification (apart from the desire to be consistent), so it will not be used in this study.

Finally, recall that all the classical nonmonotonic semantics satisfied a restricted monotonicity property according to which addition of bisequents that preserves theories leads to a growth of the corresponding nonmonotonic semantics. A partial counterpart of this property can be obtained, if we restrict possible additions to bisequents that preserve invariant bitheories.

Let us say that two bisequent theories $\Gamma$ and $\Delta$ are *invariantly equivalent*, if they determine the same invariant biconsequence relation. In other words, they are inter-derivable using the postulates for biconsequence relations and Invariance.

Clearly, two bisequent theories are invariantly equivalent if and only if they have the same invariant bitheories. Now, an addition of new bisequents to a bisequent theory results in removal of some of its bitheories. But if the invariant bitheories are preserved, any exact bitheory, partial extension or partial expansion will remain such in the new bisequent theory. Accordingly, we obtain

**Lemma 5.63** *If $\Gamma$ and $\Delta$ are invariantly equivalent bisequent theories such that $\Gamma \subseteq \Delta$, then any partial exact bitheory (partial extension, partial*

*expansion) of* $\Gamma$ *is a partial exact bitheory (respectively, partial extension, partial expansion) of* $\Delta$.

### 5.5.1 *Doubling*

Now we will describe a general translation that will transform every partial nonmonotonic semantics into the corresponding classical nonmonotonic semantics. The translation will be obtained by doubling the set of propositions of the language, and transforming the bisequents into new bisequents in the extended language. Again, the origins of this construction are in logic programming.

By a language $\mathcal{L}$ we will mean in this section simply a set of (atomic) propositions. For any proposition $A$ from $\mathcal{L}$, we will extend the language with a new proposition $A'$. $\mathcal{L}'$ will denote the set of all such new propositions, and for any $u \subseteq \mathcal{L}$, we will denote by $u'$ the set $\{A' \mid A \in u\}$. Finally, we will transform the bisequent theory $\Delta$ into a new bisequent theory $\Delta'$ in the extended language, obtained by replacing every bisequent $a{:}b \Vdash c{:}d$ from $\Delta$ with the following two bisequents:

$$a' : b \Vdash c' : d \qquad\qquad a : b' \Vdash c : d'.$$

The general effect of this translation amounts to a full separation (or 'split') between the two contexts associated with the bisequents of $\Delta$. As a result, the new bisequent theory will have especially regular logical properties.

As before, $\Vdash_{\Delta'}$ will denote the least biconsequence relation (in the extended language) that contains $\Delta'$. The next results give a description of this biconsequence relation.

**Lemma 5.64** *A pair* $(u \cup u'_1, v \cup v'_1)$ *is a bitheory of* $\Delta'$ *if and only if both* $(u_1, v)$ *and* $(u, v_1)$ *are bitheories of* $\Delta$.

***Proof.*** $(u \cup u'_1, v \cup v'_1)$ is a bitheory of $\Delta'$ if it is closed with respect to the bisequents of $\Delta'$. By the construction of $\Delta'$, this means that, for any bisequent $a{:}b \Vdash c{:}d$ from $\Delta$, if $a \subseteq u_1$ and $b \subseteq \overline{v}$, then either $c \cap u_1$, or $d \cap \overline{v}$, and if $a \subseteq u$ and $b \subseteq \overline{v}_1$, then either $c \cap u$, or $d \cap \overline{v}_1$. The latter conditions amounts to saying that both $(u_1, v)$ and $(u, v_1)$ are bitheories of $\Delta$. □

As a consequence of the above description, we immediately obtain that the bitheories of $\Delta'$ satisfy the following invariance property:

**Corollary 5.65** *If* $(u \cup u'_1, v \cup v'_1)$ *is a bitheory of* $\Delta'$, *then* $(u_1 \cup u', v_1 \cup v')$ *is also a bitheory of* $\Delta'$.

In addition, the above lemma gives the following characterization of theories of $\Delta'$:

**Corollary 5.66** *A set* $u \cup u'_1$ *is a theory of* $\Delta'$ *if and only if the pair* $(u, u_1)$ *is an invariant bitheory of* $\Delta$.

The corresponding syntactic description of $\Vdash_{\Delta'}$ is as follows:

**Lemma 5.67** *For any sets of propositions* $a, a_1, b, b_1, c, c_1, d, d_1$ *from* $\mathcal{L}$,

$$a, a'_1{:}b, b'_1 \Vdash_{\Delta'} c, c'_1{:}d, d'_1 \quad \textit{iff} \quad a_1{:}b \Vdash_\Delta c_1{:}d \ \textit{ or } \ a{:}b_1 \Vdash_\Delta c{:}d_1.$$

***Proof.*** Let us denote by $\Vdash'$ the set of bisequents in the extended language that are determined by $\Vdash_\Delta$ using the above equivalence. Then it can be easily verified that $\Vdash'$ is actually a biconsequence relation that includes $\Delta'$. Consequently, $\Vdash_{\Delta'} \subseteq \Vdash'$. In the other direction, if $a, a'_1{:}b, b'_1 \nVdash_{\Delta'} c, c'_1{:}d, d'_1$, then there exists a bitheory $(u \cup u'_1, v \cup v'_1)$ of $\Delta'$ such that $a \subseteq u$, $a_1 \subseteq u_1$, $b \subseteq \overline{v}$, $b_1 \subseteq \overline{v_1}$, $c \subseteq \overline{u}$, $c_1 \subseteq \overline{u_1}$, $d \subseteq v$ and $d_1 \subseteq v_1$. But by the preceding lemma $(u_1, v)$ and $(u, v_1)$ are bitheories of $\Delta$, which implies, respectively, that $a_1{:}b \nVdash_\Delta c_1{:}d$ and $a{:}b_1 \nVdash_\Delta c{:}d_1$. Consequently, $a, a'_1{:}b, b'_1 \nVdash' c, c'_1{:}d, d'_1$, which gives the direction from right to left. □

As a consequence of the above description, we obtain that bisequents of $\Vdash_{\Delta'}$ are invariant with respect to the $'$ operation:

**Corollary 5.68** *For any sets* $a, a_1, b, b_1, c, c_1, d, d_1$ *from* $\mathcal{L}$,

$$a, a'_1{:}b, b'_1 \Vdash_{\Delta'} c, c'_1{:}d, d'_1 \quad \textit{iff} \quad a_1, a'{:}b_1, b' \Vdash_{\Delta'} c_1, c'{:}d_1, d'.$$

Finally, the following theorem shows that the above translation transforms each partial nonmonotonic semantics into its classical counterpart.

**Theorem 5.69** *A pair* $(u, v)$ *is a partial exact bitheory (partial extension, partial expansion) of a bisequent theory* $\Delta$ *if and only if* $u \cup v'$ *is an exact theory (resp., extension, expansion) of* $\Delta'$.

***Proof.*** We will prove the result only for the (partial) exact semantics, the proof for extensions and expansions being similar.

$u \cup v'$ is an exact theory of $\Delta'$ if and only if, for any set $u_1 \cup v'_1$, the pair $(u_1 \cup v'_1, u \cup v')$ is a bitheory of $\Delta'$ iff $u_1 \cup v'_1 = u \cup v'$. By Lemma 5.64, this amounts to saying that $(u_1, v)$ and $(v_1, u)$ are bitheories of $\Delta$ if and only if $u_1 = u$ and $v_1 = v$. The latter is equivalent to the claim that $(u, v)$ is a partial exact bitheory of $\Delta$. □

The above result allows us to systematically translate all the questions and problems about partial semantics into questions about their classical counterparts. In addition, the reader should note similarity between the above doubling construction and the classical translation of four-valued logics, given in Sec. 4.1.7 of Chapter 4. The similarity suggests that partial nonmonotonic semantics can be systematically reduced to the original nonmonotonic semantics in some generalized 'partial' four-valued logical formalism. Such a formalism will be described in Chapter 8 in the framework of causal inference. For the time being, in the following sections we will give a more detailed description of the partial semantics.

### 5.5.2 *Partial exact semantics*

As follows from the above definition, a pair $(u, v)$ is a partial exact bitheory of $\Vdash$ if and only if, for any sets $u_1, v_1$ of propositions,

$$(u_1, v) \text{ is a bitheory of } \Vdash \text{ if and only if } u_1 = u, \text{ and}$$
$$(v_1, u) \text{ is a bitheory of } \Vdash \text{ if and only if } v_1 = v.$$

Thus, just as for exact theories, partial exact bitheories are bitheories, for which both $u$ and $v$, taken as assumption contexts, determine the second set as a unique objective state compatible with it. In other words, the positive $u$-reduction of $\Vdash$, $\Vdash_u^+$, is a unitary consequence relation having $v$ as its only theory, while $u$ is similarly the only theory of $\Vdash_v^+$. Consequently, Lemma 2.27 implies the following syntactic description of partial exact bitheories.

**Lemma 5.70** *A pair $(u, v)$ is a partial exact bitheory of a biconsequence relation $\Vdash$ if and only if, for any proposition $A$,*

$$A \in u \;\; \textit{iff} \;\; : \overline{v} \Vdash A : v \qquad A \in v \;\; \textit{iff} \;\; : \overline{u} \Vdash A : u$$
$$A \notin u \;\; \textit{iff} \;\; A : \overline{v} \Vdash \, : v \qquad A \notin v \;\; \textit{iff} \;\; A : \overline{u} \Vdash \, : u.$$

The corresponding description of the partial exact semantics for bisequent theories can be obtained using again Lemma 3.9.

**Lemma 5.71** *$(u, v)$ is a partial exact bitheory of a bisequent theory $\Delta$ iff $v$ is the only theory of $\Delta_u^+$, and $u$ is the only theory of $\Delta_v^+$.*

The next example shows that a bisequent theory can have partial exact models even when it does not have theories.

**Example 5.3** A bisequent theory

$$\begin{array}{ll} :B \Vdash A:A & :B \Vdash B:A \\ \Vdash A:A,B & B:\Vdash :A,B \\ :A,B \Vdash A: & :A \Vdash A:B \end{array}$$

does not have any theories. In other words, it is thoroughly classically inconsistent. Nevertheless, it has a unique partial exact bitheory $(\{A,B\},\{A\})$.

Unfortunately, the above example shows also that Regularity is no longer appropriate for partial exact semantics. Indeed, Regularity requires that $(u,v)$ is a bitheory only if $v$ is a theory of a biconsequence relation. But the above bisequent theory does not have theories, so imposing the Regularity postulate would make it inconsistent. Actually, the failure of Regularity gives a first indication of the fact that a proper description of the underlying logics for partial nonmonotonic semantics cannot be given directly in the framework of biconsequence relations. Nevertheless, the doubling construction will allow us to give a corresponding semantic description.

**Theorem 5.72** *Bisequent theories $\Gamma$ and $\Delta$ are strongly equivalent with respect to a partial exact semantics iff (i) $\Gamma$ and $\Delta$ are invariantly equivalent, and (ii) if $(u,v)$ is an invariant bitheory of $\Gamma$, then $(w,u)$ is a bitheory of $\Gamma$ iff it is a bitheory of $\Delta$.*

***Proof.*** To begin with, due to Lemma 5.64, it can be verified that the above two conditions are satisfied iff $\Gamma'$ and $\Delta'$ have the same regular bitheories. Consequently, by Theorems 5.5 and 5.69, if $\Gamma$ and $\Delta$ satisfy the above conditions, they determine the same partial exact semantics. Moreover, for any set of bisequents $\Phi$ we have also that $\Gamma' \cup \Phi'$ is regularly equivalent to $\Delta' \cup \Phi'$, and therefore $\Gamma$ and $\Delta$ will be strongly equivalent with respect to a partial exact semantics.

Assume now that the above conditions are not satisfied, and suppose first that $(u,v)$ is an invariant bitheory of $\Gamma$ that is not an invariant bitheory of $\Delta$. If $u=v$, the proof reduces to the corresponding part of the proof of Theorem 5.5. So suppose that $u \neq v$, and assume for certainty that $(u,v)$ is not a bitheory of $\Delta$ and, moreover, $u \not\subseteq v$ (the other cases being similar). Then there exists $A_0 \in u \backslash v$. For this case we denote by $\Phi$ the union of the following sets of bisequents:

$$\{A_0 :\Vdash B: \mid B \in u\} \qquad \{A_0, B :\Vdash\mid B \notin u\}$$
$$\{A_0 : B \Vdash\mid B \in v\} \qquad \{A_0 : \Vdash: B \mid B \notin v\}$$
$$\{\Vdash A_0, B: \mid B \in v\} \qquad \{B :\Vdash A_0 :\mid B \notin v\}$$
$$\{: B \Vdash A_0 :\mid B \in u\} \qquad \{\Vdash A_0 : B \mid B \notin u\}.$$

As can be verified, $(u, v)$ and $(v, u)$ are the only bitheories of $\Phi$. Now it should be clear that $(u, v)$ is a partial exact theory of $\Gamma \cup \Phi$, though it still will not be even an invariant bitheory of $\Delta \cup \Phi$.

Suppose now that $\Gamma$ and $\Delta$ are invariantly equivalent, $(u, v)$ is an invariant bitheory of both, and $(w, u)$ is a bitheory of $\Gamma$, but not of $\Delta$. If $u = v$, the proof reduces to the corresponding proof of Theorem 5.5. So assume $u \neq v$, and suppose for certainty that $v \nsubseteq u$, that is, there exists $A_0 \in v\backslash u$. Then we define $\Phi$ as the union of the following sets of bisequents:

$$\{\Vdash B{:}A_0 \mid B \in u\} \qquad \{B :\Vdash :A_0 \mid B \notin u\}$$
$$\{A, B : A_0 \Vdash \mid A \notin w, B \notin v\} \qquad \{: A_0 \Vdash A, B :\mid A \in w, B \in v\}$$
$$\{A : A_0 \Vdash B :\mid (A \notin w \,\&\, B \in v) \text{ or } (A \notin v \,\&\, B \in w)\}.$$

The first pair of sets secures that $u$ should be the only set such that $(u, v)$ is a bitheory, while the rest determine that $(x, u)$ is a bitheory only if either $x = w$ or $x = v$. As a result, both $(v, u)$ and $(w, u)$ will still be bitheories of $\Gamma \cup \Phi$, and hence $(u, v)$ will not be a partial exact theory of the latter. But $v$ will obviously be the only set such that $(v, u)$ is a bitheory of $\Delta \cup \Phi$, and therefore $(u, v)$ will be its partial exact theory. Consequently $\Gamma$ and $\Delta$ will not be strongly equivalent. This completes the proof. □

By the above result, the above conditions provide an implicit semantic description of the maximal logic adequate for the partial exact semantics. A syntactic description of this logic will be given in Chapter 8.

An instructive property of partial exact bitheories can be obtained using a *truth order* on bitheories and four-valued interpretations (see [Fitting, 1993]), which is defined as follows:

$$(u, v) \leq_t (u_1, v_1) \quad \equiv \quad u \subseteq u_1 \text{ and } v \subseteq v_1.$$

Bitheories that are smaller with respect to this order have less true propositions and more false ones. Minimal bitheories in this order will be called *t-minimal.*

Recall now that theories of a doubled bisequent theory $\Delta'$ correspond exactly to invariant bitheories of $\Delta$. Moreover, it can be easily seen that $u \cup v' \subseteq u_1 \cup v_1'$ holds if and only if $(u, v) \leq_t (u_1, v_1)$. Consequently, minimal theories of $\Delta'$ correspond precisely to t-minimal invariant bitheories of $\Delta$. In view of this correspondence, Corollary 5.13 immediately implies

**Lemma 5.73** *Any partial exact bitheory of a default bisequent theory $\Delta$ is a t-minimal invariant bitheory of $\Delta$.*

### 5.5.3 *Partial default semantics*

A pair $(u, v)$ is a partial extension of a biconsequence relation if and only if $u$ is a minimal theory of the positive reduction $\Vdash_v^+$, while $v$ is a minimal theory of $\Vdash_u^+$. This immediately implies that any partial exact theory of a biconsequence relation is a partial extension (though not vice versa).

Lemma 3.6 provides a syntactic description of partial extensions:

**Lemma 5.74** *A pair $(u, v)$ is a partial extension of $\Vdash$ if and only if $: \overline{u} \nVdash :u$, $: \overline{v} \nVdash :v$, and for any proposition $A$,*

$$A \in u \text{ iff } : \overline{v} \Vdash A, \overline{u} : v$$

$$A \in v \text{ iff } : \overline{u} \Vdash A, \overline{v} : u.$$

As in Lemma 3.6, the auxiliary conditions $: \overline{u} \nVdash :u$ and $: \overline{v} \nVdash :v$, are required,respectively, only when $v$ or $u$ is the set of all propositions. A direct consequence of the above descriptions is that partial extensions are determined by the autoepistemic subrelation of a biconsequence relation.

**Corollary 5.75** *The partial default semantics of a biconsequence relation coincides with the partial default semantics of its autoepistemic subrelation.*

For singular biconsequence relations, the above description of partial extensions is simplified as follows. The proof follows immediately from Corollary 3.36.

**Corollary 5.76** *$(u, v)$ is a partial extension of a singular biconsequence relation $\Vdash$ if and only if $u = \{: \overline{v} \Vdash A : v\}$ and $v = \{: \overline{u} \Vdash A : u\}$, and either $u, v \neq Pr$, or $\nVdash: Pr$.*

A description of the partial default semantics for a bisequent theory is given in the next lemma. The proof is immediate from the fact that $(v, u)$ is a bitheory of $\Delta$ if and only if $v$ is a theory of $\Delta_u^+$.

**Lemma 5.77** *$(u, v)$ is a partial extension of a bisequent theory $\Delta$ if and only if $u$ is a minimal theory of $\Delta_v^+$, and $v$ is a minimal theory of $\Delta_u^+$.*

As with the exact semantics, the correspondence between extensions and partial extensions cannot be extended to the corresponding logics. Thus, Consistency is clearly inappropriate for partial extensions; this follows already from the fact that the restriction to consistent bitheories reduces all invariant bitheories to ordinary theories. The failure of Consistency also abolishes a direct correspondence between expansions and exact theories for the partial case. Still, the doubling construction will give us the corresponding semantic description in this case too.

**Theorem 5.78** *Bisequent theories $\Gamma$ and $\Delta$ are strongly equivalent with respect to a partial default semantics iff (i) $\Gamma$ and $\Delta$ are invariantly equivalent, and (ii) if $(u, v)$ is an invariant bitheory of $\Gamma$, and $w \subseteq v$, then $(w, u)$ is a bitheory of $\Gamma$ iff it is a bitheory of $\Delta$.*

***Proof.*** Due to Lemma 5.64, the above two conditions are satisfied iff $\Gamma'$ and $\Delta'$ have the same consistent regular bitheories. Now, Theorem 5.36, coupled with Theorem 5.69, implies that if the above conditions are satisfied, $\Gamma$ and $\Delta$ will be strongly equivalent.

Assume now that the above conditions are not satisfied, and suppose first that $(u, v)$ is an invariant bitheory of $\Gamma$ that is not an invariant bitheory of $\Delta$. If $u = v$, the proof reduces to the corresponding part of the proof of Theorem 5.36. So suppose that $u \neq v$, and assume for certainty that $(u, v)$ is not a bitheory of $\Delta$ and, moreover, $v \not\subseteq u$ (the other cases being similar). Then there exists $A_0 \in v \backslash u$. For this case we denote by $\Phi$ the union of the following two sets of bisequents:

$$\{\Vdash B{:}A_0 \mid B \in u\} \qquad \{{:}A_0 \Vdash B{:} \mid B \in v\}.$$

As can be verified, $(u, v)$ and $(v, u)$ are positively minimal bitheories of $\Phi$, and consequently $(u, v)$ is a partial extension of $\Gamma \cup \Phi$, though it still will not be even an invariant bitheory of $\Delta \cup \Phi$.

Suppose now that $\Gamma$ and $\Delta$ are invariantly equivalent, $(u, v)$ is an invariant bitheory of both, $w \subseteq v$, and $(w, u)$ is a bitheory of $\Gamma$, but not of $\Delta$. If $u = v$, the proof reduces to the corresponding proof of Theorem 5.36. So assume $u \neq v$, and suppose again that $v \not\subseteq u$, that is, there exists $A_0 \in v \backslash u$.

Then we define $\Phi$ as the union of the following sets of bisequents:

$$\{\Vdash A : A_0 \mid A \in u\}$$
$$\{: A_0 \Vdash A :\mid A \in w\} \qquad \{A : A_0 \Vdash B :\mid A, B \in v\backslash w\}.$$

The first set secures that $(u, v)$ is a positively minimal bitheory, while the rest determine that $(x, u)$ such that $x \subseteq v$ is a bitheory only if either $x = w$ or $x = v$. As a result, both $(v, u)$ and $(w, u)$ will still be bitheories of $\Gamma \cup \Phi$, and hence $(u, v)$ will not be a partial extension of the latter. But $v$ will obviously be a minimal set such that $(v, u)$ is a bitheory of $\Delta \cup \Phi$, and therefore $(u, v)$ will be its partial extension. Consequently $\Gamma$ and $\Delta$ will not be strongly equivalent. □

Finally, as a partial counterpart of Corollary 5.40, we obtain

**Corollary 5.79** *Any partial extension of a default bisequent theory will also be its t-minimal invariant bitheory.*

### 5.5.4 *Partial supported semantics*

As we will see in due course, the partial supported semantics corresponds to three- and four-valued generalizations of the supported (or completion) semantics for logic programs.

Since partial extensions correspond to positively minimal bitheories, any partial extension of a biconsequence relation is a partial expansion, though not vice versa. A syntactic description of partial expansions is given in the next lemma. The proof is straightforward.

**Lemma 5.80** *$(u, v)$ is a partial expansion of $\Vdash$ if and only if it is an invariant bitheory of $\Vdash$ and, for any proposition $A$,*

$$A \in u \text{ iff } u\backslash\{A\} : \overline{v} \Vdash A, \overline{u} : v$$
$$A \in v \text{ iff } v\backslash\{A\} : \overline{u} \Vdash A, \overline{v} : u.$$

As in Lemma 3.6, the condition that $(u, v)$ is an invariant bitheory is needed only for the case when $u$ or $v$ is the set of all propositions.

Fortunately, the coincidence of expansions and extensions in the acyclic case holds also for their partial counterparts. Namely, Lemma 2.23 immediately implies

**Theorem 5.81** *Partial expansions of an acyclic bisequent theory coincide with its partial extensions.*

Since autoepistemic bisequent theories are acyclic, we obtain also

**Corollary 5.82** *Partial expansions of an autoepistemic bisequent theory coincide with its partial extensions.*

Finally, the doubling construction suggests that the partial supported semantics can be described via a certain completion of a bisequent theory.

**Definition 5.15** A *partial completion* of a locally finite bisequent theory $\Delta$ is the following set *compp*($\Delta$) of classical logical formulas in the extended language $\mathcal{L} \cup \mathcal{L}'$, for any $A \in \mathcal{L}$:

$$A \leftrightarrow \bigvee \{ \bigwedge (a \cup d' \cup \neg b' \cup \neg c) \mid a : b \Vdash c, A : d \in \Delta \}$$

$$A' \leftrightarrow \bigvee \{ \bigwedge (a' \cup d \cup \neg b \cup \neg c') \mid a : b \Vdash c, A : d \in \Delta \}$$

plus the set $\{ \neg \bigwedge (a' \cup d \cup \neg b) \wedge \neg \bigwedge (a \cup d' \cup \neg b') \mid a : b \Vdash : d \in \Delta \}$.

Then Theorem 5.60 immediately implies

**Theorem 5.83** *If $\Delta$ is a locally finite bisequent theory, then the classical models of compp($\Delta$) correspond exactly to partial expansions of $\Delta$.*

The above results will complete our (rather brief) preliminary description of partial nonmonotonic semantics. The study of such semantics will continue, however, in the following chapters, where they will be assigned a proper background logic.

## 5.6 Bisequent Interpretations of General Logic Programs

In this section we will describe two representations of general logic programs and their semantics in the logical formalism of biconsequence relations. These representations will establish different ways of providing (or, better, restoring) a logical basis of logic programming that will add a required support to the claim that logic programming constitutes a general-purpose computational tool for knowledge representation and reasoning.

Biconsequence relations will provide a representation of logic program rules of a most general kind, namely rules involving disjunctions and default negations in heads. Program clauses will be directly identified with bisequents, while biconsequence relations will be considered as a formalization of the *logics* corresponding to logic programs. This will give us the first basic step in restoring the connection between Logic and Logic Programming. Moreover, it will be shown that the main semantics for such general logic programs correspond precisely to the nonmonotonic semantics of biconsequence relations studied above. In addition, we will describe a general construction of nonmonotonic completion for biconsequence relations and show that it allows us to give uniform representation of various weaker semantics for general logic programs, suggested in the literature.

A *general logic program* $\Pi$ is a set of program rules of the form

$$\mathbf{not}\, d, c \leftarrow a, \mathbf{not}\, b \qquad (*)$$

where $a, b, c, d$ are finite sets of propositional atoms. Such program rules subsume practically all *structural* extensions of normal program rules suggested in the literature. They have been introduced first in [Lifschitz and Woo, 1992]; a detailed study of such programs, together with applications, can be found in [Inoue and Sakama, 1998].

A general logic program is called *disjunctive*, if its program rules do not contain **not** in heads (that is, $d = \emptyset$). Such programs are widely used now in logic programming. A disjunctive program is *normal* if its program rules contain only single propositional atoms in heads (that is, $c$ is a singleton), and *quasi-normal*, if $c$ contains no more than one atom[2].

### 5.6.1 *A default interpretation*

By the *default interpretation*, a general program rule $\mathbf{not}\, d, c \leftarrow a, \mathbf{not}\, b$ will be interpreted as a bisequent

$$a : b \Vdash c : d.$$

This interpretation will serve as our standard ('default') interpretation, since it will be shown to be adequate for the majority of logic programming semantics. We will denote by $bc(\Pi)$ the set of bisequents corresponding to a general program $\Pi$ by this interpretation.

Note that this representation treats negated atoms in program clauses simply as a new kind of propositions rather than compound literals consisting of **not** and an atom. Recall, however, that bisequents can be transformed into four-valued logical formulas (see Lemma 4.10). Thus, the above bisequent is equivalent to each of the following

$$\Vdash \bigwedge(a \cup \sim b) \to \bigvee(c \cup \sim d) :$$

$$\Vdash \bigwedge(a \cup -b) \to \bigvee(c \cup -d) :$$

[2] Such programs are often called *normal program with constraints*.

The latter bisequents give a fully transparent representation of program rules as logical formulas of a four-valued logic. Furthermore, the non-classicality of program rules is reduced on this representation to the (four-valued) interpretation of **not**, be it the global negation $\sim$, or the ht-negation $-$. As we have seen in Chapter 4, the choice between these two interpretations amounts, in effect, to stipulating whether the rule of double negation (that is, $\mathbf{not}\,\mathbf{not}\,p \equiv p$) should hold for **not**. It is interesting to note in this respect that the first interpretation above is closely related to the notion of a *nested logic program* introduced in [Lloyd and Topor, 1984], while the second one corresponds in this sense to the representation of nested logic programs in the three-valued logic of here-and-there, described in [Lifschitz *et al.*, 2001].

**Remark 5.2** *According to the view advocated in this study, a common understanding of* **not** *as 'negation by failure' (or 'negation by default') does not reflect the* declarative meaning *of the connective, but rather a particular (nonmonotonic) mechanism of obtaining negative assumptions. As we will see, however, the declarative meaning of* **not** *may have a number of different possible interpretations that agree with its procedural understanding.*

A primary justification of the above interpretation is established by the following result. It shows that the default interpretation of program rules provides an exact correspondence between stable models of a general program and extensions of the associated bisequent theory.

**Proposition 5.84** *Stable models of a general logic program* $\Pi$ *coincide with the extensions of* $bc(\Pi)$.

***Proof.*** A set of $u$ of propositions is a stable model of a general logic program $\Pi$ (see, e.g., [Inoue and Sakama, 1998]), if $u$ is a minimal model of the Gelfond-Lifschitz reduct of $\Pi$ modulo $u$. As can be easily verified, this is equivalent to the requirement that $(u, u)$ is a positively minimal bitheory of $bc(\Pi)$. □

The above correspondence allows us to analyze the properties of the stable semantics directly in the framework of biconsequence relations. Moreover, the correspondence between logic programs and biconsequence relations turns out to be bidirectional.

Recall that any bisequent in a four-valued language is logically reducible to a set of structural bisequents that do not involve connectives. Now, under the default interpretation, each such bisequent can be identified with some program rule. Accordingly, for a bisequent theory $\Delta$ in a four-valued language, we will denote by $pr(\Delta)$ the set of program rules obtained in this way from $\Delta$. Then we immediately obtain

**Proposition 5.85** *The default semantics of a bisequent theory $\Delta$ coincides with the stable semantics of the program $pr(\Delta)$.*

The importance of the above result lies in the fact that, under the default interpretation, any bisequent theory is reducible, in turn, to a logic program. Moreover, by Theorem 5.36, two bisequent theories are equivalent with respect to regular consistent biconsequence relations if and only if their corresponding programs are strongly equivalent in the sense of [Lifschitz *et al.*, 2001]. Consequently, regular consistent biconsequence relations form a maximal logic suitable for the stable semantics of general logic programs.

We will show later that the default interpretation of general program rules is adequate also for the majority of other semantics for general and disjunctive logic programs, suggested in the literature.

### 5.6.2 *An autoepistemic interpretation*

It turns out that an older, supported semantics of logic programs is based on a different understanding of program rules. Thus, it is well-known that the program rule $p \leftarrow p$ can change the set of supported models (so it has a non-trivial declarative content for the latter), but it is trivial with respect to the stable semantics. From the point of view pursued in the book, this means that program rules under the supported (or completion) semantics require a different logical interpretation. Namely, according to the *autoepistemic interpretation*, a general program rule (*) is interpreted as a bisequent

$$: b \Vdash c : d, a.$$

Clearly, the difference with the default interpretation amounts to a different understanding of the role of positive premises ($a$) in program rules: while on the default interpretation they are premises in the objective context, on the autoepistemic interpretation they serve as positive assumptions in the assumption context. It is important to observe, however, that the two interpretations coincide for program rules without positive atoms in bodies.

$abc(\Pi)$ will denote a bisequent theory corresponding to a general program $\Pi$ by the autoepistemic interpretation. As can be seen, this interpretation identifies the logical roles of positive premises and negative conclusions in program rules. In this sense, any general logic program is directly reducible under this interpretation to a disjunctive logic program. On the other hand, the autoepistemic interpretation produces only autoepistemic bisequent theories. The latter will mean that logic programs under this interpretation will admit a stronger logic.

A formal correspondence between the two interpretations of general program rules can be established using the *inverse shift* construction from [Inoue and Sakama, 1998] that transforms a logic program Π into the following program

$$invshift(\Pi) = \{\mathbf{not}\, a, \mathbf{not}\, d, c \leftarrow \mathbf{not}\, b \mid \mathbf{not}\, d, c \leftarrow a, \mathbf{not}\, b \in \Pi\}.$$

As can be seen, $invshift(\Pi)$ contains only program rules without positive premises in bodies. Moreover, it is easy to see that the autoepistemic interpretation of Π coincides with the default interpretation of $invshift(\Pi)$, that is,

$$abc(\Pi) = abc(invshift(\Pi)) = bc(invshift(\Pi)).$$

Now we are going to show that the autoepistemic interpretation of program rules is adequate for the supported semantics of general logic programs.

A generalization of supported models to disjunctive programs has been suggested in [Baral and Gelfond, 1994], while a conservative extension to programs with negation in heads has been defined in [Inoue and Sakama, 1998]. In what follows, we will use this latter definition. In particular, we will make use of the following basic fact established in [Inoue and Sakama, 1998].

**Proposition 5.86** *([Inoue and Sakama, 1998]) Supported semantics of a general program* Π *coincides with the stable semantics of* $invshift(\Pi)$.

As an immediate consequence of this reduction, the following result shows that the autoepistemic interpretation provides an adequate representation of general logic programs under the supported semantics.

**Theorem 5.87** *Supported models of a general logic program* Π *coincide with the expansions of* $abc(\Pi)$.

***Proof.*** By the preceding proposition and Proposition 5.84, the supported semantics of Π coincides with the default semantics of $abc(\Pi)$. But $abc(\Pi)$ is an autoepistemic bisequent theory, and consequently the default and supported semantics of $abc(\Pi)$ coincide by Corollary 5.55. □

An interesting consequence of the above representation result is that supported and stable semantics of general logic programs are reducible to the same (namely default) nonmonotonic semantics of biconsequence relations; the only difference amounts to a different interpretation of program rules. Note, however, that the supported semantics can also be seen, in a sense, as a common basis of the two interpretations. Recall that any biconsequence relation determines the same default semantics as its autoepistemic subrelation (see Corollary 5.28), while for the latter the default and supported semantics coincide (Corollary 5.55). As a result, the stable semantics of a general logic program $\Pi$ is reducible, in turn, to the supported semantics of a certain reduced program consisting of all the rules of the form $\mathbf{not}\, d, \leftarrow a, \mathbf{not}\, b$ that are derivable from $\Pi$. However, the transformation of this kind cannot be simple (i.e., polynomial) due to complexity considerations. Still, the construction provides logical grounds for a computational strategy that aims to reduce the computation of the stable semantics to that of a supported semantics, since the latter amounts to computing a completion of a program, and hence can be accomplished by using standard satisfiability solvers.

Since the autoepistemic interpretation turns out to be adequate for a logical representation of general programs under the supported semantics, the study of such a semantics can be transferred again to biconsequence relations. As an important illustration, we will describe now the relationship between stable and supported semantics of a program.

**Lemma 5.88** *Any stable model of a general logic program* $\Pi$ *is also a supported model of* $\Pi$*.*

***Proof.*** Note first that $\Vdash^c_{bc(\Pi)} \subseteq \Vdash^c_{abc(\Pi)}$, since, by the Negative Import rule, any bisequent from $bc(\Pi)$ is derivable from the corresponding bisequent of $abc(\Pi)$. Moreover, $bc(\Pi)$ and $abc(\Pi)$ are Scott-equivalent bisequent theories, since Positive Export gives the reverse derivations. Now by Lemma 5.33, any extension of $bc(\Pi)$ is an extension of $abc(\Pi)$. But $abc(\Pi)$ is an autoepistemic bisequent theory, and therefore its extensions coincide with expansions. Hence the result. □

The reverse inclusion does not always hold, though it holds for an important special class of logic programs described below.

**Definition 5.16** A general logic program $\Pi$ will be called *positive acyclic*, if the bisequent theory $bc(\Pi)$ is acyclic.

A more familiar equivalent description of such programs amounts to an existence of a ranking function $r$ from propositional atoms to ordinals such that, for any program rule $\mathbf{not}\, d, c \leftarrow a, \mathbf{not}\, b$ from $\Pi$, $r(A) < r(C)$, for any $A \in a$ and $C \in c$.

The next result is a generalization of the Fages' theorem for general logic programs (see [Fages, 1994; Ben-Eliyahu, 1993; Inoue and Sakama, 1998; Babovich *et al.*, 2000].

**Theorem 5.89** *If $\Pi$ is a positively acyclic logic program, then its stable models coincide with its supported models.*

***Proof.*** If $bc(\Pi)$ is acyclic, expansions of $bc(\Pi)$ coincide with its extensions by Theorem 5.53. Now, by acyclicity, $a \cap c = \emptyset$, for any bisequent $a{:}b \Vdash c{:}d$ from $bc(\Pi)$. Consequently, by Lemma 3.28(2), any bisequent of $abc(\Pi)$ is derivable from the corresponding bisequent of $bc(\Pi)$ for semi-classical biconsequence relations. Coupled with the preceding lemma, this means that in our case $bc(\Pi)$ is tightly equivalent to $abc(\Pi)$. Consequently, they have the same supported semantics by Theorem 5.52. As a result, extensions of $bc(\Pi)$ coincide with expansions of $abc(\Pi)$. □

As has been established earlier, tight biconsequence relations constitute a maximal logic suitable for the supported semantics. Moreover, it has also been shown that for such biconsequence relations any bisequent theory $\Delta$ is reducible to a certain singular autoepistemic theory $auto(\Delta)$ (see Corollary 3.31). Note now that, under the autoepistemic interpretation of program rules, any singular autoepistemic bisequent $a{:}b \Vdash A{:}$ corresponds to a unique *normal* program rule $A \leftarrow a, \mathbf{not}\, b$, while a bisequent $a{:}b \Vdash$ corresponds to a constraint $\leftarrow a, \mathbf{not}\, b$. Let us denote by $npr(\Delta)$ the logic program obtained by this procedure from an arbitrary bisequent theory $\Delta$. Then any bisequent theory is reducible, in effect, to a quasi-normal logic program:

**Lemma 5.90** *Any bisequent theory $\Delta$ is tightly equivalent to $abc(npr(\Delta))$.*

As a 'by-product' of our construction, we also obtain the result that any general logic program under the supported semantics is reducible to a normal program with constraints:

**Corollary 5.91** *Any logic program is strongly expansion-equivalent to a quasi-normal program.*

Actually, the corresponding modular transformation of logic programs can be obtained by replacing any program rule $\mathbf{not}\,d, c \leftarrow a, \mathbf{not}\,b$ such that $c \neq \emptyset$ with the set

$$\{p \leftarrow a, d, \mathbf{not}\,b, \mathbf{not}(c\backslash\{p\}) \mid p \in c\}$$

while any 'extended' constraint $\mathbf{not}\,d \leftarrow a, \mathbf{not}\,b$ is reduced to a 'normal' constraint $\leftarrow a, d, \mathbf{not}\,b$.

Among other things, the above reduction of general logic programs to normal ones displays the actual role, as well as the applicability range, of the well-known *shift operations* in logic programming that have been studied extensively in the literature—see, e.g., [Dung, 1992; Bonatti, 1993; Dix *et al.*, 1994; Schaerf, 1995]. The above results show that such an operation preserves the supported semantics, and hence is adequate for the stable semantics only for 'tight' programs where the stable and supported semantics coincide.

Finally, the above results imply also that a broad class of general logic programs, described in the next definition, can be uniformly given a default interpretation with respect to both the stable and supported semantics. Recall that the difference in understanding of program rules between stable and supported semantics emerges in the case of 'trivial' rules like $A \leftarrow A$. Now, if such rules are not present in a program, the latter can always be given a default interpretation in terms of bisequents; the difference between the two semantics will be reflected in this case as the difference between associated nonmonotonic semantics.

**Definition 5.17** A program $\Pi$ will be said to be *non-reflexive*, if it does not contain rules of the form $\mathbf{not}\,d, c, A \leftarrow A, a, \mathbf{not}\,b$.

As before, $bc(\Pi)$ denotes the bisequent theory corresponding to a program $\Pi$ by the default interpretation. Then we have

**Lemma 5.92** *If* $\Pi$ *is a non-reflexive program, then supported models of* $\Pi$ *coincide with expansions of* $bc(\Pi)$.

***Proof.*** By Lemma 3.28 (2) and the Import rule, any bisequent $a{:}b \Vdash c{:}d$ such that $a \cap c = \emptyset$ is tightly equivalent to ${:}b \Vdash c{:}a, d$. Consequently, a non-reflexive bisequent theory $bc(\Pi)$ is tightly equivalent $abc(\Pi)$, and hence they determine the same expansions. □

Thus, for non-reflexive logic programs, we can invariably use the default interpretation. This, implies, in particular, that the facts about the relation between default and supported nonmonotonic semantics of biconsequence relations, stated earlier in this chapter, are directly applicable to the correspondence between stable and supported semantics of non-reflexive logic programs.

## 5.7 Nonmonotonic Completion and Weak Semantics

Now we will describe a general approach to defining nonmonotonic semantics that will cover a wide range of semantics for logic programs suggested in the literature. The approach emerges as a combination of two principles, *circumscription* and *coherence.* Circumscription is based on the principle of minimization saying that only minimal models should count in determining the validity of propositions. The Coherence principle (see Chapter 4) amounts to the requirement that information that can be proved or refuted in a biconsequence relation should be classically consistent, that is classically true or classically false. The combination of the two principles will give us a nonmonotonic mechanism for 'jumping to conclusions'. As a result, we will obtain a new, derived biconsequence relation called the *nonmonotonic completion* of a source biconsequence relation. This nonmonotonic completion will embody all the classically coherent information that can be nonmonotonically inferred from a bisequent theory (or a logic program).

The description below will show that common kinds of reasoning about logic programs are reducible, in effect, to different kinds of logical, monotonic reasoning in a certain nonmonotonic extension of the source program. Among other things, this representation of various semantics as species of one general semantics will suggest a more tolerant view of these semantics. Instead of the question what is the best semantics in all cases, we can consider the question what expressive means are most appropriate for a particular reasoning task. On this view, the main question is an acceptable trade-off between expressive means and computational cost for a particular context of reasoning. On any choice, we are dealing, in effect, with the same semantics.

### 5.7.1 *Nonmonotonic completion*

Recall that $\Vdash^{cir}$ denotes a circumscription of a biconsequence relation $\Vdash$ (see Chapter 3).

**Definition 5.18** A proposition $A$ will be called *demonstrably true* in a biconsequence relation $\Vdash$, if $\Vdash^{cir} A :$, and *demonstrably false* in $\Vdash$, if $A : \Vdash^{cir}$.

By the definition of circumscription, a proposition $A$ is demonstrably true, if it is true in all positively minimal bitheories of $\Vdash$, while it is demonstrably false, if it is not true in every positively minimal bitheory of $\Vdash$.

According to the circumscription principle, demonstrable truth and falsity should be seen as a sufficient ground for 'jumping to conclusion' that $A$ is simply true or, respectively, false. Now, in order to be classically true (in the sense of Belnap's four-valued interpretation), a proposition should be both true and not false, while in order to be classically false, it should be false without being true. Accordingly, a demonstrably true proposition will be classically true if it is not false in any positively minimal model. But this is precisely the effect of the Positive Coherence rule, described in Chapter 4, when applied to the circumscribed biconsequence relation. Similarly, imposing Negative Coherence rule will make any demonstrably false proposition classically false. In other words, the circumscription principle for biconsequence relations can be captured by imposing the two coherence rules on the circumscribed biconsequence relation. This leads to the following definition.

**Definition 5.19** A *nonmonotonic $\mathcal{L}$-completion* of a biconsequence relation $\Vdash$ for a four-valued language $\mathcal{L}$ is the least $\mathcal{L}$-coherent biconsequence relation containing $\Vdash^{cir}$. We will denote it by $\Vdash^{cc}$.

A nonmonotonic completion of a biconsequence relation is a biconsequence relation obtained from $\Vdash$ by first circumscribing it and then closing the result with respect to the coherence rules. Note that circumscription is language independent, so the influence of the underlying language $\mathcal{L}$ amounts to imposing language restrictions on the applicability of the coherence rules. Actually, it has been shown Chapter 4 that the coherence rules in different four-valued languages can be always reduced to some structural rules. Still, the justification of the resulting nonmonotonic completion lies ultimately in its logical formulation.

In accordance with the above definition of a nonmonotonic completion, we can define a *nonmonotonic $\mathcal{L}$-semantics* of a biconsequence relation as a pair of sets of $\mathcal{L}$-propositions that are, respectively, provable and refutable in the nonmonotonic $\mathcal{L}$-completion:

**Definition 5.20** A *nonmonotonic $\mathcal{L}$-semantics of a biconsequence relation* $\Vdash$, $SEM_{\Vdash}^{\mathcal{L}}$, is a pair $\langle SEM^{+}, SEM^{-}\rangle$ of sets of $\mathcal{L}$-propositions such that

$$SEM^{+} = \{A \mid \Vdash^{cc} A : \} \qquad SEM^{-} = \{A \mid A : \Vdash^{cc}\}.$$

Due to $\mathcal{L}$-coherence, all propositions that belong to $SEM^{+}$ will be both provably true and provably non-false in the nonmonotonic completion (that is classically true), while those from $SEM^{-}$ will be provably classically false.

Finally, our representation of the nonmonotonic semantics for logic programs will be based on their default interpretation as bisequent theories, described in the preceding section. This understanding is embodied in the following definition.

**Definition 5.21** For a general program $\Pi$, let $\Vdash_{bc(\Pi)}$ be the least biconsequence relation containing $bc(\Pi)$. Then the nonmonotonic $\mathcal{L}$-semantics of $\Vdash_{bc(\Pi)}$ will be called a *nonmonotonic $\mathcal{L}$-semantics of* $\Pi$ and denoted by $SEM^{\mathcal{L}}_{\Pi}$.

Since the nonmonotonic completion is a certain extension of the circumscribed biconsequence relation corresponding to a program, programs generating the same circumscribed biconsequence relation will be always assigned the same semantics. This means, in effect, that any bisequent theory will always have the same nonmonotonic semantics as its autoepistemic reduct. Consequently, the Generalized Principle of Partial Evaluation, GPPE (see Sec. 3.3.2.2), can be seen as a general syntactic principle characterizing this feature of semantics for logic programs, a clear sign that a nonmonotonic semantics is constructed, in effect, 'on top' of the circumscribed program.

### 5.7.2 *Weak semantics*

In what follows, we will give an overview of the correspondences between different kinds of nonmonotonic completion and a number of semantics for logic programs suggested in the literature. Since the proofs of these correspondences depend heavily on the specific constructions of the particular semantics, they do not contribute to the main subject of this book, so we will omit them and refer the reader to [Bochman, 1998a] for further details.

### 5.7.2.1 *Well-founded and static semantics*

Coherence with respect to the empty language reduces the coherence rules to their structural counterparts:

$$(Positive\ Coherence)\ \frac{\Vdash A :}{: A \Vdash} \qquad (Negative\ Coherence)\ \frac{A : \Vdash}{\Vdash : A}$$

where $A$ is a propositional atom. This is a weakest form of coherence possible. Note that the Negative Coherence rule can be seen in this case as a formalization of Minker's Generalized Closed World Assumption (GCWA) (see [Lobo *et al.*, 1992]). Even in this case, however, the resulting semantics gives us the well-founded semantics for normal logic programs.

The following proposition holds for the language without connectives, that is for the case when the coherence rules (and the nonmonotonic semantics) are restricted to atomic propositions. It is actually a consequence of more general representation results given later in this section.

**Proposition 5.93** *If* $\Pi$ *is a normal program, then* $SEM_{\Pi}^{\emptyset}$ *coincides with the well-founded semantics of* $\Pi$.

Though useful for normal logic programs, such a semantics is surely too weak for disjunctive programs, since it ignores, in effect, disjunctive information. Hence, a natural first step is to extend the language by adding disjunction. In this case, Positive Coherence is already equivalent to the structural rule:

$$\frac{\Vdash a :}{: a \Vdash}$$

(where $a$ is a set of propositions), though Negative Coherence is still reducible to its singular variant. It turns out that for disjunctive programs, the resulting semantics will coincide with the *Disjunctive Well-Founded Semantics (D-WFS)*, suggested in [Brass and Dix, 1995a].

D-WFS is definable as the least semantics that is invariant under the following 'Reduction & Elimination' transformations of a disjunctive program:

- *Elimination of Tautologies*: elimination of program clauses containing common atoms in heads and bodies.
- *Elimination of Non-Minimal Rules*: if a rule $a \leftarrow b, \mathbf{not}\, c$ belongs to a program, then all rules of the form $a, a' \leftarrow b, b', \mathbf{not}\, c, \mathbf{not}\, c'$ can be eliminated.
- The *Generalized Principle of Partial Evaluation* (GPPE).

- *Positive Reduction*: if an atom $A$ does not belong to heads of clauses of a program, then all occurrences of $A$ in negative premises can be eliminated.
- *Negative Reduction*: If $a_0 \leftarrow$ belongs to a program, then all rules of the form $a \leftarrow b, \mathbf{not}\, c$ such that $a_0 \subseteq c$ can be eliminated.

All the above transformations correspond to valid rules for associated biconsequence relations. Thus, Elimination of Tautologies is actually a 'reductive' version of the Reflexivity axiom for biconsequence relations, while Elimination of Non-Minimal Rules corresponds in this sense to the Monotonicity rule. In addition, Positive Reduction follows from Negative Coherence, while Negative Reduction is a consequence of the above 'disjunctive' Positive Coherence rule. As a result, the following proposition shows that D-WFS coincides with the $\vee$-semantics of a program.

**Proposition 5.94** *If $P$ is a disjunctive program, then $SEM_P^{\vee}$ coincides with the disjunctive well-founded semantics (D-WFS) of $P$.*

Brass and Dix have shown that the construction of D-WFS can be given in the form of a *confluent calculus* in which the above reduction rules can be applied in any order. This calculus can be used as a natural computation procedure for the nonmonotonic $\vee$-semantics.

The above semantics is also closely related to Przymusinski's *static semantics* of general logic programs [Przymusinski, 1995a] (see [Brass *et al.*, 1997]). The latter semantics can also be represented as an instance of our general construction, namely as a closure of a circumscribed biconsequence relation with respect to the following coherence rule:

$$\frac{a_1 : \Vdash c :}{: c \Vdash : a_1}$$

where $a_1$ contains no more than one proposition (see [Bochman, 1997]). This rule is stronger than $\vee$-coherence, but it still does not make use of negative conjunctive information (see [Bochman, 1998a] for an example).

### 5.7.2.2 *Local completions: stationary semantics and stable classes*

Adding conjunction to the language of formulas susceptible to coherence retains the previous Positive Coherence rule, but gives a stronger, multiple variant of Negative Coherence (see Lemma 4.29):

$$\frac{a : \Vdash}{\Vdash : a}$$

This rule can be seen as a formalization of Extended Generalized Closed World Assumption (EGCWA) (see [Lobo *et al.*, 1992]), since it establishes demonstrable falsity not only for single atomic propositions, but also for sets (conjunctions) of such propositions. The resulting nonmonotonic semantics corresponds to an earlier version of the stationary semantics, suggested in [Przymusinski, 1991a]. In a later paper, [Przymusinski, 1995a], Przymusinski gave another description of a stationary semantics that amounts to the case of the local language $\{\wedge, \neg\}$ in our construction.

By Lemma 4.31, the Positive and Negative Coherence rules in the local language are already equivalent, and amount to the structural rule:

$$\frac{a : \Vdash c :}{: c \Vdash : a}$$

The rule can be informally described as saying that any data consistent with respect to non-falsity should be also consistent with respect to truth (or that an entailment with respect to truth implies an entailment with respect to non-falsity).

The correspondence with the stationary semantics is described in the following result from [Bochman, 1998a]:

**Proposition 5.95** *The local nonmonotonic completion of an affirmative program coincides with the circumscription of its stationary completion.*

The local language $\{\vee, \neg\}$ turns out also to be appropriate for describing a semantics of stable classes for normal programs suggested in [Baral and Subrahmanian, 1991; Baral and Subrahmanian, 1992]. *Stable classes* are sets of sets of propositions $S$ satisfying the following fixed-point condition:

$$S = \{\Gamma(s) \mid s \in S\},$$

where $\Gamma$ is a Gelfond–Lifschitz operator determined by a normal program. The correspondence between stable classes and our construction is based on the fact that a pair $(u, v)$ is a positively minimal bimodel of a normal program if and only if $u = \Gamma(v)$. Consequently, stable classes turn out to correspond to certain extensions of the local nonmonotonic completion (see [Bochman, 1998a] for details).

In many respects, the local nonmonotonic semantics is the largest semantics in our construction having all the good properties a reasonable semantics could have. In particular, such a semantics always exists for affirmative logic programs. However, there are some plausible desiderata for logic programs that this semantics still does not satisfy. For example, in the case of stratified disjunctive programs, it is weaker than the perfect semantics.

#### 5.7.2.3 *Invariant completion and partial stable semantics*

By Lemma 4.34, coherence for the invariant language amounts to the following structural rule:

$$\frac{a : b \Vdash c : d}{d : c \Vdash b : a} \qquad \text{(Invariance)}$$

The semantic counterpart of Invariance is a condition that if $(u, v)$ is a bitheory, then $(v, u)$ is also a bitheory of a biconsequence relation. Consequently, we immediately obtain the result that the invariant nonmonotonic completion determines the partial stable semantics of logic programs.

**Theorem 5.96** *A pair $(u, v)$ is a bitheory of an invariant completion of $\Vdash$ if and only if it is a partial extension of $\Vdash$.*

Partial extensions correspond to *p-stable models* of general logic programs, introduced in [Bochman, 1998a] as a modification of Przymusinski's disjunctive partial stable semantics (see [Przymusinski, 1991b]). The difference is due to the fact that the latter has been defined in terms of *consistent* Herbrand models. As a result, Przymusinski's semantics has a disturbing feature that the resulting models are not determined solely by positively minimal bimodels, and hence the generalized principle of partial evaluation, GPPE, fails for it.

P-stable semantics subsumes both the well-founded semantics of normal logic programs and the perfect semantics for stratified disjunctive programs. Unfortunately, it does not always exist even for disjunctive programs (see [Przymusinski, 1991b] for an example).

#### 5.7.2.4 *Classical completion and stable semantics*

The coherence with respect to the language of all classical four-valued connectives amounts to the combination of Consistency and Completeness. Accordingly, the full 'classical' completion amounts to restriction of all positively minimal bitheories of $\Vdash$ to bitheories of the form $(u, u)$. As a result, we immediately obtain

**Theorem 5.97** *The nonmonotonic completion of a biconsequence relation $\Vdash$ with respect to the full language of classical four-valued connectives*

*is a Scott biconsequence relation such that the set of its theories coincides with the default semantics of* $\Vdash$.

Thus, the stable semantics corresponds to the strongest kind of nonmonotonic semantics covered by the nonmonotonic completion scheme. Viewed the other way round, the preceding semantics could be seen as approximations of the stable semantics obtained by restricting the underlying language.

# Chapter 6

# Default Consequence Relations

In this chapter we will describe a derived formal system that is based, in effect, on singular default and autoepistemic bisequents. The importance and, in particular, sufficiency of such bisequents for representing the main nonmonotonic semantics have been shown in the preceding chapter. The formalism described in this chapter will represent both these kinds of bisequents, however, as species of the general notion of a *default rule*—a rule of the form $a : b \vdash A$, where $A$ is a proposition (the conclusion of the rule), while $a$ and $b$ are finite sets of propositions (the premises). More precisely, default rules $a : b \vdash A$ will serve as a representation for both singular default bisequents $a : b \Vdash A:$, and singular autoepistemic bisequents $:b \Vdash A : a$. The difference between the two will be reflected, however, as a difference in corresponding logics for default rules. This common representation will give us a convenient basis for a comparative study of default and autoepistemic reasoning.

A general informal interpretation of a default rule $a : b \vdash A$ will be as follows:

> 'If all propositions from $a$ are accepted (or assumed), and no proposition from $b$ is assumed, then infer $A$.'

The rules of Reiter's default logic [Reiter, 1980] can be seen as a direct counterpart of our default rules. We will explicitly use, however, 'meta-rules' allowing to infer new default rules from given ones. Sets of default rules that are closed with respect to such meta-rules will be called *default consequence relations*. The latter will provide a logical (monotonic) basis for different kinds of nonmonotonic reasoning in the framework of default consequence relations. In particular, they will allow us to give a very simple characterization of extensions and expansions.

In Chapters 9 and 10, the formalism of default consequence relations will be extended to languages that include the classical logical connectives and modal operators. The resulting systems will turn out to be an especially suitable tool for describing traditional nonmonotonic logics.

## 6.1 Default Consequence Relations

A default consequence relation will be defined below as a set of default rules satisfying certain inference rules, or postulates. In fact, it is these inference rules that will make a set of defaults a *consequence* relation. Default rules as such do not bear on their heads information about when and how they can be applied. For ordinary inference rules, this information can be embodied in the form of 'meta-rules' that produce new inference rules from given ones (this is actually the main idea behind the notion of a consequence relation). Default consequence relation is just an extension of this idea to inference rules that involve as their premises not only what is assumed to hold, but also what is assumed not to hold.

In order to enhance the expressive capabilities of default rules, as well as to provide a smooth correspondence with biconsequence relations, we will extend the notion of a default rule to include *constraint default rules* of the form $a : b \vdash$. Such rules will say that it is impossible to accept all propositions from $a$ and do not assume any proposition from $b$. Note, however, that this extension will become unnecessary for richer (e.g., classical) languages that contain the falsity constant $\mathbf{f}$; in this case, the constraint rule $a : b \vdash$ will be reducible to an ordinary default rule $a : b \vdash \mathbf{f}$.

Throughout this chapter, we will use $a{:}b \vdash \hat{A}$ as a common notation for either $a{:}b \vdash A$, or $a{:}b \vdash$.

**Definition 6.1** A set of default rules will be called a *default consequence relation* if it satisfies the following rules

**Monotonicity** If $a : b \vdash \hat{A}$ and $a \subseteq a_0$, $b \subseteq b_0$, then $a_0 : b_0 \vdash \hat{A}$.
**Constraint** If $a : b \vdash$, then $a : b \vdash A$.
**Cut** If $a : b \vdash B$ and $a, B : b \vdash \hat{A}$, then $a : b \vdash \hat{A}$.

Propositions from the first premise set of a default rule $a : b \vdash B$ will be called *positive premises*, while those from the second premise set—*negative premises*.

Monotonicity and Cut will provide a primary constraint on our understanding of default rules. Monotonicity says, in effect, that default rules are applicable in all contexts in which their premises hold. This makes a default consequence relation a fully monotonic (though somewhat unusual) inference system. The nonmonotonicity will be introduced in this framework not by the default rules themselves, but rather by choosing some intended models.

The Cut postulate is nothing other than the usual Cut rule for consequence relations, though extended to default rules. It permits the use of inferred propositions as additional positive premises in the proof. As we will see below, the postulate gives a logical basis for iterative constructions commonly used in defining nonmonotonic semantics for default theories.

A default consequence relation will be called *trivial*, if it contains all default rules of the language. Due to Monotonicity, this holds if and only if the empty constraint $\emptyset{:}\emptyset \vdash$ belongs to it.

As for (bi)consequence relations, the definition of a default consequence relation is extended to arbitrary sets of propositions in premises of default rules by stipulating that, for any sets of propositions $u$ and $v$,

$$u : v \vdash \hat{A} \quad \text{if and only if} \quad a : b \vdash \hat{A},$$

for some finite $a, b$ such that $a \subseteq u$, $b \subseteq v$. This stipulation ensures that default consequence relations will satisfy the *compactness property*.

For a given default consequence relation, we will denote by $\mathbb{C}\mathrm{n}(u{:}v)$ the set of all consequences of the pair of sets $(u, v)$, that is,

$$\mathbb{C}\mathrm{n}(u : v) = \{A \mid u : v \vdash A\}.$$

The function $\mathbb{C}\mathrm{n}$ can be considered as a provability operator corresponding to a default consequence relation. In particular, the Monotonicity and Cut postulates are expressible as the following properties of this operator:

$$\text{If } u \subseteq u_0, v \subseteq v_0, \text{ then } \mathbb{C}\mathrm{n}(u : v) \subseteq \mathbb{C}\mathrm{n}(u_0 : v_0) \qquad \text{(Monotonicity)}$$

$$\mathbb{C}\mathrm{n}(u \cup \mathbb{C}\mathrm{n}(u : v) : v) \subseteq \mathbb{C}\mathrm{n}(u : v) \qquad \text{(Cut)}$$

The above operator will help us in defining the notions of a bitheory and theory of a default consequence relation.

**Definition 6.2**

- A pair of sets of propositions $(u, v)$ will be called a *bitheory* of a default consequence relation, if $u : \overline{v} \nvdash$ and $\mathbb{C}\mathrm{n}(u : \overline{v}) \subseteq u$.
- A bitheory $(u, v)$ of a default consequence relation will be called *invariant*, if $(v, u)$ is also a bitheory.

- A set $u$ will be called a (propositional) *theory* of a default consequence relation $\vdash$, if $(u, u)$ is a bitheory of $\vdash$.

Bitheories of a default consequence relation can be seen as pairs of sets of propositions that are closed with respect to its default rules. Note that, due to the Constraint rule, the condition $u : \overline{v} \nvdash$ above is needed only for the case when $u$ is the set of all propositions.

**Definition 6.3** A bitheory $(u, v)$ will be called *consistent*, if $u \subseteq v$, and *complete*, if $v \subseteq u$.

Clearly, propositional theories correspond precisely to bitheories that are both consistent and complete.

The next result shows that default consequence relations are determined by bitheories and their consequences:

**Lemma 6.1** *If* $\vdash$ *is a default consequence relation, then* $a : b \vdash \hat{A}$ *if and only if* $u : \overline{v} \vdash \hat{A}$, *for any bitheory* $(u, v)$ *such that* $a \subseteq u$ *and* $b \subseteq \overline{v}$.

***Proof.*** Due to Monotonicity, the implication from left to right is obvious. Assume now that $a : b \nvdash \hat{A}$, and let $(u, v')$ be a maximal pair of sets of propositions that extends $(a, b)$ but still does not imply $\hat{A}$ (due to the fact that $\mathbb{C}\mathrm{n}$ is compact, such a pair always exists). Assume that $u : v' \vdash B$, for some proposition $B$. If $B \notin u$, then by the maximality of $(u, v')$ we would have $B, u : v' \vdash \hat{A}$ and hence $u : v' \vdash \hat{A}$ by Cut, in contradiction with our assumption. Hence $B \in u$ and consequently $(u, \overline{v}')$ is a bitheory. Thus, the reverse implication also holds. □

The above lemma will serve as a basis for proving the completeness of default consequence relations with respect to the default semantics, described in the next section.

### 6.1.1 *Semantics*

Despite the fact that the notion of a default consequence relation is still very abstract, it nevertheless can be given a formal semantics.

By a *default semantics* for a default consequence relation we will mean a set of models. A *model* is a triple $(w, u, v)$, where $w, u, v$ are sets of propositions such that $w \subseteq u$. We will not give an informal interpretation of such models at this point, mainly because of the diversity of their potential interpretations used in what follows.

**Definition 6.4** A default rule $a : b \vdash A$ will be said to be *valid* in a default semantics $\mathbb{S}$, if, for any model $(w, u, v)$ from $\mathbb{S}$, if $a \subseteq u$ and $b \subseteq \overline{v}$, then $A \in w$. A constraint rule $a : b \vdash$ will be said to be *valid* in $\mathbb{S}$, if $\mathbb{S}$ has no models $(w, u, v)$ such that $a \subseteq u$ and $b \subseteq \overline{v}$.

For a default semantics $\mathbb{S}$, we will denote by $\vdash_{\mathbb{S}}$ the set of all default rules that are valid with respect to $\mathbb{S}$. Then the following theorem shows that default consequence relations are complete with respect to our semantics.

**Theorem 6.2** *$\vdash$ is a default consequence relation if and only if there is a semantics $\mathbb{S}$ such that $\vdash$ coincides with $\vdash_{\mathbb{S}}$.*

***Proof.*** The direction from right to left amounts to a straightforward verification that the set of default rules $\vdash_{\mathbb{S}}$ forms a default consequence relation. In the other direction, for a default consequence relation $\vdash$, we will consider its *canonical* default semantics $\mathbb{S}_{\vdash}$ defined as the set of all models of the form $(\mathrm{Cn}(u{:}\overline{v}), u, v)$, where $(u, v)$ is a bitheory of $\vdash$. Then Lemma 6.1 shows, in effect, that $\vdash$ coincides with the set of default rules that are valid in $\mathbb{S}_{\vdash}$. □

The above completeness theorem will serve as a basis for characterizing various extensions of the notion of a default consequence relation, described in what follows.

### 6.1.2 *Default theories*

In what follows by a *default theory* we will mean an arbitrary set of default rules. As before, for any default theory $\Delta$ there exists a least default consequence relation that contains it; we will denote it by $\vdash_{\Delta}$, while $\mathrm{Cn}_{\Delta}$ will denote the corresponding provability operator. This default consequence relation can be seen as describing the logical content of the default theory $\Delta$. Accordingly, we will extend the notions of a bitheory and propositional theory to arbitrary default theories:

**Definition 6.5**

- A pair $(u, v)$ of sets of propositions will be called a *bitheory of a default theory* $\Delta$, if it is a bitheory of $\vdash_{\Delta}$.
- A set of propositions $u$ will be called a *propositional theory* of $\Delta$, if $(u, u)$ is a bitheory of $\Delta$.

For a default theory $\Delta$ and a pair of premise sets $(u, v)$, we will denote by $\Delta(u : v)$ the set of direct consequences of $(u, v)$ in $\Delta$:

$$\Delta(u : v) = \{A \mid a : b \vdash A \in \Delta \ \& \ a \subseteq u \ \& \ b \subseteq v\}$$

The next result shows that the bitheories of $\Delta$ are precisely pairs of sets of propositions that are closed with respect to the default rules from $\Delta$.

**Lemma 6.3** *A pair $(u, v)$ is a bitheory of a default theory $\Delta$ if and only if $\Delta(u{:}\overline{v}) \subseteq u$, and $\Delta$ has no constraints $a : b \vdash$ such that $a \subseteq u$ and $b \subseteq \overline{v}$.*

***Proof.*** Let $\mathbb{C}\mathrm{n}_\Delta$ denote the provability operator corresponding to $\vdash_\Delta$. Then the direction from left to right follows from the fact that $\mathbb{C}\mathrm{n}_\Delta(u{:}\overline{v}) \subseteq u$. Let $\mathcal{B}$ denote the set of all pairs $(u, v)$ that satisfy the conditions of the lemma. Then we construct the following default semantics:

$$\mathbb{S} = \{(\Delta(u : \overline{v}), u, v) \mid (u, v) \in \mathcal{B}\}.$$

Let $\vdash_\mathbb{S}$ denote the default consequence relation generated by $\mathbb{S}$, and $\mathbb{C}\mathrm{n}_\mathbb{S}$ the corresponding provability operator. It is easy to verify that if $(u, v) \in \mathcal{B}$, then $u{:}\overline{v} \nvdash_\mathbb{S}$ and $\mathbb{C}\mathrm{n}_\mathbb{S}(u{:}\overline{v}) = \Delta(u{:}\overline{v})$.

Clearly, $\Delta$ is included in $\vdash_\mathbb{S}$, and therefore $\vdash_\Delta \subseteq \vdash_\mathbb{S}$, since $\vdash_\Delta$ is a least such default consequence relation. Consequently, if $(u, v) \in \mathcal{B}$, then $u{:}\overline{v} \nvdash_\Delta$ and $\mathbb{C}\mathrm{n}_\Delta(u{:}\overline{v}) \subseteq \mathbb{C}\mathrm{n}_\mathbb{S}(u{:}\overline{v}) = \Delta(u{:}\overline{v}) \subseteq u$. This gives us the direction from right to left. □

As a by-product of the above proof, we have obtained the following property that will be used in what follows.

**Corollary 6.4** *If $(u, v)$ is a bitheory of a default theory $\Delta$, then $\mathbb{C}\mathrm{n}_\Delta(u{:}\overline{v}) = \Delta(u{:}\overline{v})$.*

Finally, we will show that the provability operator $\mathbb{C}\mathrm{n}_\Delta$ can be constructed from $\Delta$ via an iterative construction that has been commonly used in the studies of nonmonotonic reasoning.

Given a default theory $\Delta$ and a pair of sets of propositions $(u, v)$, let $\Delta_0(u : v) = \Delta(u : v)$ and, for any $j \geq 0$,

$$\Delta_{j+1}(u : v) = \Delta_j(u : v) \cup \Delta(u \cup \Delta_j(u : v) : v).$$

Then the set of *iterative consequences* of $(u, v)$ in $\Delta$ is the set

$$\Delta^{it}(u : v) =_{Df} \bigcup_j \Delta_j(u : v).$$

The obtained set has the following characteristic property:

**Lemma 6.5** $\Delta^{it}(u \cup \Delta^{it}(u:v):v) \subseteq \Delta^{it}(u:v)$.

***Proof.*** Note first that $\mathcal{F}(w) = \Delta(u \cup w : v)$ is a monotonic and continuous operator on sets of propositions, and therefore $\Delta^{it}(u:v)$ is precisely the least fixed point of $\mathcal{F}$.

It is sufficient to show that, for any $j \geq 0$, $\Delta_j(u \cup \Delta^{it}(u:v):v) \subseteq \Delta^{it}(u:v)$. The proof is by induction on $j$. For $j = 0$, we have $\Delta(u \cup \Delta^{it}(u:v):v) \subseteq \Delta^{it}(u:v)$, since $\Delta^{it}(u:v)$ is a fixed point of $\mathcal{F}$. So assume that the claim holds for $j$, and let $w$ denote $\Delta_j(u \cup \Delta^{it}(u:v):v)$. Then

$$\Delta_{j+1}(u \cup \Delta^{it}(u:v):v) = w \cup \Delta(u \cup \Delta^{it}(u:v) \cup w : v).$$

But $w \subseteq \Delta^{it}(u:v)$, so the latter set is also included in $\Delta^{it}(u:v)$. This completes the proof. □

A pair $(u,v)$ will be called $\Delta$-*inconsistent*, if $\Delta$ contains a constraint $a : b \vdash$ such that $a \subseteq \Delta^{it}(u:v)$ and $b \subseteq v$. Otherwise it will be called $\Delta$-*consistent*.

Then we have

**Lemma 6.6** *For any default theory $\Delta$ and a $\Delta$-consistent pair $(u,v)$,*

$$\mathbb{C}\mathrm{n}_\Delta(u:v) = \Delta^{it}(u:v).$$

***Proof.*** The inclusion $\Delta^{it}(u:v) \subseteq \mathbb{C}\mathrm{n}_\Delta(u:v)$ can be easily proved by induction on the construction of $\Delta^{it}(u:v)$. For the reverse inclusion, we will define an auxiliary default consequence relation $\vdash^*$ as follows:

$$a : b \vdash^* \ \text{iff } (a,b) \text{ is } \Delta\text{-inconsistent},$$
$$a : b \vdash^* A \text{ iff } A \in \Delta^{it}(a{:}b), \text{ or } (a,b) \text{ is } \Delta\text{-inconsistent}.$$

We will check first that $\vdash^*$ is indeed a default consequence relation. Monotonicity and Constraint are immediate. In order to verify Cut, assume that $a{:}b \vdash^* B$ and $a, B{:}b \vdash^* \hat{A}$. If $a : b \vdash^*$, then $a : b \vdash^* \hat{A}$ by the definition of $\vdash^*$. So assume that $B \in \Delta^{it}(a{:}b)$. Then $\Delta^{it}(a{:}b) = \Delta^{it}(a, B{:}b)$ by the preceding lemma. Consequently, if $a, B : b \vdash^*$, then $a : b \vdash^*$, while if $a, B{:}b \vdash^* A$, then $a{:}b \vdash^* A$. Thus, Cut holds for $\vdash^*$, and hence it is a default consequence relation.

Let $\mathbb{C}\mathrm{n}_*$ denote the provability operator of $\vdash^*$. Note that, if $(a,b)$ is $\Delta$-consistent, then $\mathbb{C}\mathrm{n}_*(a{:}b) = \Delta^{it}(a{:}b)$. Moreover, $\Delta$ is obviously included in $\vdash^*$, and therefore $\mathbb{C}\mathrm{n}_\Delta \subseteq \mathbb{C}\mathrm{n}_*$, since $\mathbb{C}\mathrm{n}_\Delta$ is a least such default consequence relation. Consequently, for any $\Delta$-consistent pair $(u, v)$, we have $\mathbb{C}\mathrm{n}_\Delta(u{:}v) \subseteq \Delta^{it}(u{:}v)$. This completes the proof. □

## 6.2 Extensions and Expansions

Now we will describe two main nonmonotonic semantics for default consequence relations based, respectively, on extensions and expansions[1]. As will be made clear in what follows, extensions and expansions are exact counterparts of extensions and expansions for biconsequence relations.

**Definition 6.6** A theory $u$ of a default consequence relation $\vdash$ will be called

- an *extension* of $\vdash$, if $u \subseteq \mathbb{C}\mathrm{n}(\emptyset{:}\overline{u})$;
- an *expansion* of $\vdash$, if $u \subseteq \mathbb{C}\mathrm{n}(u{:}\overline{u})$.

As can be concluded directly from the above definitions, any extension is an expansion, though not vice versa. The following lemmas provide a more transparent description of these objects.

**Lemma 6.7** *A set $u$ of propositions is an extension of a nontrivial default consequence relation if and only if $u = \mathbb{C}\mathrm{n}(\emptyset : \overline{u})$.*

***Proof.*** Since $\mathbb{C}\mathrm{n}(u{:}\overline{u}) \subseteq u$ implies $\mathbb{C}\mathrm{n}(\emptyset : \overline{u}) \subseteq u$, any extension satisfies the above condition. In the other direction, we have to show only that any set $u$ satisfying this condition will be a theory of a non-trivial default consequence relation. Now, $\mathbb{C}\mathrm{n}(u{:}\overline{u}) = \mathbb{C}\mathrm{n}(\mathbb{C}\mathrm{n}(\emptyset{:}\overline{u}){:}\overline{u}) \subseteq \mathbb{C}\mathrm{n}(\emptyset : \overline{u}) \subseteq u$, and therefore $\mathbb{C}\mathrm{n}(u{:}\overline{u}) \subseteq u$. Moreover, if $A \notin u$, for some $A$, then $u{:}\overline{u} \nvdash A$, and consequently $u{:}\overline{u} \nvdash$, as required. Therefore, $u{:}\overline{u} \vdash$ can possibly hold only if $u$ is the set of all propositions $Pr$, and $Pr{:} \vdash$. By compactness, we have $a{:} \vdash$, for some finite set $a$. But we have also $: \vdash A$, for any proposition $A$, since $Pr$ satisfies the condition of the lemma. Applying Cut a finite number of times, we obtain $\emptyset{:}\emptyset \vdash$, contrary to our assumption that the $\vdash$ is non-trivial. Hence $u$ must be a theory of $\vdash$. This completes the proof. □

An important property of extensions is that they are minimal theories of a default consequence relation.

**Lemma 6.8** *Any extension is a minimal theory of a default consequence relation.*

[1] Expansions were called weak extensions in [Marek *et al.*, 1990].

***Proof.*** Let $u$ be an extension of a default consequence relation $\vdash$, and suppose that $v \subseteq u$, for some theory $v$ of $\vdash$. Then

$$u = \mathbb{C}\mathrm{n}(\emptyset : \overline{u}) \subseteq \mathbb{C}\mathrm{n}(\emptyset : \overline{v}) \subseteq \mathbb{C}\mathrm{n}(v : \overline{v}) \subseteq v,$$

and therefore $u = v$. Hence $u$ is a minimal theory of $\vdash$. □

The corresponding description of expansions is a bit more complicated, due to the possibility that the set of all propositions can also be an expansion.

**Lemma 6.9** *A set $u$ of propositions is an expansion of a default consequence relation if and only if $u = \mathbb{C}\mathrm{n}(u{:}\overline{u})$, and either $u \neq Pr$, or $Pr{:}\nvdash$.*

***Proof.*** If $Pr$ is an expansion, then clearly $Pr{:}\nvdash$. This gives us the direction from left to right. The other direction follows from the fact that, if $u \neq Pr$, then $A \notin u$, for some $A$, and hence $u{:}\overline{u} \nvdash A$. Therefore $u{:}\overline{u} \nvdash$, as required. □

The next result states a restricted monotonicity property for expansions and extensions of default consequence relations. It says that when the set of theories is preserved, the sets of extensions and expansions grow monotonically with the growth of the default consequence relation.

**Lemma 6.10** *If $\vdash_1 \subseteq \vdash_2$ and $\vdash_1$ and $\vdash_2$ have the same theories, then any expansion of $\vdash_1$ is an expansion of $\vdash_2$, and any extension of $\vdash_1$ is an extension of $\vdash_2$.*

***Proof.*** The proof is immediate from the fact that, if $u \subseteq \mathbb{C}\mathrm{n}_1(\emptyset{:}\overline{u})$ ($u \subseteq \mathbb{C}\mathrm{n}_1(u{:}\overline{u})$), then $u \subseteq \mathbb{C}\mathrm{n}_2(\emptyset : \overline{u})$ (respectively, $u \subseteq \mathbb{C}\mathrm{n}_2(u{:}\overline{u})$), coupled with the assumption that theories are preserved. □

The above property will allow us to single out the rules for default consequence relations that are valid, respectively, for extensions and expansions.

Since default consequence relations can be viewed as 'logical closures' of default theories, the notions of expansion and extension can be extended directly to the latter.

**Definition 6.7** A set $u$ of propositions will be called an *extension* (respectively, *expansion*) of a default theory $\Delta$, if it is an extension (resp., expansion) of $\vdash_\Delta$.

The following lemma gives a constructive description of expansions and extensions of default theories.

**Lemma 6.11** *If $\Delta$ is a default theory, then a set $u$ of propositions is*

- *an extension of* $\Delta$ *iff* $u = \Delta^{it}(\emptyset{:}\overline{u})$;
- *an expansion of* $\Delta$ *iff* $u = \Delta(u{:}\overline{u})$, *and either* $u \neq Pr$, *or* $\Delta$ *does not have constraints of the form* $a :\vdash$.

***Proof.*** Immediate from, respectively, Lemma 6.6 and Corollary 6.4. □

Having at our disposal the notions of expansion and extension for arbitrary default theories, we obtain an opportunity to investigate the behavior of such models for particular kinds of default theories.

An important problem of this kind amounts to finding default theories for which expansions coincide with extensions, and a useful sufficient condition is given by a counterpart of Fages' theorem, described below.

A default theory $\Delta$ will be called *acyclic*, if there exists a ranking function $r$ from propositions to ordinals such that, for any default rule $a : b \vdash C$ from $\Delta$, $r(A) < r(C)$, for any $A \in a$.

**Theorem 6.12** *Any expansion of an acyclic default theory is its extension.*

***Proof.*** Suppose that $u$ is an expansion of an acyclic default theory $\Delta$ that is not its extension. Then $\mathbb{C}\mathrm{n}_\Delta(\emptyset{:}\overline{u}) \subset u$. Let $A$ be a proposition having a minimal rank in $u \backslash \mathbb{C}\mathrm{n}_\Delta(\emptyset{:}\overline{u})$. Since $u = \mathbb{C}\mathrm{n}_\Delta(u{:}\overline{u})$, we have $A \in \mathbb{C}\mathrm{n}(u{:}\overline{u})$. By Corollary 6.4, $A \in \Delta(u{:}\overline{u})$, and therefore $\Delta$ contains a default rule $a{:}b \vdash A$ such that $a \subseteq u$ and $b \subseteq \overline{u}$. Now, all propositions in $a$ have a lower rank than $A$, and therefore $a \subseteq \mathbb{C}\mathrm{n}_\Delta(\emptyset{:}\overline{u})$. Hence, $A \in \mathbb{C}\mathrm{n}_\Delta(\mathbb{C}\mathrm{n}_\Delta(\emptyset{:}\overline{u}) : \overline{u}) \subseteq \mathbb{C}\mathrm{n}_\Delta(\emptyset{:}\overline{u})$, contrary to our assumptions. □

We will give yet another proof of this result later, obtained as a consequence of the corresponding result for biconsequence relations.

## 6.3 Partial Expansions and Extensions

We describe now partial generalizations of the notions of expansion and extension that play an important role in logic programming.

**Definition 6.8** An invariant bitheory $(u, v)$ of a default consequence relation will be called

- a *partial expansion* if $u \subseteq \mathbb{C}\mathrm{n}(u{:}\overline{v})$ and $v \subseteq \mathbb{C}\mathrm{n}(v{:}\overline{u})$;
- a *partial extension* if $u \subseteq \mathbb{C}\mathrm{n}(\emptyset{:}\overline{v})$ and $v \subseteq \mathbb{C}\mathrm{n}(\emptyset{:}\overline{u})$.

As we will see, partial extensions and expansions, as defined above, are closely related to partial extensions and expansions of biconsequence relations described in the preceding chapter. For now, it is easy to verify that $u$ is an expansion (resp., extension) of a default consequence relation if and only if $(u, u)$ is a partial expansion (respectively, extension). In addition, the following syntactic description follows directly from the above definitions:

**Lemma 6.13**

- *$(u, v)$ is a partial expansion iff it satisfies the following conditions:*

$$u = \mathbb{C}\mathrm{n}(u{:}\overline{v}) \quad \textit{and} \quad v = \mathbb{C}\mathrm{n}(v{:}\overline{u}).$$

- *$(u, v)$ is a partial extension iff it satisfies:*

$$u = \mathbb{C}\mathrm{n}(\emptyset{:}\overline{v}) \quad \textit{and} \quad v = \mathbb{C}\mathrm{n}(\emptyset{:}\overline{u}).$$

It turns out that in our present, default setting, partial extensions and expansions have many additional properties. Most importantly, both can be characterized as fixed points of some monotonic operators.

To begin with, given a default consequence relation, let us define the following operator $\Phi$ on pairs of sets of propositions[2]:

$$\Phi(u, v) = (\mathbb{C}\mathrm{n}(u{:}\overline{v}), \mathbb{C}\mathrm{n}(v{:}\overline{u})).$$

Then we immediately obtain

**Lemma 6.14** *Partial expansions of a default consequence relation are precisely fixed points of the operator $\Phi$.*

Now, it can be verified that the operator $\Phi$ is monotonic with respect to the *knowledge order* on bitheories defined as follows (see [Fitting, 1993]):

$$(u, v) \leq_k (u_1, v_1) \quad \equiv \quad u \subseteq u_1 \text{ and } v_1 \subseteq v.$$

Bitheories that are smaller with respect to this order embody less information about both truth and falsity of propositions. Consequently, any default consequence relation has a k-least partial expansion.

Similarly, in order to describe partial extensions, let us define the following operator on sets of propositions[3]:

$$\Gamma(u) = \mathbb{C}\mathrm{n}(\emptyset : \overline{u}).$$

As can be verified, $\Gamma$ is an antimonotonic operator:

[2] Cf. [Fitting, 1985].

[3] This operator corresponds to the Gelfond-Lifschitz operator in logic programming—see [Gelfond and Lifschitz, 1988].

If $u \subseteq v$, then $\Gamma(v) \subseteq \Gamma(u)$.

Consequently, taken twice, it gives a monotonic operator. The next corollary says that partial extensions can be identified with fixed points of $\Gamma^2$, while extensions are just fixed points of $\Gamma$ itself.

**Corollary 6.15**

- *$u$ is an extension of a default consequence relation iff* $u = \Gamma(u)$.
- $(u, v)$ *is a partial extension iff* $u = \Gamma^2(u)$ *and* $v = \Gamma(u)$.

The above description obviously implies that partial extensions always exist. Moreover, there always exists a least fixed point of $\Gamma^2$; it corresponds to the well-founded model of normal logic programs (see below).

### 6.3.1 *Doubling*

Just as for biconsequence relations, partial extensions and expansions are reducible to ordinary extensions and expansions of 'doubled' default theories (see Sec. 5.5.1).

As before, we extend the source language $\mathcal{L}$ with new propositions $A'$, for every $A \in \mathcal{L}$. For any $u \subseteq \mathcal{L}$, we denote by $u'$ the set $\{A' \mid A \in u\}$. Finally, we transform a default theory $\Delta$ into a new default theory $\Delta'$ by replacing every default rule $a{:}b \vdash A$ from $\Delta$ with the following two rules:

$$a' : b \vdash A' \qquad\qquad a : b' \vdash A.$$

$\vdash_{\Delta'}$ will denote the least default consequence relation in the extended language that contains $\Delta'$.

**Lemma 6.16** *A pair* $(u \cup u_1', v \cup v_1')$ *is a bitheory of* $\Delta'$ *if and only if both* $(u_1, v)$ *and* $(u, v_1)$ *are bitheories of* $\Delta$.

***Proof.*** $(u \cup u_1', v \cup v_1')$ is a bitheory of $\Delta'$ if it is $\Delta'$-consistent and closed with respect to the bisequents of $\Delta'$. By the construction of $\Delta'$, this means that, for any $a{:}b \vdash A$ from $\Delta$, if $a \subseteq u_1$ and $b \subseteq \overline{v}$, then $A \in u_1$, and if $a \subseteq u$ and $b \subseteq \overline{v}_1$, then $A \in u$. In other words, $\Delta(u_1{:}\overline{v}) \subseteq u_1$ and $\Delta(u{:}\overline{v}_1) \subseteq u$. In addition, $(u \cup u_1', v \cup v_1')$ is $\Delta'$-consistent iff both $(u_1, v)$ and $(u, v_1)$ are $\Delta$-consistent. Hence both are bitheories of $\Delta$. □

As a consequence, we obtain that bitheories of $\Delta'$ satisfy the following invariance property:

**Corollary 6.17** *If* $(u \cup u_1', v \cup v_1')$ *is a bitheory of* $\Delta'$, *then* $(u_1 \cup u', v_1 \cup v')$ *is also a bitheory of* $\Delta'$.

In addition, we also have

**Corollary 6.18** $u \cup u_1'$ *is a theory of* $\Delta'$ *iff* $(u, u_1)$ *is an invariant bitheory of* $\Delta$.

The next result shows that derivations of atoms and tagged atoms in $\vdash_{\Delta'}$ are completely separated.

**Lemma 6.19**

$$a, a_1'{:}b, b_1' \vdash_{\Delta'} A \quad \textit{iff} \quad a{:}b_1 \vdash_\Delta A \quad \textit{or} \quad a_1{:}b \vdash_\Delta$$
$$a, a_1'{:}b, b_1' \vdash_{\Delta'} A' \quad \textit{iff} \quad a_1{:}b \vdash_\Delta A \quad \textit{or} \quad a{:}b_1 \vdash_\Delta$$
$$a, a_1'{:}b, b_1' \vdash_{\Delta'} \quad \textit{iff} \quad a_1{:}b \vdash_\Delta \quad \textit{or} \quad a{:}b_1 \vdash_\Delta .$$

***Proof.*** The implications from right to left are immediate. Let $\vdash'$ denote the set of default rules in the extended language that are determined by $\vdash_\Delta$ using the above equivalences. Then it is easy to verify that $\vdash'$ is actually a default consequence relation that includes $\Delta'$. Consequently, $\vdash_{\Delta'} \subseteq \vdash'$, which gives the direction from left to right. □

Finally, the following theorem shows that the above translation transforms each partial nonmonotonic semantics into its original counterpart.

**Theorem 6.20** $(u, v)$ *is a partial extension (partial expansion) of a default theory* $\Delta$ *if and only if* $u \cup v'$ *is an extension (resp., expansion) of* $\Delta'$.

***Proof.*** We will prove the result only for (partial) expansions, the proof for extensions being similar.

$u \cup v'$ is an expansion of $\Delta'$ if $u \cup v' = \mathrm{Cn}_{\Delta'}(u \cup v'{:}\overline{u \cup v'})$. The latter equality amounts to the following two conditions:

$$A \in u \ \text{ iff } \ u \cup v' : \overline{u \cup v'} \vdash_{\Delta'} A$$
$$A \in v \ \text{ iff } \ u \cup v' : \overline{u \cup v'} \vdash_{\Delta'} A'.$$

By the preceding lemma, these conditions amount, in turn, to

$$A \in u \ \text{ iff } \ u : \overline{v} \vdash_\Delta A \ \text{ or } \ v : \overline{u} \vdash_\Delta$$
$$A \in v \ \text{ iff } \ v : \overline{u} \vdash_\Delta A \ \text{ or } \ u : \overline{v} \vdash_\Delta .$$

Note, however, that, since $u \cup v'$ is an expansion, it is a theory of $\Delta'$, and consequently both $(u, v)$ and $(v, u)$ should be bitheories of $\Delta$ by Corollary 6.18. Consequently, the above conditions are reducible to

$$A \in u \text{ iff } u : \overline{v} \vdash_\Delta A$$
$$A \in v \text{ iff } v : \overline{u} \vdash_\Delta A.$$

which say that $(u, v)$ is a partial expansion of $\Delta$. □

As we already mentioned in the preceding chapter, a logical basis of the above doubling construction will be provided in Chapter 8 in the framework of causal inference.

## 6.4 Kinds of Default Reasoning

The general notion of a default consequence relation is rather uninformative; it is only a frame that can be filled with additional rules that would provide a more tight description of our intuitions about nonmonotonic reasoning. As we will see, however, there will be no single system that reflects adequately all our intuitions, since different nonmonotonic semantics will admit different underlying logics.

We will present now three rules for default consequence relations that will form the basis for a subsequent classification of different kinds of default reasoning.

**Reflexivity** $A :\vdash A$.
**Consistency** $A : A \vdash$.
**Factoring** If $a, B : b \vdash \hat{A}$ and $a : b, B \vdash \hat{A}$, then $a : b \vdash \hat{A}$.

A default consequence relation will be called *reflexive*, if it satisfies Reflexivity. Such consequence relation will turn out to be appropriate for nonmonotonic reasoning based on extensions. Reflexivity will be inappropriate, however, for reasoning about expansions.

A default consequence relation will be called *consistent* if it satisfies Consistency. The latter postulate states that no proposition can serve as both a positive and negative premise in a derivation.

Finally, a default consequence relation will be called *complete* if it satisfies Factoring. This postulate permits reasoning by cases with respect to positive and negative premises, and hence presumes completeness with respect to corresponding contexts. This feature turns out to be characteristic of autoepistemic reasoning.

The next definition will provide us with semantic counterparts of the above rules.

**Definition 6.9** A default semantics $\mathbb{S}$ will be called

- *reflexive*, if for any model $(w, u, v)$ from $\mathbb{S}$, $u = w$;
- *consistent*, if for any model $(w, u, v)$ from $\mathbb{S}$, $u \subseteq v$;
- *complete*, if for any model $(w, u, v)$ from $\mathbb{S}$, $v \subseteq u$.

The following result is a combined completeness theorem for the above three kinds of default consequence relations.

**Theorem 6.21** *A default consequence relation is reflexive (consistent,complete) if and only if it has a reflexive (consistent, complete) default semantics.*

***Proof.*** As in the proof of the general completeness theorem, the direction from right to left amounts to a straightforward verification that the set of default rules determined by a reflexive (consistent, complete) default semantics satisfies Reflexivity (respectively, Consistency and Factoring).

In order to provide a uniform and modular proof for the other direction, we have to restrict the canonical semantics, described in the earlier completeness proof. A bitheory $(u, v)$ of $\Vdash$ will be called *canonical*, if $(u, \overline{v})$ is a maximal pair such that $u{:}\overline{v} \nVdash \hat{A}$, for some $\hat{A}$. As shows the proof of Lemma 6.1, canonical bitheories are still sufficient for determining the source default consequence relation, and hence they also can serve as a basis for a canonical default semantics. Now, it is easy to show that if a default consequence relation $\Vdash$ is reflexive or consistent, this canonical default semantics is also, respectively, reflexive or consistent. For complete consequence relations, we have to show that if $(u, v)$ is a canonical bitheory, then $v \subseteq u$. Indeed, suppose that there exists some $B \in v \backslash u$. Then we will have $u, B{:}\overline{v} \Vdash A$ and $u{:}B, \overline{v} \Vdash A$ (since $(u, v)$ is canonical), which implies $u{:}\overline{v} \Vdash A$ by Factoring, contrary to our assumptions. Thus the canonical default semantics for $\Vdash$ is complete. □

It is important to note that the proof of the above theorem shows also that any combination of the three basic postulates is characterized semantically by the corresponding combination of semantic conditions. In the following sections we will consider in more details some important combinations of these postulates.

## 6.5 Default Scott Consequence Relations

We begin with default consequence relations that satisfy all the above rules.

**Definition 6.10** A default consequence relation will be called a *Scott* one if it satisfies Reflexivity, Consistency and Factoring.

As follows from the semantic characterization of the corresponding rules, the default semantics of a default Scott consequence relation should have only models of the form $(u, u, u)$. Moreover, the following theorem shows that such default consequence relations are actually reducible to ordinary Scott consequence relations.

**Theorem 6.22** *$\vdash$ is a default Scott consequence relation if and only if there exists a plain Scott consequence relation $\vdash_0$ such that*

$$a : b \vdash \hat{A} \text{ iff } a \vdash_0 b, \hat{A}.$$

***Proof.*** It is easy to check that if $\vdash_0$ is a Scott consequence relation, then the above description determines a default Scott consequence relation. In the other direction, if $\vdash$ is a default Scott consequence relation, let $\vdash_0$ be a consequence relation defined as follows:

$$a \vdash_0 b \;\equiv\; a : b \vdash .$$

Due to Consistency and Factoring, this is a Scott consequence relation. We will show that the condition of the theorem is satisfied for $\vdash_0$.

Assume first that $a{:}b \vdash A$. We have $A{:}A \vdash$ by Consistency, and hence $a{:}b, A \vdash$ by Cut. Assume now that $a{:}b, A \vdash$. Then $a{:}b, A \vdash A$ by Constraint. In addition, $A, a{:}b \vdash A$ by Reflexivity, and therefore $a{:}b \vdash A$ by Factoring. Hence the condition of the theorem is satisfied. □

The importance of default Scott consequence relations for our study stems from the fact that the rules Reflexivity, Consistency and Factoring preserve theories of default consequence relations.

Let us denote by $\vdash^s$ a least default Scott consequence relation containing a given default consequence relation $\vdash$.

**Lemma 6.23** *$\vdash^s$ is a greatest default consequence relation having the same theories as $\vdash$.*

***Proof.*** Let $\mathcal{T}$ be the set of all theories of $\vdash$, $\vdash_{\mathcal{T}}$ a Scott consequence relation determined by $\mathcal{T}$, and $\vdash^*$ the default Scott consequence relation corresponding to $\vdash_{\mathcal{T}}$ by Theorem 6.22. As follows from this construction, $\vdash^*$ could be defined directly as follows:

$$a : b \vdash^* A \quad \text{iff} \quad (\forall u \in \mathcal{T})(a \subseteq u \;\&\; b \subseteq \overline{u} \Rightarrow A \in u)$$
$$a : b \vdash^* \quad \text{iff} \quad \neg(\exists u \in \mathcal{T})(a \subseteq u \;\&\; b \subseteq \overline{u}).$$

It can be easily verified that $\vdash$ is included in $\vdash^*$, and they have the same theories. We will show that $\vdash^*$ coincides with $\vdash^s$. The inclusion $\vdash^s \subseteq \vdash^*$ follows from the fact that $\vdash$ is included in $\vdash^*$. Assume now that $a : b \nvdash^s A$, and let $(u, v)$ be a maximal bitheory of $\vdash^s$ such that $a \subseteq u$, $b \subseteq \overline{v}$ and $u : \overline{v} \nvdash^s A$. As in the proof of the completeness theorem, Factoring and Consistency imply that $u = v$, and hence $u$ is a theory of $\vdash^s$. Moreover, by Reflexivity, $A \notin u$. Now, since $\vdash \subseteq \vdash^s \subseteq \vdash^*$, we have that $\vdash^s$ has the same theories as $\vdash$. Hence $u$ is also a theory of $\vdash$, and consequently $a : b \nvdash^* A$. Thus, $\vdash^* \subseteq \vdash^s$, and hence $\vdash^* = \vdash^s$. □

An immediate consequence of the above result is the following

**Corollary 6.24** *Default consequence relations $\vdash$ and $\vdash_1$ have the same theories if and only if $\vdash_1^s = \vdash^s$.*

Now we will turn to the nonmonotonic semantics of default Scott consequence relations, which will be quite simple. To begin with, due to Reflexivity, any theory of such a consequence relation will already be an expansion (since we will always have $u \subseteq \mathrm{Cn}(u{:}\overline{u})$). In addition, extensions in this case will be just minimal theories.

**Lemma 6.25** *A set $u$ is an extension of a default Scott consequence relation $\vdash$ if and only if $u$ is a minimal theory of $\vdash$.*

***Proof.*** Given the representation of Theorem 6.22, the result follows immediately from Lemma 2.18. □

The above result shows that default Scott consequence relations (just as ordinary Scott consequence relations) is an appropriate framework only for a simplest kind of nonmonotonic reasoning, namely reasoning with respect to minimal models. It is interesting to note, however, that applications of default-type systems to solving traditional mathematical problems (e.g., the marriage problem—see [Marek *et al.*, 1990]) give rise to just this kind of nonmonotonic reasoning.

Though default Scott consequence relations are inappropriate for nonmonotonic reasoning in its full generality, they constitute an important upper bound on reasonable default-type systems. In other words, for reasons that will become clear in what follows, all such systems should contain only rules that are valid for default Scott consequence relations. Accordingly, the simplest way to obtain a nontrivial default consequence relation consists in rejection of one of the three rules constituting the definition of a default Scott consequence relation. In this respect, extensions and expansions give rise to two different kinds of reasoning. An extension-based reasoning is characterized by rejecting Factoring and accepting the other two rules. Such a reasoning is associated with default logic and modal nonmonotonic logics based on 'negative introspection'. An expansion-based reasoning amounts to rejection of Reflexivity, and is associated with autoepistemic logic. Below we will give a description of the corresponding systems.

## 6.6 Reflexive Default Consequence Relations

In this section we will single out the range of default consequence relations that are appropriate for reasoning with extensions.

Recall that a default consequence relation is reflexive if it satisfies Reflexivity. A convenient feature of such consequence relations is that the corresponding provability operator $\mathbb{C}\mathrm{n}(u{:}v)$ has all the usual properties of a deductive closure operator with respect to its first argument (that is, when $v$ is fixed):

C1. If $u \subseteq u_1$, then $\mathbb{C}\mathrm{n}(u : v) \subseteq \mathbb{C}\mathrm{n}(u_1 : v)$.
C2. $u \subseteq \mathbb{C}\mathrm{n}(u : v)$.
C3. $\mathbb{C}\mathrm{n}(\mathbb{C}\mathrm{n}(u : v) : v) \subseteq \mathbb{C}\mathrm{n}(u : v)$.

The semantic condition corresponding to Reflexivity is that, in any model $(w, u, v)$ of a default semantics, $w$ must coincide with $u$. This immediately suggests an alternative semantics for reflexive default consequence relations, namely the binary semantics used earlier for interpreting biconsequence relations (see Sec. 3.1.1).

**Definition 6.11** A default rule $a : b \vdash A$ will be said to be *D-valid* with respect to a binary semantics $\mathcal{B}$ if and only if, for any bimodel $(u, v)$ from $\mathcal{B}$, if $a \subseteq u$ and $b \subseteq \overline{v}$, then $A \in u$.

For a binary semantics $\mathcal{B}$, we will denote by $\vdash^D_{\mathcal{B}}$ the set of all default rules that are D-valid with respect to $\mathcal{B}$. It is easy to check that this set forms a reflexive default consequence relation. Moreover, the following result shows that reflexive consequence relations are characterized by this semantics. The proof is immediate from the general completeness result, Theorem 6.21.

**Theorem 6.26** *$\vdash$ is a reflexive default consequence relation if and only if there is a binary semantics $\mathcal{B}$ such that $\vdash$ coincides with $\vdash^D_{\mathcal{B}}$.*

As a first consequence of the above result, we conclude that reflexive default consequence relations are uniquely determined by their bitheories.

**Corollary 6.27** *If $\vdash$ is a reflexive default consequence relation, then $a : b \vdash A$ if and only if $A \in u$, for any bitheory $(u, v)$ of $\vdash$ such that $a \subseteq u$ and $b \subseteq \overline{v}$, and $a{:}b \vdash$ if and only if there is no bitheory $(u, v)$ of $\vdash$ such that $a \subseteq u$ and $b \subseteq \overline{v}$.*

Yet another important consequence of the preceding theorem is that default rules $a{:}b \vdash A$ of a reflexive default consequence relation can be viewed as singular default bisequents $a{:}b \Vdash A :$. Formally, we have

**Corollary 6.28** *A default consequence relation is reflexive if and only if it coincides with the set of singular default bisequents of some biconsequence relation.*

***Proof.*** As can be verified, the set of singular default bisequents of a biconsequence relation satisfies the postulates of a reflexive default consequence relation. Moreover, if $\vdash$ is a reflexive default consequence relation, it has some binary semantics $\mathcal{B}$. Clearly, $\vdash$ coincides with the set of singular default bisequents of the biconsequence relation generated by $\mathcal{B}$. □

It should be noted, however, that reflexive default consequence relations trivialize (partial) expansions. Namely, due to Reflexivity, we always have $u \subseteq \mathbb{C}\mathrm{n}(u{:}v)$, which immediately implies

**Lemma 6.29** *Any invariant bitheory of a reflexive default consequence relation is a partial expansion.*

In particular, we have that any theory of a reflexive default consequence relation is an expansion. Consequently, reflexive default consequence relations are already inappropriate for expansion-based nonmonotonic reasoning. Nevertheless, the following result shows that Reflexivity preserves partial extensions, so reflexive default consequence relations will be adequate for the latter.

**Theorem 6.30** *If $\vdash^i$ is a least reflexive default consequence relation that contains a default consequence relation $\vdash$, then $\vdash^i$ has the same partial extensions as $\vdash$.*

***Proof.*** Let us define the following default consequence relation:

$$a : b \vdash^* A \;\equiv\; a : b \vdash A \text{ or } A \in a.$$

It can be directly verified that $\vdash^*$ is a reflexive default consequence relation (Cut is the only nontrivial case). Moreover, $\vdash^*$ includes $\vdash$, and hence $\vdash^i \subseteq \vdash^*$. But $\vdash^*$ is clearly included in $\vdash^i$, so $\vdash^i$ coincides with $\vdash^*$.

As a consequence of the above description of $\vdash^i$, we have that, for any sets $u, v$ of propositions, $\mathbb{C}\mathrm{n}^i(u{:}v) = u \cup \mathbb{C}\mathrm{n}(u{:}v)$. In particular, we have $\mathbb{C}\mathrm{n}^i(\emptyset{:}v) = \mathbb{C}\mathrm{n}(\emptyset{:}v)$. In view of Lemma 6.13, this is sufficient for showing that $\vdash^i$ has the same partial extensions as $\vdash$. □

Now the correspondence between reflexive default consequence relations and biconsequence relations implies, in turn, the correspondence between (partial) extensions of default theories and (partial) extensions of corresponding bisequent theories.

For a default theory $\Delta$, we will denote by $\Delta_{\Vdash}$ the corresponding default bisequent theory, that is, $\Delta_{\Vdash} = \{a{:}b \Vdash \hat{A}{:} \mid a : b \vdash \hat{A} \in \Delta\}$. Then we have

**Lemma 6.31** *For any default theory $\Delta$, the bisequent theory $\Delta_{\Vdash}$ has the same extensions and partial extensions as $\Delta$.*

***Proof.*** By the preceding result, partial extensions of $\Delta$ coincide with partial extensions of $\vdash^i_\Delta$. In view of Corollary 6.28, $\vdash^i_\Delta$ coincides with the singular default subrelation of $\Vdash_{\Delta_{\Vdash}}$. Note now that, since the latter is a default biconsequence relation, Corollary 3.38 implies that $:\overline{u} \Vdash_{\Delta_{\Vdash}} A{:}u$ holds iff $:\overline{u} \Vdash_{\Delta_{\Vdash}} A{:}$. Consequently, (partial) extensions of $\Vdash_{\Delta_{\Vdash}}$ coincide with (partial) extensions of $\vdash^i_\Delta$ due to Corollary 5.76. □

The above correspondence gives us, in particular, yet another explanation why extensions are minimal theories of a default consequence relation (see Corollary 5.40).

### 6.6.1 *Regular default consequence relations*

We will describe now default consequence relations that constitute a maximal default logic suitable for nonmonotonic reasoning based on extensions. These consequence relations will also play an important role in establishing the correspondence between default logic and modal nonmonotonic logics.

It has been established in the preceding chapter that consistent regular biconsequence relations constitute a maximal logic adequate for the default nonmonotonic semantics. In order to transfer this result to default consequence relations, we have to find a default counterpart of Regularity.

**Definition 6.12** A default consequence relation will be called *regular* if it is reflexive, consistent, and satisfies the following rule:

**D-Regularity** $$\frac{c : b \vdash \quad \{a : b, C \vdash \hat{A} \mid C \in c\}}{a : b \vdash \hat{A}}$$

As follows from the semantic description below, D-Regularity is actually a default counterpart of the Regularity rule for biconsequence relations. In our present setting, however, it is a weakening of the rule Factoring. Accordingly, regular default consequence relations can be seen as a minimal weakening of default Scott consequence relations that is suitable for extension-based reasoning.

A binary semantics will be called *regular*, if it is consistent and quasi-reflexive (see Sec. 3.2.5). The following theorem establishes a completeness of regular default consequence relations with respect to this semantics.

**Theorem 6.32** *A default consequence relation is regular if and only if it has a regular binary semantics.*

***Proof.*** It can be easily verified that D-Regularity holds for a regular semantics. Consequently, any regular binary semantics produces a regular default consequence relation. In the other direction, by the general completeness theorem, it is sufficient to show that if $(u, v)$ is a canonical bitheory with respect to some $\hat{A}$, then $v$ is a theory of $\vdash$.

Assume first that $v{:}\overline{v} \vdash$. Then $c{:}\overline{v} \vdash$, for some finite $c \subseteq v$. Since $(u, v)$ is canonical with respect to $\hat{A}$, we have also $u{:}\overline{v}, C \vdash \hat{A}$, for any $C \in c$. Hence by compactness, there are finite $a \subseteq u$ and $b \subseteq \overline{v}$ such that $c{:}b \vdash$ and $a{:}b, C \vdash \hat{A}$, for any $C \in c$. Consequently, $a{:}b \vdash \hat{A}$ by D-Regularity, and therefore $u{:}\overline{v} \vdash \hat{A}$, contrary to our assumptions. Hence, $v{:}\overline{v} \nvdash$. Suppose now that $v{:}\overline{v} \vdash B$, for some $B \notin v$. Then $B{:}\overline{v} \vdash$ by Consistency, and therefore $v{:}\overline{v} \vdash$ by Cut, which is impossible. Consequently, $\mathbb{C}\mathrm{n}(v{:}\overline{v}) \subseteq v$. Thus, $v$ is a theory of $\vdash$, and therefore the canonical semantics of $\vdash$ is regular. □

The next result shows that the rules of a regular default consequence relation preserve extensions.

**Theorem 6.33** *If* $\vdash^r$ *is a least regular default consequence relation that contains a default consequence relation* $\vdash$*, then* $\vdash^r$ *has the same extensions* *as* $\vdash$.

***Proof.*** We define first a binary semantics $\mathcal{B}$ as the set of all bitheories of $\vdash$ of the form $(u, u)$ and $(\mathbb{C}\mathrm{n}(\emptyset{:}\overline{u}), u)$, where $u$ is a theory of $\vdash$. As can be verified, $\mathcal{B}$ is a regular semantics, and consequently it generates a regular default consequence relation $\vdash_{\mathcal{B}}$. Clearly, $\vdash$ is included in $\vdash_{\mathcal{B}}$, and therefore $\vdash^r \subseteq \vdash_{\mathcal{B}}$, since $\vdash^r$ is a least such consequence relation. Moreover, any theory of $\vdash$ remains a theory of $\vdash_{\mathcal{B}}$. Consequently any extension of $\vdash$ will be an extension of $\vdash_{\mathcal{B}}$ and $\vdash^r$ by Lemma 6.10.

Let $u$ be an extension of $\vdash_{\mathcal{B}}$. Since $u$ is a theory of $\vdash_{\mathcal{B}}$, it is a theory of $\vdash$, and hence $(\mathbb{C}\mathrm{n}(\emptyset{:}\overline{u}), u) \in \mathcal{B}$. Assume now that $A \in u$. Then $\emptyset : \overline{u} \vdash_{\mathcal{B}} A$ and consequently $A \in \mathbb{C}\mathrm{n}(\emptyset{:}\overline{u})$ by the definition of $\vdash_{\mathcal{B}}$. Therefore, $u \subseteq \mathbb{C}\mathrm{n}(\emptyset{:}\overline{u})$, which means that $u$ is an extension of $\vdash$. Thus, $\vdash_{\mathcal{B}}$ has the same extensions as $\vdash$, which immediately implies that both have the same extensions as $\vdash^r$ (by Lemma 6.10). □

Thus, Reflexivity, Consistency and D-Regularity are rules for default consequence relations that preserve extensions. Now we will show that regular default consequence relations constitute a maximal logic for the extension-based nonmonotonic reasoning.

**Definition 6.13** Default theories $\Gamma$ and $\Delta$ will be called *extension-equivalent*, if they have the same extensions, and *strongly extension-equivalent* if, for any set $\Phi$ of default rules, $\Gamma \cup \Phi$ is extension-equivalent to $\Delta \cup \Phi$.

The following lemma is just a reformulation of our previous result in the new terminology.

**Lemma 6.34** *Any default consequence relation* $\vdash$ *is extension-equivalent to* $\vdash^r$.

Strong extension-equivalence implicitly determines the logic of default rules that is adequate for the extension-based nonmonotonic semantics.

Let us say that default theories $\Gamma$ and $\Delta$ are *regularly equivalent*, if they determine the same regular default consequence relation. This means that each of these default theories is obtainable from the other using the postulates of regular default consequence relations. Then we have

**Theorem 6.35** *Default theories are strongly extension-equivalent if and only if they are regularly equivalent.*

***Proof.*** The following proof is similar to the proof of Theorem 5.36.

The implication from right to left follows from the preceding lemma. Assume now that $\Gamma$ and $\Delta$ are not regularly equivalent. Since reflexive default consequence relations are uniquely determined by their bitheories, we will assume for certainty that $(u, v)$ is a bitheory of $\vdash^r_\Gamma$ that is not a bitheory of $\vdash^r_\Delta$. Since our default consequence relations are regular, $u \subseteq v$, and $v$ is a theory of $\vdash^r_\Gamma$.

Suppose first that $v$ is not a theory of $\vdash^r_\Delta$, and let $\Phi = \{\vdash A \mid A \in v\}$. Then $v$ will obviously be an extension of $\vdash^r_{\Gamma\cup\Phi}$, though it will not be even a theory of $\vdash^r_{\Delta\cup\Phi}$.

Suppose now that $v$ is also a theory of $\vdash^r_\Delta$. Since $(u, v)$ is not a bitheory of $\vdash^r_\Delta$, there exists $A_0 \notin u$ such that $u{:}\overline{v} \vdash^r_\Delta A_0$. Since $v$ is a theory, however, we have $A_0 \in v$. Then we define $\Phi$ as follows:

$$\Phi = \{\vdash A \mid A \in u\} \cup \{A_0 : \vdash B \mid B \in v\}.$$

Clearly, $:\overline{v} \nvdash^r_{\Gamma\cup\Phi} A_0$, and hence $v$ will not be an extension of $\Gamma \cup \Phi$. On the other hand, $u \subseteq \mathrm{Cn}^r_{\Delta\cup\Phi}(\emptyset : \overline{v})$, and therefore

$$A_0 \in \mathrm{Cn}^r_\Delta(u{:}\overline{v}) \subseteq \mathrm{Cn}^r_{\Delta\cup\Phi}(u{:}\overline{v}) \subseteq \mathrm{Cn}^r_{\Delta\cup\Phi}(\mathrm{Cn}^r_{\Delta\cup\Phi}(\emptyset{:}\overline{v}){:}\overline{v}) \subseteq \mathrm{Cn}^r_{\Delta\cup\Phi}(\emptyset : \overline{v})$$

Hence, by the construction of $\Phi$, we finally obtain $v \subseteq \mathrm{Cn}^r_{\Delta\cup\Phi}(\emptyset : \overline{v})$, which means that $v$ is an extension of $\Vdash^r_{\Delta\cup\Phi}$. Consequently $\Gamma$ and $\Delta$ will not be strongly extension-equivalent. This completes the proof. □

The above result concludes our description of extension-based default reasoning. In the next section we are going to describe corresponding systems for default reasoning based on expansions.

## 6.7 Autoepistemic Consequence Relations

The following definition introduces the basic system of autoepistemic reasoning.

**Definition 6.14** A default consequence relation will be called *autoepistemic* if it satisfies Consistency and Factoring.

The joint effect of Consistency and Factoring amounts to a semantic requirement that, in any model $(w, u, v)$, $u$ must coincide with $v$. This means, in effect, that such models are reducible to pairs of sets $(w, u)$ such that $w \subseteq u$. This suggests that autoepistemic consequence relations can also be interpreted in terms of a binary semantics.

**Definition 6.15** A default rule $a : b \vdash A$ will be said to be *A-valid* with respect to a binary semantics $\mathcal{B}$ if and only if, for any bimodel $(u, v)$ from $\mathcal{B}$, if $a \subseteq v$ and $b \subseteq \overline{v}$, then $A \in u$.

According to an *autoepistemic interpretation of* a binary semantics, the first component, $u$, of a bimodel $(u, v)$ is an ordinary propositional interpretation describing propositions that are taken as true, while the second component represents the associated belief context, namely the propositions that are believed to hold. Accordingly, a default rule $a : b \vdash A$ is interpreted above as saying that if all propositions from $a$ are believed, while all propositions from $b$ are not believed, then $A$ should be true.

For a binary semantics $\mathcal{B}$, we will denote by $\vdash^A_{\mathcal{B}}$ the set of all default rules that are A-valid with respect to $\mathcal{B}$. It is easy to check that this set forms an autoepistemic consequence relation. Moreover, the following result shows that autoepistemic consequence relations are characterized by this semantics. The proof is immediate from Theorem 6.21.

**Theorem 6.36** *$\vdash$ is an autoepistemic consequence relation if and only if there is a consistent binary semantics $\mathcal{B}$ such that $\vdash$ coincides with $\vdash^A_{\mathcal{B}}$.*

A consequence of the above result is that default rules $a : b \vdash A$ of an autoepistemic consequence relation can be identified with singular autoepistemic bisequents $:b \Vdash A : a$ of some biconsequence relation.

**Corollary 6.37** *A default consequence relation is autoepistemic if and only if it coincides with the set of singular autoepistemic bisequents of some consistent biconsequence relation.*

***Proof.*** As can be verified, the set of singular autoepistemic bisequents of a consistent biconsequence relation satisfies the postulates of an autoepistemic consequence relation. Moreover, if $\vdash$ is an autoepistemic consequence relation, it has some binary semantics $\mathcal{B}$. Clearly, $\vdash$ coincides with the set of singular autoepistemic bisequents of the biconsequence relation generated by $\mathcal{B}$. □

The following result shows that the rules of autoepistemic consequence relations preserve expansions.

**Theorem 6.38** *If $\vdash^a$ is a least autoepistemic consequence relation containing a default consequence relation $\vdash$, then $\vdash^a$ has the same theories and expansions as $\vdash$.*

***Proof.*** Given a default consequence relation $\vdash$, we define a binary semantics $\mathcal{B}$ as the set of all pairs $(\mathbb{C}\mathrm{n}(u{:}\overline{u}), u)$ such that $u$ is a theory of $\vdash$.

This semantics is consistent, and hence generates an autoepistemic consequence relation that we will denote by $\vdash_{\mathcal{B}}$. Clearly, $\vdash$ is included in $\vdash_{\mathcal{B}}$, and therefore $\vdash^a \subseteq \vdash_{\mathcal{B}}$, since $\vdash^a$ is a least such consequence relation[4]. Moreover, any theory of $\vdash$ remains a theory of $\vdash_{\mathcal{B}}$. Consequently any expansion of $\vdash$ will be an expansion of $\vdash_{\mathcal{B}}$ and $\vdash^a$ by Lemma 6.10.

Let $u$ be an expansion of $\vdash_{\mathcal{B}}$. Since $u$ is a theory of $\vdash_{\mathcal{B}}$, it is a theory of $\vdash$, and hence $(\mathbb{C}\mathrm{n}(u{:}\overline{u}), u) \in \mathcal{B}$. Assume now that $A \in u$. Then $u{:}\overline{u} \vdash_{\mathcal{B}} A$ and consequently $A \in \mathbb{C}\mathrm{n}(u{:}\overline{u})$ by the definition of $\vdash_{\mathcal{B}}$. Therefore, $u \subseteq \mathbb{C}\mathrm{n}(u{:}\overline{u})$, which means that $u$ is an expansion of $\vdash$. Thus, $\vdash_{\mathcal{B}}$ has the same expansions as $\vdash$, which immediately implies that both have the same expansions as $\vdash^a$ (by Lemma 6.10). □

Now we will show that autoepistemic consequence relations constitute a maximal logic for the expansion-based nonmonotonic reasoning.

As before, we will say that default theories are *(strongly) expansion-equivalent*, if they are (strongly) equivalent with respect to the expansion-based nonmonotonic semantics. Then Theorem 6.38 can be reformulated as

**Corollary 6.39** *Any default consequence relation $\vdash$ is expansion-equivalent to $\vdash^a$.*

As before, strong expansion-equivalence implicitly determines the logic of default rules that is adequate for the expansion-based nonmonotonic semantics.

Let us say that default theories $\Gamma$ and $\Delta$ are *ae-equivalent*, if they determine the same autoepistemic consequence relation. Then we have

**Theorem 6.40** *Default theories are strongly expansion-equivalent if and only if they are ae-equivalent.*

***Proof.*** The implication from right to left follows from the preceding corollary. Assume now that $\Gamma$ and $\Delta$ are not ae-equivalent. By the representation theorem, an autoepistemic consequence relation $\vdash$ is uniquely determined by pairs of the form $(\mathbb{C}\mathrm{n}(v{:}\overline{v}), v)$, where $v$ is a theory of $\vdash$.

Suppose first that there exists a theory $v$ of $\vdash^a_\Gamma$ that is not a theory of $\vdash^a_\Delta$, and let $\Phi = \{\vdash A \mid A \in v\}$. Then $v$ will obviously be an expansion of $\vdash^a_{\Gamma\cup\Phi}$, though it will not be even a theory of $\vdash^a_{\Delta\cup\Phi}$.

Suppose now that $\Gamma$ and $\Delta$ have the same theories, but, for some theory $v$, $\mathbb{C}\mathrm{n}^a_\Gamma(v{:}\overline{v}) \not\subseteq \mathbb{C}\mathrm{n}^a_\Delta(v{:}\overline{v})$. Then there exists $A_0 \in \mathbb{C}\mathrm{n}^a_\Gamma(v{:}\overline{v}) \backslash \mathbb{C}\mathrm{n}^a_\Delta(v{:}\overline{v})$.

[4] Actually, $\vdash^a$ coincides with $\vdash_{\mathcal{B}}$, but we will not need this fact in the proof.

Note that, since $A_0 \in v$, we have that $v$ is not an expansion of $\Delta$. Now let $\Phi = \{A_0 : \vdash B \mid B \in v\}$. Clearly, $v{:}\overline{v} \nvdash^a_{\Delta\cup\Phi} A_0$, and hence $v$ will not be an expansion of $\Delta \cup \Phi$. On the other hand, by the construction of $\Phi$, we have $v \subseteq \mathbb{C}\mathrm{n}^a_{\Gamma\cup\Phi}(v : \overline{v})$, which means that $v$ is an expansion of $\Vdash^a_{\Gamma\cup\Phi}$. Consequently $\Gamma$ and $\Delta$ will not be strongly expansion-equivalent. This completes the proof. □

The above result demonstrates that autoepistemic consequence relations constitute a maximal logic for expansion-based reasoning.

Our next result extends the correspondence between autoepistemic consequence relations and biconsequence relations to their associated nonmonotonic semantics. The proof follows immediately from Corollary 5.37.

**Lemma 6.41** *If $\vdash$ is a singular autoepistemic subrelation of a consistent biconsequence relation $\Vdash$, then expansions of $\vdash$ coincide with the extensions of $\Vdash$.*

Recall that consistent biconsequence relations form a representative class with respect to the default nonmonotonic semantics: for any bisequent theory $\Delta$, the least consistent biconsequence relation containing $\Delta$ has the same extensions as $\Delta$. Accordingly, the above results show, in effect, that autoepistemic consequence relations are sufficiently expressive to capture the default nonmonotonic semantics of general biconsequence relations.

As an additional benefit of the above correspondence, we obtain the following simple characterization of extensions in autoepistemic consequence relations:

**Corollary 6.42** *A set $u$ is an extension of an autoepistemic consequence relation $\vdash$ if and only if $u$ is both an expansion and a minimal theory of $\vdash$.*

The proof follows directly from Lemma 5.15.

The correspondence between autoepistemic consequence relations and biconsequence relations implies, in turn, the correspondence between expansions of default theories and expansions of corresponding bisequent theories.

For a default theory $\Delta$, we will denote by $\Delta^a_{\Vdash}$ the corresponding autoepistemic bisequent theory, that is, $\Delta^a_{\Vdash} = \{:b \Vdash \hat{A}{:}a \mid a : b \vdash \hat{A} \in \Delta\}$. Then we obtain

**Lemma 6.43** *For any default theory $\Delta$, the bisequent theory $\Delta^a_{\Vdash}$ has the same expansions as $\Delta$.*

***Proof.*** In view of Corollary 6.37, $\vdash^a_\Delta$ coincides with the singular autoepistemic subrelation of $\Vdash^c_{\Delta^a_{\Vdash}}$. Since the latter is an autoepistemic biconsequence relation, its expansions coincide with its extensions, while the latter coincide with expansions of $\vdash^a_\Delta$ due to Corollary 5.29. □

Moreover, under some natural auxiliary condition, the correspondence between default theories and *default* bisequent theories, described in the preceding section, determines also an exact correspondence between expansions of the former and expansions of the latter.

**Definition 6.16** A default theory will be said to be *non-reflexive*, if it does not contain default rules $a{:}b \vdash A$ such that $A \in a$.

As before, $\Delta_{\Vdash}$ will denote the set of all *default* bisequents corresponding to default rules from $\Delta$. Then we have

**Lemma 6.44** *If $\Delta$ is a non-reflexive default theory, then expansions of $\Delta$ coincide with expansions of $\Delta_{\Vdash}$.*

***Proof.*** By Lemma 3.28, a non-reflexive default bisequent $a{:}b \Vdash A{:}$ is tightly equivalent to an autoepistemic bisequent ${:}b \Vdash A{:}a$. Consequently, expansions of $\Delta_{\Vdash}$ coincide with expansions of $\Delta^a_{\Vdash}$, and the result follows from Lemma 6.43. □

The above result shows that extensions and expansions of a non-reflexive default theory correspond, respectively, to extensions and expansions of its associated default biconsequence relation.

As an application of the above result, we obtain yet another proof of Theorem 6.12 saying that any expansion of an acyclic default theory is an extension. This time, the result follows directly from Theorem 5.53 and the fact that any positively acyclic default theory is non-reflexive.

As a final consequence of the correspondence between expansions of default consequence relations and expansions of biconsequence relations, expansions of a default theory can be computed using the classical *completion* of the latter.

**Definition 6.17** A default theory $\Delta$ will be called *locally finite*, if, for any proposition $A$, $\Delta$ has no more than a finite number of default rules with the conclusion $A$.

For locally finite default theories, the completion is definable as follows:

**Definition 6.18** A *completion* of a locally finite default theory $\Delta$ is the set $comp(\Delta)$ of the following classical logical formulas:

$$A \leftrightarrow \bigvee\{\bigwedge(a \cup \neg b) \mid a : b \vdash A \in \Delta\},$$

plus the set $\{\neg \bigwedge(a \cup \neg b) \mid a : b \vdash \in \Delta\}$.

Then we have

**Theorem 6.45** *If $\Delta$ a locally finite default theory, then the classical models of $comp(\Delta)$ correspond exactly to expansions of $\Delta$.*

The proof follows directly from Corollary 5.59.

## 6.8 Default Consequence Relations and Normal Programs

Finally, we will show that default consequence relations can serve as a logical framework for normal logic programs. The framework will allow us to give a relatively simple representation of various semantics for such programs, as well as to single out different kinds of logical reasoning that are appropriate with respect to these semantics.

Recall that a normal logic program $\Pi$ is a set of program rules

$$A \leftarrow a, \mathbf{not}\, b$$

where $a, b$ are finite sets of propositional atoms. From the very beginning (and without loss of generality) we will identify such program rules with default rules of the form $a : b \vdash A$. Normal logic programs will correspond in this sense to default theories, and we will see that the main notions defined earlier for the latter will correspond to well known logic programming constructs. Actually, this correspondence is naturally extendable to quasi-normal programs (that is, normal programs with constraints).

For a program $\Pi$ we will denote by $dtr(\Pi)$ the corresponding default theory, while $\vdash_\Pi$ will denote the least default consequence relation containing $dtr(\Pi)$. The following proposition gives a summary of correspondences between the kinds of semantics defined earlier for default consequence relations and the main semantics of normal logic programs.

**Proposition 6.46**

- *Four-valued models of $\Pi$ correspond to bitheories of $dtr(\Pi)$;*
- *Przymusinski's 3-valued models of $\Pi$ [Przymusinska and Przymusinski, 1990] correspond to consistent invariant bitheories of $dtr(\Pi)$;*

- *Supported models (= models of the completion) of* $\Pi$ *[Apt* et al., *1988] correspond to expansions of* $dtr(\Pi)$*;*
- *Three-valued models of* $Comp(\Pi)$ *[Fitting, 1985] correspond to consistent partial expansions of* $dtr(\Pi)$*;*
- *Four-valued models of* $Comp(\Pi)$ *[Fitting, 1991] correspond to partial expansions of* $dtr(\Pi)$*;*
- *Stable models of* $\Pi$ *[Gelfond and Lifschitz, 1988] correspond to extensions of* $dtr(\Pi)$*;*
- *Partial stable models of* $\Pi$ *[Przymusinski, 1990] correspond to consistent partial extensions of* $dtr(\Pi)$*.*
- *The well-founded model [Gelder* et al., *1991] coincides with the least partial extension of* $dtr(\Pi)$*.*

***Proof.*** To begin with, by Lemma 6.3, bitheories of $dtr(\Pi)$ correspond precisely to four-valued interpretations that are closed with respect to the rules of $\Pi$; in other words, they correspond to models of $\Pi$.

Recall that partial expansions are fixed points of the operator $\Phi(u, v) = (\mathbb{C}\mathrm{n}(u{:}\overline{v}), \overline{\mathbb{C}\mathrm{n}(v{:}\overline{u})})$ on the set of four-valued interpretations. Moreover, by Corollary 6.4, they coincide with the fixed points of the four-valued immediate consequence operator defined in [Fitting, 1991], and hence they are models of the four-valued completion of $\Pi$. As a consequence, we obtain also that three-valued models of $Comp(\Pi)$ (see [Fitting, 1985]) correspond to consistent partial expansions of $dtr(\Pi)$, while the ordinary classical models of the completion correspond to expansions of $dtr(\Pi)$.

The basis of the last three correspondences amounts to the fact that the operator $\Gamma$ described in Sec. 6.3 coincides with the Gelfond–Lifschitz operator of a program (see [Gelfond and Lifschitz, 1988]). Then Corollary 6.15 describes, in effect, well-known ways of defining stable, partial stable, and well-founded models of a normal program in terms of this transformation (see [Fitting, 1993; Przymusinski, 1995b]). □

The nonmonotonic semantics of extensions, expansions and their partial variants have been defined above primarily for default consequence relations, and then extended to default theories by defining a semantics of a default theory $\Delta$ as the semantics of the associated default consequence relation $\vdash_\Delta$. This implies, in particular, that all the above semantics for normal logic programs are indeed *logical* semantics, since the logic of default consequence relations turns out to be adequate for all of them. This fortunate fact is not trivial, since the common semantics for normal logic programs have originally been defined without any clear logical basis.

Due to the above correspondences, the properties of normal logic programs and their semantics can be established and proved directly in the logical framework of default consequence relations. In particular, regular default consequence relations provide an adequate and maximal logic for logic programs under the stable semantics, while autoepistemic consequence relations are suitable for logic programs under the supported semantics. Default consequence relations have provided also a convenient theoretical framework for describing the stable and supported semantics, and for proving their properties. It has been shown, in particular, that stable models of a normal logic program are always its minimal models (Lemma 6.8), any stable model is supported, as well as that supported models of an acyclic logic program coincide with its stable models (Theorem 6.12). In addition, it has been shown that supported models of a logic program coincide with the classical models of its completion (Theorem 6.45).

As a last remark, note that some alternative semantics suggested for logic programs can also be reconstructed in the framework of default consequence relations. For example, a semantics suggested in [Schlipf, 1992] was based on a principle of reasoning by cases which is in fact identical with the Factoring rule. Consequently, such a semantics can be represented in the framework of *complete* default consequence relations. As is shown by Schlipf, such models satisfy many of the desiderata for an adequate semantics of logic programs.

# Chapter 7

# Argumentation Theory

In this chapter we are going to describe yet another general formalism for nonmonotonic reasoning that is closely related to the formalisms studied earlier. The argumentation theory (as defined in [Dung, 1995b; Bondarenko *et al.*, 1997]) is based on an apparently different representation framework that consists of arguments and an attack relation describing when one argument refutes another. The task of the argumentation theory consists in finding sustainable ('defendable') sets of arguments in this setting. Such argument sets determine the associated nonmonotonic semantics. This abstract argumentation theory has proved to be a powerful framework for representing semantics for logic programs and explanatory nonmonotonic formalisms in general.

As our starting point, we will introduce a generalization of argumentation theory in which arguments will be identified with sets of *assumptions*, while the attack relation will be defined directly on such sets. This generalization naturally corresponds to the move from Tarski consequence relations to multiple-conclusion Scott consequence relations. In this generalized setting, a set of assumptions can 'collectively' attack another such set in a way that is not reducible to attacks among particular assumptions from these sets. It will be shown that, for sufficiently rich languages, the resulting collective argumentation theory will turn out to be equivalent to our basic formalisms of biconsequence relations and causal inference. These correspondences will give us yet another insight into the nature of explanatory nonmonotonic reasoning.

## 7.1 Collective Argumentation

The notion of an argument is often taken as primitive in argumentation theory. This even creates a possibility of considering arguments that are not propositional in character (e.g., arguments as inference rules, or derivations). Following [Bondarenko *et al.*, 1997], however, we will identify arguments with sets of propositions of a special kind that will be called *assumptions.* A primitive *attack relation* will be defined directly on such arguments. In the notation introduced formally below, $a \hookrightarrow b$ will denote the fact that an argument (that is, a set of assumptions) $a$ attacks an argument $b$. This fact will imply, of course, that these two arguments are incompatible. $a \hookrightarrow b$ says, however, more than that, namely that the argument $a$, being accepted, provides a reason, or explanation, for rejection of the argument $b$. Accordingly, the attack relation will not, in general, be symmetric, since acceptance of $b$ need not give reasons for rejection of $a$. In addition, we will not assume that the attack relation among arguments is reducible to attacks among individual assumptions. In other words, in full agreement with common sense, a set of assumptions can produce a nontrivial attack that is not reducible to attacks determined by individual assumptions, and an argument could be attacked in such a way that we cannot single out a particular assumption in the attacked set that could be blamed for it. For instance, we can disprove a conclusion jointly supported by a disputed set of assumptions, though no particular assumption in the set, taken alone, could be held responsible for this conclusion.

As we mentioned, assumptions will be treated as propositions of a special kind. This special role of assumptions (and thereby of arguments) will be reflected in the *default presumption*, according to which assumptions and arguments are acceptable, unless there are reasons for their rejection. As we will see in the next chapter, this default presumption constitutes yet another expression of the Closed World Assumption. As a result, assumptions will play the role of abducibles in the framework of an argumentation theory, and this understanding will serve as a guide in determining the associated nonmonotonic semantics.

**Definition 7.1**

- Let $\mathcal{A}$ be a set of propositions, called *assumptions.* Any subset of $\mathcal{A}$ will be called an *argument.*
- A (collective) *attack relation* is a relation $\hookrightarrow$ on finite arguments satisfying the following postulate:

**Monotonicity** If $a \hookrightarrow b$, then $a \cup a_1 \hookrightarrow b \cup b_1$.

Though the attack relation is defined above only on finite arguments, it can be naturally extended to arbitrary arguments by imposing the following *compactness postulate*:

**(Compactness)** $u \hookrightarrow v$ if and only if $a \hookrightarrow b$, for some finite $a \subseteq u$, $b \subseteq v$.

The attack relation can be considered as a (presumably unusual) kind of a consequence relation. Accordingly, we will use in what follows the same agreements for the attack relation as for Scott consequence relations. Thus, $a, a_1 \hookrightarrow b, b_1$ will have the same meaning as $a \cup a_1 \hookrightarrow b \cup b_1$. Similarly, $A, u \hookrightarrow v, B$ will be an alternative notation for $\{A\} \cup u \hookrightarrow \{B\} \cup v$, *etc.* Actually, it will be shown below that the similarity is not accidental, since the collective attack relation is representable as a consequence relation in a certain extended language.

An attack relation $\hookrightarrow$ will be called *trivial*, if $\emptyset \hookrightarrow \emptyset$. Due to Monotonicity, this will mean that any argument will attack any other argument. It will be assumed throughout this chapter that the attack relations are nontrivial.

The original Dung's argumentation theory can be seen as a special case of collective argumentation that satisfies a couple of further properties described in the following definition (see also [Kakas and Toni, 1999]).

**Definition 7.2** An attack relation will be called

- *affirmative* if no argument attacks the empty argument $\emptyset$;
- *local* if it satisfies the following condition:

  **(Locality)** If $a \hookrightarrow b, b_1$, then either $a \hookrightarrow b$, or $a \hookrightarrow b_1$.

- *normal* if it is both affirmative and local.

Then the following facts can be easily verified:

**Lemma 7.1**

- *If $\hookrightarrow$ is a normal attack relation, then $a \hookrightarrow b$ holds if and only if $a \hookrightarrow A$, for some $A \in b$.*
- *If $\hookrightarrow$ is a local attack relation, then $a \hookrightarrow b$ holds iff either $a \hookrightarrow \emptyset$, or $a \hookrightarrow A$, for some $A \in b$.*

Thus, the normal attack relation is reducible to the relation $a \hookrightarrow A$ between arguments and single assumptions. As we will see, the resulting theory will coincide with that given in [Dung, 1995a]. A slightly more general local attack relation admits also constraints of the form $a \hookrightarrow$. Such a constraint says that the argument $a$ is *unacceptable*.

### 7.1.1 *Argument theories*

By an *argument theory* we will mean in what follows an arbitrary set of attacks $a \hookrightarrow b$ between finite arguments. An argument theory can be viewed simply as an arbitrary relation on finite arguments. Clearly, any argument theory $\Delta$ generates a unique least attack relation that we will denote by $\hookrightarrow_\Delta$. The latter is obtained from $\Delta$ by closing it with respect to the Monotonicity rule. Accordingly, $\hookrightarrow_\Delta$ can be described directly as follows:

$$u \hookrightarrow_\Delta v \;\text{ iff }\; a_0 \hookrightarrow b_0 \in \Delta, \;\text{ for some } a_0 \subseteq u, b_0 \subseteq v.$$

An argument theory will be called *definite*, if it consists of attack rules of the form $a \hookrightarrow A$, where $A$ is a single assumption, and *singular*, if it has only attacks of the form $a \hookrightarrow b$, where $b$ contains no more than one assumption. Then the preceding lemma, coupled with the above representation, immediately implies the following simple observation:

**Lemma 7.2** *An attack relation is local (respectively, normal) if and only if it is generated by a singular (resp., definite) argument theory.*

Thus, the differences between general, local and normal argumentation are reducible to the differences between corresponding generating argument theories.

### 7.1.2 *Four-valued semantics*

Collective argumentation can be given a four-valued semantics that will be instructive in describing the meaning of the attack relation, as well as for imposing plausible constraints on argument theories and their nonmonotonic semantics.

The four-valued semantics stems from the following natural understanding of an attack $a \hookrightarrow b$:

> *If all assumptions from $a$ are accepted, then at least one of the assumptions in $b$ should be rejected.*

The expressive capabilities of the abstract argumentation theory depend, however, on the absence of usual classical constraints on the acceptance and rejection of assumptions, so it permits situations in which an assumption is both accepted and rejected, or, alternatively, neither accepted, nor rejected. Such an understanding can be captured formally by assigning any assumption a *subset* of the set $\{t, f\}$, where $t$ denotes acceptance (truth), while $f$ denotes rejection (falsity)[1]. As a result, collective argumentation acquires a four-valued semantics that is described in the following definition.

**Definition 7.3** An attack $a \hookrightarrow b$ will be said to *hold* in a four-valued interpretation $\nu$ of the set of assumptions, if either $\nu \not\models A$, for some $A \in a$, or $\nu \dashv B$, for some $B \in b$.

An interpretation $\nu$ will be called a *model* of an argument theory $\Delta$ if every attack from $\Delta$ holds in $\nu$.

Since an attack relation can be seen as a special kind of an argument theory, the above definition also determines the notion of a model for an attack relation.

Note that any pair $(u, v)$ of arguments determines a four-valued interpretation in which $u$ is the set of true (i.e., accepted) assumptions, while $\overline{v}$ is the set of assumptions that are false (rejected), and vice versa, any four-valued interpretation corresponds to such a pair of arguments. In this sense canonical models of an attack relation or an argument theory can be identified with bitheories described in the next definition.

**Definition 7.4** A pair $(u, v)$ of arguments will be called a *bitheory* of an argument theory $\Delta$, if $u \not\hookrightarrow_\Delta v$.

It can be easily verified that any bitheory of $\Delta$ corresponds to a four-valued model of the latter.

**Definition 7.5**

- A bitheory $(u, v)$ of an argument theory will be called *consistent*, if $u \subseteq v$, and *complete*, if $v \subseteq u$.
- An argument $u$ will be called *consistent*, if $u \not\hookrightarrow u$.

Consistent bitheories correspond to consistent four-valued interpretations, namely to interpretations in which no assumption is both accepted and rejected. Similarly, complete bitheories correspond to complete four-valued interpretations in which every assumption is either accepted, or rejected. Such restricted interpretations will play an important role in

[1] Cf. a similar description in [Jakobovits and Vermeir, 1999].

what follows. Finally, consistent arguments correspond exactly to bitheories that are both consistent and complete. This notion of consistency provides an appropriate generalization of the notion of a conflict-free argument in Dung's argumentation theory (see below).

For a set $I$ of four-valued interpretations, we will denote by $\hookrightarrow_I$ the set of all attacks that hold in each interpretation from $I$. Then the following result is actually a representation theorem showing that the four-valued semantics is adequate for collective argumentation.

**Theorem 7.3** *$\hookrightarrow$ is an attack relation if and only if it coincides with $\hookrightarrow_I$, for some set of four-valued interpretations $I$.*

***Proof.*** For any set $I$ of interpretations, the set of attacks $\hookrightarrow_I$ satisfies Monotonicity, so it determines an attack relation.

If $\hookrightarrow$ is an attack relation, let $I$ denote the set of all interpretations corresponding to bitheories of $\hookrightarrow$. Since $I$ consists of models of $\hookrightarrow$, we have $\hookrightarrow \subseteq \hookrightarrow_I$. Now, if $a \not\hookrightarrow b$, then $(a, b)$ is a bitheory of $\hookrightarrow$, and hence its corresponding interpretation, say $\nu$, belongs to $I$. But $a \hookrightarrow b$ clearly does not hold in $\nu$, so $a \not\hookrightarrow_I b$. This completes the proof. □

## 7.2 Argumentation vs. (Bi)consequence relations

To begin with, the four-valued semantics of an attack relation immediately suggests a representation of attacks $a \hookrightarrow b$ as bisequents of the form $a\colon \Vdash :b$, and thereby a direct connection between argumentation and biconsequence relations. Though formally adequate, this representation misses, however, the intended understanding of arguments as sets of *default assumptions*. A more adequate representation will be obtained by using the four-valued global negation connective $\sim$.

It has been shown in Chapter 4 that $\sim$ allows to transform biconsequence relations into Scott consequence relations. As we will show now, it will allow us to obtain also a similar translation for attack relations.

Let us extend the language of collective argumentation with a negation connective $\sim$ on assumptions having the following semantic interpretation:

$$\sim A \text{ is accepted iff } A \text{ is rejected}$$
$$\sim A \text{ is rejected iff } A \text{ is accepted.}$$

A syntactic characterization of this connective is obtained by adding the following set of rules for an attack relation:

$$A \hookrightarrow \sim A \qquad \sim A \hookrightarrow A$$
$$\text{If } a \hookrightarrow A, b \text{ and } a, \sim A \hookrightarrow b \text{ then } a \hookrightarrow b \tag{AN}$$
$$\text{If } a, A \hookrightarrow b \text{ and } a \hookrightarrow b, \sim A \text{ then } a \hookrightarrow b.$$

The resulting attack relations will be called *N-attack relations.* It turns out that such attack relations are interdefinable with Belnap consequence relations (see Sec. 4.1.6).

Given an attack relation $\hookrightarrow$, we can define the following consequence relation:

$$a \vdash b \equiv a \hookrightarrow \sim b. \tag{CA}$$

Similarly, for any Belnap consequence relation we can define the corresponding attack relation as follows:

$$a \hookrightarrow b \equiv a \vdash \sim b. \tag{AC}$$

Then the following result shows equivalence of the two notions.

**Theorem 7.4** *If $\hookrightarrow$ is an N-attack relation, then (CA) determines a Belnap consequence relation and vice versa, if $\vdash$ is a Belnap consequence relation, then the attack relation determined by (AC) is an N-attack relation.*

The proof presents no difficulty and amounts to a straightforward check of the corresponding rules for consequence and attack relations, respectively. Note also that if $\vdash$ is obtained from $\hookrightarrow$ by (CA), then the later can be obtained from $\vdash$ by (AC), and vice versa. This shows that the above equivalence is exact.

It should be noted, however, that N-attack relations and associated Belnap consequence relations are symmetric with respect to assumptions and their negations, so they still do not reflect the special status of assumptions, described earlier in terms of the default presumption. Speaking more formally, the intended understanding of assumptions presupposes that negations $\sim A$ of assumptions need not be assumptions by themselves. Thus, in [Bondarenko *et al.*, 1997] the assumptions have been defined as a special set of propositions, while the operation $\overline{\alpha}$, defined on assumptions only, gave the *contrary* of an assumption $\alpha$ (which does not have to be an assumption by itself). There exists, however, another fairly general way of securing the distinction.

Given an arbitrary propositional language $\mathcal{L}$ that does not contain the negation connective $\sim$, we will *define* assumptions as propositions of the form $\sim A$, where $A \in \mathcal{L}$. Then, in view of the fact that $\sim$ satisfies the double negation rule, we will obtain that a negation of an assumption is an ordinary proposition from $\mathcal{L}$. In this way, $\sim$ can serve as a faithful logical formalization of the operation of taking the contrary from [Bondarenko *et al.*, 1997]. Moreover, such a 'negative' representation of assumptions agrees with the applications of the argumentation theory to other nonmonotonic formalisms. Accordingly, Belnap consequence relations can be seen as a proper generalization of the assumption-based framework from [Bondarenko *et al.*, 1997] to Scott consequence relations.

The above negative representation of arguments as propositions of the form $\sim A$ will allow us also to establish a more adequate translation of attack relations into biconsequence relations. Namely, by the semantic definition of a global negation, an attack $\sim a \hookrightarrow \sim b$ has the same meaning as the simple bisequent $:a \Vdash b:$. Accordingly, such a representation establishes an indirect correspondence between attack relations and simple biconsequence relations from Sec. 3.3.3. Moreover, we can avoid the detour through the global negation, and give a direct *negative representation* of attack relations in terms of simple biconsequence relations as follows.

Given an argument theory $\Delta$, we will define the following simple bisequent theory $\Delta_{\Vdash}$:

$$\Delta_{\Vdash} = \{:a \Vdash b: \mid a \hookrightarrow b \in \Delta\}.$$

Then we have

**Lemma 7.5** *A pair of arguments $(u, v)$ is a bitheory of $\Delta$ if and only if $(\overline{v}, \overline{u})$ is a bitheory of $\Delta_{\Vdash}$.*

***Proof.*** It can be directly verified that $u \not\hookrightarrow_{\Delta} v$ holds if and only if $(\overline{v}, \overline{u})$ is closed with respect to all bisequents from $\Delta_{\Vdash}$. □

The above correspondence will be extended later to the correspondence between the respective nonmonotonic semantics of argument and bisequent theories.

## 7.3 Main Kinds of Argumentation

We will describe now three special kinds of collective argumentation called, respectively, classical, negative and positive argumentation. On the semantic level, these kinds of argumentation will correspond to restrictions of four-valued reasoning to two- and three-valued reasoning. For all these kinds of argumentation, the attack relation will be defined by 'borrowing' arguments of the other side in order to disprove the latter. Classical argumentation will give an abstract description of classical consistency-based reasoning. Negative argumentation will be shown to be especially appropriate for describing stable sets of arguments. Positive argumentation will also turn out to generalize some suggested semantics of argumentation.

In ordinary disputation and argumentation the parties can provisionally accept some of the assumptions defended by their adversaries in order to disprove the latter. Three basic cases of such an 'argument sharing' in attacking the opponents are described in the following definition (see also [Bondarenko *et al.*, 1997]).

**Definition 7.6** Given an attack relation $\hookrightarrow$, we will say that

- *a classically attacks b* (notation $a \hookrightarrow^{\circ} b$) if $a, b \hookrightarrow a, b$;
- *a negatively attacks b* (notation $a \hookrightarrow^{-} b$) if $a \hookrightarrow a, b$;
- *a positively attacks b* (notation $a \hookrightarrow^{+} b$) if $a, b \hookrightarrow b$.

In a classical attack, the proponent shows, in effect, that her argument is incompatible with that of the opponent. In a positive attack, the proponent temporarily accepts opponent's argument in order to disprove the latter, while in a negative attack she shows that her argument is sufficient for challenging an addition of the opponent's argument. Clearly, if $a$ attacks $b$ directly, then it attacks the latter classically, positively and negatively, though not vice versa.

As can be seen, $\hookrightarrow^{\circ}$, $\hookrightarrow^{-}$ and $\hookrightarrow^{+}$ are also attack relations. Moreover, it turns out that all of them can be given an invariant structural characterization in terms of additional rules imposed on the attack relation. For explanatory reasons, we will begin below with a simplest such kind, namely the classical argumentation. Negative and positive argumentation will be our subject in subsequent sections.

### 7.3.1 *Classical argumentation*

Classical argumentation can be seen as an 'upper bound' of collective argumentation; it is a simplest kind of argumentation which amounts, in effect, to classical consistency reasoning.

**Definition 7.7** An attack relation will be called *classical* if $a, b \hookrightarrow a, b$

always implies $a \hookrightarrow b$.

It can be easily verified that an argument theory based on a classical attack $\hookrightarrow^\circ$ will be classical. Moreover, the latter determines a least classical 'closure' of the source attack relation:

**Lemma 7.6** *$\hookrightarrow^\circ$ is a least classical attack relation containing $\hookrightarrow$.*

***Proof.*** Clearly, $\hookrightarrow^\circ$ includes $\hookrightarrow$. In addition, if $\hookrightarrow_1$ is a classical attack relation including $\hookrightarrow$, and $a \hookrightarrow^\circ b$, then $a, b \hookrightarrow a, b$, and hence $a, b \hookrightarrow_1 a, b$. But $\hookrightarrow_1$ is classical, so $a \hookrightarrow_1 b$. Thus, $\hookrightarrow_1$ should include $\hookrightarrow^\circ$, which shows that $\hookrightarrow^\circ$ is a least classical attack relation containing $\hookrightarrow$. □

An immediate consequence of the above lemma is that classical attack relations are precisely attack relations of the form $\hookrightarrow^\circ$. In other words, classical attack relations provide a canonical description of argumentation based on a classical attack.

The following result shows that classical attack relations are fully symmetric:

**Lemma 7.7** *An attack relation is classical if and only if it satisfies:*

***(Symmetry)*** $a \hookrightarrow b, c$ *iff* $a, b \hookrightarrow c$.

***Proof.*** If $a \hookrightarrow b, c$, then $a, b, c \hookrightarrow a, b, c$ by monotonicity, and hence $a, b \hookrightarrow c$. The reverse implication is similar. Now, if Symmetry holds, and $a, b \hookrightarrow a, b$, then $a, b \hookrightarrow b$, and consequently $a \hookrightarrow b$. □

As a special case of Symmetry, we have

$$u \hookrightarrow v \text{ iff } \emptyset \hookrightarrow u, v \text{ iff } u, v \hookrightarrow \emptyset.$$

This shows that a classical attack amounts to inconsistency in a fully classical sense. It should be noted in this respect that the classical closure $\hookrightarrow^\circ$ of an attack relation $\hookrightarrow$ preserves consistent arguments of the latter. Namely, the definition of $\hookrightarrow^\circ$ immediately implies that it has the same consistent arguments as $\hookrightarrow$.

As could be anticipated, classical argumentation can be characterized semantically by restricting the set of four-valued interpretations to classical two-valued ones, namely to interpretations that assign only **t** and **f** to the assumptions. This means that any assumption is either accepted or rejected in an interpretation, but not both.

**Theorem 7.8** *An attack relation is classical if and only if it is determined by a set of classical interpretations.*

***Proof.*** As can be verified, any set of classical interpretations determines a classical attack relation. Now, if $\hookrightarrow$ is a classical attack relation, let $I_c$ denote the set of (classical) interpretations corresponding to its bitheories of the form $(u, u)$. If $u \not\hookrightarrow v$, then $u, v \not\hookrightarrow u, v$, and therefore the interpretation $\nu$ corresponding to a bitheory $(u \cup v, u \cup v)$ belongs to $I_c$. But $u \hookrightarrow v$ clearly does not hold in $\nu$, so $u \not\hookrightarrow_{I_c} v$. This shows that $\hookrightarrow$ is determined by the set of classical interpretations $I_c$. □

Finally, our last result here shows that classical argumentation can be seen as a combination of positive and negative argumentation. The proof follows immediately from the definitions of respective attack relations.

**Lemma 7.9** *For any attack relation* $\hookrightarrow$, $(\hookrightarrow^-)^+ = (\hookrightarrow^+)^- = \hookrightarrow^\circ$.

The above result says, in particular, that positive and negative argumentation are incompatible on pain of collapsing to classical reasoning. This fact will have important implications in what follows.

### 7.3.2 *Negative argumentation*

The definition below provides a general description of collective argumentation based on a negative attack.

**Definition 7.8** An attack relation will be called *negative* if $a \hookrightarrow a, b$ always implies $a \hookrightarrow b$.

To begin with, it can be easily verified that any attack relation of the form $\hookrightarrow^-$ will be negative. Moreover, the latter determines a least negative closure of the source attack relation:

**Lemma 7.10** $\hookrightarrow^-$ *is a least negative attack relation containing* $\hookrightarrow$.

***Proof.*** Clearly, $\hookrightarrow^-$ is a negative attack relation containing $\hookrightarrow$. In addition, if $\hookrightarrow_1$ is a negative attack relation including $\hookrightarrow$, and $a \hookrightarrow^- b$, then $a \hookrightarrow a, b$, and hence $a \hookrightarrow_1 a, b$. But $\hookrightarrow_1$ is negative, so $a \hookrightarrow_1 b$. Thus, $\hookrightarrow_1$ should include $\hookrightarrow^-$, which shows that $\hookrightarrow^-$ is a least negative attack relation containing $\hookrightarrow$. □

An immediate consequence of the above lemma is that negative attack relations are precisely relations of the form $\hookrightarrow^-$. In other words, negative attack relations provide a canonical description of argumentation based on negative attacks.

The following result gives an important alternative characterization of negative argumentation.

**Lemma 7.11** *An attack relation is negative iff it satisfies:*

***(Import)*** *If* $a \hookrightarrow b, c$, *then* $a, b \hookrightarrow c$.

***Proof.*** If $\hookrightarrow$ is negative and $a \hookrightarrow b, c$, then $a, b \hookrightarrow a, b, c$ by monotonicity, and hence $a, b \hookrightarrow c$. The reverse implication is immediate. □

As a special case of Import, we have that if $a \hookrightarrow b$, then $a, b \hookrightarrow \emptyset$. Thus, any negative attack relation is bound to be non-affirmative. Furthermore, this implies that inconsistent arguments attack any argument:

$$\text{If } v \hookrightarrow v, \text{ then } v \hookrightarrow u.$$

This feature will be responsible for the fact that only stable sets will constitute a reasonable nonmonotonic semantics for negative argumentation.

Negative argumentation can be characterized semantically by restricting the set of possible four-valued interpretations to *consistent* ones that do not assign the set $\{t, f\}$ to assumptions. This means that no assumption can be both accepted and rejected in an interpretation.

**Theorem 7.12** *An attack relation is negative if and only if it is determined by a set of consistent interpretations.*

***Proof.*** If an attack $a \hookrightarrow b$ does not hold in a consistent interpretation $\nu$, then all assumptions in $a$ are accepted, and no assumption from $b$ is rejected in $\nu$. Since $\nu$ is consistent, no assumption in $a \cup b$ is rejected in $\nu$, so the attack $a \hookrightarrow a, b$ also does not hold in $\nu$. This shows that an attack relation determined by consistent interpretations is bound to be negative. In the other direction, if an attack relation $\hookrightarrow$ is negative, and $u \not\hookrightarrow v$, then $(u, u \cup v)$ is a consistent bitheory of $\hookrightarrow$ (since $u \not\hookrightarrow u, v$). Moreover, $u \hookrightarrow v$ does not hold in the (consistent) interpretation corresponding to this bitheory. As follows from the proof of the main representation theorem, this means that any negative attack relation is determined by a set of consistent interpretations. □

Thus, negative argumentation describes argumentation situations in which assumptions can be accepted, rejected, or neither accepted, nor rejected. A direct expression of this restriction can be given for N-attack relations. Namely, for such attack relations the rule Import is equivalent to the condition

$$A, \sim A \hookrightarrow \emptyset.$$

### 7.3.3 *Positive argumentation*

The definition below provides a structural description of positive argumentation.

**Definition 7.9** An attack relation will be called *positive* if $a, b \hookrightarrow b$ always implies $a \hookrightarrow b$.

Any attack relation $\hookrightarrow^+$ will be positive. Moreover, the latter determines a least positive extension of the source attack relation.

**Lemma 7.13** *$\hookrightarrow^+$ is a least positive argument theory containing $\hookrightarrow$.*

The proof is quite similar to the case of negative argumentation, so we will omit it. The lemma implies that positive attack relations are precisely relations of the form $\hookrightarrow^+$, and hence they give a canonical description of argumentation based on positive attacks.

Similarly to negative argumentation, positive argumentation can be characterized by the 'exportation' property described in the lemma below:

**Lemma 7.14** *An attack relation is positive iff it satisfies:*

***(Export)*** *If $a, b \hookrightarrow c$, then $a \hookrightarrow b, c$.*

Positive argumentation can also be characterized semantically by restricting the set of possible four-valued interpretations to *complete* ones, namely to interpretations that do not assign $\emptyset$ to assumptions. This means that every assumption is either accepted or rejected in an interpretation (or both).

The proof of the following theorem is similar to the two earlier representation theorems, so we also omit it.

**Theorem 7.15** *An attack relation is positive if and only if it is determined by a set of complete interpretations.*

For N-attack relations, the rule Export is equivalent to the following condition:

$$\emptyset \hookrightarrow A, \sim A.$$

The condition explicitly says that any assumption should be either rejected or accepted. As could be expected, it is equivalent also to the principle of *reasoning by cases*:

(**Factoring**) If $a, A \hookrightarrow b$ and $a, \sim A \hookrightarrow b$, then $a \hookrightarrow b$.

The rule Export implies, in particular, that inconsistent arguments are attacked by any argument:

$$\text{If } v \hookrightarrow v, \text{ then } u \hookrightarrow v.$$

So, in positive argumentation we are relieved, in effect, from the obligation to refute self-contradictory arguments. This feature can be seen as one of the main advantages of the positive argumentation. It will be shown in what follows, however, that the positive argumentation, taken in its full generality, is not appropriate for the main nonmonotonic semantics of this study, namely the stable semantics. Still, the reader can find in the literature a number of weaker argumentation systems that incorporate some of the features of positive argumentation. Just as the main kinds of argumentation, described above, such systems are based on modified definitions of an attack relation. A brief description of some such systems is given below.

#### 7.3.3.1 *Normal positive argumentation*

We will describe now positive argumentation that is determined by normal attack relations, namely, positive attack relations of the form $\hookrightarrow^+$, where $\hookrightarrow$ is a normal attack relation. The interest in this very special case of positive argumentation stems from the fact that this kind of positive argumentation has been employed in logic programming (see below).

The following definition will provide a logical characterization of such an argumentation.

**Definition 7.10** A positive attack relation will be called *n-positive* if it is affirmative and satisfies

**(Semi-locality)** If $a \hookrightarrow b, c$, then either $a, b \hookrightarrow c$ or $a, c \hookrightarrow b$.

Semi-locality could be seen as a 'non-deterministic' variant of the Import rule for negative argumentation. An interesting property of n-positive systems is that the union of two arguments is inconsistent if and only if one of them attacks the other:

$$\text{If } u, v \hookrightarrow u, v, \text{ then either } u \hookrightarrow v \text{ or } v \hookrightarrow u.$$

The following result shows that n-positive attack relations are precisely positive closures of normal attack relations.

**Theorem 7.16** *An attack relation is n-positive iff it is a relation of the form* $\hookrightarrow^+$, *for some normal attack relation* $\hookrightarrow$.

***Proof.*** Let $\hookrightarrow$ be a normal attack relation. Then $\hookrightarrow^+$ is clearly both positive and affirmative. Assume that $a \hookrightarrow^+ b, c$, that is, $a, b, c \hookrightarrow b, c$. By locality of $\hookrightarrow$, we infer that either $a, b, c \hookrightarrow b$ or $a, b, c \hookrightarrow c$. In the first case we have $a, c \hookrightarrow^+ b$, while in the second one $a, b \hookrightarrow^+ c$. Hence $\hookrightarrow^+$ is also semi-local, and therefore it is n-positive.

Assume now that $\hookrightarrow$ is an n-positive attack relation, and let $\hookrightarrow_n$ be its normal sub-relation. We will show that $\hookrightarrow$ coincides with $\hookrightarrow_n^+$.

Note first that $a \hookrightarrow_n^+ b$ holds iff $a, b \hookrightarrow A$, for some $A \in b$. Now, the latter holds only if $a, b \hookrightarrow b$, which implies $a \hookrightarrow b$ by positivity. In the other direction, if $a \hookrightarrow b$, then applying Semi-locality a sufficient number of times, we obtain $a, b \hookrightarrow A$, for some $A \in b$. Thus, $a, b \hookrightarrow_n b$, and therefore $a \hookrightarrow_n^+ b$. This concludes the proof. □

7.3.3.2 *Consistent attack relations*

A number of argumentation systems suggested in the literature (see, e.g., [Kakas *et al.*, 1994]) are based on the idea that inconsistent arguments should not form a legitimate attack on other arguments. A simplest way to incorporate this idea into an argumentation theory consists in using the following modification of an attack relation:

**Definition 7.11** Given an attack relation $\hookrightarrow$, we will say that *a consistently attacks b* (notation $a \hookrightarrow^c b$) if either $a \hookrightarrow b$, or $b \hookrightarrow b$.

It turns out that this kind of an attack relation can also be given a logical description.

**Definition 7.12** An attack relation will be called *consistent* if $b \hookrightarrow b$ implies $\emptyset \hookrightarrow b$.

As can be seen, consistent attack relations embody the most significant feature of positive argumentation, namely that inconsistent arguments are attacked by any argument. Still, consistency in the above sense is a weaker property than positivity (Export).

Clearly, any attack relation of the form $\hookrightarrow^c$ will be consistent. Moreover, the following lemma shows, as before, that consistent attack relations are precisely relations of the form $\hookrightarrow^c$.

**Lemma 7.17** *$\hookrightarrow^c$ is a least consistent attack relation containing $\hookrightarrow$.*

***Proof.*** Clearly, $\hookrightarrow^c$ includes $\hookrightarrow$. In addition, if $\hookrightarrow_1$ is a consistent attack relation including $\hookrightarrow$, and $a \hookrightarrow^c b$, then either $a \hookrightarrow b$, or $b \hookrightarrow b$. In the first case we have $a \hookrightarrow_1 b$. In the second case we have $b \hookrightarrow_1 b$, and therefore $a \hookrightarrow_1 b$, since $\hookrightarrow_1$ is consistent. Thus, $\hookrightarrow_1$ should include $\hookrightarrow^c$, and consequently it is a least consistent attack relation containing $\hookrightarrow$. □

Finally, a semantic characterization of consistent argumentation can be obtained by requiring that any inconsistent argument is rejected in at least one four-valued interpretation. This requirement is met by restricting the set of possible four-valued interpretations to *quasi-reflexive* ones, namely to sets of interpretations $I$ such that if $\nu = (\models, \dashv) \in I$, then the corresponding classical interpretation $\nu' = (\not\dashv, \dashv)$ also belongs to $I$. Accordingly, consistent attack relations correspond in this sense to regular biconsequence relations (see Section 3.2.5).

**Theorem 7.18** *An attack relation is consistent if and only if it is determined by a quasi-reflexive set of four-valued interpretations.*

***Proof.*** It can be easily verified that a quasi-reflexive set of four-valued interpretations determines a consistent attack relation. In the other direction, if $(u, v)$ is a bitheory of a consistent attack relation $\hookrightarrow$, then $(v, v)$ will also be a bitheory of $\hookrightarrow$. Indeed if $v \hookrightarrow v$, then $\hookrightarrow v$ by consistency, and hence $u \hookrightarrow v$ by monotonicity, contrary to the assumption that $(u, v)$ is a bitheory of $\hookrightarrow$. Hence the canonical semantics of a consistent attack relation will be quasi-reflexive. □

#### 7.3.3.3 *Weak positivity*

Non-affirmative argumentation systems allow to express a stronger notion of inconsistency, namely the notion of an unacceptable argument, which is expressed by an attack $u \hookrightarrow$. For negative argumentation this is equivalent to plain inconsistency, that is, to $u \hookrightarrow u$, but for general argumentation the notion of unacceptability is stronger. Note also that such unacceptable arguments naturally arise, for example, in normal logic programs with a second ('classical') negation $\neg$. More precisely, an argument will be unacceptable for such programs, if it implies both some atom $A$ and its negation $\neg A$. For systems of this kind, the following weak notion of an attack turns out to be useful:

**Definition 7.13** Given an attack relation $\hookrightarrow$, we will say that *a weakly attacks b* (notation $a \hookrightarrow^w b$) if either $a \hookrightarrow b$, or $a, b \hookrightarrow$.

The following definition provides a logical description of such an attack.

**Definition 7.14** An attack relation will be called *weakly positive* if $a, b \hookrightarrow$ implies $a \hookrightarrow b$.

The above property is again a consequence of Export, so any positive attack will be weakly positive, though not vice versa. As before, the following lemma shows that weakly positive attack relations are precisely relations of the form $\hookrightarrow^w$. The proof is similar to the preceding case, so we omit it.

**Lemma 7.19** *$\hookrightarrow^w$ is a least weakly positive attack relation containing $\hookrightarrow$.*

## 7.4 Nonmonotonic Semantics of Argumentation

In this section we are going to describe the main nonmonotonic models of argumentation. These models provide answers to the question of which arguments are sustainable in the sense that they can defend themselves against attacks by other arguments.

### 7.4.1 *Normal (Dung) argumentation*

As a convenient starting point, we will describe now a range of nonmonotonic semantics for normal argument theories suggested in [Dung, 1995b]. All these semantics will be defined in terms of the following two notions:

**Definition 7.15** Given an attack relation $\hookrightarrow$, an assumption $A$ will be called *allowable* for an argument $u$, if $u \not\hookrightarrow A$, and *acceptable* for $u$, if $u$ attacks any argument that attacks $A$.

$[u]$ will denote the set of all assumptions allowable by $u$:

$$[u] \;=\; \{A \mid u \not\hookrightarrow A\}.$$

Note that $[\,]$ is an antimonotonic operator on arguments, that is, $u \subseteq v$ implies $[v] \subseteq [u]$. In addition, this operator provides the following characterization of acceptable assumptions:

**Lemma 7.20** *If $\hookrightarrow$ is a normal attack relation, then an assumption $A$ is acceptable for an argument $u$ if and only if $A \in [[u]]$.*

***Proof.*** $A \in [[u]]$ holds iff $[u] \not\hookrightarrow A$. The latter is equivalent to the claim that $a \not\subseteq [u]$, for any argument $a$ that attacks $A$. Now, $a \not\subseteq [u]$ says that $u \hookrightarrow B$, for some $B \in a$. In the normal case, this is equivalent to $u \hookrightarrow a$. Hence the result. □

Thus, the set of assumptions that are acceptable for $u$ coincides with $[[u]]$. Note also that, since $[\,]$ is antimonotonic, $[[\,]]$ is a monotonic operator on arguments.

Using the above notions, we can give a rather simple characterization of the basic nonmonotonic models of a normal argumentation.

**Definition 7.16** For a given attack relation $\hookrightarrow$, an argument $u$ will be called

- *conflict-free* if $u \subseteq [u]$;
- *D-admissible* if it is conflict-free and $u \subseteq [[u]]$;
- a *complete extension* if it is conflict-free and $u = [[u]]$;
- a *preferred extension* if it is a maximal complete extension;
- a *stable extension* if $u = [u]$.

An argument is conflict-free if it does not attack any assumption from itself. A conflict-free set $u$ is D-admissible iff any assumption from $u$ is also acceptable for $u$, and it is a complete extension if it coincides with the set of assumptions that are acceptable with respect to it. Finally, a stable extension is a conflict-free argument that attacks any argument outside it.

Clearly, any stable extension is also a preferred extension, any preferred extension is a complete extension, and any complete extension is D-admissible. Moreover, since the operator $[[\,]]$ is monotonic, any D-admissible argument is included in some complete extension (which is a fixed point of $[[\,]]$). Consequently, preferred extensions coincide with maximal D-admissible sets. In addition, the set of complete extensions forms a complete lower semi-lattice: for any set of complete extensions, there exists a unique greatest complete extension that is included in all of them. In particular, there always exists a least complete extension of a normal attack relation (or a definite argument theory).

As has been shown in [Dung, 1995a], under a suitable translation, the above models correspond to well-known semantics for normal logic programs (see below).

### 7.4.2 *Stable and partial stable semantics*

To begin with, note that the above notions and models of Dung's argumentation theory have been defined for arbitrary collective attack relations. It should be clear, however, that they are adequate only for normal argumentation, since they are based only on definite attacks. Still, we will see that in some important cases the more general models defined below will coincide with their normal counterparts. Unfortunately, it will turn out that only a small part of the above nice and well-organized structure of nonmonotonic models for normal argumentation can be transferred into a general framework of collective argumentation.

If $(u, v)$ is a bitheory of an attack relation (that is, $u \not\hookrightarrow v$), then, due to compactness of the attack relation, $v$ is always included in a maximal set $v_1$ such $(u, v_1)$ is a bitheory. This latter bitheory will be called *negatively minimal*, since the corresponding four-valued model contains a minimal set (namely $\overline{v_1}$) of rejected assumptions for a given set $u$ of accepted ones.

For an argument $u$, we will denote by $\langle u \rangle$ the set of all maximal arguments $v$ such that $u \not\hookrightarrow v$. The operator $\langle u \rangle$ will play in what follows the same role as the operator $[u]$ in normal argumentation. In particular, using this operator, we can give the following rather simple description of stable and partial stable models of collective argumentation.

**Definition 7.17**

- An argument $u$ will be called *stable* if $u \in \langle u \rangle$.
- A bitheory $(u, v)$ will be called *partial stable* if $u \in \langle v \rangle$, and $v \in \langle u \rangle$.

To begin with, note that stable arguments correspond precisely to partial stable bitheories of the form $(u, u)$. Note also that if $(u, v)$ is a partial stable bitheory, then $(v, u)$ will also be partial stable, and vice versa. A usual additional condition imposed on partial stable models amounts, however, to requiring that $(u, v)$ should also be a consistent bitheory (that is, $u \subseteq v$). The corresponding models will be called *consistent* partial stable bitheories. In accordance with our earlier policy, however, we will not impose this condition as a general constraint. Note in this respect that the bitheories $(u, v)$ and $(v, u)$ provide the same information about 'classical' acceptance and rejection of assumptions, namely they single out the same assumptions that are accepted without being rejected, and same rejected assumptions that are not also accepted. Moreover, it will be shown below that the above models constitute argumentation counterparts of extensions and partial extensions of biconsequence relations as defined in Chapter 5.

The following lemmas give more direct, and often more convenient, descriptions of the above models.

**Lemma 7.21** *An argument $u$ is stable iff $u = \{A \mid u \not\hookrightarrow u, A\}$.*

***Proof.*** Assume first that $u$ is stable. Then $u \not\hookrightarrow u$, and consequently if $A \in u$, then $u \not\hookrightarrow u, A$. Also, if $A \notin u$, then $u \hookrightarrow u, A$, since $(u, u)$ is a negatively minimal bitheory. This gives the direction from left to right. In the other direction, suppose first that $u \hookrightarrow u$. Then $u \hookrightarrow u, A$, for any $A$, and consequently $u = \emptyset$. Thus, $\emptyset \hookrightarrow \emptyset$, which means that $\hookrightarrow$ is a trivial attack relation. Consequently, $u \not\hookrightarrow u$. Suppose now that $u \not\hookrightarrow v$, for some $v \supset u$. Then there exists $A \in v \backslash u$, and we have $u \not\hookrightarrow u, A$ by Monotonicity. But $A \notin u$, which contradicts the above description. Thus, $(u, u)$ is a negatively minimal bitheory, and therefore $u$ is a stable argument. □

The above equation says that a stable argument $u$ consists of all assumptions $A$ such that $u$ does not attack $u \cup \{A\}$. A similar description can be given for partial stable models. The proof is similar to the previous lemma, so we omit it.

**Lemma 7.22** *$(u, v)$ is a partial stable bitheory if and only if*

$$v = \{A \mid u \not\hookrightarrow v, A\} \quad \textit{and} \quad u = \{A \mid v \not\hookrightarrow u, A\}.$$

The next result shows that stable arguments and consistent partial stable bitheories of a normal attack relation coincide, respectively, with stable and complete extensions.

**Lemma 7.23** *If $\hookrightarrow$ is a normal attack relation, then*

- *stable arguments coincide with stable extensions;*
- *$(u, v)$ is a consistent partial stable bitheory iff $u$ is a complete extension, and $v = [u]$.*

***Proof.*** It can be verified that, for a normal attack relation, $[u]$ is the only argument that belongs to $\langle u \rangle$, that is, $\langle u \rangle = \{[u]\}$. Consequently, $u \in \langle u \rangle$ iff $u = [u]$, which shows that stable arguments coincide with stable extensions. In addition, $(u, v)$ is a consistent partial stable bitheory iff $u \subseteq v$, $u = [v]$ and $v = [u]$. As can be seen, the latter conditions amount to saying that $u$ is a complete extension, and $v = [u]$. □

Finally, we will show that, under the general correspondence between argument theories and simple biconsequence relations, the above models correspond precisely to (partial) extensions.

Recall that an argument theory $\Delta$ is representable as a simple bisequent theory that we denoted by $\Delta_{\Vdash}$.

**Lemma 7.24** *If $\Delta_{\Vdash}$ is a bisequent theory corresponding to an argument theory $\Delta$, then*

- *$u$ is a stable argument of $\Delta$ if and only if $\overline{u}$ is an extension of $\Delta_{\Vdash}$;*

- *$(u, v)$ is a partial stable bitheory of $\Delta$ if and only if $(\overline{v}, \overline{u})$ is a partial extension of $\Delta_{\Vdash}$;*

***Proof.*** By Lemma 7.5, bitheories of $\Delta$ stand in one-to-one correspondence with bitheories of $\Delta_{\Vdash}$. In particular, $(u, v)$ is a negatively minimal bitheory of $\Delta$ if and only if $(\overline{v}, \overline{u})$ is a positively minimal bitheory of $\Delta_{\Vdash}$. Now the result follows from the definitions of the respective models. □

Recall now that simple biconsequence relations constitute a special case of both autoepistemic and default consequence relations. Consequently, their (partial) extensions coincide with (partial) expansions. In other words, the argumentation theory does not distinguish between extensions and expansions. Note also that, due to the fact that extensions of a default biconsequence relation are also minimal theories, stable arguments are always maximal consistent.

Just as for partial extensions of biconsequence relations, it can be shown that partial stable bitheories are representable as stable arguments of some 'doubled' attack relation.

Let $\hookrightarrow$ be an attack relation on a set of assumptions $\mathcal{A}$. For each $A \in \mathcal{A}$, we introduce a new assumption $A'$. For any subset $u$ of $\mathcal{A}$, we will denote by $u'$ the set $\{A' \mid A \in u\}$. Now we define a new attack relation $\hookrightarrow_\circ$ on $\mathcal{A} \cup \mathcal{A}'$ as follows:

$$a, b' \hookrightarrow_\circ c, d' \equiv a \hookrightarrow d \text{ or } b \hookrightarrow c.$$

Then we have

**Theorem 7.25** *A bitheory $(u, v)$ is partial stable in $\hookrightarrow$ if and only if $u \cup v'$ is a stable argument in $\hookrightarrow_\circ$.*

***Proof.*** Due to Lemma 7.21, $u \cup v'$ is stable in $\hookrightarrow_\circ$ iff

$$u \cup v' = \{\tilde{A} \mid u, v' \not\hookrightarrow_\circ u, v', \tilde{A}\},$$

where $\tilde{A}$ is either $A$, or $A'$. This condition can be rewritten as the following two equalities:

$$u = \{A \mid u, v' \not\hookrightarrow_\circ u, v', A\} \quad v = \{A \mid u, v' \not\hookrightarrow_\circ u, v', A'\}.$$

Now, $u, v' \hookrightarrow_\circ u, v', A$ holds iff either $u \hookrightarrow v$ or $v \hookrightarrow u, A$. Note, however, that if $(u, v)$ is partial stable in $\hookrightarrow$, then $u \not\hookrightarrow v$ and $v \not\hookrightarrow u$. Also, if $u \cup v'$ is stable in $\hookrightarrow_\circ$, then it is conflict-free, that is $u, v' \not\hookrightarrow_\circ u, v'$, which immediately implies $u \not\hookrightarrow v$ and $v \not\hookrightarrow u$. Consequently, $u, v' \hookrightarrow_\circ u, v', A$ holds iff $v \hookrightarrow u, A$. Similarly, it can be shown that $u, v' \hookrightarrow_\circ u, v', A'$ holds iff $u \hookrightarrow v, A$. As a result, the above two equalities turn out to be equivalent to the two conditions for partial stable bitheories stated in Lemma 7.22. □

The above theorem shows, in effect, that partial stable models are essentially stable arguments 'in disguise'. Unfortunately, in the case of collective argumentation they lack most of the structural properties they had in the normal case of Dung's theory. Most importantly, they do not form a lower semilattice and, in particular, there may be no least partial stable model. In fact, unlike the normal case, collective argument theories may have no partial stable models at all.

**Example 7.1** (1) It can be verified that the argument theory $\{\hookrightarrow A, B, C;\ A \hookrightarrow B;\ B \hookrightarrow C;\ C \hookrightarrow A\}$ does not have any partial stable bitheories.

(2) the argument theory $\{\hookrightarrow A, B;\ A \hookrightarrow A;\ B \hookrightarrow B\}$ does not have consistent partial stable models, though $(\{A\}, \{B\})$ and $(\{B\}, \{A\})$ are its partial stable bitheories.

Now we turn to describing the logics of argumentation appropriate for the stable semantics. To begin with, positive argumentation turns out to be inadequate for the latter. Moreover, the following result shows that already consistent attack relations trivialize stable arguments; namely, they reduce the latter to maximal consistent ones.

**Lemma 7.26** *If $\hookrightarrow$ is a consistent attack relation, then*

- *stable arguments coincide with maximal consistent arguments;*
- *consistent partial stable bitheories are bitheories of the form $(u, u)$, where $u$ is a stable argument.*

***Proof.*** It is easy to verify that any stable argument is always maximal consistent. In the other direction, assume that $u$ is a maximal consistent argument of a consistent attack relation $\hookrightarrow$, and suppose that $(u, v)$ is a bitheory of $\hookrightarrow$ such that $u \subset v$. Then $(v, v)$ is also a bitheory of $\hookrightarrow$, that is, $v \not\hookrightarrow v$, and hence $u \not\hookrightarrow v$ by monotonicity, contrary to our assumption that $(u, v)$ is a bitheory of $\hookrightarrow$. Thus, $u$ is actually a stable argument of $\hookrightarrow$.

If $(u, v)$ is a consistent partial stable bitheory of $\hookrightarrow$, then $u \not\hookrightarrow v$, and hence $v \not\hookrightarrow v$. But $u \subseteq v$, and therefore $u = v$ (since $u \in \langle v \rangle$). Hence the result. □

Thus, the only nontrivial partial stable models of a consistent attack relation should be neither consistent, nor complete. This does not leave us much opportunity for a useful (partial) stable nonmonotonic semantics.

It turns out, however, that negative argumentation constitutes an adequate and very convenient framework for studying stable arguments. As a first step, the following result shows that stable arguments of an attack relation are precisely stable extensions of its negative closure.

**Lemma 7.27** *Stable arguments of an attack relation $\hookrightarrow$ coincide with stable extensions of $\hookrightarrow^{-}$.*

***Proof.*** By Lemma 7.21, the characteristic condition of stable arguments can be written as follows: $u = \{A \mid u \not\hookrightarrow^{-} A\}$. The latter condition coincides with the definition of stable extensions with respect to $\hookrightarrow^{-}$. □

The above result shows once more that stable extensions and stable arguments of collective argumentation are indeed close relatives. As a consequence, we immediately obtain

**Corollary 7.28**

- *Stable arguments of a negative attack relation coincide with its stable extensions.*
- *Any attack relation $\hookrightarrow$ has the same stable arguments as $\hookrightarrow^{-}$.*

The second claim above implies that Import is an argumentation rule that preserves stable arguments, and hence negative argumentation turns out to be appropriate for the stable nonmonotonic semantics. An additional consequence of the above results is the eventual reduction of stable arguments to stable extensions of Dung's argumentation theory. Lemma 7.27 says, in effect, that, after extending a given attack relation to a negative one (by closing it with respect to Import), we can restrict ourselves to its normal sub-relation; stable extensions of the resulting normal attack relation will coincide with stable arguments of the original attack relation.

Our next result shows, however, that negative argumentation trivialize partial stable models, so it is inappropriate for the latter.

**Lemma 7.29** *Partial stable bitheories of a negative attack relation are bitheories of the form $(u, u)$, where $u$ is a stable argument.*

***Proof.*** By the rule Import, if $v \not\hookrightarrow u$, then $v \not\hookrightarrow u, v$. Consequently, $(u, v)$ is a negatively minimal bitheory only if it is consistent. As a result, both $(u, v)$ and $(v, u)$ will be negatively minimal only if $u = v$. □

Thus, just as classical argumentation, negative argumentation reduces partial stable models to stable ones. As we will see in the next section, negative argumentation seems to exclude all nonmonotonic semantics other than the stable one.

### 7.4.3 *Admissibility semantics*

Finally we will briefly consider collective counterparts of D-admissible arguments in normal argumentation. Recall that the latter have been defined as conflict-free arguments that counterattack any argument against them. This definition can be generalized to collective argumentation as follows:

**Definition 7.18** A consistent argument $u$ will be called *admissible* if, for any $v$, if $v \hookrightarrow u$, then $u \hookrightarrow v$.

Admissible arguments can also be described in terms of the $\langle\ \rangle$ operator. Namely, $u$ is admissible if no argument from $\langle u \rangle$ attacks $u$. Clearly, admissibility reduces to D-admissibility for normal attack relations. Unfortunately, in the context of collective argumentation the notion of admissibility behaves in a much less ordered fashion than D-admissibility in Dung's theory. Note, in particular, that even stable arguments need not be admissible in this sense:

**Example 7.2** Let us consider an argument theory $\{A \hookrightarrow B \hookrightarrow A, B\}$. As can be seen, $\{B\}$ is a stable argument of this theory, but it is not admissible: we have $A \hookrightarrow B$, though $B \not\hookrightarrow A$.

It turns out, however, that consistent stable extensions are always both admissible and stable.

**Lemma 7.30** *Any consistent stable extension of an attack relation is both an admissible and stable argument.*

***Proof.*** If $v \hookrightarrow u$, then $v \not\subseteq u$ (since $u$ is consistent), and therefore there exists $A \in v \backslash u$. But $u$ is a stable extension, so $u \hookrightarrow A$, and therefore $u \hookrightarrow v$. This shows that $u$ is an admissible set of $\hookrightarrow$. Also, if $A \notin u$ then $u \hookrightarrow A$, and hence $u \hookrightarrow u, A$. Thus, $u$ is stable. □

The following result shows that admissible arguments play an important role in negative argumentation.

**Theorem 7.31** *Let $\hookrightarrow$ be a negative attack relation.*

- *If $u$ is an admissible argument in $\hookrightarrow$, and $v$ a consistent argument that includes $u$, then $v$ is also admissible in $\hookrightarrow$.*
- *Stable arguments of $\hookrightarrow$ coincide with maximal admissible arguments.*

***Proof.*** (1) Assume that $u$ is admissible, $u \subseteq v$ and $w \hookrightarrow v$. Then $w \hookrightarrow v, u$, and hence $w, v \hookrightarrow u$ by Import. Since $u$ is admissible, we obtain $u \hookrightarrow w, v$, and hence $u, v \hookrightarrow w$ by Import. But the latter amounts to $v \hookrightarrow w$, which shows that $v$ is also admissible.

(2) Let $u$ be a stable argument, and $v \hookrightarrow u$. Then $v$ is not a subset of $u$ (since $u$ is consistent), and hence $u \hookrightarrow u, v$, since $u$ is a maximal set that is not attacked by $u$. Applying Import, we obtain $u \hookrightarrow v$, which shows that any stable argument is admissible. Moreover, any superset of a stable argument will not already be consistent. Consequently stable arguments are maximal admissible.

If $u$ is a maximal admissible argument and $A \notin u$, then $u \cup \{A\}$ will not be consistent by the preceding claim, and hence $u, A \hookrightarrow u, A$. Consequently $u, A \hookrightarrow u$, and therefore $u \hookrightarrow u, A$ (since $u$ is admissible). This shows that $u$ is actually a stable argument. □

The above theorem demonstrates that the structure of admissible and stable arguments in negative argumentation is very simple. Namely, they behave much like logically consistent sets. There is, however, a crucial difference: the empty set $\emptyset$ is not, in general, admissible. Moreover, a negative attack relation may have no admissible arguments at all; this happens precisely when it has no stable arguments.

Turning to positive argumentation, let us say that an argument is *positively admissible* for an attack relation $\hookrightarrow$, if it is an admissible argument in $\hookrightarrow^+$. As a matter of fact, such arguments were introduced in [Kakas and Mankarella, 1991] for normal programs under the name *weakly stable sets.* The following observation establishes an equivalence between our definition and the characterization of weakly stable sets, given in [Kakas and Toni, 1999]:

**Lemma 7.32** *If $\hookrightarrow$ is affirmative, then an argument $u$ is positively admissible if and only if $u, v \hookrightarrow v \backslash u$, for any $v$ that attacks $u$.*

***Proof.*** Assume first that $u$ is positively admissible, and $v \hookrightarrow u$, for some $v$. Then $u, v\backslash u \hookrightarrow u$, that is, $v\backslash u \hookrightarrow^+ u$. Consequently $u \hookrightarrow^+ v\backslash u$, and therefore $u, v \hookrightarrow v\backslash u$. In the other direction, if the above condition is satisfied, and $u \hookrightarrow u$, them $u \hookrightarrow \emptyset$, which is impossible, since $\hookrightarrow$ is affirmative. Consequently, $u$ is a consistent argument. Also, if $v \hookrightarrow^+ u$, then $u, v \hookrightarrow u$, which implies $u, v \hookrightarrow v\backslash u$, and hence $u, v \hookrightarrow v$. Thus, $u \hookrightarrow^+ v$, and therefore $u$ is positively admissible. □

Note also that normal logic programs determine normal attack relations. Consequently, a study of weakly stable sets reduces to a study of admissible arguments for what we have called n-positive attack relations. Actually, a large part of Dung's argumentation theory can be reproduced in this setting (see [Bochman, 2003] for further details).

It turns out that many other semantics of argumentation, suggested in the literature, are representable as admissibility semantics for particular kinds of attack relations. As an illustration, we will describe below the admissibility semantics for consistent and weakly positive argumentation.

An argument will be called *consistently* admissible, if it is admissible in $\hookrightarrow^c$, and *weakly positively* admissible, if it is admissible in $\hookrightarrow^w$. The following observation gives a direct description of such arguments.

**Lemma 7.33** *A consistent argument $u$ is*

- *consistently admissible iff $u \hookrightarrow v$, for any consistent argument $v$ that attacks $u$;*
- *weakly positively admissible iff either $u \hookrightarrow v$, or $u, v \hookrightarrow$, for any argument $v$ that attacks $u$.*

In addition to the above proliferation of admissibility semantics, it should be noted that all these semantics are in general incomparable, even when the underlying attack relations are comparable logically. All this makes the study of admissibility semantics for different kinds of argumentation a wide and largely unexplored area.

### 7.4.4 *Argumentation in logic programming*

A general abductive argumentation framework used for interpreting normal logic programs (see, e.g., [Dung, 1995a; Kakas and Toni, 1999]) consists of a set of assumptions (abducibles) of the form $\mathbf{not}\, p$ and the attack relation defined as a relation between sets of abducibles and particular abducibles they attack. A set of abducibles $\mathbf{not}\, a$ attacks an abducible $\mathbf{not}\, p$ in the abductive theory associated with a normal logic program $P$ if $P$, taken together with $\mathbf{not}\, a$ as a set of additional assumptions, allows to derive $p$. For example, the program rule $r \leftarrow \mathbf{not}\, p, \mathbf{not}\, q$ implies that the set of abducibles $\{\mathbf{not}\, p, \mathbf{not}\, q\}$ attacks the abducible $\mathbf{not}\, r$.

As has been shown in [Dung, 1995a], under this correspondence, stable extensions correspond to stable models, complete extensions correspond to partial stable models, preferred extensions correspond to regular models, while the least complete extension corresponds in this sense to the well-founded semantics (WFS). These results have shown, in effect, that the abstract argumentation theory successfully captures the essence of logical reasoning behind normal logic programs.

The above correspondence between normal logic programs and normal argumentation immediately suggests a generalization according to which any disjunctive logic program $P$ determines an attack relation among sets of abducibles as follows:

$$\mathbf{not}\, a \text{ attacks } \mathbf{not}\, b \text{ iff } P \cup \mathbf{not}\, a \text{ derives } \bigvee b.$$

As can be easily verified, the above defined attack relation satisfies all the properties of collective argumentation. However, it is in general not local: $P \cup \mathbf{not}\, a$ may derive $p \vee q$ without deriving either $p$ or $q$. Still, it will be affirmative for disjunctive logic programs without constraints.

The appropriateness of the original argumentation theory for representing semantics of normal logic programs was based, ultimately, on the fact that these semantics are completely determined by rules of the form $p \leftarrow \mathbf{not}\, b$ that are derivable from a program. Note that the principle of partial deduction, GPPE (see Sec. 3.3.2.2), is valid also for the majority of semantics suggested for disjunctive logic programs. According to this principle, semantics of such programs should be completely determined by rules $c \leftarrow \mathbf{not}\, b$ without positive atoms in bodies that are derivable from the source program.

The following proposition establishes the correspondence between the nonmonotonic semantics of collective argumentation theory and the main semantics for disjunctive logic programs. The proof is immediate from the biconsequence representation of logic programs, described in Chapter 5, and Lemma 7.24.

**Proposition 7.34** *If $\mathbb{A}_\Pi$ is a collective argument theory corresponding to a disjunctive program $\Pi$, then*

- *$u$ is a stable model of $\Pi$ iff $\mathbf{not}\, \overline{u}$ is a stable set in $\mathbb{A}_\Pi$.*
- *$(u, v)$ is a p-stable model of $\Pi$ iff $(\mathbf{not}\, \overline{u}, \mathbf{not}\, \overline{v})$ is p-stable in $\mathbb{A}_P$.*

## 7.5 Propositional Argumentation

In this section we will show how argumentation theories can be extended to a full classical propositional language. The material of this section will serve as a natural link to the next chapter, where we will establish a close connection between argumentation and causal inference.

Since we have decided from the very beginning to adhere to a propositional understanding of arguments as sets of assumptions, there is no conceptual obstacle in extending the language of argumentation to arbitrary classical formulas. Actually, the four-valued interpretation of attack relations suggests a natural way of doing this, namely an extension of the language with the local classical connectives $\{\neg, \wedge\}$. Moreover, just as for biconsequence relations, we can introduce and characterize these connectives separately, which will give us an opportunity to consider argumentation theories in different languages.

To begin with, recall that the four-valued conjunction is defined by the following conditions:

$$A \wedge B \text{ is accepted iff } A \text{ is accepted and } B \text{ is accepted}$$
$$A \wedge B \text{ is rejected iff } A \text{ is rejected or } B \text{ is rejected.}$$

A syntactic characterization of this connective for attack relations is obtained by the following two conditions:

$$a, A \wedge B \hookrightarrow b \;\text{ iff }\; a, A, B \hookrightarrow b$$
$$a \hookrightarrow A \wedge B, b \;\text{ iff }\; a \hookrightarrow A, B, b. \qquad (A_\wedge)$$

**Corollary 7.35** *An attack relation $\hookrightarrow$ satisfies $(A_\wedge)$ if and only if it coincides with $\hookrightarrow_I$, for some set of four-valued interpretations $I$ in a language with a four-valued conjunction $\wedge$.*

***Proof.*** It can be directly verified that if $I$ is a set of four-valued interpretations in a language with a four-valued conjunction $\wedge$, then the attack relation $\hookrightarrow_I$ satisfies the above conditions. In the other direction, it is sufficient to notice that if $I$ is the set of all interpretations corresponding to bitheories of $\hookrightarrow$ that satisfies $(A_\wedge)$, then conjunctions $A \wedge B$ satisfy the characteristic conditions for a four-valued conjunction. Consequently, the result follows from Theorem 7.3. □

An immediate benefit of introducing conjunction in the language of argumentation consists in the possibility of representing any finite argument $a$ by a single proposition $\bigwedge a$:

$$a \hookrightarrow b \quad \text{iff} \quad \bigwedge a \hookrightarrow \bigwedge b.$$

This obliterates, in effect, the distinction between (finite) arguments and assumptions.

Further expressive capabilities will be acquired with adding the local negation $\neg$ to the language that has the following interpretation:

$$\neg A \text{ is accepted iff } A \text{ is not accepted}$$
$$\neg A \text{ is rejected iff } A \text{ is not rejected.}$$

A syntactic characterization of the local negation is obtained by imposing the following set of rules on an attack relation:

$$A, \neg A \hookrightarrow \qquad \hookrightarrow A, \neg A$$
$$\text{If } a, A \hookrightarrow b \text{ and } a, \neg A \hookrightarrow b \text{ then } a \hookrightarrow b \qquad (A_{\neg})$$
$$\text{If } a \hookrightarrow b, A \text{ and } a \hookrightarrow b, \neg A \text{ then } a \hookrightarrow b.$$

The following corollary shows that the above conditions provide an adequate syntactic description of the argumentation in a local four-valued language. The proof is similar to the preceding one.

**Corollary 7.36** *An attack relation* $\hookrightarrow$ *satisfies* $(A_{\wedge})$ *and* $(A_{\neg})$ *if and only if it coincides with* $\hookrightarrow_I$, *for some set of four-valued interpretations* $I$ *in a local classical language.*

Since finite arguments are reducible to single propositions using the conjunction $\wedge$, an attack relation in a local classical language can be viewed simply as a certain relation on the set of classical propositions. The following definition gives a direct description of such a relation.

**Definition 7.19** A relation $\hookrightarrow$ on a set of classical propositions will be called a *propositional attack relation*, if it satisfies the following rules:

**(Left Strengthening)** If $A \vDash B$ and $B \hookrightarrow C$, then $A \hookrightarrow C$;
**(Right Strengthening)** If $A \hookrightarrow B$ and $C \vDash B$, then $A \hookrightarrow C$;
**(Left Or)** If $A \hookrightarrow C$ and $B \hookrightarrow C$, then $A \vee B \hookrightarrow C$;
**(Right Or)** If $A \hookrightarrow B$ and $A \hookrightarrow C$, then $A \hookrightarrow B \vee C$;
**(Truth)** $\mathbf{t} \hookrightarrow \mathbf{f}$;
**(Falsity)** $\mathbf{f} \hookrightarrow \mathbf{t}$.

Now, it can be verified that, for any attack relation $\hookrightarrow$ in a local classical language, the set of all attacks of the form $A \hookrightarrow B$ constitutes a propositional attack relation. Moreover, the original attack relation can be 'restored' from the latter due to the fact that $a \hookrightarrow b$ is equivalent to $\bigwedge a \hookrightarrow \bigwedge b$.

Consequently, propositional attack relations turn out to provide an adequate description of attack relations in a (local) classical language[2].

Finally, for a local classical language, attack relations become fully equivalent to biconsequence relations. Indeed, given an attack relation in such a language, we can define the following biconsequence relation:

$$a{:}b \Vdash c{:}d \;\equiv\; \neg b, d \hookrightarrow a, \neg c.$$

It can be verified that the above relation satisfies all the postulates of biconsequence relations in the local classical language. Moreover, given an arbitrary biconsequence relation $\Vdash$ in such a language, we can define the following attack relation:

$$a \hookrightarrow b \;\equiv\; b{:} \Vdash {:}a.$$

The above attack relation satisfies the conditions $(A_\wedge)$ and $(A_\neg)$, so it will correspond to an attack relation in a classical language. Moreover, it can be easily verified that the above pair of definitions are perfect duals, which will show an exact equivalence between the two notions.

The correspondence between propositional argumentation and biconsequence relations could, of course, be extended to associated nonmonotonic semantics. We have refrained from doing this, however, since at this point of our development, it would amount simply to a reformulation of our previous results in a new terminology. Still, a propositional generalization of the stable argumentation semantics will turn out to be instructive for our subsequent study.

**Definition 7.20** A set $u$ of propositions will be called a *stable extension* of a propositional attack relation $\hookrightarrow$, if $u = \{A \mid u \not\hookrightarrow A\}$.

As can be seen, the above notion of a stable extension agrees with our earlier definition, though it is defined now on the set of all propositions (instead of just arguments). In the next chapter, this argumentation semantics will be shown to correspond to the main nonmonotonic semantics of causal inference.

[2] An alternative, indirect proof of this correspondence will be given in the next chapter.

# Chapter 8

# Production and Causal Inference

In the preceding chapters we have given a structural description of explanatory nonmonotonic reasoning, namely a description that essentially does not involve propositional connectives and full-fledged logics. In this chapter we will introduce what could be seen as a primary *logical* system for such a reasoning.

The systems of production and causal inference, described below, can be viewed as a most natural and immediate generalization of classical logic that allows to express nonmonotonic reasoning. Basically, this generalization amounts to dropping the Reflexivity postulate of classical inference. The logical foundations of these inference systems will be built in the framework of a logical system for production rules, called *production inference relations*, that originates in input/output logics of [Makinson and van der Torre, 2000]. It turns out, however, that the latter logics can be assigned both a standard monotonic semantics (that gives a semantic interpretation to production rules) and a natural nonmonotonic semantics, which will allow us to give a fully logical representation framework for the explanatory nonmonotonic reasoning studied in previous chapters. Moreover, it will be shown that biconsequence relations constitute a structural counterpart of this logical formalism.

From the point of view of this study, production and causal reasoning constitute the main logical formalisms for explanatory nonmonotonic reasoning. Unlike the epistemic formalisms of default and modal nonmonotonic logics, described later in this study, they are based on a direct and transparent description of factual and causal (explanatory) information about the world. In a hindsight, it even seems strange that the majority of the initial nonmonotonic formalisms suggested in the literature were of epistemic kind, while the causal reasoning has been introduced into nonmonotonic reasoning only recently. Anyway, with the addition of causal logics, the picture of explanatory nonmonotonic reasoning will become complete and well-balanced.

Our basic language in this chapter will be a classical propositional language with the usual classical connectives and constants $\{\wedge, \vee, \neg, \rightarrow, \mathbf{t}, \mathbf{f}\}$. $\vDash$ will stand for the classical entailment, while Th will denote the associated classical provability operator. As before, $p, g, r, \ldots$ will denote propositional atoms, and $A, B, C, \ldots$ arbitrary classical propositions.

## 8.1 Production Inference

Production inference relations, introduced below, are based on conditionals of the form $A \Rightarrow B$ that hold among classical propositions. A general informal interpretation of such conditionals will be '*A produces, or explains, B*'. Accordingly, such conditionals will be called *production rules*. It is worth mentioning that this terminology reflects our conviction that the production rules and associated inference relations constitute a reasonable logical formalization of the well-known, though notoriously vague, notion of production as it has been used in AI. Moreover, we will introduce later a particular, objective interpretation of production rules, according to which the latter will be considered as truly *causal* rules giving a formal representation of causal reasoning.

Though driven by very different considerations and objectives, production inference relations have originated in input-output logics from [Makinson and van der Torre, 2000]. Many results from the latter study will be used in what follows. Moreover, our description of different kinds of production relations in this chapter will closely follow the classification of input-output logics suggested by Makinson and van der Torre.

**Definition 8.1** A *production inference relation* is a binary relation $\Rightarrow$ on the set of classical propositions satisfying the following postulates:

**(Strengthening)** If $A \vDash B$ and $B \Rightarrow C$, then $A \Rightarrow C$;
**(Weakening)** If $A \Rightarrow B$ and $B \vDash C$, then $A \Rightarrow C$;
**(And)** If $A \Rightarrow B$ and $A \Rightarrow C$, then $A \Rightarrow B \wedge C$;
**(Truth)** $\mathbf{t} \Rightarrow \mathbf{t}$;
**(Falsity)** $\mathbf{f} \Rightarrow \mathbf{f}$.

From a logical point of view, the most significant 'omission' of the above set of postulates is the absence of the reflexivity postulate $A \Rightarrow A$. As we will see in what follows, it is precisely this feature of production and causal rules that will create a possibility of nonmonotonic reasoning in this framework.

Production inference relations almost coincide with general input/output logic, except for the last postulate, Falsity. The latter makes the production relations inconsistency-preserving, which amounts, in effect, to restricting the universe of discourse to classically consistent theories. This will give us more smooth semantic characterizations, as well as some additional important properties of production inference. On the other hand, input/output logics constitute, in turn, a special kind of general *expectation relations* studied in [Bochman, 2001]; the latter have been required to satisfy only Strengthening and Weakening.

As a first step, we will extend production rules to rules having arbitrary sets of propositions as premises using the familiar compactness recipe: for any set $u$ of propositions, we define $u \Rightarrow A$ as follows:

$$u \Rightarrow A \;\equiv\; \bigwedge a \Rightarrow A, \text{ for some finite } a \subseteq u.$$

For a set $u$ of propositions, $\mathcal{C}(u)$ will denote the set of propositions 'produced' by $u$, that is

$$\mathcal{C}(u) = \{A \mid u \Rightarrow A\}.$$

As could be expected, the production operator $\mathcal{C}$ will play much the same role as the usual derivability operator for consequence relations. In particular, it satisfies the following important monotonicity property:

**Monotonicity** If $u \subseteq v$, then $\mathcal{C}(u) \subseteq \mathcal{C}(v)$.

Thus, $\mathcal{C}$ is a monotonic operator. Actually, due to compactness, $\mathcal{C}$ is not only monotonic, but also a continuous operator. Note also that $\mathcal{C}(u)$ is always a deductively closed set:

**Lemma 8.1** *For any $u$, $\mathcal{C}(u) = \mathrm{Th}(\mathcal{C}(u))$.*

***Proof.*** If $u \Rightarrow A$ and $A \vDash B$, then $\bigwedge a \Rightarrow A$, for some $a \subseteq u$, and therefore $\bigwedge a \Rightarrow B$ by Weakening, that is, $u \Rightarrow B$. In addition, if $A, B \in \mathcal{C}(u)$, then $\bigwedge a \Rightarrow A$ and $\bigwedge b \Rightarrow B$, for some $a, b \subseteq u$, and consequently $\bigwedge(a \cup b) \Rightarrow A \wedge B$ by Strengthening and And. The latter implies $A \wedge B \in \mathcal{C}(u)$. □

Still, $\mathcal{C}$ is not inclusive, that is, $u \subseteq \mathcal{C}(u)$ does not always hold. Also, it is not idempotent, that is, $\mathcal{C}(\mathcal{C}(u))$ can be distinct from $\mathcal{C}(u)$.

The following fact will be used in proving completeness theorems for different kinds of production inference.

**Lemma 8.2** *If $A \notin \mathcal{C}(u)$, then there exists a consistent deductively closed set $v$ such that $u \subseteq v$, $A \notin \mathcal{C}(v)$, and $A \in \mathcal{C}(v')$, for any $v' \supset v$.*

***Proof.*** If $\mathcal{U}$ is a family of sets that do not produce $A$, and $\mathcal{U}$ is linearly ordered by inclusion, then a usual compactness argument shows that $\bigcup \mathcal{U}$ also does not produce $A$. Consequently, $u$ is included in some maximal set $v$ that does not produce $A$. Suppose now that $v \vDash B$, though $B \notin v$. Then $A \in \mathcal{C}(v, B)$ due to maximality of $v$, and hence $V \wedge B \Rightarrow A$, where $V$ is a conjunction of some propositions from $v$. But $v$ implies $V \wedge B$, and hence $V_0 \vDash V \wedge B$, where $V_0$ is again a conjunction of some propositions from $v$. Then $V_0 \Rightarrow A$ holds by Strengthening, and therefore $A \in \mathcal{C}(v)$—a contradiction. Consequently, $v$ is a deductively closed set. Moreover, $\mathbf{f} \notin v$, since $\mathbf{f} \Rightarrow A$ by Falsity. Therefore, $v$ is also consistent. □

The reader should note that the theory $v$ in the formulation of the above lemma need not be a world, that is, a complete deductively closed set.

### 8.1.1 *Semantics*

We will describe now a general semantic framework for production relations. Our basic semantic object will be a pair of deductively closed theories that will be called, as before, a bimodel. In accordance with the 'input-output' understanding of productions, a bimodel will represent an initial state (input) and a possible final state (output) of a production derivation based on a given set of production rules. The set of such bimodels will give a semantic description for these production rules.

**Definition 8.2** A pair of consistent deductively closed sets will be called a *classical bimodel*. A set of classical bimodels will be called a *classical binary semantics*.

Classical bimodels have been defined above in a syntactic fashion, namely as pairs of theories of the language. This formulation will make subsequent constructions simpler and more transparent. Still, any such bimodel $(u, v)$ can be safely equated with a pair of sets of worlds (or propositional interpretations):

$$(u, v) \equiv (\{\alpha \mid u \text{ is valid in } \alpha\}, \{\beta \mid v \text{ is valid in } \beta\}).$$

All our subsequent constructions will permit such a purely semantic reformulation.

A classical binary semantics can also be viewed as a *binary relation* on the set of deductive theories. Accordingly, given a set of bimodels (semantics) $\mathcal{B}$, we will write $u\mathcal{B}v$ to denote the fact that the a bimodel $(u, v)$ belongs to $\mathcal{B}$. These descriptions will be used interchangeably in what follows.

Now we will define the notion of validity of production rules with respect to a classical binary semantics.

**Definition 8.3** A production rule $A \Rightarrow B$ will be said to be *valid* in a classical binary semantics $\mathcal{B}$ if, for any bimodel $(u, v)$ from $\mathcal{B}$, $A \in v$ only if $B \in u$.

We will denote by $\Rightarrow_{\mathcal{B}}$ the set of all production rules that are valid in a semantics $\mathcal{B}$. It can be easily verified that this set is closed with respect to the rules for production relations, and hence we have

**Lemma 8.3** *For a classical binary semantics $\mathcal{B}$, $\Rightarrow_{\mathcal{B}}$ is a production relation.*

In order to prove completeness, for any production relation $\Rightarrow$ we will construct its *canonical semantics* $\mathcal{B}_{\Rightarrow}$ as the set of all classical bimodels of the form $(\mathcal{C}(w), w)$, where $w$ is an arbitrary consistent and deductively closed theory. Then the following result is actually a representation theorem showing that this semantics is strongly complete for the source production relation.

**Theorem 8.4** *If $\mathcal{B}_{\Rightarrow}$ is the canonical semantics for a production relation $\Rightarrow$, then, for any set of propositions $u$ and any $A$,*

$$u \Rightarrow A \text{ iff } A \in w, \text{ for any bimodel } (w, v) \in \mathcal{B}_{\Rightarrow} \text{ such that } u \subseteq v.$$

***Proof.*** If $u \Rightarrow A$ and $u \subseteq v$, for some deductively closed set $v$, then clearly $A \in \mathcal{C}(v)$. In the other direction, if $u \not\Rightarrow A$, then by Lemma 8.2, $u$ is included in some theory $v$ such that $v \not\Rightarrow A$. Clearly, $(\mathcal{C}(v), v)$ is a bimodel from $\mathcal{B}_{\Rightarrow}$ such that $u \subseteq v$ and $A \notin \mathcal{C}(v)$. This completes the proof. □

As an immediate consequence of the above results, we obtain the basic completeness result:

**Corollary 8.5** *A binary relation $\Rightarrow$ on the set of propositions is a production inference relation if and only if it is determined by a classical binary semantics.*

### 8.1.2 *Causal theories*

In what follows, by a *causal theory* we will mean an arbitrary set of production rules. Since all the postulates for production relations are Horn ones, for any causal theory $\Delta$ there exists a least production relation that includes $\Delta$. We will denote it by $\Rightarrow_\Delta$, while $\mathcal{C}_\Delta$ will denote the corresponding derivability operator. Clearly, $\Rightarrow_\Delta$ is the set of all production rules that can be derived from $\Delta$ using the postulates for production relations.

It is important to note that causal theories are undistinguishable, as such, from *conditional theories* defined in Sec. 2.5 of Chapter 2; the only difference is that causal theories are governed by only a small subset of the classical inference rules. Still, this correspondence will be extensively exploited in what follows when we consider some stronger kinds of production inference.

For any set $u$ of propositions, we will denote by $\Delta(u)$ the set of all propositions that can be directly produced from $u$ by $\Delta$, that is

$$\Delta(u) = \{A \mid B \Rightarrow A \in \Delta, \text{ for some } B \in u\}.$$

The following explicit description of $\Rightarrow_\Delta$ has been given in [Makinson and van der Torre, 2000]:

**Proposition 8.6** $\mathcal{C}_\Delta(u) = \mathrm{Th}(\Delta(\mathrm{Th}(u)))$.

***Proof.*** Let us define the following production relation:

$$u \Rightarrow A \;\equiv\; \Delta(\mathrm{Th}(u)) \vDash A.$$

It can be verified that this relation includes $\Delta$ and satisfies all the properties of a production inference relation, and hence we have $\mathcal{C}_\Delta(u) \subseteq \mathrm{Th}(\Delta(\mathrm{Th}(u)))$, for any $u$, since $\Rightarrow_\Delta$ is a least such relation. In the other direction, assume $\Delta(\mathrm{Th}(u)) \vDash A$. Then $\Delta$ contains a finite set of rules $\{B_i \Rightarrow A_i\}$ such that $\bigwedge A_i \vDash A$ and $u \vDash \bigwedge B_i$. Consequently $\bigwedge b \vDash \bigwedge B_i$, for some finite $b \subseteq u$. Now we have $\bigwedge B_i \Rightarrow_\Delta \bigwedge A_i$ by Strengthening and And, which implies $\bigwedge b \Rightarrow_\Delta A$ by Strengthening and Weakening. Consequently, $u \Rightarrow_\Delta A$, and therefore $\mathcal{C}_\Delta(u) = \mathrm{Th}(\Delta(\mathrm{Th}(u)))$. □

The above description will be used quite often in what follows.

### 8.1.3 *Regular production inference*

A production inference relation will be called *regular* if it satisfies the following well-known rule:

**(Cut)** If $A \Rightarrow B$ and $A \wedge B \Rightarrow C$, then $A \Rightarrow C$.

Cut is one of the basic rules for ordinary consequence relations. In the context of production inference it plays the same role, namely, allows for a reuse of produced propositions as premises in further productions[1]. It corresponds to the following characteristic property of the production operator:

$$\mathcal{C}(u \cup \mathcal{C}(u)) \subseteq \mathcal{C}(u).$$

Regular production relations have a number of additional properties. Thus, any such relation will already be transitive, that is, it will satisfy

**(Transitivity)** If $A \Rightarrow B$ and $B \Rightarrow C$, then $A \Rightarrow C$.

Transitivity corresponds to the following familiar property of the production operator:

$$\mathcal{C}(\mathcal{C}(u)) \subseteq \mathcal{C}(u).$$

Note, however, that Transitivity is a weaker postulate than Cut, since it does not imply the latter (see below).

A production rule of the form $A \Rightarrow \mathbf{f}$ will be called a *constraint*. Such rules can be used for incorporating a purely factual information into causal theories: a rule $A \Rightarrow \mathbf{f}$ says, in a sense, that $A$ is production- or explanatory inconsistent, and hence it should not hold in any intended model.

Now, an important property of regular relations is that any production rule implies the corresponding constraint:

**(Constraint)** If $A \Rightarrow B$, then $A \wedge \neg B \Rightarrow \mathbf{f}$.

(Indeed, if $A \Rightarrow B$, then $A \wedge \neg B \Rightarrow B$ by Strengthening and $A \wedge B \wedge \neg B \Rightarrow \mathbf{f}$ by Falsity. Hence $A \wedge \neg B \Rightarrow \mathbf{f}$ by Cut[2].)

In particular, we have that $\mathbf{t} \Rightarrow A$ implies $\neg A \Rightarrow \mathbf{f}$. Note, however, that the reverse entailment does not hold even in the latter special case.

As a special case of Constraint, we have also the rule

**(Coherence)** If $A \Rightarrow \neg A$, then $A \Rightarrow \mathbf{f}$.

that says that if a proposition produces propositions that are incompatible with it, then it is explanatory inconsistent. Actually, Coherence turns out

[1] Such production relations correspond to input-output logics with reusable output in [Makinson and van der Torre, 2000].

[2] Note that the use of Falsity is essential here.

to be equivalent to Constraint for all production inference relations (see Lemma 8.50 below).

**Remark 8.1** *Regular production inference sanctions, in effect, an* atemporal *understanding of the notion of production. For example, the rule* $p \wedge q \Rightarrow \neg q$ *cannot be understood as saying that* $p$ *and* $q$ *jointly produce* $\neg q$ *(afterwards) in a temporal sense; instead, by Coherence it implies* $p \wedge q \Rightarrow \mathbf{f}$, *which means, in effect, that* $p \wedge q$ *cannot hold. Speaking generally, production-consistent propositions cannot produce a result incompatible with them. Just as in classical logic, however, a representation of temporal domains in this formalism can be obtained by adding explicit temporal arguments to propositions; this is what has actually been done in [McCain and Turner, 1997].*

Regular production relations can already be described in terms of a usual notion of a theory.

**Definition 8.4** A set $u$ of propositions will be called a *theory* of a production relation, if it is deductively closed, and $\mathcal{C}(u) \subseteq u$.

$u$ will be called a *theory* of a causal theory $\Delta$, if it is a theory of $\Rightarrow_\Delta$.

A theory of a production relation is a set of propositions that is closed both deductively and with respect to its production rules, namely, if $A \in u$ and $A \Rightarrow B$, then $B \in u$. Accordingly, such theories have much the same properties as ordinary theories of consequence relations. Note, in particular, that the set of theories of a production inference relation is closed with respect to arbitrary intersections, and consequently any set of propositions is included in some least such theory. In addition, theories that are worlds have a very simple characterization:

**Lemma 8.7** *A world* $\alpha$ *is a theory of a regular production relation if and only if* $\alpha \not\Rightarrow \mathbf{f}$.

***Proof.*** Clearly, if $\alpha \Rightarrow \mathbf{f}$, then $\mathcal{C}(\alpha)$ is an inconsistent theory, and hence $\mathcal{C}(\alpha) \subseteq \alpha$ cannot hold. Assume now that a world $\alpha$ is not a theory. Then $A, \neg B \in \alpha$, for some propositions $A, B$ such that $A \Rightarrow B$. But then we have also $A \wedge \neg B \Rightarrow \mathbf{f}$ by Constraint, and therefore $\alpha \Rightarrow \mathbf{f}$. □

As could be expected, theories of a causal theory $\Delta$ are the sets of propositions that are closed with respect to the rules of $\Delta$. Thus, the following description follows immediately from Proposition 8.6.

**Lemma 8.8** *A deductively closed set* $u$ *is a theory of a causal theory* $\Delta$ *if and only if* $\Delta(u) \subseteq u$.

Theories of a regular production relation will determine its canonical semantics, described in the proof of the completeness theorem below. Note, however, that the regular production relation will be determined not only by what its theories are, but also by what they produce.

The semantic characterization of regular production relations can be obtained by considering only classical bimodels $(u, v)$ such that $u \subseteq v$. We will call such bimodels (and the corresponding semantics) *consistent* ones.

**Theorem 8.9** *$\Rightarrow$ is a regular production relation if and only if it is generated by a consistent classical binary semantics.*

***Proof.*** It can be verified that the production relation generated by a consistent semantics will satisfy Cut. In the other direction, for a regular production relation $\Rightarrow$, we will construct a canonical semantics as the set of bimodels of the form $(\mathcal{C}(w), w)$, where $w$ is a theory of $\Rightarrow$. Clearly, if $u \Rightarrow A$ and $u \subseteq w$, then $A \in \mathcal{C}(w)$. In the other direction, if $u \not\Rightarrow A$, then by Lemma 8.2, $u$ is included in some maximal deductively closed set $w$ such that $w \not\Rightarrow A$. Assume that $w \Rightarrow B$, for some $B$, though $B \notin w$. Due to maximality of $w$, we have $w \cup \{B\} \Rightarrow A$. Since $w$ is deductively closed, there are propositions $C, D \in w$ such that $C \Rightarrow B$ and $D \wedge B \Rightarrow A$. But then by Strengthening and Cut we obtain $C \wedge D \Rightarrow A$, contrary to our assumption that $w \not\Rightarrow A$. Hence $w$ is a theory of $\Rightarrow$, and therefore $(\mathcal{C}(w), w)$ is a consistent bimodel that invalidates $u \Rightarrow A$. □

The above proof contains, in effect, the following characterization of regular production inference relations in terms of their theories:

**Corollary 8.10** *$\Rightarrow$ is a regular production inference relation if and only if, for any set $v$ and any $A$,*

$$v \Rightarrow A \text{ iff } A \in \mathcal{C}(u), \text{ for any theory } u \text{ of} \Rightarrow \text{ that contains } v.$$

We will denote by $\Rightarrow^r_\Delta$ the least regular production relation containing a causal theory $\Delta$. As a consequence of the above characterization, we obtain a constructive characterization of $\Rightarrow^r_\Delta$, given in [Makinson and van der Torre, 2000].

**Proposition 8.11** *$v \Rightarrow^r_\Delta A$ iff $A \in \mathrm{Th}(\Delta(u))$, for any theory $u$ of $\Delta$ that contains $v$.*

As a last result in this section, we will show that regular production relations allow to define an appropriate notion of equivalence among propositions such that equivalent propositions would be substitutable in any production rule. Namely, let us say that propositions $A$ and $B$ are *production equivalent* with respect to a production inference relation, if $\mathbf{t} \Rightarrow (A \leftrightarrow B)$ holds. Then we have

**Lemma 8.12** *Propositions A and B are production-equivalent with respect to a regular production relation* $\Rightarrow$ *if and only if any occurrence of A can be replaced by B in the rules of* $\Rightarrow$.

***Proof.*** If $A$ can be replaced by $B$ in any rule of $\Rightarrow$, then it can be replaced also in $\mathbf{t} \Rightarrow (A \leftrightarrow A)$, which holds by Truth. Hence, $\mathbf{t} \Rightarrow (A \leftrightarrow B)$ holds in $\Rightarrow$.

We will denote by $X(A/B)$ an arbitrary formula obtained from a formula $X$ by replacing some of the occurrences of $A$ in it by $B$. Clearly, $A \leftrightarrow B \vDash X \leftrightarrow X(A/B)$. Assume now that $A$ and $B$ are production-equivalent, and $X \Rightarrow Y$. Then $X \Rightarrow (A \leftrightarrow B)$ by Strengthening, and hence $X \Rightarrow (Y \leftrightarrow Y(A/B))$ by Weakening. Consequently, $X \Rightarrow Y(A/B)$ by And and Weakening. Thus, $B$ can replace $A$ in the heads of the rules from $\Rightarrow$. In addition, we have $X(A/B), A \leftrightarrow B \vDash X$, and therefore $X(A/B) \wedge (A \leftrightarrow B) \Rightarrow Y$ by Strengthening. But we have also $X(A/B) \Rightarrow (A \leftrightarrow B)$, so we can apply Cut and obtain $X(A/B) \Rightarrow Y$. This shows that $A$ can be replaced by $B$ also in the bodies of the rules from $\Rightarrow$. □

Due to the above result, production-equivalence can be used, in particular, to describe definitional extensions of the underlying language with new propositions (cf. [Turner, 1999]).

### 8.1.4 *Production inference vs. consequence relations*

A further insight into the properties of regular production inference can be obtained by comparing it with associated consequence relations.

It can be easily discerned from the description of supraclassical Tarski consequence relations, given in Sec. 2.5, that the only difference between the latter and regular production inference relations amounts to the Reflexivity postulate. Note also that any causal theory, and hence any production inference relation, can also be considered as an ordinary conditional theory (a set of inference rules), so it determines a corresponding supraclassical consequence relation. The following construction gives a direct description of this consequence relation in terms of the corresponding production relation. Namely, for a (regular) production relation $\Rightarrow$, we will define the following consequence relation:

$$A \vdash_{\Rightarrow} B \equiv A \Rightarrow (A \rightarrow B).$$

**Theorem 8.13** *If $\Rightarrow$ is a regular production relation, then $\vdash_{\Rightarrow}$ is a least supraclassical consequence relation containing $\Rightarrow$.*

***Proof.*** We will show first that $\vdash_{\Rightarrow}$ is a supraclassical consequence relation, namely it satisfies Dominance, Transitivity and And (see Sec. 2.5). If $A \vDash B$, then $A \to B$ is a tautology, and hence $A \Rightarrow (A \to B)$ holds by Truth and Strengthening. Thus, Dominance is satisfied. Assume now that $A \Rightarrow (A \to B)$ and $B \Rightarrow B \to C$. Then $A \wedge B \Rightarrow B \to C$ by Strengthening, and hence $A \Rightarrow (B \to C)$ by Cut. Together with $A \Rightarrow (A \to B)$, this gives $A \Rightarrow (A \to C)$ by And and Weakening. Thus, Transitivity holds. Finally, And for $\vdash_{\Rightarrow}$ follows directly from the And postulate for $\Rightarrow$. Consequently, $\vdash_{\Rightarrow}$ is a supraclassical consequence relation.

Clearly, $\Rightarrow$ is included in $\vdash_{\Rightarrow}$. Let $\vdash_1$ be any supraclassical consequence relation that includes $\Rightarrow$, and $A \vdash_{\Rightarrow} B$. Then $A \Rightarrow A \to B$, and hence $A \vdash_1 (A \to B)$. But $A \vdash_1 A$, and hence $A \vdash_1 B$. Thus, $\vdash_{\Rightarrow}$ is included in $\vdash_1$, and therefore it is a least consequence relation containing $\Rightarrow$. □

Let $\mathrm{Cn}_{\Rightarrow}$ denote the provability operator corresponding to $\vdash_{\Rightarrow}$. Then the above description can be extended to the following equality, for any set $u$ of propositions:

$$\mathrm{Cn}_{\Rightarrow}(u) = \mathrm{Th}(u \cup \mathcal{C}(u)).$$

The equality shows, in effect, that $\mathcal{C}(u)$ captures practically all nontrivial consequences included in $\mathrm{Cn}_{\Rightarrow}(u)$, except for $u$ itself.

As a first consequence of the above correspondence, we obtain

**Lemma 8.14** *Theories of $\Rightarrow$ coincide with the theories of $\vdash_{\Rightarrow}$.*

***Proof.*** $u$ is a theory of $\vdash_{\Rightarrow}$ iff $u = \mathrm{Cn}_{\Rightarrow}(u)$. By the above equality, this holds if and only if $u$ is deductively closed and $\mathcal{C}(u) \subseteq u$. □

Since theories of $\vdash_{\Rightarrow}$ are exactly sets of propositions of the form $\mathrm{Cn}_{\Rightarrow}(u)$, the above result implies that such sets are precisely theories of $\Rightarrow$.

As yet another consequence of the above equation, we obtain the following alternative characterization of regular inference:

$$\mathcal{C}(u) = \mathcal{C}(\mathrm{Cn}_{\Rightarrow}(u)).$$

Note that we have also $\mathcal{C}(u) = \mathrm{Cn}_{\Rightarrow}(\mathcal{C}(u))$, so the production operator absorbs $\mathrm{Cn}_{\Rightarrow}$ on both sides: $\mathrm{Cn}_{\Rightarrow} \circ \mathcal{C} = \mathcal{C} \circ \mathrm{Cn}_{\Rightarrow} = \mathcal{C}$.

The above description of associated consequence relations can be immediately generalized to arbitrary causal (= conditional) theories. Thus, if $\mathrm{Cn}_\Delta$ denotes the least supraclassical consequence relation containing a causal theory $\Delta$, while $\mathcal{C}^r_\Delta$ is the production operator of the least regular production relation containing $\Delta$, then we have

$$\mathrm{Cn}_\Delta(u) = \mathrm{Th}(u \cup \mathcal{C}^r_\Delta(u)).$$

Moreover, Proposition 8.11 will immediately imply the following simplified characterization of $\mathcal{C}^r_\Delta$:

**Corollary 8.15** $\mathcal{C}^r_\Delta(u) = \mathrm{Th}(\Delta(\mathrm{Cn}_\Delta(u)))$.

This characterization will also be used in what follows.

## 8.2 Nonmonotonic Production Semantics

In the preceding sections, we have given a formalization and standard (monotonic) semantics for the logical system of production inference. It turns out, however, that production inference relations determine also a natural nonmonotonic semantics, and provide thereby a logical basis for nonmonotonic reasoning. Namely, the fact that the production operator $\mathcal{C}$ is not reflexive creates an important distinction among theories of a production relation.

**Definition 8.5** For a production inference relation $\Rightarrow$,

- A set $u$ of propositions will be called *explanatory closed*, if $u \subseteq \mathcal{C}(u)$.
- A theory $u$ of $\Rightarrow$ will be called *exact*, if it is consistent and explanatory closed, that is, $u = \mathcal{C}(u)$.
- A set $u$ of propositions is an *exact theory of a causal theory* $\Delta$, if it is an exact theory of $\Rightarrow_\Delta$.

An exact theory describes an informational state in which every proposition is produced, or *explained*, by other propositions accepted in this state. Accordingly, restricting our universe of discourse to exact theories amounts to imposing a kind of an explanatory closure assumption on a production relation. Namely, it amounts to requiring that any accepted proposition should also have reason, or explanation, for its acceptance. This suggests the following notion of a nonmonotonic semantics:

**Definition 8.6** A *nonmonotonic production semantics* of a production inference relation or a causal theory is the set of all its exact theories.

The nonmonotonic production semantics, as defined above, is a certain set of propositional theories. As for biconsequence relations, this abstract definition leaves us much freedom in determining what can be seen as *nonmonotonic consequences* of a causal theory. The most obvious choice consists in taking propositions that belong to all exact theories. As we will see, however, this means that we accept only propositions that belong to the least exact theory. But we can also choose propositions that belongs to all *maximal* exact theories. Similarly, we can consider all propositions that do not belong to any such theory as nonmonotonically *rejected*. All these options determine useful variants of a *sceptical*, or cautious, nonmonotonic semantics. A *credulous* nonmonotonic semantics can be defined by considering propositions that belong (or not belong) to at least one exact theory. As studies in nonmonotonic reasoning show, each of these options could be appropriate for particular reasoning tasks. Again, it could be safely argued that all the information that can be discerned from the nonmonotonic production semantics of a causal theory, or a production inference relation, can be seen as nonmonotonically implied by the latter.

The nonmonotonic production semantics for causal theories is indeed nonmonotonic in the sense that adding new rules to the production relation may lead to a nonmonotonic change of the associated semantics, and thereby to a nonmonotonic change in the derived information (a number of examples will be presented below). This happens even though production rules themselves are monotonic, since they satisfy Strengthening (the Antecedent).

Exact theories are precisely fixed points of the production operator $\mathcal{C}$. Since the latter operator is monotonic and continuous, exact theories (and hence the nonmonotonic semantics) always exist. Also, the general properties of monotonic operators imply the following properties of exact theories:

**Lemma 8.16**

*(1) Any production relation has a least exact theory.*
*(2) Any theory of a production relation contains a greatest exact theory.*
*(3) The union of any chain of exact theories (with respect to set inclusion) is an exact theory.*
*(4) Any exact theory is included in a maximal exact theory.*

***Proof.*** (1) The least fixed point of $\mathcal{C}$ determines a least exact theory.

(2) If $\mathcal{C}(u) \subseteq u$, then iterating $\mathcal{C}$ starting from $u$ will give us a greatest fixed point of $\mathcal{C}$ that is included in $u$.

(3) Let $\{u_i\}$ be a set of exact theories of $\Rightarrow$ linearly ordered by inclusion, and $u = \bigcup u_i$. Since each $u_i$ is a theory of $\Rightarrow$, the usual compactness argument implies that $u$ will also be a theory of $\Rightarrow$, that is $\mathcal{C}(u) \subseteq u$. In addition, by the monotonicity of $\mathcal{C}$, we immediately have that $u$ is explanatory closed, that is, $u \subseteq \mathcal{C}(u)$. Hence $u = \mathcal{C}(u)$.

(4) Follows from (3). □

Unfortunately, the following example shows that exact theories are not closed with respect to arbitrary intersections.

**Example 8.1** Let us consider a causal theory $\Delta = \{p_i \Rightarrow p_i, p_i \Rightarrow q \mid i \geq 0\}$. Then, for any natural $n$, the set $u_n = \mathrm{Th}(q, p_n)$ is an exact theory of $\Rightarrow_\Delta$. However, $\bigcap u_n = \mathrm{Th}(q)$ is not an exact theory of $\Rightarrow_\Delta$.

As a result, a least exact theory containing a given set of propositions does not always exist.

The following simple lemma gives a constructive description of the nonmonotonic production semantics of a causal theory. The proof is immediate by Proposition 8.6.

**Lemma 8.17** *$u$ is an exact theory of a causal theory $\Delta$ iff $u = \mathrm{Th}(\Delta(u))$.*

We are going to show now that regular production inference provides an adequate and maximal logical framework for reasoning with exact theories.

**Definition 8.7** Two causal theories will be called *(strongly) nonmonotonically equivalent* if they are (strongly) equivalent with respect to the nonmonotonic production semantics.

Note that production inference relations can also be considered as (rather big) causal theories. As before, let $\Rightarrow^r_\Delta$ denote the least regular production relation that contains a causal theory $\Delta$. Then we have

**Lemma 8.18** *A causal theory $\Delta$ is nonmonotonically equivalent to $\Rightarrow^r_\Delta$.*

***Proof.*** If $v$ is a theory of $\Delta$, then $v = \mathrm{Cn}_\Delta(v)$, and hence $\mathrm{Th}(\Delta(v)) = \mathrm{Th}(\Delta(\mathrm{Cn}_\Delta(v)))$. Consequently, $v = \mathrm{Th}(\Delta(v))$ iff $v = \mathrm{Th}(\Delta(\mathrm{Cn}_\Delta(v)))$. By Corollary 8.15, this implies that $v$ is an exact theory of $\Delta$ if and only if it is an exact theory of $\Rightarrow^r_\Delta$. □

The above lemma implies that the postulates of regular inference are adequate for reasoning with exact theories, since they preserve the latter. Moreover, we will show now that regular inference relations constitute a maximal logic suitable for the nonmonotonic production semantics.

Let us say that causal theories $\Delta$ and $\Gamma$ are *regularly equivalent*, if each can be obtained from the other using the postulates of regular production inference. Or, equivalently, when $\Rightarrow^r_\Delta = \Rightarrow^r_\Gamma$.

Strong nonmonotonic equivalence can be seen as an equivalence with respect to the background monotonic logic of causal theories. And the next result shows that this logic is precisely the logic of regular production relations.

**Theorem 8.19** *Two causal theories are strongly nonmonotonically equivalent if and only if they are regularly equivalent.*

***Proof.*** To simplify notation, $\Rightarrow_\Psi$ below will denote the least regular production relation containing a causal theory $\Psi$, while $\mathcal{C}_\Psi$ will denote the associated production operator.

The direction from right to left follows from the preceding lemma and the fact that, if $\Delta$ and $\Gamma$ are regularly equivalent, then, for any $\Phi$, $\Delta \cup \Phi$ and $\Gamma \cup \Phi$ are also regularly equivalent.

Assume now that $\Delta$ is not regularly equivalent to $\Gamma$. Then we may assume for certainty that there are propositions $A, B$ such that $A \Rightarrow_\Delta B$ and $A \not\Rightarrow_\Gamma B$. The latter fact means that there is a theory $u$ of $\Gamma$ such that $A \in u$ and $B \notin \mathcal{C}_\Gamma(u)$. Let us consider two cases.

Suppose first that $u$ is not a theory of $\Delta$. Then we choose $\Phi = \{C \Rightarrow C \mid C \in u\}$. Clearly, $u$ is an exact theory for $\Gamma \cup \Phi$, though not for $\Delta \cup \Phi$.

Suppose now that $u$ is a theory of $\Delta$. Since $B \in \mathcal{C}_\Delta(u)$, we have $B \in u$. Let $\beta$ be a world that includes both $\mathcal{C}_\Gamma(u)$ and $\neg B$ (since $B \notin \mathcal{C}_\Gamma(u)$, such a world should exist). Then we define $\Phi$ as $\{C \Rightarrow C \mid C \in u \cap \beta\}$. Note first that $\mathcal{C}_{\Gamma \cup \Phi}(u) = u \cap \beta$, and hence $u$ is not an exact theory for $\Gamma \cup \Phi$. But $u$ is the least theory that contains both $\mathcal{C}_\Delta(u)$ and $u \cap \beta$, and hence it is an exact theory for $\Delta \cup \Phi$. Indeed, if $C \in u$, then $B \to C \in u \cap \beta$, and therefore $B \to C \in \mathcal{C}_{\Delta \cup \Phi}(u)$. In addition, $B \in \mathcal{C}_{\Delta \cup \Phi}(u)$ (since $B \in \mathcal{C}_\Delta(u)$). Consequently, $C \in \mathcal{C}_{\Delta \cup \Phi}(u)$, and therefore $u \subseteq \mathcal{C}_{\Delta \cup \Phi}(u)$. □

The above result implies, in effect, that regular production relations are maximal inference relations that are adequate for nonmonotonic production reasoning in causal theories: any postulate that is not valid for regular production relations can be 'falsified' by finding a suitable extension of two causal theories that would determine different nonmonotonic semantics, and hence would produce different nonmonotonic conclusions.

Note that discriminating sets of causal rules $\Phi$ were restricted in the proof to rules of the form $C \Rightarrow C$. Such rules will play an important role later in representing abductive reasoning in the framework of production inference.

Now we will show that production inference relations also satisfy a restricted monotonicity property with respect to the nonmonotonic semantics.

**Definition 8.8** Causal theories $\Gamma$ and $\Delta$ will be called *supraclassically equivalent*, if they determine the same supraclassical consequence relation.

Supraclassical equivalence amounts, in effect, to the equivalence of $\Delta$ and $\Gamma$ viewed as sets of ordinary rules of a (supraclassical) consequence relation (see Chapter 2). Consequently, $\Delta$ and $\Gamma$ are supraclassically equivalent if and only if they have the same theories.

**Lemma 8.20** *If causal theories $\Gamma$ and $\Delta$ are supraclassically equivalent, and $\Gamma \subseteq \Delta$, then any exact theory of $\Gamma$ is an exact theory of $\Delta$.*

***Proof.*** If $u = \mathcal{C}_\Gamma(u)$, then clearly $u \subseteq \mathcal{C}_\Delta(u)$. But $u$ is a theory of $\Gamma$, and hence it is a theory of $\Delta$, that is, $\mathcal{C}_\Delta(u) \subseteq u$. Therefore $u = \mathcal{C}_\Delta(u)$, and consequently $u$ is an exact theory of $\Delta$. □

The above result clarifies the reasons why the semantics of exact theories is nonmonotonic. Indeed, if the production rules added to a causal theory do not change the set of theories of the latter, then they extend, in general, the set of its exact theories, and therefore not all the sceptical conclusions made earlier will be preserved.

To end this section, we will present some useful properties of exact theories for regular production relations.

To begin with, we will give a number of equivalent descriptions for explanatory closed sets in regular production relations. To simplify the notation, $\mathcal{C}$ below will denote the production operator of a regular production relation, while Cn—the associated supraclassical consequence relation.

**Lemma 8.21** *For a regular production relation, the following conditions are equivalent:*

- *$u$ is an explanatory closed set;*
- *$\mathcal{C}(u) = \mathrm{Cn}(u)$;*
- *$\mathrm{Cn}(u)$ is an exact theory.*

***Proof.*** Since $\mathrm{Cn}(u) = \mathrm{Th}(u \cup \mathcal{C}(u))$, it is easy to see that $\mathcal{C}(u) = \mathrm{Cn}(u)$ holds if and only if $u \subseteq \mathcal{C}(u)$. Note also that $\mathcal{C}(u) = \mathcal{C}(\mathrm{Cn}(u))$, and therefore the second condition above is equivalent also to the third one, namely to $\mathrm{Cn}(u) = \mathcal{C}(\mathrm{Cn}(u))$. □

As a consequence of the above lemma, we obtain

**Corollary 8.22** *If $u$ is an explanatory closed set of a regular production relation, then $\mathcal{C}(u)$ is an exact theory.*

This implies, in particular,

**Corollary 8.23** *$\mathcal{C}(\mathbf{t})$ is the least exact theory of a regular production relation.*

***Proof.*** Clearly, the set $\{\mathbf{t}\}$ is explanatory closed (by Truth), so $\mathcal{C}(\mathbf{t})$ is an exact theory. Moreover, by monotonicity of $\mathcal{C}$, $\mathcal{C}(\mathbf{t})$ is included in any theory of a production relation. □

It is important to note, however, that $\mathcal{C}(u)$ being an exact theory does not imply, in general, that $u$ is explanatory closed, though it clearly implies that $\mathcal{C}(u)$ is explanatory closed.

As a preparation for what follows, we will now introduce the following special kind of production inference relations:

**Definition 8.9** A production inference relation will be called *dense* if $A \Rightarrow B$ holds only if $A \Rightarrow C$ and $C \Rightarrow B$, for some proposition $C$.

The above property is trivial, of course, for ordinary consequence relations (due to Reflexivity), but it is nontrivial for production relations. It corresponds to the following characteristic property of the production operator:

$$\mathcal{C}(u) \subseteq \mathcal{C}(\mathcal{C}(u)).$$

The above property says, in effect, that any set of propositions of the form $\mathcal{C}(u)$ is explanatory closed. But any such set is also a theory of a regular production relation. Consequently, the set of exact theories of a dense regular production relation has an especially simple structure:

**Lemma 8.24** *The nonmonotonic semantics of a dense regular production relation coincides with the set of all sets of propositions of the form $\mathcal{C}(u)$.*

Dense production relations will play an important role in the next section.

## 8.3 Production Inference and Abduction

Systems of abductive reasoning provide a primary example of nonmonotonic formalisms that are based on the explanatory closure assumption.

Such systems are designed to capture the relation between facts and their admissible explanations. In this section we will show that production inference relations, coupled with the nonmonotonic production semantics, allow us to provide a formal representation of abductive reasoning. In addition to specific results, this will give us also a broader perspective on the representation capabilities of production inference relations as a general-purpose formalism for nonmonotonic reasoning.

### 8.3.1 *Abductive systems and abductive semantics*

We will describe below a general formal representation of abductive reasoning that subsumes the majority of abductive frameworks suggested in the literature. It will serve as a basis for our subsequent constructions.

A general *abductive system* can be defined as a pair $\mathbb{A} = (\mathrm{Cn}, \mathcal{A})$, where Cn is a supraclassical Tarski consequence relation, while $\mathcal{A}$ is a distinguished set of propositions called *abducibles*. A proposition $A$ is *explainable* in an abductive system $\mathbb{A}$ if there exists a consistent set of abducibles $a \subseteq \mathcal{A}$ such that $A \in \mathrm{Cn}(a)$; in this case the set $a$ is called *an explanation* of $A$. Clearly, $A$ may have, in general, a number of different (and even incompatible) explanations.

In practical applications, the supraclassical consequence relation Cn is usually given indirectly by a generating conditional theory $\Delta$, namely by a set of inference rules of the form $a \vdash A$. A corresponding abductive system can be represented in this case by a pair $(\Delta, \mathcal{A})$. However, given a conditional theory $\Delta$, we can identify Cn with $\mathrm{Cn}_\Delta$—the least supraclassical consequence relation containing $\Delta$. Then $A \in \mathrm{Cn}(a)$ will hold if and only if $A$ is derivable from $a$ using the classical entailment and the rules from $\Delta$. Accordingly, the pair $(\Delta, \mathcal{A})$ can be faithfully represented by an abductive system $(\mathrm{Cn}_\Delta, \mathcal{A})$ as defined above.

In abductive systems, acceptance of propositions depends on existence of explanations, and consequently such systems sanction not only forward inferences determined by the associated consequence relation, but also backward inferences from facts to their possible explanations, as well as combinations of both. All these kinds of abductive inference can be captured formally by considering only theories of Cn that are generated by the abducibles. This suggests the following notion of an abductive semantics:

**Definition 8.10** The *abductive semantics* $\mathcal{S}_\mathbb{A}$ of an abductive system $\mathbb{A}$ is the set of theories $\{\mathrm{Cn}(a) \mid a \subseteq \mathcal{A}\}$.

Note that a consequence relation Cn is uniquely determined by the set of *all* its theories. Accordingly, by restricting the set of these theories to theories generated by abducibles, we obtain a semantic framework containing more information. Generally speaking, all the information that can be discerned from the abductive semantics of an abductive system can be seen as abductively implied by the latter. Recall, however, that any set of deductively closed theories determines a unique supraclassical Scott consequence relation. Moreover, in many cases the correspondence between sets of theories and Scott consequence relations is one-to-one (e.g., in a finite case—see Lemma 2.9). Accordingly, in most cases, the information embodied in the abductive semantics can be made explicit by considering the associated Scott consequence relation.

**Definition 8.11** An *abductive consequence relation* associated with an abductive system $\mathbb{A}$ is a supraclassical Scott consequence relation $\vdash_{\mathbb{A}}$ determined by the abductive semantics $\mathcal{S}_{\mathbb{A}}$.

The abductive consequence relation associated with an abductive system can be defined explicitly as follows:

$$b \vdash_{\mathbb{A}} c \;\equiv\; (\forall a \subseteq \mathcal{S}_{\mathbb{A}})(b \subseteq \mathrm{Cn}(a) \;\rightarrow\; c \cap \mathrm{Cn}(a) \neq \emptyset).$$

By the above description, $b \vdash_{\mathbb{A}} c$ holds if any set $a$ of abducibles that explains $b$ explains also at least one proposition from $c$.[3] In other words, $b \vdash_{\mathbb{A}} c$ holds if any explanation of $b$ is also an explanation of some $C \in c$.

The abductive consequence relation $\vdash_{\mathbb{A}}$ is an extension of Cn obtained by restricting the set of its theories. As a result, it describes not only forward explanatory relations, but also abductive inferences from propositions to their explanations. For example, if $C$ and $D$ are the only abducibles that imply $A$ in an abductive system, then we will have $A \vdash_{\mathbb{A}} C, D$. Speaking generally, the abductive consequence relation describes the *explanatory closure*, or *completion*, of an abductive system, and allows thereby to capture abduction by deduction (see [Console *et al.*, 1991; Konolige, 1992]).

**Example 8.2** The following abductive system describes a variant of the well-known example from [Pearl, 1987]. Assume that an abductive system

[3] A Tarski consequence relation of this kind has been used for the same purposes in [Lobo and Uzcátegui, 1997].

$\mathbb{A}$ is determined by the set $\Delta$ of rules

$$Rained \vdash Grasswet$$
$$Sprinkler \vdash Grasswet$$
$$Rained \vdash Streetwet,$$

and the set abducibles

$$\mathcal{A} = \{Rained, \neg Rained, Sprinkler, \neg Sprinkler, \neg Grassswet\}.$$

By stipulating that both *Rained* and $\neg$*Rained* are abducibles, we make *Rained* an independent (exogenous) parameter (and similarly for *Sprinkler*). However, since only $\neg$*Grassswet* is an abducible, non-wet grass does not require explanation, but wet grass does. Thus, any theory of $\mathcal{S}_{\mathbb{A}}$ that contains *Grasswet* should contain either *Rained*, or *Sprinkler*, and consequently we have

$$Grasswet \Vdash_{\mathbb{A}} Rained, Sprinkler.$$

Similarly, *Streetwet* implies in this sense both its only explanation *Rained* and a collateral effect *Grasswet*.

By the above construction, abductive reasoning with respect to a supraclassical consequence relation amounts to extending the latter to the corresponding abductive consequence relation. It turns out that this transformation is quite similar to circumscription of a consequence relation studied in Chapter 2.

Let us say that two consequence relations are $\mathcal{A}$-*equivalent*, for a set of abducibles $\mathcal{A}$, if they have the same rules of the form $a \vdash A$, where $a \subseteq \mathcal{A}$. Clearly, two consequence relations are $\mathcal{A}$-equivalent, if they provide precisely the same explanations. Consequently, $\mathcal{A}$-equivalence amounts to coincidence with respect to theories generated by abducibles. Moreover, as for circumscription, the associated abductive consequence relation is precisely the greatest consequence relation that produces the same explanations as the source consequence relation.

**Lemma 8.25** *Two consequence relations are $\mathcal{A}$-equivalent iff they determine the same abductive semantics. If $\mathbb{A} = (\mathrm{Cn}, \mathcal{A})$ is an abductive system, then $\vdash_{\mathbb{A}}$ is a greatest consequence relation among $\mathcal{A}$-equivalents of* Cn.

### 8.3.2 Abductive production inference

In order to translate abductive reasoning into the framework of production inference, we will slightly extend the relevant notion of explanation and say that an arbitrary set $u$ of propositions *explains* a proposition $A$ in an abductive system, if $A$ is explainable by the abducibles that are implied by $u$. Then the set of propositions that are explainable by $u$ will coincide with $\mathrm{Cn}(\mathrm{Cn}(u) \cap \mathcal{A})$.

Now, the main idea behind the following representation consists in viewing this latter notion of an explanation as a particular kind of production inference. In other words, $u$ will be taken to produce $A$ if it explains $A$.

**Definition 8.12** A *production inference relation associated with an abductive system* $\mathbb{A}$ is a production relation $\Rightarrow_{\mathbb{A}}$ determined by all bimodels of the form $(u, \mathrm{Cn}(u \cap \mathcal{A}))$, where $u$ is a consistent theory of Cn.

Note that the classical binary semantics described in the above definition is consistent, and therefore the associated production inference relation will always be regular.

To simplify the subsequent representation, we will assume that the set of abducibles $\mathcal{A}$ of an abductive system is closed with respect to conjunctions, that is, if $A$ and $B$ are abducibles, then $A \wedge B$ is also an abducible. In addition, in order to deal with limit cases, we will also assume that the constants $\mathbf{t}$ and $\mathbf{f}$ are abducibles. Then it turns out that the above defined production inference relation admits a very simple syntactic characterization. According to the description that follows, $A \Rightarrow_{\mathbb{A}} B$ holds if and only if $A$ implies some abducible that explains $B$.

**Lemma 8.26** *If* $\Rightarrow_{\mathbb{A}}$ *is a production inference relation associated with an abductive system* $\mathbb{A}$, *then*

$$A \Rightarrow_{\mathbb{A}} B \quad \textit{iff} \quad (\exists C \in \mathcal{A})(C \in \mathrm{Cn}(A) \ \& \ B \in \mathrm{Cn}(C)).$$

***Proof.*** Assume first that $C \in \mathrm{Cn}(A)$ and $B \in \mathrm{Cn}(C)$, for some $C \in \mathcal{A}$. Let $u$ be a Cn-theory such that $A \in u$. Then $C \in u$, and hence $C \in u \cap \mathcal{A}$. Consequently $B \in \mathrm{Cn}(u \cap \mathcal{A})$. This shows that $A \Rightarrow_{\mathbb{A}} B$ holds.

Assume now that $A \Rightarrow_{\mathbb{A}} B$ holds, and suppose first that $\mathbf{f} \in \mathrm{Cn}(A)$. But $\mathbf{f}$ is an abducible, and we have also $B \in \mathrm{Cn}(\mathbf{f})$, so the implication from left to right holds in this case. So, assume now that $\mathbf{f} \notin \mathrm{Cn}(A)$, and consider a consistent Cn-theory $\mathrm{Cn}(A)$. Then it must be the case that $B \in \mathrm{Cn}(\mathrm{Cn}(A) \cap \mathcal{A})$. If $\mathrm{Cn}(A) \cap \mathcal{A}$ is empty, we have $B \in \mathrm{Cn}(\mathbf{t})$ and $\mathbf{t} \in \mathrm{Cn}(A)$, for an abducible $\mathbf{t}$. Otherwise, since $\mathcal{A}$ is closed with respect to conjunctions, there must exist $C \in \mathcal{A}$ such that $C \in \mathrm{Cn}(A)$ and $B \in \mathrm{Cn}(C)$, as required. □

As a consequence of the above description, abducibles of an abductive system correspond precisely to 'reflexive' propositions of the associated production inference relation.

**Corollary 8.27** *If $\Rightarrow_{\mathbb{A}}$ is a production inference relation associated with an abductive system $\mathbb{A}$, then $C \Rightarrow_{\mathbb{A}} C$ if and only if $C$ is* Cn*-equivalent to an abducible from $\mathcal{A}$.*

Due to this correspondence, reflexive (self-explanatory) propositions of a production relation can be seen as abducibles, and hence we introduce the following definition:

**Definition 8.13** A proposition $A$ will be called an *abducible* of a production relation $\Rightarrow$, if $A \Rightarrow A$.

Note that the set of abducibles of a production inference relation conforms to our earlier agreement, namely it is closed with respect to conjunctions, and both **t** and **f** are abducibles.

Another important fact about abducibles of a production relation is that any set of abducibles is obviously explanatory closed. As a result, Lemma 8.21 implies

**Corollary 8.28** *If $a$ is a set of abducibles of a regular production relation $\Rightarrow$, then $\mathcal{C}(a) = \mathrm{Cn}_{\Rightarrow}(a)$, and $\mathcal{C}(a)$ is an exact theory of $\Rightarrow$.*

It turns out that production inference relations corresponding to abductive systems form a special class that is described in the next definition.

**Definition 8.14** A production inference relation will be called *abductive* if it is regular and satisfies

**(Abduction)** If $B \Rightarrow C$, then $B \Rightarrow A \Rightarrow C$, for some abducible $A$.

As can be seen, production inference in abductive production relations is always mediated by abducibles. Consequently, for such production relations, propositions are produced, in effect, by the derived set of abducibles: for any set $u$ of propositions,

$$\mathcal{C}(u) = \mathcal{C}(\mathcal{C}(u) \cap \mathcal{A}),$$

where $\mathcal{A}$ is the set of abducibles of $\Rightarrow$.

Clearly, any abductive production relation is dense, and consequently its exact theories are sets of the form $\mathcal{C}(u)$. Moreover, in our case we have that all exact theories are produced by abducibles:

**Lemma 8.29** *The nonmonotonic semantics of an abductive production relation is the set of all sets of propositions of the form $\mathcal{C}(u)$, for $u \subseteq \mathcal{A}$.*

***Proof.*** By Lemma 8.24, exact theories of an abductive production relation are the sets of the form $\mathcal{C}(u)$. But by the above equality, the latter sets coincide with $\mathcal{C}(\mathcal{C}(u) \cap \mathcal{A})$, and hence they are produced by abducibles. □

Now we will show that abductive production relations are precisely production inference relations that are generated by abductive systems.

**Theorem 8.30** *A production inference relation is abductive if and only if it is generated by an abductive system.*

***Proof.*** To begin with, we will verify that any production relation generated by an abductive system satisfies Abduction. Note first that if $C \in \mathcal{A}$, then, for any proposition $A$, $A \Rightarrow C$ holds iff $C \in \mathrm{Cn}(A)$, while $C \Rightarrow A$ holds iff $A \in \mathrm{Cn}(C)$. In addition, as we have mentioned, if $C \in \mathcal{A}$, then $C \Rightarrow C$. Given these facts, Abduction follows directly from Lemma 8.26.

In the other direction, assume that $\Rightarrow$ is an abductive production relation. Then we construct a *canonical* abductive system $\mathbb{A} = (\mathrm{Cn}, \mathcal{A})$ by taking $\mathcal{A}$ to be the set of abducibles of $\Rightarrow$, and Cn the least supraclassical consequence relation containing $\Rightarrow$. By Theorem 8.13, this consequence relation is definable as follows: $B \in \mathrm{Cn}(A) \equiv A \Rightarrow (A \rightarrow B)$.

Assume first that $A \Rightarrow B$. By Abduction, there is some $C$ such that $A \Rightarrow C$, $C \Rightarrow C$ and $C \Rightarrow B$. Consequently, $A \Rightarrow (A \rightarrow C)$ and $C \Rightarrow (C \rightarrow B)$, and therefore $C \in \mathcal{A}$, $C \in \mathrm{Cn}(A)$ and $B \in \mathrm{Cn}(C)$. In the other direction, if there exists $C \in \mathcal{A}$ such that $C \in \mathrm{Cn}(A)$ and $B \in \mathrm{Cn}(C)$, then $A \Rightarrow (A \rightarrow C)$, $C \Rightarrow (C \rightarrow B)$ and $C \Rightarrow C$. The last two rules imply $C \Rightarrow B$, and hence $A \wedge C \Rightarrow B$. Combined with the first rule, this gives us $A \Rightarrow B$ by Cut. Now the claim follows from Lemma 8.26. □

Finally, the following basic result shows that the abductive semantics of an abductive system coincides with the nonmonotonic production semantics of the associated abductive production relation.

**Theorem 8.31** *If $\Rightarrow_{\mathbb{A}}$ is a production inference relation corresponding to an abductive system $\mathbb{A}$, then the abductive semantics of $\mathbb{A}$ coincides with the nonmonotonic production semantics of $\Rightarrow_{\mathbb{A}}$.*

***Proof.*** By Lemma 8.26, $\mathcal{C}_{\mathbb{A}}(u) = \mathrm{Cn}(\mathrm{Cn}(u) \cap \mathcal{A})$, for any set $u$. If we take $u$ to be a set of abducibles from $\mathbb{A}$, we obtain $\mathcal{C}_{\mathbb{A}}(u) = \mathrm{Cn}(u)$. Now the result follows from Lemma 8.29. □

Due to the above results, abductive production relations, coupled with the nonmonotonic production semantics, can be seen as a faithful logical representation of abductive reasoning. Note that abductive production relations provide in this sense a syntax-independent description of abduction, since the set of abducibles is determined as a set of propositions having certain logical properties with respect to the production relation (namely reflexivity).

**Example 8.3** (*continued*) The following causal theory determines the abductive production relation corresponding to the Pearl's example, described earlier.

$$Rained \Rightarrow Grasswet \quad Sprinkler \Rightarrow Grasswet \quad Rained \Rightarrow Streetwet$$
$$Rained \Rightarrow Rained \qquad \neg Rained \Rightarrow \neg Rained$$
$$Sprinkler \Rightarrow Sprinkler \qquad \neg Sprinkler \Rightarrow \neg Sprinkler$$
$$\neg Grasswet \Rightarrow \neg Grasswet \qquad \neg Streetwet \Rightarrow \neg Streetwet$$

As follows from the preceding results, the nonmonotonic production semantics of this causal theory coincides the abductive semantics of the original abductive system, and hence it determines the same abductive inferences.

### 8.3.3 *Quasi-abductive production inference*

Now we are going to show that any production inference relation includes an important abductive subrelation; as we will see, in many regular situations the latter subrelation will determine the same nonmonotonic semantics.

Given a regular production relation $\Rightarrow$, we will define the following production relation:

$$A \Rightarrow^a B \equiv (\exists C)(A \Rightarrow C \Rightarrow C \Rightarrow B).$$

Then we have

**Theorem 8.32** *If $\Rightarrow$ is a regular production relation, then $\Rightarrow^a$ is the greatest abductive production relation included in $\Rightarrow$.*

***Proof.*** We need to check first that $\Rightarrow^a$ satisfies the postulates of regular production inference. Strengthening, Weakening, Truth and Falsity are obvious.

*And.* Assume that $A \Rightarrow^a B$ and $A \Rightarrow^a D$. Then there are $C_1$ and $C_2$ such that $A \Rightarrow C_1 \Rightarrow C_1 \Rightarrow B$ and $A \Rightarrow C_2 \Rightarrow C_2 \Rightarrow D$. Note that $C_1 \wedge C_2 \Rightarrow C_1 \wedge C_2$ holds by Strengthening and And, as well as $A \Rightarrow C_1 \wedge C_2$ and $C_1 \wedge C_2 \Rightarrow B \wedge D$. Hence $A \Rightarrow^a B \wedge D$. Thus, And holds.

*Cut.* Assume that $A \Rightarrow^a B$ and $A \wedge B \Rightarrow^a D$. Then there are $C_1$ and $C_2$ such that $A \Rightarrow C_1 \Rightarrow C_1 \Rightarrow B$ and $A \wedge B \Rightarrow C_2 \Rightarrow C_2 \Rightarrow D$. As before, we have $C_1 \wedge C_2 \Rightarrow C_1 \wedge C_2$. In addition, since $A \Rightarrow B$ (by Transitivity) and $A \wedge B \Rightarrow C_2$, we have $A \Rightarrow C_2$ by Cut, and therefore $A \Rightarrow C_1 \wedge C_2$. Also, $C_2 \Rightarrow D$ implies $C_1 \wedge C_2 \Rightarrow D$. Therefore, $A \Rightarrow^a D$, which shows that Cut holds for $\Rightarrow^a$.

Thus, $\Rightarrow^a$ is an abductive production relation. Moreover, if $A \Rightarrow^a B$, then $A \Rightarrow B$ by Transitivity, so $\Rightarrow^a$ is included in $\Rightarrow$.

Let $\Rightarrow_1$ be some abductive production relation that is included in $\Rightarrow$, and $A \Rightarrow_1 B$. By Abduction, there is $C$ such that $A \Rightarrow_1 C \Rightarrow_1 C \Rightarrow_1 B$. But $\Rightarrow_1$ is included in $\Rightarrow$, and therefore $A \Rightarrow C \Rightarrow C \Rightarrow B$. The latter implies $A \Rightarrow^a B$, which shows that $\Rightarrow_1$ is included in $\Rightarrow^a$. Thus, $\Rightarrow^a$ is the greatest abductive production relation included in $\Rightarrow$. □

It turns out that the above abductive subrelation of a production relation preserves many properties of the latter. For example, both have the same constraints, that is, $A \Rightarrow \mathbf{f}$ holds if and only if $A \Rightarrow^a \mathbf{f}$. Similarly, both have the same 'axioms': $\mathbf{t} \Rightarrow A$ holds iff $\mathbf{t} \Rightarrow^a A$. Last but not least, both have the same abducibles. The latter fact implies, in particular,

**Lemma 8.33** *The nonmonotonic semantics of $\Rightarrow^a$ is the set of all theories of $\Rightarrow$ of the form $\mathcal{C}(u)$, where $u$ is a set of abducibles of $\Rightarrow$.*

***Proof.*** By the definition of $\Rightarrow^a$, if $u$ is a set of abducibles, then $\mathcal{C}^a(u) = \mathcal{C}(u)$. Consequently, the result follows from Lemma 8.29. □

Let $\mathcal{A}_{\Rightarrow}$ denote the set of abducibles of $\Rightarrow$, and $\mathrm{Cn}_{\Rightarrow}$ the least supraclassical consequence relation including $\Rightarrow$. Then the following result shows that the abductive system $(\mathrm{Cn}_{\Rightarrow}, \mathcal{A}_{\Rightarrow})$ generates $\Rightarrow^a$ as its associated production relation.

**Lemma 8.34** *If $\Rightarrow$ is a regular production relation, then its abductive subrelation $\Rightarrow^a$ is generated by an abductive system* $(\mathrm{Cn}_{\Rightarrow}, \mathcal{A}_{\Rightarrow})$.

***Proof.*** We have to show that $A \Rightarrow^a B$ holds if and only if $C \in \mathrm{Cn}_{\Rightarrow}(A)$ and $B \in \mathrm{Cn}_{\Rightarrow}(C)$, for some $C$ such that $C \Rightarrow C$.

If $A \Rightarrow^a B$, then $A \Rightarrow C \Rightarrow B$, for some abducible $C$. Consequently, $A \Rightarrow (A \to C)$ and $C \Rightarrow (C \to B)$ by Weakening, and hence $C \in \mathrm{Cn}_{\Rightarrow}(A)$ and $B \in \mathrm{Cn}_{\Rightarrow}(C)$. This gives us the direction from left to right.

Assume now that $C \Rightarrow C$, $A \Rightarrow (A \to C)$ and $C \Rightarrow (C \to B)$. Then $A \wedge C \Rightarrow C$ by Strengthening, and hence $A \Rightarrow C$ by Cut. Also, $C \Rightarrow B$ by And and Weakening. Consequently, $A \Rightarrow^a B$. □

The nonmonotonic production semantics is based on the explanation closure assumption, according to which any accepted proposition should be produced, or explained, by other accepted propositions. But the latter should also be explained by accepted propositions, and so on. It should be clear that if our 'explanatory resources' are limited (for example, if our language is finite), such an explanation process should stop somewhere. More exactly, it should reach abducible (self-explanatory) propositions. This indicates that in many regular cases the nonmonotonic semantics of a production relation should coincide with the nonmonotonic semantics of its abductive subrelation. Below we will make this claim precise.

**Definition 8.15** A production relation will be called *quasi-abductive* if it is nonmonotonically equivalent to its abductive subrelation.

The next definition will give us an important sufficient condition for quasi-abductivity.

**Definition 8.16** A production relation $\Rightarrow$ will be called *well-founded* if any infinite sequence $\{A_0, A_1, A_2, \dots\}$ of propositions such that $A_{n+1} \Rightarrow A_n$, for every $n \geq 0$, contains an abducible.

The above definition describes a variant of a standard notion of well-foundedness with respect to the partial order determined by a production relation. Namely, it says that any infinite descending sequence of productions should always contain reflexive elements. The following lemma provides an alternative description of well-foundedness.

**Lemma 8.35** *A production relation is well-founded if and only if any explanatory closed set of propositions contains an abducible.*

***Proof.*** A chain $\{A_0, A_1, A_2, \dots\}$ of propositions such that $A_{n+1} \Rightarrow A_n$ is clearly explanatory closed; this gives us the direction from right to left. In the other direction, if $A \in u \subseteq \mathcal{C}(u)$, then $u$ contains an infinite chain $\{A, A_1, A_2, \dots\}$ such that $A_1 \Rightarrow A$ and $A_{n+1} \Rightarrow A_n$, for any $n$. If $\Rightarrow$ is well-founded, this chain should contain an abducible that belongs to $u$. □

It should be clear that any production relation in a finite language is well-founded. Moreover, let us say that a regular production relation is *finitary*, if it is a least regular production relation containing some finite causal theory. Then we have

**Theorem 8.36** *Any finitary regular production relation is well-founded.*

***Proof.*** Let $\Rightarrow$ be a regular production relation determined by a finite causal theory $\Delta$, and assume that $\{A_i \mid i \geq 0\}$ is an infinite sequence of propositions such that $A_{n+1} \Rightarrow A_n$, for any $n \geq 0$.

Let us say that a proposition $C$ is *explicit* with respect to $\Rightarrow$ if it is a conjunction of heads of some rules from $\Delta$. Since $\Delta$ is finite, the set of explicit propositions will also be finite (up to logical equivalence). Moreover, Proposition 8.11 implies that $A \Rightarrow B$ holds only if $A \Rightarrow C$, for some explicit C such that $C \vDash B$. This means, in particular, that in the above infinite production sequence, any production is 'mediated' by an explicit proposition: $A_{i+1} \Rightarrow C_i \vDash A_i$.

Since the set of explicit propositions is finite, there must exist at least two propositions $A_j, A_k$ in the sequence such that $j > k$, $A_{j+1} \Rightarrow C \vDash A_j$ and $A_{k+1} \Rightarrow C \vDash A_k$, for some explicit $C$. Then we have $C \vDash A_j$ and $A_j \Rightarrow C$ (by Transitivity), and hence $A_j \Rightarrow A_j$ by Weakening. Hence, any sequence of productions in $\Rightarrow$ should be well-founded. □

Finally, the following result shows that a well-founded production relation determines precisely the same nonmonotonic production semantics as its abductive subrelation.

**Theorem 8.37** *Any well-founded regular production relation is quasi-abductive.*

***Proof.*** By Lemma 8.33, any exact theory of $\Rightarrow^a$ is an exact theory of $\Rightarrow$. Assume that $u$ is an exact theory of $\Rightarrow$, that is, $u = \mathcal{C}(u)$. Clearly $\mathcal{C}^a(u) \subseteq u$. Let $A_0 \in u$. Then $A_0 \in \mathcal{C}(u)$, and hence there must exist $A_1 \in u$ such that $A_1 \Rightarrow A_0$. Repeating this argument, we obtain an infinite chain $\{A_0, A_1, A_2, \dots\}$ of propositions such that all $A_i$ belong to $u$ and $A_{i+1} \Rightarrow A_i$, for any $i \geq 0$. But our production relation is well-founded, so there must exist some abducible $A_n$ in the chain. Clearly, $A_n \in u$ and $A_n \Rightarrow A_n \Rightarrow A_0$ (by Transitivity). Hence $A_n \Rightarrow^a A_0$, and therefore $A_0 \in \mathcal{C}^a(u)$. This shows that $u \subseteq \mathcal{C}^a(u)$, and hence $u$ is an exact theory of $\Rightarrow^a$. □

Since abductive production relations correspond exactly to abductive systems, the above result shows that in the well-founded case the nonmonotonic production semantics of a regular production relation is describable by some abductive system, and vice versa. As a general conclusion, however, we can say that production inference constitutes a proper generalization of abductive reasoning, a generalization that goes beyond well-foundedness.

### 8.3.4 *Abduction in literal causal theories*

It turns out that a certain well-known class of abductive systems can be directly interpreted as causal theories. The description below will show, in effect, that the production (or explanatory) reading of abductive systems has long been present in the study of abduction and diagnosis.

By a *literal* inference rule we will mean a rule of the form $a \vdash l$, where $l$ is a propositional literal, and $a$ a set of literals. In what follows, the constants **t** and **f** will also be treated as literals. A conditional theory $\Delta$ will be called *literal* one, if it consists only of literal rules. Finally, an abductive system $\mathbb{A} = (\Delta, \mathcal{A})$ will be called *literal* one, if $\Delta$ is a literal conditional theory, and the set of abducibles $\mathcal{A}$ is also a set of literals.

The above simplified abductive framework has been extensively studied and used in the theory of diagnosis under the name 'causal theory' (see, e.g., [Console *et al.*, 1991; Konolige, 1992; Konolige, 1994; Poole, 1994]). The name has a different meaning in our study, namely it denotes an arbitrary set of production rules. It will be shown, however, that the these two notions of a causal theory are closely related.

Recall that any conditional theory can also be viewed as a causal theory in our sense. Moreover, it has been shown earlier that abducibles can be incorporated into causal theories by accepting corresponding reflexive rules $A \Rightarrow A$. Accordingly, for an abductive system $(\Delta, \mathcal{A})$, we will introduce a causal theory $\Delta_{\mathcal{A}}$ which is the union of $\Delta$ (viewed as a set of production rules) and the set $\{l \Rightarrow l \mid l \in \mathcal{A}\}$. In addition, $\Rightarrow_{\Delta_{\mathcal{A}}}$ will denote the least regular production relation containing $\Delta_{\mathcal{A}}$.

To begin with, it is easy to verify that the abductive semantics of $\mathbb{A}$ is included in the nonmonotonic production semantics of $\Rightarrow_{\Delta_{\mathcal{A}}}$.

**Lemma 8.38** *If $a \subseteq \mathcal{A}$, then $\mathrm{Cn}_{\Delta}(a)$ is an exact theory of $\Rightarrow_{\Delta_{\mathcal{A}}}$.*

***Proof.*** Note that $\Delta$ and $\Delta_{\mathcal{A}}$ are equivalent as conditional theories, that is, $\mathrm{Cn}_{\Delta}(u) = \mathrm{Cn}_{\Delta_{\mathcal{A}}}(u)$, for any $u$. Also, any proposition from $\mathcal{A}$ is clearly an abducible in $\Rightarrow_{\Delta_{\mathcal{A}}}$. Now the result follows from Corollary 8.28. □

However, the reverse inclusion in the above lemma does not hold, even in our present, literal case, and it is important to clarify the reasons why this happens. First of all, the production relation $\Rightarrow_{\Delta_\mathcal{A}}$ is not well-founded, in general, so it may have exact theories that are not generated by abducibles. Second, even in the well-founded case, the causal theory $\Delta_\mathcal{A}$ may create new abducibles of its own, if some of the propositions happen to be interderivable. Taking a simplest example, if we have that both $p \vdash q$ and $q \vdash p$ belong to $\Delta$, then both $p$ and $q$ will be abducibles of $\Rightarrow_{\Delta_\mathcal{A}}$.

Both the above reasons for a discrepancy will disappear, however, if $\Delta$ is an *acyclic* conditional theory. As a matter of fact, a restriction of this kind has been used extensively in the literature—see, e.g., [Console *et al.*, 1991; Poole, 1994]. Pearl's belief networks [Pearl, 1988] can also be seen as belonging to this class, because they are defined in terms of directed acyclic graphs of dependencies.

By a (literal) *dependency graph* of a literal conditional theory $\Delta$ we will mean the directed graph such that its nodes are the literals occurring in $\Delta$, while the arcs are the pairs of literals $(l, m)$, for which $\Delta$ contains a rule of the form $l, a \vdash m$. As usual, a literal conditional theory $\Delta$ will be called *acyclic*, if its dependency graph does not contain infinite descending paths. In what follows, we will use, however, a weaker condition that will be sufficient for our purposes.

**Definition 8.17** A literal abductive system $\mathbb{A} = (\Delta, \mathcal{A})$ will be called *abductively well-founded*, if any infinite descending path in the dependency graph of $\Delta$ contains an abducible from $\mathcal{A}$.

As can be seen from the above definition, an abductive system is abductively well-founded, if it does not have infinite descending chains of dependencies that consist of non-abducibles only. This implies, in particular, that non-abducibles do not form loops of dependencies. Clearly, any acyclic theory will also be abductively well-founded. Note also that we do not require that abducibles should not appear in heads of the rules, a condition often imposed on such abductive systems.

The following result shows that in this case the causal theory $\Delta_\mathcal{A}$ captures the 'abductive content' of the source abductive system.

**Theorem 8.39** *If $\mathbb{A}$ is an abductively well-founded literal abductive system, then the abductive semantics of $\mathbb{A}$ coincides with the nonmonotonic semantics of $\Rightarrow_{\Delta_\mathcal{A}}$.*

***Proof.*** In view of the preceding lemma, we have to show only that any exact theory of $\Rightarrow_{\Delta_\mathcal{A}}$ belongs to the abductive semantics of $\mathbb{A}$. Let $u$ be an exact theory of $\Rightarrow_{\Delta_\mathcal{A}}$, that is, $u = \mathcal{C}_{\Delta_\mathcal{A}}(u)$. We will show first that $u$

coincides with $\mathcal{C}_{\Delta_\mathcal{A}}(u \cap \mathcal{A})$. Note that, due to the literal form of the rules from $\Delta_\mathcal{A}$, $u$ is actually a logical closure of some set of literals. So assume that $u$ is not included in $\mathcal{C}_{\Delta_\mathcal{A}}(u \cap \mathcal{A})$. Then there is a literal $l \in u$ such that $l \notin \mathcal{C}_{\Delta_\mathcal{A}}(u \cap \mathcal{A})$. This is possible only if $l$ is not an abducible. But $l \in \mathcal{C}_{\Delta_\mathcal{A}}(u)$, so by Corollary 8.15, $\Delta$ must contain a rule $a \Rightarrow l$ such that $a \subseteq u$. Clearly, $a \nsubseteq u \cap \mathcal{A}$, so $a$ should contain a non-abducible, say $l_1$. Repeating this argument, we obtain an infinite descending path of non-abducibles $l_i$, for $i > 0$, contrary to our assumption that $\mathbb{A}$ is abductively well-founded. Hence $u$ coincides with $\mathcal{C}_{\Delta_\mathcal{A}}(u \cap \mathcal{A})$. But any set of abducibles is explanatory closed, so by Lemma 8.21, $u$ coincides with $\mathrm{Cn}_{\Delta_\mathcal{A}}(u \cap \mathcal{A})$, and hence with $\mathrm{Cn}_\Delta(u \cap \mathcal{A})$ (since $\Delta$ and $\Delta_\mathcal{A}$ determine the same consequence relation), which shows that $u$ belongs to the abductive semantics of $\mathbb{A}$. □

The above result shows that, from the perspective of abductive reasoning, abductively well-founded literal conditional theories can be viewed directly as causal theories.

## 8.4 Basic and Causal Production Inference

Following [Makinson and van der Torre, 2000], a production inference relation will be called *basic* if it satisfies

**(Or)** If $A \Rightarrow C$ and $B \Rightarrow C$, then $A \vee B \Rightarrow C$.

The above inference rule sanctions reasoning by cases, and hence basic production relations can already be seen as systems of *objective* production inference, namely as systems of reasoning about complete worlds.

The Or postulate corresponds to the following characteristic condition on derivability: for any deductively closed sets $u, v$:

$$\mathcal{C}(u \cap v) = \mathcal{C}(u) \cap \mathcal{C}(v).$$

As a consequence of this condition, the set of propositions produced by a theory $u$ coincides with the set of propositions that are produced by every world containing $u$:

$$\mathcal{C}(u) = \bigcap\{\mathcal{C}(\alpha) \mid u \subseteq \alpha\}.$$

Let us say that a production rule is *clausal*, if it has the form $\bigwedge l_i \Rightarrow \bigvee l_j$, where $l_i, l_j$ are classical literals. A causal theory will be called *clausal*, if it contains only clausal rules.

Note that, for any production inference relation, a rule $A \Rightarrow B \wedge C$ is equivalent to the pair of rules $A \Rightarrow B$ and $A \Rightarrow C$ (due to And and Weakening). Now, for basic production inference, a rule $A \vee B \Rightarrow C$ is equivalent to the pair of rules $A \Rightarrow C$ and $B \Rightarrow C$ (by Or and Strengthening). Consequently, we obtain the following important fact about basic production inference:

**Lemma 8.40** *For a basic production inference, any causal theory is reducible to a clausal causal theory.*

For any causal theory $\Delta$, a least basic production relation containing $\Delta$ will be denoted by $\Rightarrow^b_\Delta$. The following characterization of this relation has been obtained in [Makinson and van der Torre, 2000]:

**Proposition 8.41** *For any set of propositions $u$ and any proposition $A$,*

$$u \Rightarrow^b_\Delta A \textit{ if and only if } A \in \mathrm{Th}(\Delta(\alpha)), \textit{ for every world } \alpha \supseteq u.$$

The proof of this result can be obtained from the proof of the completeness theorem, given in the next section.

### 8.4.1 *Possible worlds semantics*

The semantic characterization of basic production relations can be obtained from the general classical binary semantics by restricting the set of bimodels to world-based ones, namely to bimodels of the form $(\alpha, \beta)$, where $\alpha, \beta$ are worlds. Generalizing this setting a little, the corresponding binary semantics can be defined as a usual *relational possible worlds model* $\mathbb{W} = (W, \mathcal{B}, V)$, where $W$ is a set of possible worlds, $\mathcal{B}$ is a binary accessibility relation on $W$, and $V$ is a valuation function assigning each possible world a propositional interpretation. The following definition provides the corresponding notion of validity for productions:

**Definition 8.18** A production rule $A \Rightarrow B$ will be said to be *valid* in a possible worlds model $(W, \mathcal{B}, V)$ if, for any pair of worlds $\alpha, \beta \in W$ such that $\alpha\mathcal{B}\beta$, if $A$ holds in $\alpha$, then $B$ holds in $\beta$.

We will denote by $\Rightarrow_{\mathbb{W}}$ the set of all productions that are valid in a possible worlds model $\mathbb{W}$. It can be easily verified that this set is already closed with respect Or, so it forms a basic production relation. In order to prove completeness, for any basic production relation $\Rightarrow$ we will construct its *canonical possible worlds model* $\mathbb{W}_{\Rightarrow}$ as a triple $\mathbb{W}_{\Rightarrow} = (W, \mathcal{B}, V)$ such that $W$ is a set of all worlds (maximal classically consistent sets), $V$ is a function assigning each world its corresponding classical interpretation, while $\mathcal{B}$ is a relation on $W$ defined as follows:

$$\alpha\mathcal{B}\beta \equiv \mathcal{C}(\alpha) \subseteq \beta.$$

Then the following result shows that this semantics is strongly complete for the source production relation.

**Lemma 8.42** *If $\mathbb{W}_{\Rightarrow}$ is the canonical semantics of a basic production relation $\Rightarrow$, then, for any set $u$ of propositions and any $A$,*

$$u \Rightarrow A \textit{ iff } A \in \beta, \textit{ for any } \alpha, \beta \in W \textit{ such that } \alpha\mathcal{B}\beta \textit{ and } u \subseteq \alpha.$$

***Proof.*** If $u \Rightarrow A$ and $u \subseteq \alpha$, for a world $\alpha$, then $A \in \mathcal{C}(\alpha)$, and therefore $A \in \beta$, for any world $\beta$ that includes $\mathcal{C}(\alpha)$. Thus, $u \Rightarrow A$ is valid in the canonical semantics. In the other direction, if $u \not\Rightarrow A$, then by Lemma 8.2, $u$ is included in a maximal deductively closed set $\alpha$ that does not produce $A$. Now, by the rule Or, $B \vee C \in \alpha$ only if either $B \in \alpha$ or $C \in \alpha$. Hence $\alpha$ should be a world. Now since $\mathcal{C}(\alpha)$ is deductively closed, there must exist a world $\beta$ containing $\mathcal{C}(\alpha)$ and such that $A \notin \beta$. Clearly, $(\alpha, \beta)$ is a bimodel that refutes $u \Rightarrow A$. □

As a general conclusion, we obtain

**Corollary 8.43** *$\Rightarrow$ is a basic production relation if and only if it has a possible worlds semantics.*

The above semantics immediately suggests a modal translation of production rules described in [Makinson and van der Torre, 2000] (see also [Turner, 1999]). Namely, let $\Box$ be the usual modal operator definable in a possible worlds model: $\Box A$ holds in $\alpha$ iff $A$ holds in all $\beta$ such that $\alpha R\beta$. Then the validity of $A \Rightarrow B$ in a possible worlds model is equivalent to validity of the formula $A \rightarrow \Box B$. Consequently, causal rules are representable by modal formulas of the latter form.

#### 8.4.1.1 *D-validity*

It turns out that basic production inference relations can be given an alternative semantic representation in the framework of arbitrary classical binary semantics. This semantic representation will turn out to be instructive in comparing production inference and default logic in Chapter 9.

**Definition 8.19** A production rule $A \Rightarrow B$ will be said to be *d-valid* in a classical binary semantics $\mathcal{B}$ if, for any bimodel $(u, v) \in \mathcal{B}$, either $\neg A \in v$, or $B \in u$. $\Rightarrow^d_{\mathcal{B}}$ will denote the set of all production rules that are d-valid in $\mathcal{B}$.

Note that d-validity coincides with plain validity for possible worlds models. Moreover, the following lemma shows that the above notion of d-validity always determines a basic production relation.

**Lemma 8.44** *If $\mathcal{B}$ is a classical binary semantics, then $\Rightarrow^d_{\mathcal{B}}$ is a basic production relation.*

***Proof.*** Truth, Falsity, And and Weakening are immediate, so we will check only Strengthening and Or.

Assume that $A \vDash B$ and $B \Rightarrow^d_{\mathcal{B}} C$, and let $(u, v)$ be a bimodel from $\mathcal{B}$ such that $\neg A \notin u$. Since $u$ is deductively closed, we have $\neg B \notin u$, and therefore $B \Rightarrow^d_{\mathcal{B}} C$ implies $C \in v$. Consequently, $A \Rightarrow C$ is also d-valid in $\mathcal{B}$, and hence Strengthening holds.

Assume now that $A \Rightarrow^d_{\mathcal{B}} C$ and $B \Rightarrow^d_{\mathcal{B}} C$, and let $(u, v)$ be an arbitrary bimodel from $\mathcal{B}$ such that $\neg(A \vee B) \notin v$. Since $v$ is deductively closed, we have that either $\neg A \notin v$, or $\neg B \notin v$. In the first case $A \Rightarrow^d_{\mathcal{B}} C$ implies $C \in u$, while in the second one the same result follows from $B \Rightarrow^d_{\mathcal{B}} C$. Consequently $A \vee B \Rightarrow C$ is d-valid in $\mathcal{B}$, and therefore Or also holds. □

The following result shows that basic production relations are actually complete for this semantics. The proof is immediate from the preceding lemma and the fact that, for possible worlds models, d-validity coincides with plain validity.

**Lemma 8.45** *A production relation is basic iff it coincides with the set of productions that are d-valid in some classical binary semantics.*

The reader should be warned at this point that we do not have strong completeness here (cf. Lemma 8.42). The reason is that the extension of production rules to rules with *sets* of premises does not yield a transparent semantic description in terms of d-validity.

### 8.4.2 *Production inference vs. biconsequence relations*

Recall that the binary semantics of biconsequence relations is a set of bimodels that can be viewed as pairs of propositional interpretations. In other words, a binary semantics is just a binary relation on the set of classical interpretations. Furthermore, the local four-valued connectives behave just as ordinary classical connectives with respect to these interpretations. Accordingly, the above possible worlds semantics of basic production inference demonstrates, in effect, that basic production inference relations constitute a logical counterpart of biconsequence relations for the language of local classical connectives. This correspondence can be made precise as follows.

For any biconsequence relation $\Vdash$ in the language containing the local classical connectives, we define the following set of production rules:

$$\Rightarrow_{\Vdash} = \{A \Rightarrow B \mid \Vdash B : A\}$$

$\Rightarrow_{\Vdash}$ will be called the *production subrelation* of $\Vdash$.

**Theorem 8.46**

- $\Rightarrow_{\Vdash}$ *is a basic production inference relation.*
- *For any basic production inference relation* $\Rightarrow$ *there exists a unique biconsequence relation in the language with the local connectives that has* $\Rightarrow$ *as its production subrelation.*

***Proof.*** The fact that $\Rightarrow_{\Vdash}$ is a production inference relation follows immediately from the semantic characterization of the bisequents $\Vdash B : A$ in the canonical semantics for biconsequence relations.

Given a production inference relation $\Rightarrow$, we can construct the associated biconsequence relation directly as the following set of bisequents:

$$\{a : b \Vdash c : d \mid \bigwedge(\neg b \cup d) \Rightarrow \bigvee(\neg a \cup c)\}.$$

It can be verified that the above set constitutes a biconsequence relation satisfying all the rules for the local classical connectives. In addition, we have that $A \Rightarrow B$ holds if and only if $\Vdash B{:}A$, so $\Rightarrow$ is a production subrelation of $\Vdash$. Moreover, for any biconsequence relation in the language with the local connectives, we have that $a : b \Vdash c : d$ is inter-derivable with $\Vdash \bigvee(\neg a \cup c) : \bigwedge(\neg b \cup d)$ (see Lemma 4.10), so such a biconsequence relation is uniquely determined by its production subrelation. □

The above correspondence shows, in effect, that production inference relations constitute a logical formalism that is fully equivalent to biconsequence relations with local classical connectives. By this correspondence, a production rule $A \Rightarrow B$ can be seen as a general assumption-based conditional saying that if $A$ is assumed, then $B$ should (objectively) hold.

Recall now that any biconsequence relation in a language with only four-valued connectives is equivalent to a unique biconsequence relation without connectives, and therefore it is equivalent to a unique biconsequence relation in the language with the local connectives. In this sense, any biconsequence relation in a four-valued language will be equivalent to some basic production relation.

Among many other things, the correspondence between biconsequence relations and basic production relations immediately suggests that basic production inference relations can also serve as a fully representative formalism for four-valued reasoning. The description that follows makes this idea precise.

Let us treat production rules as rules in the four-valued language of local classical connectives. Then we can directly define the notion of validity of production rules with respect to a four-valued semantics:

**Definition 8.20** A production rule $A \Rightarrow B$ will be said to be *valid* in a set of four-valued interpretations **I** when

$$\nu \dashv A \text{ or } \nu \models B, \text{ for any } \nu \in \mathbf{I}.$$

Let us denote by $\Rightarrow_{\mathbf{I}}$ the set of all production rules that are valid in **I**. Then, as an immediate consequence of the above correspondence between basic production relations and biconsequence relations, we obtain

**Theorem 8.47** *A set of rules* $\Rightarrow$ *is a basic production inference relation iff* $\Rightarrow = \Rightarrow_{\mathbf{I}}$, *for some set of four-valued interpretations* **I**.

The above result shows that the four-valued semantics gives a complete semantic characterization of basic production inference relations. In particular, we can freely use any four-valued connective in this setting by supplying appropriate axioms that are 'translations' of the corresponding rules for this connective in biconsequence relations. Thus, the following rules provide a complete characterization of the global negation and ht-negation in the framework of production inference:

$$\neg A \Rightarrow \sim A \qquad \sim A \Rightarrow \neg A$$
$$A \Rightarrow \neg\!\sim\! A \qquad \neg\!\sim\! A \Rightarrow A$$
$$\neg A \Rightarrow -A \qquad -A \wedge A \Rightarrow \mathbf{f}$$
$$A \Rightarrow \neg - A \qquad \neg - A \wedge \neg A \Rightarrow \mathbf{f}.$$

A similar axiomatization can be given for all the other four-valued connectives of interest for our study.

Recall now that all the four-valued connectives are eliminable in the framework of biconsequence relations. This fact can now be used to show that *all the non-local four-valued connectives are eliminable in the context of production inference relations.* Thus, the following equivalences show how we can eliminate the global and ht-negation:

$$A\wedge \sim C \Rightarrow B \;\equiv\; A \Rightarrow B \vee C \qquad A \Rightarrow B \vee \sim C \;\equiv\; A \wedge C \Rightarrow B$$
$$A \wedge \neg\sim C \Rightarrow B \;\equiv\; A \Rightarrow C \to B \qquad A \Rightarrow B \vee \neg\sim C \;\equiv\; A \wedge \neg C \Rightarrow B$$

$$A \wedge -C \Rightarrow B \;\equiv\; A \wedge \neg C \Rightarrow B \qquad A \Rightarrow B \vee -C \;\equiv\; A \wedge C \Rightarrow B$$
$$A \wedge \neg - C \Rightarrow B \;\equiv\; A \wedge C \Rightarrow B \qquad A \Rightarrow B \vee \neg - C \;\equiv\; A \wedge \neg C \Rightarrow B.$$

The above equivalences show, in effect, that both these negation connectives behave similarly in heads of the production rules, and that $-$ reduces to the classical negation in the bodies of such rules[4]. On the other hand, they show also that using each of these negations, we can move all premises to heads of production rules, and hence reduce any such rule to a rule of the form $\mathbf{t} \Rightarrow A$:

$$A \Rightarrow B \;\equiv\; \mathbf{t} \Rightarrow -A \vee B \;\equiv\; \mathbf{t} \Rightarrow \sim A \vee B.$$

The above equivalences provide, in effect, possible ways of translating basic production inference into ordinary four-valued logics.

As a last application of the correspondence between basic production inference and four-valued logics, recall that four-valued logics can be translated into classical logic by doubling the set of atoms (see Sec. 4.1.7). This translation can now be immediately transferred to basic production inference relations.

For a classical formula $A$, we will denote by $A'$ the result of replacing each propositional atom $p$ with a new atom $p'$. Then, for a production rule $\rho = A \Rightarrow B$, we will denote by $[\rho]$ the classical formula $A \to B'$. Similarly, for a causal theory $\Delta$, we will denote by $[\Delta]$ the corresponding set of classical translations. Then Theorem 4.11 implies[5]

**Corollary 8.48** *A rule $A \Rightarrow B$ is derivable from a causal theory $\Delta$ with respect to a basic production inference if and only if $[\Delta] \vDash A \to B'$.*

8.4.2.1 *Production inference as argumentation*

Due to the established correspondence between basic production inference, on the one hand, and biconsequence relations and four-valued semantics,

[4] Note that $- - A$ is equivalent to $\neg - A$.
[5] Cf. [Makinson and van der Torre, 2000].

on the other hand, we also obtain an amazingly simple correspondence between production inference and argumentation. Namely, given a basic production relation $\Rightarrow$, we can define the associated (propositional) attack relation as follows:

$$A \hookrightarrow B \;\equiv\; A \Rightarrow \neg B. \tag{PA}$$

In addition, given a propositional attack relation, we can define the corresponding production relation:

$$A \Rightarrow B \;\equiv\; A \hookrightarrow \neg B. \tag{AP}$$

**Lemma 8.49** *If $\Rightarrow$ is a basic production relation, then the relation $\hookrightarrow$ defined by (PA) is a propositional attack relation, and vice versa, if $\hookrightarrow$ is a propositional attack relation, then the relation $\Rightarrow$ defined by (AP) is a basic production relation.*

***Proof.*** Immediate from the fact that, under the above translations, the axiomatization of a propositional attack relation (see Definition 7.19) corresponds precisely to the axiomatization of basic production inference. □

The above correspondences show, in effect, that basic production inference and (propositional) argumentation are just terminological variants of the same basic notion of explanation. This correspondence is extendable also to the associated nonmonotonic semantics.

### 8.4.3 *Causal inference*

Now we will consider production relations that are both basic and regular.

**Definition 8.21** A production relation will be called *causal* if it satisfies Or and Cut.

Causal inference relations enjoy the properties of both basic and regular production relations. In particular, since they are basic, causal inference can also be considered as a particular (namely, regular) kind of objective production inference. Moreover, production rules of a causal inference relation can already be interpreted as truly *causal rules*, since they provide a natural formal representation of ordinary causal assertions.

An interesting syntactic fact about causal inference relations is that the Cut rule turns out to be equivalent to Coherence (see Sec. 8.1.3).

**Lemma 8.50** *For basic production relations, Cut is equivalent to Coherence.*

***Proof.*** It has been shown earlier that, for any production relation, Cut implies Constraint (and hence Coherence). Assume now that Coherence holds, and we have $A \Rightarrow B$ and $A \wedge B \Rightarrow C$. Then the former implies $A \wedge \neg B \Rightarrow \neg(A \wedge \neg B)$ by Strengthening and Weakening, and therefore $A \wedge \neg B \Rightarrow \mathbf{f}$ by Coherence[6]. Consequently, $A \wedge \neg B \Rightarrow C$ by Weakening, and therefore $A \Rightarrow C$ by Or. Thus, Cut holds. □

Another important fact about causal relations is the following decomposition of causal rules:

**Lemma 8.51** *Any causal rule $A \Rightarrow B$ is equivalent to a pair of rules $A \wedge \neg B \Rightarrow \mathbf{f}$ and $A \wedge B \Rightarrow B$.*

***Proof.*** The direction from left to right is immediate. In the other direction, if $A \wedge \neg B \Rightarrow \mathbf{f}$ and $A \wedge B \Rightarrow B$, then $A \wedge \neg B \Rightarrow B$ by Weakening, and hence $A \Rightarrow B$ by Or. □

Causal rules of the form $A \wedge B \Rightarrow B$ are logically trivial, but they play an important explanatory role in causal reasoning. Namely, they say that, in any causally explained interpretation in which $A$ holds, we can freely accept $B$, since it is self-explanatory in this context. Accordingly, such rules will be called *explanatory rules* in what follows.

Since causal inference is a special kind of an objective (world-based) inference, a constraint $A \wedge \neg B \Rightarrow \mathbf{f}$ says, in effect, that the classical implication $A \to B$ should hold in any causally consistent world.

Now the above lemma says that any causal rule can be decomposed into a constraint and an explanatory rule. This decomposition neatly delineates two kinds of information conveyed by causal rules. One is a factual information that constraints the set of admissible models, while the other is an explanatory information describing what propositions are caused (explainable) in such models[7]. As we will see later, this decomposition allows to give a more concise description of the informational content of causal theories.

Now we will turn to a semantic description of causal inference. It has been shown earlier that possible worlds models with arbitrary accessibility relations provide a semantics for basic production relations. It turns out that causal inference relations are determined by possible worlds models in which the accessibility relation is *quasi-reflexive*, that is, satisfies the following condition for any two worlds:

[6] This shows, in effect, that Constraint and Coherence are equivalent rules.
[7] Cf. a similar decomposition of causal rules in [Thielscher, 1997].

(Quasi-Reflexivity) If $\alpha R\beta$, then $\alpha R\alpha$.

The next lemma shows that quasi-reflexive models determine causal inference relations.

**Lemma 8.52** *A production relation determined by a quasi-reflexive possible worlds model is causal.*

***Proof.*** Suppose that $(W, R, V)$ is a quasi-reflexive model in which $A \Rightarrow B$ and $A \wedge B \Rightarrow C$ are valid, while $A \Rightarrow C$ is not valid. Then there are worlds $\alpha, \beta$ such that $\alpha R\beta$, $A \in \alpha$ and $C \notin \beta$. Consequently, $\alpha R\alpha$ by quasi-reflexivity, and hence $A \Rightarrow B$ implies that $B \in \alpha$. Thus, $A \wedge B \in \alpha$, and therefore $A \wedge B \Rightarrow C$ gives us that $C$ should hold in $\beta$, contrary to our assumptions. Hence, production relations generated by quasi-reflexive models are causal. □

The following theorem shows that causal relations are actually complete for such models.

**Theorem 8.53** *A production relation is causal iff it is determined by a quasi-reflexive possible worlds model.*

***Proof.*** Given a causal relation $\Rightarrow$, we construct the corresponding canonical model $(W, R_c, V)$ by defining $R_c$ as follows:

$$\alpha R_c \beta \ \equiv \ \mathcal{C}(\alpha) \subseteq \alpha \cap \beta.$$

Note that this definition directly implies quasi-reflexivity of $R_c$.

As in the proof of Lemma 8.42, it can be shown that if $A \Rightarrow B$ holds, then it is valid in $(W, R_c, V)$. Now if $A \not\Rightarrow B$, the same proof shows that there are worlds $\alpha, \beta$ such that $A \in \alpha$, $B \notin \beta$ and $\mathcal{C}(\alpha) \subseteq \beta$. Moreover, we will show that $\mathcal{C}(\alpha) \subseteq \alpha$.

Suppose that $\mathcal{C}(\alpha) \not\subseteq \alpha$. This means that there are propositions $C, D$ such that $D \in \alpha$ and $D \Rightarrow C$, but $C \notin \alpha$. Now, $\alpha$ has been defined in the proof of Lemma 8.42 as a maximal set that does not produce $B$. Consequently, $B \in \mathcal{C}(\alpha, C)$, and hence there must exist $E \in \alpha$ such that $C \wedge E \Rightarrow B$. The latter implies $D \wedge C \wedge E \Rightarrow B$. In addition, $D \Rightarrow C$ implies $D \wedge E \Rightarrow C$. Hence $D \wedge E \Rightarrow B$ by Cut. But $D \wedge E \in \alpha$, and therefore $B \in \mathcal{C}(\alpha)$, contrary to the definition of $\alpha$. Thus, $\mathcal{C}(\alpha) \subseteq \alpha$.

By the definition of $R_c$, we have now $\alpha R_c \beta$, and therefore $A \Rightarrow B$ is not valid in $(W, R_c, V)$. This completes the proof. □

It is interesting to note that the above semantic interpretation gives clear semantic reasons why the transitivity of production relation is a weaker property that Cut. Indeed, it is easy to verify that Transitivity holds for all production relations determined by possible world models with a *dense* accessibility relation, that is, a relation satisfying the condition that if $\alpha R\beta$, then there exists $\gamma$ such that $\alpha R\gamma$ and $\gamma R\beta$. Clearly, quasi-reflexivity is a stronger property than density.

As for basic production relation, there is an alternative semantics for causal relations that is based on d-validity (see Definition 8.19).

**Lemma 8.54** *A production relation is causal if and only if it coincides with the set of productions that are d-valid with respect to a consistent classical binary semantics.*

***Proof.*** The proof of Theorem 8.53 shows, in effect, that a canonical semantics for a causal relation can be defined also as the set of all bimodels of the form $(\alpha, \mathcal{C}(\alpha))$, where $\mathcal{C}(\alpha) \subseteq \alpha$. Moreover, for such bimodels d-validity coincides with plain validity. Hence the result. □

In what follows, $\Rightarrow^c_\Delta$ will denote the least causal inference relation containing a causal theory $\Delta$. In addition, $\overrightarrow{\Delta}$ will denote the set of material implications corresponding to the production rules from $\Delta$, namely

$$\overrightarrow{\Delta} = \{A \to B \mid A \Rightarrow B \in \Delta\}.$$

As for all the kinds of productions considered earlier, [Makinson and van der Torre, 2000] contains a constructive description of the least causal inference relation containing a given causal theory. Such a description can be obtained from the corresponding description for regular production relations, given in Proposition 8.11, simply by restricting the set of theories of $\Delta$ to worlds. Note, however, that a world $\alpha$ is theory of $\Delta$ if and only if $\overrightarrow{\Delta} \subseteq \alpha$. Consequently, we obtain

**Proposition 8.55** *If* $\Rightarrow^c_\Delta$ *is the least causal relation containing a causal theory* $\Delta$, *then*

$$u \Rightarrow^c_\Delta A \text{ iff } A \in \mathrm{Th}(\Delta(\alpha)), \text{ for any world } \alpha \supseteq u \cup \overrightarrow{\Delta}.$$

Thus, derivability in causal inference relations is reducible, in effect, to derivability in basic production relations with an additional set of assumptions $\overrightarrow{\Delta}$. This fact implies that the material implications corresponding to the production rules can be used as auxiliary assumptions in making derivations. In other words, causal inference relations make valid the following rule:

If $A \Rightarrow B$ and $C \wedge (A \rightarrow B) \Rightarrow D$, then $C \Rightarrow D$.

In the general correspondence between production inference and biconsequence relations, causal inference relations correspond to regular biconsequence relations. This fact is established formally in the following lemma.

**Lemma 8.56**

- *The production subrelation of a regular biconsequence relation in the local language forms a causal inference relation.*
- *The (unique) biconsequence relation corresponding to a causal inference relation is regular.*

***Proof.*** In the general correspondence between production rules and bisequents, described in the proof of Theorem 8.46, the Regularity rule for biconsequence relations corresponds precisely to the Constraint rule for production relations. Hence the result follows from Lemma 8.50. □

As a consequence of the above correspondence, we conclude that causal inference relations can also be translated into classical logic by doubling the atoms. More exactly, for a causal rule $\rho = A \Rightarrow B$, we will denote by $[\rho]^c$ the classical formula $A \rightarrow (B \wedge B')$, while $[\Delta]^c$ will denote by the corresponding translation of a causal theory $\Delta$. Then Corollary 4.12 implies

**Corollary 8.57** *A causal rule $A \Rightarrow B$ is derivable from a causal theory $\Delta$ with respect to a causal inference if and only if $[\Delta]^c \vDash A \rightarrow B \wedge B'$.*

The above result implies, in particular, that causal theories $\Delta$ and $\Gamma$ are equivalent with respect to causal inference if and only if their corresponding translations are classically equivalent (cf. [Turner, 2004]).

8.4.3.1 *Abductive causal inference*

In this section we will consider abductive systems that correspond to causal inference relations.

To begin with, the following result shows that the abductive subrelation of a causal inference relation is also causal.

**Lemma 8.58** *If $\Rightarrow$ is a causal inference relation, then its abductive subrelation $\Rightarrow^a$ is causal.*

***Proof.*** It is sufficient to show that $\Rightarrow^a$ satisfies Or. Assume that $A \Rightarrow^a D$ and $B \Rightarrow^a D$. Then there are abducibles $C_1$ and $C_2$ such that $A \Rightarrow C_1 \Rightarrow D$ and $B \Rightarrow C_2 \Rightarrow D$. But now we have $C_1 \vee C_2 \Rightarrow C_1 \vee C_2$ by Weakening and Or, and hence $C_1 \vee C_2$ is an abducible. Also, $A \vee B \Rightarrow C_1 \vee C_2$ and $C_1 \wedge C_2 \Rightarrow D$ (by Or). Hence $A \vee B \Rightarrow^a D$. Thus, Or holds for $\Rightarrow^a$, and hence it is a causal inference relation. □

By the way, the above proof shows that the set of abducibles of a causal inference relation is closed with respect to disjunctions.

It might be tempting to suppose that causal inference relations correspond to classical abductive systems $(\mathrm{Cn}, \mathcal{A})$, where Cn is a classical consequence relation. Indeed, it is easy to verify that any abductive production relation generated by such an abductive system will already be causal. Still, the reverse claim turns out to be wrong, since classical abductive systems correspond in this sense to a stronger, quasi-classical production inference described later in this chapter. An adequate abductive setting for causal inference is described in the next definition.

**Definition 8.22** An abductive system $\mathbb{A} = (\mathrm{Cn}, \mathcal{A})$ will be called $\mathcal{A}$-*disjunctive* if $\mathcal{A}$ is closed with respect to disjunctions, and Cn satisfies the following two conditions, for any abducibles $A, A_1 \in \mathcal{A}$, and arbitrary $B, C$:

- If $A \in \mathrm{Cn}(B)$ and $A \in \mathrm{Cn}(C)$, then $A \in \mathrm{Cn}(B \vee C)$;
- If $B \in \mathrm{Cn}(A)$ and $B \in \mathrm{Cn}(A_1)$, then $B \in \mathrm{Cn}(A \vee A_1)$.[8]

The following result shows that $\mathcal{A}$-disjunctive systems are precisely abductive systems that generate causal abductive production relations.

**Theorem 8.59** *An abductive production relation is causal if and only if it is generated by an $\mathcal{A}$-disjunctive abductive system.*

***Proof.*** Assume first that an abductive system $\mathbb{A}$ is $\mathcal{A}$-disjunctive, and we have $C \Rightarrow_{\mathbb{A}} B$ and $D \Rightarrow_{\mathbb{A}} B$. Then $A_1 \in \mathrm{Cn}(C)$, $B \in \mathrm{Cn}(A_1)$, $A_2 \in \mathrm{Cn}(D)$ and $B \in \mathrm{Cn}(A_2)$, for some abducibles $A_1, A_2$. We apply the rules of $\mathcal{A}$-disjunctivity and obtain $A_1 \vee A_2 \in \mathrm{Cn}(C \vee D)$ and $B \in \mathrm{Cn}(A_1 \vee A_2)$. But $A_1 \vee A_2$ is also an abducible, so $C \vee D \Rightarrow_{\mathbb{A}} B$. Thus, $\Rightarrow_{\mathbb{A}}$ satisfies Or, and hence it is causal.

As has been established earlier, any abductive production relation $\Rightarrow$ is generated by a canonical abductive system $(\mathrm{Cn}_{\Rightarrow}, \mathcal{A}_{\Rightarrow})$. So, it is sufficient to show that if $\Rightarrow$ is causal, the latter system will be $\mathcal{A}$-disjunctive.

Assume that $A \Rightarrow A$, $B \Rightarrow (B \to A)$ and $C \Rightarrow (C \to A)$. Then we have also $B \wedge A \Rightarrow A$ and $C \wedge A \Rightarrow A$. Hence, $B \Rightarrow A$ and $C \Rightarrow A$ by Cut, and therefore $(B \vee C) \Rightarrow A$ by Or. Consequently, $(B \vee C) \Rightarrow ((B \vee C) \to A)$, that is, $A \in \mathrm{Cn}_{\Rightarrow}(B \vee C)$. This gives the first condition of $\mathcal{A}$-disjunctivity.

[8] This rule corresponds to the rule Ab-Or in [Lobo and Uzcátegui, 1997].

Assume that $A \Rightarrow A$, $A_1 \Rightarrow A_1$, $A \Rightarrow (A \to B)$ and $A_1 \Rightarrow (A_1 \to B)$. Then we have $A \Rightarrow B$ and $A_1 \Rightarrow B$ by And and Weakening, and therefore $(A \vee A_1) \Rightarrow B$ by Or. Consequently, $B \in \mathrm{Cn}_{\Rightarrow}(A \vee A_1)$, which shows the validity of the second condition of $\mathcal{A}$-disjunctivity. □

## 8.5 Causal Nonmonotonic Semantics

If we concentrate on an objective understanding of causal rules as rules acting in world-based contexts, it is only natural to also consider the corresponding restriction of the nonmonotonic production semantics to exact theories that are worlds. In this case, the principle of explanatory closure can be justifiably called the *principle of universal causation* (see [Turner, 1999]), since it says, in effect, that any fact should have a cause.

**Definition 8.23** A *causal nonmonotonic semantics* of a production inference relation or a causal theory is the set of all its exact worlds.

Since the causal nonmonotonic semantics forms a subset of the nonmonotonic production semantics, it produces, in general, a larger set of nonmonotonic consequences. Moreover, the causal semantics is just a set of worlds, so its logical content is exhausted by the classical propositional theory that is uniquely associated with this set of worlds. Note, however, that, unlike the nonmonotonic production semantics, the causal nonmonotonic semantics is not guaranteed to exist for any causal theory.

The following lemma gives a useful description of exact worlds.

**Lemma 8.60** *A world $\alpha$ is an exact world of a production inference relation if and only if, for any propositional atom $p$,*

$$p \in \alpha \quad \textit{iff} \quad \alpha \Rightarrow p$$
$$p \notin \alpha \quad \textit{iff} \quad \alpha \Rightarrow \neg p.$$

***Proof.*** For worlds, the above conditions are sufficient for $\alpha = \mathcal{C}(\alpha)$. □

By Lemma 8.17, the causal nonmonotonic semantics of a causal theory $\Delta$ is the set of worlds $\alpha$ such that $\alpha = \mathrm{Th}(\Delta(\alpha))$. Such worlds coincide with *causally explained interpretations* of [McCain and Turner, 1997], which determine the nonmonotonic semantics of their causal theories. Consequently the causal nonmonotonic semantics provides an adequate representation for this nonmonotonic system.

A description of exact worlds for causal theories is given below.

**Corollary 8.61** *A world $\alpha$ is an exact world of a causal theory $\Delta$ if and only if, for any propositional atom $p$,*

$$p \in \alpha \quad \textit{iff} \quad \Delta(\alpha) \vDash p$$
$$p \notin \alpha \quad \textit{iff} \quad \Delta(\alpha) \vDash \neg p.$$

***Proof.*** The above conditions are clearly equivalent to $\alpha = \mathrm{Th}(\Delta(\alpha))$. □

Now we will show that causal inference relations provide an adequate framework of reasoning with respect to the causal nonmonotonic semantics. As before, we will introduce first the following definitions:

**Definition 8.24** Causal theories $\Gamma$ and $\Delta$ will be called

- *(strongly) objectively equivalent* if they are (strongly) equivalent with respect to the causal nonmonotonic semantics;
- *causally equivalent* if $\Rightarrow^c_\Delta = \Rightarrow^c_\Gamma$.

Two causal theories are causally equivalent if each theory can be obtained from the other using the inference postulates of causal relations.

**Lemma 8.62** *Any causal theory $\Delta$ is objectively equivalent to $\Rightarrow^c_\Delta$.*

***Proof.*** By Proposition 8.55, for any causally consistent world $\alpha$, $\mathcal{C}^c_\Delta(\alpha) = \mathrm{Th}(\Delta(\alpha))$. Consequently, $\alpha = \mathcal{C}^c_\Delta(\alpha)$ if and only if $\alpha = \mathrm{Th}(\Delta(\alpha))$. □

The above lemma says that the postulates of causal inference relations are adequate for reasoning with exact worlds, since they preserve the latter. Moreover, the next theorem shows that causal inference relations constitute a maximal logic suitable for the causal nonmonotonic semantics.

**Theorem 8.63** *Two causal theories are strongly objectively equivalent if and only if they are causally equivalent.*

***Proof.*** Coincides with the proof of Theorem 8.19, once we note that, for our present case, the theory $u$ in this proof is a world. □

Finally, just as for the nonmonotonic production semantics, under some conditions, the causal nonmonotonic semantics grows monotonically with the growth of these causal theories.

**Definition 8.25** Causal theories $\Gamma$ and $\Delta$ will be called *classically equivalent*, if $\overrightarrow{\Delta}$ is logically equivalent to $\overrightarrow{\Gamma}$.

Causal theories are classically equivalent if they are logically equivalent when viewed as sets of classical material implications. Recall now that causally consistent worlds of a causal theory $\Delta$ are the worlds satisfying $\overrightarrow{\Delta}$. Consequently, classically equivalent causal theories have the same causally consistent worlds, and hence as a consequence of Lemma 8.20, we obtain the corresponding restricted monotonicity property:

**Corollary 8.64** *If causal theories $\Gamma$ and $\Delta$ are classically equivalent, and $\Gamma \subseteq \Delta$, then any exact world of $\Gamma$ is an exact world of $\Delta$.*

As a particular application of the above result, suppose that we add a new inference rule for production relations that corresponds to a valid rule of classical logic. Such a rule will not change the causally consistent worlds of a production relation, and consequently the new causal nonmonotonic semantics will include the original one (see below for an example).

It turns out that, in the general correspondence between basic production relations and biconsequence relations, established earlier, the causal semantics corresponds to the exact nonmonotonic semantics of biconsequence relations.

**Lemma 8.65** *If $\Rightarrow$ is a basic production relation corresponding to a biconsequence relation $\Vdash$, then the exact semantics of $\Vdash$ correspond precisely to the causal semantics of $\Rightarrow$.*

***Proof.*** Exact worlds of a production relation are complete and consistent sets of propositions $\alpha$ such that $\alpha = \mathcal{C}(\alpha)$. Let us denote by $u_\alpha$ the set of propositional atoms in $\alpha$. Then it can be easily verified that the latter equality holds if and only if the following two conditions are satisfied, for any propositional atom $p$:

$$p \in u_\alpha \quad \text{iff} \quad u_\alpha, \neg\overline{u}_\alpha \Rightarrow p$$

$$p \notin u_\alpha \quad \text{iff} \quad u_\alpha, \neg\overline{u}_\alpha \Rightarrow \neg p.$$

Now, by Lemma 5.1, $u_\alpha$ is an exact theory of $\Vdash$. Consequently, exact worlds of $\Rightarrow$ correspond precisely to exact theories of $\Vdash$. □

As a general consequence of the above result, most of the properties of the exact semantics for biconsequence relations can be translated into the corresponding results for the causal semantics of production relations. For example, the above result that causal theories are strongly objectively equivalent if and only if they are causally equivalent can be obtained also as a consequence of Theorem 5.5 for biconsequence relations. Additional implications of this correspondence will be described below.

Finally, in the correspondence between production inference and argumentation, exact worlds correspond precisely to stable extensions.

**Lemma 8.66** *If $\hookrightarrow$ is a propositional attack relation corresponding to a basic production relation $\Rightarrow$ by (PA), then the causal nonmonotonic semantics of $\Rightarrow$ coincides with the set of stable extensions of $\hookrightarrow$.*

***Proof.*** Definition 7.20 of stable extensions for propositional attack relations corresponds to the following condition for the production relation: $u = \{A \mid u \not\Rightarrow \neg A\}$. This condition can be reformulated as follows:

$$\mathcal{C}(u) = \{A \mid \neg A \notin u\}.$$

Note, however, that the set of propositions compatible with $u$ can be deductively closed only when $u$ is a world, in which case the latter condition reduces to $\mathcal{C}(u) = u$. Hence the result. □

### 8.5.1 *Factual and explanatory content of causal theories*

Since causal inference relations form a maximal logic with respect to the causal nonmonotonic semantics, the *informational (or logical) content* of a causal theory $\Delta$ with respect to the latter semantics can be identified with $\Rightarrow^{c}_{\Delta}$, that is, with the set of causal rules that are derivable from $\Delta$ by the rules of causal inference. For causal theories there exists, however, a more fine-grained description of this informational content.

Recall that causal rules serve in causal inference simultaneously two informational roles. One consists in determining causally consistent worlds, while the other in establishing explanatory relations between propositions. Fortunately, these two roles can be neatly separated by decomposing any causal rule into a constraint and an explanation (see Lemma 8.51). This suggests the following definition.

**Definition 8.26**

- The set of constraints $A \Rightarrow \mathbf{f}$ belonging to a causal relation will be called its *factual content*.
- The *explanatory content* of a causal relation is the set of its *explanatory rules*, namely the rules $A \Rightarrow B$ such that $A \vDash B$.

Constraints restrict the set of worlds that are admissible (causally consistent) with respect to a causal theory. In this sense they play the role of ordinary classical formulas, namely they just express facts about the world. However, they do not explain anything, and hence they can be seen as devoid of explanatory content. The later is expressed, however, by explanatory causal rules. Such rules are 'factually trivial', since they do not impose restrictions on admissible worlds; their only role consists in determining what explains what in admissible worlds. Consequently, the factual and explanatory contents are not only disjoint, but are actually independent of each other. Moreover, due to the above-mentioned decomposition of causal rules, the informational content of causal theories can be safely represented as a union of a factual and explanatory contents.

The interplay of the factual and explanatory contents determines, eventually, the nonmonotonic semantics, and it is responsible, in particular, for the nonmonotonic properties of the latter. Namely, the nonmonotonicity arises from the fact that the two kinds of content have opposite impacts on derivability. Thus, addition of constraints leads, as expected, to reduction of the set of admissible worlds (and hence to increase of factual information). However, the addition of explanatory rules leads, in general, to *increase* of exact worlds, and hence to decrease of nonmonotonically derived information (cf. Corollary 8.64). But in all cases, one of the effects of growth in informational content is a monotonic *reduction of the set of non-exact (unexplained) worlds.*

### 8.5.2 *Determinate theories and completions*

To begin with, we will show that any causal theory is objectively equivalent to a causal theory of a special kind, called determinate one.

A production rule will be called *determinate*, if it has the form $A \Rightarrow l$, where $l$ is either a literal or a falsity constant $\mathbf{f}$[9]. A causal theory will be called *determinate*, if it contains only determinate rules. Finally, causal theories $\Delta$ and $\Gamma$ will be called *determinately equivalent*, if $\Rightarrow_\Delta$ and $\Rightarrow_\Gamma$ have the same determinate rules.

Causal theories are determinately equivalent, if they derive the same determinate rules. Now, Lemma 8.60 shows that the exact worlds of a production relation are uniquely determined by the determinate rules that belong to it. Consequently, we obtain

**Lemma 8.67** *Determinately equivalent causal theories are objectively equivalent.*

The above result implies that the causal nonmonotonic semantics of a

[9]Note that any constraint is a determinate rule by this definition.

causal theory is determined ultimately by the determinate rules that are derivable from the theory. This immediately suggests that any causal theory can be transformed into a determinate theory that is objectively equivalent to it. Such a transformation is provided below[10].

For a causal theory $\Delta$, let us denote by $\Delta_d$ the set of all determinate rules of the form $\bigwedge A_i \Rightarrow l$, for which $\Delta$ contains a (minimal) set of rules $\{A_i \Rightarrow B_i\}$ such that $\bigwedge B_i \vDash l$. Then the following result shows that $\Delta_d$ embodies the 'determinate content' of $\Delta$.

**Lemma 8.68** *$\Delta$ is determinately equivalent to $\Delta_d$.*

***Proof.*** Note first that any production rule from $\Delta_d$ is derivable from $\Delta$ by Strengthening, And and Weakening. Assume now that $A \Rightarrow_\Delta l$, for some literal $l$. Then $\Delta(\mathrm{Th}(A)) \vDash l$ by Proposition 8.6. This can hold only if $\Delta$ contains a set of rules $A_i \Rightarrow B_i$ such that $A_i \in \mathrm{Th}(A)$, for any $i$, and $\bigwedge B_i \vDash l$. But then $\bigwedge A_i \Rightarrow l$ belongs to $\Delta_d$, and therefore $A \Rightarrow_{\Delta_d} l$ by Strengthening. This shows that $\Rightarrow_{\Delta_d}$ includes all determinate production rules from $\Rightarrow_\Delta$, and consequently $\Delta$ and $\Delta_d$ are determinately equivalent. □

As a consequence, $\Delta_d$ turns out to be a determinate causal theory that is objectively equivalent to $\Delta$.

Unfortunately, the above algorithm is neither modular, nor polynomial. Moreover, the complexity considerations confirm that this is as it should be, due to the difference in complexity between arbitrary and determinate causal theories, established in [Giunchiglia *et al.*, 2004]. Still, in many cases the algorithm gives a convenient recipe for transforming an arbitrary causal theory into an objectively equivalent determinate theory. It should be kept in mind, however, that we do not have strong equivalence here. The following example illustrates this.

**Example 8.4** (*Two gears*) This is a simplified atemporal version of the example due to Marc Denecker that was described in [McCain, 1997]. Two gears are powered by separate motors that can turn them in opposite (i.e., compatible) directions. In addition, when the gears are connected, each can also turn the other. Let us assume that this domain is given the following causal representation $\Delta$:

$$Connected \Rightarrow Turning1 \leftrightarrow Turning2$$
$$Motor1 \Rightarrow Turning1 \qquad Motor2 \Rightarrow Turning2,$$

[10] A similar algorithm has been suggested earlier by Norman McCain (V. Lifschitz, personal communication).

plus the assumptions that $(\neg)Motor1$, $(\neg)Motor2$ and $(\neg)Connected$ are abducibles.

The causal theory $\Delta$ is not determinate (due to the first rule), but by the above algorithm, it can be reduced to a determinate theory $\Delta_d$ obtained from $\Delta$ by replacing the first rule with the following two determinate rules:

$$Connected \land Motor1 \Rightarrow Turning2 \qquad Connected \land Motor2 \Rightarrow Turning1$$

$\Delta$ and $\Delta_d$ have, of course, the same causal nonmonotonic semantics, namely the worlds where both gears are turning, and either both motors are working, or else one of them is working, and the gears are connected. Let us add, however, a causal rule $\neg Turning2 \Rightarrow \neg Turning2$ to each of these causal theories. Since the added rule is purely explanatory, it can only extend the set of exact worlds. And indeed, being added to $\Delta$, it creates a new exact world $\alpha$ in which the gears are connected, the two motors are not working, and both gears are not turning. This is because $\neg Turning2$ is now self-explanatory, while $\neg Turning1$ is explained by the rule $Connected \land \neg Turning2 \Rightarrow \neg Turning1$ that is derivable from the first rule of $\Delta$ and $\neg Turning2 \Rightarrow \neg Turning2$. However, if the latter rule is added to $\Delta_d$, the world $\alpha$ will not be an exact world of the resulting theory. As a result, we can still nonmonotonically infer from the second theory that both gears are turning.

As has been established in [McCain and Turner, 1997], for a special kind of determinate theories, the causal nonmonotonic semantics coincides with the classical semantics of their completions.

**Definition 8.27** A causal theory will be called

- *locally finite* if any propositional atom appears in heads of no more than a finite number of its causal rules.
- *definite* if it is determinate and locally finite.

Any finite causal theory will be locally finite, though not vice versa. Similarly, any finite determinate theory will be definite.

Given a definite causal theory $\Delta$, we will define its *completion*, $comp(\Delta)$, as the set of all classical formulas of the forms

$$p \leftrightarrow \bigvee\{A \mid A \Rightarrow p \in \Delta\}$$
$$\neg p \leftrightarrow \bigvee\{A \mid A \Rightarrow \neg p \in \Delta\},$$

for any propositional atom $p$, plus the set $\{\neg A \mid A \Rightarrow \mathbf{f} \in \Delta\}$.

Note that if $\Delta$ does not have rules with the head $p$, then $comp(\Delta)$ contains the formula $p \leftrightarrow \bigvee \emptyset$, which amounts to $\neg p$ (and similarly for $\neg p$).

The following result shows that the classical models of $comp(\Delta)$ precisely correspond to exact worlds of $\Delta$. The proof follows readily from Corollary 8.61. It will follow also from a more general result proved later.

**Proposition 8.69** *The causal nonmonotonic semantics of a definite causal theory coincides with the classical semantics of its completion.*

**Example 8.5** (*Reiter's simple solution*). As an illustration, we will use the framework of [McCain and Turner, 1997] in order to give a toy causal representation of the well-known Reiter's simple solution to the frame problem (see [Reiter, 1991; Reiter, 2001]). Despite its simplicity, the representation contains the main ingredients of causal reasoning in temporal domains.

We consider a small causal theory for a single propositional fluent $F$. The temporal behavior of $F$ is described using two propositional atoms $F_0$ and $F_1$ saying, respectively, that $F$ holds now and $F$ holds in the next moment.

$$
\begin{array}{cc}
C^+ \Rightarrow F_1 & C^- \Rightarrow \neg F_1 \\
F_0 \wedge F_1 \Rightarrow F_1 & \neg F_0 \wedge \neg F_1 \Rightarrow \neg F_1 \\
F_0 \Rightarrow F_0 & \neg F_0 \Rightarrow \neg F_0.
\end{array}
$$

The first pair of causal rules describes the factors (actions or natural causes) that can cause $F$ and, respectively, $\neg F$ ($C^+$ and $C^-$ can be arbitrary formulas, but they normally describe the present situation). Such rules correspond to Reiter's *effect axioms for fluent* $F$, though in our description they are not relativized to particular actions. Second, instead of Reiter's explanatory closure axioms, we have a pair of *inertia axioms.* The latter are instances of explanatory production rules stating that if $F$ holds (does not hold) now, then it is self-explanatory that it will hold (respectively, not hold) in the next moment. The last pair of *initial axioms* states, in effect, that the truth-value of $F_0$ is an independent (exogenous) parameter.

The above causal theory is clearly definite, and its completion (with respect to $F$) is as follows:

$$
\begin{array}{c}
F_1 \leftrightarrow C^+ \vee (F_0 \wedge F_1) \\
\neg F_1 \leftrightarrow C^- \vee (\neg F_0 \wedge \neg F_1).
\end{array}
$$

Now, it can be easily verified that the latter formulas are logically equivalent to the following two:

$$\neg(C^+ \wedge C^-)$$
$$F_1 \leftrightarrow C^+ \vee (F_0 \wedge \neg C^-).$$

The above formulas provide, in effect, an abstract description of Reiter's simple solution: the first formula corresponds to his *consistency condition*, while the second one—to the *successor state axiom* for $F$, since it describes the conditions for $F$ to hold in the next state.

As can be seen, Proposition 8.69 is a causal counterpart of Corollary 5.11 stating that the exact nonmonotonic semantics of a definite bisequent theory corresponds precisely to the classical semantics of its pointwise completion. And just as for the latter, the notion of completion can be extended to a broader class of causal theories using the corresponding generalized notion of loop-completion.

Let us say that a causal theory is *semi-clausal*, if it consists of production rules of the form $A \Rightarrow C$, where $C$ is a clause (disjunction of literals). Note that any production rule of a production inference relation can be reduced to a set of such semi-clausal rules. For a semi-clausal causal theory $\Delta$, let $\Delta^+$ denote the set of all clauses appearing in heads of the rules from $\Delta$. The set of clauses $\Delta^+$ can be viewed as a sequent theory, so we can extend to it the notions of a literal dependency graph and literal loop. As before, we will say that a semi-clausal theory $\Delta$ is *finitary*, if $\Delta^+$ is finitary (see Definition 2.9).

By a *causal completion* of a finitary causal theory $\Delta$ we will mean a classical theory, denoted by $ccomp(\Delta)$, that consists of the following formulas:

- $A \rightarrow C$, for any rule $A \Rightarrow C$ from $\Delta$;
- $\bigwedge l \rightarrow \bigvee\{A \wedge \neg \bigvee(c \backslash l)) \mid A \Rightarrow \bigvee c \in \Delta \ \&\ l \cap c \neq \emptyset \ \&\ \neg l \cap c = \emptyset\}$, for any literal loop $l$ of $\Delta^+$.

The following result[11] shows that the causal completion provides a concise description of the causal nonmonotonic semantics of $\Delta$. The proof is immediate from Theorem 5.9.

**Theorem 8.70** *The causal nonmonotonic semantics of a finitary causal theory coincides with the classical semantics of its causal completion.*

[11] Which is a reformulation of the result obtained in [Lee, 2004].

Thus, for a broad class of causal theories, the causal nonmonotonic semantics is reducible to a classical semantics of their causal completions.

### 8.5.3 *Partial exact semantics*

Now we will describe a partial counterpart of the causal nonmonotonic semantics. As we will see below, the following definition will give us precisely the production equivalent of partial exact bitheories for biconsequence relations.

**Definition 8.28**

- A pair $(\alpha, \beta)$ of worlds will be called *exact* with respect to a production inference relation $\Rightarrow$, if $\mathcal{C}(\alpha) = \beta$ and $\mathcal{C}(\beta) = \alpha$.
- A world pair $(\alpha, \beta)$ will be called *exact* for a causal theory $\Delta$, if it is an exact pair of $\Rightarrow_\Delta$.
- A *partial exact semantics* of a production inference relation or a causal theory is the set of all its exact world pairs.

An exact world pair describes an explanatory situation in which each of the two worlds explains the other one. Whether or not such a situation admits a direct physical reading, it has a plausible epistemic understanding that is based on viewing the pair $(\alpha, \beta)$ as a *partial description of a world.* Namely, propositions from $\alpha \cap \beta$ can be seen as definitely holding in such a world, while the rest of propositions is undetermined. Under this reading, exact pairs can be viewed as determining explanatory closed 'partial worlds'. It should be noted also that a pair of the form $(\alpha, \alpha)$ is exact if and only if $\alpha$ is an exact world. Consequently, the partial exact semantics subsumes the causal nonmonotonic semantics.

The following lemma gives an alternative description of exact world pairs. The proof is immediate.

**Lemma 8.71** *A pair of worlds $(\alpha, \beta)$ is exact if and only if, for any propositional atom $p$,*

$$p \in \alpha \;\; \textit{iff} \;\; \beta \Rightarrow p \qquad p \notin \alpha \;\; \textit{iff} \;\; \beta \Rightarrow \neg p$$
$$p \in \beta \;\; \textit{iff} \;\; \alpha \Rightarrow p \qquad p \notin \beta \;\; \textit{iff} \;\; \alpha \Rightarrow \neg p.$$

In addition, Proposition 8.6 gives the following description of the partial exact semantics for causal theories.

**Corollary 8.72** *A pair of worlds $(\alpha, \beta)$ is exact for a causal theory $\Delta$ if and only if, for any propositional atom $p$,*

$$p \in \alpha \text{ iff } \Delta(\beta) \vDash p \qquad p \notin \alpha \text{ iff } \Delta(\beta) \vDash \neg p$$
$$p \in \beta \text{ iff } \Delta(\alpha) \vDash p \qquad p \notin \beta \text{ iff } \Delta(\alpha) \vDash \neg p.$$

Unfortunately, the Cut rule will no longer be adequate for the partial exact semantics. This follows already from the fact that if $(\alpha, \beta)$ is a non-trivial exact pair, then neither $\alpha$, nor $\beta$ can be a theory of a production relation, which contradicts Lemma 8.7. Consequently, only basic production relations will be admissible for the latter.

**Lemma 8.73** *Any causal theory $\Delta$ has the same partial exact semantics as $\Rightarrow^b_\Delta$.*

***Proof.*** By Proposition 8.41, for any world $\alpha$, $\mathcal{C}^b_\Delta(\alpha) = \mathrm{Th}(\Delta(\alpha))$. Now the result follows from the preceding corollary. □

The above lemma says that the postulates of basic inference relations are adequate for reasoning with the partial exact semantics, since they preserve the latter. A maximal underlying logic for this semantics will be given later in this chapter.

The following simple lemma provides further support to the understanding of exact world pairs as descriptions of explanatory closed partial worlds:

**Lemma 8.74** *If a pair $(\alpha, \beta)$ is exact for a basic production relation $\Rightarrow$, then $\alpha \cap \beta$ is an exact theory of $\Rightarrow$.*

***Proof.*** If a pair $(\alpha, \beta)$ is exact, then $\mathcal{C}(\alpha \cap \beta) \subseteq \alpha \cap \beta$ by monotonicity of $\mathcal{C}$. Assume now that $C \in \alpha \cap \beta$. Then $\alpha \Rightarrow C$ and $\beta \Rightarrow C$, and hence there exist $A \in \alpha$ and $B \in \beta$ such that $A \Rightarrow C$ and $B \Rightarrow C$. Consequently, $A \vee B \Rightarrow C$ by Or. But $A \vee B \in \alpha \cap \beta$, and therefore $C \in \mathcal{C}(\alpha \cap \beta)$. Thus, $\alpha \cap \beta = \mathcal{C}(\alpha \cap \beta)$. □

In view of the above result, the partial exact semantics can be seen as an intermediate semantics between the nonmonotonic production and causal nonmonotonic semantics. Finally, the next result shows that the general correspondence between basic production relations and biconsequence relations extends to a correspondence between their partial exact semantics.

**Lemma 8.75** *If $\Rightarrow$ is a basic production relation corresponding to a biconsequence relation $\Vdash$, then the partial exact semantics of $\Vdash$ corresponds precisely to the partial exact semantics of $\Rightarrow$.*

***Proof.*** Let $u_\alpha$ denote the set of propositional atoms of a world $\alpha$. Then it can be verified that $(\alpha, \beta)$ is an exact world pair iff the following conditions are satisfied, for any propositional atom $p$:

$$p \in u_\alpha \text{ iff } u_\beta, \neg\overline{u}_\beta \Rightarrow p \qquad p \notin u_\alpha \text{ iff } u_\beta, \neg\overline{u}_\beta \Rightarrow \neg p$$
$$p \in u_\beta \text{ iff } u_\alpha, \neg\overline{u}_\alpha \Rightarrow p \qquad p \notin u_\beta \text{ iff } u_\alpha, \neg\overline{u}_\alpha \Rightarrow \neg p.$$

Now the result follows from Lemma 5.70. □

Our next result shows that the partial exact semantics is also uniquely determined by the determinate production rules that are derivable from a causal theory. Namely, Lemma 8.71 implies

**Lemma 8.76** *Determinately equivalent causal theories have the same partial exact semantics.*

Moreover, the algorithm of transforming a given causal theory $\Delta$ into a determinate theory $\Delta_d$, described earlier, is appropriate also in our present case.

We will continue the study of the partial nonmonotonic semantics later in this chapter.

## 8.6 Negative Closure and Tightness

In this section we will describe production inference relations that are relevant to logic programming. We will begin with negatively closed production relations that give a logical expression to the closed world assumption.

**Definition 8.29** A production relation will be called *negatively closed*, if it satisfies

**(Default Negation)** $\neg p \Rightarrow \neg p$, for any propositional atom $p$.

The Default Negation postulate stipulates, in effect, that negations of atomic propositions do not require explanation, since they are self-explanatory. This means that the explanatory closure assumption is reduced in such systems to the necessity of explaining only positive facts. The postulate can be seen as giving a formal expression to Reiter's *Closed World Assumption* [Reiter, 1978]. Accordingly, it reflects the main distinctive feature of logical reasoning behind logic programs and databases.

It can be easily verified that, in the general correspondence between biconsequence relations and (basic) production inference relations, Default

Negation corresponds exactly to the Consistency postulate for biconsequence relations. Accordingly, we have

**Corollary 8.77**

- *The production subrelation of a consistent biconsequence relation in the local language forms a negatively closed production relation.*
- *The (unique) biconsequence relation corresponding to a negatively closed basic production relation is consistent.*

It is important to observe, however, that Default Negation is not a fully logical postulate in the framework of production inference, since propositional atoms $p$ in it cannot be replaced by arbitrary formulas (on pain of transforming a causal inference relation into an ordinary reflexive consequence relation)[12].

Consistency is equivalent to each of the two Import rules (see Sec. 3.2.1). These rules correspond to the following postulates for production inference: for any atom $p$ and arbitrary propositions $A$ and $B$:

If $A \wedge p \Rightarrow B$, then $A \Rightarrow p \to B$;
If $A \Rightarrow B \vee p$, then $A \wedge \neg p \Rightarrow B$.

For a world $\alpha$, we will denote by $At(\alpha)$ the set of propositional atoms that belong to $\alpha$. The next definition provides a semantics for negatively closed production relations.

**Definition 8.30** A possible worlds semantics $\mathbb{W} = (W, R, V)$ will be called *inclusive*, if, for any $\alpha, \beta \in W$, $\alpha R \beta$ holds only if $At(\beta) \subseteq At(\alpha)$.

It can be verified that inclusive possible worlds semantics correspond to consistent binary semantics for biconsequence relations, so, as a consequence of the completeness theorem for consistent biconsequence relations (see Theorem 3.12), we obtain

**Theorem 8.78** *A basic production relation is negatively closed if and only if it has an inclusive possible worlds semantics.*

Recall now that the correspondence between basic production inference and biconsequence relations extends to a correspondence between their non-monotonic semantics. Moreover, it has been shown in Chapter 5 that exact

---

[12]For biconsequence relations, this amounts to an observation that Consistency extended to all formulas in a local classical language reduces biconsequence relations to Scott ones.

theories of a consistent biconsequence relation coincide with its extensions. Accordingly, the causal nonmonotonic semantics of negatively closed causal relations describes, in effect, the default nonmonotonic semantics of biconsequence relations. This correspondence can be described as follows.

**Definition 8.31** A world $\alpha$ will be called an *extension* of a production relation $\Rightarrow$, if it is a theory of $\Rightarrow$ and, for any world $\beta$ such that $\mathcal{C}(\alpha) \subseteq \beta$, if $At(\beta) \subseteq At(\alpha)$, then $At(\beta) = At(\alpha)$.

A world $\alpha$ is an extension if it is a theory of $\Rightarrow$ that has a minimal number of propositional atoms among the worlds consistent with $\mathcal{C}(\alpha)$. Clearly, any exact world will be an extension, though not vice versa.

It can be easily verified that extensions of a causal relation correspond precisely to extensions of the associated biconsequence relation.

**Lemma 8.79** *If* $\Vdash$ *is a biconsequence relation corresponding to a basic production relation* $\Rightarrow$, *then extensions of* $\Rightarrow$ *coincide with extensions of* $\Vdash$.

As a result, Theorem 5.31 immediately implies the following

**Corollary 8.80** *A world* $\alpha$ *is an exact world of a negatively closed causal relation* $\Rightarrow$ *if and only if it is an extension of* $\Rightarrow$.

Moreover, Theorem 5.36 implies that negatively closed causal relations constitute a maximal causal logic suitable for extensions. These facts will be used later in establishing correspondence between causal inference relations and logic programs.

Now we will describe causal relations that correspond to semi-classical biconsequence relations.

**Definition 8.32** A production relation will be called *semi-classical*, if it satisfies

**(Semi-Classicality)** $l \wedge m \Rightarrow l \vee m$, for distinct literals $l$ and $m$.

and *tight* if it is semi-classical and negatively closed.

Semi-classical causal relations are 'highly explanatory', since they automatically explain disjunctions of any two distinct literals that hold in a given world. As a result, only single literals have to be explained in such causal systems. As with Default Negation, however, Semi-Classicality is not a structural postulate, since it does not hold for arbitrary propositions. Note also that, for negatively closed causal relations, Semi-Classicality is reducible to its positive instance, namely to

**(Tightness)** $p \wedge q \Rightarrow p \vee q$, for any two distinct atoms $p, q$.

In the correspondence between biconsequence relations and production inference relations, Semi-Classicality corresponds exactly to the postulates defining a semi-classical biconsequence relation. Consequently, we have

**Corollary 8.81**

- *The production subrelation of a semi-classical [tight] biconsequence relation in the local language forms a semi-classical [tight] causal relation.*
- *The (unique) biconsequence relation corresponding to a semi-classical [tight] causal inference relation is semi-classical [tight].*

As a result, it can be easily verified that the following definition gives a semantic description of semi-classical causal relations.

**Definition 8.33** A possible world semantics will be called *pointwise*, if, for any worlds $\alpha, \beta \in W$, $\alpha R \beta$ holds only if $At(\beta) \triangle At(\alpha)$ contains no more than one propositional atom, and *tight*, if it is pointwise and inclusive.

**Corollary 8.82** *A causal relation is semi-classical [tight] if and only if it has a pointwise [tight] quasi-reflexive possible worlds semantics.*

An important reduction property of semi-classical biconsequence relations, stated as Corollary 3.29, translates into the following reduction property of causal relations:

**Lemma 8.83** *If $c$ is a consistent set of literals, then a semi-clausal rule $A \Rightarrow \bigvee c$ of a semi-classical causal relation is equivalent to the following set of determinate rules:*

$$\{A, \neg(c \backslash \{l\}) \Rightarrow l \mid l \in c\}.$$

As a consequence, we conclude that, for semi-classical causal inference, any causal theory is *logically* reducible to a determinate theory.

For tight causal relations, Corollary 3.31 suggests the following strengthening of the reduction property:

**Lemma 8.84** *If $a, c$ are disjoint sets of propositional atoms, and $c \neq \emptyset$, then a rule $A \Rightarrow \bigvee(\neg a \cup c)$ of a tight causal relation is equivalent to the following set of rules:*

$$\{A, a, \neg(c \backslash \{p\}) \Rightarrow p \mid p \in c\}.$$

A determinate causal theory will be called *positive*, if it contains only rules of the form $A \Rightarrow \tilde{p}$, where $\tilde{p}$ is either an atom, or the falsity constant $\mathbf{f}$. Then the above result implies the following

**Corollary 8.85** *For tight causal inference, any causal theory is equivalent to some positive determinate theory.*

Since semi-classical causal relations correspond to semi-classical biconsequence relations, the causal nonmonotonic semantics of semi-classical causal relations corresponds to the singular semantics for biconsequence relations. Similarly, since tight causal relations correspond to tight biconsequence relations, the causal nonmonotonic semantics of tight causal relations corresponds to the semantics of expansions. The latter are definable in the framework of production inference as follows:

**Definition 8.34** A world $\alpha$ is an *expansion* of a production relation $\Rightarrow$ if it is a theory of $\Rightarrow$, and there is no world $\beta$ consistent with $\mathcal{C}(\alpha)$ that has precisely one atom less than $\alpha$.

Comparing the above description with the definition of expansions for biconsequence relations, we immediately obtain

**Lemma 8.86** *If $\Vdash$ is a biconsequence relation corresponding to a basic production relation $\Rightarrow$, then expansions of $\Rightarrow$ coincide with expansions of $\Vdash$.*

As a result, Corollary 5.50 implies the following

**Corollary 8.87** *A world $\alpha$ is an exact world of a tight causal relation $\Rightarrow$ if and only if it is an expansion of $\Rightarrow$.*

In addition, Theorem 5.52 implies that tight causal relations constitute a maximal causal logic suitable for extensions. These facts will also be used in establishing correspondence between causal inference relations and logic programs.

## 8.7 Quasi-Classicality

We now consider production relations that will be shown to correspond to abductive systems based on classical consequence relations.

**Definition 8.35** A production relation will be called *quasi-classical*, if it satisfies the rule

**(Weak Deduction)** If $A \Rightarrow B$, then $\mathbf{t} \Rightarrow (A \to B)$.

Weak Deduction says, in effect, that material implications corresponding to production rules can be seen as universally valid propositions in production inference. The following lemma provides two alternative descriptions of quasi-classicality.

**Lemma 8.88** *A production relation is quasi-classical if and only if it satisfies one the following conditions:*

**(Dual Cut)** *If $A \Rightarrow B$ and $C \Rightarrow A \lor B$, then $C \Rightarrow B$.*
**(Contradiction)** *If $\neg A \Rightarrow A$, then $\mathbf{t} \Rightarrow A$.*

***Proof.*** If $A \Rightarrow B$ and $C \Rightarrow A \lor B$, then $\mathbf{t} \Rightarrow A \to B$ by Weak Deduction, and hence $C \Rightarrow A \to B$ by Strengthening. Consequently $C \Rightarrow B$ by And. Thus, Weak Deduction implies Dual Cut.

Assume $\neg A \Rightarrow A$. We have $\mathbf{t} \Rightarrow A \lor \neg A$ by Truth, and hence $\mathbf{t} \Rightarrow A$ by Dual Cut. Thus, Dual Cut implies Contradiction.

Finally, if $A \Rightarrow B$, then $A \land \neg B \Rightarrow \neg A \lor B$ by Strengthening and Weakening, and hence $\mathbf{t} \Rightarrow A \to B$ by Contradiction. Thus, Contradiction implies Weak Deduction. □

Note that Dual Cut also implies Transitivity, so any quasi-classical production relation will already be transitive.

A semantic interpretation of basic quasi-classical production relations can be obtained by requiring *right reflexivity* of the accessibility relation: if $\alpha R \beta$, then $\beta R \beta$.

**Theorem 8.89** *A production relation is quasi-classical if and only if it is determined by a right reflexive possible worlds model.*

***Proof.*** It can be verified that any right reflexive possible worlds model determines a quasi-classical production relation. Hence we have to show only that the canonical semantics for basic productions is right reflexive in our case. Suppose that $\mathcal{C}(\alpha) \subseteq \beta$ and $A \Rightarrow B$. Then $\mathbf{t} \Rightarrow A \to B$ by Weak Deduction, and therefore $A \to B \in \mathcal{C}(\alpha)$. Consequently $A \to B \in \beta$, which means that $\beta$ is closed with respect to the production rules, that is $\mathcal{C}(\beta) \subseteq \beta$. Thus, the canonical accessibility relation is right reflexive. □

Taken together with quasi-reflexivity, right reflexivity gives a full reflexivity of the accessibility relation:

**Corollary 8.90** *A causal relation is quasi-classical if and only if it is determined by a reflexive possible worlds model.*

A constructive description of the least quasi-classical production relation containing a causal theory is given in the next lemma.

**Lemma 8.91** *If $\Rightarrow^q_\Delta$ is the least quasi-classical production relation containing a causal theory $\Delta$, then $\mathcal{C}^q_\Delta(u) = \mathrm{Th}(\overrightarrow{\Delta} \cup \Delta(\mathrm{Th}(u)))$.*

***Proof.*** Clearly, $\mathcal{C}^q_\Delta(u)$ should include both $\Delta(\mathrm{Th}(u))$ and $\overrightarrow{\Delta}$ (by Weak Deduction). Hence, $\mathrm{Th}(\overrightarrow{\Delta} \cup \Delta(\mathrm{Th}(u))) \subseteq \mathcal{C}^q_\Delta(u)$. Moreover, it can be directly verified that the right side of the above equality determines a quasi-classical production relation containing $\Delta$. Since $\Rightarrow^q_\Delta$ is a least such relation, this gives us $\mathcal{C}^q_\Delta(u) \subseteq \mathrm{Th}(\overrightarrow{\Delta} \cup \Delta(\mathrm{Th}(u)))$. □

The above description shows that quasi-classical production inference amounts to a general production inference which is based, in a sense, on a modified background logic Th that includes $\overrightarrow{\Delta}$ as the set of axioms. As a consequence, we obtain the following description of the associated causal nonmonotonic semantics.

**Corollary 8.92** *A world $\alpha$ is an exact world of $\Rightarrow^q_\Delta$ iff $\alpha = \mathrm{Th}(\overrightarrow{\Delta}, \Delta(\alpha))$.*

Recall that causally consistent worlds are precisely the worlds that satisfy $\overrightarrow{\Delta}$. Accordingly, the above description says that $\alpha$ is an exact world of $\Rightarrow^q_\Delta$ if and only if it is the only *causally consistent* world containing $\Delta(\alpha)$.

Despite apparent plausibility, the following example shows, however, that quasi-classical inference produces seemingly unexpected results.

**Example 8.6** A causal theory $\Delta = \{p \Rightarrow q,\ \neg q \Rightarrow \neg q\}$ has an empty causal semantics. However, $p \Rightarrow q$ implies $\mathbf{t} \Rightarrow (p \to q)$ by Weak Deduction, and then $\neg q \Rightarrow (p \to q)$ by Strengthening. Coupled with $\neg q \Rightarrow \neg q$, this gives us $\neg q \Rightarrow \neg p$, namely the contraposition of $p \Rightarrow q$. As a result, $\Rightarrow^q_\Delta$ already has an exact world, namely $\{\neg p, \neg q\}$.

The above example shows, of course, that quasi-classical inference can change the causal nonmonotonic semantics. It still does not show, however, that such an inference can produce downright wrong results. Note in this respect that, since Weak Deduction is a classically valid rule, quasi-classical inference can only add new exact worlds, and never eliminates them (cf. Corollary 8.64). Accordingly, the nonmonotonic conclusions obtained by this inference will always be valid with respect to the 'standard' causal nonmonotonic semantics of causal theories.

An additional attractive feature of quasi-classical inference can be found in the fact that it corresponds to abductive reasoning based on classical consequence relations. To begin with, the following result shows that the least supraclassical consequence relation $\vdash_{\Rightarrow}$ containing a quasi-classical regular relation $\Rightarrow$ is fully classical.

**Lemma 8.93** *If $\Rightarrow$ is a regular production relation, then $\vdash_{\Rightarrow}$ is a classical consequence relation if and only if $\Rightarrow$ is quasi-classical.*

***Proof.*** Let $\Rightarrow$ be a quasi-classical and regular production relation. If $A \wedge B \vdash_{\Rightarrow} C$, then $A \wedge B \Rightarrow (A \wedge B) \rightarrow C$. Consequently, $\mathbf{t} \Rightarrow (A \wedge B) \rightarrow C$ by Weak Deduction, and therefore $A \Rightarrow (A \wedge B) \rightarrow C$, that is, $A \vdash_{\Rightarrow} (B \rightarrow C)$. This shows that Deduction holds for $\vdash_{\Rightarrow}$, and therefore it is a classical consequence relation.

Assume now that $\vdash_{\Rightarrow}$ is a classical consequence relation, and $B \Rightarrow C$. Then $B \vdash_{\Rightarrow} C$, and therefore $\mathbf{t} \vdash_{\Rightarrow} B \rightarrow C$ by Deduction, which is equivalent to $\mathbf{t} \Rightarrow B \rightarrow C$. Hence Weak Deduction holds for $\Rightarrow$ and therefore it is quasi-classical. □

An abductive system $(\mathrm{Cn}, \mathcal{A})$ will be called *classical* if Cn is a classical consequence relation (see Chapter 2). A classical consequence relation can be seen as a classical entailment augmented with a set of nonlogical axioms. Consequently, a classical abductive system can be safely equated with a pair $(\Sigma, \mathcal{A})$, where $\Sigma$ is a set of classical propositions (the domain theory), and $\mathcal{A}$ a set of abducibles. Moreover, the associated Scott consequence relation $\vdash_{\mathbb{A}}$ will be a consequence relation that is base-generated by $\mathcal{A}$ in the sense of [Bochman, 2001].

The following result establishes the correspondence between classical abductive systems and quasi-classical causal relations.

**Theorem 8.94** *An abductive production relation is generated by a classical abductive system if and only if it is causal and quasi-classical.*

***Proof.*** Note first that a classical abductive system is already $\mathcal{A}$-disjunctive, so its associated production relation will be causal. Also, it can be verified that $\neg A \Rightarrow_{\mathbb{A}} \mathbf{f}$ holds for the production relation associated with an arbitrary abductive system $\mathbb{A} = (\mathrm{Cn}, \mathcal{A})$ if and only if $\mathrm{Cn}(\neg A)$ is an inconsistent theory. Now, if Cn is classical, this is equivalent to $A \in \mathrm{Cn}(\mathbf{t})$ (by Deduction), while the latter immediately implies $\mathbf{t} \Rightarrow_{\mathbb{A}} A$. This shows that the associated production relation will be quasi-classical.

Assume now that $\Rightarrow$ is a quasi-classical abductive production relation. By Theorem 8.30, it is generated by an abductive system $(\mathrm{Cn}_{\Rightarrow}, \mathcal{A}_{\Rightarrow})$, where $\mathrm{Cn}_{\Rightarrow}$ is the least supraclassical consequence relation containing $\Rightarrow$. Moreover, by Lemma 8.93, $\mathrm{Cn}_{\Rightarrow}$ is actually a classical consequence relation. As a result, $\Rightarrow$ is generated by a classical abductive system. □

To end this section, note that a natural further strengthening of Weak Deduction is full Contraposition:

**(Contraposition)** If $A \Rightarrow B$, then $\neg B \Rightarrow \neg A$.

As can be verified, Contraposition is valid for all symmetric accessibility relations. Note, however, that even this property still does not transform production relations into (reflexive) consequence relations.

## 8.8 Partial Production Inference

In this section we are going to describe a logical formalism of partial production relations. The formalism will provide, in particular, a logical representation for partial nonmonotonic semantics, studied earlier.

At first glance, the idea of giving a partial (namely four-valued) generalization of causal relations does not look promising since, as has been shown earlier, causal relations are already four-valued in some sense. Fortunately, there exists an elegant way of separating the two kinds of partiality, which is based on an invariant possible worlds semantics described in Chapter 4.

As our basic logical language we will take below the invariant four-valued language, obtained from the classical language by adding the negation connective $\sim$ (see Sec. 4.3). The new negation connective will be called a *relevant negation*, and it will function as a global negation with respect to theories and worlds of an invariant four-valued logic on which the production relation will be defined. Accordingly it will be distinct from the global negation, studied earlier as part of the four-valued representation of the production relation itself (see Sec. 8.4.2). In particular, it will not satisfy the characteristic rules of the latter negation, such as $\neg A \Rightarrow \sim A$ and $\sim A \Rightarrow \neg A$. As a result, the relevant negation will not be eliminable in the context of production relations.

An axiomatization of the partial production inference will be obtained by considering production relations that are based on the invariant four-valued logic $\mathbb{L}_4^i$ instead of the classical logic. As before $\mathbf{t}$ ($\mathbf{f}$) will denote an arbitrary classical tautology (respectively, contradiction).

**Definition 8.36** A relation $\Rightarrow$ on the set of invariant propositions will be called a *partial production relation* if it satisfies the following postulates:

**(I-Strengthening)** If $A \vDash_4 B$ and $B \Rightarrow C$, then $A \Rightarrow C$;
**(I-Weakening)** If $A \Rightarrow B$ and $B \vDash_4 C$, then $A \Rightarrow C$;
**(And)** If $A \Rightarrow B$ and $A \Rightarrow C$, then $A \Rightarrow B \wedge C$;
**(Truth)** $\mathbf{t} \Rightarrow \mathbf{t}$;
**(Falsity)** $\mathbf{f} \Rightarrow \mathbf{f}$.

As can be seen from the above description, partial production relations constitute a direct generalization of ordinary production relations to the language of invariant propositions. Moreover, most of the results and notions, described earlier, can be easily transferred to this generalized setting. That is why we will concentrate below only on the results and constructions that will make a difference.

As in the standard setting, a partial production relation will be called *regular*, if it satisfies Cut, *basic*, if it satisfies Or, and *causal*, if it satisfies both. Similarly, all the other notions defined earlier for production relations will be extended to partial ones, with the proviso that the classical entailment $\vDash$ and associated provability operator Th should be systematically replaced with the four-valued entailment $\vDash_4$ and corresponding provability operator that will be denoted by $\mathrm{Th}_4$. In addition, the notions of a literal or a world should be replaced with 4-literals and 4-worlds, *etc.*

In what follows, by a *partial causal theory* we will mean an arbitrary causal theory in the invariant language. As an immediate generalization of Proposition 8.6, we will have the following description of the least partial production relation containing a partial causal theory $\Delta$.

**Lemma 8.95** $\mathcal{C}_\Delta(u) = \mathrm{Th}_4(\Delta(\mathrm{Th}_4(u)))$.

Recall now that four-valued logics can be translated into classical logic by doubling the set of atoms (see Sec. 4.1.7). This translation can now be transferred to partial production relations, which will give us a translation of the latter into ordinary production relations. More exactly, given a partial causal theory $\Delta$, we will define the following causal theory $|\Delta|$ in the classical language:

$$|\Delta| = \{|A| \Rightarrow |B| \mid A \Rightarrow B \in \Delta\},$$

where $|\ |$ is the classical translation defined in Sec. 4.1.7. Then we obtain

**Lemma 8.96** *A partial production rule $A \Rightarrow B$ is derivable from $\Delta$ iff $|A| \Rightarrow |B|$ is derivable from $|\Delta|$.*

Furthermore, Corollary 8.48 allows us to translate $|\Delta|$ into a classical theory, which gives us a two-step translation of partial causal theories into ordinary classical theories.

Finally note that an alternative axiomatization of partial regular and partial causal inference can be obtained simply by taking the corresponding postulates for ordinary production relations and adding to them the following postulates for the relevant negation:

**(Double Negation)** $\mathbf{t} \Rightarrow {\sim\sim}A \leftrightarrow A$;
**(de Morgan)** $\mathbf{t} \Rightarrow {\sim}(A \wedge B) \leftrightarrow ({\sim}A \vee {\sim}B)$;
**(Commutativity)** $\mathbf{t} \Rightarrow {\sim}\neg A \leftrightarrow \neg{\sim}A$.

Note that the above postulates correspond to the axioms of the logic $\mathbb{L}_4^i$ from Sec. 4.3. In addition, due to Lemma 8.12, a rule $\mathbf{t} \Rightarrow A \leftrightarrow B$ implies that $A$ and $B$ can replace each other both in heads and bodies of production rules. As a result, the postulates I-Strengthening and I-Weakening can now be derived from plain Strengthening and Weakening.

### 8.8.1 *Possible worlds semantics*

The semantic characterization of partial basic and partial causal relations can be obtained in terms of possible worlds models defined below.

**Definition 8.37**

- A *relational possible worlds $*$-model* is a quadruple $\mathbb{W} = (W, R, ^*, V)$, where $(W, ^*, V)$ is a $*$-model, while $R$ is a binary relation on $W$.
- A relational $*$-model will be called *regular*, if $R$ is quasi-reflexive.

As has been shown in Sec. 4.3.2, $*$-models provide a representation for the invariant language, so relational $*$-models constitute a natural partial generalization of possible worlds semantics for basic and causal production inference.

Retaining the previous definition of validity for causal rules, let us denote by $\Rightarrow_{\mathbb{W}}$ the set of all productions that are valid in a relational $*$-model $\mathbb{W}$. It can be easily verified that this set is closed with respect to the postulates for partial basic productions, and hence we have

**Lemma 8.97** *If $\mathbb{W}$ is a relational $*$-model, then $\Rightarrow_{\mathbb{W}}$ is a partial basic production relation. Moreover, if $\mathbb{W}$ is regular, then $\Rightarrow_{\mathbb{W}}$ is a partial causal relation.*

In order to prove completeness, for any partial basic production relation $\Rightarrow$ we will construct its *canonical possible worlds model* $\mathbb{W}_{\Rightarrow}$ as a quadruple $\mathbb{W}_{\Rightarrow} = (W, \mathcal{B}, {}^*, V)$ such that $W$ is a set of all 4-worlds of the language, $V$ is a function assigning each 4-world its corresponding four-valued interpretation, $^*$ is a function assigning each 4-world its dual $\alpha^*$, while, as before, $\mathcal{B}$ is a relation on $W$ defined as follows:

$$\alpha\mathcal{B}\beta \equiv \mathcal{C}(\alpha) \subseteq \beta.$$

Then the next result shows that this semantics is strongly complete for the source partial causal relation.

**Lemma 8.98** *If $\mathbb{W}_{\Rightarrow}$ is the canonical semantics of a partial causal relation $\Rightarrow$, then, for any set $u$ of propositions and any $A$,*

$$u \Rightarrow A \textit{ iff } A \in \beta, \textit{ for any } \alpha, \beta \in W \textit{ such that } \alpha\mathcal{B}\beta \textit{ and } u \subseteq \alpha$$

As a conclusion, we obtain

**Theorem 8.99** *$\Rightarrow$ is a partial basic production relation if and only if it has a relational possible worlds $*$-model.*

Similarly, it can be shown that partial causal relations are determined by quasi-reflexive $*$-models.

### 8.8.2 *Partial nonmonotonic semantics*

For partial production relations, we adopt practically the same definition of the causal nonmonotonic semantics, namely the set of all 4-worlds (i.e., maximal consistent sets of propositions in the language $\{\wedge, \neg, \sim\}$) that are fixed points of $\mathcal{C}$.

**Definition 8.38** A *partial nonmonotonic semantics* of a partial production relation or a partial causal theory is the set of all its exact 4-worlds.

Since 4-world is a syntactic counterpart of a four-valued interpretation, it is uniquely determined by the literals of the form $p, \neg p, \sim p, *p$. This immediately gives us the following description of exact 4-worlds.

**Lemma 8.100** *A 4-world $\alpha$ is an exact world of a partial production relation if and only if, for any propositional atom $p$,*

$$p \in \alpha \textit{ iff } \alpha \Rightarrow p \qquad p \notin \alpha \textit{ iff } \alpha \Rightarrow \neg p$$
$$*p \in \alpha \textit{ iff } \alpha \Rightarrow *p \qquad *p \notin \alpha \textit{ iff } \alpha \Rightarrow \sim p.$$

By Lemma 8.95, the partial nonmonotonic semantics of a causal theory $\Delta$ is the set of 4-worlds $\alpha$ such that $\alpha = \mathrm{Th}_4(\Delta(\alpha))$. Again, this description can be reformulated as follows:

**Corollary 8.101** *A 4-world $\alpha$ is an exact world of a partial causal theory $\Delta$ if and only if, for any propositional atom $p$,*

$$p \in \alpha \ \ \textit{iff} \ \ \Delta(\alpha) \vDash_4 p \qquad p \notin \alpha \ \ \textit{iff} \ \ \Delta(\alpha) \vDash_4 \neg p$$
$$*p \in \alpha \ \ \textit{iff} \ \ \Delta(\alpha) \vDash_4 *p \qquad *\,p \notin \alpha \ \ \textit{iff} \ \ \Delta(\alpha) \vDash_4 \sim p$$

As in the standard case, it turns out that partial causal relations provide an adequate framework for reasoning with respect to the partial nonmonotonic semantics.

**Definition 8.39** Partial causal theories $\Gamma$ and $\Delta$ will be called *p-causally equivalent* if they determine the same partial causal relation.

Two partial causal theories are p-causally equivalent if each theory can be obtained from the other using the inference postulates of partial causal relations. Then the following theorem shows that partial causal relations constitute a maximal logic suitable for the partial nonmonotonic semantics. The proof practically coincides with the proofs of Theorems 8.63 and 8.19.

**Theorem 8.102** *Partial causal theories are strongly equivalent with respect to the partial nonmonotonic semantics if and only if they are p-causally equivalent.*

Finally, it can be shown that any partial causal theory is nonmonotonically equivalent to a determinate causal theory having the rules of the form $A \Rightarrow l$, where $l$ is either a 4-literal or $\mathbf{f}$. Namely, Lemma 8.100 shows that exact 4-worlds are uniquely determined by determinate rules. Consequently, any causal theory can be transformed into a partially equivalent determinate theory. Actually, the algorithm used earlier for transforming a causal theory $\Delta$ into a determinate theory $\Delta_d$ can be immediately adapted to the case of partial production relations.

### 8.8.3 *Invariance*

As we will see in what follows, partial semantics for biconsequence relations are reducible to special instances of the partial nonmonotonic semantics. Moreover, these special instances actually admit a stronger underlying causal logic that we are going to describe now.

**Definition 8.40** A partial production relation will be called *invariant*, if it satisfies the following postulate:

**(Invariance)** If $\neg A \Rightarrow \neg B$, then $\sim A \Rightarrow \sim B$.

The Invariance postulate is similar to the rule of L-Invariance that characterizes invariant four-valued inference (see Sec. 4.3.3), but it acts on production rules. Roughly, it says that production inference is invariant with respect to taking duals of invariant propositional formulas. A semantic description of this invariant inference will be given below. For now note that, since $A$ and $B$ above are arbitrary propositions, Invariance is equivalent to each of the following rules:

If $A \Rightarrow B$, then $*A \Rightarrow *B$.
If $*A \Rightarrow *B$, then $A \Rightarrow B$.
If $\sim A \Rightarrow \sim B$, then $\neg A \Rightarrow \neg B$.

Thus, Invariance implies, ultimately, that $\neg A \Rightarrow \neg B$ is equivalent to $\sim A \Rightarrow \sim B$ and $A \Rightarrow B$ is equivalent to $*A \Rightarrow *B$.

A semantic characterization of invariance for partial basic production inference is given in the next definition.

**Definition 8.41** A relational $*$-model will be called *invariant*, if the accessibility relation satisfies the following condition, for any worlds $\alpha, \beta$:

$$\text{If } \alpha R \beta, \text{ then } \alpha^* R \beta^*.$$

Taking into account the intended meaning of pairs $(\alpha, \alpha^*)$ as representing four-valued interpretations, the above condition says, in effect, that production inference is invariant with respect to taking duals of four-valued interpretations.

**Theorem 8.103** *A partial basic production relation is invariant if and only if it has an invariant relational $*$-model.*

***Proof.*** It can be directly verified that partial production relation generated by an invariant relational $*$-model satisfies the Invariance postulate. In the other direction, it is sufficient to check that the canonical relational $*$-model of an invariant basic production relation is invariant. Indeed, assume that $\mathcal{C}(\alpha) \subseteq \beta$, and $\alpha^* \Rightarrow A$. Then $\alpha \Rightarrow *A$ by Invariance, and hence $*A \in \beta$, that is, $A \in \beta^*$. Consequently $\mathcal{C}(\alpha^*) \subseteq \beta^*$, which means that the canonical model is invariant. □

Invariance implies the following property of the partial nonmonotonic semantics. The proof is immediate

**Lemma 8.104** *If $\alpha$ is an exact 4-world of an invariant production relation $\Rightarrow$, then $\alpha^*$ is also an exact 4-world of $\Rightarrow$.*

For a partial causal theory $\Delta$, we will denote by $\Delta^i$ the union of $\Delta$ and the following set of dual rules:

$$\{*A \Rightarrow *B \mid A \Rightarrow B \in \Delta\}.$$

Let $\Rightarrow^i_\Delta$ denote by the least invariant partial production relation including $\Delta$. Then we have

**Lemma 8.105** $\Rightarrow^i_\Delta = \Rightarrow_{\Delta^i}$.

***Proof.*** Due to Invariance, $\Delta^i$ is obviously included in $\Rightarrow^i_\Delta$, which gives us $\Rightarrow_{\Delta^i} \subseteq \Rightarrow^i_\Delta$. In the other direction, it is sufficient to show that $\Rightarrow_{\Delta^i}$ is an invariant production relation. By Lemma 8.95, if $A \Rightarrow_{\Delta^i} B$, then $B \in \mathrm{Th}_4(\Delta^i(\mathrm{Th}_4(A)))$, and hence there exist finite sets $\{A_i\}$ and $\{B_i\}$ of propositions such that, for any $i$, $A \vDash_4 A_i$, $A_i \Rightarrow B_i \in \Delta^i$, and $\bigwedge B_i \vDash_4 B$. By the construction of $\Delta^i$, we have $*A_i \Rightarrow *B_i \in \Delta^i$. But $\vDash_4$ is an invariant four-valued inference, so we have also $*A \vDash_4 *A_i$ and $\bigwedge *B_i \vDash_4 *B$. Consequently $*B \in \mathrm{Th}_4(\Delta^i(\mathrm{Th}_4(*A)))$, which implies $*A \Rightarrow_{\Delta^i} *B$. Thus, $\Rightarrow_{\Delta^i}$ is invariant, and therefore $\Rightarrow^i_\Delta \subseteq \Rightarrow_{\Delta^i}$. This completes the proof. □

The above result shows, in effect, that the invariant production inference with respect to a partial causal theory $\Delta$ amounts to a general partial production inference with respect to a 'doubled' theory $\Delta^i$. This fact will be used in the next section.

### 8.8.4 *Doubling*

Finally we will show that the partial exact semantics of ordinary production inference can be viewed as a special case of a partial nonmonotonic semantics. The following construction can also be seen as a logical basis of doubling used earlier for describing partial nonmonotonic semantics for biconsequence relations (see Sec. 5.5.1).

Given a causal theory $\Delta$ in a classical language, we define an associated partial causal theory $\Delta^*$ as the set of all rules of the form $A \Rightarrow *B$ and $*A \Rightarrow B$ such that $A \Rightarrow B$ belongs to $\Delta$.

The partial causal theory $\Delta^*$ has a special feature, namely no 4-literal appears both in the head and body of a production rule. This feature implies the following *split property* of the associated partial production relation:

**Lemma 8.106** *If $u, v, A, B$ are classical propositions, then*

$$u, *v \Rightarrow_{\Delta^*} A \vee *B \quad \textit{iff} \quad u \Rightarrow_{\Delta} B \text{ or } v \Rightarrow_{\Delta} A.$$

***Proof.*** For a direction from right to left, we will show that $A \Rightarrow_{\Delta} B$ implies both $A \Rightarrow_{\Delta^*} *B$ and $*A \Rightarrow_{\Delta^*} B$. By Lemma 8.95, if $A \Rightarrow_{\Delta} B$, then $B \in \mathrm{Th}_4(\Delta(\mathrm{Th}_4(A)))$, and hence there exist finite sets $\{A_i\}$ and $\{B_i\}$ such that, for any $i$, $A \vDash_4 A_i$, $A_i \Rightarrow B_i \in \Delta$, and $\bigwedge B_i \vDash_4 B$. Then $A_i \Rightarrow *B_i \in \Delta^*$ and $\bigwedge *B_i \vDash_4 *B$, and therefore $A \Rightarrow_{\Delta^*} *B$. Similarly, it can be proved that $*A \Rightarrow_{\Delta^*} B$.

Assume now that $u \not\Rightarrow_{\Delta} B$ and $v \not\Rightarrow_{\Delta} A$. Then by Lemma 8.6 there are worlds $\alpha, \beta$ such that $\Delta(\mathrm{Th}(u)) \subseteq \alpha$, $B \notin \alpha$, $\Delta(\mathrm{Th}(v)) \subseteq \beta$ and $A \notin \beta$. Let $\nu$ be a four-valued interpretation determined by (the classical interpretations corresponding to) the pair $(\beta, \alpha)$. Clearly, $\nu \not\vDash A \vee *B$. We will show, however, that $\nu$ is a model of $\Delta^*(\mathrm{Th}_4(u \cup *v))$. If $C \in \Delta^*(\mathrm{Th}_4(u \cup *v))$, then $\Delta^*$ contains a rule $D \Rightarrow C$ such that $u, *v \vDash_4 D$. Assume for certainty that $D \Rightarrow C$ has the form $D_0 \Rightarrow *C_0$, where $D_0 \Rightarrow C_0 \in \Delta$ (the second case, namely $*D_0 \Rightarrow C_0$, is similar). Then $u, *v \vDash_4 D_0$, where $D_0$ is a classical proposition, and hence $u \vDash D_0$ by Corollary 4.19 (note that $v$ is classically consistent, since $v \not\Rightarrow_{\Delta} A$). Consequently $C_0 \in \Delta(\mathrm{Th}(u))$, and therefore $C_0 \in \alpha$. By the definition of $\nu$, we have $\nu \vDash *C_0$, and consequently $\nu \vDash C$. Thus, $\nu$ is a model of $\Delta^*(\mathrm{Th}_4(u \cup *v))$, which gives us $u, *v \not\Rightarrow_{\Delta^*} A \vee *B$ by Lemma 8.95. □

Now we have all that is necessary for the basic result showing that the partial exact semantics is representable as a special case of the partial nonmonotonic semantics.

**Theorem 8.107** *Let $\Delta$ be a causal theory in a classical language. Then a world pair $(\alpha, \beta)$ is exact for $\Delta$ if and only if $\mathrm{Th}_4(\alpha \cup *\beta)$ is an exact 4-world of $\Delta^*$.*

***Proof.*** $\mathrm{Th}_4(\alpha \cup *\beta)$ is an exact 4-world of $\Delta^*$ if and only if $\mathrm{Th}_4(\alpha \cup *\beta) = \mathcal{C}_{\Delta^*}(\alpha \cup *\beta)$. By Corollary 4.19, this is reducible to the following two equivalences, for any classical proposition $A$:

$$A \in \alpha \quad \text{iff} \quad \alpha, *\beta \Rightarrow_{\Delta^*} A$$
$$A \in \beta \quad \text{iff} \quad \alpha, *\beta \Rightarrow_{\Delta^*} *A.$$

But by the preceding lemma we have

$$\alpha, *\beta \Rightarrow_{\Delta^*} A \quad \text{iff} \quad \beta \Rightarrow_{\Delta} A$$
$$\alpha, *\beta \Rightarrow_{\Delta^*} *A \quad \text{iff} \quad \alpha \Rightarrow_{\Delta} A.$$

Consequently, the above two equivalences are reducible to

$$A \in \alpha \quad \text{iff} \quad \beta \Rightarrow_{\Delta} A$$
$$A \in \beta \quad \text{iff} \quad \alpha \Rightarrow_{\Delta} A.$$

The above two conditions say, however, that $(\alpha, \beta)$ is an exact pair. □

Finally, we will show that the above doubling construction can be simplified if we take an invariant production inference as an underlying logic.

For a causal theory $\Delta$ in a classical language, let us introduce now the following partial causal theory:

$$\Delta_* = \{A \Rightarrow *B \mid A \Rightarrow B \in \Delta\}.$$

As can be seen, the earlier doubled partial causal theory $\Delta^*$ is nothing other than the invariant closure of $\Delta_*$, that is, $\Delta^* = \Delta_*^i$. In view of Lemma 8.105, this implies, in particular, that $\Rightarrow_{\Delta^*}$ is an invariant production relation. Moreover, we immediately have

**Corollary 8.108** *A world pair $(\alpha, \beta)$ is exact for a causal theory $\Delta$ iff* $\mathrm{Th}_4(\alpha \cup *\beta)$ *is an exact 4-world of the least invariant production relation containing $\Delta_*$.*

### 8.8.4.1 *Partial extensions and expansions*

The above doubling construction has actually a much wider scope than what has been stated so far. To see this, note that it is similar to the doubling construction for biconsequence relations, described in Sec. 5.5.1. In fact, this similarity can be turned into an exact equivalence when we note that, if a bisequent theory $\Delta$ corresponds to an ordinary causal theory $\Delta_c$, then the doubled bisequent theory $\Delta'$ corresponds to the classical translation $|\Delta_c^*|$ of the partial causal theory $\Delta_c^*$ (see Lemma 8.96).

Abusing our terminology somewhat, for a *bisequent* theory $\Delta$, we will denote by $\Delta^*$ the partial causal theory obtained by doubling the causal theory that corresponds to $\Delta$. In other words, for each bisequent $a{:}b \Vdash c{:}d$ of $\Delta$, the theory $\Delta^*$ will contain the following two production rules:

$$\neg b, d \Rightarrow \bigwedge *a \to \bigvee *c \quad \text{and} \quad \sim b, *d \Rightarrow \bigwedge a \to \bigvee c.$$

In addition, given a pair $(u, v)$ of sets of propositional atoms, we will denote by $\alpha_{(u,v)}$ the unique 4-world determined by the set of 4-atoms $u \cup *v$. Then the correspondence between the two doubling constructions, coupled with Theorems 5.69 and 8.107, will give us

**Corollary 8.109** *A pair $(u, v)$ is a partial exact bitheory of a bisequent theory $\Delta$ if and only if $\alpha_{(u,v)}$ is an exact 4-world of $\Delta^*$.*

By the above result, the partial exact semantics of a bisequent theory $\Delta$ corresponds precisely to the partial nonmonotonic semantics of $\Delta^*$. Moreover, Theorem 5.69 can now be used for providing a logical basis for the partial stable and partial supported semantics of biconsequence relations. Namely, these semantics will be represented, respectively, as partial nonmonotonic semantics of negatively closed and tight partial causal relations.

As before, a partial production relation will be called *negatively closed*, if it satisfies Default Negation, and *tight*, if it is negatively closed and satisfies Semi-Classicality. Note that, for invariant partial production relations, Default Negation is equivalent to $\sim p \Rightarrow \sim p$, for any propositional atom $p$ (and similarly for Semi-Classicality).

Now as a consequence of Theorem 5.31 and Corollary 5.50, we obtain, respectively,

**Theorem 8.110** *A pair $(u, v)$ is a partial extension [partial expansion] of a bisequent theory $\Delta$ if and only if $\alpha_{(u,v)}$ is an exact 4-world of the least negatively closed [resp. tight] partial production relation containing $\Delta^*$.*

By the above result, the partial stable and partial supported semantics of a bisequent theory $\Delta$ correspond, respectively, to the partial nonmonotonic semantics of the least negatively closed and least tight partial production relations containing $\Delta^*$.

As for the partial exact semantics, the associated partial production relations are implicitly invariant, which immediately suggests the following simplified representation.

For a bisequent theory $\Delta$, we will denote by $\Delta_*$ the following partial causal theory:

$$\Delta_* = \{\sim b, *d \Rightarrow \bigwedge a \to \bigvee c \mid a{:}b \Vdash c{:}d \in \Delta\}.$$

**Corollary 8.111** *A pair $(u, v)$ is a partial extension [expansion] of a bisequent theory $\Delta$ iff $\alpha_{(u,v)}$ is an exact 4-world of the least negatively closed [tight] invariant production relation containing $\Delta_*$.*

The above descriptions will be used in the next section for a causal interpretation of logic programs.

## 8.9 Causal Interpretation of Logic Programs

In this section we are going to show that causal inference relations provide a natural logical basis for logic programming. More exactly, on the causal interpretation, any general logic program can be seen as a causal theory satisfying the Negation As Default principle (alias Closed World Assumption). As for the biconsequence interpretation, the correspondence between logic programs and causal theories will turn out to be bidirectional in the sense that, for an appropriate causal logic, any causal theory will be reducible to a logic program. Moreover, the correspondence will be shown to be adequate for a broad range of logic programming semantics, including stable, supported and partial stable models.

Speaking generally, the causal interpretation is based on a recurrent idea that logic program rules express causal, or explanatory, relationship between propositional atoms (see, e.g., [Dix *et al.*, 1994; Schubert, 1994]). The declarative meaning of logic programs contains, however, an additional component, namely, an asymmetric treatment of positive and negative information, which is reflected in viewing **not** as *negation as failure*. It turns out that such an understanding can be uniformly captured in causal logic by accepting the Default Negation postulate that gives a formal expression to the Closed Word Assumption.

In what follows, we will denote by $DN$ the set of causal rules $\neg p \Rightarrow \neg p$, for all propositional atoms $p$ of the underlying language.

### 8.9.1 *The stable interpretation*

The *stable (causal) interpretation* amounts to interpreting a program rule $\mathbf{not}\, d, c \leftarrow a, \mathbf{not}\, b$ as the following causal rule:

$$d, \neg b \Rightarrow \bigwedge a \to \bigvee c.$$

The interpretation gives a classical understanding to **not**, but makes the relevant classical literals $\neg b$ explanatory assumptions. As a result, the non-classicality of this representation amounts solely to the non-classicality of $\Rightarrow$.

For a program $\Pi$, we will denote by $st(\Pi)$ the set of causal rules corresponding by this interpretation to the rules of $\Pi$, while $ST(\Pi)$ will denote the union of $st(\Pi)$ and $DN$. Then we have

**Theorem 8.112** *The nonmonotonic semantics of $ST(\Pi)$ coincides with the stable semantics of $\Pi$.*

***Proof.*** By Proposition 5.84, stable models of $\Pi$ coincide with extensions of $bc(\Pi)$. By Lemma 8.79, the latter coincide with extensions of $st(\Pi)$, and hence with exact worlds of $ST(\Pi)$ by Corollary 8.80. □

The above result[13] shows that the stable causal interpretation of program rules provides an adequate description of logic programs under the stable semantics. Moreover, negatively closed causal relations constitute a precise causal logic behind stable logic programming. Indeed, if $\Rightarrow^c_\Delta$ is the least negatively closed causal relation containing a causal theory $\Delta$, then Theorem 8.112 gives us

**Corollary 8.113** *The stable semantics of a program $\Pi$ coincides with the nonmonotonic semantics of $\Rightarrow^c_{st(\Pi)}$.*

Thus, negatively closed causal relations can be seen as a causal logic of logic programs under the stable semantics. Moreover, since such causal relations are maximal for extensions, they constitute actually a maximal causal logic for the stable semantics.

Recall now that any causal rule is reducible to a set of 'clausal' causal rules $\bigwedge a \Rightarrow \bigvee b$, where $a$ and $b$ are sets of classical literals. Moreover, under the stable interpretation of logic programs, each such causal rule can be identified with some program rule. Accordingly, for a causal theory $\Delta$, we will denote by $pr(\Delta)$ the set of program rules obtained in this way from $\Delta$. Then the following result can be shown:

**Corollary 8.114** *For any causal theory $\Delta$, the nonmonotonic semantics of $\Rightarrow^c_\Delta$ coincides with the stable semantics of the program $pr(\Delta)$.*

***Proof.*** By Theorem 8.112, the stable semantics of $pr(\Delta)$ coincides with the nonmonotonic semantics of $\Rightarrow^c_{\Delta'}$, where $\Delta'$ is a clausal reduction of $\Delta$. But $\Delta'$ is causally equivalent to $\Delta$, hence the result. □

Thus, under the stable causal interpretation, any causal theory is reducible, in turn, to a logic program.

[13] For the case of disjunctive programs, this result has actually been proved as an auxiliary lemma in [Giunchiglia *et al.*, 2004].

### 8.9.2 *The supported interpretation*

Since stable and supported semantics of logic programs are based on a different understanding of program rules, the latter should have a different causal interpretation under the supported semantics. The corresponding causal interpretation of logic programs can be obtained by interpreting a program rule $\mathbf{not}\, d, c \leftarrow a, \mathbf{not}\, b$ as the following causal rule:

$$a, d, \neg b \Rightarrow \bigvee c.$$

We will call this causal interpretation a *supported interpretation* of program rules. The only difference with the stable interpretation, described earlier, amounts to treating positive premises in $a$ as additional assumptions (causal explanations), rather than as part of what is explained.

Let us denote by $su(\Pi)$ the set of causal rules corresponding by this interpretation to the rules of a program $\Pi$. As we already mentioned, however, a full meaning of a logic program presupposes also the principle of Default Negation. Accordingly, let us denote by $SU(\Pi)$ a causal theory which is the union of $su(\Pi)$ and the set $DN$ of default negation rules. Then we obtain

**Theorem 8.115** *The nonmonotonic semantics of $SU(\Pi)$ coincides with the set of supported models of $\Pi$.*

***Proof.*** By Proposition 5.87, supported models of $\Pi$ coincide with expansions of $abc(\Pi)$. By Lemma 8.86, the latter coincide with expansions of $su(\Pi)$, and hence with exact worlds of $SU(\Pi)$ by Corollary 8.87. □

The above result shows that the supported causal interpretation of program rules provides an adequate description of logic programs under the supported semantics.

It is interesting to observe that the admissibility of the Cut rule for the supported semantics (that follows from the above theorem) immediately implies the correctness of the principle of partial evaluation for logic programs under the completion semantics (see [Lloyd and Shepherdson, 1991]).

Note now that the supported causal interpretation produces only head-positive causal rules. As has been shown earlier, the reasoning with such rules admits a stronger causal logic of tight causal relations. As a consequence, tight causal relations constitute an adequate causal logic for logic programs under the supported semantics. Moreover, tight causal relations constitute a maximal causal logic for the supported semantics.

Let us say that two causal theories are *tightly equivalent*, if they determine the same tight causal relation (that is, each can be obtained from the other using the postulates of causal relations, Default Negation and Semi-Classicality). Then we have

**Lemma 8.116** *Programs $\Pi_1$ and $\Pi_2$ are strongly expansion-equivalent if and only if $su(\Pi_1)$ and $su(\Pi_2)$ are tightly equivalent.*

The above result implies that tight causal relations are maximal causal relations that are adequate for the supported semantics of the associated logic programs. Furthermore, any causal theory is tightly equivalent, in a sense, to some logic program.

By Lemma 8.84, any causal theory is reducible to a set of rules of the form $a, \neg b \Rightarrow \hat{p}$, where $a$ and $b$ are sets of atoms, while $\hat{p}$ is either an atom $p$, or the falsity constant $\mathbf{f}$. Note now that, under the supported interpretation of program rules, any causal rule $a, \neg b \Rightarrow p$ corresponds to a unique normal program rule $p \leftarrow a, \mathbf{not}\, b$, while a causal rule $a, \neg b \Rightarrow \mathbf{f}$ corresponds to a constraint $\leftarrow a, \mathbf{not}\, b$. Let us denote by $npr(\Delta)$ the logic program obtained by this procedure from an arbitrary causal theory $\Delta$. Then we obtain

**Corollary 8.117** *Any causal theory $\Delta$ is tightly equivalent to $su(npr(\Delta))$.*

### 8.9.3 *Partial causal interpretations*

Now we are going to show that partial causal relations provide a logical representation for the main partial semantics of logic programs.

#### 8.9.3.1 *Partial supported interpretation*

A *partial supported interpretation* of logic programs is obtained by interpreting a program rule $\mathbf{not}\, d, c \leftarrow a, \mathbf{not}\, b$ as the following causal rule:

$$a, *d, \sim b \Rightarrow \bigvee c.$$

By Invariance, the above rule is equivalent to

$$*a, d, \neg b \Rightarrow \bigvee *c.$$

As a matter of fact, the above two causal rules correspond precisely to the *split*, or *doubling*, of program rules used in [Drabent and Martelli, 1991; Wallace, 1993; Gelder and Schlipf, 1993] for representing 3-completion. Note also that, as has been shown in [Stärk, 1996], three- and four-valued consequences of such a completion coincide, so we can freely use our general four-valued representation.

Since the three-valued completion has been defined so far only for normal logic programs, let $PSU(\Pi)$ denote the causal theory containing the above translation of all the rules of a *normal* program $\Pi$, plus the set $DN$ of default negation rules. Then we obtain

**Theorem 8.118** *The nonmonotonic semantics of* $PSU(\Pi)$ *coincides with the set of partial supported models of* $\Pi$.

The above result can be obtained directly from the doubling transformation of Theorem 5.69, coupled with Theorem 8.115. The result implies that negatively closed partial causal relations constitute an adequate causal logic for logic programs under the four-valued supported semantics.

#### 8.9.3.2 *The partial stable interpretation*

Just as in the main case, the distinction between the partial supported and partial stable interpretations will amount to treating positive premises in bodies of program rules not as causal assumptions, but as conditions on conclusions. More exactly, a *partial stable interpretation* interprets a program rule $\mathbf{not}\, d, c \leftarrow a, \mathbf{not}\, b$ as a causal rule

$$*d, {\sim}b \Rightarrow \bigwedge a \to \bigvee c.$$

The above rule clearly shows that partial stable interpretation is just a four-valued version of a stable interpretation. Again, due to Invariance, the above causal rule is equivalent to

$$d, \neg b \Rightarrow \bigwedge *a \to \bigvee *c.$$

This immediately suggests that the partial stable interpretation can be seen as a stable interpretation of a *doubled* logic program (cf. [Wallace, 1993]). An abstract, argumentation-theoretic formulation of this construction has been given in Chapter 7.

$PST(\Pi)$ will denote the causal theory containing the above translations of all the program rules from $\Pi$, plus $DN$. Then the next result shows that the nonmonotonic semantics of this causal theory determines precisely the p-stable semantics of the source logic program. As before, it follows directly from the doubling construction of Theorem 5.69 and Theorem 8.112.

**Theorem 8.119** *The nonmonotonic semantics of* $PST(\Pi)$ *coincides with the set of p-stable models of* $\Pi$.

We already mentioned earlier that p-stable semantics differs from the original Przymusinski's partial stable semantics for disjunctive logic programs, suggested in [Przymusinski, 1991b]. The main distinction amounts to the difference in their underlying logics. Namely, Przymusinski's construction of partial stable models is based on *consistent* partial interpretations, and hence presupposes a three-valued logic, while the construction of p-stable models is thoroughly four-valued. Accordingly, a representation of partial stable models can be obtained by adding a condition that restricts possible partial interpretations to consistent ones. The consistency condition is captured by the following postulate:

**(P-consistency)** $\mathbf{t} \Rightarrow {\sim}p \rightarrow \neg p$, for any propositional atom $p$.

Actually, the corresponding doubling construction for Przymusinski's semantics has already been described in [Janhunen *et al.*, 2000], so we refer the reader to the latter paper for further details.

## Chapter 9

# Epistemic Consequence Relations

A distinctive feature of both default and modal nonmonotonic logics is that they are inherently epistemic formalisms. Namely, they primarily describe our beliefs and knowledge, unlike the extensional classical logic and the formalisms described earlier in this book that are normally used for a direct representation of objective facts about the world. In this chapter we will introduce a corresponding epistemic generalization of biconsequence relations and show that these 'traditional' nonmonotonic logics will find their natural place in this framework. In many other respects, however, the descriptions below will largely repeat the story already told in Chapters 3–6 in an abstract setting.

An epistemic understanding of biconsequence relations is naturally obtained by treating the objective and assumption contexts, respectively, as the contexts of knowledge and belief. In other words, propositions that hold in the objective context can be viewed as known, while propositions belonging to the assumption context can be seen as forming the set of associated beliefs. This understanding will be given a fully explicit formal representation in the next chapter, where we will consider the modal extensions of the formalism. Already at this stage, however, the epistemic reading imposes an essential change in the semantic representation of biconsequence relations, since our knowledge and beliefs are usually incomplete. Consequently, both the objective and assumption contexts of bimodels will correspond in this case not to complete worlds, but to incomplete deductive theories (sets of worlds). Accordingly, epistemic biconsequence relations will belong to the next, epistemic level of logical reasoning.

## 9.1 General Epistemic Biconsequence Relations

We will begin with a general notion of an epistemic biconsequence relation. The latter notion constitutes a generalization similar to the move from classical to supra-classical consequence relations, and is driven by the same considerations. Namely, such biconsequence relations should provide a formalism of reasoning about possibly incomplete knowledge and beliefs, rather than a direct representation of reasoning about the world. Accordingly, our basic sematic objects will correspond to 4-bitheories (see Sec. 4.2) and *sets* of four-valued interpretations.

Note first that an epistemic biconsequence relation will be defined as a biconsequence relation in some four-valued language $\mathcal{L}$, but it will not be assumed to satisfy all the introduction and elimination rules for the four-valued connectives in $\mathcal{L}$, described in Chapter 4. In order to prevent possible confusion, the earlier biconsequence relations will be called *extensional* in what follows. As before, $\|\!\models$ will denote the least extensional biconsequence relation (for a given four-valued language).

**Definition 9.1** A biconsequence relation $\Vdash$ in a four-valued language $\mathcal{L}$ will be called *weakly $\mathcal{L}$-epistemic*, if it satisfies the following rules:

$$\frac{a : \|\!\models A : d}{a : \Vdash A : d} \qquad\qquad \frac{a : A \|\!\models : d}{a : A \Vdash : d}$$

and *(strongly) $\mathcal{L}$-epistemic*, if it satisfies, in addition

$$\frac{a : \|\!\models : d}{a : \Vdash : d} \qquad\qquad \frac{a : \|\!\models : d}{a : \Vdash : d}$$

Clearly, any extensional biconsequence relation in the language $\mathcal{L}$ will be $\mathcal{L}$-epistemic, though not vice versa. Still, $\mathcal{L}$-epistemic biconsequence relations can be seen as inference relations that subsume the four-valued entailment for the language $\mathcal{L}$. Accordingly, 4-equivalent propositions can replace each another in bisequents. This means, in particular, that (for sufficiently rich languages) any propositional formula can be reduced to one of the normal forms described in Sec. 4.1.5. In addition, if $\wedge$ belongs to the language, sets of positive premises and negative conclusions can be replaced by their conjunctions:

$$a : b \Vdash c : d \;\equiv\; \bigwedge a : b \Vdash c : \bigwedge d,$$

though positive conclusion sets and negative premise sets are not replaceable by their classical disjunctions.

Recall that a binary semantics for biconsequence relations is a set of bimodels (see Sec. 3.1.1). Now, a binary semantics $\mathcal{B}$ for a language $\mathcal{L}$ will be called *4-closed*, if all its bimodels are consistent 4-bitheories in $\mathcal{L}$. Then we have

**Theorem 9.1** *A biconsequence relation is $\mathcal{L}$-epistemic if and only if it is determined by a 4-closed binary semantics.*

***Proof.*** Assume first that $\Vdash$ is determined by a 4-closed binary semantics, and $a\colon \nVdash A{:}d$. Then there exists a 4-bitheory $(u, v) \in \mathcal{B}$ such that $a \subseteq u$, $A \notin u$, and $d \subseteq v$. By Lemma 4.13, this implies that there exists a four-valued interpretation $\nu$ such that $\nu \models B$, for any $B \in a$, $\nu \not\models A$, and $\nu \not\dashv D$, for any $D \in d$. Consequently, $a\colon |\!\not\models A{:}d$. Similarly, it can be shown that if $a{:}A \nVdash {:}d$, then $a{:}A\,|\!\not\models {:}d$. Hence $\Vdash$ is an epistemic biconsequence relation. In the other direction, it is sufficient to show that the canonical semantics (i.e., the set of bitheories) of an epistemic biconsequence relation is 4-closed.

Let $(u, v)$ be a bitheory of $\Vdash$, and $A \notin u$. Then $u\colon \nVdash A{:}v$, and consequently $u\colon |\!\not\models A{:}v$, since $\Vdash$ is epistemic. Similarly, if $A \notin v$, we have $u{:}A\,|\!\not\models {:}v$, which shows that $(u, v)$ is a 4-bitheory. □

Finally, if the language $\mathcal{L}$ contains, e.g., the conflation connective $*$, then due to the properties of 4-bitheories (see Lemma 4.14), epistemic biconsequence relations are reducible to Scott consequence relations:

$$a : b \Vdash c : d \;\equiv\; a, *d :\Vdash *b, c : .$$

More exactly, such biconsequence relations will be equivalent to Scott consequence relations in $\mathcal{L}$ that subsume the positive four-valued entailment $\models_4$. Such Scott consequence relations could be justifiably called *supra-four-valued.*

The above descriptions provide a general idea of what we mean by an epistemic generalization of logical formalisms. In the rest of the book, however, we will restrict our discussion to the very special case of epistemic biconsequence relations in a (local) classical language and its modal extensions. It should be noted, however, that this restriction is to some extent arbitrary, since it leaves outside the scope of the study a number of natural, almost anticipated generalizations of the formal systems described in the preceding chapters (such as partial generalizations of nonmonotonic semantics). Worse still, it excludes some interesting systems of nonmonotonic reasoning suggested in the literature (such as [Gelfond, 1994; Denecker *et al.*, 2003]). The only excuse we have for this is that even the remaining 'classical' area is still quite rich and demanding.

## 9.2 Supraclassical Biconsequence Relations

Supraclassical biconsequence relations, defined below, coincide, in effect, with $\mathcal{L}$-epistemic biconsequence relations for the case when $\mathcal{L}$ is a local classical language. These biconsequence relations can already be viewed as biconsequence relations in a plain classical language such that both its component contexts respect classical entailment.

**Definition 9.2** A biconsequence relation in a classical language will be called *weakly supraclassical*, if it satisfies

**Supraclassicality** $\dfrac{a \vDash A}{a : \Vdash A :}$ $\dfrac{a \vDash A}{: A \Vdash : a}$

and *(strongly) supraclassical*, if it satisfies also

**Positive Falsity** $\mathbf{f} : \Vdash$ **Negative Falsity** $\Vdash : \mathbf{f}$.

The most important consequence of Supraclassicality is the possibility of replacement of classically equivalent formulas in bisequents. In addition, it allows us to replace positive premises and negative conclusions by their conjunctions, but positive conclusion sets and negative premise sets are not replaceable in this way by their classical disjunctions. Speaking more generally, supraclassical biconsequence relations are only *supra*-classical, which means, in particular, that the deduction theorem, contraposition, and disjunction in the antecedent are not valid, in general, for each of the two contexts. As before, strong supraclassicality amounts to a restriction to classically consistent contexts.

A semantics of supraclassical biconsequence relations can be obtained from the general binary semantics by requiring that bimodels are pairs of consistent deductively closed sets. Such bimodels and semantics have already been used in Chapter 8 and called *classical*. Then, as an immediate consequence of the general Theorem 9.1 for epistemic biconsequence relations, we obtain

**Corollary 9.2** *A biconsequence relation is supraclassical if and only if it has a classical binary semantics.*

In the next chapter, the above classical binary semantics will be transformed into a full-fledged possible worlds semantics.

Structural rules for biconsequence relations, described in Chapter 3, will be used also in the supraclassical case, with the obvious distinction that the propositional variables in these rules will now range over classical propositions. Moreover, they will have the same semantic interpretation. Thus, Consistency will correspond to the requirement that $u \subseteq v$, for any bimodel $(u, v)$, while Completeness will amount to the reverse inclusion $v \subseteq u$. As before, supraclassical biconsequence relations that are both consistent and complete will be reducible to (supraclassical) Scott consequence relations. Similarly, regular biconsequence relations will be determined by quasi-reflexive binary semantics, *etc.* Only Semi-Classicality will be replaced with a more appropriate Saturation condition for the supraclassical case (see below).

By a *bisequent theory* we will mean in this chapter an arbitrary set of bisequents in the classical language, while $\Vdash_\Delta$ will invariably denote the least supraclassical biconsequence relation containing $\Delta$. Moreover, by a *bitheory* or a *propositional theory* of $\Delta$ we will mean a bitheory or a propositional theory of $\Vdash_\Delta$. Accordingly, bitheories of a bisequent theory will be pairs of consistent deductively closed sets. More precisely, such bitheories will be pairs of consistent deductively closed sets that will also be closed with respect to the bisequents of a bisequent theory.

If we compare supraclassical biconsequence relations with extensional biconsequence relations in the local classical language, we can immediately see that the classical conjunction satisfies all the rules and conditions for the four-valued conjunction (cf. Lemma 4.14). This means, in particular, that the distinction between the two kinds of biconsequence relations can be reduced to a new, weaker interpretation of the classical negation $\neg$.

As a first useful consequence of strong supraclassicality, we have the following simplified description of positively minimal bitheories:

**Lemma 9.3** *A pair $(u, v)$ of consistent deductively closed sets is a positively minimal bitheory of a supraclassical biconsequence relation $\Vdash$ if and only if, for any proposition $A$,*

$$A \in u \textit{ iff } : \overline{v} \Vdash A, \overline{u} : v.$$

The additional condition $: \overline{v} \nVdash : v$ (cf. Lemma 3.6) is no longer needed due to Falsity.

### 9.2.1 *Supraclassical relations and production inference*

Recall that the classical binary semantics is identical with the binary semantics used in Chapter 8 for interpreting production inference. Accordingly, general production rules $A \Rightarrow B$ (that earlier had no counterpart in biconsequence relations) are representable as bisequents $\Vdash B : A$ of a supraclassical biconsequence relation.

As in Sec. 8.4.2, the *production subrelation* $\Rightarrow_{\Vdash}$ of a biconsequence relation $\Vdash$ will be defined as the set of production rules

$$\{A \Rightarrow B \mid \Vdash B : A\}.$$

Then we have the following embedding.

**Lemma 9.4** *$\Rightarrow$ is a (regular) production inference relation iff it is a production subrelation of some (consistent) supraclassical biconsequence relation.*

***Proof.*** A bisequent $\Vdash B{:}A$ is valid in a classical binary semantics iff, for any classical bimodel $(u, v)$, $A \in v$ only if $B \in u$. Accordingly, the production subrelation of a (consistent) supraclassical biconsequence relation will obviously form a (regular) production inference relation. Moreover, for a production inference relation $\Rightarrow$, let us consider a biconsequence relation $\Vdash_{\Rightarrow}$ determined by the canonical classical binary semantics of $\Rightarrow$. Clearly, $\Rightarrow$ will be the production subrelation of $\Vdash_{\Rightarrow}$. Moreover, if the classical binary semantics is consistent, $\Vdash_{\Rightarrow}$ will be a consistent biconsequence relation. □

The above correspondence will be extended later to the correspondence between the associated nonmonotonic semantics. Note, however, that, unlike the correspondence between basic production relations and extensional biconsequence relations (see Theorem 8.46), supraclassical biconsequence relations are not determined uniquely by their production subrelations, and hence constitute a more general logical formalism.

We will define now a class of supraclassical biconsequence relations related to basic and causal production inference from Chapter 8.

**Definition 9.3** A supraclassical biconsequence relation will be called

- *negatively classical* if it satisfies

  **(Negative Completeness)** $: A, \neg A \Vdash$.
- *causal* if it is negatively classical, regular and consistent.

Negative Completeness restricts the assumption contexts to worlds, and hence a semantic representation of negatively classical biconsequence relations can be given in terms of bimodels of the form $(u, \alpha)$ with single worlds as assumption contexts. This implies, in particular, that any theory of a negatively classical biconsequence relation should be a world.

Negatively classical biconsequence relations satisfy all the rules and conditions for classical inference with respect to the negative premises and conclusions of bisequents. As a consequence, we have the following reductions:

$$a : b \Vdash c : d \;\equiv\; a : \bigwedge d \to \bigvee b \Vdash c : \;\equiv\; a : \Vdash c : \bigwedge (d \cup \neg b).$$

The above reductions show, in particular, that negatively classical biconsequence relations are uniquely determined by their default bisequents.

Causal biconsequence relations are determined by bimodels $(u, \alpha)$ such that $u \subseteq \alpha$, and $(\alpha, \alpha)$ is also a bimodel. Such biconsequence relations provide a non-modal logical formalism for Turner's logic of universal causation (UCL) from [Turner, 1999] (see below).

The next result generalizes the corresponding result for extensional biconsequence relations (Theorem 8.46) and shows that any negatively classical biconsequence relation generates a basic production inference.

**Lemma 9.5** *$\Rightarrow$ is a basic (respectively, causal) production inference relation iff it is a production subrelation of some negatively classical (resp., causal) biconsequence relation.*

***Proof.*** It is easy to verify that if $\Vdash$ is negatively classical, then $\Rightarrow_{\Vdash}$ satisfies Or. The other direction is immediate from Theorem 8.46. □

The above embedding demonstrates that the formalism of supraclassical biconsequence relations subsumes also basic and causal production inference as special cases. This correspondence will also be extended in what follows to the associated nonmonotonic semantics.

### 9.2.2 *Saturated biconsequence relations*

The definition of a semi-classical biconsequence relation in Chapter 3 was based, in effect, on the same idea as the notion of a supported (pointwise-minimal) theory for Scott consequence relations. Accordingly, a proper modification of this notion for the supraclassical case can be obtained by analogy with classically supported theories (see Definition 2.15 from Chapter 2).

**Definition 9.4** A supraclassical biconsequence relation will be called *saturated*, if it is consistent, regular, and satisfies the following postulate:

**Saturation** $\Vdash A \vee B, \neg A \vee B : B.$

Recall that $u\bot$ denotes the set of all maximal sub-theories of $u$, plus $u$ itself. Then the next definition provides a semantic description of Saturation.

**Definition 9.5** A classical bimodel $(u, v)$ will be called *saturated*, if $u \in v\bot$. A classical binary semantics $\mathcal{B}$ will be called *saturated* if it is regular, and all its bimodels are saturated.

According to the above definition, a bimodel $(u, v)$ is saturated, if $u$ either coincides with $v$, or is a maximal theory included in $v$. Clearly, any saturated binary semantics will be consistent.

The next theorem establishes a completeness of saturated biconsequence relations with respect to a saturated binary semantics.

**Theorem 9.6** *A biconsequence relation is saturated if and only if it has a saturated binary semantics.*

***Proof.*** If $(u, v)$ is a saturated bimodel, then $u = v \cap \alpha$, for some world $\alpha$. For any proposition $A$, we have $A \in \alpha$ or $\neg A \in \alpha$. Consequently, if $B \in v$, then either $A \vee B \in u$, or $\neg A \vee B \in u$. This shows that $\Vdash A \vee B, \neg A \vee B : B$ is always valid in a saturated semantics. In the other direction, we have to show that the canonical semantics of a saturated biconsequence relation is saturated.

Let $(u, v)$ be a bitheory of a saturated biconsequence relation $\Vdash$. Since $\Vdash$ is consistent, we have $u \subseteq v$. Assume that $u \neq v$. Then there exists a proposition $B \in v \backslash u$. Now, by Saturation, we have that, for any proposition $A$, either $A \vee B \in u$, or $\neg A \vee B \in u$. This implies that $\mathrm{Th}(u, \neg B)$ is a world; we will denote it by $\alpha$. Then it is easy to verify that $u = v \cap \alpha$, and consequently $u \in v\bot$. Thus, the canonical semantics of $\Vdash$ is saturated. □

The next lemma describes some characteristic properties of saturated biconsequence relations. All these properties can be easily verified semantically, so we omit a syntactic proof.

**Lemma 9.7** *If* $\Vdash$ *is a saturated biconsequence relation, then*

*(1)* $\Vdash A, A \to B : A, B$;
*(2)* $A \vee B :\Vdash A, B : A, B$;
*(3) If* $a : b \Vdash c, C \vee D : d$, *then* $a : b \Vdash c, C, D : d, C, D$;
*(4) If* $a : b \Vdash \bigvee c_0, c : d$, *then* $a : b \Vdash c_0, c : d, c_0$;
*(5)* $a : b \Vdash c : d$ *iff* $a : b, c\backslash c_0 \Vdash \bigvee c_0 : d$, *for any* $c_0 \subseteq c$;
*(6)* $A, a : b \Vdash c : d$ *iff* $a : b \Vdash \{A \to C \mid C \in c\} : d, A$.

The last two properties above imply the following reduction:

**Corollary 9.8** $a{:}b \Vdash c{:}d$ *iff* $: b, c\backslash c_0 \Vdash \bigwedge a \to \bigvee c_0 : a, d$, *for any* $c_0 \subseteq c$.

The most important consequence of the above reduction is that saturated biconsequence relations are also uniquely determined by their singular autoepistemic bisequents.

Note now that saturated biconsequence relations that are also negatively classical are already causal, and hence are determined by bimodels of the form $(\alpha \cap \beta, \alpha)$, where $\alpha, \beta$ are worlds. As we are going to show, such biconsequence relations are already equivalent to extensional (classical) biconsequence relations, as well as to causal inference relations from Chapter 8.

Given an extensional biconsequence relation $\Vdash$, we define the corresponding causal saturated biconsequence relation as follows:

$$a : b \Vdash_C c : d \;\equiv\; a : b, c\backslash c_0 \Vdash c_0 : a, d, \text{ for every } c_0 \subseteq c.$$

In addition, for a causal saturated biconsequence relation $\Vdash$, we define the corresponding extensional biconsequence relation as

$$a : b \Vdash_E c : d \;\equiv : b \Vdash \bigwedge a \to \bigvee c : d.$$

Then we have the following exact correspondence:

**Theorem 9.9** *If* $\Vdash$ *is a causal saturated biconsequence relation, then* $\Vdash_E$ *is an extensional regular biconsequence relation, and* $\Vdash_{EC} = \Vdash$. *Conversely, if* $\Vdash$ *is an extensional regular biconsequence relation, then* $\Vdash_C$ *is a causal saturated biconsequence relation, and* $\Vdash_{CE} = \Vdash$.

***Proof.*** Instead of a straightforward syntactic check, we will consider the corresponding semantic interpretations.

A bisequent $:b \Vdash \bigwedge a \to \bigvee c{:}d$ holds in a causal saturated bimodel $(\alpha \cap \beta, \alpha)$ iff the bisequent $a{:}b \Vdash c{:}d$ holds both in $(\beta, \alpha)$ and in $(\alpha, \alpha)$. Consequently, if $\Vdash$ is a causal saturated biconsequence relation determined by a semantics $\mathcal{B}$, then $\Vdash_E$ is determined by the set of all bimodels $(\beta, \alpha)$ and $(\alpha, \alpha)$ such that $(\alpha \cap \beta, \alpha) \in \mathcal{B}$, and hence it is an extensional regular biconsequence relation. Conversely, it can be verified that the set of bisequents $\{a{:}b, c\backslash c_0 \Vdash c_0{:}a, d \mid c_0 \subseteq c\}$ holds in a bimodel $(\beta, \alpha)$ iff $a{:}b \Vdash c{:}d$ holds in $(\alpha \cap \beta, \alpha)$. Consequently, if $\Vdash$ is an extensional regular biconsequence relation determined by a semantics $\mathcal{B}$, then $\Vdash_C$ is determined by the set of all saturated bimodels $(\alpha \cap \beta, \alpha)$ such that $(\beta, \alpha) \in \mathcal{B}$, and hence it is a causal saturated biconsequence relation. □

Extensional biconsequence relations are equivalent, in turn, to causal inference relations (see Lemma 8.56). Moreover, it can easily be seen that the above correspondences between causal saturated and extensional biconsequence relations preserve the production subrelation. Consequently, we immediately obtain

**Corollary 9.10** *Any causal inference relation is a production subrelation of a unique causal saturated biconsequence relation.*

A direct correspondence between causal saturated biconsequence relations and causal inference relations can be established as follows. To begin with, any bisequent of a saturated biconsequence relation is reducible to a set of singular autoepistemic bisequents, that is, to bisequents of the form $:b \Vdash C{:}d$, while any such bisequent in a negatively classical biconsequence relation is reducible to $\Vdash C{:} \bigwedge(d \cup \neg b)$. Thus, any bisequent of a causal saturated biconsequence relation is reducible to bisequents of the form $\Vdash A{:}B$, and hence such biconsequence relations are uniquely determined by their production subrelations. In the other direction, given a causal inference relation $\Rightarrow$, we can define $\Vdash$ as the biconsequence relation determined by all bitheories $(\alpha \cap \beta, \alpha)$ such that $(\beta, \alpha)$ is a bitheory of $\Rightarrow$. An explicit description of this biconsequence relation is as follows:

$$a{:}b \Vdash c{:}d \;\equiv\; a, d, \neg b, \neg(c \backslash c_0) \Rightarrow \bigwedge a \to \bigvee c_0, \text{ for any } c_0 \subseteq c.$$

As can be verified, the production subrelation of $\Vdash$ is precisely $\Rightarrow$.

## 9.3 Classical Nonmonotonic Semantics

The notions of an exact theory and extension from Chapter 5 can be directly extended to supraclassical consequence relations, with the only, though important, qualification that they form now deductively closed sets.

**Definition 9.6** A set $u$ of propositions will be called a *classical exact theory* (respectively, *classical extension*) of a bisequent theory $\Delta$, if it is an exact theory (resp., extension) of $\Vdash_\Delta$.

Recall that $\Vdash_\Delta$ denotes in this chapter the least *supraclassical* biconsequence relation containing $\Delta$. Consequently, classical exact theories and classical extensions are deductively closed sets. Still, practically all the results about such semantics, described in Chapter 5 remain valid for the supraclassical case. For instance, a syntactic characterization of exact theories, given by Lemma 5.1, remains the same, provided that $A$ below ranges over classical propositions:

**Lemma 9.11** *A set $u$ of propositions is an exact theory of a supraclassical biconsequence relation $\Vdash$ if and only if, for any proposition $A$,*

$$A \in u \textit{ iff } :\overline{u} \Vdash A : u \quad \textit{and} \quad A \notin u \textit{ iff } A : \overline{u} \Vdash : u.$$

Regular supraclassical biconsequence relations will still constitute a maximal logic suitable for the exact semantics (see Theorem 5.5). Finally, we still have that the default subrelation of a biconsequence relation determines precisely the subset of the exact semantics that consists of minimal theories (Theorem 5.12). As a consequence (cf. Corollary 5.13), exact theories of a default bisequent theory will always be minimal.

As we will see, the default nonmonotonic semantics of supraclassical biconsequence relations constitutes a proper generalization of Reiter's default logic. As a consequence of Lemma 5.27, we have the following description of extensions in our present case:

**Lemma 9.12** *A set $u$ is an extension of a supraclassical biconsequence relation if and only if $u = \{A \mid : \overline{u} \Vdash A, \overline{u} : u\}$.*

Consequently, extensions are determined by the autoepistemic subrelation of a biconsequence relation. In addition, supraclassical biconsequence relations that are consistent and regular will now be shown to constitute a maximal logic adequate for extensions (cf. Theorem 5.36).

**Definition 9.7** Bisequent theories $\Gamma$ and $\Delta$ in a classical language will be called *classically default equivalent*, if they determine the same supraclassical regular consistent biconsequence relation.

**Theorem 9.13** *Bisequent theories are strongly equivalent with respect to the classical default semantics if and only if they are classically default equivalent.*

***Proof.*** The implication from right to left is immediate. Assume that $\Gamma$ and $\Delta$ are strongly equivalent with respect to a classical default semantics, and let $\Sigma$ denote the set of all bisequents of the form $a\!: \Vdash A\!:$ and $:\!A \Vdash :\!a$ such that $a \vDash A$, plus the two 'falsity' bisequents $\mathbf{f}\!: \Vdash$ and $\Vdash :\!\mathbf{f}$. As follows from the definition of a supraclassical biconsequence relation, $\Gamma$ and $\Delta$ determine the same classical extensions only if $\Gamma \cup \Sigma$ and $\Delta \cup \Sigma$ determine the same extensions. Consequently, $\Gamma$ and $\Delta$ are strongly equivalent only if $\Gamma \cup \Sigma$ and $\Delta \cup \Sigma$ are strongly extension-equivalent. The latter gives us that $\Gamma \cup \Sigma$ and $\Delta \cup \Sigma$ are default equivalent (by Theorem 5.36), and hence $\Gamma$ and $\Delta$ are classically default equivalent. $\square$

Corollary 5.37 gives us the following description of classical extensions in the consistent case:

**Corollary 9.14** *A set $u$ is an extension of a supraclassical consistent biconsequence relation $\Vdash$ if and only if*

$$u = \{A \mid\, : \overline{u} \Vdash A : u\}.$$

Thus, an extension can be seen as a set of formulas that are provable on the basis of taking precisely itself as the set of assumptions. The description also shows that extensions of consistent biconsequence relations are determined by their singular autoepistemic bisequents.

Since the default subrelation of a biconsequence relation determines precisely the extensions that are also minimal theories (Theorem 5.39), classical extensions of a default bisequent theory will always be minimal. Actually, default bisequent theories, coupled with the classical default nonmonotonic semantics, give an exact representation for the *disjunctive default logic* from [Gelfond *et al.*, 1991].

Finally, in the correspondence between supraclassical biconsequence relations and general production inference (Lemma 9.4), classical extensions of the former correspond to exact theories of the latter.

Below, for a causal theory $\Delta$, we will denote by $\Delta_{\Vdash}$ the corresponding bisequent theory $\{\Vdash B{:}A \mid A \Rightarrow B \in \Delta\}$.

**Lemma 9.15** *If $\Delta$ is a causal theory, then exact theories of $\Delta$ coincide with extensions of $\Delta_{\Vdash}$.*

***Proof.*** Bitheories of $\Delta_{\Vdash}$ are pairs $(u, v)$ of deductively closed sets that are closed with respect to bisequents of $\Delta_{\Vdash}$. In our case, this holds iff $\Delta(v) \subseteq u$. Now, a deductively closed set $u$ is a classical extension of $\Delta_{\Vdash}$ if $u$ is a theory of $\Delta_{\Vdash}$, that is, $\Delta(u) \subseteq u$, and there is no deductive theory $v \subset u$ such that $(v, u)$ is a bitheory of $\Delta_{\Vdash}$, that is, $\Delta(u) \subseteq v$. As can be seen, this holds iff $u = \mathrm{Th}(\Delta(u))$, and hence the claim follows from Lemma 8.17. $\square$

### 9.3.1 *Classical expansions*

Just as the notion of tightness had to be modified in the supraclassical case to that of Saturation, the notion of expansion for supraclassical biconsequence relations will be modified to the notion of a classical expansion, defined below. The resulting nonmonotonic semantics will be called autoepistemic due to its tight connection with autoepistemic logic.

**Definition 9.8** A theory $u$ of a supraclassical biconsequence relation $\Vdash$ will be called a *classical expansion* of $\Vdash$, if, for any $v \in u\bot$ that is distinct from $u$, the pair $(v, u)$ is not a bitheory of $\Vdash$. The set of classical expansions will determine the *(classical autoepistemic semantics* of $\Vdash$.

Clearly, any extension of a supraclassical biconsequence relation will also be a classical expansion, though not vice versa.

The following result shows that classical expansions can be precisely characterized as extensions of saturated biconsequence relations.

**Theorem 9.16** *If* $\Vdash'$ *is a least saturated biconsequence relation that contains* $\Vdash$, *then classical expansions of* $\Vdash$ *coincide with extensions of* $\Vdash'$.

***Proof.*** Bitheories of $\Vdash'$ are exactly regular saturated bitheories of $\Vdash$. Consequently, $u$ is an extension of $\Vdash'$ precisely when there is no $v \in u\bot$ such that $u \neq v$ and $(v, u)$ is a bitheory of $\Vdash$. □

As a consequence, we obtain

**Corollary 9.17** *Classical expansions of a saturated biconsequence relation coincide with its extensions.*

Moreover, since extensions of a consistent biconsequence relation coincide with exact theories, we actually have

**Corollary 9.18** *If* $\Vdash$ *is a saturated biconsequence relation, then the sets of its exact theories, extensions and classical expansions coincide.*

Thus, the rules of saturated biconsequence relations are admissible for classical expansions. Moreover, we will show that such biconsequence relations constitute a maximal logic for the latter.

**Theorem 9.19** *Bisequent theories are strongly equivalent with respect to the classical autoepistemic semantics if and only if they are equivalent in saturated biconsequence relations.*

***Proof.*** The implication from right to left is immediate. Assume now that $\Gamma$ and $\Delta$ are strongly equivalent with respect to the classical autoepistemic semantics, and let $\Sigma$ denote the set of all bisequents of the form $\Vdash A \vee B, \neg A \vee B : B$. Note that $\Gamma$ and $\Delta$ determine the same classical expansions only if $\Gamma \cup \Sigma$ and $\Delta \cup \Sigma$ determine the same classical extensions. Consequently, $\Gamma$ and $\Delta$ are strongly equivalent with respect to the classical autoepistemic semantics only if $\Gamma \cup \Sigma$ and $\Delta \cup \Sigma$ are strongly equivalent with respect to a classical default semantics. The latter gives us that $\Gamma \cup \Sigma$ and $\Delta \cup \Sigma$ are classically default equivalent (by Theorem 9.13), which is reducible to the claim that $\Gamma$ and $\Delta$ determine the same saturated biconsequence relation. □

Our next result states two important sufficient conditions for coincidence of classical expansions and extensions of a bisequent theory.

A bisequent theory $\Delta$ will be called *positively simple*, if positive premises and positive conclusions of any bisequent from $\Delta$ are sets of classical literals. Then we have[1]

**Theorem 9.20** *If a bisequent theory is autoepistemic or positively simple, then classical expansions of $\Delta$ coincide with its classical extensions.*

The proof follows immediately from Theorem 2.45.

As a first application of the above result, we infer that exact theories of a general production inference relation coincide also with expansions of the associated biconsequence relation.

**Corollary 9.21** *If $\Delta$ is a causal theory, then exact theories of $\Delta$ coincide with classical expansions of $\Delta_{\Vdash}$.*

***Proof.*** Follows from Lemma 9.15 due to the fact that $\Delta_{\Vdash}$ is an autoepistemic bisequent theory. □

In view of the above result, production inference relations are insensitive to the distinction between classical extensions and expansions.

Finally, for an autoepistemic nonmonotonic semantics, any bisequent theory is logically reducible to a singular autoepistemic theory.

For a bisequent theory $\Delta$, we will define *cauto*($\Delta$) as the following set of singular autoepistemic bisequents:

$$\{: b, c \backslash c_0 \Vdash \bigwedge a \to \bigvee c_0 : a, d \mid a : b \Vdash c : d \in \Delta \ \&\ c_0 \subseteq c\}.$$

[1] The origins of this result are in the Main Lemma from [Lifschitz and Schwarz, 1993].

Now, Corollary 9.8 implies that, for saturated biconsequence relations, any bisequent theory $\Delta$ is equivalent to $cauto(\Delta)$. Moreover, $cauto(\Delta)$ is an autoepistemic bisequent theory, and therefore we conclude with

**Corollary 9.22** *Classical autoepistemic semantics of* $\Delta$ *coincides with the classical default semantics of* $cauto(\Delta)$.

The above results establish an eventual reduction of biconsequence relations under the autoepistemic nonmonotonic semantics to autoepistemic default consequence relations considered later in this chapter.

### 9.3.2 *Extended programs and classical negation*

A bisequent $a{:}b \Vdash c{:}d$ will be called a *literal* one, if $a, b, c, d$ are sets of classical literals. It turns out that literal bisequent theories can be seen as logical counterparts of extended logic programs with classical negation (see [Gelfond and Lifschitz, 1991]).

An *extended logic program* $\Pi$ is a set of program rules of the form

$$\mathbf{not}\, d, c \leftarrow a, \mathbf{not}\, b \qquad (*)$$

where $a, b, c, d$ are finite sets of classical literals. The nonmonotonic semantics of such programs is determined by *answer sets* which are sets of classical literals defined just as stable models, subject to an additional requirement that they should be classically consistent.

A *default interpretation* of general program rules from Chapter 5 can be extended directly to the above rules, so the rule (*) will be interpreted as a bisequent

$$a : b \Vdash c : d.$$

As before, $bc(\Pi)$ will denote the set of bisequents corresponding to an extended logic program $\Pi$ by this interpretation.

A deductively closed theory will be called a *literal* one, if it is a logical closure of some set of literals. Any such theory is uniquely determined, of course, by its literals.

Now, extensions of a literal bisequent theory will clearly be literal theories. Moreover, the next result shows that extensions of the literal bisequent theory $bc(\Pi)$ correspond to sets of literals that are answer sets of the program $\Pi$.

**Proposition 9.23** *Answer sets of an extended logic program* $\Pi$ *correspond exactly to extensions of* $bc(\Pi)$.

***Proof.*** We will denote by $l(u)$ the set of literals in a set $u$ of propositions.

Bitheories of $bc(\Pi)$ are pairs of consistent deductively closed sets that are closed also with respect to the bisequents of $bc(\Pi)$. Now a bitheory $(v, u)$ will be positively minimal only if $v$ is a literal theory (since $bc(\Pi)$ is a literal bisequent theory). Consequently, extensions of $bc(\Pi)$ will be literal deductive theories. Moreover, it can be easily verified that a literal theory $u$ is an extension of $bc(\Pi)$ if and only if $l(u)$ is a minimal model of the Gelfond–Lifschitz reduct of $\Pi$ modulo $l(u)$. Hence the result. □

Thus, answer sets of extended logic programs correspond to extensions of literal bisequent theories. Moreover, literal bisequent theories are obviously positively simple, so Theorem 9.20 gives us that extended logic programs also obliterate the distinction between extensions and classical expansions.

**Corollary 9.24** *Answer sets of an extended logic program* $\Pi$ *correspond exactly to classical expansions of* $bc(\Pi)$.

The above result provides logical grounds for representing extended logic programs in autoepistemic logic (see [Lifschitz and Schwarz, 1993]).

The above representation strongly indicates that the extended logical programs, unlike general logic programs, considered earlier, require already an epistemic understanding as descriptions of our knowledge. This epistemic understanding perfectly agrees with the intended use of such programs, suggested in [Gelfond and Lifschitz, 1991], such as legal or administrative regulations, including extreme cases like

$$Interview(x) \leftarrow \mathbf{not}\, Eligible(x), \mathbf{not}\, \neg Eligible(x),$$

or rules for actions like $Cross \leftarrow \neg Train$ (versus $Cross \leftarrow \mathbf{not}\, Train$). All such examples presuppose an epistemic understanding and, in particular, an epistemic reading of $\mathbf{not}\, p$ as '*p is not known to hold*'.

The epistemic interpretation of logic programs is more general, and it allows us to give a proper representation of the above epistemic descriptions. It has, however, the price of weakening the underlying logic. In particular, the arrow $\leftarrow$ can no longer be seen as a logical implication (even for programs without **not**), but only as an inference rule, and reasoning by cases is no longer valid. In addition, this interpretation influences the interpretation of disjunctions in heads of the program rules, making them epistemic.

Moreover, it has been rightly argued in [Gelfond, 1994] that a comprehensive representation of epistemic reasoning in logic programming requires a further extension of the language with proper epistemic operators as well. The corresponding modal logical formalisms for nonmonotonic reasoning will be our subject in the next chapter.

### 9.3.3 *Complete extensions and expansions*

As a special case, the nonmonotonic semantics of supraclassical biconsequence relations also subsume the causal nonmonotonic semantics of production inference relations, described in Sec. 8.5. It turns out that the latter semantics corresponds simply to the restriction of the above semantics to worlds.

In what follows, classical extensions and expansions that are worlds will be called *complete* extensions and expansions, respectively. The corresponding restrictions of classical default and autoepistemic semantics will also be called *complete.*

The next claim states that, in the general correspondence between production inference and biconsequence relations, exact worlds correspond to complete extensions. The proof is immediate from Lemma 9.15.

**Corollary 9.25** *If* $\Delta$ *is a causal theory, then exact worlds of* $\Delta$ *coincide with complete extensions of* $\Delta_{\Vdash}$.

Now we are going to show that causal biconsequence relations (see Definition 9.3) constitute a maximal logic adequate for complete extensions.

**Definition 9.9** Bisequent theories $\Gamma$ and $\Delta$ will be called *causally equivalent*, if they determine the same causal biconsequence relation.

To begin with, due to negative classicality, any theory of a causal biconsequence relation is a world, and hence we have

**Lemma 9.26** *Any extension of a causal biconsequence relation is a complete extension.*

In addition, the next result shows that the rules of a causal biconsequence relation preserve complete extensions.

**Lemma 9.27** *If* $\Vdash^{ca}$ *is a least causal biconsequence relation containing* $\Vdash$, *then* $\Vdash^{ca}$ *has the same complete extensions as* $\Vdash$.

***Proof.*** Bitheories of $\Vdash^{ca}$ are precisely bitheories of $\Vdash$ of the form $(u, \alpha)$, where $\alpha$ is a world. Consequently, $\alpha$ is a positively minimal bitheory of $\Vdash$ if and only if it is a positively minimal bitheory of $\Vdash^{ca}$. □

Moreover, we also have

**Theorem 9.28** *Bisequent theories are strongly equivalent with respect to complete default semantics if and only if they are causally equivalent.*

***Proof.*** The implication from right to left is immediate by the preceding lemma. Assume that $\Gamma$ and $\Delta$ are strongly equivalent with respect to complete extensions, and let $\Sigma$ denote the set of all bisequents of the form $:A, \neg A \Vdash$. Then $\Gamma$ and $\Delta$ determine the same complete extensions only if $\Gamma \cup \Sigma$ and $\Delta \cup \Sigma$ determine the same classical extensions. Consequently, $\Gamma$ and $\Delta$ are strongly equivalent with respect to complete extensions only if $\Gamma \cup \Sigma$ and $\Delta \cup \Sigma$ are strongly equivalent with respect to a classical default semantics. The latter gives us that $\Gamma \cup \Sigma$ and $\Delta \cup \Sigma$ are classically default equivalent (by Theorem 9.13), which amounts to the causal equivalence of $\Gamma$ and $\Delta$. □

The above result shows that causal biconsequence relations constitute a maximal underlying logic for complete extensions. Note now that, if $\Vdash^{ca}_{\Delta}$ is a least causal biconsequence relation containing a bisequent theory $\Delta$, then bitheories of $\Vdash^{ca}_{\Delta}$ are precisely pairs $(u, \alpha)$ of deductively closed sets such that $u \subseteq \alpha$, and both $(u, \alpha)$ and $(\alpha, \alpha)$ are closed with respect to $\Delta$. Such bitheories correspond precisely to SE-models of Turner's logic of universal causation UCL, and hence the above result can be seen as a syntactic counterpart of the semantic characterization of strong equivalence of UCL theories, given in [Turner, 2004].

Finally Corollary 9.14 gives us the following description of (complete) extensions for causal biconsequence relations:

**Lemma 9.29** *A world $\alpha$ is an extension of a causal biconsequence relation $\Vdash$ if and only if*

$$\alpha = \{A \mid \Vdash A : \alpha\}.$$

***Proof.*** By negative classicality, $:\overline{\alpha} \Vdash A : \alpha$ is equivalent to $\Vdash A : \alpha, \neg\overline{\alpha}$, while the latter is equivalent to $\Vdash A : \alpha$, since $\neg\overline{\alpha} \subseteq \alpha$. Hence the result.□

As a consequence, we immediately obtain

**Corollary 9.30** *Extensions of a causal biconsequence relation coincide with exact worlds of its production subrelation.*

***Proof.*** By the preceding lemma, $\alpha$ is an extension of $\Vdash$ iff, for any $A$, $A \in \alpha$ iff $\alpha \Rightarrow A$ for the production subrelation of $\Vdash$. □

Turning now to complete expansions, we will show that saturated causal biconsequence relations constitute an adequate logic for the latter. First, by negative classicality, we have

**Lemma 9.31** *Any expansion of a causal biconsequence relation is a complete expansion.*

Moreover, for saturated biconsequence relations, expansions coincide with extensions, so for causal saturated biconsequence relations, all the nonmonotonic semantics coincide.

**Lemma 9.32** *For saturated causal biconsequence relations, extensions, expansions, complete extensions and complete expansions coincide.*

The next result shows that the rules of a saturated causal biconsequence relation preserve complete expansions.

**Lemma 9.33** *If* $\Vdash^{sc}$ *is a least saturated causal biconsequence relation containing* $\Vdash$*, then* $\Vdash^{sc}$ *has the same complete expansions as* $\Vdash$.

***Proof.*** Bitheories of $\Vdash^{sc}$ are precisely bitheories of $\Vdash$ of the form $(\alpha \cap \beta, \alpha)$. Consequently, $\alpha$ is an expansion of $\Vdash$ if and only if it is an expansion of $\Vdash^{sc}$. □

Moreover, we have also

**Theorem 9.34** *Bisequent theories are strongly equivalent with respect to complete autoepistemic semantics if and only if they are equivalent in saturated causal biconsequence relations.*

***Proof.*** As before, the proof follows from Theorem 9.19 and the fact that $\Gamma$ and $\Delta$ are strongly equivalent with respect to complete autoepistemic semantics if and only if $\Gamma \cup \Sigma$ and $\Delta \cup \Sigma$ are strongly equivalent with respect to the classical autoepistemic semantics, where $\Sigma$ is the set of all bisequents of the form $:A, \neg A \Vdash$. □

Recall now that, for saturated causal biconsequence relations, any bisequent is reducible to a set of 'production' bisequents $\Vdash B{:}A$. Accordingly, for a bisequent theory $\Delta$, we will define the following causal theory:

$$caus(\Delta) = \{a, d, \neg b, \neg(c \backslash c_0) \Rightarrow \bigwedge a \rightarrow \bigvee c_0 \mid a{:}b \Vdash c{:}d \in \Delta \ \&\ c_0 \subseteq c\}.$$

**Theorem 9.35** *The set of complete expansions of a bisequent theory* $\Delta$ *coincides with the set of exact worlds of* $caus(\Delta)$.

***Proof.*** By Corollary 9.22, complete expansions of $\Delta$ coincide with complete extensions of $cauto(\Delta)$, while the latter coincide with exact worlds of $caus(\Delta)$ by Corollary 9.30. □

The above theorem demonstrates, in effect, that supraclassical biconsequence relations under the nonmonotonic semantics of complete expansions is fully equivalent to (causal) production inference under the causal nonmonotonic semantics.

## 9.4 Supraclassical Default Consequence Relations

Default consequence relations, described in Chapter 6, can also be extended to inference relations that subsume classical inference.

To begin with, we will no longer need default constraints $a{:}b \vdash$, since the latter are representable by 'ordinary' default rules $a{:}b \vdash \mathbf{f}$. Accordingly, by a default rule we will mean in what follows only rules of the form $a : b \vdash A$.

The corresponding notion of a supraclassical default consequence relation is given in the next definition.

**Definition 9.10** A set $\vdash$ of default rules in a classical language will be called a *supraclassical default consequence relation*, if it satisfies the following postulates:

**Monotonicity** If $a : b \vdash A$ and $a \subseteq a_0$, $b \subseteq b_0$, then $a_0 : b_0 \vdash A$.
**Cut** If $a : b \vdash B$ and $a, B : b \vdash A$, then $a : b \vdash A$.
**C-Closure** If $c \vDash A$ and $a : b \vdash C_i$, $\forall C_i \in c$, then $a : b \vdash A$.

C-Closure implies that $\mathbb{C}\mathrm{n}(u{:}v)$ is always a deductively closed set. Accordingly, it can be replaced with the following two rules:

**And** If $a : b \vdash A$ and $a : b \vdash B$, then $a : b \vdash A \wedge B$.
**Weakening** If $a : b \vdash A$ and $A \vDash B$, then $a : b \vdash B$.

A default semantics will be called *supraclassical*, if it consists of models $(w, u, v)$ such that $w$ is a consistent deductively closed set. Then as a consequence of the general completeness result, Theorem 6.2, we obtain

**Theorem 9.36** *$\vdash$ is a supraclassical default consequence relation if and only if it is determined by a supraclassical default semantics.*

***Proof.*** Clearly, any supraclassical default semantics validates C-Closure, so it determines a supraclassical default consequence relation. The other direction follows directly from the proof of Theorem 6.2, since the canonical default semantics of a supraclassical default consequence relation will be supraclassical. □

By a *classical default theory* we will mean an arbitrary set of default rules in a classical language. Moreover, in this chapter $\vdash_\Delta$ will invariably denote the least supraclassical default consequence relation that contains a (classical) default theory $\Delta$, while $\mathbb{C}\mathrm{n}_\Delta$ will denote the corresponding provability operator.

A slight adaptation of Lemma 6.3 to the supraclassical case will give us

**Lemma 9.37** *$(u, v)$ is a bitheory of a default theory $\Delta$ iff $\Delta(u{:}\overline{v}) \subseteq u$.*

In addition, we have the following analogue of Corollary 6.4:

**Corollary 9.38** *If $(u, v)$ is a bitheory of a default theory $\Delta$, then $\mathbb{C}\mathrm{n}_\Delta(u{:}\overline{v}) = \mathrm{Th}(\Delta(u{:}\overline{v}))$.*

Finally, the corresponding modification of the iterative construction for the operator $\mathbb{C}\mathrm{n}_\Delta$ in the supraclassical case is as follows (cf. [Reiter, 1980]):

$\Delta_0(u : v) = \Delta(u : v)$ and, for any $j \geq 0$,

$$\Delta_{j+1}(u : v) = \mathrm{Th}(\Delta_j(u : v)) \cup \Delta(u \cup \Delta_j(u : v) : v).$$

As before, we define the set of *iterative consequences* of $(u, v)$ in $\Delta$ as

$$\Delta^{it}(u : v) =_{Df} \bigcup_j \Delta_j(u : v).$$

Then an obvious modification of the proof of Lemma 6.6 will give us

**Lemma 9.39** $\mathbb{C}\mathrm{n}_\Delta(u : v) = \Delta^{it}(u : v)$.

The earlier definitions of extensions and expansions of a default consequence relation or a default theory will be directly extended to supraclassical relations. Moreover, we can now define them directly as follows:

- A set $u$ of propositions is a (classical) *extension* of a supraclassical default consequence relation $\vdash$, if $u = \mathbb{C}\mathrm{n}(\emptyset{:}\overline{u})$.
- A set $u$ a (classical) *expansion* of $\vdash$, if $u = \mathbb{C}\mathrm{n}(u{:}\overline{u})$.

As can be verified, both extensions and expansions are now deductively closed sets. As before, we have that any extension is an expansion, though not vice versa, and that any extension is a minimal (classical) theory of a default consequence relation (cf. Lemma 6.8). As we will see, classical extensions correspond precisely to extensions of Reiter's default logic, while classical expansions correspond to nonmodal counterparts of stable expansions in autoepistemic logic (and to *weak extensions* from [Marek and Truszczyński, 1989]).

The following lemma gives a constructive description of expansions and extensions of default theories. The proof is immediate from Lemma 9.39 and Corollary 9.38, respectively.

**Lemma 9.40** *If $\Delta$ is a default theory, then a set $u$ of propositions is*

- *an extension of $\Delta$ iff $u = \Delta^{it}(\emptyset{:}\overline{u})$;*
- *an expansion of $\Delta$ iff $u = \mathrm{Th}(\Delta(u{:}\overline{u}))$.*

As a first illustration of the acquired expressive power, we will show now that the expansion-based semantics of supraclassical default consequence relations provides a natural representation for parallel circumscription.

The framework of (propositional) *parallel circumscription* [Lifschitz, 1985] is a triple $\Pi = (P, F, T)$ such that $T$ is a classical propositional theory, while $P$ and $F$ are disjoint sets of atoms of the language. The task of parallel circumscription consists in finding $(P, F)$-minimal models of $T$, namely propositional models that have a minimal set of atoms from $P$, provided the atoms from $F$ are fixed. The rest of the atoms may vary freely.

Given a circumscription framework $\Pi$, we define the corresponding default theory $\Delta_\Pi$ as the set containing default rules $\vdash A$, for any $A \in T$, combined with the following 'circumscription rules':

$$\{: p \vdash \neg p \mid p \in P \cup F\} \bigcup \{: \neg p \vdash p \mid p \in F\}.$$

Then we obtain

**Lemma 9.41** *A model $\alpha$ is a $(P, F)$-minimal model of a theory $T$ if and only if it is a model of some expansion of $\Delta_\Pi$.*

***Proof.*** To begin with, note that if $u$ is an extension of $\Delta_\Pi$, it should be closed with respect to the above circumscription rules, which immediately implies that either $p \in u$, or $\neg p \in u$, for any $p \in P \cup F$. In addition, by Lemma 9.40, $u$ is an expansion of $\Delta_\Pi$ iff $u = \mathrm{Th}(\Delta_\Pi(u{:}\overline{u}))$. As can be verified, in our case $\Delta_\Pi(u{:}\overline{u})$ is the union of $T$, $\neg(P \backslash u)$, $\neg(F \backslash u)$, and $F \cap u$.

We will identify below propositional models with corresponding sets of propositions (worlds). Assume first that $u$ is an expansion of $\Delta_\Pi$, while $\alpha, \beta$ are models of $T$ such that $u \subseteq \alpha$, $\alpha \cap F = \beta \cap F$, and $\beta \cap P \subseteq \alpha \cap P$. By the above description, $\Delta_\Pi(u{:}\overline{u}) \subseteq \beta$, and therefore $u \subseteq \beta$. But $u$ is complete on P-literals, and therefore $\beta \cap P = \alpha \cap P$. This shows that $\alpha$ is a $(P, F)$-minimal model of $T$.

Assume now that $\alpha$ is a $(P, F)$-minimal model of $T$, and consider the set $u = \mathrm{Th}(T \cup L)$, where $L$ is a set of all literals from $\alpha$ based on the atoms of $P \cup F$. We will show that $u$ is an expansion of $\Delta_\Pi$. Indeed, it is easy to verify that $\Delta_\Pi(u{:}\overline{u}) \subseteq u$, and hence $u$ is a theory of $\Delta_\Pi$. Suppose that $u$ is not included in $\mathrm{Th}(\Delta_\Pi(u{:}\overline{u}))$. By the composition of $\Delta_\Pi(u{:}\overline{u})$, this is possible only if there exists $p \in P \cap u$ such that $\Delta_\Pi(u{:}\overline{u}) \nvdash p$. But then there exists a model $\beta$ of $T$ such that $\alpha \cap F = \beta \cap F$, and $\beta \cap P \subset \alpha \cap P$, contrary to the assumption that $\alpha$ is a $(P, F)$-minimal model of $T$. Thus, $u$ is an extension, and $u \subseteq \alpha$. This completes the proof. □

As we will see later, expansions of prerequisite-free default theories coincide with extensions, so the above result will also hold for the usual extension-based semantics.

### 9.4.1 *Reiter's default logic*

In the original formulation of default logic, given in [Reiter, 1980], a default theory was defined as a pair $\Delta = (W, D)$, where $W$ is a set of propositions and $D$ a set of default rules of the form[2] $A : B_1, \ldots, B_k/C$ having the following informal interpretation:

*If $A$ holds, and each of $B_i$ can be consistently assumed, then infer $C$.*

The connection between our default theories and that of Reiter can be established by representing propositions from $W$ as default rules $:\vdash A$, and translating the rules $A : B_1, \ldots, B_k/C$ into the following default rules:

$$A : \neg B_1, \ldots, \neg B_k \vdash C.$$

This translation will be denoted by $rtr(\Delta)$. As can be seen, it agrees with the above informal meaning of Reiter's default rules. Note also that the translation is reversible: a default rule $a{:}b \vdash C$ corresponds exactly to the Reiter's default rule $\bigwedge a : \neg b/C$. Accordingly, the two versions of default theory can be seen as notational variants.

It turns out that, under the above translation, extensions of Reiter's default theories correspond precisely to extensions of corresponding default theories. The proof of this fact could be obtained from a slight generalization of the iterative construction described in Lemma 6.6. Below we will give, however, a short direct proof.

[2] It is interesting to note that a 'pseudo-modal' operator **M** that appeared in the original formulation was later removed by Reiter as unnecessary.

**Theorem 9.42** *Extensions of a Reiter default theory $\Delta$ coincide with the classical extensions of $rtr(\Delta)$.*

***Proof.*** By Definition 1 from [Reiter, 1980], extensions are fixed points of an operator $\Gamma$ such that, for any set $u$ of propositions, $\Gamma(u)$ is the least deductively closed set that includes $W$ and such that, if $A : b/C$ is a default rule, $A \in \Gamma(u)$ and $\neg b \subseteq \overline{u}$, then $C \in \Gamma(u)$.

To simplify the presentation, $\vdash$ below will denote $\vdash_{rtr(\Delta)}$, while $\mathbb{C}\mathrm{n}$ will be the corresponding provability operator. Then we will show that, for any set $u$ of propositions, $\mathbb{C}\mathrm{n}(\emptyset{:}\overline{u})$ coincides with $\Gamma(u)$.

Clearly, $\mathbb{C}\mathrm{n}(\emptyset{:}\overline{u})$ is a deductively closed set that contains $W$. In addition, if $A : b/C$ is a default rule such that $A \in \mathbb{C}\mathrm{n}(\emptyset{:}\overline{u})$ and $\neg b \subseteq \overline{u}$, then we have $:\overline{u} \vdash C$ by Cut, and consequently $\mathbb{C}\mathrm{n}(\emptyset{:}\overline{u})$ is closed with respect to the default rules of $\Delta$. Now, since $\Gamma(u)$ is the least such set, we obtain $\Gamma(u) \subseteq \mathbb{C}\mathrm{n}(\emptyset, \overline{u})$.

In order to prove the reverse inclusion, let us denote by $\mathbb{S}$ a supraclassical default semantics that consists of all models of the form $(\Gamma(u), \Gamma(u), u)$, for any set $u$. It can be easily verified that all rules from $rtr(\Delta)$ are valid in $\mathbb{S}$, and hence $rtr(\Delta) \subseteq \vdash_{\mathbb{S}}$. Consequently, $\vdash \subseteq \vdash_{\mathbb{S}}$, since $\vdash$ is the least such relation. Finally, if $:\overline{u} \vdash_{\mathbb{S}} A$, then $A \in \Gamma(u)$ (since $(\Gamma(u), \Gamma(u), u) \in \mathbb{S}$). Thus, $\mathbb{C}\mathrm{n}_{\mathbb{S}}(\emptyset{:}\overline{u}) \subseteq \Gamma(u)$, and consequently $\mathbb{C}\mathrm{n}(\emptyset{:}\overline{u}) \subseteq \Gamma(u)$, as required.

Now, since $\mathbb{C}\mathrm{n}(\emptyset, \overline{u}) = \Gamma(u)$, we immediately obtain that fixed points of $\Gamma$ coincide with the extensions of $rtr(\Delta)$. □

Due to the above result, supraclassical default consequence relations constitute an appropriate underlying monotonic logic for Reiter's default logic. The above proof indicates, however, that this logic is far from being a maximal one. The latter will be described in the next section.

### 9.4.2 *Kinds of supraclassical default consequence relations*

In this section we will describe the main kinds of supraclassical default consequence relations that will play key roles in representing nonmonotonic reasoning with default rules.

#### 9.4.2.1 *Introspective consequence relations*

As we have already seen, both reasoning with extensions and reasoning with expansions admit richer underlying logics of default rules. As we will see in due course, supraclassical default consequence relations described in the next definition provide a common core of such logics.

**Definition 9.11** A supraclassical default consequence relation will be called

- *strongly supraclassical* if it satisfies the following postulates:

  **Positive Closure** If $a \vDash A$ and $a, A : b \vdash B$, then $a : b \vdash B$.
  **Negative Closure** If $c \vDash B$ and $a{:}b, C_i \vdash A$, $\forall C_i \in c$, then $a{:}b, B \vdash A$.
  **Positive Falsity** $\mathbf{f} : \vdash \mathbf{f}$.
  **Negative Falsity** If $a : b, \mathbf{f} \vdash A$, then $a : b \vdash A$.

- *introspective*, if it is strongly supraclassical, and satisfies Consistency and D-Regularity.

The two Closure postulates above secure that classical inference can be used also in premises of default rules. They allow, in particular, replacement of classically equivalent formulas. In addition, sets of positive premises can be replaced by their conjunctions, while negative premises leading to the same conclusion can be conjoined:

$$\frac{a : b, A \vdash C \qquad a : b, B \vdash C}{a : b, A \wedge B \vdash C}$$

Finally, the two Falsity postulates impose an eventual exclusion of inconsistent sets of positive or negative premises.

Let us say that a default semantics is *classical*, if its models $(w, u, v)$ are triples of consistent deductive theories. The next result shows that such a semantics determines precisely strongly supraclassical default consequence relations.

**Corollary 9.43** *A default consequence relation is strongly supraclassical if and only if it has a classical default semantics.*

***Proof.*** It can be directly verified that a classical default semantics makes valid all the postulates of strong supraclassicality. In the other direction, it is sufficient to show that the canonical default semantics constructed in the proof of Theorem 6.21 is classical in our case.

Let $(u, v)$ be a canonical bitheory for some $A$. Then Positive Closure implies that $u$ is deductively closed, while Positive Falsity implies that it is consistent. Similarly, Negative Closure implies that $v$ is deductively closed, while Negative Falsity gives $\mathbf{f} \notin v$, so $v$ will also be consistent. □

Finally, given strong supraclassicality, the D-Regularity rule of regular consequence relations can be simplified to the following weakening of Factoring:

**CD-Regularity** $$\frac{a, B : b \vdash \mathbf{f} \quad a : b, B \vdash A}{a : b \vdash A}$$

**Lemma 9.44** *A supraclassical default consequence relation is introspective iff it is strongly supraclassical, consistent and satisfies CD-Regularity.*

***Proof.*** Assume that the default consequence relation is introspective, and we have $a, B{:}b \vdash \mathbf{f}$ and $a{:}b, B \vdash A$. Then by Consistency $a{:}b, C \vdash A$, for any $C \in a$, so $a{:}b \vdash A$ by D-Regularity. Hence CD-regularity holds.

Assume now that CD-Regularity holds, $c{:}b \vdash \mathbf{f}$ and $a{:}b, C \vdash A$, for any $C \in c$. Then $\bigwedge c{:}b \vdash \mathbf{f}$ by Positive Closure, and $a{:}b, \bigwedge c \vdash A$ by Negative Closure. Consequently, $a{:}b \vdash A$ by CD-Regularity. Thus, D-regularity holds. □

9.4.2.2 *Regular consequence relations*

As has been shown in Chapter 6, the default rules of reflexive default consequence relations correspond to singular default bisequents $a{:}b \Vdash A :$. This correspondence is directly extendable to the supraclassical case. As a result, we immediately obtain that reflexive supraclassical default relations correspond to supraclassical singular default biconsequence relations, and hence they have the same extensions (Lemma 6.31). Moreover, we still have that the maximal logic of default rules suitable for classical extensions is a logic of regular default consequence relations. This observation follows immediately from the fact that Theorems 6.33 and 6.35 (as well as their proofs) still hold in the supraclassical case.

Recall that a semantic representation of regular default consequence relations is given by a regular binary semantics (see Theorem 6.32). The following result shows that regular supraclassical consequence relations are complete with respect to the corresponding *classical* binary semantics.

**Theorem 9.45** *A supraclassical default consequence relation is regular if and only if it has a regular classical binary semantics.*

***Proof.*** Since a classical binary semantics obviously validates C-Closure, Theorem 6.32 implies that any regular classical binary semantics determines a regular supraclassical consequence relation. In the other direction, if $\vdash$ is a regular supraclassical consequence relation, then by the same theorem it is sufficient to show that if $(u, v)$ is a canonical bitheory for some $A$, then both $u$ and $v$ are consistent deductively closed sets. But $\vdash$ is reflexive, so $(u, v)$ is a bitheory of $\vdash$ iff $u = \mathbb{C}\mathrm{n}(u{:}\overline{v})$, which immediately implies that $u$ is deductively closed and, moreover, consistent (since $A \notin u$). In addition, $v$ should be a theory of $\vdash$, that is $v = \mathbb{C}\mathrm{n}(v{:}\overline{v})$, so $v$ is also deductively closed. Finally, the proof of Theorem 6.32 shows, in effect, that consistency of $v$ follows from Regularity. □

As follows from the above semantic representation, regular supraclassical consequence relations are precisely introspective default consequence relations that are also reflexive.

#### 9.4.2.3 *Saturated consequence relations*

Now we will describe default consequence relations that correspond to saturated biconsequence relations.

**Definition 9.12** A supraclassical default consequence relation will be called *saturated*, if it is regular and satisfies

**Conditional Factoring** $$\frac{a, B : b \vdash A \qquad a : b, B \vdash A}{a : b \vdash B \to A}$$

The next result shows that such consequence relations are determined precisely by saturated binary semantics.

**Theorem 9.46** *A default consequence relation is saturated if and only if it has a saturated binary semantics.*

***Proof.*** Let us verify first that a saturated semantics validates Conditional Factoring. Assume that $a{:}b \vdash B{\to}A$ is not valid in a saturated semantics $\mathcal{B}$. Then there exists a bimodel $(u, v) \in \mathcal{B}$ such that $a \subseteq u$, $B{\to}A \notin u$ and $b \subseteq \overline{v}$. Since $\mathcal{B}$ is saturated, $(v, v) \in \mathcal{B}$ and $u = v \cap \alpha$, for some world $\alpha$. If $B \notin v$, then $(u, v)$ invalidates $a{:}b, B \vdash A$, and we are done. So assume $B \in v$. Now, if $A \notin v$, then $(v, v)$ invalidates $B, a{:}b \vdash A$, as required, so assume $A \in v$. In this case $B{\to}A \in v$ and $B{\to}A \notin u$, and consequently $B{\to}A \notin \alpha$. But then we have $B \in u$, and consequently $(u, v)$ invalidates $B, a{:}b \vdash A$. Therefore saturated semantics determines a saturated default consequence relation.

In the other direction, it is sufficient to show that the canonical binary semantics of a saturated default consequence relation $\vdash$ is saturated.

Let $(u, \overline{v})$ be a maximal pair such that $u{:}\overline{v} \nvdash A$, for some $A$. Since $\vdash$ is regular, $(v, v)$ is also a canonical bimodel. We show first that in our case there are no other bimodels $(u', v')$ such that $u \subseteq u'$ and $v' \subseteq v$. Indeed, an instance of Conditional Factoring is the following rule

$$\frac{A \to B, a : b \vdash A \qquad a : b, A \to B \vdash A}{a : b \vdash A}$$

(substitute $A{\to}B$ for $B$). Consequently, for any $B$, either $A \to B \in u$ or $A \to B \in \overline{v}$. Now let $(u', v')$ be another canonical model such that $u \subseteq u'$ and $v' \subseteq v$. Due to maximality of $(u, v)$, we have $u' : \overline{v}' \vdash A$, and hence $A \in u'$. Now if $B \in v$, then $A{\to}B \in v$ and hence $A{\to}B \in u$. Consequently $A{\to}B \in u'$ and therefore $B \in u'$ (since $u'$ is deductively closed). Thus, $v \subseteq u'$, and consequently $(u', v')$ coincides with $(v, v)$.

Now we will show that the set $w = u \cup \neg(v \setminus u)$ is consistent. Indeed, otherwise $v \backslash u$ contains a finite subset $c$ such that $\bigvee c \in u$. Clearly, $c$ contains at least one pair of propositions $C, D$ such that $C{\to}D \notin u$ (otherwise $c$ is included in $u$). Now $u : \overline{v} \nvdash C \to D$, and Conditional Factoring implies that either $C, u : \overline{v} \nvdash D$ or $u : \overline{v}, C \nvdash D$. In the first case we have that there exists a canonical model $(x, y)$ that extends $(u, \overline{v})$ and such that $C \in x$ but $D \notin x$. However, this is impossible since neither $C$ nor $D$ belong to $u$, and both belong to $v$. Similarly, in the second case we would have $C \in \overline{v}$. Thus, $w$ is consistent.

Since $w$ is consistent, it can be extended to a world, say $\beta$. It is easy to see that $u = \beta \cap v$. Indeed, assume that $C \in \beta \cap v$, but $C \notin u$. Then $C \in v \backslash u$ and hence $\neg C \in \neg(v \backslash u)$. Consequently $\neg C \in \beta$, which is impossible. Thus, $(u, v)$ is a saturated bimodel, which shows that the canonical semantics of $\vdash$ is saturated. □

#### 9.4.2.4 *Classical autoepistemic consequence relations*

Turning to autoepistemic reasoning, we will extend the notion of an autoepistemic consequence relation from Chapter 6 to a supraclassical one. As we will show formally in the next chapter, the resulting formalism will capture precisely the non-modal part of the autoepistemic logic. Moreover, this non-modal part will uniquely determine the latter.

**Definition 9.13** An autoepistemic consequence relation in a classical language will be called *classical*, if it is strongly supraclassical.

Note that, given the postulates of an autoepistemic consequence relation, Positive Closure is equivalent for them to Negative Closure, while Positive Falsity is equivalent to Negative Falsity. Accordingly, the corresponding classical relation can be defined as an autoepistemic consequence relation that satisfies only Positive Closure and Positive Falsity. As for production inference relations, described in Chapter 8, a distinctive feature of autoepistemic rules is that they do not satisfy Reflexivity.

As before, a semantic representation of classical autoepistemic consequence relations is provided by a *classical* binary semantics (see Theorem 6.36).

**Corollary 9.47** *$\vdash$ is a classical autoepistemic consequence relation if and only if there is a consistent classical binary semantics $\mathcal{B}$ such that $\vdash$ coincides with $\vdash^{A}_{\mathcal{B}}$.*

Now, Theorem 6.40 and its proof remain valid in the classical case, so classical autoepistemic consequence relations constitute a maximal logic for reasoning with classical expansions.

We will establish now a partial correspondence between the nonmonotonic semantics of saturated and autoepistemic consequence relations.

For a default theory $\Delta$, we will define the following new default theory

$$\Delta^a = \{a : b \vdash (\bigwedge a \to C) \mid a : b \vdash C \in \Delta\}.$$

Note that if $\Delta$ contains only prerequisite-free rules, then $\Delta^a$ coincides with $\Delta$.

**Theorem 9.48** *If $\vdash^{st}_{\Delta}$ is the least saturated default consequence relation containing $\Delta$, then the default semantics of $\vdash^{st}_{\Delta}$ coincides with the autoepistemic semantics of $\Delta^a$.*

***Proof.*** Let $\Delta_d$ denote the default bisequent theory corresponding to $\Delta$. Clearly, the default semantics of $\vdash^{st}_{\Delta}$ coincides with the default semantics of $\vdash^{st}_{\Delta_d}$. Moreover, by Theorem 9.19, $\Delta_d$ has the same expansions as $\Delta'_d = \{:b \Vdash \bigwedge a \to C : a \mid a : b \vdash C \in \Delta\}$ (see Lemma 9.7(6)). Finally, the autoepistemic bisequent theory $\Delta'_d$ clearly has the same expansions as the default theory $\Delta^a$. Hence the result. □

As a consequence of the above result, we obtain

**Corollary 9.49** *If $\Delta$ is a literal or a prerequisite-free default theory, then classical extensions of $\Delta$ coincide with classical expansions of $\Delta^a$.*

***Proof.*** Follows from the fact that, by Theorem 9.20, extensions of $\Delta_d$ coincide with its expansions. □

The example below shows that the restriction to literal or prerequisite-free default theories cannot be dropped.

**Example 9.1** Consider a default theory $\Delta = \{p{:}\vdash q,\ q{:}\vdash p,\ \vdash p \vee q\}$ that is neither prerequisite-free, nor literal one. Then

$$\Delta^a = \{p :\vdash p{\to}q,\ q :\vdash q{\to}p,\ \vdash p \vee q\}.$$

It can be verified that $\mathrm{Th}(p,q)$ is an expansion of $\Delta^a$, though it is not an extension (= minimal theory) of $\Delta$.

The above result gives a description of a default semantics in terms of an autoepistemic semantics of some modified default theory. Note, however, that the reverse description is impossible, in general, due to the fact that extensions are always minimal theories and hence, unlike expansions, they are always incomparable with respect to set inclusion.

### 9.4.3 *Default relations vs. production inference*

As we have seen earlier, general production rules $A \Rightarrow B$ are representable as bisequents $\Vdash B : A$ of a supraclassical biconsequence relation. It turns out that production rules admit both a default and autoepistemic interpretation in the framework of default consequence relations. The two interpretations reveal, respectively, the connections of production inference to default and autoepistemic logic.

#### 9.4.3.1 *Autoepistemic representation of general productions*

A more specific framework for general production inference is provided by the classical autoepistemic logic, in which production rules $A \Rightarrow B$ can be identified with default rules $A :\vdash B$. The adequacy of this representation can be demonstrated as follows.

Given a causal theory $\Delta$, let us define the following default theory

$$\Delta_A = \{A :\vdash B \mid A \Rightarrow B \in \Delta\}.$$

Then the following result shows precise correspondence between the exact semantics of $\Delta$ and the autoepistemic semantics of $\Delta_A$.

**Theorem 9.50** *Exact theories of a causal theory $\Delta$ coincide with expansions of $\Delta_A$.*

***Proof.*** By Lemma 9.40, $u$ is an expansion of $\Delta_A$ iff $u = \mathrm{Th}(\Delta_A(u{:}\overline{u}))$. In our case, however, $\Delta_A(u{:}\overline{u}) = \Delta_A(u{:}\emptyset) = \Delta(u)$. Consequently, $u = \mathrm{Th}(\Delta(u))$, and hence the claim follows from Lemma 8.17. □

Due to the above correspondence, classical autoepistemic consequence relations turn out to constitute an adequate (and maximal) logic for general production inference and its nonmonotonic production semantics. This shows, in effect, that the nonmonotonic formalism of production inference is a special case of autoepistemic reasoning that is based on positive introspection only.

### 9.4.3.2 *Default representation of causal productions*

It turns out that basic and causal production relations admit yet another representation in the framework of default logic. Moreover, this latter representation, though partial, will imply that, in certain cases, default logic can simulate the representation capabilities of causal inference.

If we compare the semantic representation of production rules based on d-validity (see Definition 8.19) with the D-representation of reflexive default consequence relations (Definition 6.11), we immediately note that a basic production rule $A \Rightarrow B$ can also be viewed as a default rule $:\neg A \vdash B$ that is prerequisite-free and has a single justification[3].

For a causal theory $\Delta$, we define this time the following default theory

$$\Delta_D = \{: \neg A \vdash B \mid A \Rightarrow B \in \Delta\}.$$

Also, $\dot{u}$ will denote the set of propositions that are compatible with $u$:

$$\dot{u} = \{A \mid u \cup \{A\} \text{ is consistent}\}.$$

Given this notation, we have

**Lemma 9.51** *A set $u$ is an extension of $\Delta_D$ iff $u = \mathrm{Th}(\Delta(\dot{u}))$.*

***Proof.*** Since $\Delta_D$ is prerequisite-free, its extensions and expansions coincide by Corollary 9.49. Now, by Lemma 9.40, $u$ is an expansion of $\Delta_D$ iff $u = \mathrm{Th}(\Delta_D(u{:}\overline{u}))$. It is easy to see, however, that $\Delta_D(u{:}\overline{u}) = \Delta_D(\emptyset{:}\overline{u}) = \Delta(\dot{u})$. Hence the result. □

As a consequence of the above result, we obtain the following correspondence between the causal semantics of $\Delta$ and default semantics of $\Delta_D$ (cf. [McCain and Turner, 1997]):

**Corollary 9.52** *A world $\alpha$ is an exact world of a causal theory $\Delta$ if and only if it is an extension of $\Delta_D$.*

***Proof.*** Since $\alpha = \dot{\alpha}$, the result follows from Lemma 8.17. □

[3] Such rules correspond to Reiter's default rules of the form $:A/B$.

The significance of the above result amounts to the observation that, despite the fact that default logic is a more general (and thereby a weaker) formalism than causal inference, in many simple cases it is nevertheless capable of representing the nonmonotonic inferences determined by the latter. This might serve as a possible explanation of why causal inference has been discovered so late in the history of nonmonotonic reasoning.

# Chapter 10

# Modal Nonmonotonic Logics

The modal approach to nonmonotonic reasoning was initiated in [McDermott and Doyle, 1980]. This and subsequent paper [McDermott, 1982] gave rise to a study of autoepistemic logic [Moore, 1985] and to a whole range of modal nonmonotonic logics based on 'negative introspection' in the works of Marek, Truszczyński and Schwarz (see, e.g., [Marek and Truszczyński, 1993; Marek *et al.*, 1993; Schwarz, 1992a; Schwarz and Truszczyński, 1994]).

Despite the difference in the underlying language, the similarity between default and modal nonmonotonic logics was noticed early, and a number of attempts has been made to clarify their relationship (see, e.g., [Konolige, 1988]). An adequate translation of default logic into a broad range of modal nonmonotonic logics has been given by Truszczyński in [Truszczyński, 1991b; Truszczyński, 1991a].

In this chapter we introduce the notion of a modal (bi)consequence relation. Such consequence relations will be defined in a modal language, but otherwise will involve the same rules as general consequence relations. Modal consequence relations will turn out to be an especially suitable tool for studying modal nonmonotonic reasoning. Thus, both autoepistemic reasoning and reasoning with negative introspection will acquire a natural characterization in this framework.

As we will see, under certain reasonable conditions modal consequence relations will be reducible to nonmodal consequence relations in a way that preserves the associated nonmonotonic semantics. These results will be used for establishing a two-way correspondence between modal and nonmodal formalizations. Thus, for a number of modal nonmonotonic logics that appear in the literature, we will give a representation in terms of modal default consequence relations. We will show also how and under what conditions objective default consequence relations can be faithfully embedded into modal ones. Finally, we will demonstrate that the modal logic S4F (or S4.3.2) can be seen as a 'canonical' modal logic for extension-based non-monotonic reasoning, while the modal logics SW5 and KD45 play the same role for autoepistemic reasoning.

Both modal and nonmodal formalisms for nonmonotonic reasoning have advantages of their own. For nonmodal systems it is mainly conceptual simplicity and avoidance of nested modalities (as we will see, nested modalities of depth more than two will be largely irrelevant). For modal formalisms, it is a convenience of working with familiar modal formulas, for which the underlying theory and semantics already exist. As the results below show, in most cases we can freely choose each of these formalisms. Moreover, it will be shown that different modal axioms influence nonmonotonic reasoning only to the extent they change the structural properties of the corresponding consequence relation. The results will also show why such otherwise esoteric modal logics as KD4G, KD45, S4.2, S4F and SW5 occupy a special place in the study of modal nonmonotonic reasoning.

In this chapter we will use a lot of standard modal terminology. Most of it can be found, e.g., in [Bull and Segerberg, 1984].

Let $\mathcal{L}_L$ be a classical propositional language with a modal operator $L$. As usual, $M$ will denote the corresponding possibility operator, that is, $MA \equiv \neg L \neg A$. In the context of modal nonmonotonic logics, the operator $L$ is usually interpreted as an *epistemic* operator, that is, either as an operator of belief (see, e.g., [Moore, 1985]) or an operator of knowledge (e.g., in [Schwarz and Truszczyński, 1994]). Both these interpretations will be used in this chapter.

In what follows, propositions without the modal operator $L$ will be called *objective*. $\mathcal{L}_o$ will denote the subset of $\mathcal{L}_L$ consisting of all objective propositions. For any set of propositions $u$ from $\mathcal{L}_L$, we let $u_o$ denote the set $u \cap \mathcal{L}_o$ and $\overline{u}_o$ the set $\mathcal{L}_o \setminus u$. Note that if $\Vdash$ is a biconsequence relation in $\mathcal{L}_L$, its restriction to $\mathcal{L}_o$ is an objective biconsequence relation having the same structural rules as $\Vdash$. We will denote this objective subrelation by ${}_o\Vdash$.

If $\mathcal{M}$ is a modal logic containing the necessitation rule $A/LA$, then $u \vdash_{\mathcal{M}} A$ will denote the fact that $A$ is derivable from $u$ and axioms of $\mathcal{M}$ using modus ponens and necessitation[1]. In addition, $\mathrm{Cn}_{\mathcal{M}}$ will denote the corresponding derivability operator. N will denote the least modal logic of this kind, namely the modal logic without proper modal axioms and

[1] which means that we are using the notion of a *global* modal consequence.

necessitation as the only modal inference rule (see [Fitting *et al.*, 1992]).

A set $u$ of propositions in a modal language is called a *stable theory* ([Moore, 1985]), if it is a deductively closed set that satisfies the following two conditions:

- If $A \in u$, then $LA \in u$;
- If $A \notin u$, then $\neg LA \in u$.

In what follows, we will extensively use the following well known properties of stable theories (see, e.g., [Moore, 1985; Konolige, 1988; Schwarz, 1990]):

**Proposition 10.1**

- *Stable theories are uniquely determined by their objective parts;*
- *Stable theories are incomparable: if $u \subseteq v$, then $u = v$;*
- *$u$ is a stable theory if and only if $u = \mathrm{Cn}_{\mathbf{N}}(u_o \cup \neg L\overline{u})$.*

## 10.1 Modal Biconsequence Relations

As we already said in the preceding chapter, an epistemic understanding of biconsequence relations is naturally obtained by treating the positive and assumption contexts, respectively, as the contexts of knowledge and belief. Now, the role of the modal operator $L$ in this setting will consist in expressing (or reflecting) this knowledge and belief as propositions in the object language. Accordingly, modal biconsequence relations will be defined as biconsequence relations in a classical modal language that satisfy certain reflection and introspection principles with respect to the modal operator. The interplay of these principles will determine the characteristic features of modal nonmonotonic reasoning.

In what follows, we will use two informal epistemic interpretations of the modal operator $L$. The first, simpler interpretation will consist in viewing $L$ as a pure *operator of belief*. On this reading, $LA$ will invariably mean that $A$ is believed, that is, belongs to the current set of assumptions. On the second interpretation, $L$ will be treated as the *knowledge operator*. Accordingly, in the positive context, $LA$ will mean that $A$ is known, while in the belief (assumption) context it will mean that $A$ is believed. This knowledge operator will already satisfy the modal T axiom $LA \rightarrow A$. Moreover, the intended interpretation of this operator will incorporate a rather strong epistemic assumption that the derived operator $ML$ will express precisely the corresponding belief operator. In other words, a proposition $A$ will be believed (that is, assumed) if and only if $MLA$ will hold in either the positive, or assumption context.

Both the above epistemic interpretations are admissible with respect to the general notion of a modal biconsequence relation, described in the next definition.

**Definition 10.1** A supraclassical biconsequence relation in $\mathcal{L}_L$ will be called *modal* if it satisfies the following postulates:

**Positive Reflection** $A : \Vdash LA:$,
**Negative Reflection** $: LA \Vdash :A$,
**Negative Introspection** $: A \Vdash \neg LA:$.

The first thing that should be noted about modal biconsequence relations is that Positive Reflection and Negative Introspection jointly imply $A{:}A \Vdash$, for any $A$, and hence we have

**Lemma 10.2** *Any modal biconsequence relation is consistent.*

Also, given Cut, Positive Reflection is equivalent to the following rule:

**Necessitation** If $a : b \Vdash A, c{:}d$, then $a : b \Vdash LA, c{:}d$.

In this sense, Positive Reflection captures the effect of the necessitation rule $A/LA$ in modal logics.

An important property of modal biconsequence relations is described in the next lemma.

**Lemma 10.3** *If $(u, v)$ is a bitheory of a modal biconsequence relation, then $v$ is a stable theory, and*

$$A \in v \quad \textit{iff} \quad \neg LA \notin u \quad \textit{iff} \quad MLA \in u.$$

***Proof.*** If $(u, v)$ is a bitheory of a modal biconsequence relation $\Vdash$, then $v$ is deductively closed. In addition, if $A \in v$, then $LA \in v$ by Negative Reflection, and if $A \notin v$, then $\neg LA \in u$ by Negative Introspection, and hence $\neg LA \in v$ by Consistency. Thus, $v$ is a modal stable theory. Now if $A \in v$, then $\neg LA \notin v$, since $v$ is stable. This implies $MLA \in u$ by Negative Introspection, and hence $L\neg LA \notin u$ by consistency of $u$. Therefore $\neg LA \notin u$ by Positive Reflection, and hence $A \in v$ by Negative Introspection. This shows that all the above equivalences hold. □

As a first consequence of the above result, we immediately obtain

**Corollary 10.4** *Any theory of a modal biconsequence relation is a stable theory.*

The above fact will imply, in particular, that extensions and expansions of modal biconsequence relations will always be stable theories.

The description of the above lemma also implies that the assumption context of a modal biconsequence relation is uniquely determined by the (modal formulas from the) positive context. This implies, in turn, that corresponding bisequents are reducible to positive bisequents. Namely, the reductions below follow directly from the equivalences of the preceding lemma.

**Corollary 10.5** *Any bisequent $a{:}b \Vdash c{:}d$ of a modal biconsequence relation is equivalent to each of the following:*

*(1)* $a{:}b, \neg Ld \Vdash c{:},$
*(2)* $a, \neg Lb{:} \Vdash c, \neg Ld{:},$
*(3)* $a, \neg Lb, \neg L\neg Ld{:} \Vdash c{:},$
*(4)* $a{:} \Vdash c, \neg L\neg Lb, \neg Ld{:}.$

For singular bisequents, we have also the following reduction:

**Lemma 10.6** *Any singular bisequent $a{:}b \Vdash C{:}d$ of a modal biconsequence relation is equivalent to* $a{:} \Vdash \bigwedge L\neg Lb \wedge \bigwedge \neg L\neg Ld \to C{:}.$

***Proof.*** The above reduction stems from the following two equivalences:

$a{:}b, B \Vdash C{:}d$ is equivalent to $a{:}b \Vdash L\neg LB \to C{:}d$;
$a{:}b \Vdash C{:}d, D$ is equivalent to $a{:}b \Vdash \neg L\neg LD \to C{:}d$.

Now, $a{:}b, B \Vdash C{:}d$ follows from $a{:}b \Vdash L\neg LB \to C{:}d$, since ${:}B \Vdash L\neg LB{:}$ by Negative Introspection and Necessitation. In the other direction, if $a{:}b, B \Vdash C{:}d$, then $a{:}b, B \Vdash L\neg LB \to C{:}d$. In addition, $a{:}b, \neg LB \Vdash L\neg LB \to C{:}d$ by Negative Introspection, and hence $a{:}b \Vdash L\neg LB \to C{:}d, B$ by the preceding corollary. Now $a{:}b \Vdash L\neg LB \to C{:}d$ follows by Negative Cut.

The proof of the second equivalence is similar. □

The above reduction implies, in particular, that any singular autoepistemic bisequent is reducible to a modal formula. This fact will play an important role in what follows.

Another useful property of such biconsequence relations stems from the fact that stable theories are uniquely determined by their objective (non-modal) parts. More exactly, modal biconsequence relations sanction the following reductions of modal operators in assumption contexts:

**Lemma 10.7** *If $\Vdash$ is a modal biconsequence relation, then*

- *any bisequent $a{:}b, LA \vee B \Vdash c{:}d$ is equivalent to $a{:}b, A, B \Vdash c{:}d$;*
- *a bisequent $a{:}b, \neg LA \vee B \Vdash c{:}d$ is equivalent to $a{:}b, B \Vdash c{:}d, A$;*
- *$a{:}b \Vdash c{:}d, LA \vee B$ is equivalent to $a{:}b \Vdash c{:}d, A$ and $a{:}b \Vdash c{:}d, B$;*
- *$a{:}b \Vdash c{:}d, \neg LA \vee B$ is equivalent to $a{:}b, A \Vdash c{:}d$ and $a{:}b \Vdash c{:}d, B$.*

***Proof.*** The proof follows from the fact that if $v$ is a stable theory, then $LA \vee B \in v$ iff $A \in v$ or $B \in v$, and $\neg LA \vee B \in v$ iff $A \notin v$ or $B \in v$. □

Recall now that conjunction can be eliminated in the context of supraclassical biconsequence relations. Consequently, using the above reductions, any bisequent can be reduced to a set of bisequents without modal operators in negative premises and conclusions.

**Corollary 10.8** *Any bisequent $a{:}b \Vdash c{:}d$ of a modal biconsequence relation is reducible to a set of bisequents of the form $a{:}b_i \Vdash c{:}d_i$, where $b_i, d_i$ are sets of objective propositions.*

Yet another consequence of the above reductions is the following fact that will turn out to be useful:

**Lemma 10.9** *If $u$ is a stable set, then $a{:}\overline{u} \Vdash c{:}u$ iff $a{:}\overline{u}_o \Vdash c{:}u_o$.*

***Proof.*** If $a{:}\overline{u}_o \nVdash c{:}u_o$, then $a \subseteq w$ and $u \cap c = \emptyset$, for some bitheory $(w, v)$ of $\Vdash$ such that $u_o = v_o$. Since $v$ is stable, we have $u = v$, since both are stable theories having the same objective part. Thus, $a{:}\overline{u} \nVdash c{:}u$. □

By a (modal) *bisequent theory* we will mean below an arbitrary set of bisequents in the modal language. Moreover, we will often identify plain modal theories, that is, sets of modal propositions, with corresponding bisequent theories containing bisequents of the form $\Vdash A{:}$. Note in this respect that, due to Lemma 10.6, any singular autoepistemic bisequent theory will be equivalent to a modal theory in this sense.

### 10.1.1 *Normal biconsequence relations*

If we are taking seriously the idea of viewing the modal operator $L$ as an epistemic operator representing our knowledge or beliefs, we should consider the question to what extent the modal axioms usually imposed on such epistemic operators influence the properties of the corresponding biconsequence relations and associated nonmonotonic semantics.

**Definition 10.2** For a modal logic $\mathcal{M}$, a modal biconsequence relation $\Vdash$ will be called an *$\mathcal{M}$-biconsequence relation*, if $\Vdash A{:}$, for any (instance of a) modal axiom of $\mathcal{M}$.

To begin with, already general modal biconsequence relations are modally nontrivial. More exactly, they imply both the modal D axiom, and the Geach axiom G.

**Lemma 10.10** *If $\Vdash$ is a modal biconsequence relation, then, for any $A$,*

**D** $\Vdash LA \to MA :;$
**G** $\Vdash MLA \to LMA :.$

***Proof.*** Note first that $:A \Vdash \neg LA{:}$ by negative introspection, and hence $:A \Vdash L\neg LA{:}$ by Necessitation. Similarly, we have $:\neg A \Vdash \neg L\neg A{:}$, and hence $:\neg A \Vdash LMA{:}$. Since $\Vdash$ is supraclassical, we obtain, respectively, $:A \wedge \neg A \Vdash \neg LA \vee \neg L\neg A{:}$ and $:A \wedge \neg A \Vdash L\neg LA \vee LMA{:}$, and therefore $\Vdash \neg LA \vee \neg L\neg A{:}$ and $\Vdash L\neg LA \vee LMA{:}$ by Negative Falsity. □

Still, modal biconsequence relations need not satisfy, in general, the modal K axiom $L(A{\to}B) \wedge LA{\to}LB$. Adding the latter will give us a broad class of 'normal' modal biconsequence relations that can already be given an instructive possible worlds semantics.

A possible worlds semantics for K-biconsequence relations is obtainable in terms of Kripke models having a last cluster, namely models of the form $M = (W, R, F, V)$, where $(W, R, V)$ is an ordinary Kripke model with a set of worlds $W$, an accessibility relation $R$ and a valuation function $V$, while $F$ is a *last cluster* of the model, that is, a non-empty subset of $W$ satisfying the following conditions (see [Segerberg, 1971]):

- If $\alpha R\beta$ and $\alpha \in F$, then $\beta \in F$;
- $\alpha R\beta$, for any $\beta \in F$ and $\alpha \in W$.

Note that, if a Kripke model has a last cluster, it is unique. We will call such models *final Kripke models*, while a set of such models will be called a *final possible worlds semantics*. The relevance of such semantics for modal nonmonotonic reasoning has been shown already in [Schwarz, 1992a].

For a final Kripke model $M = (W, R, F, V)$, we will denote by $|M|$ the set of modal propositions that are valid in $M$, while $||M||$ will denote the set of propositions that are valid in the submodel of $M$ generated by $F$. Note that the latter is actually an S5-model. Clearly, $|M| \subseteq ||M||$.

For a final possible worlds semantics $\mathcal{S}$, we define the associated binary semantics $\mathcal{B}_{\mathcal{S}}$ as the set of all bimodels of the form $(|M|, ||M||)$, for $M \in \mathcal{S}$.

**Definition 10.3** A bisequent $a{:}b \Vdash c{:}d$ will be said to be *valid* in a final possible worlds semantics $\mathcal{S}$, if it is valid in $\mathcal{B}_{\mathcal{S}}$.

**Remark 10.1** *The above semantic framework corresponds to a unimodal BK-semantics from [Schwarz and Truszczyński, 1994] (cf. also [Bochman, 1995]). The latter semantics constituted, in turn, a conceptual simplification of bimodal semantics and associated bimodal nonmonotonic logics suggested in [Lin and Shoham, 1992; Lifschitz, 1994]. The possibility of this unimodal simplification was due to the fact that the second modal operator used in these systems has turned out to be definable as $ML$.*

$\Vdash_{\mathcal{S}}$ will denote the set of all bisequents that are valid in $\mathcal{S}$ according to the above definition. Then the following generic result shows that K-biconsequence relations are complete with respect to this notion of validity.

**Theorem 10.11** *$\Vdash$ is a K-biconsequence relation if and only if it coincides with $\Vdash_{\mathcal{S}}$, for some final possible worlds semantics $\mathcal{S}$.*

***Proof.*** We verify first that $\Vdash_{\mathcal{S}}$ is a K-biconsequence relation. Since $\mathcal{B}_{\mathcal{S}}$ is a classical consistent binary semantics, $\Vdash_{\mathcal{S}}$ will be consistent and supraclassical. In addition, if $M$ is a final model, and $A \in |M|$, then clearly $LA \in |M|$, and if $A \in \|M\|$, then $LA \in \|M\|$ . This gives the two Reflection postulates. Similarly, if $A \notin \|M\|$, then $\neg A$ holds in some world $\alpha \in F$. But $\alpha$ is accessible from any world of $M$, and hence $\neg LA \in |M|$. Thus, Negative Introspection is also valid, so $\Vdash_{\mathcal{S}}$ is a modal biconsequence relation. Finally, the validity of K amounts to the validity of the modal K axiom in Kripke models.

In the other direction, for a K-biconsequence relation $\Vdash$, we construct a canonical final semantics as follows. If $(u, w)$ is a bitheory of $\Vdash$, let $U$ be the set of all modal worlds (maximal classically consistent sets of modal propositions) containing $u$, while $W$ the set of worlds containing $w$. Then the associated Kripke model will be defined as a canonical model $(U, R, V)$, where $V$ is a valuation function assigning each canonical world $\alpha$ the set of its propositional atoms, while R is a relation defined in the usual way:

$$\alpha R \beta \equiv (\forall A)(LA \in \alpha \rightarrow A \in \beta).$$

To begin with, we will show that the above model is a final model with $W$ as the last cluster. Since $w$ is a stable theory, If $A \in w$, then $LA \in w$, and hence $LA \in \alpha$, for any $\alpha \in W$. Consequently, if $\alpha R \beta$, then $A \in \beta$. This shows that $w \subseteq \beta$, and consequently, if $\alpha \in W$ and $\alpha R \beta$, then $\beta \in W$. For the second property of clusters, if $LA \in \alpha \in U$, then $\neg LA \notin u$, and hence

$A \in w$ by negative introspection. Consequently, $A \in \beta$, for any $\beta \in W$, and therefore $\alpha R \beta$, for any $\beta \in W$. Thus, $W$ is the last cluster of the model. Accordingly, we define $\mathcal{S}_{\Vdash}$ as the set of all final models corresponding in this sense to bitheories of $\Vdash$.

As in standard completeness proofs in modal logic, the main step consists in showing that an arbitrary proposition $A$ holds in a world $\alpha$ of a canonical model if and only if $A \in \alpha$. This can be done by induction on the complexity of $A$, the only nontrivial case being the claim that, if $A \in \beta$, for any $\beta$ accessible from $\alpha$, then $LA \in \alpha$.

Assume that $LA \notin \alpha \in U$. Then the set $v = u \cup \{B \mid LB \in \alpha\} \cup \{\neg A\}$ is consistent. Indeed, otherwise there exists a finite set $b$ of propositions such that $Lb \subseteq \alpha$ and $\bigwedge b \to A \in u$. By the first introspection axiom we have $L(\bigwedge b \to A) \in u$ and consequently $\bigwedge Lb \to LA \in u$ by the K postulate. But then $\bigwedge Lb \to LA \in \alpha$, and hence $LA \in \alpha$, contrary to our assumption. Thus, $v$ is consistent, and hence it can be extended to a world, say $\beta$. Clearly $\alpha R \beta$ and $A \notin \beta$, as required. As a result, an arbitrary proposition $A$ holds in $\alpha$ if and only if $A \in \alpha$.

Now, $a{:}b \nVdash_{\mathcal{S}_{\Vdash}} c{:}d$ iff there exists a bitheory $(u, w)$ of $\Vdash$ such that, for the associated model $M$, $a \subseteq |M|$, $b \subseteq \overline{\|M\|}$, $c \subseteq \overline{|M|}$ and $d \subseteq \|M\|$. By the preceding claim we have, however, that $A \in |M|$ iff $A \in u$, and $A \in \|M\|$ iff $A \in w$. Consequently $a \subseteq u$, $b \subseteq \overline{w}$, $c \subseteq \overline{u}$ and $d \subseteq w$, which is equivalent to $a{:}b \nVdash c{:}d$. Thus, $\Vdash$ coincides with $\Vdash_{\mathcal{S}_{\Vdash}}$. □

Adding further modal axioms will give us modal biconsequence relations based on particular normal modal logics. The corresponding completeness proofs for most of them are easily obtainable from the construction of the canonical semantics, given in the above proof, coupled with corresponding standard completeness proofs in modal logic. In this way we can obtain, in particular, the completeness results given in the following Corollary (we omit the proofs, since they are not essential for the further exposition). Note, however, that the formalism of modal biconsequence relations is more expressive than axiomatic modal logics (mainly because it represents multiple-conclusion derivations), and hence it allows us to express syntactically more fine-grained semantic distinctions than the latter.

**Corollary 10.12** *A modal biconsequence relation $\Vdash$ is a*

- *K4-biconsequence relation iff it is determined by a set of final Kripke models with a transitive accessibility relation;*
- *S4-biconsequence relation iff it is determined by a set of final Kripke*

*models with a transitive and reflexive accessibility relation;*

- *S4F-biconsequence relation iff it is determined by final Kripke models $(W, R, F, V)$ such that $R$ restricted to $W \backslash F$ is an equivalence relation.*

Due to Lemma 10.10, K4-biconsequence relations actually include all the axioms of KD4G (alias D4.2 -see [Segerberg, 1971]), while S4-biconsequence relations include all the axioms of S4.2. This fact will imply that these modal logics will determine the same modal nonmonotonic semantics.

The modal logic S4F (see [Segerberg, 1971]) is obtained from S4 by adding the axiom $(A \wedge MLB) \rightarrow L(MA \vee B)$. Note that the above semantics is more general than the standard possible worlds semantics given to this logic. The difference will turn out to be important, since the latter semantics will actually determine a stronger F-biconsequence relation, described in the next section.

* * *

For a modal logic $\mathcal{M}$, we will denote by $\Vdash_{\Delta}^{\mathcal{M}}$ the least $\mathcal{M}$-biconsequence relation containing a bisequent theory $\Delta$. In accordance with this terminology, the least modal biconsequence relation containing $\Delta$ can be identified with $\Vdash_{\Delta}^{N}$, where $N$ is a pure logic of necessitation. Moreover, by a *modal theory* of $\Delta$ we will mean a propositional theory of $\Vdash_{\Delta}^{N}$. As follows from Corollary 10.4, any modal theory of $\Delta$ will be a stable theory. A more constructive description of these modal theories will be given later in this chapter.

#### 10.1.1.1 *Weak, positive and reflexive introspection*

In this section we will describe a number stronger modal biconsequence relations that will play an important role in what follows. These biconsequence relations can already be described using certain additional introspection principles.

We begin with biconsequence relations based on the modal logic D4.4 in the classification of [Segerberg, 1971], namely the modal logic obtained from KD4 by adding the weak 5 axiom W5: $A \wedge \neg LA \rightarrow L \neg LA$. It turns out that corresponding biconsequence relations can be described as K-biconsequence relations that satisfy the following introspection principle:

**Weak Introspection** $\Vdash A \rightarrow LA : A$.

Note that the above introspection principle still allows for either belief or knowledge interpretations of the modal operator. It turns out that Weak Introspection is equivalent to W5 and, taken together with K, implies the rest of the axioms of D4.4.

**Theorem 10.13** *The following conditions are equivalent:*

*(1)* $\Vdash$ *is a K-biconsequence relation satisfying Weak Introspection;*
*(2)* $\Vdash$ *is a D4.4-biconsequence relation;*
*(3)* $\Vdash$ *is determined by final Kripke models* $(W, R, F, V)$ *such that* $\alpha R\beta$*, for* $\alpha \neq \beta$*, holds only if* $\beta \in F$*.*

***Proof.*** (1) $\leftrightarrow$ (2). If $\Vdash A \wedge MLA \to LA$, then $:\neg LA \Vdash A \to LA$ by negative introspection, and hence $\Vdash A \to LA : A$ by Corollary 10.5(1). In the other direction, given Weak Introspection, we have $\Vdash W_5{:}A$, where $W_5$ denotes the formula $A \wedge MLA \to LA$. But $:A \Vdash L\neg LA$: by Negative Introspection and necessitation, and hence $:A \Vdash W_5{:}$. Therefore $\Vdash W_5{:}$ by Negative Cut. In addition, $\Vdash LA \to LLA{:}LA$ by Weak Introspection, and hence $\Vdash LA \to LLA{:}A$ by Negative Reflection. In addition, $:A \Vdash LA \to LLA$ by Negative Introspection. Consequently, $\Vdash LA \to LLA{:}$ by Negative Cut. This shows that $\Vdash$ is a D4.4-biconsequence relation.

(2) $\leftrightarrow$ (3). The possible worlds semantics from (3) clearly validates D4.4. In the other direction, consider the canonical model from the proof of Theorem 10.11, and assume that $\alpha R\beta$, for some $\alpha \neq \beta$. Then there exists a proposition $A$ such that $A \in \alpha$ and $\neg A \in \beta$, and consequently $\neg LA \in \alpha$ by the definition of $R$. Now if $B \in w$, then $A \vee B \in w$, and hence $(A \vee B) \to L(A \vee B) \in u$ by Weak Introspection. Consequently, $(A \vee B) \to L(A \vee B) \in \alpha$ and hence $L(A \vee B) \in \alpha$, since $A \in \alpha$. Now we have $A \vee B \in \beta$ by the definition of $R$, and therefore $B \in \beta$. This shows that $w \subseteq \beta$, that is, $\beta \in W$. Thus, $\alpha R\beta$, $\alpha \neq \beta$, holds only if $\beta \in W$, as required. This completes the proof. □

Now we will consider two maximal reasonable modal logics for our study, namely KD45 and SW5. Note that both these logics include D4.4. Moreover, we will show that the corresponding biconsequence relations can be described using the following stronger introspection principles:

**Positive Introspection** $\Vdash LA : A$,
**Reflexive Introspection** $\Vdash A \leftrightarrow LA : A$.

The above two introspection principles already clearly differentiate the two possible epistemic interpretations of the operator $L$ that has been described at the beginning of this chapter. Namely, Positive Introspection determines the belief interpretation of $L$, while Reflexive Introspection expresses the corresponding knowledge interpretation.

Positive Introspection turns out to be equivalent to the modal 5 axiom $MLA \to LA$, and implies, in effect, all the axioms of KD45.

**Theorem 10.14** *The following conditions are equivalent:*

*(1)* $\Vdash$ *is a modal biconsequence relation satisfying Positive Introspection;*
*(2)* $\Vdash$ *is a 5-biconsequence relation;*
*(3)* $\Vdash$ *is a KD45-biconsequence relation;*
*(4)* $\Vdash$ *is determined by final Kripke models* $(W, R, F, V)$ *such that* $R$ *is empty on* $W \backslash F$, *that is,* $\alpha R \beta$ *iff* $\beta \in F$.

***Proof.*** (1) $\leftrightarrow$ (2). If $\Vdash MLA \to LA$, then $:\neg LA \Vdash LA$ by negative introspection, and hence $\Vdash LA : A$ by Corollary 10.5(1). In the other direction, we have $:A \Vdash L\neg LA$ by negative introspection and necessitation, and hence $\Vdash L\neg LA \vee LA$ by Positive Introspection and Negative Cut.

(2) $\leftrightarrow$ (3). Since Positive Introspection implies Weak Introspection, we have to prove only the modal K axiom. Let K denote the formula $LA \wedge L(A \to B) \to LB$. We have $:A \Vdash K:$ and $:A \to B \Vdash K:$ by negative introspection, and hence $:A \wedge (A \to B) \Vdash K:$ by Negative Closure, which implies $:A \wedge B \Vdash K:$. But we have also $\Vdash LB{:}B$ by Positive Introspection, and hence $\Vdash K{:}A \wedge B$ by supraclassicality. Therefore, $\Vdash K:$ by Negative Cut.

(3) $\leftrightarrow$ (4). It is easy to verify that the possible worlds semantics from (4) validates 5. In the other direction, let us consider the canonical model constructed in the proof of Theorem 10.11. If $A \in w$, then $LA \in u$ by Positive Introspection, and hence $LA \in \alpha$, for any $\alpha \in U$. Consequently, if $\alpha R \beta$, then $A \in \beta$, which implies $w \subseteq \beta$, that is, $\beta \in W$. Thus, $R$ is empty on $U \backslash W$, as required. This completes the proof. □

Our next result provides a similar description for biconsequence relations based on the modal logic SW5 (known also as S4.4—see [Segerberg, 1971]), namely the modal logic obtained from S4 by adding W5. This time Reflexive Introspection turns out to be equivalent to the combination of W5 and the T axiom $LA \to A$, and implies the rest of the axioms of SW5.

**Theorem 10.15** *The following conditions are equivalent:*

*(1)* $\Vdash$ *is a modal biconsequence relation satisfying Reflexive Introspection;*
*(2)* $\Vdash$ *is a TW5-biconsequence relation;*
*(3)* $\Vdash$ *is an SW5-biconsequence relation;*

*(4)* $\Vdash$ *is determined by final Kripke models* $(W, R, F, V)$ *such that* $R$ *restricted to* $W\backslash F$ *is identity:* $\alpha R\beta$ *iff* $\alpha = \beta$ *or* $\beta \in F$.

***Proof.*** (1) $\leftrightarrow$ (2). Since Reflexive Introspection implies Weak Introspection, while the latter is equivalent to W5, it is sufficient to show that the modal T axiom $\Vdash LA\rightarrow A$: follows from $\Vdash LA\rightarrow A{:}A$. Indeed, since $:A \Vdash LA\rightarrow A$ by negative introspection, we obtain $\Vdash LA\rightarrow A$: by Negative Cut.

(2) $\leftrightarrow$ (3). As before, we have to prove only the modal K axiom. We have $:A \Vdash K$: and $:A\rightarrow B \Vdash K$: by negative introspection, which implies $:A \wedge B \Vdash K$:. But Positive Introspection implies $\Vdash A\leftrightarrow LA{:}A \wedge B$, $\Vdash B\leftrightarrow LB{:}A \wedge B$, and $\Vdash (A\rightarrow B)\leftrightarrow L(A\rightarrow B){:}A \wedge B$, and hence $\Vdash K{:}A \wedge B$ by supraclassicality and the fact that $\Vdash A \wedge (A\rightarrow B)\rightarrow B$:. Therefore, $\Vdash K$: by Negative Cut.

(3) $\leftrightarrow$ (4). The possible worlds semantics from (4) clearly validates SW5. In the other direction, since $\Vdash$ is a D4.4-biconsequence relation, we have that in its canonical model $\alpha R\beta$ holds only if either $\alpha = \beta$, or $\beta \in W$. But $R$ is now reflexive, and $W$ is a last cluster, so if either $\alpha = \beta$, or $\beta \in W$, then $\alpha R\beta$, as required. This completes the proof. □

Again, the above semantics for KD45 and SW5-biconsequence relations are more general than the standard possible worlds semantics for these logics. As we will see later, the latter semantics will determine precisely corresponding saturated biconsequence relations.

As a consequence of the above two descriptions, we conclude that S5-biconsequence relations already coincide with (modal) Scott biconsequence relations (see Sec. 3.2.3).

**Corollary 10.16** *A modal biconsequence relation is an S5-biconsequence relation if and only if it is Scott biconsequence relation.*

***Proof.*** Recall that a Scott biconsequence relation is a biconsequence relation that is both consistent and complete, that is, $\Vdash A{:}A$ holds for any proposition $A$. Now, if $\Vdash A{:}A$, then $\Vdash LA{:}A$ by necessitation, and hence $\Vdash A\leftrightarrow LA{:}A$. Thus, both Positive and Reflexive Introspection hold, and therefore $\Vdash$ includes all the axioms of S5. In the other direction, if $\Vdash$ is an S5-biconsequence relation, then both Positive and Reflexive Introspection hold, and therefore $\Vdash A{:}A$ follows by supraclassicality. □

The above result implies, in particular, the well-known claim that the modal logic S5 is already inappropriate for representing nonmonotonic reasoning. Still, the result implies also that S5-biconsequence relations play the same role in modal nonmonotonic reasoning as Scott biconsequence relations.

As has been established already in [Lenzen, 1979] (see also [Schwarz, 1992b]), the modal logics KD45 and SW5 are in some sense interdefinable. This correspondence will be extended below to the correspondence between associated biconsequence relations.

Following [Schwarz, 1992b], for a modal formula $A$, we will denote by $A^B$ the result of replacement of each sub-formula $LC$ in $A$ by $LC \wedge C$, while $A^K$ will denote the result of replacing each occurrence of $L$ in $A$ with $\neg L \neg L$. For a set $u$ of propositions, $u^B$ will denote the set $\{A^B \mid A \in u\}$, and similarly for $u^K$. Finally, given a modal biconsequence relation $\Vdash$, we will define the following biconsequence relations:

$$a : b \Vdash_B c : d \;\equiv\; a^B : b \Vdash c^B : d$$
$$a : b \Vdash_K c : d \;\equiv\; a^K : b \Vdash c^K : d.$$

**Theorem 10.17** *If $\Vdash$ is a KD45-biconsequence relation, then $\Vdash_B$ is an SW5-biconsequence relation, and $\Vdash_{BK} = \Vdash$. Conversely, if $\Vdash$ is an SW5-biconsequence relation, then $\Vdash_K$ is a KD45-biconsequence relation, and $\Vdash_{KB} = \Vdash$.*

***Proof.*** To begin with, note that the formulas $A^B$ and $A^K$ are S5-equivalent to $A$, and hence they are equivalent with respect to any stable theory. Consequently, the above derived biconsequence relations can be described alternatively as follows:

$$a : b \Vdash_B c : d \;\equiv\; a^B : b^B \Vdash c^B : d^B$$
$$a : b \Vdash_K c : d \;\equiv\; a^K : b^K \Vdash c^K : d^K.$$

Now, it can be easily verified that $\Vdash_B$ is a supraclassical biconsequence relation. Also, Positive and Negative Reflection are immediate, while Negative Introspection for $\Vdash_B$ amounts to $:A^B \Vdash \neg(LA^B \wedge A^B):$, which follows from Negative Introspection for $\Vdash$. In addition, Reflexive Introspection for $\Vdash^B$ amounts to $\Vdash A^B \rightarrow LA^B{:}A$, which follows from $\Vdash LA^B{:}A^B$. Thus, if $\Vdash$ is a KD45-biconsequence relation, then $\Vdash_B$ is an SW5-biconsequence relation. Finally, $\Vdash_{BK} = \Vdash$ follows from the fact that any proposition $A$ is equivalent to $A^{KB}$ in KD45 (cf. Proposition 4.6 in [Schwarz, 1992b]).

The proof of the second claim is similar, but this time Negative Introspection for $\Vdash_K$ amounts to $:A^K \Vdash L\neg LA^K:$, which follows again from Negative Introspection for $\Vdash$. Also, Positive Introspection for $\Vdash^K$ amounts to $\Vdash \neg L \neg LA^K{:}A^K$, which holds for any modal biconsequence relation. Thus, if $\Vdash$ is an SW5-biconsequence relation, then $\Vdash_K$ is a KD45-biconsequence relation. Finally, $\Vdash_{KB}=\Vdash$ follows from the fact that any proposition $A$ is equivalent to $A^{BK}$ in SW5 (Proposition 4.4 in [Schwarz, 1992b]). □

Now we are going to show that both KD45- and SW5-biconsequence relations are uniquely determined by their objective, nonmodal sub-relations. We will begin with a simpler case of KD45-biconsequence relations that support the following reductions:

**Lemma 10.18** *If $\Vdash$ is a KD45-biconsequence relation, then*

- $a, LA \vee B{:}b \Vdash c{:}d$ *iff* $a{:}b \Vdash c{:}d, A$ *and* $a, B{:}b \Vdash c{:}d$;
- $a{:}b \Vdash c, LA \vee B{:}d$ *iff* $a{:}b, A \Vdash c, B{:}d$;
- $a, \neg LA \vee B{:}b \Vdash c{:}d$ *iff* $a{:}b, A \Vdash c{:}d$ *and* $a, B{:}b \Vdash c{:}d$;
- $a{:}b \Vdash c, \neg LA \vee B{:}d$ *iff* $a{:}b \Vdash c, B{:}d, A$.

***Proof.*** As can be verified, for any KD45-model $M$,

$$LA \vee B \in |M| \text{ iff } A \in ||M|| \text{ or } B \in |M|;$$
$$\neg LA \vee B \in |M| \text{ iff } A \notin ||M|| \text{ or } B \in |M|.$$

The above reductions follow directly from these equivalences. □

Together with the modal reductions from Lemma 10.7, the above reductions immediately imply the following

**Corollary 10.19**

- *Any bisequent of a KD45-biconsequence relation is reducible to a set of objective bisequents.*
- *KD45-biconsequence relations having the same objective subrelations coincide.*

Using the above equivalences, any modal bisequent theory $\Delta$ is reducible (in a modular way) to an objective bisequent theory that is equivalent to $\Delta$ with respect to KD45-biconsequence relations. We will call this objective bisequent theory the *objective belief reduct* of $\Delta$, and denote it by $B(\Delta)$. As we will see, this objective reduct embodies all the information necessary for determining the associated modal nonmonotonic semantics.

Since KD45 and SW5 are interdefinable, it should not be surprising that similar, though more complex, reductions hold also for SW5-biconsequence relations.

**Lemma 10.20** *If $\Vdash$ is an SW5-biconsequence relation, then*

- $a, LA \vee B{:}b \Vdash c{:}d$ *iff* $a, A \vee B{:}b \Vdash c{:}d, A$ *and* $a, B{:}b \Vdash c{:}d$;
- $a{:}b \Vdash c, LA \vee B{:}d$ *iff* $a{:}b \Vdash c, A \vee B{:}d$ *and* $a{:}b, A \Vdash c, B{:}d$;
- $a, \neg LA \vee B{:}b \Vdash c{:}d$ *iff* $a{:}b, A \Vdash c{:}d$ *and* $a, A \to B{:}b \Vdash c{:}d$;
- $a{:}b \Vdash c, \neg LA \vee B{:}d$ *iff* $a{:}b \Vdash c, A \to B{:}d, A$.

***Proof.*** Follows from the fact that, for any SW5-model $M$,

$LA \vee B \in |M|$ iff $A \vee B \in |M|$, and either $B \in |M|$ or $A \in \|M\|$;
$\neg LA \vee B \in |M|$ iff $A \to B \in |M|$ or $A \notin \|M\|$.

□

Combined with Lemma 10.7, the above reductions imply this time

**Corollary 10.21**

- *Any bisequent of an SW5-biconsequence relation is reducible to a set of objective bisequents.*
- *SW5-biconsequence relations having the same objective subrelations coincide.*

Again, using the above equivalences, any modal bisequent theory $\Delta$ is reducible to an objective bisequent theory that is equivalent to $\Delta$ with respect to SW5-biconsequence relations. We will call this objective bisequent theory the *objective knowledge reduct* of $\Delta$, and denote it by $K(\Delta)$.

In fact, the correspondence between KD45 and SW5 is extendable also to the correspondence between the knowledge and belief reducts of a bisequent theory. Let $\Delta^K$ denote the set of bisequents $a^K{:}b \Vdash c^K{:}d$ such that $a{:}b \Vdash c{:}d$ belongs to $\Delta$, and similarly for $\Delta^B$. Then the following equalities can be easily inferred from the corresponding reductions for SW5 and KD45 biconsequence relations:

**Lemma 10.22** *If $\Delta$ is a modal bisequent theory, then*

$$B(\Delta) = K(\Delta^K) \quad \textit{and} \quad K(\Delta) = B(\Delta^B).$$

As a final result in this section, we will show that modal biconsequence relations are conservative with respect to derivability of objective bisequents. More precisely, we will show that, for a broad range of modal logics $\mathcal{M}$, any objective biconsequence relation that is consistent and supraclassical can be conservatively embedded into some $\mathcal{M}$-biconsequence relation.

**Theorem 10.23** *Any objective consistent supraclassical biconsequence relation is an objective subrelation of some $\mathcal{M}$-biconsequence relation, for any modal logic $\mathcal{M}$ such that $\mathcal{M} \subseteq KD45$ or $\mathcal{M} \subseteq SW5$.*

***Proof.*** It is sufficient to prove the claim for the two maximal modal logics in this set, namely KD45 and SW5. We will prove it only for KD45, the proof for SW5 being perfectly similar.

Given an objective biconsequence relation $\Vdash$, we construct the corresponding final KD45-semantics as follows. If $(u, w)$ is a bitheory of $\Vdash$, let $U$ be the set of all *objective* worlds (maximal consistent sets of objective propositions) containing $u$, while $W$ the set of objective worlds containing $w$. Then the associated Kripke model will be defined as the tuple $(U, R, W, V)$, where $V$ assigns each canonical world the set of its propositional atoms, while $R$ is defined as follows: $\alpha R \beta$ iff $\beta \in W$. Let $\mathcal{S}_{\Vdash}$ be the set of all models corresponding in this sense to bitheories of $\Vdash$, and $\Vdash^m$ the modal biconsequence relation determined by $\mathcal{S}_{\Vdash}$. By Theorem 10.14, this is a KD45-biconsequence relation. It should be clear, however, that an objective bisequent is valid in $\mathcal{S}_{\Vdash}$ if and only if it belongs to $\Vdash$. Consequently, $\Vdash$ is precisely the objective subrelation of $\Vdash^m$. □

The above result will be used later in showing that the nonmonotonic semantics of objective bisequent theories will coincide with the objective part of the corresponding modal nonmonotonic semantics.

### 10.1.2 *F-biconsequence relations and S4F*

Biconsequence relations described in the next definition will play a crucial role in a modal representation of extension-based nonmonotonic reasoning.

**Definition 10.4** A modal biconsequence relation will be called an *F-biconsequence relation*, if it is regular and satisfies

**F** $\Vdash A, LA \to B : B.$

To begin with, we are going to show that F-biconsequence relations provide, in effect, an alternative, more concise representation for the modal logic S4F.

A standard semantic characterization of S4F (see [Segerberg, 1971]) is given in terms of final Kripke models $(W, R, F, V)$, such that $\alpha R \beta$ iff either $\beta \in F$, or $\alpha \notin F$. Note that $R$ is uniquely determined by $F$, so we will occasionally omit it in what follows. Clearly, such models form a subclass of general models for S4F, described in Corollary 10.12, in that in standard S4F-models $W \backslash F$ forms a single equivalence class with respect to $R$.

We will say that a final possible worlds semantics $\mathcal{S}$ is *regular*, if, for any final model $(W, R, F, V)$ from $\mathcal{S}$, its (S5-)submodel determined by $F$

also belongs to $\mathcal{S}$.

**Theorem 10.24** *A biconsequence relation is an F-biconsequence relation iff it coincides with* $\Vdash_{\mathcal{S}}$*, for some standard regular S4F-semantics* $\mathcal{S}$.

***Proof.*** By Theorem 10.11, $\Vdash_{\mathcal{S}}$ is a modal biconsequence relation, and it is clearly regular in our case. In addition, if $B \in \|M\|$ and $LA \to B \notin |M|$, then $LA \wedge \neg B$ holds in some world $\alpha$. But $B$ holds in all worlds from $F$, so $\alpha \notin F$. Now, by the definition of the accessibility relation, since $LA$ holds in $\alpha$, we have that $A$ should hold in all worlds of the model, that is $A \in |M|$. Consequently, $\Vdash A, LA \to B{:}B$ is valid in $\mathcal{S}$, and therefore $\Vdash_{\mathcal{S}}$ is an F-biconsequence relation.

In the other direction, for an F-biconsequence relation $\Vdash$, we construct a canonical S4F semantics just as in the proof of Theorem 10.11 with the only distinction that $\alpha R \beta$ is now defined directly as holding iff either $\alpha \notin W$, or $\beta \in W$. Hence we have to show that, under the new definition, $LA \in \alpha$ iff $A \in \beta$, for any world $\beta$ accessible from $\alpha$.

Assume first that $LA \in \alpha$. If $\beta \in W$ (that is, $v \subseteq \beta$) then, since $u \subseteq \alpha$, we have $\neg LA \notin u$, and hence $A \in v$ by negative introspection. Consequently $A \in \beta$, as required. Assume now that $\alpha \in U \backslash W$. Since $\alpha \notin W$, there exists a proposition $B \in w$ such that $\neg B \in \alpha$. Consequently, $LA \to B \notin u$, $B \in w$, and therefore $A \in u$ by the postulate F. Thus, $A \in \beta$, for any world $\beta$ of the model. This shows that if $LA \in \alpha$, then $A$ belongs to all worlds accessible from $\alpha$.

Assume now that $LA \notin \alpha$. If $A \notin w$, then $A \notin \beta$, for some $\beta \in W$, in which case the claim holds, since $\beta$ is accessible from $\alpha$. So assume that $A \in w$. Then $LA \in w$, since $w$ is a stable theory, and consequently $\alpha \in U \backslash W$. In addition, since $u \subseteq \alpha$, we have $LA \notin u$, and hence $A \notin u$ by Positive Reflection. Therefore there exists $\beta \in U$ such that $A \notin \beta$. Moreover, $\beta \notin W$ (since $A \in w$), and consequently $\beta$ is accessible from $\alpha$, as required.

The rest of the proof proceeds as in the proof of Theorem 10.11. □

It follows from the above representation result that any F-biconsequence relation is an S4F-relation, though not vice versa, since the postulate F is not valid in general models of S4F, only in standard ones. As a result, F-biconsequence relations posses some additional properties. Thus, any bisequent of an F-biconsequence relation is already reducible to a provable modal formula.

**Corollary 10.25** *Any bisequent* $a{:}b \Vdash c{:}d$ *of an F-biconsequence relation is equivalent to* $\Vdash \bigwedge(La \cup L\neg Lb) \to \bigvee(Lc \cup L\neg Ld) :$.

The proof follows immediately from the semantic equivalence of these two bisequents in standard regular S4F-semantics. Note also that, under this translation, the postulate F corresponds exactly to the characteristic modal axiom F of the logic S4F.

The importance of the above result lies in the fact that sufficiently rich modal biconsequence relations are representable by modal formulas, and hence any bisequent theory in such a logic is reducible to the corresponding ordinary modal theory.

For a bisequent $r = a{:}b \Vdash c{:}d$ in the modal language, let us denote by $\tilde{r}$ the formula

$$\bigwedge(La \cup L\neg Lb) \to \bigvee(Lc \cup L\neg Ld).$$

Similarly, for a bisequent theory $\Delta$, let $\tilde{\Delta}$ denote the set of corresponding modal formulas. The latter modal theory will be called a *modal knowledge reduct* of $\Delta$. As follows from the preceding corollary, any bisequent theory is equivalent to its modal reduct in the logic of F-biconsequence relations.

Extending our earlier terminology, $\Vdash^F_\Delta$ will denote the least F-biconsequence relation containing a bisequent theory $\Delta$. Then the following result shows that F-biconsequence relations constitute a kind of a sequent calculus for the modal logic S4F.

**Corollary 10.26** $\Vdash^F_\Delta = \{r \mid \tilde{\Delta} \vdash_{S4F} \tilde{r}\}$.

***Proof.*** Let $\Vdash_0$ denote the set of bisequents $\{r \mid \tilde{\Delta} \vdash_{S4F} \tilde{r}\}$. It can be directly verified that this is an F-biconsequence relation containing $\Delta$ (the modal F axiom implies the postulate F in this case), which gives us $\Vdash^F_\Delta \subseteq \Vdash_0$. Assume now that a bisequent $r = a{:}b \Vdash c{:}d$ does not belong to $\Vdash^F_\Delta$. Then there exists a standard S4F model $M$ of $\Delta$ in which $r$ is not valid. By the preceding corollary, $\tilde{\Delta}$ is valid in $M$, while $\tilde{r}$ is not valid in $M$, and hence $\tilde{\Delta} \nvdash_{S4F} \tilde{r}$. □

The above result shows that a bisequent is derivable from a bisequent theory $\Delta$ by the postulates of F-biconsequence relations if and only if its modal reduct is derivable from $\tilde{\Delta}$ in S4F. As an immediate consequence, we infer that two bisequent theories determine the same F-biconsequence relation if and only if their modal reducts are equivalent in S4F.

Our next result shows that any objective biconsequence relation that is consistent and supraclassical can be conservatively embedded into an

F-biconsequence relation.

**Lemma 10.27** *Any objective supraclassical biconsequence relation that is regular and consistent coincides with the objective subrelation of some F-biconsequence relation.*

***Proof.*** The proof coincides with the proof of Theorem 10.23, with the only distinction that $\alpha R \beta$ is now defined as holding iff either $\alpha \notin W$, or $\beta \in W$. Then we obtain a standard and regular S4F-semantics, and hence it will determine an F-biconsequence relation. □

The above result will serve as a basis of the correspondence between objective and modal default nonmonotonic semantics. As the main step, the following corollary shows that classical default equivalence of objective bisequent theories (see Definition 9.7) is reducible to S4F-equivalence of their modal reducts.

**Corollary 10.28** *Objective bisequent theories* $\Gamma$ *and* $\Delta$ *are classically default equivalent if and only if* $\tilde{\Gamma}$ *and* $\tilde{\Delta}$ *are S4F-equivalent.*

***Proof.*** If $\Gamma$ and $\Delta$ are classically default equivalent, they determine the same supraclassical regular consistent biconsequence relation, and consequently the same F-biconsequence relation. Due to Corollary 10.26, the latter implies that $\tilde{\Gamma}$ and $\tilde{\Delta}$ are S4F-equivalent. In the other direction, let $\Vdash^F_\Delta$ be the least F-biconsequence relation containing $\Delta$, while $\Vdash^{rc}_\Delta$ the least supraclassical regular and consistent biconsequence relation containing $\Delta$. Clearly, $\Vdash^{rc}_\Delta \subseteq \Vdash^F_\Delta$. Moreover, Theorem 10.27 implies that $\Vdash^{rc}_\Delta$ actually coincides with the objective part of $\Vdash^F_\Delta$. Now, if $\tilde{\Gamma}$ and $\tilde{\Delta}$ are S4F-equivalent, then $\Vdash^F_\Delta = \Vdash^F_\Gamma$, and consequently the two F-biconsequence relations should have the same objective subrelations, that is, $\Vdash^{rc}_\Delta = \Vdash^{rc}_\Gamma$. The latter means that $\Gamma$ and $\Delta$ are classically default equivalent. □

As we will see, the above result will imply that S4F constitutes a maximal modal logic suitable for representing objective extension-based nonmonotonic semantics (cf. [Schwarz and Truszczyński, 1994]).

It should be noted, however, that F-biconsequence relations are not determined, in general, by their objective subrelations. The following example illustrates this.

**Example 10.1** Let us consider the following two standard S4F-models in a language generated by propositional atoms $\{p, q\}$. The first is $M_1 = (\{\alpha, \beta\}, \{\beta\}, V)$, where $V(\alpha) = \{q\}$, $V(\beta) = \{p\}$. The second is $M_2 = (\{\alpha, \beta, \beta'\}, \{\beta\}, V)$, where $V$ associates the same interpretations to $\alpha$ and

$\beta$, while $V(\beta') = \{p\}$. Then it can be verified that $Lp \vee q$ is valid in $M_1$, though it is not valid in $M_2$. Consequently, $\Vdash Lp \vee q$: will hold in the F-biconsequence relation determined by $M_1$, but it will not hold in the F-biconsequence relation determined by $M_2$. Note, however, that these two models determine the same objective bisequents, due to the fact that the worlds $\beta$ and $\beta'$ have the same interpretation. Consequently, these two different F-biconsequence relations will have the same objective subrelation.

The technical result below establishes a restricted correspondence between F-biconsequence relations and S4F-biconsequence relations. It will be used in what follows.

**Lemma 10.29** *If $\Delta$ is a plain modal theory, then $\Vdash^F_\Delta$ and $\Vdash^{S4F}_\Delta$ have the same singular bisequents.*

***Proof.*** We have to show only that if $a{:}b \Vdash^F_\Delta C{:}d$, then $a{:}b \Vdash^{S4F}_\Delta C{:}d$. Assume that $a{:}b \nVdash^{S4F}_\Delta C{:}d$. Then there exists a general S4F-model $M = (W, R, F, V)$ of $\Delta$ such that $a \subseteq |M|$, $d \subseteq ||M||$, $b \cap ||M|| = \emptyset$ and $C \notin |M|$. The latter implies that $\neg C$ holds in some world $\alpha \in W$. Let $W_0$ be the equivalence class (cluster) of $\alpha$ with respect to $R$, and consider the submodel $M_1$ of $M$ that is generated by $W_0 \cup F$. Clearly, $M_1$ is a standard S4F-model. Moreover, since $\Delta$ is an ordinary modal theory, $M_1$ is also a model of $\Delta$, and hence $M_1$ determines a bitheory of $\Vdash^F_\Delta$. But $M_1$ still invalidates the bisequent $a{:}b \Vdash C{:}d$, and therefore $a{:}b \nVdash^F_\Delta C{:}d$. This completes the proof□

Note that, due to Lemma 10.6, the above result holds actually for arbitrary autoepistemic bisequent theories $\Delta$.

### 10.1.3 *Modal saturated biconsequence relations*

To begin with, note that, for saturated biconsequence relations, any bisequent theory $\Delta$ is reducible to a singular autoepistemic bisequent theory $cauto(\Delta)$ (see Corollary 9.8). Combined with Lemma 10.6, this gives us

**Lemma 10.30**

- *Any bisequent of a modal saturated biconsequence relations is reducible to a set of provable modal formulas.*
- *Modal saturated biconsequence relations containing the same modal formulas coincide.*

Two principal kinds of modal saturated biconsequence relations are described in the next definition.

**Definition 10.5** A modal saturated biconsequence relation will be called an *A-biconsequence relation*, if it satisfies Positive Introspection, and an *R-biconsequence relation*, if it satisfies Reflexive Introspection.

As we will see in what follows, the above two kinds of biconsequence relations constitute, respectively, maximal logics for ordinary ([Moore, 1985]) and reflexive ([Schwarz, 1992b]) autoepistemic nonmonotonic reasoning.

Now, the correspondence between KD45- and SW5-biconsequence relations, established in Theorem 10.17, immediately extends to the correspondence between A- and R-biconsequence relations.

**Corollary 10.31** *If* $\Vdash$ *is an A-biconsequence relation, then* $\Vdash_B$ *is an R-biconsequence relation, and* $\Vdash_{BK}=\Vdash$*. Conversely, if* $\Vdash$ *is an R-biconsequence relation, then* $\Vdash_K$ *is an A-biconsequence relation, and* $\Vdash_{KB}=\Vdash$*.*

As follows from Theorem 10.14, A-biconsequence relations coincide with saturated KD45-biconsequence relations. Unlike the general possible worlds semantics for KD45-biconsequence relations, described earlier, the standard modal semantics for KD45 consists of final Kripke models of the form $(F \cup \{\gamma\}, R, F, V)$, where $\alpha R \beta$ holds iff $\beta \in F$. The following result shows that this standard semantics provides a representation for A-biconsequence relations.

**Theorem 10.32** *A biconsequence relation is an A-biconsequence relation if and only if it coincides with* $\Vdash_{\mathcal{S}}$*, for some regular standard KD45-semantics* $\mathcal{S}$*.*

***Proof.*** It can be verified that a regular standard KD45-semantics $\mathcal{S}$ determines a saturated binary semantics, so $\Vdash_{\mathcal{S}}$ will be saturated, and hence an A-biconsequence relation by Theorem 10.14. In the other direction, we have only to show that if $\Vdash$ is an A-biconsequence relation, its canonical semantics given in the proof of Theorem 10.14 is actually standard, that is, $U = \{\alpha\} \cup W$, for some world $\alpha$.

Suppose that $(u, w)$ is a bitheory of $\Vdash$ such that $u \subset w$. Then there exists a proposition $B \in w \backslash u$. Let $\alpha = \mathrm{Th}(u, \neg B)$; by Saturation, we have that either $A \in \alpha$, or $\neg A \in \alpha$, for any $A$, so $\alpha$ is a world, and $\alpha \in U \backslash W$. Let us take now an arbitrary world $\beta \in U \backslash W$. Since $\beta \notin W$, $\neg C \in \beta$, for some $C \in w$. Then $B \wedge C \in w$, and consequently $B \to C \in u$ by Lemma 9.7(1). Hence $\neg B \in \beta$, which implies $\alpha = \mathrm{Th}(u, \neg B) \subseteq \beta$, that is $\alpha = \beta$. Thus, $U = \{\alpha\} \cup W$, and therefore the corresponding model is a standard KD45-model. □

A direct reduction of bisequents of an A-biconsequence relation to modal formulas is described below.

**Corollary 10.33** *Any bisequent $a{:}b \Vdash c{:}d$ of an A-biconsequence relation is equivalent to* $\Vdash \bigwedge(La \cup a \cup \neg Lb \cup Ld) \to \bigvee\{LC \wedge C \mid C \in c\}$ :.

The above reduction follows from the semantic equivalence of these bisequents in standard regular KD45-semantics.

For a bisequent $r = a{:}b \Vdash c{:}d$, let $\breve{r}$ denote the formula

$$\bigwedge(La \cup a \cup \neg Lb \cup Ld) \to \bigvee\{LC \wedge C \mid C \in c\}.$$

Similarly, for a bisequent theory $\Delta$, let $\breve{\Delta}$ be the set of corresponding modal formulas. This modal theory will be called the *modal belief reduct* of $\Delta$. As follows from the preceding corollary, any bisequent theory is equivalent to its modal belief reduct in the logic of A-biconsequence relations.

Let $\Vdash^A_\Delta$ denote the least A-biconsequence relation containing a bisequent theory $\Delta$. Then the following result shows that A-biconsequence relations constitute a sequent calculus for the modal logic KD45.

**Corollary 10.34** $\Vdash^A_\Delta = \{r \mid \breve{\Delta} \vdash_{KD45} \breve{r}\}$.

***Proof.*** It can be directly verified that the set of bisequents $\{r \mid \breve{\Delta} \vdash_{KD45} \breve{r}\}$ is an A-biconsequence relation containing $\Delta$ (Negative Introspection amounts to the modal 5 axiom, while the rest of the postulates follow from KD4). Assume now that a bisequent $r = a{:}b \Vdash c{:}d$ does not belong to $\Vdash^A_\Delta$. Then there exists a standard KD45 model $M$ of $\Delta$ in which $r$ is not valid. By the preceding corollary, $\breve{\Delta}$ is valid in $M$, while $\breve{r}$ is not valid in $M$, and hence $\breve{\Delta} \nvdash_{KD45} \breve{r}$. □

As an immediate consequence, we conclude that two bisequent theories $\Gamma$ and $\Delta$ determine the same A-biconsequence relation if and only if the modal theories $\breve{\Gamma}$ and $\breve{\Delta}$ are equivalent in KD45.

An additional relation between A- and KD45-biconsequence relations is established in the next lemma.

**Lemma 10.35** *If $\Delta$ is a modal theory, then $\Vdash^A_\Delta$ and $\Vdash^{KD45}_\Delta$ have the same singular bisequents.*

***Proof.*** Assume that $a{:}b \nVdash^{KD45}_\Delta C{:}d$. Then there exists a general KD45-model $M = (W, R, F, V)$ of $\Delta$ such that $a \subseteq |M|$, $d \subseteq ||M||$, $b \cap ||M|| = \emptyset$ and $C \notin |M|$. The latter implies that $\neg C$ holds in some world $\alpha \in W$. Let us consider the submodel $M_1$ of $M$ that is generated by $\{\alpha\} \cup F$. Clearly,

$M_1$ is a standard KD45-model. Moreover, since $\Delta$ is a modal theory, $M_1$ is also a model of $\Delta$, and hence $M_1$ determines a bitheory of $\Vdash^A_\Delta$. But $M_1$ still invalidates the bisequent $a{:}b \Vdash C{:}d$, and therefore $a{:}b \nVdash^A_\Delta C{:}d$. This completes the proof. □

Finally, as a special case of Theorem 10.23, we obtain

**Lemma 10.36** *Any objective saturated biconsequence relation is an objective subrelation of some A-biconsequence relation.*

***Proof.*** As can be immediately verified, if $\Vdash$ is an objective saturated biconsequence relation, then the possible worlds semantics constructed in the proof of Theorem 10.23 is actually a standard KD45 semantics. □

Since an A-biconsequence relation is a KD45-biconsequence relation, it is uniquely determined by its objective subrelation. Moreover, due to Corollary 9.8, we obtain

**Corollary 10.37**

- *Any bisequent of an A-biconsequence relation is reducible to a set of objective singular autoepistemic bisequents.*
- *A-biconsequence relations having the same objective singular autoepistemic subrelations coincide.*

Thus, the logic of A-biconsequence relations is quite rich and allows for both modal and objective reductions. Namely, any bisequent theory $\Delta$ is reducible to a modal theory $\breve{\Delta}$, as well as to an objective bisequent theory $B(\Delta)$; moreover, due to the above corollary, the latter can actually be reduced further to a set of singular autoepistemic bisequents.

Now we turn to R-biconsequence relations. To begin with, such relations can be described alternatively as biconsequence relations that are simultaneously F- and SW5-biconsequence relations.

**Lemma 10.38** *A modal biconsequence relation is an R-biconsequence relation iff it satisfies Reflexive Introspection and the postulate F.*

***Proof.*** Given Reflexive Introspection, the postulate F, $\Vdash A, LA{\to}B{:}B$ is equivalent to $\Vdash A, A{\to}B{:}A, B$ (see the last reduction in Lemma 10.20). Now, the latter bisequent holds in saturated biconsequence relations (see Lemma 9.7(1)). Moreover, replacing $A$ with $A \vee B$ in the latter, we immediately obtain Saturation. Consequently, given Positive Introspection, Saturation is equivalent to the postulate F. Hence the result. □

As follows from Theorem 10.15, R-biconsequence relations coincide with saturated SW5-biconsequence relations. As before, the standard modal semantics for SW5 consists of final Kripke models of the form $(F \cup \{\gamma\}, R, F, V)$, where $\alpha R \beta$ holds iff $\alpha = \beta$ or $\beta \in F$. The following result shows that this standard semantics provides a representation for R-biconsequence relations. The proof is similar to that of Theorem 10.32 (based this time on Theorem 10.15), so we omit it.

**Theorem 10.39** *A biconsequence relation is an R-biconsequence relation if and only if it coincides with* $\Vdash_{\mathcal{S}}$*, for some regular standard SW5-semantics* $\mathcal{S}$.

As for F-biconsequence relations, the above representation implies that R-biconsequence relations express derivability in SW5. Let $\Vdash^R_\Delta$ denote the least R-biconsequence relation containing a bisequent theory $\Delta$.

**Corollary 10.40** $\Vdash^R_\Delta = \{r \mid \tilde{\Delta} \vdash_{SW5} \tilde{r}\}$.

***Proof.*** It is easy to check that the set of bisequents $\{r \mid \tilde{\Delta} \vdash_{SW5} \tilde{r}\}$ forms an R-biconsequence relation containing $\Delta$ (W5 implies Saturation). In the other direction, if $r = a{:}b \Vdash c{:}d$ does not belong to $\Vdash^R_\Delta$, there exists a standard SW5 model $M$ of $\Delta$ in which $r$ is not valid. Then, as before, $\tilde{\Delta}$ is valid in $M$, while $\tilde{r}$ is not valid in $M$, and hence $\tilde{\Delta} \nvdash_{SW5} \tilde{r}$. □

In addition, as for A-biconsequence relations, we have the following correspondence between R- and SW5-biconsequence relations. The proof is similar to that of Lemma 10.35.

**Lemma 10.41** *If* $\Delta$ *is a modal theory, then* $\Vdash^R_\Delta$ *and* $\Vdash^{SW5}_\Delta$ *have the same singular bisequents.*

As a special case of Theorem 10.27, we have that any objective saturated biconsequence relation can be conservatively embedded also into an R-biconsequence relation.

**Lemma 10.42** *Any objective saturated biconsequence relation is an objective subrelation of some R-biconsequence relation.*

***Proof.*** If $\Vdash$ is an objective saturated biconsequence relation, then the modal biconsequence relation constructed in the proof of Theorem 10.27 is also saturated. □

Since an R-biconsequence relation is an SW5-biconsequence relation, it is uniquely determined by its objective subrelation. Furthermore, due to Corollary 9.8, we have

**Corollary 10.43**

- *Any bisequent of an R-biconsequence relation is reducible to a set of objective singular autoepistemic bisequents.*
- *R-biconsequence relations having the same objective singular autoepistemic subrelations coincide.*

Thus, just as A-biconsequence relations, the logic of R-biconsequence relations allows for both modal and objective reductions of arbitrary bisequent theories. This fact will turn out to be useful in what follows.

As a final result in this section, we will show that a broad class of saturated K-biconsequence relations can be represented as intersections of A-biconsequence relations and R-biconsequence relations.

**Lemma 10.44** $\Vdash$ *is a saturated K-biconsequence relation if and only if* $\Vdash = \Vdash^A \cap \Vdash^R$, *where* $\Vdash^A$ *and* $\Vdash^R$ *are, respectively, an A-biconsequence relation and an R-biconsequence relation.*

***Proof.*** Note first that both A- and R-biconsequence relations are saturated K-biconsequence relations, which gives us the direction from right to left. In the other direction, suppose that $\Vdash$ is a saturated K-biconsequence relation, and $\mathcal{S}$ its canonical possible worlds semantics. It should be clear that each model in $\mathcal{S}$ is either a standard KD45-model, or a standard SW5-model. Let $\Vdash^A$ and $\Vdash^R$ be biconsequence relations determined, respectively, by all the KD45-models and all the SW5-models from $\mathcal{S}$. Then we immediately obtain that $\Vdash$ is an intersection of $\Vdash^A$ and $\Vdash^R$. □

The above result shows that saturated biconsequence relations do not leave much room for proliferation of modal reasoning. Note, in particular, that both A- and R-biconsequence relations satisfy Weak Introspection, and hence Theorem 10.13 immediately implies

**Corollary 10.45** *Any saturated K-biconsequence relation is a D4.4-biconsequence relation.*

## 10.2 Modal Nonmonotonic Semantics

We turn now to describing the nonmonotonic semantics of modal biconsequence relations and bisequent theories.

To begin with, note that, since modal biconsequence relations are consistent, exact theories of such biconsequence relations will already coincide with extensions. Consequently, we can restrict our attention to modal counterparts of extensions and expansions. Modal biconsequence relations may have, however, a nontrivial modal content, so by varying the underlying modal logic, we obtain a whole range of new, *modal* nonmonotonic semantics of bisequent theories.

**Definition 10.6** For a bisequent theory $\Delta$ and a modal logic $\mathcal{M}$, a set of modal propositions will be called an *$\mathcal{M}$-extension* (*$\mathcal{M}$-expansion*) of a bisequent theory $\Delta$, if it is an extension (resp. expansion) of $\Vdash^{\mathcal{M}}_{\Delta}$.

In what follows, we will use the same terminology also for F-, A- an R-biconsequence relations. As we will see later, if $\Delta$ is a plain modal theory, then $\mathcal{M}$-extensions of $\Delta$ will coincide with *$\mathcal{S}$-expansions* in the sense of [Marek *et al.*, 1993][2].

Given a bisequent theory $\Delta$, let us denote by $\Delta^{\mathcal{M}}$ a bisequent theory obtained from $\Delta$ by adding (all instances of) the modal reflection and introspection postulates, as well as all modal axioms of $\mathcal{M}$. Then the following simple observation follows directly from the definition of a modal biconsequence relation.

**Lemma 10.46** *A set $u$ is an $\mathcal{M}$-extension ($\mathcal{M}$-expansion) of a bisequent theory $\Delta$ iff it is a classical extension (respectively, expansion) of $\Delta^{\mathcal{M}}$.*

The above result implies that modal extensions and expansions should have much the same properties as classical extensions and expansions. Thus, we still have a *restricted monotonicity* property, according to which stronger biconsequence relations should have larger nonmonotonic semantics so far as they do not change the set of theories. Due to Corollary 10.16, however, two modal biconsequence relations (or bisequent theories) have the same theories if and only if they determine the same S5-biconsequence relation. Accordingly, the restricted monotonicity property implies, in particular, the following observation (cf. [McDermott, 1982]):

**Lemma 10.47** *If $\mathcal{M}_1$ and $\mathcal{M}_2$ are modal logics such that $\mathcal{M}_1 \subseteq \mathcal{M}_2 \subseteq S5$, then any $\mathcal{M}_1$-extension ($\mathcal{M}_1$-expansion) of $\Delta$ is an $\mathcal{M}_2$-extension (resp., $\mathcal{M}_2$-expansion) of $\Delta$.*

As yet another consequence of the above correspondence between modal and classical nonmonotonic semantics, we immediately obtain a characterization of the maximal logics suitable for modal nonmonotonic semantics.

---

[2] This creates, of course, an unfortunate terminological discrepancy, which is compensated, however, by the conformity of our terminology with the rest of this study.

**Theorem 10.48** *Bisequent theories are strongly equivalent with respect to*

- $\mathcal{M}$*-extensions if and only if they are equivalent in regular* $\mathcal{M}$*-biconsequence relations;*
- $\mathcal{M}$*-expansions if and only if they are equivalent in saturated* $\mathcal{M}$*-biconsequence relation.*

***Proof.*** In both cases, the implication from right to left is immediate. If $\Gamma$ and $\Delta$ are strongly equivalent with respect to $\mathcal{M}$-extensions, then $\Gamma^{\mathcal{M}}$ and $\Delta^{\mathcal{M}}$ are strongly equivalent with respect to a classical default semantics by Lemma 10.46, and hence they are classically default equivalent by Theorem 9.13, which implies, in turn, that $\Gamma$ and $\Delta$ determine the same regular $\mathcal{M}$-biconsequence relation. The proof for modal expansions is similar, based on Theorem 9.19. □

Finally, recall that both extensions and expansions are theories of a biconsequence relation, while theories of modal biconsequence relations are stable. Consequently, we obtain the following characteristic property of modal extensions and expansions:

**Corollary 10.49** *Modal extensions and expansions are modal stable theories.*

As is well-known, stable theories are uniquely determined by their objective subsets. This suggests a possibility of reducing modal nonmonotonic reasoning to a nonmodal one or, alternatively, representing (or embedding) of nonmodal nonmonotonic reasoning in a modal one. In what follows, we will explore both these possibilities.

### 10.2.1 *Modal extensions*

As a first step, the following lemma shows that modal extensions have a very simple syntactic characterization.

**Lemma 10.50** *A set* $u$ *is an extension of a modal biconsequence relation* $\Vdash$ *if and only if* $u = \{A \mid : \overline{u} \Vdash A :\}$.

***Proof.*** Note first that, if $u$ satisfies the above condition, it is a stable theory. Indeed, if $A \in u$, then $:\overline{u} \Vdash A:$, and hence $:\overline{u} \Vdash LA:$ by necessitation, which implies $LA \in u$. Also, if $A \notin u$, then $:\overline{u} \Vdash \neg LA:$ by negative introspection, and hence $\neg LA \in u$.

Since $\Vdash$ is consistent, Corollary 9.14 implies that $u$ is an extension iff $u = \{A \mid :\overline{u} \Vdash A{:}u\}$. Note also that any extension is a theory of a biconsequence relation, and hence it is a stable set in our case. Hence, in order to obtain the above characterization of extensions, it is sufficient to show that, if $u$ is a stable theory, then $:\overline{u} \Vdash A{:}$ if and only if $:\overline{u} \Vdash A{:}u$. Indeed, if $:\overline{u} \Vdash A{:}u$, then $:\overline{u}, \neg Lu \Vdash A{:}$ by Corollary 10.5(1). But since $u$ is stable, we have $\neg Lu \subseteq \overline{u}$, and therefore $:\overline{u} \Vdash A{:}$, as required. □

Actually, the above description of modal extensions could be obtained directly from Lemma 5.15 from Chapter 5, due to the fact that theories of a modal biconsequence relation are stable, which implies that they are incomparable and therefore are always minimal. This description will imply also that modal default consequence relations, described in what follows, will constitute a fully expressive formalism for the extension-based modal nonmonotonic semantics.

Since extensions of a modal biconsequence relation are uniquely determined by its autoepistemic bisequents, Lemma 10.6 implies

**Corollary 10.51** *Extensions of a modal biconsequence relation are determined by the set of its provable formulas.*

Thus, two modal biconsequence relations containing the same provable formulas should have the same extensions.

Recall now that $_o\Vdash$ denotes the objective subrelation of a modal biconsequence relation $\Vdash$. The following theorem establishes a direct correspondence between modal theories and extensions, and their objective counterparts:

**Theorem 10.52** *If $\Vdash$ is a modal biconsequence relation, and $u$ a stable theory, then*

*(1) $u$ is a theory of $\Vdash$ if and only if $u_o$ is a theory of $_o\Vdash$;*
*(2) $u$ is an extension of $\Vdash$ if and only if $u_o$ is an extension of $_o\Vdash$.*

***Proof.*** (1) If $u$ is a theory of $\Vdash$, then $u{:}\overline{u} \nVdash \overline{u}{:}u$, and hence $u_o{:}\overline{u}_o \nVdash \overline{u}_o{:}u_o$, which implies that $u_o$ is a theory $_o\Vdash$. In the other direction, if $u_o{:}\overline{u}_o \nVdash \overline{u}_o{:}u_o$, then there is a bitheory $(v, u')$ of $\Vdash$ such that $v_o = u'_o = u_o$. Now, since $u'$ is stable, we have $u = u'$. In addition, $u_o \subseteq v \subseteq u$, $v$ is closed with respect to necessitation (by Positive Reflection) and contains $\neg L\overline{u}$ by negative introspection. Consequently, $\mathrm{Cn}_{\mathbf{N}}(u_o \cup \neg L\overline{u}) \subseteq v$, and therefore $u = v$ (see Proposition 10.1). Thus, $u{:}\overline{u} \nVdash \overline{u}{:}u$, and hence $u$ is a theory of $\Vdash$.

(2) If $u$ is an extension of $\Vdash$, it is a stable theory, and hence, for any objective proposition $A$, $A \in u_o$ iff $A \in u$ iff $:\overline{u} \Vdash A{:}u$ iff $:\overline{u}_o \Vdash A{:}u_o$ by Lemma 10.9. Thus, $u_o$ is an extension of ${}_o\Vdash$. In the other direction, if $u_o$ is an extension of ${}_o\Vdash$, then it is a theory of ${}_o\Vdash$, and hence $u$ is a theory of $\Vdash$ by the first claim. Consequently, if $:\overline{u} \Vdash A{:}u$, then $A \in u$. Let $v = \{A \mid :\overline{u} \Vdash A{:}u\}$. Then, as before, we have $u_o \subseteq v \subseteq u$, $v$ is closed with respect to necessitation (by Positive Reflection) and contains $\neg L\overline{u}$ by negative introspection. Consequently, $\mathrm{Cn}_{\mathbf{N}}(u_o \cup \neg L\overline{u}) \subseteq v$, and therefore $u = v$ by Proposition 10.1, which amounts to saying that $u$ is an extension of $\Vdash$. □

According to the above result, theories and extensions of an objective subrelation of a modal biconsequence relation $\Vdash$ are precisely objective parts of the corresponding modal theories and extensions of $\Vdash$. Moreover, since the later are stable sets, they are uniquely determined by their objective parts, which means that the objective biconsequence relation ${}_o\Vdash$ embodies all the information about the modal nonmonotonic semantics of $\Vdash$. In other words, for the modal extension-based nonmonotonic semantics, the net effect of modal reasoning in biconsequence relations can be measured by the set of derived objective bisequents; the latter are sufficient for determining the nonmonotonic consequences of a modal biconsequence relation.

As a consequence of the above result, non-modal supraclassical biconsequence relations turn out to be sufficiently expressive to capture extension-based modal nonmonotonic reasoning. This reduction should also be combined with the following result showing that a broad class of modal biconsequence relations is conservative, in a sense, with respect to the objective default nonmonotonic semantics.

**Corollary 10.53** *If $\Delta$ is an objective bisequent theory, then classical extensions of $\Delta$ are precisely objective parts of $\mathcal{M}$-extensions of $\Delta$, for any modal logic $\mathcal{M}$ included in either KD45 or SW5.*

***Proof.*** By Theorem 10.23, the objective part of $\Vdash^{\mathcal{M}}_{\Delta}$, for any modal logic $\mathcal{M}$ in this range, coincides with the least consistent supraclassical biconsequence relation containing $\Delta$. Now the result follows from the preceding theorem. □

Theorem 10.52 suggests that, as a way of computing the set of modal extensions of a modal bisequent theory $\Delta$, we could determine first the set ${}_o\Delta$ of objective bisequents that are derivable from $\Delta$, using a given modal logic $\mathcal{M}$, and then determine the set of classical extensions of ${}_o\Delta$.

Now, while finding ${}_o\Delta$ is a difficult task in general, for the two maximal logics KD45 and SW5 it is straightforward, since in both these logics any bisequent theory $\Delta$ has an objective reduct that can be obtained by a direct and modular transformation of the bisequents from $\Delta$.

**Lemma 10.54** *If $B(\Delta)$ and $K(\Delta)$ are, respectively, the objective belief reduct and objective knowledge reduct of a bisequent theory $\Delta$, then*

- *Classical extensions of $B(\Delta)$ coincide with objective parts of KD45-extensions of $\Delta$.*
- *Classical extensions of $K(\Delta)$ coincide with objective parts of SW5-extensions of $\Delta$.*

Moreover, the following result shows that, just as the source modal logics, these nonmonotonic semantics are also interdefinable. This result generalizes the corresponding result proved in [Schwarz, 1992b] for modal theories.

**Corollary 10.55** *For any bisequent theory $\Delta$,*

- *KD45-extensions of $\Delta$ coincide with SW5-extensions of $\Delta^K$;*
- *SW5-extensions of $\Delta$ coincide with KD45-extensions of $\Delta^B$.*

***Proof.*** By Lemma 10.22, $B(\Delta) = K(\Delta^K)$ and $K(\Delta) = B(\Delta^B)$. Now the above two claims are immediate by the preceding lemma. □

Finally, the next result shows that, for plain modal theories, A-, R- and F-extensions are reducible to their appropriate modal logic counterparts.

**Lemma 10.56** *If $\Delta$ is a modal theory, then*

- *KD45-extensions of $\Delta$ coincide with A-extensions of $\Delta$;*
- *SW5-extensions of $\Delta$ coincide with R-extensions of $\Delta$;*
- *S4F-extensions of $\Delta$ coincide with F-extensions of $\Delta$.*

***Proof.*** Since extensions are determined by singular autoepistemic bisequents of a biconsequence relation, the claims are immediate from Lemmas 10.6 ,10.35, 10.41, and 10.29. □

Our results so far have been mainly reductive, and hence they have not shown yet the advantages of modal nonmonotonic reasoning as compared with the non-modal one. However, it has been established earlier that modal F-biconsequence relations allow to transform any bisequent theory into a usual modal theory. As we will see, this creates a possibility of using ordinary modal logical formalisms in representing and describing nonmonotonic reasoning.

Recall that $\tilde{\Delta}$ denotes the modal reduct of a bisequent theory $\Delta$. Then we have

**Theorem 10.57** *F-extensions of a bisequent theory $\Delta$ coincide with S4F-extensions of $\tilde{\Delta}$.*

***Proof.*** By Corollary 10.25, F-extensions of $\Delta$ coincide with F-extensions of $\tilde{\Delta}$. But $\tilde{\Delta}$ is a set of modal propositions, so it determines an autoepistemic bisequent theory. Recall now that extensions of a consistent biconsequence relation are determined by the set of its singular autoepistemic bisequents. Consequently, F-extensions of $\tilde{\Delta}$ coincide with S4F-extensions of $\tilde{\Delta}$ by Lemma 10.29. Hence the result. □

As a consequence of the above result, the modal logic S4F turns out to be suitable for a modal representation of objective bisequent theories. Thus, the following result provides a generalization of the corresponding result about a modal embedding of (disjunctive) default theories, established first in [Truszczyński, 1991b].

**Corollary 10.58** *If $\Delta$ is an objective bisequent theory, then classical extensions of $\Delta$ are precisely objective parts of S4F-extensions of $\tilde{\Delta}$.*

***Proof.*** By Lemma 10.27, we have that classical extensions of $\Delta$ are also objective parts of F-extensions of $\Delta$. Consequently, the result follows from the preceding theorem. □

By the above result, the classical nonmonotonic semantics of a nonmodal bisequent theory is equivalent, in a sense, to a modal nonmonotonic semantics of some plain propositional modal theory. This result should also be combined with the following observation that shows, in effect, that the modal logic S4F constitutes a maximal logic for an adequate embedding of objective bisequent theories under the extension-based nonmonotonic semantics. The proof is immediate from Theorem 9.13 and Corollary 10.28.

**Lemma 10.59** *Objective bisequent theories $\Gamma$ and $\Delta$ are strongly equivalent with respect to a classical default semantics if and only if $\tilde{\Gamma}$ and $\tilde{\Delta}$ are S4F-equivalent.*

As has been shown in [Truszczyński, 1991a], the full strength of S4F is not actually needed for the special case of ordinary, singular, default theories. Slightly generalized, this result can be described as follows.

To begin with, the modal reduct $\tilde{r}$ of a singular bisequent $r = a{:}b \Vdash C{:}d$ can be simplified to the formula

$$\bigwedge(La \cup L\neg Lb \cup \neg L\neg Ld) \to C.$$

As can be seen, the latter formula is provably equivalent to $\tilde{r}$ for any T-biconsequence relation. So, somewhat abusing our terminology, for a singular bisequent theory $\Delta$, we will still denote by $\tilde{\Delta}$ the set of the above modal reducts of all the bisequents in $\Delta$. Then we have

**Corollary 10.60** *If $\Delta$ is a singular objective bisequent theory, then classical extensions of $\Delta$ are precisely objective parts of $\mathcal{M}$-extensions of $\tilde{\Delta}$, for any modal logic $\mathcal{M} \subseteq S4F$.*

***Proof.*** If $\Vdash$ is a modal biconsequence relation, and $\Vdash \tilde{r}{:}$, for a singular bisequent $r = a{:}b \Vdash C{:}d$, then $:b \Vdash \bigwedge La{\to}C{:}d$ by Lemma 10.6, and hence $a{:}b \Vdash C{:}d$ by Positive Reflection. This shows that $\Delta \subseteq \Vdash^{\mathcal{M}}_{\tilde{\Delta}}$, for any logic $\mathcal{M}$ in the above range, and hence $\Vdash^{\mathcal{M}}_{\Delta} \subseteq \Vdash^{\mathcal{M}}_{\tilde{\Delta}}$. By restricted monotonicity, this implies that any $\mathcal{M}$-extension of $\Delta$ is an $\mathcal{M}$-extension of $\tilde{\Delta}$. But we have also $\Vdash^{\mathcal{M}}_{\tilde{\Delta}} \subseteq \Vdash^{S4F}_{\tilde{\Delta}}$, which means that $\Vdash^{\mathcal{M}}_{\tilde{\Delta}}$ and $\Vdash^{S4F}_{\tilde{\Delta}}$ should have the same extensions. Hence the result. □

### 10.2.2 *Modal expansions*

It turns out that the structure of expansions in the modal case is quite different from the structure of extensions, as well as from the structure of classical expansions. So we will start with pointing out two main differences.

To begin with, expansions of modal biconsequence relations do not stand in one-to-one correspondence with their objective counterparts. Thus, the example below shows that a modal biconsequence relation $\Vdash$ may have an expansion $u$ such that $u_o$ is not an expansion of ${}_o\Vdash$.

**Example 10.2** Let us return to Example 10.1 on page 360 that describes an F-biconsequence relation $\Vdash$ determined by a single standard S4F-model $M_2 = (\{\alpha, \beta, \beta'\}, \{\beta\}, V)$, where $V(\alpha) = \{q\}$ and $V(\beta) = V(\beta') = \{p\}$. Then the stable theory containing $\mathrm{Th}(p \wedge \neg q)$ is clearly an expansion of $\Vdash$, but $\mathrm{Th}(p \wedge \neg q)$ is not an expansion of ${}_o\Vdash$, since $(\mathrm{Th}(\neg(p \leftrightarrow q)), \mathrm{Th}(p \wedge \neg q))$ is a saturated bitheory of ${}_o\Vdash$.

Still, the next result shows that the reverse implication holds.

**Lemma 10.61** *If $\Vdash$ is a modal biconsequence relation, $u$ a stable theory, and $u_o$ is an expansion of ${}_o\Vdash$, then $u$ is an expansion of $\Vdash$.*

***Proof.*** If $u_o$ is an expansion of ${}_o\Vdash$, then $u$ is a theory of $\Vdash$ by Theorem 10.52. Suppose that $u$ is not an expansion of $\Vdash$. Then there exists a world $\alpha$ (in a modal language) such that $u \not\subseteq \alpha$, and $(u \cap \alpha, u)$ is a bitheory of $\Vdash$, that is, $u \cap \alpha{:}\overline{u} \nVdash \overline{u \cap \alpha}{:}u$. Note that $\alpha_o$ is an objective world, and, moreover, we have $u_o \cap \alpha_0{:}\overline{u}_0 \nVdash \overline{u_o \cap \alpha_o}{:}u_o$. But then $(u_o \cap \alpha_o, u_o)$ is a bitheory of ${}_o\Vdash$, and consequently $u_o$ is not an expansion of ${}_o\Vdash$, contrary to our assumption. Hence $u$ is an expansion of $\Vdash$. □

A second important discrepancy is that modal expansions of autoepistemic bisequent theories do not coincide, in general, with extensions. This property has played an important role in our descriptions of general and classical nonmonotonic semantics (cf. Theorem 9.20), and its invalidity in the modal case significantly changes the resulting picture.

As a starting point in a positive description of modal expansions, we have that Theorem 9.16 remains valid in the modal case, and hence obtain

**Lemma 10.62** *Expansions of a modal saturated biconsequence relation coincide with its extensions.*

As has been shown earlier (see Theorem 10.48), saturated $\mathcal{M}$-biconsequence relations provide a maximal logic for $\mathcal{M}$-expansions. This fact will give us an opportunity to provide an exhaustive description of expansions for normal modal logics $\mathcal{M}$. To begin with, as a consequence of Lemma 10.30, we have that expansions of bisequent theories are always reducible to expansions of plain modal theories.

**Lemma 10.63** *For modal saturated biconsequence relations, any bisequent theory is reducible to some modal theory.*

For a bisequent theory $\Delta$, the corresponding modal theory is obtainable by applying the reduction of Lemma 10.6 to $cauto(\Delta)$. Thus, in studying modal expansions, we can restrict our attention to expansions of modal theories.

Two particular kinds of expansions will turn out to be important for a general description of the modal autoepistemic semantics. The first kind includes 5-expansions, that is expansions of biconsequence relations containing the modal axiom 5. We will call them *stable expansions*, since they will correspond to Moore's stable expansions. A detailed description of such expansions is given in the next theorem.

**Theorem 10.64** *If $\Delta$ is a modal bisequent theory, and $u$ a stable theory, then the following conditions are equivalent:*

*(1) u is a stable expansion of* $\Delta$*;*
*(2) u is an A-expansion of* $\Delta$*;*
*(3) u is an* $\mathcal{M}$*-expansion of* $\Delta$*, for any* $\mathcal{M}$ *in the range* $5 \subseteq \mathcal{M} \subseteq KD45$*;*
*(4) u is a KD45-extension of* $\breve{\Delta}$*;*
*(5)* $u_o$ *is a classical extension of* $B(\Delta)$*.*

***Proof.*** $1 \leftrightarrow 2$. By Theorem 10.14, any 5-biconsequence relation is a KD45-biconsequence relation, and hence any saturated 5-biconsequence relation is already an A-biconsequence relation. Consequently, $\Vdash^5_\Delta$ has the same expansions as $\Vdash^A_\Delta$.

$1 \leftrightarrow 3$. If $5 \subseteq \mathcal{M} \subseteq$ KD45, then by restricted monotonicity, any 5-expansion of $\Delta$ is an $\mathcal{M}$-expansion of $\Delta$, and any $\mathcal{M}$-expansion of $\Delta$ is an A-expansion of $\Delta$. But 5-expansions of $\Delta$ coincide with A-expansions of $\Delta$, hence the result.

$2 \leftrightarrow 4$. Since A-biconsequence relations are saturated, A-expansions of $\Delta$ coincide with A-extensions of $\Delta$. The latter coincide with A-extensions of $\breve{\Delta}$ by Corollary 10.33. Finally, $\breve{\Delta}$ corresponds to an autoepistemic bitheory, and hence A-extensions of $\breve{\Delta}$ coincide with KD45-extensions of $\breve{\Delta}$ by Lemma 10.35.

$3 \leftrightarrow 5$. Follows from Lemma 10.54. □

If we combine Definition 9.8 of expansions with the possible worlds semantics of A-biconsequence relations, we immediately obtain the semantic definition of stable expansions in Moore's autoepistemic logic [Moore, 1985]. Consequently,

**Corollary 10.65** *Stable expansions of a modal theory coincide with Moore's stable expansions.*

The above theorem provides us with two alternative ways of computing stable expansions for arbitrary bisequent theories. The first amounts to transforming a bisequent theory $\Delta$ into a modal theory $\breve{\Delta}$, and then computing KD45-extensions of the latter. This task amounts to the standard problem of finding stable expansions in autoepistemic logic. The second way consists in reducing $\Delta$ to an objective bisequent theory $B(\Delta)$ and computing classical extensions of the latter. It is interesting to note in this respect that if $\Delta$ is an objective bisequent theory, then $B(\breve{\Delta})$ amounts precisely to the autoepistemic reduction of $\Delta$ described in Corollary 9.8.

The next theorem provides a detailed description of the second important kind of expansions, namely expansions based on the normal modal logic KT. We will call them *reflexive expansions*, since they will correspond to expansions of Schwarz' reflexive autoepistemic logic.

**Theorem 10.66** *If $\Delta$ is a modal bisequent theory, and u a stable theory, then the following conditions are equivalent:*

*(1) u is a reflexive expansion of $\Delta$;*
*(2) u is an R-expansion of $\Delta$;*
*(3) u is an $\mathcal{M}$-expansion of $\Delta$, for any $\mathcal{M}$ in the range $KT \subseteq \mathcal{M} \subseteq SW5$;*
*(4) u is an SW5-extension of $\tilde{\Delta}$;*
*(5) $u_o$ is a classical extension of $K(\Delta)$.*

***Proof.*** $1 \leftrightarrow 2$. Any saturated KT-biconsequence relation is an SW5-biconsequence relation by Corollary 10.45, and hence is an R-biconsequence relation. Consequently, $\Vdash_\Delta^{KT}$ has the same expansions as $\Vdash_\Delta^{R}$.

$1 \leftrightarrow 3$. Follows by restricted monotonicity from the fact that KT-expansions of $\Delta$ coincide with R-expansions of $\Delta$.

$2 \leftrightarrow 4$. Since R-biconsequence relations are saturated, R-expansions of $\Delta$ coincide with R-extensions of $\Delta$. The latter coincide with R-extensions of $\tilde{\Delta}$ by Corollary 10.25. Finally, R-extensions of $\tilde{\Delta}$ coincide with SW5-extensions of $\tilde{\Delta}$ by Lemma 10.41.

$3 \leftrightarrow 5$. Follows from Lemma 10.54. □

This time, the definition of an R-expansion is directly equivalent to the semantic definition of reflexive expansion from [Schwarz, 1992b], and hence we have

**Corollary 10.67** *Reflexive expansions of a modal theory coincide with Schwarz's reflexive expansions.*

As with stable expansions, the above theorem provides two alternative ways of computing reflexive expansions for arbitrary bisequent theories, namely either as SW5-expansions of the modal theory $\tilde{\Delta}$, or as classical extensions of $K(\Delta)$. Moreover, Corollary 10.55 implies the following correspondence between stable and reflexive expansions (cf. [Schwarz, 1992b]):

**Corollary 10.68** *For any bisequent theory $\Delta$,*

- *stable expansions of $\Delta$ coincide with reflexive expansions of $\Delta^K$;*
- *reflexive expansions of $\Delta$ coincide with stable expansions of $\Delta^B$.*

Finally, the following theorem provides a description of 'normal' expansions in general.

**Theorem 10.69** *A set of propositions is a K-expansion of a modal bisequent theory $\Delta$ iff it is both a stable and reflexive expansion of $\Delta$.*

***Proof.*** If $\Vdash^{sK}_{\Delta}$ is a least saturated K-biconsequence relation containing $\Delta$, then by Lemma 10.44, $\Vdash^{sK}_{\Delta}=\Vdash^{A}_{\Delta} \cap \Vdash^{R}_{\Delta}$. In other words, $(u,v)$ is a bitheory of $\Vdash^{sK}_{\Delta}$ if and only if it is either a bitheory of $\Vdash^{A}_{\Delta}$, or a bitheory of $\Vdash^{R}_{\Delta}$. Accordingly, $u$ is an expansion (=extension) of $\Vdash^{sK}_{\Delta}$ if and only if it is an expansion of both $\Vdash^{A}_{\Delta}$ and $\Vdash^{R}_{\Delta}$. Hence the result. □

The above result completes our description of normal modal expansions. The example below shows, however, that not all modal expansions are K-expansions.

**Example 10.3** We will use Example 7 from [Marek *et al.*, 1993]. Let us consider a bisequent theory $\Delta = \{\Vdash Lp{\to}p :, \Vdash \neg LLp{\to}p :\}$. It can be shown that $\Vdash^{K}_{\Delta} p :$, and therefore the stable theory $E(p)$ determined by Th($p$) is a K-expansion of $\Delta$. Still, we will show that it is not an N-expansion of $\Delta$.

Let $v$ be the set of all propositions of the form $LA$ such that $A \in E(p)$ and $A \neq p$. We will treat $v$ as a set of atomic propositions in the modal language, so $v$ corresponds in this sense to a unique maximal classically consistent set that we will denote by $\alpha$. Note that $E(p) \not\subseteq \alpha$, since $p \notin \alpha$. Now it can be verified that $(E(p) \cap \alpha, E(p))$ is a bitheory of $\Vdash^{N}_{\Delta}$, and consequently $E(p)$ is not an N-expansion of $\Delta$.

## 10.3 Modal Default Consequence Relations

In this section we will introduce the notion of a modal default consequence relation that will provide a natural logical representation for the main modal nonmonotonic logics.

**Definition 10.7** A default consequence relation in a modal language will be called *modal* if it is supraclassical and satisfies the following postulates:

**(Positive) Reflection** $A :\vdash LA$,
**(Negative) Introspection** $: A \vdash \neg LA$.

As for modal biconsequence relations, the above two postulates jointly imply Consistency, that is, $A{:}A \vdash \mathbf{f}$, for any $A$. In addition, Reflection, together with Cut, implies

**Necessitation** If $a : b \vdash A$, then $a : b \vdash LA$.

A modal default consequence relation $\vdash$ will be called an $\mathcal{M}$-*consequence relation*, if $\vdash A$, for any (instance of a) modal axiom from $\mathcal{M}$. Note, in particular, that the least modal consequence relation coincides with the default N-consequence relation, where N is a pure logic of necessitation.

As for biconsequence relations, if a modal default consequence is supraclassical with respect to its negative premises, it includes the modal axioms D and G. Thus, the proof of the following lemma repeats that of Lemma 10.10.

**Lemma 10.70** *If a modal default consequence relation* $\vdash$ *satisfies Negative Closure and Negative Falsity, then, for any* $A$,

**D** $\vdash LA \to MA$;
**G** $\vdash MLA \to LMA$.

Recall that propositional theories of a default consequence relation are deductive theories $u$ such that $\mathbb{C}\mathrm{n}(u{:}\overline{u}) \subseteq u$. Consequently, due to the modal postulates, theories of a modal default consequence relation will be modal *stable theories* in the usual sense of [Moore, 1985].

**Lemma 10.71** *Any theory of a modal default consequence relation is a stable theory.*

A first link between modal default consequence relations and modal biconsequence relations can be established on the level of regular default consequence relations.

**Theorem 10.72** *A default consequence relation* $\vdash$ *is modal and regular if and only if it is a singular default subrelation of some modal regular biconsequence relation.*

***Proof.*** It can be easily verified that the set of bisequents of the form $a{:}b \Vdash A{:}$ belonging to a regular modal biconsequence relation forms a modal regular default consequence relation. In the other direction, let $\mathcal{B}$ be the set of bitheories of a modal regular default consequence relation $\vdash$, and $\Vdash_{\mathcal{B}}$ a biconsequence relation determined by the binary semantics $\mathcal{B}$. Clearly, $\Vdash_{\mathcal{B}}$ is a consistent regular biconsequence relation, and its singular default subrelation coincides with $\vdash$. The latter fact implies, in particular, that $\Vdash_{\mathcal{B}}$ satisfies Positive Reflection and Negative Introspection. Moreover, since $\vdash$ is regular, if $(u, v)$ is a bitheory of $\vdash$, then $v$ is a theory of $\vdash$ and hence it is stable. Consequently, if $A \in v$, then $LA \in v$, which implies that $\Vdash_{\mathcal{B}}$ satisfies Negative Reflection, and therefore it is a modal biconsequence relation. □

The first consequence of the above correspondence is that regular $\mathcal{M}$-consequence relations posses a possible worlds semantics in the framework of (regular) final Kripke models.

Combined with Theorems 10.14 and 10.15, the above theorem implies

**Corollary 10.73**

- *Any regular 5-consequence relation is a KD45-consequence relation;*
- *Any regular TW5-consequence relation is an SW5-consequence relation.*

In addition, the correspondence implies that, for a broad range of modal logics $\mathcal{M}$, any objective regular default consequence relation can be conservatively embedded into some modal regular $\mathcal{M}$-consequence relation.

**Theorem 10.74** *Any objective regular default consequence relation is an objective subrelation of some regular* $\mathcal{M}$*-consequence relation, for any modal logic* $\mathcal{M}$ *such that* $\mathcal{M} \subseteq KD45$ *or* $\mathcal{M} \subseteq SW5$.

***Proof.*** Any objective regular default consequence relation $\vdash$ is a singular default subrelation of some objective supraclassical biconsequence relation that is consistent and regular, while the latter is an objective subrelation of some $\mathcal{M}$-biconsequence relation, for any modal logic $\mathcal{M}$ in the above range (by Theorem 10.23). Now, the singular default subrelation of the latter is clearly a regular default $\mathcal{M}$-consequence relation, whereas $\vdash$ is precisely its objective subrelation. □

As a special case, the correspondence between regular default consequence relations and biconsequence relations is extendable also to the correspondence between relevant saturated consequence relations.

**Corollary 10.75** *A default consequence relation is modal and saturated if and only if it is a singular default subrelation of some modal saturated biconsequence relation.*

***Proof.*** The set of bisequents of the form $a{:}b \Vdash A{:}$ belonging to a saturated modal biconsequence relation clearly forms a modal saturated default consequence relation. In the other direction, let $\mathcal{B}$ be the canonical saturated semantics of $\vdash$ constructed in the proof of Theorem 9.46, and $\Vdash_{\mathcal{B}}$ the biconsequence relation determined by $\mathcal{B}$. Then as in the proof of Theorem 10.72, it can be verified that $\Vdash_{\mathcal{B}}$ is a modal saturated biconsequence relation such that its singular default subrelation coincides with $\vdash$. □

The second important link between modal default consequence relations and biconsequence relations can be established for autoepistemic consequence relations.

**Definition 10.8** A modal default consequence relation will be called *autoepistemic*, if it is a classical autoepistemic consequence relation.

**Theorem 10.76** *A modal default consequence relation is autoepistemic if and only if it is a singular autoepistemic subrelation of some KD45-biconsequence relation.*

***Proof.*** Let $\vdash$ be the set of default rules $a{:}b \vdash A$ corresponding to bisequents $:b \Vdash A{:}a$ of a KD45-biconsequence relation $\Vdash$. Clearly, $\vdash$ is a classical autoepistemic consequence relation satisfying Introspection. In addition, Reflection for $\vdash$ follows from Positive Introspection for $\Vdash$ (see Theorem 10.14). Thus, $\vdash$ is a modal autoepistemic consequence relation.

In the other direction, if $\vdash$ is a modal autoepistemic consequence relation, it is classical autoepistemic, and hence it has a classical canonical binary semantics $\mathcal{B}$. Let $\Vdash_{\mathcal{B}}$ be the biconsequence relation determined by $\mathcal{B}$. Clearly, the singular autoepistemic subrelation $\Vdash_{\mathcal{B}}$ coincides with $\vdash$. Moreover, if $(u, v)$ is a bitheory of $\vdash$, then $Lv \subseteq u$ by Reflection and $\neg L\overline{v} \subseteq u$ by Introspection, and consequently $\Vdash_{\mathcal{B}}$ satisfies both Negative and Positive Introspection. Note also that if $A \in u$, then $A \in v$ (by Consistency), and hence $LA \in u$ by Reflection, which implies that Positive Reflection is also valid for $\Vdash_{\mathcal{B}}$. Thus, $\Vdash_{\mathcal{B}}$ is modal biconsequence relation that satisfies Positive Introspection, and consequently it is a KD45-biconsequence relation by Theorem 10.14. □

The above correspondence immediately implies that modal autoepistemic consequence relations have a very simple structure. To begin with, any modal default rule is reducible for them to a set of objective default rules.

**Lemma 10.77** *If $\vdash$ is a modal autoepistemic consequence relation, then*

- $a, LA \vee B{:}b \vdash C$ *iff* $a, A{:}b \vdash C$ *and* $a, B{:}b \vdash C$;
- $a, \neg LA \vee B{:}b \vdash C$ *iff* $a{:}b, A \vdash C$ *and* $a, B{:}b \vdash C$;
- $a{:}b, LA \vee B \vdash C$ *iff* $a{:}b, A, B \vdash C$;
- $a{:}b, \neg LA \vee B \vdash C$ *iff* $a, A{:}b, B \vdash C$;
- $a{:}b \vdash LA \vee B$ *iff* $a{:}b, A \vdash B$;
- $a{:}b \vdash \neg LA \vee B$ *iff* $a, A{:}b \vdash B$.

The proof is immediate from the preceding theorem, combined with Lemma 10.7 and 10.18. Now, since conjunction can be eliminated in the context of strongly supraclassical default consequence relations, we obtain

**Corollary 10.78**

- *Any rule of a modal autoepistemic consequence relation is reducible to a set of objective default rules.*

• *Modal autoepistemic consequence relations with the same objective subrelations coincide.*

As can be seen from the above equivalences, any default rule $a{:}b \vdash C$ is reducible also to $\vdash \bigwedge La \wedge \bigwedge \neg Lb \to C$. Consequently, we have

**Corollary 10.79** *For modal autoepistemic consequence relations, any default theory is reducible to a modal theory.*

For a default theory $\Delta$, the set of modal formulas $\vdash \bigwedge La \wedge \bigwedge \neg Lb \to C$ such that $a{:}b \vdash C$ belongs to $\Delta$, will be called a *modal autoepistemic reduct* of $\Delta$ and denoted by $\breve{\Delta}$.

Further properties of modal autoepistemic consequence relations can be obtained from the fact that KD45-biconsequence relations coincide with A-biconsequence relations on singular autoepistemic bisequents.

**Lemma 10.80** *Any modal autoepistemic consequence relation is a singular autoepistemic subrelation of some A-biconsequence relation.*

***Proof.*** If $\vdash$ is a modal autoepistemic consequence relation, let $\Vdash_{\vdash}$ be the least KD45-biconsequence relation containing all autoepistemic bisequents $:b \Vdash C{:}a$ such that $a{:}b \vdash C$ belongs to $\vdash$. By Theorem 10.76, $\vdash$ corresponds precisely to the singular autoepistemic subrelation of $\Vdash_{\vdash}$. Now let $\Vdash^{A}_{\vdash}$ the least A-biconsequence relation containing $\vdash$ (in the same sense). Then Lemma 10.35 implies that the singular autoepistemic subrelation of $\Vdash^{A}_{\vdash}$ is precisely $\vdash$. □

As a consequence of the above embedding, Corollary 10.34 immediately implies that derivability of default rules in modal autoepistemic consequence relations amounts to a modal entailment in KD45.

**Corollary 10.81** *If $\vdash^{ae}_{\Delta}$ is a least modal autoepistemic consequence relation containing a default theory $\Delta$, then $\vdash^{ae}_{\Delta} = \{r \mid \breve{\Delta} \vdash_{KD45} \breve{r}\}$.*

For any modal default consequence relation $\vdash$, its restriction to the non-modal language $\mathcal{L}_o$ is clearly an objective default consequence relation having the same structural rules as $\vdash$. We will denote this objective subrelation by ${}_o\vdash$.

The following auxiliary lemma will be used in what follows.

**Lemma 10.82** *If $\vdash$ is a modal introspective consequence relation, and $u$ a stable theory, then*

*(1)* $\mathbb{C}\mathrm{n}(u{:}\overline{u}) = \mathbb{C}\mathrm{n}(u_o{:}\overline{u}_o)$;

*(2)* $\mathbb{C}\mathrm{n}(\emptyset:\overline{u}) = \mathbb{C}\mathrm{n}(\emptyset:\overline{u}_o, \neg Lu_o)$*;*
*(3)* $u$ *is a theory of* $\vdash$ *if and only if* $u_o$ *is a theory of* ${}_o\vdash$.

***Proof.*** (1) Note first that $\mathbb{C}\mathrm{n}(\mathrm{Cn}_{\mathbf{N}}(v){:}w) \subseteq \mathbb{C}\mathrm{n}(v{:}w)$ by Reflection and Cut. Consequently, $\mathbb{C}\mathrm{n}(u{:}\overline{u}) = \mathbb{C}\mathrm{n}(\mathrm{Cn}_{\mathbf{N}}(u_o \cup \neg L\overline{u}){:}\overline{u}) \subseteq \mathbb{C}\mathrm{n}(u_o \cup \neg L\overline{u}{:}\overline{u})$. In addition, $\neg L\overline{u} \subseteq \mathbb{C}\mathrm{n}(u_o{:}\overline{u})$ by Introspection. Therefore,

$$\mathbb{C}\mathrm{n}(u_o \cup \neg L\overline{u}{:}\overline{u}) \subseteq \mathbb{C}\mathrm{n}(u_o \cup \mathbb{C}\mathrm{n}(u_o{:}\overline{u}){:}\overline{u}) \subseteq \mathbb{C}\mathrm{n}(u_o{:}\overline{u})$$

by Cut. Thus, $\mathbb{C}\mathrm{n}(u{:}\overline{u}) \subseteq \mathbb{C}\mathrm{n}(u_o{:}\overline{u})$.

Assume now that $u_o{:}\overline{u}_o \nvdash A$. Then there exists a bitheory $(v, w)$ of $\vdash$ such that $u_o \subseteq v \subseteq w$, $\overline{u}_o \subseteq \overline{w}$, $v{:}\overline{w} \nvdash A$, and $w$ is a consistent theory of $\vdash$. As can be seen, $w_o = u_o$, and therefore $u = w$, since both are stable theories having the same objective part. Consequently $u_o{:}\overline{u} \nvdash A$, and therefore $\mathbb{C}\mathrm{n}(u_o{:}\overline{u}) \subseteq \mathbb{C}\mathrm{n}(u_o{:}\overline{u}_o)$. Hence $\mathbb{C}\mathrm{n}(u{:}\overline{u}) \subseteq \mathbb{C}\mathrm{n}(u_o{:}\overline{u}_o)$ by the preceding claim.

(2) Since $\overline{u}_o \cup \neg Lu_o \subseteq \overline{u}$, we have $\mathbb{C}\mathrm{n}(\emptyset{:}\overline{u}_o, \neg Lu_o) \subseteq \mathbb{C}\mathrm{n}(\emptyset{:}\overline{u})$. Now if ${:}\overline{u}_o, \neg Lu_o \nvdash A$, there exists a stable theory $w$ such that $\overline{u}_o \cup \neg Lu_o \subseteq \overline{w}$ and ${:}\overline{w} \nvdash A$. But $\neg Lu_o \subseteq \overline{w}$ iff $u_o \subseteq w$, and therefore $u = w$, since $u$ and $w$ have the same objective part. Thus, ${:}\overline{u} \nvdash A$, and hence $\mathbb{C}\mathrm{n}(\emptyset{:}\overline{u}) \subseteq \mathbb{C}\mathrm{n}(\emptyset{:}\overline{u}_o, \neg Lu_o)$.

(3) Clearly, if $u$ is a theory of $\vdash$, then $\mathbb{C}\mathrm{n}(u_o{:}\overline{u}_o)_o \subseteq u_o$, and hence $u_o$ is a theory of ${}_o\vdash$. In the other direction, if $\mathbb{C}\mathrm{n}(u_o{:}\overline{u}_o)_o \subseteq u_o$, then $\mathbb{C}\mathrm{n}(u{:}\overline{u})_o \subseteq u_o$ by (1). If $u_o$ is consistent, we have $u{:}\overline{u} \nvdash \mathbf{f}$, and hence $u$ is a theory of $\vdash$.□

### 10.3.1 *Prime modal consequence relations*

The correspondence between modal default consequence relations and common modal nonmonotonic logics can be established by restricting the former to default consequence relations that are generated by modal theories.

**Definition 10.9** A modal default consequence relation will be called *prime* if it is a least such consequence relation containing some set of (modal) propositions.

For any set $m$ of propositions, $\vdash^{\mathcal{M}}_m$ will denote be the least $\mathcal{M}$-consequence relation containing $m$. The next lemma gives a direct description of this default consequence relation.

**Lemma 10.83** $a : b \vdash^{\mathcal{M}}_m A$ *if and only if* $A \in \mathrm{Cn}_{\mathcal{M}}(m \cup La \cup \neg Lb)$.

***Proof.*** It can be easily verified that the description on the right side of the above equivalence determines a modal default $\mathcal{M}$-consequence relation that contains $m$. Let us denote it by $\vdash_0$. Then clearly $\vdash_m^{\mathcal{M}} \subseteq \vdash_0$. Moreover, if $\vdash$ is an arbitrary $\mathcal{M}$-consequence relation containing $m$, then, for any $a$ and $b$, $\mathbb{C}\mathrm{n}(a{:}b)$ is an $\mathcal{M}$-theory containing $m \cup La \cup \neg Lb$ (by the modal postulates), and hence $\mathbb{C}\mathrm{n}_0(a{:}b) \subseteq \mathbb{C}\mathrm{n}(a{:}b)$. Consequently, $\vdash_0 = \vdash_m^{\mathcal{M}}$. □

An important question that arises here is to what extent the modal axioms of $\mathcal{M}$ influence the general properties of the corresponding default consequence relation. In the rest of this section we will give representation results for a number of modal logics in this setting. It will turn out that most of them possess a simple characterization in terms of structural rules for the associated default consequence relations.

The following theorem provides a description of prime default consequence relations based on the modal logic KD4G (=D4.2)[3].

**Theorem 10.84** *The following conditions are equivalent:*

*(1)* $\vdash$ *is a prime KD4G-consequence relation;*
*(2)* $\vdash$ *is a modal default consequence relation that satisfies Positive Closure, and the following two deduction rules:*

**Positive Deduction** *If* $A, a : b \vdash B$, *then* $a : b \vdash LA \to B$;
**Negative Deduction** *If* $a{:}A, b \vdash B$, *then* $a{:}b \vdash L\neg LA \to B$.

*(3)* $\vdash$ *is introspective and satisfies Positive Deduction.*

***Proof.*** *From (1) to (3).* If $\vdash$ is a prime KD4G-consequence relation, then Lemma 10.83 immediately implies that $\vdash$ is strongly supraclassical. For CD-Regularity, assume $a{:}b \nvdash A$. Then by Lemma 10.83, there is a KD4G-model $M$ such that all formulas from $La \cup \neg Lb$ are valid in $M$, but $A$ is not valid in $M$. Now if $\neg LB$ is valid in $M$, then $a{:}b, B \nvdash A$. Otherwise $LB$ holds in some world $\alpha$ from $M$. In this case the sub-model of $M$ generated by $\alpha$ invalidates $a, B{:}b \vdash \mathbf{f}$. Thus, CD-regularity holds, and hence $\vdash$ is an introspective consequence relation. For Positive Deduction, assume $a{:}b \nvdash LA \to B$. Then there is a KD4G-model $M$ such that all formulas from $La \cup \neg Lb$ are valid in $M$, but there is a world $\alpha \in M$ such that $LA \to B$ is false in $\alpha$. Let $M_\alpha$ be the submodel of $M$ generated by $\alpha$. Clearly, $LA$ and all formulas from $La \cup \neg Lb$ are valid in $M_\alpha$, while $B$ is still not valid. Consequently we have $A, a : b \nvdash B$. Therefore, Positive Deduction is satisfied.

*From (3) to (2).* We only need to show Negative Deduction. Assume that $a{:}b, A \vdash B$. We have $A, \neg LA{:} \vdash LA$ by Reflection, and $LA, A, \neg LA{:} \vdash$

[3] A description for some weaker modal logics can be found in [Bochman, 1998b].

$\mathbf{f}$ by Consistency. Applying Cut, we obtain $A, \neg LA{:} \vdash \mathbf{f}$, and therefore $A, \neg LA, a{:}b \vdash \mathbf{f}$. Then $\neg LA, a{:}b \vdash B$ by CD-Regularity, and hence $a{:}b \vdash L\neg LA \to B$ by Positive Deduction. Thus, Negative Deduction is valid.

*From (2) to (1).* We prove first the axioms of KD4G. By Reflection, $A, A \to B, B{:} \vdash LB$, and hence $A, A \to B{:} \vdash LB$ by Positive Closure. Applying Positive Deduction to the latter, we obtain the axiom K. Similarly, since $A{:} \vdash LA$, we have $A{:} \vdash LLA$ by Necessitation and consequently $\vdash LA \to LLA$ by Positive Deduction. This gives the axiom 4. Finally, the proofs for D and G follow from the proof of Lemma 10.10.

In order to prove primeness, it is sufficient to show that both deduction rules are reversible, that is, the following rules are always valid:

$$\frac{a : b \vdash La \to B}{A, a : b \vdash B} \qquad \frac{a : b \vdash L\neg LA \to B}{a : b, A \vdash B}$$

The first rule immediately follows from Reflection, while the second rule is valid, since $:A \vdash L\neg LA$ holds by Introspection and Necessitation.

Now let $\vdash'$ be an arbitrary modal default relation that includes $\mathbb{C}\mathrm{n}(\emptyset{:}\emptyset)$, and assume that $a{:}b \vdash C$ holds. Applying the two deduction rules, we obtain $\vdash \bigwedge(La \cup L\neg Lb) \to C$ and consequently $\vdash' \bigwedge(La \cup L\neg Lb) \to C$. By the above reverse deduction rules $a{:}b \vdash' C$ and hence $\vdash \subseteq \vdash'$. Thus, $\vdash$ is a prime consequence relation. □

The above theorem gives a first example of the correspondence between rules for default consequence relations and usual modal axioms.

Since the two deduction rules have been shown to be reversible, we immediately conclude that any default rule can be transformed to a provable proposition:

**Corollary 10.85** *Any default rule $a{:}b \vdash C$ of a prime KD4G-consequence relation is equivalent to a provable formula $\bigwedge(La \cup L\neg Lb) \to C$.*

Given the correspondence between default rules in our sense and the rules of Reiter's default logic (see Sec. 9.4.1), the above transformation of default rules into modal formulas is in fact identical with the modal translation of defaults suggested by Truszczyński in [Truszczyński, 1991a].

Replacing D with a stronger T axiom $LA \to A$, we obtain a representation for prime S4.2-consequence relations.

**Corollary 10.86** *$\vdash$ is a prime S4.2-consequence relation iff it is a modal regular default consequence relation satisfying Positive Deduction.*

***Proof.*** The result follows immediately from Theorem 10.84 if we note that, given Positive Deduction, $A\colon\vdash A$ is equivalent to $\vdash LA\to A$. □

Moving beyond regular consequence relations, we will now consider the modal counterpart of saturated default consequence relations. It turns out that the latter correspond precisely to the modal logic SW5.

**Theorem 10.87** *$\vdash$ is a prime SW5-consequence relation if and only if it is a modal saturated consequence relation satisfying Positive Deduction.*

***Proof.*** Using an appropriate Kripke model for SW5, it can be shown that any prime SW5-consequence relation satisfies Conditional Factoring. In the other direction, by the preceding corollary we only need to prove W5. We have $A :\vdash LA \lor L\neg LA$ by Reflection, and $:A \vdash LA \lor L\neg LA$ by Introspection, Necessitation and C-Closure. Applying Conditional Factoring to these two rules, we obtain $\vdash LA\to(LA \lor L\neg LA)$, which is equivalent to W5. □

The following simple example shows that even regular SW5-consequence relations do not satisfy, in general, Positive Deduction, so not all of them are prime.

**Example 10.4** Let us consider a general SW5-model $M = (\{\alpha,\beta,\gamma\}, R, \{\gamma\}, V)$ (see Theorem 10.15) such that $V(\alpha) = \{p\}$, $V(\beta) = \{q\}$, and $V(\gamma) = \{p,q\}$. This model generates an SW5-biconsequence relation, and thereby a default SW5-consequence relation $\vdash$. Now, we trivially have $p :\vdash q$, though $\vdash Lp\to q$ does not hold, since $Lp \land \neg q$ holds in $\alpha$. Thus, Positive Deduction is not valid for $\vdash$.

The next example shows that saturated KD45-consequence relations need not satisfy Positive Deduction, so they are also not prime, in general.

**Example 10.5** Let us consider a standard KD45-model $M = (\{\alpha,\beta\}, R, \{\beta\}, V)$, where $V(\alpha) = \{p\}$ and $V(\beta) = \{q\}$. The corresponding default consequence relation will clearly be a saturated KD45-consequence relation. Moreover, we have $q :\vdash q$ by Reflexivity, but $\vdash Lq\to q$ does not hold, since $Lq \land \neg q$ holds in $\alpha$. Thus, Positive Deduction is not valid for $\vdash$.

The above examples show that, for all modal logics $\mathcal{M}$ that are included in either SW5, or KD45, there is an essential difference between general and prime $\mathcal{M}$-consequence relations. The latter means that default rules of general $\mathcal{M}$-consequence relations are not reducible to modal formulas, and hence corresponding default theories are not reducible, in general, to modal theories.

Now we turn to autoepistemic reasoning. For prime K4-consequence relations, the modal 5 axiom is equivalent to the rule Factoring, which is characteristic of autoepistemic reasoning. Moreover, we have that prime KD45-consequence relations actually coincide with modal autoepistemic consequence relations.

**Theorem 10.88** *The following conditions are equivalent:*

*(1)* $\vdash$ *is a prime KD45-consequence relation;*

*(2)* $\vdash$ *is a modal consequence relation that satisfies Positive Deduction and*

**Strong Negative Deduction** *If* $a{:}A, b \vdash B$, *then* $a{:}b \vdash \neg LA \to B$.

*(3)* $\vdash$ *is a modal autoepistemic consequence relation.*

***Proof.*** From (1) to (3). Theorem 10.84 implies that prime KD45-consequence relations satisfy Positive Closure and Positive Falsity, while the validity of Factoring can be easily checked using an appropriate Kripke model.

From (3) to (2). If $A, a{:}b \vdash B$, then $A, a{:}b \vdash LA \to B$. In addition, $a{:}b, A \vdash LA \to B$ by Introspection. Applying Factoring, we obtain $a{:}b \vdash LA \to B$. Thus, Positive Deduction is satisfied. In the same way, $a{:}b, A \vdash B$ implies $a{:}b, A \vdash \neg LA \to B$, while $A, a{:}b \vdash \neg LA \to B$ follows from Reflection. Applying Factoring, we obtain $a{:}b \vdash \neg LA \to B$. Hence, Strong Negative Deduction also holds.

From (2) to (1). In view of Theorem 10.84, we only need to prove the 5 axiom. Applying Necessitation to Introspection, we obtain $:A \vdash L\neg LA$, and hence by Strong Negative Deduction $\vdash \neg LA \to L\neg LA$. □

The above result provides yet another proof of the fact that any default rule $a{:}b \vdash C$ of a modal autoepistemic (= prime KD45) consequence relation is equivalent to a provable formula $\bigwedge(La \cup \neg Lb) \to C$. The replacement of $L\neg L$ with a simpler $\neg L$ in the modal translation of default rules amounts precisely to admitting Factoring as an additional rule appropriate for autoepistemic reasoning.

As a final step, the next result provides a description of prime S5-consequence relations.

**Lemma 10.89** $\vdash$ *is a prime S5-consequence relation if and only if it is a modal Scott default consequence relation.*

***Proof.*** Modal Scott default consequence relations are precisely autoepistemic modal consequence relations that are reflexive. Now, the result follows from the fact that, given Positive Deduction, $A\colon \vdash A$ is equivalent to $\vdash LA \to A$. □

The equivalence of prime S5 and default Scott consequence relations can now be combined with Theorem 6.22, and we obtain that prime S5-consequence relations are equivalent to Scott consequence relations. This fact can be seen as the source of collapse of modal nonmonotonic reasoning based on S5 to monotonic one ([McDermott, 1982; Tiomkin and Kaminski, 1991]). Actually, the next lemma shows that S5-consequence relations are good only for describing associated stable theories. The proof is immediate from the preceding lemma and Lemma 6.24.

**Corollary 10.90** *Two modal theories are S5-equivalent if and only if they determine the same stable theories.*

The above results have shown that there is a remarkable correspondence between the main types of default consequence relations and well-known modal nonmonotonic logics. This correspondence can also be considered as a justification of the claim that particular modal axioms are important for modal nonmonotonic reasoning only to the extent they influence the structural properties of the associated default consequence relations.

### 10.3.2 *Nonmonotonic semantics*

Now we turn to describing the two nonmonotonic semantics of modal default consequence relations, namely the default and autoepistemic semantics. It will be shown, in particular, that these modal nonmonotonic semantics correspond, respectively to two well known nonmonotonic systems, namely modal nonmonotonic logics based on negative introspection, and Moore's autoepistemic logic.

#### 10.3.2.1 $\mathcal{M}$-*extensions*

By an $\mathcal{M}$-*extension* of a default theory $\Delta$ we will mean an extension of the least default $\mathcal{M}$-consequence relation containing $\Delta$. In addition, by a *modal extension* of $\Delta$ we will mean an extension of the least modal default consequence relation containing $m$. Clearly, if $Ax_{\mathcal{M}}$ is the set of the modal axioms of a modal logic $\mathcal{M}$, then $\mathcal{M}$-extensions of $\Delta$ coincide with modal extensions of $\Delta \cup Ax_{\mathcal{M}}$. Note that Lemma 6.10, taken together with Corollary 10.90, implies the well-known result from [McDermott, 1982] that stronger modal logics produce larger sets of extensions.

**Corollary 10.91** *If $\mathcal{M}$ and $\mathcal{T}$ are modal logics such that $\mathcal{M} \subseteq \mathcal{T} \subseteq S5$, then any $\mathcal{M}$-extension is a $\mathcal{T}$-extension.*

As before, Theorems 6.33 and 6.35 imply that the maximal logic of default rules suitable for modal extensions is a logic of modal regular default consequence relations. This fact can now be combined with the correspondence between regular default consequence relations and modal biconsequence relations (Theorem 10.72), and we conclude that $\mathcal{M}$-extensions of modal default consequence relations correspond precisely to $\mathcal{M}$-extensions of modal biconsequence relations.

Given a default theory $\Delta$, let us denote by $\Delta_{\Vdash}$ the corresponding default bisequent theory, that is, $\Delta_{\Vdash} = \{a{:}b \Vdash A{:} \mid a{:}b \vdash A \in \Delta\}$.

**Lemma 10.92** *$\mathcal{M}$-extensions of a default theory $\Delta$ coincide with $\mathcal{M}$-extensions of the corresponding bisequent theory $\Delta_{\Vdash}$.*

***Proof.*** $\Delta$ has the same $\mathcal{M}$-extensions as the least modal regular $\mathcal{M}$-consequence relation containing $\Delta$. By Theorem 10.72, the latter coincides with the singular default subrelation of $\Vdash^{\mathcal{M}}_{\Delta_{\Vdash}}$. Finally, by Lemma 10.50, extensions of the latter are precisely $\mathcal{M}$-extensions of $\Delta$. □

It is also important to observe that the extension-based semantics of an arbitrary modal biconsequence relation is uniquely determined by its singular default subrelation (by Lemma 10.50), and hence coincides with the nonmonotonic semantics of the corresponding modal default consequence relation. In other words, unlike the non-modal default semantics described in the preceding chapters, in the modal setting we already have a bidirectional correspondence between extension-based nonmonotonic semantics of default and biconsequence relations.

The above correspondence implies that extensions of modal default consequence relations should have much the same structure as extensions of modal biconsequence relations. Thus, Corollary 10.53 immediately implies

**Corollary 10.93** *Classical extensions of an objective default theory $\Delta$ are precisely objective parts of $\mathcal{M}$-extensions of $\Delta$, for any modal logic $\mathcal{M}$ included in either KD45 or SW5.*

Similarly, Corollary 10.60 gives us a correspondence between objective extensions of a default theory and extensions of its modal reduct.

As in Corollary 10.60, the modal reduct $\tilde{\Delta}$ of a default theory $\Delta$ is defined as the set of formulas $\{\bigwedge(La \cup L\neg Lb \cup \neg L\neg Ld) \to C \mid a : b \vdash C\}$.

**Corollary 10.94** *If $\Delta$ is an objective default theory, then classical extensions of $\Delta$ are precisely objective parts of $\mathcal{M}$-extensions of $\tilde{\Delta}$, for any modal logic $\mathcal{M} \subseteq S4F$.*

In addition to the above correspondence, the semantics of $\mathcal{M}$-extensions is related also to the standard semantics of modal nonmonotonic logics. Thus, as a consequence of Lemma 10.83, we have

**Lemma 10.95** *A set $u$ of propositions is an $\mathcal{M}$-extension of a modal theory $m$ iff $u = \mathrm{Cn}_{\mathcal{M}}(m \cup \neg L\overline{u})$.*

Due to this description, $\mathcal{M}$-extensions of modal theories correspond to models suggested already in [McDermott, 1982]; they have been called $\mathcal{S}$-extensions in [Schwarz, 1990], but renamed into *$\mathcal{S}$-expansions* in [Marek *et al.*, 1993] and subsequent literature. It follows that modal nonmonotonic logics based on 'negative introspection' are directly representable in the formalisms of modal default consequence relations and modal biconsequence relations in general.

Now we will describe the relation between modal extensions and their objective counterparts. Unfortunately, for default consequence relations, this correspondence is only partial, because extensions of the objective subrelation ${}_o\vdash$ should also be its *minimal* theories. Hence, following [Konolige, 1988], we introduce the following definition.

**Definition 10.10** Let $\vdash$ be a modal default consequence relation.

- A theory $u$ of $\vdash$ will be called *ground*, if $\vdash$ does not have theories $v$ such that $v_o \subset u_o$.
- An extension $u$ of $\vdash$ will be called *ground*, if it is a ground theory of $\vdash$.

Thus, ground theories and extensions of a modal default consequence relation correspond to its objectively minimal theories. And the following theorem establishes a one-to-one correspondence between ground extensions and objective extensions.

**Theorem 10.96** *If $\vdash$ is a modal introspective consequence relation, then a stable theory $u$ is a ground extension of $\vdash$ if and only if $u_o$ is an extension of ${}_o\vdash$.*

***Proof.*** We will prove first that if $u$ is a ground theory of $\vdash$, then $\mathbb{C}\mathrm{n}(\emptyset{:}\overline{u}) = \mathbb{C}\mathrm{n}(\emptyset{:}\overline{u}_o)$. Assume that $:\overline{u}_o \nvdash A$. Then there exists a theory $w$ of $\vdash$ such that $\overline{u}_o \subseteq \overline{w}$ and $:\overline{w} \nvdash A$. Since $u$ is a ground theory, and $w_o \subseteq u_o$, we have $u = w$ and hence $:\overline{u} \nvdash A$. Thus $\mathbb{C}\mathrm{n}(\emptyset{:}\overline{u}) \subseteq \mathbb{C}\mathrm{n}(\emptyset{:}\overline{u}_o)$.

Now if $u$ is a ground extension of $\vdash$, we have $u = \mathbb{C}\mathrm{n}(\emptyset{:}\overline{u}_o)$, and hence $u_o = \mathbb{C}\mathrm{n}(\emptyset{:}\overline{u}_o)_o$. Thus, $u_o$ is an extension of ${}_o\!\vdash$.

Assume now that $u_o$ is an extension of ${}_o\!\vdash$. Then $u_o$ is a theory of ${}_o\!\vdash$, and therefore $u$ is a theory of $\vdash$. Now let $v$ be a theory of $\vdash$ such that $v_o \subseteq u_o$. By Lemma 10.82, we have that $v_o$ is a theory of ${}_o\!\vdash$, and hence

$$u_o = \mathbb{C}\mathrm{n}(\emptyset{:}\overline{u}_o)_o \subseteq \mathbb{C}\mathrm{n}(\emptyset{:}\overline{v}_o)_o \subseteq \mathbb{C}\mathrm{n}(v_o{:}\overline{v}_o)_o \subseteq v_o.$$

Thus, $u_o = v_o$, and consequently $u$ is a ground theory of $\vdash$. In addition, $u_o \subseteq \mathbb{C}\mathrm{n}(\emptyset{:}\overline{u})$, and hence $\mathbb{C}\mathrm{n}_{\mathbf{N}}(u_o \cup \neg L\overline{u}) \subseteq \mathbb{C}\mathrm{n}(\emptyset{:}\overline{u})$. Consequently, $u \subseteq \mathbb{C}\mathrm{n}(\emptyset{:}\overline{u})$. But $\mathbb{C}\mathrm{n}(\emptyset{:}\overline{u}) \subseteq u$, since $u$ is a theory of $\vdash$. Thus, $u = \mathbb{C}\mathrm{n}(\emptyset{:}\overline{u})$, and hence $u$ is an extension of $\vdash$. □

As to modal extensions in general, we have the following result:

**Lemma 10.97** *A stable theory $u$ is an extension of an introspective consequence relation $\vdash$ if and only if $u_o = \mathbb{C}\mathrm{n}(\emptyset : \overline{u}_o, \neg L u_o)_o$.*

***Proof.*** The direction from left to right follows from by Lemma 10.82(2).

If $u_o = \mathbb{C}\mathrm{n}(\emptyset{:}\overline{u}_o, \neg L u_o)_o$, then $:\overline{u}_o, \neg L u_o \nvdash \mathbf{f}$, since $u$ is consistent. Hence there exists a consistent theory $w$ of $\vdash$ such that $(\overline{u}_o \cup \neg L u_o) \subseteq \overline{w}$. Since $w$ is a stable theory, $\neg L u_o \subseteq \overline{w}$ iff $u_o \subseteq w$. But then $u = w$, since both are stable theories having the same objective part. Thus, $u$ is a theory of $\vdash$, and hence $\mathbb{C}\mathrm{n}(\emptyset{:}\overline{u}) \subseteq u$. Moreover, we have $\mathbb{C}\mathrm{n}(\emptyset{:}\overline{u}_o, \neg L u_o) \subseteq \mathbb{C}\mathrm{n}(\emptyset{:}\overline{u})$, and therefore $u_o \subseteq \mathbb{C}\mathrm{n}(\emptyset{:}\overline{u})$. Now $\mathbb{C}\mathrm{n}_{\mathbf{N}}(u_o \cup \neg L\overline{u}) \subseteq \mathbb{C}\mathrm{n}(\emptyset{:}\overline{u})$, due to Introspection and Necessitation, and consequently $u \subseteq \mathbb{C}\mathrm{n}(\emptyset{:}\overline{u})$. Thus, $u = \mathbb{C}\mathrm{n}(\emptyset : \overline{u})$ and therefore $u$ is an extension of $\vdash$. □

The above result can be seen as a default counterpart of the corresponding result for biconsequence relations stated in Theorem 10.52.

#### 10.3.2.2 *Modal expansions*

By a *modal expansion* of a default theory $\Delta$ we will mean an expansion of the least modal default consequence relation containing $\Delta$. We will show first that such modal expansions correspond to Moore's stable expansions. To begin with, as a consequence of Lemma 10.83, we have

**Lemma 10.98** *A set $u$ of propositions is a modal expansion of a modal theory $m$ iff $u = \mathrm{Cn}_N(m \cup Lu \cup \neg L\overline{u})$.*

Now the following result shows that modal expansions are precisely stable expansions of Moore's autoepistemic logic [Moore, 1985].

**Corollary 10.99** *Modal expansions of a modal theory $m$ coincide with Moore's stable expansions of $m$.*

***Proof.*** Stable expansions of $m$ can be defined syntactically as sets $u$ satisfying the equality $u = \mathrm{Th}(m \cup Lu \cup \neg L\overline{u})$, while by the preceding lemma, modal expansions are sets $u$ such that $u = \mathrm{Cn}_{\mathbf{N}}(m \cup Lu \cup \neg L\overline{u})$. Note that, in both cases, $u$ is a stable theory containing $m$.

Now, for a stable theory $u$ that contains $m$, let $u_m$ denote the set $\mathrm{Th}(m \cup Lu \cup \neg L\overline{u})$. Clearly, $u_m \subseteq u$. Moreover, $u_m$ is closed with respect to necessitation. Indeed, if $A \in u_m$, then $A \in u$, and hence $LA \in Lu$, which implies $LA \in u_m$. Consequently, $u_m \supseteq \mathrm{Cn}_{\mathbf{N}}(m \cup Lu \cup \neg L\overline{u})$, since the latter is a least deductively closed set that contains $m \cup Lu \cup \neg L\overline{u}$ and is closed with respect to necessitation. Consequently, $\mathrm{Th}(m \cup Lu \cup \neg L\overline{u}) = \mathrm{Cn}_{\mathbf{N}}(m \cup Lu \cup \neg L\overline{u})$, which immediately implies the result. □

Thus, expansions of modal default consequence relations provide a formalization of Moore's autoepistemic logic.

The next result already shows that for introspective consequence relations, we have a perfect match between modal and objective expansions.

**Theorem 10.100** *If $\vdash$ is a modal introspective consequence relation, and $u$ a stable theory, then $u$ is an expansion of $\vdash$ iff $u_o$ is an expansion of ${}_o\vdash$.*

***Proof.*** If $u$ is an expansion of $\vdash$, then $\mathbb{C}\mathrm{n}(u{:}\overline{u})_o = u_o$, and hence $u_o$ is an expansion of ${}_o\vdash$ by Lemma 10.82. In the other direction, if $u_o$ is an expansion of ${}_o\vdash$, then it is a theory of ${}_o\vdash$, and hence $u$ is a theory of $\vdash$. Moreover, since $u_o \subseteq \mathbb{C}\mathrm{n}(u{:}\overline{u})$, we have $\mathrm{Cn}_{\mathbf{N}}(u_o \cup \neg L\overline{u}) \subseteq \mathbb{C}\mathrm{n}(u{:}\overline{u})$, due to Introspection and Necessitation. Consequently, $u \subseteq \mathbb{C}\mathrm{n}(u{:}\overline{u})$ by Proposition 10.1, and hence $u$ is an expansion of $\vdash$. □

Since introspective consequence relations form a representative class of consequence relations with respect to both nonmonotonic semantics, the above result, combined with Theorem 10.96, completes a partial reduction of modal nonmonotonic logics to objective default logics.

As before, Theorem 6.40 implies that modal autoepistemic consequence relations constitute a maximal logic for modal expansions. The latter consequence relations provide us with two convenient representations for modal expansions, one purely modal, the other purely objective.

To begin with, by Corollary 10.78 any modal default theory $\Delta$ is reducible to an objective default theory that we will denote by $B(\Delta)$. Then we have

**Lemma 10.101** *For any default theory $\Delta$, classical expansions of $B(\Delta)$ are precisely objective parts of modal expansions of $\Delta$.*

***Proof.*** Note that, for any objective default theory $\Delta_o$, the least classical autoepistemic consequence relation containing $\Delta_o$ is precisely the objective part of the least modal autoepistemic consequence relation containing $\Delta_o$ (this fact can be obtained, e.g., from Theorems 10.76 and 10.74). Now the result follows from the preceding theorem. □

By the above result, modal autoepistemic reasoning is completely reducible to the non-modal classical autoepistemic reasoning.

On the other hand, in modal autoepistemic consequence relations, any default theory $\Delta$ is reducible also to a purely modal theory $\breve{\Delta}$ (see Corollary 10.78). As a consequence, default theories under the classical autoepistemic semantics are translatable into modal theories in Moore's autoepistemic logic, and vice versa.

As an illustration, the representation of parallel circumscription in default theories (see Lemma 9.41 on page 330) can be transformed into a representation of parallel circumscription in autoepistemic logic. More precisely, given a circumscription framework $\Pi$, we define the corresponding modal theory $m_\Pi$ as the set containing $T$ and the following modal formulas:

$$\{\neg Lp \to \neg p \mid p \in P \cup F\} \bigcup \{\neg L \neg p \to p \mid p \in F\}.$$

Then we obtain the following result from [Niemelä, 1992]:

**Corollary 10.102** *A model $\alpha$ is a $(P, F)$-minimal model of a theory $T$ iff it is a model of the objective part of some stable expansion of $m_\Pi$.*

By Theorem 10.88, modal autoepistemic consequence relations coincide with prime KD45-consequence relations. As we are going to show, this reduces modal expansions to KD45-extensions.

To begin with, by Theorem 10.88, modal expansions of a modal theory $m$ coincide with expansions of $\vdash_m^{KD45}$. Accordingly, by restricted monotonicity property of expansions, we have

**Lemma 10.103** *Modal expansions of a modal theory $m$ coincide with expansions of $\vdash_m^{\mathcal{M}}$, for any modal logic $\mathcal{M} \subseteq KD45$.*

Now, the following result shows that the modal 5 axiom $\neg LA \to L\neg LA$ reduces expansions to extensions[4]:

[4]Cf. Theorem 4.2 in [Marek *et al.*, 1993].

**Lemma 10.104** *Any consistent expansion of a prime 5-consequence relation is an extension.*

***Proof.*** If $u$ is a consistent expansion of a prime 5-consequence relation $\vdash$, then it is a stable theory. Consequently, if $A \in u$, then $LA \in u$, and hence $\neg LA \notin u$. Therefore, $\neg L \neg LA \in \neg L\overline{u}$, and by 5 we have $LA \in \mathrm{Cn}_5(\neg L\overline{u})$. Thus, $Lu \subseteq \mathrm{Cn}_5(\neg L\overline{u})$, and hence $\mathrm{Cn}_5(m \cup Lu \cup \neg L\overline{u}) = \mathrm{Cn}_5(m \cup \neg L\overline{u})$. Due to Lemmas 10.98 and 10.95, this implies that u is an extension of $\vdash$□

Combined with the preceding lemma, this implies the well-known result established in [Schwarz, 1990]:

**Corollary 10.105** *Modal expansions coincide with KD45-extensions.*

Actually, the above lemma implies that modal expansions coincide with $\mathcal{M}$-extensions, for any modal logic $\mathcal{M}$ in the range $5 \subseteq \mathcal{M} \subseteq$ KD45. The latter fact suggests, in turn, the simplest way of embedding an autoepistemic logic into a modal default logic: stable expansions of a modal theory $m$ coincide with modal extensions of the modal theory obtained from $m$ by adding the instances of the axiom 5 (cf. [Janhunen, 1996]).

Finally, the correspondence between modal autoepistemic and KD45-consequence relations implies also that KD45 is a maximal modal logic adequate for modal autoepistemic reasoning.

**Definition 10.11** Default theories $\Gamma$ and $\Delta$ will be called *mae-equivalent*, if they have the same modal expansions, and *strongly mae-equivalent* if, for any set $\Phi$ of default rules, $\Gamma \cup \Phi$ is mae-equivalent to $\Delta \cup \Phi$.

**Theorem 10.106** *Default theories $\Gamma$ and $\Delta$ are strongly mae-equivalent if and only if $\breve{\Gamma}$ and $\breve{\Delta}$ are KD45-equivalent.*

***Proof.*** By Theorem 10.88, modal theories $\breve{\Gamma}$ and $\breve{\Delta}$ are KD45-equivalent if and only if they determine the same modal autoepistemic consequence relation. Now the result follows from Theorem 6.40. □

This result completes our study.

# Bibliography

C. Alchourrón, P. Gärdenfors, and D. Makinson. On the logic of theory change: Partial meet contraction and revision functions. *Journal of Symbolic Logic*, 50:510–530, 1985.

K. R. Apt and R. N. Bol. Logic programming and negation: A survey. *Journal of Logic Programming*, 19,20:9–71, 1994.

K. Apt, H. Blair, and A. Walker. Towards a theory of declarative knowledge. In J. Minker, editor, *Foundations of Deductive Databases and Logic Programming*, pages 89–148. Morgan Kaufmann, San Mateo, CA, 1988.

O. Arieli and A. Avron. Reasoning with logical bilattices. *Journal of Logic, Language, and Information*, 5:25–63, 1996.

Y. Babovich, E. Erdem, and V. Lifschitz. Fages' theorem and answer set programming. In *Proceedings of the Nonmonotonic Reasoning Workshop, NMR-2000*, 2000.

C. Baral and M. Gelfond. Logic programming and knowledge representation. *Journal of Logic Programming*, 19,20:73–148, 1994.

C. Baral and V. S. Subrahmanian. Dualities between alternative semantics for logic programming and nonmonotonic reasoning (extended abstract). In *Proc. 1st Int. Worksop on Logic Programming and Nonmonotonic Reasoning*, pages 69–86, 1991.

C. Baral and V. S. Subrahmanian. Stable and extension class theory for logic programs and default logics. *J. of Automated Reasoning*, 8:345–366, 1992.

C. Baral. *Knowledge Representation, Reasoning and Declarative Problem Solving.* Cambridge UP, 2003.

N. D. Belnap, Jr. A useful four-valued logic. In M. Dunn and G. Epstein, editors, *Modern Uses of Multiple-Valued Logic*, pages 8–41. D. Reidel, 1977.

R. Ben-Eliyahu. From program completion to default logic. In *Proc. 10th Israeli Symp. On Artificial Intelligence, Computer Vision, and Neural Networks*, Ramat Gan, 1993.

S. Blamey. Partial logic. In D. M. Gabbay and F. Guenthner, editors, *Handbook of Philosophical Logic, Vol. III*, pages 1–70. D. Reidel, 1986.

A. Bochman. On bimodal nonmonotonic logics and their unimodal and non-modal equivalents. In *Proc. IJCAI'95*, pages 1518–1524, 1995.

A. Bochman. A study of Przymusinski's static semantics. In *Proc. Int. Conf. On Logic Programming and Nonmonotonic Reasoning, LPNMR'97, LNAI 1265*, pages 170–184. Springer, 1997.

A. Bochman. A logical foundation for logic programming, I and II. *Journal of Logic Programming*, 35:151–194, 1998.

A. Bochman. On the relation between default and modal nonmonotonic reasoning. *Artificial Intelligence*, 101:1–34, 1998.

A. Bochman. *A Logical Theory of Nonomonotonic Inference and Belief Change*. Springer, 2001.

A. Bochman. Collective argumentation and disjunctive logic programming. *Journal of Logic and Computation*, 9:55–56, 2003.

P. Bonatti. Shift-based semantics: General results and applications. Technical Report CD-TR-93-59, Technical University of Vienna, 1993.

A. Bondarenko, P. M. Dung, R. A. Kowalski, and F. Toni. An abstract, argumentation-theoretic framework for default reasoning. *Artificial Intelligence*, 93:63–101, 1997.

S. Brass and J. Dix. Disjunctive semantics based upon partial and bottom-up evaluation. In L. Sterling, editor, *Proc. 12Th Int. Conf. On Logic Programming*, pages 199–213. MIT Press, 1995.

S. Brass and J. Dix. A general approach to bottom-up computation of disjunctive semantics. In J. Dix, L. Pereira, and T. Przymusinski, editors, *Nonmonotonic Extensions of Logic Programming*, volume 927 of *LNAI*, pages 127–155. Springer, 1995.

S. Brass, J. Dix, I. Niemelä, and T. Przymusinski. Comparison and efficient computation of the static and the disjunctive WFS. In G. Brewka, E. Weydert, and C. Witteveen, editors, *Proceedings of the third Dutch-German Workshop on Nonmonotonic Reasoning and its Applications*, pages 37–42, 1997.

R. A. Bull and K. Segerberg. Basic modal logic. In D. Gabbay and F. Guenthner, editors, *Handbook of Philosophical Logic*, pages 1–88. Dordrecht: D. Reidel, 1984.

K. Clark. Negation as failure. In H. Gallaire and J. Minker, editors, *Logic and Data Bases*, pages 293–322. Plenum Press, 1978.

L. Console, D. Theseider Dupre, and P. Torasso. On the relationship between abduction and deduction. *Journal of Logic and Computation*, 1:661–690, 1991.

M. Denecker, V. W. Marek, and M. Truszczyński. Uniform semantic treatment of default and autoepistemic logics. *Artificial Intelligence*, 143:79–122, 2003.

J. Dix and M. Müller. Partial evaluation and relevance for approximations of the stable semantics. In Z. W. Raz and M. Zemankova, editors, *Methodologies of Intelligent Systems, ISMIS'94*, volume 869 of *LNAI*, pages 511–520. Springer, 1994.

J. Dix, G. Gottlob, and V. Marek. Causal models for disjunctive logic programs. In P.Van Hentenryck, editor, *Proc. 11th Int. Conf. On Logic Programming, S. Margherita Ligure*, pages 290–302. MIT Press, 1994.

J. Dix. Classifying semantics of logic programs. In A. Nerode, W. Marek, and V. S.

Subrahmanian, editors, *Proceedings 1st International Workshop on Logic Programming and Nonmonotonic Reasoning*, pages 166–180, Cambridge, Mass., 1991. MIT Press.

W. Drabent and M. Martelli. Strict completion of logic programs. *New Generation Computing*, 9:69–79, 1991.

P. M. Dung. Acyclic disjunctive programs with abductive procedure as proof procedure. In *Proc. Int. Conference on Fifth Generation Computer Systems*, pages 555–561. ICOT, 1992.

P. M. Dung. An argumentation-theoretic foundation for logic programming. *J. of Logic Programming*, 22:151–177, 1995.

P. M. Dung. On the acceptability of arguments and its fundamental role in nonmonotonic reasoning, logic programming and n-persons games. *Artificial Intelligence*, 76:321–358, 1995.

J. M. Dunn. Intuitive semantics for first-degree entailment and coupled trees. *Philosophical Studies*, 29:149–168, 1976.

F. Fages. Consistency of Clark's completion and existence of stable models. *Journal of Methods of Logic in Computer Science*, 1:51–60, 1994.

R. Fagin, J. Y. Halpern, and M. Y. Vardi. A nonstandard approach to the logical omniscience problem. *Artificial Intelligence*, 79, 1995.

M. C. Fitting, W. Marek, and M. Truszczyński. The pure logic of necessitation. *Journal of Logic and Computation*, 2:349–373, 1992.

M. C. Fitting. A Kripke-Kleene semantics for logic programs. *Journal of Logic Programming*, 2:295–312, 1985.

M. C. Fitting. Bilattices and the theory of truth. *Journal of Philosophical Logic*, 18:225–256, 1989.

M. C. Fitting. Bilattices and the semantics of logic programming. *Journal of Logic Programming*, 11:91–116, 1991.

M. C. Fitting. The family of stable models. *Journal of Logic Programming*, 17:197–225, 1993.

D. M. Gabbay. *Investigations in Modal and Tense Logics*. D. Reidel, 1976.

D. M. Gabbay. *Semantical Investigations in Heyting's Intuitionistic Logic*. D. Reidel, 1981.

D. M. Gabbay. *Fibring Logics*. Oxford University Press, 1998.

A. Van Gelder and J. S. Schlipf. Commonsense axiomatizations for logic programs. *Journal of Logic Programming*, 17:161–196, 1993.

A. Van Gelder, K. A. Ross, and J. S. Schlipf. The well-founded semantics for general logic programs. *J. ACM*, 38:620–650, 1991.

M. Gelfond and V. Lifschitz. The stable model semantics for logic programming. In R. Kowalski and K. Bowen, editors, *Proc. 5th International Conf./Symp. on Logic Programming*, pages 1070–1080, Cambridge, MA, 1988. MIT Press.

M. Gelfond and V. Lifschitz. Classical negation and disjunctive databases. *New Generation Computing*, 9:365–385, 1991.

M. Gelfond, V. Lifschitz, H. Przymusińska, and M. Truszczyński. Disjunctive defaults. In *Proc. Second Int. Conf. on Principles of Knowledge Representation and Reasoning, KR'91*, pages 230–237, Cambridge, Mass., 1991.

M. Gelfond. Logic programming and reasoning with incomplete information.

*Annals of Mathematics and Artificial Intelligence*, 12:89–116, 1994.

E. Giunchiglia, J. Lee, V. Lifschitz, N. McCain, and H. Turner. Nonmonotonic causal theories. *Artificial Intelligence*, 153:49–104, 2004.

A. Grove. Two modelings for theory change. *Journal of Philosophical Logic*, 17:157–170, 1988.

H. E. Hendry. Minimally incomplete sets of Lukasiewiczean truth-functions. *Notre Dame Journal of Formal Logic*, 24:146–150, 1983.

K. Inoue and C. Sakama. Negation as failure in the head. *Journal of Logic Programming*, 35:39–78, 1998.

H. Jakobovits and D. Vermeir. Robust semantics for argumentation frameworks. *Journal of Logic and Computation*, 9:215–261, 1999.

T. Janhunen, I. Niemelä, P. Simons, and J.-H. You. Unfolding partiality and disjunctions in stable model semantics. In F. Giunchiglia and B. Selman, editors, *Proc. Int. Conference on Principles of Knowledge Representation and Reasoning, KR'00*, pages 411–424, Breckenridge, Co., 2000. Morgan Kaufmann.

T. Janhunen. Representing autoepistemic introspection in terms of default rules. In *Proc. European Conf. on AI, ECAI-96*, pages 70–74, Budapest, 1996. John Wiley & Sons.

A. C. Kakas and P. Mankarella. Stable theories for logic programs. In V. Saraswat and K. Ueda, editors, *Proc. Int. Symp. On Logic Programming*, pages 85–100. MIT Press, 1991.

A. C. Kakas and F. Toni. Computing argumentation in logic programming. *Journal of Logic and Computation*, 9:515–562, 1999.

A. C. Kakas, P. Mancarella, and P. M. Dung. The acceptability semantics for logic programs. In P. Van Hentenryck, editor, *Proceedings Int. Conf. on Logic Programming, ICLP-94*, pages 504–519, Camb., MA, 1994. MIT Press.

K. Konolige. On the relation between default and autoepistemic logic. *Artificial Intelligence*, 35:343–382, 1988.

K. Konolige. Abduction versus closure in causal theories. *Artificial Intelligence*, 53:255–272, 1992.

K. Konolige. Using default and causal reasoning in diagnosis. *Annals of Mathematics and Artificial Intelligence*, 11:97–135, 1994.

S. Kraus, D. Lehmann, and M. Magidor. Nonmonotonic reasoning, preferential models and cumulative logics. *Artificial Intelligence*, 44:167–207, 1990.

T. Langholm. How different is partial logic? In P. Doherty, editor, *Partiality, Modality, and Nonmonotonicity*, pages 3–43. CSLI, Stanford, 1996.

J. Lee and V. Lifschitz. Loop formulas for disjunctive logic programs. In *Proc. Nineteenth Int. Conference on Logic Programming*, pages 451–465, 2003.

J. Lee. Nondefinite vs. definite causal theories. In V. Lifschitz and I. Niemelä, editors, *Proc. 7th Int. Conference on Logic Programming and Nonmonotonic Reasoning, LPNMR 2004*, pages 141–153, Fort Lauderdale, FL, USA, 2004. Springer. LNAI 2923.

D. Lehmann. Another perspective on default reasoning. *Annals of Mathematics and Artificial Intelligence*, 15:61–82, 1995.

W. Lenzen. Epistemologische betrachtungen zu [s4,s5]. *Erkenntnis*, 14:33–56,

1979.

V. Lifschitz and G. Schwarz. Extended logic programs as autoepistemic theories. In L. M. Pereira and A. Nerode, editors, *Proc. Second Int. Workshop on Logic Programming and Nonmonotonic Reasoning*, pages 101–114. MIT Press, 1993.

V. Lifschitz and T. Woo. Answer sets in general nonmonotonic reasoning (preliminary report). In *Proc. Third Int. Conf. on Principles of Knowledge Representation and Reasoning, KR'92*, pages 603–614. Morgan Kauffman, 1992.

V. Lifschitz, D. Pearce, and A. Valverde. Strongly equivalent logic programs. *ACM Transactions on Computational Logic*, 2:526–541, 2001.

V. Lifschitz. Computing circumscription. In *Proc. 9th Int. Joint Conf. on Artificial Intelligence, IJCAI-85*, pages 121–127. Morgan Kaufmann, 1985.

V. Lifschitz. Pointwise circumscription. In M. Ginsberg, editor, *Readings in Non-Monotonic Reasoning*, pages 179–193. Morgan Kaufmann, San Mateo, CA, 1987.

V. Lifschitz. Minimal belief and negation as failure. *Artificial Intelligence*, 70:53–72, 1994.

F. Lin and Y. Shoham. A logic of knowledge and justified assumptions. *Artificial Intelligence*, 57:271–289, 1992.

F. Lin and Y. Zhao. ASSAT: Computing answer sets of a logic program by SAT solvers. In *Proceedings AAAI-02*, 2002.

J. W. Lloyd and J. C. Shepherdson. Partial evaluation in logic programming. *Journal of Logic Programming*, 11:217–242, 1991.

J. Lloyd and R. Topor. Making Prolog more expressive. *Journal of Logic Programming*, 3:225–24–, 1984.

J. Lobo and C. Uzcátegui. Abductive consequence relations. *Artificial Intelligence*, 89:149–171, 1997.

J. Lobo, J. Minker, and A. Rajasekar. *Foundations of Disjunctive Logic Programming.* MIT Press, Cambridge, Mass., 1992.

D. Makinson and L. van der Torre. Input/Output logics. *Journal of Philosophical Logic*, 29:383–408, 2000.

D. Makinson. General theory of cumulative inference. In M. Reinfrank, editor, *Nonmonotonic Reasoning*, volume 346 of *LNAI*, pages 1–18. Springer, 1989.

W. Marek and M. Truszczyński. Relating autoepistemic and default logics. In *Int. Conf. on Principles of Knowledge Representation and Reasoning, KR'89*, pages 276–288, San Mateo, Calif., 1989. Morgan Kaufmann.

W. Marek and M. Truszczyński. *Nonmonotonic Logic, Context-Dependent Reasoning.* Springer, 1993.

W. Marek, A. Nerode, and J. Remmel. A theory of nonmonotonic rule systems. *Annals of Mathematics and Artificial Intelligence*, 1:241–273, 1990.

V. W. Marek, G. F. Schwarz, and M. Truszchinski. Modal nonmonotonic logics: ranges, characterization, computation. *Journal of ACM*, 40:963–990, 1993.

N. McCain and H. Turner. Causal theories of action and change. In *Proceedings AAAI-97*, pages 460–465, 1997.

N. McCain. *Causality in Commonsense Reasoning About Actions.* PhD thesis,

University of Texas at Austin, 1997.

D. McDermott and J. Doyle. Nonmonotonic logic. *Artificial Intelligence*, 13:41–72, 1980.

D. McDermott. Nonmonotonic logic II: Nonmonotonic modal theories. *Journal of the ACM*, 29:33–57, 1982.

R. C. Moore. Semantical considerations on non-monotonic logic. *Artificial Intelligence*, 25:75–94, 1985.

R. Muskens. On partial and paraconsistent logics. *Notre Dame Journal of Formal Logic*, 40:352–374, 1999.

I. Niemelä. A unifying framework for nonmonotonic reasoning. In *Proc. 10th European Conference on Artificial Intelligence, ECAI-92*, pages 334–338, Vienna, 1992. John Wiley.

D. Pearce. A new logical characterization of stable models and answer sets. In J. Dix, L. M. Pereira, and T. Przymusinski, editors, *Non-Monotonic Extensions of Logic Programming*, volume 1216 of *LNAI*, pages 57–70. Springer, 1997.

J. Pearl. Embracing causality in formal reasoning. In *Proceedings AAAI-87*, pages 369–373, Seattle, 1987.

J. Pearl. *Probabilistic Reasoning in Intelligent Systems: Networks of Plausible Inference*. Morgan Kaufmann, 1988.

D. Poole. Explanation and prediction: An architecture for default and abductive reasoning. *Computational Intelligence*, 5:97–110, 1989.

D. Poole. A methodology for using a default and abductive reasoning system. *Int. Journal of Intelligent Systems*, 5:521–548, 1990.

D. Poole. Representing diagnosis knowledge. *Annals of Mathematics and Artificial Intelligence*, 11:33–50, 1994.

H. Przymusinska and T. Przymusinski. Semantic issues in deductive databases and logic programs. In R. Benerji, editor, *Formal Techniques in Artificial Intelligence*, pages 321–367. North-Holland, Amsterdam, 1990.

T. C. Przymusinski. The well-founded semantics coincides with the three-valued stable semantics. *Fundamenta Informaticae*, 13:445–464, 1990.

T. C. Przymusinski. Semantics of disjunctive logic programs and deductive databases. In *Proc. Second Int. Conf. On Deductive and Object-Oriented Databases*, pages 85–107. Springer, 1991.

T. C. Przymusinski. Stable semantics for disjunctive programs. *New Generation Computing*, 9:401–424, 1991.

T. C. Przymusinski. Semantics of normal and disjunctive programs: A unifying framework. In J. Dix, L. Pereira, and T. Przymusinski, editors, *Proc. Workshop on Non-Monotonic Extensions of Logic Programming*, pages 43–67. Springer, 1995. LNAI.

T. C. Przymusinski. Static semantics for normal and disjunctive logic programs. *Annals of Mathematics and Artificial Intelligence*, 1995.

R. Reiter. On closed world data bases. In H. Gallaire and J. Minker, editors, *Logic and Data Bases*, pages 119–140. Plenum Press, 1978.

R. Reiter. A logic for default reasoning. *Artificial Intelligence*, 13:81–132, 1980.

R. Reiter. The frame problem in the situation calculus: A simple solution (sometimes) and a completeness result for goal regression. In V. Lifschitz, editor, *Artificial Intelligence and Mathematical Theory of Computation: Papers in Honor of Lohn McCarthy*, pages 318–420. Academic Press, 1991.

R. Reiter. *Knowledge in Action: Logical Foundations for Specifying and Implementing Dynamic Systems.* MIT Press, 2001.

R. Routley, V. Plumwood, R. Meyer, and R. Brady. *Relevant Logics and their Rivals.* Ridgeview, Ca., 1982.

C. Sakama and H. Seki. Partial deduction of disjunctive logic programs: A declarative approach. In L. Fribourg and F. Turini, editors, *Logic Program Synthesis and Transformation – Meta-Programming in Logic*, volume 883 of *LNCS*, pages 170–181. Springer, 1994.

M. Schaerf. Negation and minimality in disjunctive databases. *Journal of Logic Programming*, 23:63–86, 1995.

J. S. Schlipf. Formalizing a logic for logic programming. *Annals of Mathematics and Artificial Intelligence*, 5:279–302, 1992.

L. K. Schubert. Explanatory closure, action closure and the Sandewall test suite for reasoning about change. *Journal of Logic and Computation*, 4:679–700, 1994.

G. Schwarz and M. Truszczyński. Minimal knowledge problem: a new approach. *Artificial Intelligence*, 67:113–141, 1994.

G. Schwarz. Autoepistemic modal logics. In R. Parikh, editor, *Theoretical Aspects of Reasoning about Knowledge, TARK-90*, pages 97–109, San Mateo, CA, 1990. Morgan Kaufmann.

G. Schwarz. Minimal model semantics for nonmonotonic modal logics. In *Proceedings LICS-92*, pages 34–43, Santa Cruz, CA., 1992.

G. Schwarz. Reflexive autoepistemic logic. *Fundamenta Informaticae*, 17:157–173, 1992.

D. Scott. Completeness and axiomatizability in many-valued logic. In *Proc. Symp. In Pure Math., No. 25*, pages 431–435, 1974.

K. Segerberg. *An Essay in Classical Modal Logic*, volume 13 of *Filosofiska Studier.* Uppsala University, 1971.

K. Segerberg. *Classical Propositional Operators.* Clarendon Press, 1982.

M. P. Shanahan. *Solving the Frame Problem.* The MIT Press, 1997.

J. C. Shepherdson. Negation in logic programming. In J. Minker, editor, *Deductive Databases and Logic Programming*, pages 19–88. M. Kaufmann, 1988.

D. J. Shoesmith and T. J. Smiley. *Multiple-Conclusion Logic.* Cambridge University Press, 1978.

Y. Shoham. *Reasoning about Change.* Cambridge University Press, 1988.

R. F. Stärk. From logic programs to inductive definitions. In W. A. Hodges et al., editors, *Logic: From Foundations to Applications, European Logic Colloquium'93*, pages 453–481, Oxford, 1996. Clarendon Press.

M. Thielscher. Ramification and causality. *Artificial Intelligence*, 89:317–364, 1997.

M. Tiomkin and M. Kaminski. Nonmonotonic default modal logics. *Journal of the ACM*, 38:963–984, 1991.

M. Truszczyński. Embedding default logic into modal nonmonotonic logics. pages

151–165, Cambridge Mass., 1991. The MIT Press.

M. Truszczyński. Modal interpretations of default logic. In J. Myopoulos and R. Reiter, editors, *Proceedings Int. Joint Conf. on Artificial Intelligence, IJCAI'91*, pages 393–398, San Mateo, Calif., 1991. Morgan Kaufmann.

H. Turner. A logic of universal causation. *Artificial Intelligence*, 113:87–123, 1999.

H. Turner. Strong equivalence for causal theories. In V. Lifschitz and I. Niemelä, editors, *Proc. Int. Conf. on Logic Programming and Nonmonotonic Reasoning, LPNMR 2004*, volume 2923 of *LNAI*, pages 289–301, Fort Lauderdale, FL, 2004. Springer.

J Van Benthem. *A Manual of Intensional Logic*. CSLI, Stanford, second edition, 1988.

M. H. van Emden and R. A. Kowalski. The semantics of predicate logic as a programming language. *J. of ACM*, 23:733–742, 1976.

M. Wallace. Tight, consistent, and computable completions for unrestricted logic programs. *Journal of Logic Programming*, 15:243–273, 1993.

L. Wittgenstein. *Tractatus Logico-Philosophicus*. Routledge & Kegan Paul, London, 1961. English translation by D. F. Pears and B. F. McGuinness.

L. Y. Yuan and J.-H. You. Autoepistemic circumscription and logic programming. *J. of Automated Reasoning*, 10:143–160, 1993.

# Index